Creating a More Perfect Slaveholders' Union

CONSTITUTIONAL THINKING

Sanford Levinson
Jeffrey K. Tulis
Emily Zackin
Mariah Zeisberg
Editors

Creating a More Perfect Slaveholders' Union

Slavery, the Constitution, and Secession in Antebellum America

Peter Radan

School of Law, Macquarie University

UNIVERSITY PRESS OF KANSAS

Published by the University Press of Kansas (Lawrence, Kansas 66045), which was organized by the Kansas Board of Regents and is operated and funded by Emporia State University, Fort Hays State University, Kansas State University, Pittsburg State University, the University of Kansas, and Wichita State University.

Library of Congress Cataloging-in-Publication Data

Names: Radan, Peter, author.
Title: Creating a more perfect slaveholders' Union: slavery, the Constitution, and secession in antebellum America / Peter Radan.
Description: Lawrence: University Press of Kansas, 2023. | Series: Constitutional thinking | Includes bibliographical references and index.
Identifiers: LCCN 2023004236 (print) | LCCN 2023004237 (ebook)
ISBN 9780700635801 (cloth)
ISBN 9780700635818 (paperback)
ISBN 9780700635825 (ebook)
Subjects: LCSH: Secession—United States—History. | Constitutional history—United States. | States' rights (American politics)—History. | Nullification (States' rights) | Slavery—Law and legislation—United States—History—18th century. | Slavery—Law and legislation—United States—History—19th century. | United States—History—Revolution, 1775–1783. | United States—History—1783–1815. | BISAC: LAW / Legal History | HISTORY / United States / Civil War Period (1850-1877)
Classification: LCC KF4613 .R33 2024 (print) | LCC KF4613 (ebook) | DDC 342.7304/2—dc23/eng/20230728
LC record available at https://lccn.loc.gov/2023004236.
LC ebook record available at https://lccn.loc.gov/2023004237.

British Library Cataloguing-in-Publication Data is available.

Printed in the United States of America

10 9 8 7 6 5 4 3 2 1

The paper used in this publication is acid free and meets the minimum requirements of the American National Standard for Permanence of Paper for Printed Library Materials Z39.48–1992.

CONTENTS

FOREWORD

You hold in your hand a remarkable book! I first read it as a dissertation submitted to the University of Technology in Sydney, Australia. I quickly realized that it was easily tied for first among all dissertations I had read in nearly a fifty-year academic career. This is no surprise, because in fact it is Radan's second PhD; he is already a mature scholar in every way. I am, therefore, absolutely delighted to write this foreword on its well-deserved publication in the Constitutional Thinking series, for which I am privileged to serve as a coeditor, by the University Press of Kansas. This will rapidly take its place as an absolutely essential book for any academic interested in what I personally believe to remain the most important questions raised by the American Constitution. In fact, the quality of his prose and accessibility of his argument should make it essential reading for any general reader interested in what is labeled today "American constitutional development."

So what are these essential questions? The first one may appear abstract, though it ultimately provides the basis for war in 1861 and much of the "polarization" that characterizes American politics today. It involves the conceptualization of American identity, whether in 1787 or today. Did a single unified people come together to "ordain" a new Constitution (and government) or, instead, were they members of discrete "sovereign states" located along the Atlantic from Massachusetts down to Georgia, who joined together to negotiate a quasi-treaty that would nonetheless continue to recognize the dissimilarity and ultimate priority of these state identities? The most obvious dissimilarity, as recognized by Madison at the Philadelphia Convention, involved the presumptive legitimacy of enslaving other human beings, where the basis of such enslavement, incidentally, had become thoroughly racialized by the eighteenth century. So to what degree was the Constitution designed to preserve, protect, and defend the system of chattel slavery that most certainly existed in the United States at the time of its drafting and ratification in 1787–1788? The final question is whether the Constitution, albeit silently, offered the option to states to unilaterally withdraw from the Union, as obviously was attempted by eleven states in 1860–1861, should they come to the conclusion that the ostensible commitments of 1787 were not being respected.

These questions, in many ways, divide us, at least intellectually, almost as much in 2023 as in the mid-nineteenth century. One need only refer to the acrimonious debate engendered by the so-called 1619 Project and its insistence that the real "founding" of America occurred with the arrival in Jamestown, Virginia of the first Black slaves. What constitutes the "authentic" America and its legacy, including that of the Constitution? The Texas legislature, bitterly antagonistic to the 1619 Project, nonetheless requires that all children be taught "the history of white supremacy, including the institution of slavery . . . and the ways in which it is morally wrong." Presumably no one objects to this requirement, including the premise that students should be taught by their teachers (speaking in behalf of the State) that both are "morally wrong." Radan surely does not disagree. There is not an ounce of sympathy in his book for the "Lost Cause" narrative that continues to be evoked to apologize for the Confederacy.

But he is asking a profoundly different question. Does the fact that slavery is—and always was—"morally wrong" mean that it was not, from the perspective of a thoughtful legal analyst, protected by the United States Constitution? Thus Joseph Story, one of the greatest members of the antebellum Supreme Court—and, as well, a leading professor at the Harvard Law School and author of an authoritative three-volume "commentary" on the Constitution—wrote as follows in 1842 to a friend: "You know full well that I have ever been opposed to slavery. But I take my standard of duty as a judge from the Constitution." What this signifies, in fact, was that Story wrote an opinion that year in *Prigg v. Pennsylvania* upholding the Fugitive Slave Law of 1793, along the way declaring that slavecatchers had a constitutional right to capture their alleged fugitive without going to any court at all so long as the capture was "peaceful" (itself a euphemism, at least from the perspective of the person being captured). William Lloyd Garrison notably described the Constitution as a "covenant with death and agreement with hell"; others, of course, disagreed, including Abraham Lincoln and Frederick Douglass after he had broken with Garrison early in the 1850s. This remains a subject of bitter contention, with some scholars like Sean Wilentz and Randy Barnett emphasizing the importance of so-called "anti-slavery constitutionalism," a notion certainly never supported by the Supreme Court itself.

But where the rubber truly hits the road is whether the slaveholding states could ultimately assert their retained sovereign right to secede—to withdraw from the Union—should they plausibly assert that the commitments made to protect the "peculiar institution," whether or not considered just, were being ignored by their purported partners. This is the most fundamental question that Radan wrestles with, and his answer will surely displease—indeed outrage—many readers who will certainly not be contented with the moral denunciation of slavery and slavery-based secession; they want to be reassured as well that the Confederates were unfaithful to the Constitution as well as to what we might like to believe are the claims of morality.

Radan believes that secession was perfectly constitutional, that the arguments offered by Jefferson Davis and others were considerably stronger than the answers given by Abraham Lincoln and other opponents of the Confederacy. He unfolds his argument in three extraordinarily thorough and carefully argued chapters that build on one another with the skill of someone using Lego blocks to create a truly complex structure. No one will be able to dismiss his meticulously presented arguments whatever the degree of discomfort they might cause.

The first chapter (following a remarkably comprehensive introductory overview of the existing secondary literature) concerns the nature of the Union itself, what I sometimes identify to my students as the "metaphysics" of the American constitutional order. The Preamble indicates that "We the People of the United States" do "ordain" the Constitution. But who, exactly, is "the People" in whose name, and on the basis of whose authority, the inert words drafted in Philadelphia are given juridical life? One answer is that there is a singular collective entity, which we might call "the people of the United States." That scarcely answers the question as to whether *everyone* living within the United States is part of the "American people." Think only of Indigenous Nations and enslaved persons, not to mention those "people," like white women, who were clearly thought to be citizens but without any right (save in New Jersey until 1807) to participate in any public decisionmaking.

But what Radan focuses on, understandably enough, is the argument that the Constitution was "ordained" by the plural *peoples* of the separate states that were declared "independent" by the Declaration of Independence and whose sovereignty as separate entities was acknowledged by Great Britain in the Treaty of Paris of 1783. Before one points out that the Preamble includes the singular "people" and not the plural "peoples," consider that everything may turn on how one inflects the words "United States." If one chooses to inflect the latter, then one might well accept Radan's argument that the Constitution is best understood as a "compact" among the several independent states exercising their sovereignty to form what they hoped would be a "more perfect Union." But they did not give up their sovereignty. They might have become what Thomas Hobbes called "sleeping sovereigns" if satisfied by the actions of the new government established by the Constitution; they could, however, always awaken and reassert their sovereignty should the government betray its essential promises.

As one should by now expect, Radan offers a thorough examination of the arguments made at the time of the formation and adoption of the Constitution in order to establish which were predominant, and he strongly affirms the priority of the "compact" argument made most memorably in the 1798 Kentucky and Virginia Resolutions authored by Thomas Jefferson and James Madison, respectively. There were those, to be sure, who were "nationalists," evoking the existence of a singular "American people," but, Radan believes, on the basis of strong evidence, that they were a minority. More to the point, perhaps, many aspects of the Constitution, including the Senate and the procedures for amending the Constitution, must be read against the background of recognition of the continued importance, indeed priority, of state political identity and power.

He then moves on to the second central issue: Was the Constitution in fact "pro-slavery"? He is certainly not ignorant of the fact that some people, both then and now, have argued just the opposite, that, closely read, especially if combined with a sympathetic reading of the Declaration of Independence—a document that Lincoln believed was in fact more important than the Constitution—the Constitution should be considered "anti-slavery." There is, of course, a third possibility, argued by Lincoln's great adversary, Illinois senator Stephen A. Douglas, that the Constitution is basically neutral on the issue, leaving it up to "popular sovereignty" state by state to decide. After full examination, he determines that the unlikely bedfellows of John C. Calhoun and William

Lloyd Garrison were correct, that the Constitution, best analyzed, was designed to protect slavery, which means, among other things, that so-called "slave states" were entitled to expect a good-faith recognition of this fact, however unhappy, and enforcement of the rights held by slave-owners and the states recognizing slavery.

Lincoln himself recognized the validity of the so-called "federal consensus," which held that Congress was without power to affect slavery in any of the states where it already existed. The sticking point was expansion of slavery into the territories owned by the United States that had not yet become states. Did citizen-slaveowners have a right to settle on equal terms with non-slaveowning citizens, which would mean having the right to bring with them into territories their lawful property recognized in, say, Missouri or Tennessee or Texas? Or, as Lincoln argued, did the United States have the right to bar slavery in any of its territories not yet admitted to statehood? *That* was the issue upon which the "house divided" collapsed. This is, of course, also a central topic of the notorious *Dred Scott* case in 1857, where Chief Justice Taney, for the majority, held that the Missouri Compromise of 1820 was unconstitutional because Congress had attempted to bar slavery in most of the territories. As Justice John Catron notably argued, with capital letters, this failed to protect the EQUALITY of all citizens, including slaveowners, to be welcome, with their property, in all federal territories that Congress was holding and regulating in behalf of *all* citizens and not only those whose behavior it might favor.

By now one should not be surprised that Radan finds that the "pro-slavery" description of the Constitution is stronger than the more comforting views of the Constitution we might prefer to endorse (and to teach to the young). One might choke at the paradox of South Carolina accusing Northern states of attempting to "nullify" the Fugitive Slave Act of 1850, passed as part of the Compromise of 1850 and endorsed as legal even if lamentable by Abraham Lincoln, but the Charlestonians had a point. Part of Radan's overall argument is that "nullification" and "secession" are not so completely sectional as many might think. New England Federalists bitterly opposed to Jefferson's and Madison's policies, including the War of 1812, spoke of the possibility of seceding from a Republican-dominated Union. Garrison himself advocated "no Union with slaveholders" and burnt what he considered the pro-slavery Constitution. One can only wonder what "our" reaction might have been to a counterfactual history in which New England is successfully induced by abolitionists to accept Garrison's argument. But, of course, for almost all Americans, secession immediately conjures the Confederate States of America.

The final chapter, therefore, considers whether the would-be C.S.A. could legitimately claim a right to secede from the Union that was, if one accepts Radan's scholarship, founded on the basis of individual decisions by the constituent States to enter the Union on the basis of solemn promises that certain essential interests would be recognized and protected. Radan argues that the answer is yes. As Cynthia Nicoletti argued several years ago in a fine book on whether Jefferson Davis committed treason—he was indicted but never tried, and President Andrew Johnson pardoned Davis on Christmas in 1868—the question is truly complicated, turning on answers to the questions so well laid out by Radan. What is *not* complicated, at least for us, is to denounce him—and Robert E. Lee and all other Confederate leaders—for their commitment to protecting chattel slavery, but it should be obvious that that elides the central *legal* set of questions.

Ironically or not, several modern analysts of the legality of secession, such as Harvard Law School's eminent professor Laurence Tribe, suggest that the question was in effect answered on the grounds of battle. Paul Finkelman, perhaps the leading living legal historian of American slavery, likes to refer to the case of Grant v. Lee, whose verdict was announced at Appomattox Courthouse in April of 1865. Nicoletti, in her book, notes that several writers at the time reverted to the medieval theory of "trial by battle" to determine who was right, acknowledging that the abstract issue was not subject to a clear legal determination. But lawyers must be embarrassed by such a reliance inasmuch as they like to argue that legal argument serves as a substitute for force rather than a handmaiden. "Might makes right" is not a view comfortably accepted in the classroom or, one suspects, around most dinner tables. We are almost desperately eager to believe that legal right accompanied Northern might in overcoming the Confederacy.

My own proclivity, as a long-time legal academic, is to steer away from confident pronouncements as to which, within a set of arguments, is "right" or "wrong." Generally, I try to encourage students to understand why arguments they may well (and rightly) be offended by made "perfectly good sense" within the context of legal possibility as understood at the time. (And, of course, that is true today as well.) To say that we find an argument repellent, because of its consequences, is not evidence for the proposition that denizens of the legal profession (including, say, Joseph Story) might not have what they considered good reasons for coming to the opposite conclusions. In some sense, Radan is more of a lawyer—or, perhaps more accurately, a *judge*—than I am; he wants to resolve legal controversies that I prefer to leave hanging. But for me it is more than enough to say of Radan's book that he establishes beyond reasonable doubt that the arguments for Confederate secession were completely plausible and in no way subject to the dismissal that one sometimes finds even from eminent scholars determined to defend Lincoln. As someone who considers himself knowledgeable about the issues addressed by Radan, I was truly embarrassed at how much I learned from reading the original dissertation and then this polished final book. He has truly mastered all of the relevant primary and secondary literature and integrated them into a stunning and accessible narrative.

As an academic, I have an obligation to teach *both* Lincoln and Davis as offering thoroughly defensible theories of the 1787 Constitution. That being said, I must confess that if forced to "grade" the arguments, then Radan does persuade me that many of the Confederate arguments were, on balance, stronger than those of their adversaries. Once again, this in no way requires that one offer even the slightest trace of sympathy for the underlying causes of secession, the desire to maintain racially based enslavement. The war, and the slaughter of 750,000 persons, was perhaps a form of "humanitarian intervention" both necessary and proper to overcome the reality of chattel slavery. The Thirteenth Amendment formally abolishing slavery never would have been added to the Constitution in 1865 without the war. But no one should any longer believe that Abraham Lincoln had "no choice," in terms of his constitutional duties, when deciding how to respond to South Carolina and other states claiming their sovereign right to withdraw from a Union they no longer trusted (in part because of Lincoln's election itself). We may wish to continue celebrating Lincoln as a "Great Emancipationist," but Radan makes clear that that is altogether different from celebrating him as well as a "Great Constitutionalist."

As noted at the outset, this book is part of a series devoted to "constitutional thinking." Thinking should beget argument, sometimes heated and even acrimonious. I expect that Radan's book will quickly become the subject of deserved scrutiny, and many reviewers, because of its completely uncomfortable conclusions, will try to demonstrate its weaknesses. I believe that there are few, if any, weaknesses in this truly stunning book. But, at the very least, the ball is now in the court of those who wish to reassure us that (1) the Constitution was "ordained" by a singular and unified American people; (2) the document is not fairly interpreted as significantly pro-slavery; and that (3) the "union" created by the Constitution is more akin to a traditional Catholic marriage, with no divorce being possible, whatever betrayals one partner might commit against the other, than to a "Protestant marriage," treated as a contract that allows unilateral divorce under at least some circumstances. I personally doubt that they will be able to overcome Radan's extraordinary scholarship and sheer skill in lawyerly argument, but let the debates begin!

Sanford Levinson
Coeditor, Constitutional Thinking

ACKNOWLEDGMENTS

Although it would never have occurred to me at the time, the roots of this book took hold in the late 1960s when, with three fellow students, the last two of our high school years involved weekly modern history classes studying the origins of the American Civil War. This topic was chosen for us by a wonderful teacher, Mrs. Janet Kingsbury. I was then bitten by the Civil War bug and, with varying degrees of intensity, have been scratching that itch ever since. It certainly prompted my interest in the topic of secession which, in due course, became the primary research focus during my life as an academic.

This book has its more immediate origins in my doctoral dissertation undertaken at the University of Technology Sydney, under the supervision of my colleagues and friends, Professors Brian Opeskin, Shaunnagh Dorsett, and Katherine Biber. I was indeed privileged to have the benefit of their keen and critical eyes as they read through various drafts of the dissertation as well as their guidance, advice, and continued encouragement, not only in completing the doctorate, but also getting a revised version of it published. To both the examiners of my dissertation and the reviewers of the manuscript of this book, I owe heartfelt thanks for their incisive and constructive comments and suggestions that contributed to making this book better than it otherwise would have been. I also owe an enormous debt to my long-time friend and colleague at Macquarie University, Aleksandar Pavković, for the countless hours we spent over the years discussing secession, as well as the time he spent providing valuable feedback on the various drafts of both my dissertation and the manuscript for this book. Finally, I would like to thank Professor Sanford Levinson for, unbeknownst to him, encouraging me to believe, at a time when my belief was wavering, that what has turned out to be this book was worthy of publication.

At the University Press of Kansas, I would like to thank David Congdon, for his help, guidance, and support in transforming a proposed manuscript into a book.

Writing this book would not have been possible without the commitment of various institutions and individuals who have, over the years, put in a massive amount of time and effort in digitising almost any pre–Civil War written materials that any researcher could possibly need to access. Without the availability of materials that digitization enabled, this book could not have been written, at least not by one working from a desk in Sydney, Australia.

However, my greatest debt is to my family. Without their love, encouragement, and, perhaps, most of all, understanding and patience, this book would not have ever seen the light of day. This is particularly so in relation to my wonderful and loving wife, Sybil, who has been a rock in terms of support throughout our more than four decades together. Our three now-adult children, Rade, Andrija, and Aleksandra, grew up in a state of bemused wonderment as they watched an expanding collection of books and materials on pre–Civil War America occupy an increasing number of rooms in our home, as did, more recently, our wonderful daughter-in-law, Ellie. In mid-2021, as the writing of this book was being finalised, Rade and Ellie produced an addition to the family, and it is to my beautiful grand-daughter, Giselle, that this book is dedicated.

Peter Radan
Honorary Professor of Law, Macquarie University
Fellow of the Australian Academy of Law
2 April 2023

GLOSSARY

In this book, except in the case of direct quotations from sources, unless the context clearly indicates otherwise:

"Articles of Confederation" means The Articles of Confederation and Perpetual Union that were agreed to on 15 November 1777 and which came into effect on 1 March 1781

"Civil War" means the armed conflict between the forces of the Union and Confederacy in the years 1861 to 1865

"Confederacy" means the Confederate States of America that was proclaimed on 11 March 1861

"Confederation" means the confederation that came into operation on 1 March 1781 and was governed by the Articles of Confederation

"Confederation Congress" means the Continental Congress that met pursuant to the Article of Confederation

"Congress" means the Congress referred to in the Constitution

"Constitution" means the Constitution of the United States of America that was drafted at the Philadelphia Convention in 1787, ratified on 21 June 1788, and came into practical operation in March 1789

"Philadelphia Convention" means the convention of delegates that met in Philadelphia in 1787 and drafted the Constitution

"Representative" means an elected member of Congress's House of Representatives

"State" means an independent, territorially–based political entity that operates on the international plane

"state" means territorially-based political entity that forms a federal unit within a State and is not an independent actor on the international plane

"Supreme Court" means the United States Supreme Court

"Union" means the United States of America formed pursuant to the Constitution

Note on Quotations

Quotations from primary and secondary sources are reproduced as they appear in the relevant source. No corrections or changes to spelling, punctuation, or grammar have been made. Emphasis in the quotations by way of italics is by the author(s) of the quotation, unless otherwise indicated.

PROLOGUE

In the first sentence of his book *America Aflame*, David Goldfield asks the question: "Can anyone say anything new about the Civil War?"[1] This book seeks to do so by answering in the affirmative what Sanford Levinson suggests was "probably the most fundamental constitutional question of [America's] entire history as a country,"[2] namely, whether or not the eleven Southern slave states that unilaterally seceded from the Union and formed the Confederacy during the great secession winter of 1860–1861 had a constitutional right to do so.

Americans have long regarded that the answer to Levinson's "most fundamental constitutional question" was provided by the Supreme Court's decision in 1869, in *Texas v. White*, where Chief Justice Salmon P. Chase, in delivering the opinion of the court, asserted that the secession of a state from the Union "for any cause, regarded by herself as sufficient" was unconstitutional because "[t]he Constitution, in all its provisions, looks to an indestructible Union, composed of indestructible States" and that, therefore, once a state became part of the Union, "[t]here was no place for reconsideration, or revocation, except through revolution, or through consent of the States."[3] Such is the acceptance of the correctness of Chase's opinion that Cass Sunstein cites *Texas v. White* as authority for the proposition that "no serious scholar or politician now argues that a right of secession exists under American constitutional law."[4] And according to Akhil Reed Amar, those who suggest otherwise are to be dismissed as "constitutional flat-earthers."[5]

If, as the Southern poet and novelist Robert Penn Warren wrote, the Civil War was "for the American imagination, the great single event of our history,"[6] what is surprising is that the issue of the constitutional validity of the Confederate secessions barely features in the vast literature on that "great single event." Perhaps this is why Kermit Roosevelt refers to the issue as "a bit arcane."[7] Given that in antebellum America, as Dumas Malone points out, "there was nothing particularly startling in the idea that the Union was dissoluble,"[8] this is especially remarkable. Secession was, as Niels Eichhorn notes, "a universal experience across the Atlantic World during the middle decades of the nineteenth century . . . [and] Southern secession in 1861 was just the latest manifestation."[9] And, as James Crawford notes, during the nineteenth century, "secession was the most conspicuous and probably the most common method of the creation of new States."[10] Indeed, the examples that he uses to illustrate this point, namely, the States that emerged from the American Revolution, the States created from former Spanish colonies in Central and South America, and the secessions of Greece from the Ottoman Empire and of Belgium from the Netherlands, all occurred before 1860.[11] Thus, it was unsurprising that Alexis de Tocqueville, in his observations on America, concluded that "[i]f one of the states chose to withdraw its name from the [Union], it would be difficult to disprove its right of doing so, and the federal government would have no means of maintaining its claims directly, either by force or by right."[12]

As to why discussion of the constitutionality of the Confederate secessions has been neglected, Mark Brandon suggests three causative factors. One is that secession is viewed as disloyalty to the United States, bordering on treason. Another is that secession led to the most destructive war in the Union's history to that point of time. The final, and arguably the most important, factor is that the Confederate secessions were associated with the evil of slavery.[13] Nevertheless, the lack of detailed studies on the issue of the constitutional legality of the Confederate secessions is surprising, given that, as G. Edward White states:

> It is necessary to recognize that the constitutional argument on behalf of secession was very far from a marginal oddity in early- and mid-nineteenth century jurisprudence. The constitutional logic that led to a "right" in states to secede from the Union was straight-forward enough for mid-nineteenth century jurists. . . . . A "compact" theory of sovereignty . . . was especially self-evident if one believed, as many early nineteenth century Americans did, that the primary loyalty of individual citizens was to their states and localities.[14]

Other legal scholars agree with White. Thus, Daniel Farber concedes that the case mounted by the secessionists "was not a frivolous one."[15] And although Sanford Levinson sees both the arguments for and against the constitutional validity of the Confederate secessions as "a series of question-begging, more-than-a-bit tendentious arguments that ultimately persuade only those who wish to be persuaded in the first place,"[16] he nevertheless concedes that, in the case of President Abraham Lincoln's arguments against secession, they had "more than a trace of 'union mysticism' that led him to underestimate the theoretical force of the Southern argument for voluntary dissolution of the Union"[17] and, furthermore, that "[t]he arguments for secession were not stupid."[18] Indeed, he goes on to state that "we should, if we are honest, recognize profound elements of constitutional merit" in both the arguments for and against the Confederate secessions.[19] However, he goes on to suggest that "[a] decision as to which [argument] should prevail is as much a 'leap of faith' as a submission to the claims of logic or reason."[20]

Given the paucity of any detailed analysis of the arguments concerning the constitutional legality of the Confederate secessions that were articulated during the great secession winter of 1861–1862, this book fills this gap in the scholarly legal literature. Furthermore, its conclusion is that the pro-secessionist argument mounted in 1860–1861 is one that can be sustained, not, as Levinson suggests, based upon a "leap of faith," but rather, as a matter of "logic and reason." In what Linda Colley refers to as "a country which has made a cult of its own written constitutions,"[21] such a conclusion, as Roman Hoyos points out, involves conceding that it "risks rendering the U.S. Constitution a charter of slavery."[22] But, as Paul Finkelman, arguably the leading scholar on the issue of slavery and the Constitution, asserts: "Slavery was a central issue of the American Founding." He goes on to state that, if so, "the stain of racism and the legacy of slavery do not, after all, make pleasant reading."[23] Although Finkelman recognizes that one of the legacies of the constitutional entrenchment of slavery was the Civil War, he vigorously rejects the argument that the secessions of the Confederate states were constitutionally valid.[24] In parting company with Finkelman on this issue, this book makes for further unpleasant reading.

In the debate in the scant literature since the Civil War on the issue of the constitutional validity of the Confederate secessions, arguments that maintain that the Confederate secession were unconstitutional exhibit two broad schools of thought. The first is that they were illegal because, as a matter of fact, they failed. The second is that they were unlawful as a matter of constitutional law.

The first approach is evidenced in George Ticknor Curtis's 1896 history of American constitutional law, where he wrote that the illegality of secession was "determined by a resort to physical force, or by a trial of strength between the states which had seceded and those which still adhered to the Federal Government."[25] Cynthia Nicoletti suggests that "[h]istorians . . . have universally assumed that the war led inexorably to the demise of secession as a constitutional argument."[26] A significant body of scholarly historical literature reflects this "trial by battle" argument. For example, Daniel Wait Howe writes that whether there existed a legal right of secession "was finally settled, not by arguments, but by the Civil War."[27] Legal scholars have also propounded this argument. For example, Laurence Tribe encapsulates this approach when he writes that "none would be so bold as to pretend to 'read' [a right of secession] into our Constitution's written words" and that the prohibition of secession from the Union was "an axiom written in blood rather than ink."[28]

The implication of this approach is that had the Confederacy emerged as the Civil War's victor, the Confederate secessions would have been constitutionally legal, a point made in the Virginia Court of Appeal's decision in 1871 in *Walker v. Christian*, where Judge Richard Moncure said:

> Suppose the decision by this wager of battle had been different from what it was, as it well might have been; how would this case then have stood? Could it then have been said that the Confederate government was not a government?[29]

However, other scholars reject the "trial by battle" argument because, as Nicoletti points out, for them "[t]he Civil War did not definitively resolve the question of secession's constitutionality."[30] What can be said is that the Civil War and the enormous human suffering that it witnessed meant that secession was thereafter dead and buried as a political issue. This is why Brandon states that "[t]he Civil War did decide the secessions of 1861 as a matter of raw force; but it did not—it *could not*—decide secession as a matter of constitutional authority."[31]

The second approach against the legality of the Confederate secessions is based on the Constitution, which, according to Akhil Reed Amar, "emphatically denied state authority to unilaterally secede."[32] In reaching this conclusion, scholars commonly refer to Abraham Lincoln's First Inaugural Address on 4 March 1861[33] and his Message to Congress in Special Session on 4 July 1861[34] as the principal sources for this argument. Amar, who regards Lincoln as "the most significant constitutional interpreter and decision-maker of the past two centuries,"[35] provides a generally supportive analysis of Lincoln's arguments.[36] Although he concedes that "Lincoln got some things right and some things wrong," he nevertheless goes on to say that Lincoln "was right when it counted."[37] And Herman Belz writes that "[t]he brevity of Lincoln's argument detracts nothing from its substance and persuasiveness."[38] Other scholars, generally, and at times uncritically, refer to Lincoln's arguments as support for the proposition that the Confederate secessions were unconstitutional. For example, Laurence Tribe, in addition to his "written in blood" reasoning, states that, on the basis of Lincoln's arguments on the issue, "the Constitution forbids secession from the Union by any state."[39] On the other hand, Peter Lindsay and Christopher Wellman find Lincoln's arguments unsatisfactory, but nevertheless conclude that the Confederate states' argument in favor of unilateral secession "was disqualified by its interest in preserving the institution of slavery."[40]

Lincoln's reasoning was significantly echoed in Chief Justice Chase's opinion in *Texas v. White*. Although Chase was proud of his opinion and regarded it as the most important that he ever wrote,[41] it attracted only scant and superficial analysis in the legal literature at the time.[42] The few scholars who have since analyzed it have broadly supported its reasoning and conclusion. Thus, Harold Hyman concludes that *Texas v. White* "enjoys landmark status in America's constitutional history."[43] For Charles Fairman, Chase's opinion was "justified quite simply" because the Constitution, "framed in high hope, allowed for amendment but not for dissolution."[44] And Herman Belz argues that Chase's opinion constituted an attempt to resolve the issue of secession "in a principled and prudential way."[45] On the other hand, Thomas Cooley,[46] the prominent nineteenth-century constitutional law scholar and later judge, simply accepts that secession was unconstitutional because *Texas v. White* said so. Cooley's approach of eschewing "discussing or even designing to allude to any abstract theories as to the precise position and actual power of the several States"[47] stemmed from his view that discussions on sovereignty, rather than being based upon historical facts, rested upon a "sort of philosophical mysticism, which forms a general theory first and then undertakes the impossible task of making the diverse systems of different nations conform to it."[48] Other scholars have since adopted the same approach as Cooley.[49] The same can be said for scholars who detail the facts of *Texas v. White* and, without comment, outline Chase's reasoning.[50] However, as is detailed in this book, Chase's opinion in *Texas v. White* has not met with universal acclaim. Nevertheless, as Brandon aptly points out, "the Supreme Court's confused benediction [in *Texas v. White*], has made national perpetuity and the illegitimacy of secession appear to be brute constitutional facts." He goes on to posit that the elevated status of the ruling in *Texas v. White* stemmed from "[t]he emphatic character of the military solution, the ascent of the myth that the forces of the Union had fought the Civil War to free the slaves, and the martyrdom of Father Abraham" and thereby "tended to obscure the constitutional weakness of Lincoln's claims."[51]

On the other hand, the few scholars who argue that the Confederate secessions were constitutionally legal, while forcefully arguing that such a right existed, nevertheless overwhelmingly reject that they had anything to do with slavery. Rather, they claim that the secessions were based upon infringements of, and in defense of, the rights of states under the Constitution.[52] Their denial that the preservation and perpetuation of slavery was the impulse for secession is a central element of the apologia developed after the Civil War that is known as "the Lost Cause," which negated the defeat of the Confederacy, extolled its values, and supported the resurrection of the antebellum social contract between former master and former slave in a Jim Crow world.[53]

Arguably the most prominent exponent of the Lost Cause claim is the Confederacy's president, Jefferson Davis, who asserted, as an "intact and incontrovertible truth," that "the existence of African servitude was in no way the cause of the conflict, but only an incident."[54] The argument, as detailed by Davis and replicated in most of the Lost Cause literature, has been critiqued and rejected by scholars such as Thomas Cooley,[55] Daniel Farber,[56] and Stephen Neff.[57]

Although this book argues that the arguments that the unilateral secessions of the Confederate states were better than those against them being constitutionally valid, it should not be taken as in any way endorsing or condoning race-based slavery, an institution that, in the words of Kris Manjapra, "stripped [Africans] of their person and family names, obliterated their kinship ties, and assigned them a market price as atomized pieces of human property."[58] Rather, it documents how what James Madison recognized to be "the most oppressive dominion ever exercised by man over man"[59] led to the secessions of eleven of the Union's slave states during the great secession winter of 1861–1862. As this book details, slavery was of vital importance when what the nineteenth-century English social theorist Harriet Martineau described as "[a] social neighborhood of colonies, all suffering under colonial grievances"[60] proclaimed their independence from their imperial master on 4 July 1776. The culmination of this pivotal event took place at Philadelphia in the summer of 1787 when fifty-five white men, thirty-one of whom were lawyers, drafted a Constitution in which, as Gouverneur Morris said at that time, "domestic slavery is the most prominent feature."[61] As John Quincy Adams wrote in his diary in March 1820, the Constitution "sanctioned a dishonourable compromise with slavery" in which "the bargain between freedom and slavery contained in [it] . . . is morally and politically vicious, [and] inconsistent with the principles upon which alone our Revolution can be justified."[62] And, when speaking of the Constitution's slavery provisions in 1847 in *Jones v. Van Zandt*, Justice Levi Woodbury referred to "the right of property in persons which they recognize."[63] That the Philadelphia Convention produced a Constitution that, as Manisha Sinha writes, "gave slavery ironclad guarantees,"[64] stemmed from the reality that, as William Wiecek, puts it, "in 1787 slavery was wholly compatible with the American constitutional order; indeed, was an essential element of it." Wiecek goes on to state that "America was then a racist, slaveholding society, and its constitutional order conformed to that fundamental characteristic."[65] To similar effect, James Kloppenberg writes that the Convention "naturalized oppression and inequality, fixing in place a regime of white supremacy that encouraged white males to see all nonwhites, including not only slaves but also free blacks and Indians, as their inferiors" and "produced a document that made possible the emergence of . . . a culture of domination, dependency, and inequality."[66] This culture was effectively entrenched because, as Douglas Egerton points out, "the requirement [in Article V of the Constitution] that it take three-quarters of the states to ratify an amendment all but gave the slaveholding states a veto over any future attempts to alter the protections granted in the constitution."[67] When writing to Marquis de Lafayette on the day after the conclusion of the Philadelphia Convention, this reality was arguably on George Washington's mind when, after pondering over whether the Constitution was good or bad, he conceded that "if bad it will recoil on the Framers."[68]

That the Philadelphia Convention produced a Constitution that, according to Noah Feldman, "contained and continued a deep moral wrong"[69] was in spite of the fact that many of its delegates, including the most prominent, knew that slavery was morally indefensible. It was for this reason that, as James Madison observed, the Convention's delegates "had scruples against admitting the terms 'Slaves' into the [Constitution]."[70] However, only a handful of delegates, namely Gouverneur Morris,[71] Rufus King,[72] and Luther Martin,[73] expressed opposition to slavery.[74] This led Martin, when addressing the Maryland legislature in November 1787, to observe that although the American Revolution presented the Convention with the opportunity to draft a constitution "grounded upon the preservation of *those rights* which God and nature had entitled *us*, not in *particular*, but *common* with *all the rest of mankind*," it ended up drafting a constitution that "ought to be considered as a *solemn mockery of*, and *insult to that God* . . . who views with equal eye the poor *African slave* and his *American master.*"[75] It was for this reason that various delegates to the ratification conventions opposed ratification of the Constitution. For example, New Hampshire's Joshua Atherton, when speaking in reference to the Constitution's provision that prevented Congress from banning the importation of slaves prior to 1808, implored his fellow delegates to "not lend the aid of our ratification to this cruel and inhuman merchandise, not for even a day."[76] It was because of such a Constitution that, in 1829, William Lloyd Garrison felt compelled to proclaim: "I am ashamed of my country. I am sick of our unmeaning declamation in praise of liberty and equality, our hypocritical cant about the inalienable rights of man."[77]

Although Convention delegates, as Feldman writes, "felt ashamed of their association with slavery . . . [t]hey just did not feel sufficiently ashamed to do anything about it, at least not while their livelihoods and those of their families depended upon the labor of enslaved persons. They could compromise on slavery in the constitution—because they always compromised on slavery in their own lives."[78] This constituted what the eminent revolutionary-era historian Gordon Wood refers to as "[t]he great aberration amidst all the Revolutionary talk of equality, voting and representation."[79] This dismissal of the principle of equality enshrined in the opening paragraphs of the Declaration of Independence was echoed by pro-secessionists in the great secession winter of 1860–1861, as is evidenced in Texas's Louis Trezevant Wigfall's speech to the Senate on 12 December 1860, with its reference to "the clap-trap of 4th of July froth."[80] Thus, in 1864, the self-educated former slave and prominent abolitionist Frederick Douglass observed that if a constitutional right of unilateral secession did exist, the fact that the antebellum Union stood on an "accursed corner-stone" built with "Fugitive Slave laws, Slavery extension law, and Dred Scott," meant that the stance taken by the Confederate states was "logical and consistent." In this respect he said:

> [The secessionists'] two great all-commanding ideas are, first, that Slavery is right; and second, that the slaveholders are a superior order or class. . . . . Slavery being right, all that is inconsistent with its entire security is necessarily wrong, and of course ought to be put down. There is no flaw in their logic.[81]

That, in these circumstances, the secessions of the great secession winter were, as Douglass put it, "logical and consistent," was the consequence of a history which the historian Imani Perry describes as one in which race was "at the heart of the nation" in which "the creation of racial slavery in the colonies was a gateway to habits and dispositions that ultimately became commonplace ways of doing things."[82] Thus, as Gerald Horne writes, because "slavery [in 1776] was a lineal ancestor of 1861 . . . [d]efenders of the so-called Confederate States of America were far from bonkers when they argued passionately that their revolt was consistent with the animating and driving spirit of 1776."[83] Edward Larson makes the same point when he writes that the Constitution's "[d]ecorous words did not hide nefarious acts or prevent monstrous consequences."[84]

This book does not defend the "habits and dispositions" that shaped a history that led to what Mark Graber has labelled as a "constitutional evil," thereby rendering the Constitution a flawed document because of its rejection of the principle of equality enshrined in the opening paragraphs of the Declaration of Independence.[85] It merely details how and why the "constitutional evil" that those "habits and dispositions" created made the unilateral secessions of the Confederate states "logical and consistent."

In assessing the legacy of the Civil War for African Americans, the American historian David Blight writes that "[i]n our national memory today we much prefer narratives of America as a nation that freed its slaves to the more troubled story of America as the nation that sanctioned one of the largest, most enduring slave societies in modern history." He then goes on to pose the following question:

> Just how do we explain that among all the nations and empires in which slaves were freed by some legal means in the nineteenth century, only in the divided United States did it occur in a bloody, all-encompassing civil war?[86]

This book seeks, in part, to address that question.

Introduction

On 9 April 1865, at Appomattox Court House in Virginia, Ulysses S. Grant, the commanding general of the Union's armed forces, accepted the surrender of the Confederacy's Army of Northern Virginia under the command of General Robert E. Lee. Although Civil War hostilities only came to an end with the surrender of the Confederate ship C.S.S. Shenandoah on 6 November 1865, Lee's surrender at Appomattox effectively marked the end of the Civil War as an armed conflict which, according to recent scholarship, led to the loss of at least 750,000 lives.[1]

However, the Civil War was more than just an armed conflict. As Arthur Bestor points out, the unilateral secessions of the eleven southern slave states that subsequently formed the Confederacy, during what Henry Adams then referred to as "the great secession winter" of 1860–1861,[2] were a "constitutional catastrophe," and the ensuing Civil War was a "constitutional crisis."[3] It raised the constitutional question, as formulated by Representative Lucius Q. C. Lamar—the "soul of secession at [Mississippi's secession] convention"[4]—of whether "the South was right in asserting the . . . authority to secede, or the Republican party was right in denying the right to secede and asserting the power to coerce."[5] This question, as Akhil Reed Amar suggests, "was probably the most serious constitutional question ever to arise in America."[6]

At the Philadelphia Convention that drafted the Constitution in 1787, the issue of secession, as Max Farrand points out, was "not even seriously discussed" because "[i]t would have been inexpedient to have forced this issue in 1787, when the fate of any sort of central government was doubtful."[7] Farrand also notes that "there is certainly no record of [it] being mentioned" at the Convention.[8] Thus, and unsurprisingly, the Constitution contained no provision dealing with secession. This silence meant that, in the decades preceding the Civil War, secession was, as Mark Brandon points out, "a recurrent theme of constitutional arguments."[9] These arguments revealed that, as Andrew Delbano observes, "[n]ot only was secession conceivable . . . it was by no means clear that the Constitution did not permit it."[10]

In what is, in this book, referred to as "the nationalist theory" of the Constitution, the unilateral secession of a state was constitutionally impossible. This theory rested principally on the notion that the Constitution was, as stated in its Preamble, ordained and established by the "People of the United States," considered as a single American people. This meant that the secession of a state could only be sanctioned by the "People of the United States" and not by the people or legislature of that state. On the basis of this theory, the unilateral secessions of the Confederate states were unconstitutional. The main expositor of the nationalist theory during the great secession winter was President Abraham Lincoln.

The counterargument to the nationalist theory of the Constitution is, in this book, referred to as "the compact theory" of the Constitution. This theory was anchored in the notion that the Constitution was ratified by the separate peoples of the Confederation's States that formed the Union, with the consequence that the Constitution was a compact or contract between those States. Furthermore, if a state or states committed certain breaches of the constitutional compact, affected states could terminate the compact by unilaterally seceding from the Union. On the basis of this theory, secessionists alleged that breaches relating to constitutional obligations concerning race-based slavery were such breaches and had been committed by some non-slave states and the federal government, thereby entitling the Confederate states to unilaterally secede from the Union. At that time, the arguments propounding the constitutional validity of these secessions were principally articulated in various formal declarations and statements issued by these states.

Of these competing theories and their implications for the legality of the unilateral secessions of the Confederate states, Kenneth Stampp writes that it was "uncertain whether in 1865 reason and logic were . . . indisputably on either side."[11] Two matters arising in the immediate wake of the Civil War amply illustrate this uncertainty.

The first was the implicit requirement placed upon all eleven defeated Confederate states except Tennessee[12] to formally renounce secession as a condition of readmission to the Union. This requirement stemmed from Section 5 of the First Reconstruction Act of 1867, which mandated that the "rebel States" organize conventions to adopt, for approval by Congress, constitutions that were in "conformity with the Constitution of the United States in all respects."[13] To meet this requirement, all ten "rebel States" adopted constitutions which expressly prohibited secession.[14] Given that there was no explicit prohibition in the Constitution against the unilateral secession of a state from the Union, even if one believed that such a secession was unconstitutional, it may have been prudent to have the Confederate states explicitly include such provisions in their state constitutions. Nevertheless, these state constitutional provisions, at the very least, suggest that the Confederate states may have had a constitutional right to unilaterally secede from the Union.[15]

The second matter confirming the uncertainty surrounding the legality of unilateral secession stemmed from the capture and arrest, on 10 May 1865, of Jefferson Davis, the president of the defeated Confederacy. Davis was indicted to stand trial charged with various "traitorous compassings, imaginations, and intentions."[16] Counsel for both the prosecutor and Davis recognized that, if the secessions of the Confederate states were constitutionally legal, Davis was not guilty of committing treason against the United States. As the then chief justice of the Supreme Court, Salmon P. Chase, wrote in a private communication in 1867: "If the rebels levying war against the Government [of the United States] were not traitors, secession was a valid act, and our war was one of conquest."[17] Davis was confident that he would be vindicated and wanted the trial to go ahead.[18] His prosecutors, fearing that Davis's confidence was not misplaced and that he would be acquitted on the ground that the Confederate states had legally seceded from the Union, led President Andrew Johnson to issue a proclamation on Christmas Day 1868 that granted Davis a "full pardon and amnesty for the offence of treason against the United States."[19] The pardon and ensuing formal withdrawal of proceedings against Davis, on 11 February 1869,[20] meant that the issue of the legality of the secessions of the Confederate states was not litigated.

However, on 12 April 1869, a mere two months after the Davis trial was formally aborted, the uncertainty that Stampp refers to was seemingly resolved by the Supreme Court in *Texas v. White*. In delivering the opinion of the Court, Chief Justice Chase decreed that the *unilateral* secession of a state "for any cause, regarded by herself as sufficient," was unconstitutional because "[t]he Constitution, in all its provisions, looks to an indestructible Union, composed of indestructible States," and therefore, once a state became part of the Union, "[t]here was no place for reconsideration, or revocation, except through revolution, or through consent of the States."[21]

This book's argument is that, on the basis of American constitutional law as it stood at the time, the claim that the Confederate states had a constitutional right to unilaterally secede from the Union is to be preferred to the claim that they did not have such a right. If so, then, by extension, *Texas v. White* was wrongly decided. In so arguing, this book goes beyond merely addressing a question of constitutional legal history. It is also of continuing practical relevance, because federal authorities and state courts have consistently relied upon the decision in *Texas v. White* to deny any current right of secession from the Union. For example, in the immediate wake of President Barack Obama's reelection as president in 2012, petitions from groups within fifty states were received on the federal government's petitions website seeking permission for their state to secede from the United States. The White House's response to all of them was that, on the basis of the decision in *Texas v. White*, the United States was perpetual and secession from it was impossible.[22] Furthermore, in 2010, the Supreme Court of Alaska, in *Kohlhaas v. State of Alaska*, ruled against the holding of a referendum on the secession of Alaska from the Union because "while a state's ability to secede was an unsettled question before the end of the Civil War," *Texas v. White* "concluded that secession is clearly unconstitutional."[23]

The basis upon which the Confederate states argued that they had a constitutional right to unilaterally secede from the Union was articulated by South Carolina as early as April 1852, when a convention of delegates from the Palmetto State resolved that South Carolina had the right to do so because of breaches of constitutional obligations concerning race-based slavery. The resolution read as follows:

> *Resolved by the people of South Carolina in Convention assembled*, That the frequent violations of the Constitution of the United States by the Federal Government, and its encroachments upon the reserved rights of the sovereign States of this Union, especially in relation to slavery, amply justify this State, so far as any duty or obligation to her confederates is involved, in dissolving at once all political connection with her co-States.[24]

This statement raises three critical questions that are central to the issue of whether, from the perspective of the Union's constitutional law at the time of the great secession winter, the unilateral secessions of the Confederate states were lawful. The first, and pivotal, question relates to whether, in the absence of any express provision related to secession, the Constitution nevertheless allowed a state, in particular circumstances, to unilaterally secede from the Union. This question requires a resolution of the merits of the competing nationalist and compact theories of the Constitution.

The second question relates to race-based provisions concerning slavery in the Constitution that Mark Graber describes as "a constitutional text. . . . saturated with concessions to evil."[25] The four major provisions in the Constitution that, either expressly or impliedly, dealt with slavery were the three-fifths clause (Article I, Section 2, Clause 3), the slave importation clause (Article I, Section 9, Clause 1), the fugitive slave clause (Article IV, Section 2, Clause 3), and the new states and territories clauses (Article IV, Section 3). For unilateral secession to be constitutionally upheld pursuant to the compact theory of the Constitution, these obligations had to be essential or fundamental in the sense that a constitution without them would not have been ratified by all the States that ratified it and became state members of the Union that, as the Constitution's Preamble states, was formed by the ratification of the Constitution. The third, and final, question relates to whether any of these four constitutional obligations concerning race-based slavery were breached and thereby gave an affected state the right to unilaterally secede from the Union.

This book, thus, deals with two important, but separate, constitutional issues. The first is whether, in 1860–1861, a state had, in particular circumstances, a constitutional right to unilaterally secede from the Union, an issue that was heatedly debated in the antebellum period. The second is the significance of the Constitution's provisions on race-based slavery, also heatedly debated in the antebellum period. As to this issue it can, at this stage, be noted that the nationalist lawyer and political essayist from Philadelphia, Sidney George Fisher, correctly observed in 1862 that slavery did "deface the fair Constitution" and had the effect that "slavery . . . was protected . . . forever."[26] Akhil Reed Amar recognizes this when he writes that "[s]lavery was the original sin of the New World Garden, and the Constitution did more to feed the serpent than to crush it."[27] And, as Paul Starr explains, during the antebellum era slavery was "entrenched through the political power of the South, constitutional law, and the staggering costs of emancipation, as those costs appeared at the time."[28] Slavery was, as James Buchanan put it in 1836, "the weak point in [the Union's] institutions."[29] Its presence in the Constitution was, therefore, what Mark Graber refers to as a "constitutional evil" which rendered it a flawed document because of its rejection of the principle of equality enshrined in the opening paragraphs of the Declaration of Independence.[30] The role of the Supreme Court in entrenching slavery, in what George van Cleve aptly refers to as "a slaveholders' union,"[31] stemmed from its approach to interpreting the Constitution. This approach was made clear in its decision in 1825 in *The Antelope*, in which Chief Justice John Marshall, although denouncing the morality of slavery, drew a distinction between morality and law when he said: "This court must not yield to feelings which might seduce it from the path of duty, and must obey the mandate of the law."[32] The constitutional entrenchment of slavery also allowed Marshall, in his personal life, to buy and sell slaves. As Paul Finkelman points out, Marshall "actively participated in the business of human bondage . . . accumulating more than one hundred and fifty [slaves] by 1830." Furthermore, when Marshall died, "he did not free the dozen or so personal slaves who had loyally served him for so long, much less any of those toiling on his plantations."[33]

What joined the constitutional issues of secession and slavery was the unilateral secessions of the Confederate states during the great secession winter of 1860–1861. The essence of their claim to have legally seceded from the Union was clearly articulated by Jefferson Davis, in February 1862, in his Inaugural Address as president of the Confederacy. Davis stated that, in the face of breaches of the entrenched constitutional obligations concerning race-based slavery, "[t]he experiment instituted by [the Union's] revolutionary fathers, of a voluntary Union of sovereign states for purposes specified in a solemn compact, had been perverted" and that the Union "had ceased to answer the ends for which it was ordained and established." In such circumstances, Davis went on to say, the only option for the slave states was "to preserve in spirit, as well as in form, a system of government [they] believed to be peculiarly fitted to [their] condition."[34] In effect, he claimed that, if the Constitution formed, as its Preamble asserted, a "more perfect Union" as compared to the union of the Articles of Confederation, and its slavery provisions made it a slaveholders' union, the Confederate states sought to create a more perfect slaveholders' union, as compared to the Union formed by the Constitution. This the secessionist states of the great secession winter sought to do by unilaterally declaring their independence and coming together to form the Confederacy so that they could, just like Chief Justice Marshall before them, continue to participate, unhindered, in the business of human bondage.[35]

Secession as a Revolutionary Act

Although the focus of this book is on whether the unilateral secessions of the Confederate states were constitutionally valid, a brief discussion is warranted of an alternative basis of secession, namely, secession as a revolutionary right. Such a right, based upon the text and spirit of the Declaration of Independence of 1776, was at times raised by some pro-secessionists in addition to legal arguments justifying secession.[36] In doing so, as William Freehling observes, they made "a shrewd polemical decision," given that "[t]he narrowly constitutional and suffocating legalist justification was drier than dust," in contrast to "the natural and nonconstitutional right of revolution argument [that] provoked a seductive call for freedom."[37] However, in the secession ordinances and formal justifications for secession, secession was overwhelmingly justified on constitutional, rather than revolutionary, grounds.[38]

Whether the secession of the Confederate states was justified on revolutionary grounds was contested by opponents of secession, such as Abraham Lincoln. He did not deny the existence of a revolutionary right of secession. In his First Inaugural Address, he reaffirmed his long-held view of a revolutionary right to secession,[39] when he said that if a majority deprived a minority of a "vital" and "clearly written constitutional right," this would, from "a moral point of view, justify revolution."[40] Lincoln argued that the seven slave states that had, to that point, seceded, had not suffered the deprivation of any vital constitutional right,[41] and therefore that their secessions were not justified revolutionary acts because they were not in pursuit of "a morally justifiable cause," but rather "a wicked exercise of physical power" which would, if not thwarted, "put an end to free government upon the earth."[42]

Although Lincoln regarded slavery as "a moral, social and political wrong" and an "unqualified evil to the negro,"[43] he did not base his argument against the revolutionary right of secession on this ground.[44] Nor could he do so, given that he proposed[45] and, in his First Inaugural Address,[46] supported, albeit reluctantly,[47] the so-called Corwin Amendment that, if ratified, would have amended the Constitution so as to preclude Congress from abolishing a state's "domestic institutions . . . including that of persons held to labor or service by the laws" of that state.[48] On the other hand, as already noted, there were some pro-secessionists who argued that the slave states had a revolutionary right to unilaterally secede from the Union. Most relevantly, the Tennessee General Assembly, in its "Address to the People of Tennessee," anchored Tennessee's right to secede on "the right of a people to *revolutionize*" that would "sever the ties that bind Tennessee to her enemies and oppressors."[49]

Since the Civil War, scholars have argued that the Confederate states' secessions could not be justified on revolutionary grounds because of their association with the immoral institution of slavery. For example, Sanford Levinson argues that "[t]he failure of the white South to recognize the claim to equality and self-determination of black slaves . . . invalidates the appeal to the principles of the Declaration of Independence that might, in another context, have justified secession and against Union efforts to prevent it."[50]

The problem with this view is that in 1861, few Americans viewed the immorality of slavery as a reason for its abolition. Abolitionists who opposed slavery on moral grounds constituted only a small, but vocal, minority of the population, of whom Harriet Martineau, the English social theorist, observed during her sojourn in the United States in the mid-1830s that "[a]ll who are not with [them] are against them."[51] Anti-slavery sentiment in non-slave states existed and was articulated by the Republican Party, not in relation to ending slavery, but merely to opposing its spread into the Union's territories. As Daniel Crofts points out: "Racial justice and emancipation were not part of the mainstream agenda—or Lincoln's agenda—even though he and his fellow Republicans disliked slavery and hoped it would eventually disappear."[52] Indicative of this approach to slavery was the proposed Corwin Amendment, which, if ratified, would have prevented Congress from enacting legislation to abolish slavery in the states where it existed. The proposed amendment was approved on the eve of Lincoln's inauguration as president by the two-thirds majorities of both houses of Congress[53] as required by Article V of the Constitution and then ratified by Kentucky, Ohio, Rhode Island, Maryland, Illinois, and the legislature of the emerging state of West Virginia.[54] Had the Civil War not intervened, it would likely have become the thirteenth amendment to the Constitution.[55]

Finally, whether or not a moral justification for secession based upon the revolutionary right of secession existed at that time was irrelevant simply because it, like any revolutionary act, would either succeed or fail as a matter of fact. This was implicitly recognized by Justice Samuel Chase in 1798 when, in *Calder v. Bull*, he said: "I admit, an act *unlawful* in the beginning may, in some cases, become lawful *by matter of after fact*."[56] And in 1877, in the context of discussing the validity of acts "where a portion of the inhabitants of a country have separated themselves from the parent State and established an independent government," Justice Stephen Field, speaking for a unanimous Supreme Court in *Williams v. Bruffy*, said:

> The validity of its acts, both against the parent State and its citizens or subjects, depends entirely upon its ultimate success. If it fail to establish itself permanently, all such acts perish with it. If it succeed, and become recognized, its acts from the commencement of its existence are upheld as those of an independent nation.[57]

That both sides of the Civil War recognized the essential truth of Field's statement is reflected in the priority they gave to diplomatic efforts on the issue of international recognition of the Confederacy. For the Confederacy, recognition by Great Britain in particular may well have led to France and other States following suit and would have been a major boost in the Confederacy's effort to establish itself on a permanent basis. For the Union, Lincoln was prepared to risk war with Great Britain, if necessary, in order to prevent it recognizing the Confederacy.[58]

The Structure of This Book

In detailing this book's central argument, Chapter 1 will outline the historical context in which the issue of unilateral secession from the Union arose. This chapter focuses on the related issues of slavery and the Union's territorial expansion during the antebellum period. Charting this history is necessary in order to understand the emergence and application of the legal rules and principles that are discussed in the ensuing three chapters and which relate to the issue of whether or not the Confederate states had, and, if so, had validly exercised, a constitutional right to unilaterally secede from the Union.

Chapter 2 evaluates whether, in particular circumstances, a state had a constitutional right to unilaterally secede from the Union. This entails an evaluation of the merits of the competing nationalist and compact theories of the Constitution and argues that the latter theory is to be preferred. Although an argument can be mounted that, pursuant to the compact theory, a state could unilaterally secede from the Union simply because it chose to do so, the argument is not evaluated because it was not raised by the Confederate states as a basis upon which they claimed to have exercised a constitutional right to unilaterally secede from the Union.

Chapter 3, building upon the conclusion reached in Chapter 2, details and evaluates how race-based slavery featured in the Constitution and argues that its provisions relating to the federal government's powers concerning the Union's territories and the admission of new states into the Union and fugitive slaves gave rise to obligations that were essential or fundamental in the sense that the Constitution would not have been ratified without these provisions.

Chapter 4, building upon the conclusions reached in Chapters 2 and 3, argues that breaches of the Constitution's provisions relating to new states and territories and fugitive slaves occurred and that, therefore, pursuant to the compact theory of the Constitution, the Confederate states were entitled to exercise their constitutional right to unilaterally secede from the Union.

Given that the Constitution contained no express provision concerning secession from the Union, the questions raised in Chapters 2, 3, and 4 required a careful interpretation of a number of its provisions. In undertaking this task, the approach taken was that expounded by arguably the three most influential judges of the antebellum period, namely Chief Justices John Marshall and Roger Taney and Justice Joseph Story. Marshall articulated the approach in 1824, in *Gibbons v. Ogden*, when, in relation to the wording of the Constitution, he said that its framers "must be understood to have employed words in their natural sense, and to have intended what they have said."[59] Similarly, in 1842, in *Prigg v. Pennsylvania*, in ruling that the Fugitive Slave Act of 1793 was a constitutionally valid exercise by Congress of its plenary power to enforce the Constitution's fugitive slave clause, Story asserted that this reflected the meaning of the Constitution as understood and accepted by "those who were its immediate framers, or intimately connected with its adoption."[60] And, finally, in 1857, in *Dred Scott v. Sandford*, in ruling that African Americans were not entitled to the Declaration of Independence's "unalienable rights," Taney said that this was on the basis of "the language as understood in that day" and that the Declaration's framers "perfectly understood the meaning of . . . and how it would be understood by others."[61] And, in relation to the Constitution, he observed that it was to be interpreted "according to its true intent and meaning when it was adopted."[62]

However, given the occasional absence or abstruseness of words in the Constitution that touch upon some issues analyzed in this book, this approach to constitutional interpretation is not without its difficulties. That this would be so was recognized from the outset. In his letter of 17 September 1787, forwarding the proposed Constitution to the Confederation Congress, George Washington noted that it was one in which it was "difficult to draw with precision the line between those rights which must be surrendered, and those which must be reserved" and that interpretation of the Constitution will "depend as well on situation and circumstance, as on the object to be obtained."[63] At the Pennsylvania ratification convention, James Wilson recognized that the Constitution contained some "inaccuracy of language" and was not "drawn with mathematical precision."[64] James Madison referred to the Constitution's "imperfection of language"[65] which meant that it was "always liable . . . to discordant interpretations."[66] Chief Justice Marshall made a similar point in 1819, in *McCulloch v. Maryland*, when, in the context of the Constitution, he said that "[s]uch is the character of human language, that no word conveys to the mind, in all situations, one single definite idea."[67] And in 1816, in *Martin v. Hunter's Lessee*, Justice Story observed that the Constitution's "language is essentially defective in precision."[68]

In construing the Constitution where there is, as Madison put it, an "imperfection of language," clarification can be sought in other documents, such as the Declaration of Independence, the Articles of Confederation, the records of the Philadelphia Convention, the Constitution's ratification debates, decisions of the courts, the speeches and writings of persons who played a part in the creation of these documents, and various other writings of the time.

As important and helpful as these materials are, their use must be conditioned upon an understanding of their purpose and the circumstances that gave rise to them. For example, in relation to the eighty-five articles known as *The Federalist*, it is important to know that, although fifty-one were written by Alexander Hamilton, twenty-nine by James Madison, and five by John Jay, they were published anonymously under the pseudonym of "Publius" and that they were, as Richard Beeman points out, "first and foremost, political propaganda aimed at persuading undecided voters and convention delegates to support the Constitution."[69] Because of this, Madison cautioned against their uncritical use in interpreting the Constitution.[70]

The book's final chapter explains why, on the basis of the argument that the Confederate states' claim to a constitutional right to unilateral secession from the Union, anchored upon the compact theory of the Constitution, was superior to the competing nationalist theory argument against such a right, the Supreme Court's decision in *Texas v. White* was wrongly decided and, therefore, cannot be the basis for asserting that unilateral secession from the United States today is unconstitutional. Thus, support for such an assertion must be located elsewhere in the Constitution. Possible sources of support, grounded in the Constitution's Fourteenth Amendment, are briefly discussed. Finally, given that *Texas v. White* recognized that secession by agreement can occur, ways by which that may possibly be accomplished are also briefly detailed.

1

"An Irrepressible Conflict"
Slavery and the Union's Territorial Expansion

This chapter outlines the necessary historical context to the critical legal issues to be analyzed in the ensuing three chapters on the issue of whether or not the Confederate states had a constitutional right to unilaterally secede from the Union. The historical background to these legal issues concerns the related matters of slavery and the Union's territorial expansion during the antebellum era. For this reason, this chapter's contextual material will focus on these matters.

At the time that South Carolina declared its independence from the Union in December 1860, the Union consisted of thirty-three states and a significant expanse of territories. The Union had its genesis in the American Revolution, during which thirteen colonies on the eastern seaboard of North America, all of which at that time sanctioned slavery, declared their independence from the British Empire. This collective act of secession, which the influential revolutionary writer and activist Thomas Paine[1] viewed as "in great measure the cause of all mankind,"[2] was proclaimed in the Declaration of Independence on 4 July 1776, in which the colonies announced that they were thereafter "Free and Independent States."[3] In 1783, by the terms of Article I of the Treaty of Paris which ended the war between the British and their colonies, Great Britain formally recognized each of the colonies as "free sovereign and independent States."[4] In the meantime, pursuant to the Articles of Confederation and Perpetual Union which came into force on 1 March 1781, these thirteen States entered into a loose alliance known as "The United States of America," which, in Article II, stipulated that each State retained its "sovereignty, freedom and independence."[5]

The Confederation created by the Articles of Confederation proved to be inadequate and in need of reform. According to James Madison, reform and the creation of the Union was a

> necessity . . . as our bulwark against foreign danger, as the conservator of peace among ourselves, as the guardian of our commerce and other common interests, as the only substitute for those military establishments which have subverted the liberties of the Old World, and as the proper antidote for the diseases of faction, which have proved fatal to other popular governments, and of which alarming symptoms have been betrayed by our own.[6]

Gordon Wood suggests that another contributing factor to this reform was the "excessive democracy" of the States of the Confederation, whose legislatures had, according to New York's Robert R. Livingston, become full of men "unimproved by education and unreformed by honor."[7] In July 1787, this led Henry Knox, the Confederation's secretary of war, to assert that the "vile State governments" would "contaminate the American name" and to argue that it was time to "smite them in the name of God and the people."[8] Thus, the Confederation did not live up to its self-proclaimed perpetuity and was replaced by a new political entity, also known as "The United States of America," which came into operation in March 1789[9] pursuant to the Constitution, which had been drafted in 1787 by delegates from twelve of the Confederation's member States and, by then, ratified by eleven of them. Although by then, slavery had been either abolished or was on the path towards abolition in most of the northern States, it remained legal and of utmost importance to the economic prosperity of other States and their white populations, especially for those in the South. The trebling of the number of states in the Union by 1860 and, in particular, whether many of the new states would be slave states, were critical factors that ultimately led to secessionist disunion in the wake of the election to the presidency of the Union, in November 1860, of the Republican Party's standard bearer, Abraham Lincoln.

The first part of this chapter outlines the place of slavery in Great Britain's colonies in North America from the start of the American Revolution to when the Constitution came into operation in March 1789. This forms the necessary background to the place of slavery in the Constitution. The second part, covering the period from 1789 to Lincoln's electoral triumph, focuses on slavery's growth within the Union and the economic issues that this gave rise to. The chapter's third part, covering the same period, focuses on the emergence and growth of secessionist sentiment occasioned by the Union's territorial expansion west across the North American continent to the Pacific Ocean. The second and third parts of this chapter provide the context in which constitutional obligations associated with the expansion of slavery into the territories and fugitive slaves were allegedly breached and, according to the Confederate states, legally sanctioned their unilateral secessions from the Union.

Slavery from Colonial Times to March 1789

The arrival of a shipment of approximately twenty Africans at Jamestown, Virginia, in August 1619[10] represented the first instance of what, two centuries later, James Madison referred to as "the dreadful fruitfulness of the original sin of the African [slave] trade."[11] Whether, at this time, the Africans became slaves or indentured servants is not altogether clear. However, by the mid-seventeenth century, imported Africans were held in slave bondage.[12] A critical factor in this transformation was the increase in their longevity, which reversed the earlier preference for indentured servants over slaves that flowed from the simple proposition that "there could be no great advantage in owning a man for a lifetime rather than for a period of years, especially since a slave cost roughly twice as much as an indentured servant."[13]

By 1770, slaves constituted approximately 30 percent of all private wealth in the southern colonies and were therefore a crucial component of their economies. Georgia, Virginia, North and South Carolina, and Maryland accounted for the great bulk of slaves, constituting 41 percent of their total population.[14] These five southern colonies also accounted for over 50 percent of the total population and total wealth of all the American colonies, giving them significant political and economic advantages over the remaining eight northern colonies.[15] These advantages stemmed from having a climate that was conducive to growing crops such as tobacco, for which the use of slave labor, rather than free labor or indentured servants, enabled the maximization of profits. This is not to deny the importance of slavery for the economies of the northern colonies, where, as Gavin Wright writes, it "was central to [their] economies . . . not mainly through the direct presence of slave labor, but indirectly, through sales to markets that originated with slave-based production . . . [where] [a]s late as 1768–1772, the British West Indies were the largest single market for northern-colony exports, accounting for more than half the overall total and dominating sales of such items as wood products, fish, and meat."[16]

Although the American colonies were the final destination for only 5.6 percent of the estimated 11.5 million slaves that arrived into the New World during the colonial era, Rhode Island shippers controlled about two-thirds of that number.[17] This was so despite the fact that Rhode Island passed laws in 1652 and 1659 that, respectively, declared slavery to be illegal and banned the slave trade. The trade in slaves continued unhampered because these laws were not enforced.[18] In summing up the significance of slavery for colonial Rhode Island, Christy Clark-Pujara writes that "the business of slavery undergirded the entire economy: it was not just central to the economy, it *was* the economy."[19] New York was another important and profitable point through which African slaves were processed.[20] There was nothing "peculiar" about this at that time, given that "[s]lave-trading carried no social stigma because slavery was widely accepted and because the leading slave-traders in America were men of high social and political stature."[21]

In the American colonies, slavery differed significantly from the slavery that had previously existed for thousands of years in many cultures.[22] Although race had, to some degree, always been a factor in slavery, historically slaves were nevertheless able to participate in many aspects of the social life of the society in which they found themselves. However, this was not so in the United States, especially in the southern slave colonies (later states), where the racial distinction between slaveholders (white) and slaves (black) was clear and where the latter suffered an unprecedented level of social isolation and contempt from the former. As James Rawley and Stephen Behrendt point out, "[r]acial bias was the main reason why black Africans remained in perpetual servitude. British Americans inherited deeply rooted notions that blackness of skin color connoted filthiness, sin, baseness, ugliness, evil, and the devil. Blacks were heathens, lechers, and barbarians."[23]

That slavery was race-based in the American colonies is most clearly evidenced in the view of slaves sketched by Thomas Jefferson. During his lifetime, Jefferson harbored differing views on what he professed were the evils of slavery. In 1784, he came close to having the

Continental Congress adopt a proposal directed towards the eventual abolition of slavery. Jefferson's proposal was that, as of 1800, slavery was to be banned in the then Confederation's territories. However, with the Union's territorial expansion during his presidency, as an adherent of the so-called diffusion theory,[24] Jefferson believed the best way to eliminate slavery was to permit its spread into all of the Union's territories,[25] on the basis that, through diffusion, the slaves' "happiness would be increased, & the burthen of their future liberation lightened by bringing a greater number of shoulders under it."[26] Although he professed slavery to be evil, Jefferson was, as Dennis Rasmussen points out, "a major slaveholder who bought, sold, bred, punished, hunted down, and (in at least one case) slept with his chattel," who, despite his protestations of the evils of slavery, was "profoundly racist, even when judged by the standards of his time."[27] This racism was vividly displayed in his influential *Notes on the State of Virginia*, first published in 1785, which, as Robert Pierce Forbes points out, "contains Jefferson's most passionate indictments of slavery and his most blatant expressions of racism."[28] After referring to the "numberless afflictions" of African American slaves such as their "colour," "strong and disagreeable odor," "want of forethought," and tendency "to participate more in sensation than reflection," Jefferson went on to write:

> Comparing them by their faculties of memory, reason, and imagination, it appears to me that in memory they are equal to the whites; in reason much inferior . . . and . . . in imagination they are dull, tasteless, and anomalous. . . . . [I know of no instance] that a black had uttered a thought above the level of plain narration. . . . . [H]is imagination is wild and extravagant, escapes incessantly from every restraint of reason and taste, and, in the course of its vagaries, leaves a tract of thought as incoherent and eccentric, as is the course of a meteor through the sky.[29]

Jefferson's influential musings about African Americans "provided an authoritative framework and conceptual language for marking racial difference, which would justify the evils he thought unfortunate and hoped were remediable."[30] Thus, Jefferson's fellow slaveholder, Virginian, and chief justice of the Supreme Court, John Marshall, in writing to the Virginia legislature in 1831 in relation to "the miseries of the condition, and the vices of the life of the free person of colour," wrote the following:

> The *one* is an anomaly of wretchedness; the *other* a vegetation of sloth, or

> an activity of mischief and roguery. In Richmond . . . it would be hazarding little to say, that half the criminals tried in the City for the offence of Larceny, are free persons of colour. Their idleness is proverbial. . . . . Their rate of increase far exceeds even that of the slaves, and in a higher degree than of the whites; and whatever energy can be spared from annoying both classes, appears to be expended in multiplying their own number. If it be fixed as destiny, that the slave on the day of his subjection loses half his worth, it seems equally certain that the free negro on the day of his emancipation, loses all. . . . . Recent occurrences present him also, in a new and formidable light. Although deplorably ignorant himself, yet less so than the slave, he exercises great influence over his enslaved brother.[31]

With these words, both Jefferson and Marshall would have found themselves in agreement with their fellow slaveholder from South Carolina, Senator John C. Calhoun when, in his *Disquisition on Government*, he wrote that the Declaration of Independence's assertion that "all Men are created equal" was "unfounded and false" and "destitute of all sound reason."[32]

A significant event that impacted slavery in the American colonies was Lord Mansfield's decision, in 1772, in the English case of *Somerset v. Stewart*.[33] In this case, James Somerset was a slave owned by Charles Stewart, formerly of Virginia. In November 1769, Somerset and his master arrived in England. After briefly escaping in early October 1771, Somerset was recaptured and, in late November 1771, delivered to John Knowles, the captain of the ship *Ann and Mary*, to be transported to Jamaica to be sold on behalf of Stewart.[34] Somerset then sought a writ of habeas corpus which, if granted, would prevent him being removed from England against his will. In this process he was aided by Granville Sharp, a British abolitionist who, in 1769, had presciently argued that any slave brought to Great Britain should be confiscated like contraband goods and set free.[35] Although Lord Mansfield ruled in favor of Somerset,[36] his decision did not challenge the legitimacy of the international slave trade, nor did it abolish slavery in the British Empire, where it continued until 1833.[37] However, as William Wiecek points out, "Many contemporaries . . . thought *Somerset* abolished slavery in England; a few thought it challenged slavery in the colonies as well."[38] These fears stemmed from Mansfield's description of slavery as being "so odious, that nothing can be suffered to support it, but positive law."[39] This statement accepted freedom as the natural condition of humans and reversed the previous understanding of a natural or common law right to property in man in the form of slavery. The only way in which slavery could be supported, as the Maryland Court of Appeals conceded in *Mahoney v. Ashton* in 1799, was by positive law. The court went on to note that "[b]y a positive law of this State in 1715, then the Province of Maryland, the relation of master and slave is recognized."[40] What is clear, as Wiecek points out, is that *Somerset v. Stewart* did not abolish slavery in the colonies, notwithstanding the belief of some, and the fear of others, that it did.[41]

Aziz Rana argues that, for pro-slavery American colonists, *Somerset v. Stewart* had three consequences.[42] First, in casting a cloud over the legitimacy of slavery, it was viewed as a threat to the social supremacy of the colonies' white populations. Second, it threatened the economic well-being of slaveholders. Third, and more worryingly for them, it raised anxieties about possible slave revolts,[43] such as the one that threatened to take place, in 1774, in Virginia, a colony in which slaves constituted approximately 42 percent of its population.[44] Virginian slaveholders were deeply concerned by this possible revolt, fearing that it could inspire other such revolts elsewhere. Indeed, one of them, James Madison, counselled that knowledge of the attempted revolt not be circulated, arguing that "[i]t is prudent that such attempts should be concealed as well as suppressed."[45] In short, the self-interest of colonial elites meant that *Somerset v. Stewart* was, as Gerald Horne concludes, the catalyst of a policy of defending slavery.[46]

SLAVERY AND THE DECLARATION OF INDEPENDENCE

It was in this context that the Continental Congress adopted the Declaration of Independence on 4 July 1776. Of its fifty-six signatories, two-thirds (38) were slaveholders,[47] including its principal author, Thomas Jefferson.[48] Thus, in stark contrast to the Declaration of the Rights of Man and the Citizen that was approved by the National Assembly of France on 26 August 1789 and which, in its first Article, declared that "[m]en are born and remain free,"[49] the Declaration, in its second paragraph, merely declared that "all Men are created equal." In what was, for Jefferson's contemporaries, its most important part,[50] the Declaration then went on to list the grievances against King George III that justified the claim for independence. The list was deliberately ordered to start with the less significant grievances for which George III was indicted with relatively mild verbs such as "obstructed," refused," and "affected." The latter grievances were the more significant and saw the use of more evocative verbs such as "plundered," "ravaged," and "destroyed."[51] It was no coincidence that this order of grievances was, as Pauline Maier points out, "carefully considered," with the grievances dealing with "domestic Insurrections" being last because it was "meant to be the emotional climax of [the] case against the King."[52] This grievance, as George Anastaplo observes, "condemned . . . the slave uprisings that the British were believed to be inciting."[53] In what Robert Parkinson demonstrates was regarded by American rebels as Britain's "most serious crime,"[54] but would also "cast a long shadow over the idea of who was part of the new republic and who was not,"[55] this grievance read as follows:

> He [i.e., George III] has excited domestic Insurrections amongst us, and has endeavoured to bring on the Inhabitants of our frontiers, their merciless Indian Savages, whose known rule of warfare, is an undistinguished destruction, of all ages, sexes and conditions.[56]

Although slave revolts had occurred in the past, the first recorded one taking place in Gloucester County, Virginia, in 1663,[57] they rose significantly in the decades preceding the American Revolution. One of the more prominent of these was Stono's Revolt in South Carolina in September 1739, which, as Gerald Horne notes, "struck terror in the hearts and minds of settlers, solidifying the perception that though enslaved Africans were necessary for development, their presence was dangerous and, therefore, they must be brutally suppressed."[58] George Washington voiced this fear of slave revolts when, one week after the signing of the Declaration of Independence, in his letter to the General Court of Massachusetts Bay, he referred to "a crisis like the present, when our Enemies are prosecuting a War with unexampled severity—When they have called upon foreign mercenaries, and have excited Slaves and Savages to arms against us."[59] Fears of slave insurrections led Virginia, in January 1776, to issue a proclamation which stipulated that slaves who conspired "to rebel or make insurrection, shall suffer death" unless they voluntarily surrendered themselves to the commanders of Virginia's armed forces.[60] Furthermore, South Carolina and Virginia echoed the Declaration's grievance about "domestic insurrections" in the constitutions they adopted in 1776. South Carolina's Preamble stated that the

British had "excited domestic insurrections; proclaimed freedom to servants and slaves, enticed or stolen them from, and armed them against their masters."[61] Virginia's Preamble referred to George III as having "prompt[ed] our negroes to rise in arms against us."[62]

The use of the political euphemism "domestic Insurrections"[63] in the Declaration masked, to some extent, the anomaly between its preambular reference to the "self-evident" truth "that all men are created equal" and "endowed . . . with . . . [the] unalienable Rights . . . [of] Life, Liberty and the Pursuit of Happiness" and the reality of slavery in the American colonies. Most of the leaders of the American Revolution owned slaves and many of them recognized that slavery was immoral, but, as Joseph Ellis points out, none of them "ever attempted to argue that slavery was morally compatible with the values of the Declaration of Independence."[64] In reality, the Declaration reflected what the overwhelming majority of the founding generation knew was, as Kermit Roosevelt describes it, "a world of dominant and pervasive white supremacy."[65] This was confirmed by the "Report" of the seven, now independent States, that met at New Haven in January 1778, which asserted that it was "[t]he *free-born inhabitants* of America opprest by the tyranny of Great Britain, [who] found it necessary for the support of their liberties to declare themselves independent" (emphasis added).[66] At best, if at all, the American revolutionaries regarded the Declaration's promise of equality, as Abraham Lincoln put it "[f]our score and seven years" later at Gettysburg, as merely a "proposition" to which they were "dedicated."[67] In a speech in 1857, Lincoln conceded that the Declaration's "assertion that "all men are created equal" was of no practical use in effecting our separation from Great Britain," and that "it was placed in the Declaration, nor for that, but for future use." This stemmed from the fact that the signatories to the Declaration "meant simply to declare the *right*, so that the *enforcement* of it might follow as fast as circumstances should permit."[68] However, in the meantime, as he observed in 1854, when delivering his eulogy for his political hero, the slaveholder Henry Clay, the Declaration constituted "the white-man's charter of freedom."[69] Given that slavery was legal in all thirteen colonies at the time of the Declaration of Independence, it was thus unsurprising that the constitutions of six of the thirteen "free and independent" States that emerged as a result of the American Revolution were derived from, or declared in the name of, their "freemen."[70] This hypocrisy did not go unnoticed at that time. For example, in 1774, Nathaniel Miles, a Congregationalist minister from Connecticut, wrote : "For shame, let us either cease to enslave our fellow-men, or else let us cease to complain of those that would enslave us."[71] Similarly, in 1777, Ebenezer Hazard, soon to be the Confederation's Postmaster General, while travelling through Maryland, wrote in his journal that "[e]very argument which can be argued in favor of our liberties will certainly operate with equal force in favor of that of the Negroes" and that "we [can] not with propriety contend for the one while we withhold the other."[72] And in a letter to her husband John Adams, Abigail Adams wrote: "It always seemed a most iniquitous Scheme to me, fight ourselfs for what we are daily robbing and plundering from those who have as good a right to freedom as we have."[73]

The Declaration's grievance concerning "domestic Insurrections" was vital in securing support for the Revolutionary War's objectives of independence and freedom. To achieve these objectives, the Declaration had to "highlight the depravity of their enemies," which it did by "dredg[ing] up colonists' deepest fears about what slaves, savages, and mercenaries, 'instigated,' 'tampered with,' or 'excited' by evil agents of the king, might do to their loved ones."[74]

These fears, in fact, preceded the proclamation of the Declaration of Independence. For example, in private correspondence, in June 1775, James Madison recognized the danger posed by possible slave insurrections when he wrote that British "tampering with the Slaves . . . to make great Use of them in case of a war in [Virginia] . . . is the only part in which this Colony is vulnerable; & if we should be subdued, we will fall like Achilles by the hand of one that knows that secret."[75] In the same month, James Iredell, a future justice of the Supreme Court, denounced the British and their "more than diabolical purpose of exciting our own domestics (Domestics they forced upon us) to cut our throats, and involve Men, Women and children in one universal massacre."[76]

Fears of slave insurrections were first formally voiced by the Continental Congress on 6 July 1775 in its "Declaration of the Causes and Necessity of Taking Up Arms," which listed as the last of its grievances against the British, fears that the British were hatching "schemes . . . to excite domestic enemies against us."[77] What Benjamin Franklin, on the following day, angrily referred to as the British aim of having "Domestic Slaves, [the British] have sold us, to cut their Master's Throats" by means of "exciting an Insurrection among Blacks,"[78] was most prominently put into effect on 7 November 1775, when the Earl of Dunmore, Great Britain's governor of Virginia, seeking to exploit existing unrest amongst Virginia's slave population,[79] issued a proclamation offering liberty to "all *indented servants*, *negroes*, or *others*, (appertaining to Rebels)," but not those of loyalists, who fled their masters and joined the effort to suppress the colonial revolt against the British.[80] The number of slaves that fled and joined the British is not precisely known. However, estimates range from 20,000[81] to 100,000.[82] According to Gary Nash, of the slaves who fled to the British, "disease turned out to be their worst enemy . . . [and] that not more than one-third . . . survived the Revolution."[83]

Prior to Dunmore's proclamation, on 8 October 1775, the colonial military leadership "agreed Unanimously to reject all Slaves from enlisting" in the rebel armed forces and further agreed by "a great Majority to reject [free] Negroes altogether" from enlisting or re-enlisting.[84] Later that month the Continental Congress resolved that free African Americans and slaves "be rejected altogether."[85] In his initial response to Dunmore's proclamation, George Washington, who had assumed command of the Continental Army in July 1775, urged that Dunmore's "diabolical Schemes" be crushed so as to "convince the Slaves and Servants of the Impotency of His designs."[86] Towards achieving this objective, on 14 December 1775, Virginia's General Convention of delegates adopted a resolution which, after referring to existing legislation in Virginia that stipulated "that all negro or other slaves, conspiring to rebel or make insurrection, shall suffer death, and be excluded all benefit of Clergy," went on to state "that all slaves, who have been, or shall be seduced by his Lordship's proclamation, or other acts to desert their masters' service, and take up arms against the inhabitants of this Colony shall be liable to such punishments as shall hereafter be directed by the General Convention."[87] Given this state of affairs, it is easy to see why the last and most important of the grievances against the King in the Declaration of Independence was that he had "excited domestic Insurrections" against his colonial subjects.

However, Dunmore's proclamation also forced a change in official policy toward African Americans. In order to forestall the recruitment of free African Americans into the British armed forces,[88] on 16 January 1776, the Continental Congress resolved that "free negroes who have served faithfully in the army at Cambridge may be re-enlisted, but no others."[89] Slaves, however, were still unable to join. This aspect of the policy was subsequently reversed, when, starting with Rhode Island in early 1778,[90] some colonies began to allow slaves into the Continental Army.[91] In the case of South Carolina, allowing slaves to join the rebel forces was, as Alexander Hamilton noted, deemed "expedient" given the then "state of Southern affairs," namely that "the enemy's operations there [were] growing infinitely serious and formidable" and had to be pursued, notwithstanding that it would be met by "much opposition from prejudice and self-interest," because slaves would "probably" end up fighting on the British side.[92] This reversal of policy resulted in approximately 6,600 slaves obtaining their freedom in return for fighting with the American rebels,[93] approximately one-third of the number that fought on the British side.[94]

On the other hand, Dunmore's proclamation had the effect of convincing many uncommitted white colonists to join and support the rebellion against the British. As Thomas Jefferson wrote at the time, the proclamation "raised our country into perfect phrensy."[95] On the same day, his fellow Virginian, Richard Henry Lee, wrote that Dunmore's "unparalleled conduct in Virginia has, a few Scotch excepted, united every Man in that large Colony."[96] And, in South Carolina, although the fear of slave insurrections had initially inclined its slaveholders to remain loyal to the British, Dunmore's proclamation saw them switch to supporting independence from the British.[97] Gerald Horne observes that the effect of this increase in support for the American rebels "effectively barred any possibility of rebel reconciliation with London,"[98] and that Dunmore's proclamation, coupled with the impact of *Somerset v. Stewart*, were "powerfully important landmarks on the road to 4 July 1776."[99]

SLAVERY AND THE ARTICLES OF CONFEDERATION AND PERPETUAL UNION

In 1781, the thirteen self-proclaimed independent States eventually agreed to come together in a confederation by ratifying the Articles of Confederation and Perpetual Union, which, in Article IV, indirectly but significantly, protected the institution of slavery. Article IV secured important privileges and immunities to the "people of the different States." However, because these privileges and immunities only extended to "free inhabitants" of member States, they did not extend to slaves. Furthermore, in preventing member States from imposing restrictions on free inhabitants that would "prevent the removal of property imported into in any State," Article IV effectively negated the decision in *Somerset v. Stewart*. This consequence flowed from the reality that "property" was understood to include slaves.[100] Finally, Article IV required persons guilty of, or charged with, "treason, felony, or other high misdemeanor" and who had fled the State in which such offences had been committed to "be delivered up and removed to the State having jurisdiction of [the] offense." Given that various member States made slave rebellion a felony and that a declaration of outlawry against a fugitive slave was generally regarded as the equivalent of a charge of a "felony, or other high misdemeanor," this provision amounted to what George Van Cleve describes as a "proto-fugitive slave clause."[101]

ANTI-SLAVERY SENTIMENT

Notwithstanding the significance of the slavery provisions in the both the Declaration of Independence and the Articles of Confederation, the revolutionary period witnessed the emergence of America's first abolitionist movement. It was the product of three major factors. First, there was opposition to slavery based upon religious principles, especially from the Quakers and New England Calvinists.[102] Second, there was the impact of Enlightenment ideas about human equality. For example, in 1761, in his widely publicized legal challenge to British writs that were imposed to strictly enforce trade and navigation laws, James Otis, a lawyer and political activist from Massachusetts, asserted that "black and white, born here, are free-born British subjects, and entitled to all essential civil rights of such" and that pursuant to the British constitution, "every man in the dominions is a free man."[103] Third, following the Declaration of Independence, many recognized the inconsistency between its assertion of the right to liberty and equality, on the one hand, and the institution of slavery, on the other.[104] The antislavery sentiment that this inspired was, however, one that "reflected more a concern for the reputation of Americans than a concern for the welfare of enslaved Africans."[105]

James Oakes identifies four abolitionist achievements of the eleven years between the Declaration of Independence and the Philadelphia Convention in 1787. The first was the movement towards abolition of slavery or gradual emancipation of slaves in several northern States such as Massachusetts, New Hampshire, Rhode Island, and Pennsylvania.[106] However, this process was, as John Adams pointed out, largely driven by

> the multiplication of labouring White People, who, would no longer suffer the Rich to employ these Sable Rivals, so much to their Injury. . . . . The common People would not Suffer, the Labour by which alone they could obtain a subsistance, to be done by Slaves. If the gentlemen had been permitted by Law to hold Slaves, the common white People would have put the Negroes to Death, and their Masters too perhaps.[107]

This process of abolition in the northern States continued after the American Revolution so that by 1850, slavery had been formally abolished in the Union's northern states.[108] The second was the manumission of thousands of slaves in individual States, especially in slave States such as Virginia and Maryland.[109] By the time of the first census in 1790, there were more free African Americans in the slave States and territories in the South (32,457) than in the northern non-slave states (27,054).[110] However, these emancipation laws and manumissions imposed significant burdens on slaves affected by them. Thus, gradual emancipation laws usually "stipulated that emancipated people should pay compensation to slave-owners in the form of sentences of unpaid labor" which meant that "in reality . . . [they] continued to live as enslaved people for decades afterward."[111] And manumission usually required the slave "to make long-term debt payments, in cash or labor, to their former enslavers."[112]

The third, partly inspired by the oversupply of slaves in many slave markets in the colonies,[113] was the various measures taken by individual States to ban the importation of slaves. Thus, by Article II of the Articles of Association, adopted by the First Continental Congress on 20 October 1774, the colonies agreed to "wholly discontinue the slave trade."[114] Although such laws passed by New York, New Jersey, Rhode Island, Virginia, North Carolina, and South Carolina[115] were sometimes ignored and not enforced, they did result in a reduction of the volume of slaves traded through these States.[116] Furthermore, States such as Virginia, Pennsylvania, and Maryland sought to diminish the extent of the slave trade by imposing high import duties on slaves.[117] By the time of the Philadelphia Convention, only Georgia had failed to institute any measures to restrict the slave trade.[118]

The final achievement identified by Oakes was the Northwest Ordinance, adopted by the Confederation Congress in July 1787, which, in Article VI, prohibited slavery in territory north of the Ohio River (the Northwest Territory). This prohibition was significant in the context of the later sectional divide over slavery, because "but for that prohibition it is not improbable that both Indiana and Illinois, which were largely peopled by settlers from Kentucky, Tennessee, Virginia, and North Carolina, would have established slavery" when admitted to the Union in 1816 and 1818 respectively.[119] However, the effect of the Ordinance's Article VI should not be overstated because, as Paul Finkelman notes, although its words "sounded idealistic, [they] had little force." Its prohibition of slavery in the Northwest Territory did not mean that slavery was entirely abolished in the Northwest Territory. This was because slaves present in the Northwest Territory prior to the passage of the Ordinance were not affected by Article VI. In fact, slavery continued in this territory in the states subsequently carved out of it.[120] For example, although Illinois was admitted as a nominally non-slave state in 1818, Article VI, Section 1 of its 1818 Constitution only prohibited the further introduction of slavery into that state. Illinois' existing slave population remained enslaved for the rest of their lives, although Article VI, Section 3 stipulated that their female children at the age of eighteen and male children at age twenty-one would become free.[121] It was only with Article XIII, Section 16 of its 1848 Constitution that slavery was completely abolished in Illinois.[122] However, Article VI, Section 1 denied Illinois' free African Americans the right to vote.[123] Furthermore, Article XIV required Illinois' legislature to pass legislation to prohibit "free persons of color from immigrating and settling in [Illinois]."[124] Reflecting John Quincy Adams's 1837 observation that "[i]n the North the people favor the whites and fear the blacks of the South,"[125] this provision, restated Illinois' earlier legislative enactments—similar to those adopted in Ohio and Indiana—and was targeted at formerly enslaved African Americans that had been freed under manumission laws in slave states, especially Virginia.[126] Thus, in 1853, the Illinois legislature passed the so-called Logan Law that rendered free or enslaved African Americans who entered and stayed in Illinois for more than ten days guilty of a high misdemeanor. If the offender could not pay the scheduled fine of fifty dollars, he or she was subjected to imprisonment and sale to any person prepared to pay the fine, with the purchaser being able to compel "the said negro or mulatto" to work without pay for a period of time determined by a justice of the peace. However, a consequence of passage of the Logan Law was that it energized antislavery activists in Illinois in their campaign to repeal anti–African American laws and secure fair and equal treatment for them.[127] A critical factor driving the passage of legislation such as the Logan Law was the fact that manumission laws in ten slave states required the emancipated slave to leave the state within periods ranging from immediately to twelve months.[128] De Tocqueville observed that, as a result of these laws, "the prejudice which repels the Negroes seems to increase in proportion as they are emancipated."[129]

SLAVERY AND THE PHILADELPHIA CONVENTION

Within a few years of the Confederation's formation, economic difficulties, flowing from the absence of a functioning internal market, and social disorder, most notably evidenced by Shays's Rebellion of 1786–1787,[130] combined with threatened international intervention by external powers, convinced many members of its political elite of the need to restructure the relationship between its member States.[131] With the Confederation, in the words of Massachusetts' delegate to the Philadelphia Convention, Nathaniel Gorham, "near its exit,"[132] the legislatures of twelve of the Confederation's thirteen "free sovereign and independent States" elected fifty-five white men to meet in Philadelphia during the summer of 1787 in what Thomas Jefferson then called an "assembly of demigods."[133] The Convention constituted what has been described as "an international conference, conducted . . . among diplomatic plenipotentiaries of the states" to negotiate a peace pact in the form of a "reasoned response to a serious security problem that espied a sequence in which internal division and the intervention of external powers would create the same whirlwind in America that had undone Europe."[134] Against a background in which there existed a widespread belief that the Articles of Confederation were no longer binding because of numerous breaches of its provisions,[135] what emerged in the summer of 1787 was a proposed Constitution which, upon ratification, formed a new and more centralized union that came into operation in March 1789. In *Federalist 41*, James Madison, who has been widely,[136] but not universally, acclaimed as the "father of the Constitution,"[137] listed the Constitution's various objectives, the first of which was "security against foreign danger," followed by "regulation of the intercourse with foreign nations."[138] Slaveholders, such as Charles Pinckney, a delegate to the Convention from South Carolina, had a particular interest in supporting these objectives. They feared a possible international intervention that would adopt something akin to Dunmore's proclamation during the American Revolution that would lead to the abolition of slavery.[139] For them, the Confederation, viewed by Pinckney as a "miserable, feeble mockery of Government,"[140] was incapable of fending off any such intervention. Thus, in coming to the Convention, as George Washington later opined, the issue was whether the Americans would "survive as an independent Republic, or decline from our foederal dignity into insignificant & wretched fragments of Empire," and the debate over the proposed Constitution and the ratification conventions that followed was a contest not "so much for glory" but for "existence."[141]

Slavery was extensively debated at the Philadelphia Convention, notwithstanding that it was a matter regulated by the laws of individual States. The majority of the Convention's delegates, in the words of Maryland's Luther Martin, regarded slavery as "odious" and "*inconsistent* with the *genius* of *republicanism*."[142] Nevertheless, as William L. Yancey correctly pointed out at Alabama's secession convention in 1861, the Convention's debates on slavery "were based upon utilitarian, and not on moral views."[143] As James Madison explained, these debates stemmed from the reality that under the Constitution slaves were "with great propriety" viewed "in the mixt character of persons and property," that is, as he put it, "considered by our laws, in some respects, as persons, and in other respects as property."[144]

In what Madison, in 1819, referred to as the Union's "national evil,"[145] the Constitution contained a number of provisions that Paul Finkelman concludes "gave slave owners . . . virtually everything they asked for"[146] in terms of protecting and preserving the institution of slavery.[147] The three-fifths clause (Article I, Section 2, Clause 3) counted free persons as well as three-fifths of "other," that is enslaved, persons for the purposes of representation in the House of Representatives and the Electoral College, and taxation; the fugitive slave clause (Article IV, Section 2, Clause 3) dealt with the rendition of runaway slaves; and the slave importation clause (Article I, Section 9, Clause 1) prohibited Congress from banning the importation of slaves into the Union prior to 1808. In addition to these express provisions, the new states and territories clauses (Article IV, Section 3), by saying nothing about whether or not slavery would be permitted to expand into the Union's territories and the states that emerged from them, implicitly endorsed the further expansion of slavery beyond those states where it existed at the time the Constitution was ratified. As Micah Alpaugh concludes, the Philadelphia Convention produced a Constitution that "restrained a growing abolitionist cause and gave hated institutions new legitimacy."[148]

The Constitution also excluded slaves from the Declaration of Independence's assertions that "all Men are created equal" and are "endowed . . . with certain unalienable Rights" such as "Life, Liberty and the Pursuit of Happiness." When the Declaration referred to the "Right of the People" to "alter or to abolish" any "Form of Government" that threatened to destroy a man's right to "Life, Liberty and the pursuit of Happiness," it did not include African Americans as part of that "People."[149] They were, as Thomas Jefferson referred to them in the deleted parts of his draft of the Declaration, "a distant people."[150] This exclusion stemmed from the reality that America's Founding Fathers did not view the Declaration as a legally binding document. Rather, as Richard Brown observes, they regarded it as nothing more than "a political instrument to rally Americans by appealing to their ideals and reminding them of British insults."[151] Thus, in 1788, in written reflections on the Constitution, John Jay, soon to be the Union's first chief justice, noted that the signatories to the Declaration were "undoubtedly very inconsistent with . . . declarations on the subject of human rights," because they and "the great majority or rather the great body of our people had been so long accustomed to the practice and convenience of having slaves, that very few among them even doubted the propriety and rectitude of it."[152] In 1857, in the Supreme Court decision in *Dred Scott v. Sandford*, Chief Justice Roger B. Taney, in delivering the opinion of the court, pointed to the Constitution's fugitive slave and slave importation clauses as proof that "the negro race as a separate class of persons . . . were not regarded as a portion of the people or citizens of the Government then formed."[153] In 1862, the nationalist lawyer and political essayist from Philadelphia, Sidney George Fisher, echoed Taney's opinion when he wrote that "[t]he [Preamble's] "we the people," with which the [Constitution] begins, do not apply to him [the African American]."[154]

Robert Parkinson is substantially, but not completely, correct in assessing Taney's opinion in *Dred Scott v. Sandford* as "a codification, a formalization of the notion of exclusion, first raised in 1775–1776,"[155] because, as is discussed below in more detail, although free African Americans were treated much like slaves, a few northern non-slave states did allow, for example, free African Americans the right to vote. The radical abolitionist William Lloyd Garrison put it correctly when, in his analysis of the Constitution, after referring to the Preamble's aspirational statement that the Constitution would "secure the Blessings of Liberty to ourselves and our posterity," he went on to write:

> Nothing is more certain than that the preamble . . . never included, in the minds of those who framed it, those who were then pining in bondage. . . . . The [preamble's words] . . . assuredly did not mean to include the slave population. The truth is, our fathers were intent on securing liberty to themselves, without being scrupulous as to the means they used to accomplish their purpose. They were not actuated by the spirit of universal philanthropy; and though in words they recognized occasionally the brotherhood of the human race, in practice they continually denied it. They did not blush to enslave a portion of their fellow men, and to buy and sell them as cattle in the market, while they were fighting against oppression of the mother country and boasting their regard for the rights of man.[156]

Many contemporaries to the ratification of the Constitution predicted that a great national tragedy awaited the Union that it formed. For example, towards the end of the Philadelphia Convention, George Mason astutely observed that "[b]y an inevitable chain of causes & effects providence punishes national sins, by national calamities."[157] The national calamity foreseen by Mason was more directly articulated by Samuel Hopkins, a prominent abolitionist and theologian, who, on 29 January 1788, presciently forecast that "civil war will not be avoided."[158]

Slavery during the Antebellum Era

The importance of slavery during the antebellum era related to the agricultural economy of the Union's slave states. Prior to the American Revolution, slavery was of major importance to the agricultural economies of the southern colonies where slave labor was used primarily to grow tobacco, rice, and indigo.[159] At that time, many people thought that slavery was on an inevitable path towards extinction.[160] For example, at the Philadelphia Convention, Oliver Ellsworth urged the Convention not to "intermeddle" with the existence of slavery because "[s]lavery in time will not be a speck in our Country."[161] However, as Gordon Wood observes, this was "the most fatal of the Founders' many illusions," the reality being that "slavery . . . was on the verge of its greatest expansion."[162] In fact, crops produced with slave labor were profitable and, as Paul Finkelman notes, "Southern politicians from the 1770s through to the 1790s jealously protected their interest in slave property, because they knew it was the central institution of their economy."[163]

The realization that states such as Georgia and South Carolina had an ideal climate for growing cotton led George Washington, a few weeks before his inauguration as the Union's first President, to observe that "the most excellent quality" of South Carolina's cotton, grown "in abundt quantities," would prove to be "a more profitable species of agriculture, than any other Crop," which in turn meant that "the encrease of that new material . . . must be of almost infinite consequence to the prosperity of America."[164] The combination of several factors proved Washington to be right. In 1793, Eli Whitney patented a new type of cotton gin that "[o]vernight . . . increased ginning productivity by a factor of fifty."[165] His gin, together with other bigger and more productive gins, led to dramatic increases in annual cotton production. In 1790, prior to Whitney's invention, total cotton production in the Union was 1.5 million pounds. In 1800, it increased to 36.5 million pounds and, in 1820, to 167.5 million pounds.[166] This technological advance, when coupled with the increased demand for cotton from the English textile industry—cloth being the industrial revolution's first mass-produced product—transformed the growing of cotton into a very profitable business enterprise. Given the "hot and hellish" climate in the South, slavery has been described as "a horrific response to a basic climatic fact," because it was generally believed that "you could not get free men to harvest labor-intensive crops in the heat and humidity."[167] Indicative of the importance of slavery to the production of cotton was Article VII of Kentucky's Constitution of 1792, which stipulated that its legislature had "no power to pass laws for the emancipation of slaves without the consent of their owners or without paying their owners, previous to such emancipation, a full equivalent of money for the slaves so emancipated."[168] Georgia, in Article IV, Section 11 of its Constitution of 1798, included a similar provision together with a further provision that prohibited its legislature from preventing settlers into Georgia from bringing their slaves with them.[169] And, in a debate over a petition presented to Congress in 1790 for the abolition of the slave trade, Representative Thomas Tudor Tucker from South Carolina was prescient in his warning that "a general emancipation of slaves by law" was something that "would never be submitted to by the Southern States without a civil war."[170]

The growing demand for southern cotton witnessed a corresponding growing demand for slaves and, according to official census figures, resulted in the Union's slave population of 694,207 in 1790 (17.83 percent of the total population) ballooning to 3,950,546 in 1860 (12.67 percent of the total population).[171] African Americans born into slavery in the southern slave states accounted for the bulk of this growth. The legal importation of slaves prior to 1808, and to a lesser extent, illegal importation thereafter, accounted for a relatively minor portion of this growth.[172] This growth in slave numbers provided the workforce that led to an increase in the production of cotton from 3,000 bales in 1790 to 3,841,000 bales in 1860,[173] the substantial majority of which was produced on territory acquired by the Union after ratification of the Constitution.[174] Slave-state cotton growers captured almost 45 percent of the British market for raw cotton[175] and accounted for more than half of America's exports between 1815 and 1860.[176]

The value and significance of cotton to the South engendered a confidence in the minds of the secessionists of 1860–1861 that they would prevail in any conflict over their claims to independence.[177] To this effect, in 1858, in his notorious Mudsill Speech to the Senate, South Carolina's James Henry Hammond boasted: "[W]ould any sane nation make war on cotton? Without firing a gun, without drawing a sword, should they make war on us we could bring the whole world to our feet. . . . . No power on earth dares make war upon it. Cotton is King."[178]

Hammond's boast was echoed by Texas's Louis Trezevant Wigfall, who, on 12 December 1860, in his speech to the Senate, proclaimed: "I say that cotton is king, and that he waves his sceptre not only over these thirty-three States, but over the Island of Great Britain and over continental Europe, and that there is no crowned head upon that island, or upon the continent, that does not bend the knee in fealty and acknowledge allegiance to the monarch."[179]

Underpinning these boasts was the fact that in 1861, the Confederate states, taken as whole, constituted the fourth most prosperous economy in the world, in which, albeit inequitably distributed, "per capita incomes (even including the slave population) . . . were higher than those of Belgium, France, the Netherlands and Germany, and were only exceeded by those of the Australian colonies, the Northern United States and Britain."[180] Also indicative of the wealth of the Confederate states, as compared to the rest of the Union, was the ranking of the Union's states in 1861 according to the per capita wealth of their white populations, where eight of the top ten states (included the top four) were Confederate states.[181]

Apart from being exported, the South's cotton provided the raw material for the manufacturing of cotton textiles in the Union's northern non-slave states.[182] The significance of this cotton manufacturing was that "[b]y 1860 . . . making cotton textiles [was] the United States' most important manufacturing industry in terms of capital invested, workers employed, and net value of its product."[183] Furthermore, cotton production was vital to the economies of northern states such as New York, where its banks helped finance production of cotton, the acquisition of plantations in the South, and the purchase of slaves. The port in New York also served as a major port for the shipment of cotton to Europe.[184]

SLAVERY AND THE CONFLICT OVER TARIFFS

For most of the period from 1820 to 1860, tariffs accounted for approximately 85 percent of federal revenues. Other revenues came principally from sales of public lands.[185] During this period, the most significant federal expenditure items were associated with funding federal government expenditures, especially on the military, as well as interest on the national debt. Other expenditure, at times significant, was on what became known as "the American System," which involved supporting nascent manufacturing industries through subsidies and spending on infrastructure such as roads, railways, and bridges. By the 1850s, this area of expenditure slightly exceeded military expenditure.[186] Given the importance of tariffs to federal coffers, a significant by-product of the South's slave-based agricultural economy was the sectional conflict over the levels of tariffs that Congress should impose.

In this sectional divide, northern states generally favored higher tariffs, whereas the southern states, who viewed tariffs as the keystone of the American System, generally campaigned for lower tariffs. The most influential proponent of tariffs in the Union's early days was its first secretary of the treasury, Alexander Hamilton, who proposed the first tariff legislation that was enacted in July 1789.[187] Subsequently, during his long and influential political career, Henry Clay, a slaveholding southerner from the border state of Kentucky, was the leading champion of tariffs. For him, tariffs supplied the funds for federal government assistance to support nascent manufacturing enterprises in the northern states so as to enable them to compete with less expensive imported products.[188] Northern non-agricultural workers also supported higher tariffs because they protected northern industries that provided them with employment.

In the nascent manufacturing economy in their region, northern mills competed with British factories in relation to the purchase of southern cotton and the sale of clothes, tools, and shackles to southerners who had to purchase such goods either from overseas or northern manufacturers.[189] In either case, higher tariffs increased the price for such goods. Furthermore, increases in the level of tariffs threatened the viability of the South's slave-based economy because its agricultural products, especially cotton, were then more likely to face tariffs in foreign ports. Thus, the use of federal revenues in support of the emerging manufacturing industries and infrastructure was overwhelmingly more beneficial to the economic interests in the North than to most slaveholders in the South.[190] These southerners complained that the effect of higher tariffs was that the South, through the higher prices it paid for goods and equipment as a result of tariffs, was subsidizing northern economic development.[191] Thus, the approach of most southern slaveholders towards tariff policy was to keep tariffs down to levels that would raise no more revenue than was needed to meet necessary government expenditures. An exception to southern state opposition to higher tariffs came from Louisiana, where tariffs protected the local sugar industry from competition from cheaper imported sugar.[192]

DIVERGENT ATTITUDES TOWARDS SLAVERY

As noted above, in the early years of the Union, many, primarily in the North, took a negative attitude towards slavery and believed, or hoped, that it would gradually die away. However, by the 1830s, a number of factors led to the transformation of public opinion in the South towards viewing, in positive terms, what was increasingly referred to by both northerners and southerners as the South's "peculiar institution."[193]

The first was the importance of slave labor needed for the dramatically increased production of cotton for a growing world market. What this meant, as Richard Brown emphasizes, was that in the South, when the Declaration of Independence's assertion that "all Men are created equal" came up against property rights in slavery, the latter always prevailed.[194] This confirmed the reality that, during the eighteenth century and the first half of the nineteenth, slavery in the Union's slaveholding regions had "shifted from a peripheral influence on economic and social orders to a central organizing feature, and much of the American South came to be structured around enslaved production."[195]

The second factor was a "fear of a revolt being mounted by the enslaved [which] became a defining characteristic of the slaveholding South."[196] The most significant slave revolt of the time started in 1791 in the French colony of Saint-Domingue in the Caribbean Sea, at that time "the undisputed crown jewel of all European colonies anywhere."[197] Despite the Union's significant assistance to French planters to suppress the slave revolt in the form of provisions, arms, and ammunition,[198] the revolt resulted in most whites being either killed or fleeing. Thousands of those who fled settled in the southern slave states, including over eight thousand in New Orleans.[199] The revolt "convinced southerners that the only thing they could expect from freed slaves was vicious retaliation . . . [and] supported their conviction that blacks were incapable of civilization on their own."[200] These fears were rekindled by occasional threatened slave revolts such as those in Virginia in 1800 (Gabriel's Rebellion)[201] and South Carolina in 1822 (Vesey's Rebellion),[202] as well as actual slave revolts such as the German Coast Slave Rebellion in Louisiana in 1811[203] and, most notably, Nat Turner's Rebellion in Virginia in 1831.[204]

The perceived threat flowing from possible slave revolts was used to garner support for the secession of the Confederate states, just as was, as previously noted, the threat of "domestic Insurrections" set out in the Declaration of Independence used to secure support for independence during the American Revolution. For example, Georgia alleged that "Northern states [had] been engaged in constant efforts to subvert our institutions and to excite insurrection and servile war against us."[205] Mississippi condemned the abolitionist movement from the North because it "advocates negro equality, socially and politically, and promotes insurrection and incendiarism in our midst."[206] South Carolina accused northern states of inciting "servile insurrection."[207] And Texas claimed that northern abolitionists had "hired emissaries . . . to stir up servile insurrection and bring blood and carnage to our firesides" and "hired emissaries among us to burn our towns and distribute arms and poison to our slaves for the same purpose."[208]

The third factor contributing towards public opinion in the South viewing slavery in positive terms was the emergence, especially in the northern non-slave states, of the second wave of abolitionism, ironically at a time when, as Alexis de Tocqueville observed, "the prejudice of race appears to be stronger in the states that have abolished slavery than in those where it still exists; and nowhere is it so intolerant as in those states where servitude has never been known."[209] A number of factors contributed to the emergence of this movement. The first was Nat Turner's Rebellion, which "affected white opinion in the North by undermining the claim that slaves were contented,"[210] and thereby "opened a national debate that fuelled regional rivalries and triggered a wide-ranging discussion over what to do about slavery in Virginia."[211] The second was the British Slavery Abolition Act of 1833, which "played a critical role in mobilizing southern thinkers to formulate an ever-bolder argument that alleged black slavery to be a humane and modern institution" because British abolitionism was viewed as "a radical act—the unjust appropriation of property by a tyrannical government and the ultimate demonstration of the potency of abolitionist thought."[212] The third was the passage of the so-called Indian Removal Act in 1830,[213] which facilitated the forced resettlement of Native American tribes to federal territory west of the Mississippi River. Linda Kerber notes that abolitionists such as William Lloyd Garrison were "sensitive to the Indian question because they saw in it analogies to the problem of slavery."[214] Indeed, Garrison held proslavery advocates as largely responsible for this policy.[215] The hostility of antislavery advocates to this policy had the consequence that, as Kerber writes, "abolitionism became more vigorous."[216] Finally, the Second Great Awakening, the Protestant revival movement of the early decades of the nineteenth century that was anchored in a belief in the perfectibility of man, "energized abolitionism, as well as sustaining the slaves themselves."[217] Importantly, this abolitionism was not confined to whites. It included African Americans, such as David Walker, Sojourner Truth (born Isabella Baumfree), and, most famously, the former slave Frederick Douglass.[218]

These events led to a two-pronged response to slavery in the southern slave states. The first was a "stiffening southern resistance to even the faintest hint of antislavery activity in Congress."[219] This resistance was strongest in South Carolina, whose legislature, for example, passed a resolution in 1835 which asserted that "the formation of abolition societies, and the acts and doings of certain fanatics, calling themselves abolitionists, in non-slaveholding states . . . are in direct violation of the compact of union."[220]

The second response was a casting of slavery as a benevolent institution and a "positive good,"[221] or as John S. Carlile, a delegate to Virginia's secession convention, put it, "a social, political and religious blessing."[222] The roots of the positive good thesis can be traced as far back as 1696 when Cotton Mather, an influential Puritan minister from Massachusetts, wrote of slaves: "You are better *Fed* & better *Clothed*, & better *Managed* by far, than you would be, if you were your *Own men*."[223] John C. Calhoun was a key figure in this nineteenth century recasting of slavery. Although Calhoun extolled the ideals of liberty and equality set out in the Declaration of Independence, in 1820, he told John Quincy Adams that it applied "only to white men" and that slavery was "the best guarantee to equality among the whites."[224] For Calhoun, whom Adams later privately referred to as "the high-priest of Moloch—the embodied spirit of slavery,"[225] only "the Caucasian race" was "incorporat[ed] into the Union." African Americans were excluded because, according to him, "Ours . . . is the Government of the white man."[226]

In February 1837, in what Robert Elder refers to as "the most famous defence of slavery in American history," Calhoun delivered a speech in the Senate which "[i]n its force, clarity, and content . . . marked a significant departure in the political debate over slavery."[227] In that speech, Calhoun said that "where two races of different origin, and distinguished by color, and other physical differences, as well as intellectual, are brought together, the relation now existing in the slave-holding States between the two, is, instead of an evil, a good—a positive good." Furthermore, slavery was justified, according to Calhoun, because there had never "existed a wealthy and civilized society in which one portion of the community did not . . . live on the labor of the other."[228] What this meant for American democracy was, as Harriet Martineau recorded following her travels through the United States in the mid-1830s, that "the true enthusiastic love of freedom could exist in a republic, only in the presence of a servile class."[229]

Calhoun's "positive good" thesis was echoed in the writings of others, such as the social theorist George Fitzhugh[230] and professor of history and political economy Thomas Dew.[231] Their writings, and those of others, were popularized in the slave states by publication in the influential *De Bow's Review*,[232] which declared that "civilization itself may almost be said to depend upon the continual servitude of blacks in America."[233] South Carolina's James Henry Hammond voiced this sentiment in 1858 in his Mudsill Speech to the Senate, when he said:

> In all social systems there must be a class to do the menial duties, to perform the drudgery of life. That is, a class requiring but a low order of intellect and but little skill. Its requisites are vigor, docility, fidelity. Such a class you must have, or you would not have that other class which leads progress, civilization, and refinement. It constitutes the very mud-sills of society and of political government; and you might as well attempt to build a house in the air, as to build either the one or the other, except on the mud-sills. Fortunately for the South, she found a race adapted to that purpose to her hand. A race inferior to her own, but eminently qualified in temper, in vigor, in docility, in capacity to stand the climate, to answer all her purposes. We use them for our purpose, and call them slaves. . . . . Our slaves are black, of another and inferior race. The *status* in which we have placed them is an elevation. They are elevated from the condition in which God first created them, by being made our slaves. None of that race on the whole face of the globe can be compared with the slaves of the South, and they know it. They are happy, content, unaspiring, and utterly incapable, from intellectual weakness, ever to give us any trouble by their aspirations.[234]

As George Fredrickson points out, these views posited "a democratic and egalitarian society for whites, [while] denying that blacks were in any real sense at all, part of the human community," thereby creating a political democracy for a white master race, or what has been called a "*Herrenvolk* democracy."[235]

The positive good thesis was often articulated during the secession conventions of 1860–1861.[236] A stark illustration of this was voiced by Richard K. Call, twice former governor of the Territory of Florida, who wrote as follows:

> To . . . make America the home of civilization, *human labor was indispensably necessary*. . . . . The experiment with African labor proved

eminently successful. Here was an animal, in the form of a man, possessing the greatest physical power, and the greatest capacity for labor and endurance, without one principle of his nature, one faculty or his mind or feeling of heart, without spirit or pride of character, to enable him to regard slavery as a degradation. A wild barbarian, to be tamed and civilized by the discipline of slavery. Here was the discovery of an animal power almost as essential as the discovery of the new continent, to bring forth the vegetable, animal, and mineral productions of America, to supply the wants and relieve the necessities of Europe. . . . . This race, so distinctly marked by nature with inferiority, physical, moral and mental, as forever to forbid amalgamation, and keep it distinct from our own, has become a great class of laboring, civilized people, domesticated with the white race, and dependent on the discipline of that race for the preservation of the civilization it has acquired. . . . . The African seems designed by the Creator for a slave; docile and humble, with a heart full of the kindest sensibilities, generally grateful and affectionate, and with a mind incapable of a higher elevation than that which is required to direct the machinery of his limbs to useful action. . . . . You may give him physical liberty, but it will be only the liberty of indulgence in sloth and indolence—the liberty of gratification in animal passions and propensities. No human power can ever liberate his mind. It is enslaved in the despotism of superstition and ignorance, of natural imbecility and inertness. It can never be elevated to the comprehension of the dignity and sublimity of that human liberty which, with all its imperfections and inferiority, approaches nearest to the liberty and power of God. . . . . Whether physically bound or free, *mentally* he must remain in bondage. He has animal courage as high and as fierce as the energy of a beast, when driven to desperation; but he is docile and submissive, with a moral timidity arising from his instinctive knowledge of natural inferiority, which makes him ever yield passive obedience to every reasonable will of his master. He looks on the master as a superior being, depends upon him for instruction and direction in all things, and looks to him for support and protection. Though naturally indolent and improvident, he works cheerfully for his master (*even without compulsion*) much better than *he does for himself*. . . . . The black race *must remain forever where it is*. . . . . Search through the history of all time, and you will search in vain to find *any portion of the African race, from its first appearance on record until the present day, in the aggregate, so elevated,*

> *intelligent, enlightened, civilized, comfortable, and happy, as that portion of this degraded race* found as slaves in our country.[237]

On the other hand, northern non-slave states were, with some exceptions, virulently racist in terms of their attitude towards the relatively small numbers of free African Americans within their borders.[238] Indeed, the gradual emancipation of laws in these states and the consequential increase in the number of free African Americans resulted in an intensification of this racism.[239] A key manifestation of this racism was anti-immigration articles in some state constitutions, such as those of Illinois in 1848,[240] Indiana in 1851,[241] and Oregon in 1857,[242] that were targeted against free African Americans. Other states, such as Ohio in 1803–1804,[243] achieved the same objective by legislation. These provisions were fundamentally directed towards keeping these states populated only by white people. Indeed, as Donald Yacovone notes, "[T]he more immigration made the North heterogenous, the more intense became the ideas of white supremacy."[244] Thus, in relation to the free African Americans in northern non-slave states, Ira Berlin notes that "in many places, [they] continued to be governed by the same regulations as slaves, subjected to curfews, restricted in their travels, and denied the right to vote, sit on juries, testify in court, and stand in the militia."[245] In relation to voting rights, although the right to vote was extended to all white adult males in all northern states by 1860, free African Americans were denied that right in all but five of them.[246] In justifying this policy, in 1860, Sidney George Fisher, wrote that "[t]he white [race] alone possesses the intellectual and moral energy which creates that development of free government, industry, science, literature, and the arts, which we call civilization. The black can neither originate, maintain, nor comprehend civilization." This meant for Fisher that "[t]he white race must of necessity, by reason of its superiority, govern the negro."[247] The logical consequence of this was, as he wrote in 1862, that "[t]he principles of democracy do not apply to the negro [because he] is not capable of thinking at all on the political questions or the great interests of a civilized community."[248] This was so because, according to James Madison, writing in 1823, free African Americans were "[g]enerally idle & depraved; appearing to retain the bad qualities of the slaves with whom they continue to associate, without acquiring any of the good ones of the Whites."[249] The consequence of such measures was that white supremacy in the North became, as Yacovone states, an "enduring cultural binding force" that "suffused Northern religion, high culture, literature, education, politics, music, law, and science."[250]

What the denial of basic rights to free African Americans in northern non-slave states demonstrated was, as Senator John Pettit from Illinois asserted in his speech to the Senate on 20 February 1854, that the Declaration of Independence's claim that it was a "self-evident" truth "that all men are created equal" was for both him and in reality "a self-evident lie." As Pettit went on to say to those who believed otherwise, "[G]o, if you will, to the States of Indiana, Ohio, New York, or any other free State, and show me that the Negro race, or the negro man, is upon an equality with the white man, and you show me what does not exist."[251]

It can be noted that the views of Fisher, Madison, and Pettit were consistent with the sentiments of southern pro-secessionists such as William L. Harris, who, on 17 December 1860, in addressing Georgia's General Assembly in his capacity as Mississippi's secession commissioner to Georgia, said:

> Our fathers made this a government for the white man, rejecting the negro, as an ignorant, inferior, barbarian race, incapable of self-government, and not, therefore, entitled to be associated with the white man upon terms of civil, political, or social equality.[252]

Popular sentiment behind disenfranchising free African Americans is evidenced by a statement of a delegate to Pennsylvania's constitutional convention in 1837 who said that if blacks were entitled to vote, "every negro in the State, worthy and worthless—degraded and debased, as nine-tenths of them are, will rush to the polls in senseless and unmeaning triumph."[253] In effect, African Americans were excluded from democracy in America, because, in the words of the Pennsylvania Supreme Court, in 1837: "No coloured race was party to [America's] social compact" and that there was no basis upon which "to raise this depressed race to the level of the white one."[254] Free African Americans in the North were, as Alexis de Tocqueville observed, "condemned by the law and public opinion to a hereditary state of misery and degradation."[255]

However, the North was also home to a small but vocal group of abolitionists, both black and white, who demanded the emancipation of slaves and equality for free African Americans.[256] For them, in the words of William Lloyd Garrison, delivered in a speech in January 1845, America's Constitution was a "covenant with death" and "an agreement with hell."[257] His fellow abolitionist Wendell Phillips asserted that it was "the duty of each individual to trample [the Constitution] under his feet."[258] Not all abolitionists viewed the Constitution as proslavery. Some saw it as grounding an antislavery constitutionalism.[259] However, for all abolitionists, their response to the policies of non-slave states towards African Americans was summarized by Gerrit Smith, a long-term friend and supporter of Frederick Douglass, a founder of the abolitionist Liberty Party in 1840, and a one-term representative from New York in the 1850s,[260] who, in an August 1844 letter that was published in Garrison's influential weekly abolitionist newspaper, *The Liberator*, wrote:

> The laws and usages, by which free people of color in the Northern States, are vexed, hampered, outraged, crushed, constitute so gratuitous, so wantonly wicked, a chiming with the slaveholding policy of the South, and so indispensable a prop of this policy, as to make them not less guilty than the bloodiest slave codes.[261]

The abolitionists were part of what Kate Masur refers to, and documents in detail, as a "sustained struggle . . . for racial equality . . . [that] encompassed pastors, journalists, lawyers, politicians, and countless ordinary citizens who demanded that the nation's white majority reject racist laws and join the struggle for a better, more just society." Although this movement included white northerners, African Americans were at its forefront. In pressing for what Masur refers to as "new ideas about citizenship, individual rights, and the proper scope of state power," its real success and significance was not in the limited success in getting racist laws and constitutional provisions repealed, such as occurred in Ohio in 1849,[262] but rather that "their arguments informed the remarkable congressional debates of the 1860s."[263]

Although there was widespread sympathy in the northern non-slave states for the enslaved population in the southern slave states, there was very little support for abolitionism.[264] Northern whites generally opposed the further expansion of slavery into the territories, rather than slavery itself.[265] This sentiment was bluntly expressed by Thomas Day in an editorial in the *Hartford Courant* in 1856 in which he asserted: "We resist the progress of Slavery in this country, not because we feel any burning zeal in the black man's cause," but because "[we support] the rights of the white man, to labor on his own farm, uncontaminated by the insulting contiguity of black slaves, laboring in the adjoining field."[266] Abraham Lincoln expressed the same sentiment as a means of achieving the American Dream when, in October 1854, he said: "We want [the territories] for the homes of white people. This they cannot be, to any considerable extent, if slavery shall be planted within them. Slave States are places for poor white people to remove FROM; not to remove TO. New free States are the places for poor people to go to and better their condition."[267] And, in 1858, he said that "irrespective of the moral aspect as to whether there is a right or wrong in enslaving a negro," he favored the territories to be free of slavery so they could serve as "an outlet for *free white people everywhere*" to enable them to "find new homes and better their conditions in life."[268]

Slavery, Territorial Expansion, and the Emergence of Sectionalism

Because cotton growth exhausted the soil after a few years, those engaged in the cotton industry were constantly on the lookout for new lands into which cotton could be planted. The territorial expansion of the United States during the antebellum period was, therefore, strongly supported by southern elites, and implemented by what Sven Beckett describes as "the military-cotton complex"[269] that had been created by the federal government. This territorial expansion was accompanied by the spread of slavery to the south and west of the states in the Southeast, such as South Carolina and Virginia, into states in the Southwest, such as Alabama, Georgia, Louisiana, Mississippi, Arkansas, and Texas. By 1860, cotton grown in the Southwest more than tripled that grown in the Southeast.[270]

SLAVERY AND THE TERRITORIAL EXPANSION OF THE UNION TO 1820

That the Union and, indeed, its predecessor, the Confederation, were intent on territorial expansion is clear. The Articles of Confederation made this explicit in Article XI, which provided for Canada's possible accession to the Confederation and further stipulated that other colonies could also be admitted to the Confederation. The prospect of territorial expansion was also evident at the Philadelphia Convention.[271] For example, in a letter in 1803, Gouverneur Morris, one of the Convention's most influential delegates, articulated what later became known as the

Union's "manifest destiny"[272] when he wrote: "I knew as well then as I do now that North America must at length be annexed to us."[273] This expansionist intent was, in due course, fulfilled to a significant extent.[274] Although Canada never became part of the Union, by the end of the nineteenth century the Union consisted of a vast tract of North America's land mass stretching from the Atlantic Ocean to the Pacific Ocean and had jurisdiction over Hawaii and other islands in the Pacific Ocean as well as Puerto Rico and other islands in the Caribbean Sea. This territorial expansion was complemented by the Monroe Doctrine of 1823, which proclaimed to Europe's imperial powers that the rest of the "New World" was within the Union's sphere of influence. The critical impetus for this territorial expansion was the desire to create a powerful Union whose territorial scope was continental and whose international influence was hemispheric.[275]

On the domestic level, maintaining a sectional balance between non-slave states and slave states carved out of newly acquired territory was a major issue for the Congress. The sectional conflict over this issue was one of the two critical issues that led to the secessions of eleven slave states in 1860–1861. The major objective of southern slave states in this sectional conflict was to block or minimize the scope of any legislation that would prohibit slavery in any states carved out of the Union's newly acquired territories. Southern plantation owners and farmers needed land in order to maintain the slave-based agricultural economy upon which their prosperity was based. This need for new land was driven by the practice of "shifting cultivation," which John Majewski describes as follows:

> Farmers and planters who used shifting cultivation burned forest growth to quickly release nutrients into the soil. After five or six years, when the nutrients had been exhausted, the old field was abandoned until it cleared in twenty years. Given the constraints of the southern environment—the region's poor soils and inhospitable climate—shifting cultivation worked well for individual farmers and planters. The drawback of shifting cultivation, though, was that southerners had to hold large tracts of unimproved land in prolonged fallow for up to twenty years.[276]

Thus, as John Stuart Mill pointed out in 1862, the slaveholders in the southern slave states knew that it was "a matter of life and death to find fresh fields for the employment of slave labor" and that "[t]he day when slavery can no longer extend itself, is the day of its doom."[277] With the outbreak of the Civil War, it was thus logical that the Confederacy sought and expected to get what it considered its rightful share of the Union's territories.[278]

On the other hand, for non-slave states, especially those from New England, preventing too many slave states being carved out of the new territories acquired by the Union was critical in preventing Congress being dominated by slave state members that could enact legislation that was inimical to their sectional interests.

Of the thirteen States that had wrested their independence from the British and joined the Union by 1790, the six southern States of Delaware, Georgia, Maryland, North Carolina, South Carolina, and Virginia were slave states and were the home to the great majority of the Union's slaves. Of the remaining seven northern States, Massachusetts and New Hampshire had amended their constitutions, and Connecticut, Pennsylvania, and Rhode Island had enacted legislation that either abolished slavery or provided for the gradual emancipation of slaves. The other two states, New York and New Jersey, enacted gradual emancipation legislation in 1799 and 1804 respectively.[279]

The first new states to be admitted to the Union were Vermont as a non-slave state, in 1791, and Kentucky as a slave state, in 1792. The significance of maintaining a sectional balance between slave and non-slave states at this time is reflected in Alexander Hamilton's letter to Nathan Chipman in July 1788, in which he wrote:

> One of the first subjects of deliberation with the new Congress will be the independence of Kentucky for which the Southern States will be anxious. The Northern will be glad to send a counterpoise in Vermont. Their mutual interests and inclinations will facilitate a proper result.[280]

Hamilton reiterated this point a few months later when, in relation to Vermont's admission to the Union, he wrote to Chipman stating that "in several of the Southern states a jealousy of Northern influence will prevent any great zeal for increasing in the national councils the number of Northern Voters."[281]

Vermont and Kentucky were states carved out of the territory that the Union had at the time the Constitution was ratified in 1788. Prior to 1820, the remainder of that territory provided all, or the bulk, of the territory of three slave states, namely, Tennessee (1796), Mississippi (1817), and Alabama (1819); and three non-slave states, namely, Ohio (1803), Indiana (1816), and Illinois (1818).[282] Thus, prior to 1820, there existed eleven non-slave and ten slave states from within the Union's geographical extent as at 1788. However, the acquisition of further territories after 1788 resulted in the admission of Louisiana as a slave state in 1812. Thus, in 1820, there was an equal number of slave and non-slave states.

The Union's territorial expansion prior to 1820 brought into sharp focus the delicate issue of maintaining a sectional balance between the number of slave and non-slave states. In 1819, Spain ceded its colonial territory in Florida to the Union pursuant to Article II of the Treaty of Adams-Onis.[283] Western parts of the Florida cession became parts of Louisiana, Mississippi, and Alabama, with the remainder forming the state of Florida, which was admitted to the Union as a slave state in 1845.

However, the major territorial acquisition prior to 1820 was the Louisiana Purchase, consummated in July 1803, by which a vast tract of territory west of the Mississippi River was acquired from France.[284] According to Henry Adams, this territorial acquisition, which doubled the territorial scope of the Union, "ranked in historical importance next to the Declaration of Independence and the adoption of the Constitution . . . [and of] which it was the logical outcome."[285]

The Louisiana Purchase prompted a secessionist movement within some New England states, where the Federalist Party was dominant, but a powerless minority in Congress. A section of the Federalist Party viewed this acquisition of territory as part of a plan to further marginalize the Federalists by the admission of additional slave states from the territory so acquired.[286] In late December 1803, New Hampshire's Senator William Plumer explained the reason for the proposed secession as follows:

> All the great measures of Congress are tending to one point—to build up & aggrandize . . . the States south of the Potomac. . . . . The weight, influence & votes of New England will soon be of little avail in the National legislature.[287]

This fear of loss of influence was more explicitly voiced by Representative William Ely from Massachusetts, who asserted that, due to the effect of the Constitution's three-fifths clause, the Louisiana Purchase would lead to "an extensive country, which will require a great number of slaves for its cultivation, and when admitted into the Union . . . will contribute, by the number of its slaves, to destroy the real influence of the Eastern States in the National Government."[288] Similar concerns were articulated by others, such as Timothy Pickering from Massachusetts,[289] who had previously held the federal offices of postmaster general, secretary of state, and secretary of war; and Representative Roger Griswold from Connecticut.[290]

The secessionist plans in these northern states were, as Kevin Gannon notes, "not a curiosity nor a product of irrational, paranoid cranks," but rather "a legitimate expression of political grievances that had a potentially wide base of support."[291] The Northern Confederation that they envisaged was to be one in which "[n]either slavery nor slave representation would mar their economic progress or threaten political equity in their new splinter Republic."[292] However, their efforts were effectively blocked by fellow Federalists such as Alexander Hamilton and John Quincy Adams.[293]

New England states were the source of another secessionist movement triggered by their refusal to comply with President James Madison's demand that they place their militias under federal command during the War of 1812 with Great Britain. Compliance with this demand would have required New England troops to serve elsewhere, leaving New England vulnerable to attack by the British. In 1814, in response to this situation, a report by a committee of the Massachusetts legislature stated:

> We spurn the idea that the free, sovereign, and independent State of Massachusetts is reduced to a mere municipal corporation, without power to protect its people or to defend them from oppression, from whatever quarter it comes. Whenever the national compact is violated, and the citizens of this State are oppressed by cruel and unauthorized enactments, this Legislature is bound to interpose its power, and to wrest from the oppressor its victim. This is the spirit of our Union, and thus it has been explained by the very man [James Madison], who now sets at defiance all the principles of his early political life. The question, then, is not a question of power or right, but of TIME AND EXPEDIENCY.[294]

In relation to proposed, but subsequently not enacted, legislation to give effect to Madison's demands, in December 1814, Daniel Webster, then a representative from New Hampshire, voiced strong opposition to it and indicated what New England would do if it was enacted, when he said:

> The operation of measures thus unconstitutional and illegal ought to be prevented by a resort to other measures which are both constitutional and legal. It will be the solemn duty of the State Governments to protect their own authority over their own militia, and to interpose between their citizens and arbitrary power. These are among the objects for which the State Governments exist, and their highest obligations bind them to the preservation of their own rights and liberties of their people.[295]

Webster's speech echoed sentiments first enunciated in the Virginia and Kentucky Resolutions of 1798, authored by James Madison and Thomas Jefferson respectively. These resolutions were adopted in response and opposition to the federal Alien and Sedition Acts of the same year. Although there were differences between the two resolutions in terms of what a state could do in response to federal legislation that it deemed unconstitutional, both were anchored in the theory that the Constitution was a compact entered into between the states. Webster's invocation of this basal idea underpinning the 1798 resolutions was an early example of their use by states from both the North and the South. Indeed, during the antebellum era, "[t]he strongest expression of [this] states' rights sentiment was not in the South but in New England."[296]

Against this background and the feeling that the Madison administration had abandoned their economic and defensive needs, public opinion clamored for secession from the Union. In May 1813, the *Boston Centinel* asserted that "[t]he determination that was necessary in 1776 is necessary now."[297] Boston's New England Federalists called for a convention of delegates from Massachusetts, Connecticut, and Rhode Island to gather at Hartford, Connecticut, in December 1814.[298] According to Henry Adams, the Convention's objectives were "the restoration of peace and . . . the establishment of a new Federal compact comprising either the whole or a portion of the actual Union."[299] The majority of New England Federalists at that time viewed the Union as a collection of sovereign states which had merely delegated a portion of their sovereign powers to the federal government, and believed that secession was constitutionally legal and did not amount to treason.[300] For example, Thomas Pickering said that "[i]f the great objects of union are utterly abandoned" or "wantonly, corruptly, and treacherously sacrificed . . . let the Union be severed."[301] And for Gouverneur Morris, the circumstances at that time were such that led him to write that "we of the North and East, may save ourselves by a severance of the Union."[302]

However, Morris, and the more radical defenders of New England were not delegates at the Hartford Convention and were critical of what Morris referred to as its "modest propositions."[303] The Convention merely resolved to demand various constitutional amendments aimed at protecting New England's sectional interests. What New England states feared was the admission of new slave states from the Louisiana Purchase territory. Two amendments to the Constitution were proposed with this fear in mind. The first was to delete the Constitution's three-fifths clause and have representation in the House of Representatives based only upon a state's free population, thereby diluting slave state representation in the lower chamber of Congress. The second was that no new state could be admitted into the Union without the approval of two-thirds of both houses of Congress.[304] These amendments would have enabled New England states to effectively veto the admission of new states from the Louisiana Purchase territory whose interests were inimical to theirs. Furthermore, the Convention resolved to reconvene "if . . . the defence of [the Harford Convention] states should be neglected" and "if . . . the situation of the country shall urgently require it."[305] It was clear that, in such a situation, a reconvened Convention was likely to move towards secession. Although not a delegate to the Convention, Daniel Webster greeted the Convention's demands as "moderate, temperate & judicious."[306]

At the conclusion of the Convention, a delegation of three commissioners was appointed to go to Washington to seek implementation of its recommendations. However, the signing of the Treaty of Ghent in December 1814,[307] which ended the war with the British, meant that the anticipated negotiations for implementation of the Convention's demands never got underway,[308] and the Convention was never reconvened. What was, at its core, an attempt to revive the political role and influence in national politics of New England states ended in failure and witnessed the demise of the Federalist Party.[309]

THE MISSOURI COMPROMISE OF 1820

The sectional conflicts triggered by the Louisiana Purchase and the War of 1812 were temporarily laid to rest with the passage of legislation in 1820 giving effect to what is known as the "Missouri Compromise." In the words of Robert Pierce Forbes, the debates over the Union's territories and the states to be carved out of them that preceded the enactment of the Missouri Compromise "exposed the hold that slavery had acquired over the process of national decision making."[310] These issues, of paramount importance in terms of maintaining a sectional balance between the number of slave and non-slave states, were debated against the reality that by 1820, the population in the North was growing at a much faster rate than in the South. This gave northern states the preponderant position in the House of Representatives, with the consequence that the Senate, where each state had equal representation of two senators, would be the key federal institution through which a sectional balance could be maintained.

The Missouri Compromise arose in the context of the admission of Missouri into the Union and was triggered by a proposal by James Tallmadge Jr., a representative from New York. The so-called Tallmadge Amendment, which did not affect slaves already living in Missouri, would have prohibited the "further introduction of slavery" into Missouri and required slaves subsequently born there to be freed upon attaining the age of twenty-five.[311] Tallmadge and most of his northern colleagues all argued that Congress could prohibit the expansion of slavery into the Louisiana Purchase territory on the basis that it had the right and power to prohibit slavery in the Union's territories and any states carved out of them. Southern members of Congress, already fearful of the possible threat to the institution of slavery posed by the expansive interpretation of federal legislative power sanctioned by the Supreme Court decision in 1819 in *McCulloch v. Maryland*,[312] vehemently rejected this assertion.[313] Although the House of Representatives twice passed the Tallmadge Amendment, the Senate rejected it.[314] The compromise that resolved the issue over Missouri's application for admission to statehood was orchestrated by Henry Clay, the speaker of the House of Representatives, with the considerable backing and support of President James Monroe.[315] Its critical components were: (1) the admission of the northern part of Massachusetts as the free state of Maine;[316] (2) the admission, in due course, of Missouri as a slave state without the Tallmadge proviso;[317] and (3) the prohibition of slavery in the Louisiana Purchase territory north of latitude 36 degrees 30 minutes north.[318] Missouri was subsequently admitted to the Union as a slave state on 2 March 1821.[319] However, in the words of Representative Thomas Cobb of Georgia, the Tallmadge Amendment "kindled a fire which all the waters of the ocean cannot put out, which seas of blood can only extinguish."[320] It, and the

Missouri Compromise which it spawned, led William Henry Trescot, a South Carolina planter, to state that they marked "a broad declaration that in the American Union there are two people, differing in intentions, feelings, and in the basis of their political faith . . . and . . . that as to certain matters of political interest, they must, by an imaginary line, be separated."[321] And John Quincy Adams, then the Union's secretary of state, although accepting of the Missouri Compromise, feared the dissolution of the Union and wrote in his diary that "[i]f the Union must be dissolved, slavery is precisely the question upon which it ought to break."[322]

THE EXACERBATION OF SECTIONALISM IN THE 1830S

Sectional tensions flared again in the late 1820 and early 1830s, this time over the issue of tariffs. The dispute erupted in the wake of Congress enacting the so-called Tariff of Abominations in 1828, which significantly increased tariffs over a range of imported products.[323] Formal protests again this legislation were passed by the legislatures in South Carolina, Georgia, Alabama, Mississippi, and Virginia.[324] These protests elicited formal measures in support of the legislation by a number of states, most notably Kentucky, Louisiana, and Pennsylvania.[325] The leading opponent of the significant increase in tariff levels that this legislation imposed was John C. Calhoun, who at that time was vice-president of the United States and who subsequently served as a senator from South Carolina, for all but two years, until his death in 1850. Calhoun argued that the 1828 legislation was "unconstitutional, unequal, and oppressive" because it was imposed "not for revenue, but the protection of one branch of industry at the expense of others."[326] For him, the practical effect of the tariff was that it unfairly favored northern manufacturing interests at the expense of the southern agricultural economy built upon the institution of slavery.

Some of the "abominations" were removed by legislation passed in 1832.[327] However, in November 1832, South Carolina responded to this legislation by adopting an ordinance nullifying the tariff. The ordinance, drawing inspiration from the Virginia and Kentucky Resolutions, declared (1) that the 1828 and 1832 tariff legislation was "null, void and no law, nor binding upon [South Carolina], its officers, or citizens"; (2) that legislation would be passed to prevent collection of the tariff in South Carolina after 1 February 1833; (3) that South Carolina's public officials would be required to take "an oath, well and truly to obey, execute and enforce [the] Ordinance"; (4) that South Carolina would "not submit to the application of force, on the part of the federal government, to reduce [it] to obedience"; and (5) that any federal legislation or action against South Carolina would lead to the following consequence:

> The People of [South Carolina] will thenceforth hold themselves absolved from all further obligation to maintain or preserve their political connexion with the people of other States, and will forthwith proceed to organize a separate Government, and to do all other acts and things which sovereign and independent States may of right do.[328]

On 10 December 1832, President Andrew Jackson issued a proclamation that rejected nullification as "plainly unconstitutional" and threatened federal military intervention if South Carolina proceeded to act in defiance of federal law.[329] The crisis was defused when Congress passed two pieces of legislation on 2 March 1833. The first foreshadowed a progressive lowering of tariffs through to 1842, by which stage there would be a uniform rate of 20 percent on dutiable imports.[330] The second, commonly known as the Force Bill, authorized the use of force against South Carolina if it persisted with any act of nullification of federal legislation.[331] Calhoun, by then a senator from South Carolina, declared that, despite minor objections to the tariff reduction legislation, he supported it because anyone who "loves the Union must desire to see this agitating question brought to a termination."[332] Indeed, most nullifiers saw the legislation as a victory for South Carolina because it achieved, in great measure, what they wanted, namely, a lowering of the tariff. This support led, in turn, to South Carolina's state convention rescinding its Ordinance of Nullification by a vote of 153 to 4 on 15 March 1833.[333] However, the Force Bill, which had been widely denounced, most notably in the Senate by Calhoun,[334] as an attack on South Carolina's freedom was, three days later, declared "null and void, within the limits of [South Carolina]" by the state convention, by a vote of 132 to 19, on the ground that it was "unauthorized by the Constitution of the United States, subversive to that Constitution, and destructive of public liberty."[335]

Although tariffs ceased to be an issue of any great significance in the political debates leading up to the outbreak of the Civil War, the crisis instigated by the Tariff of Abominations was a key causative factor in the articulation of the anti-secession nationalist theory of the Constitution. Prior to then, in the sectional tensions that arose, both the northern non-slave states and southern slave states embraced the compact theory of the Constitution as the legal basis for their claims. As Henry James wrote of this period, the compact theory was "in itself a sound and true doctrine; as a starting point of American history and constitutional law there is no other which will bear a moment's examination; it was as dear to New England as to Virginia."[336] To similar effect, Charles Francis Adams wrote that, prior to the 1830s, "the belief was nearly universal that in the case of a final, unavoidable issue, sovereignty resided in the State, and to the State its citizens' allegiance was due."[337]

In early 1830, in his celebrated Senate debate with South Carolina's Robert Hayne, Daniel Webster, "the erstwhile New England particularist"[338] who had previously advocated interposition and supported the Hartford Convention resolutions, as senator from Massachusetts, emerged as the leading spokesman for the nationalist theory of the Constitution. Webster's argument that the Constitution did not permit a state to legally secede from the Union was significantly influenced by the writings of his friend, Supreme Court justice and Harvard law professor Joseph Story. Story's subsequently published treatise on constitutional law[339] was written in part to refute the doctrines of nullification and interposition and construct a nationalist interpretation of the Constitution anchored in expansive federal power and federal judicial supremacy.[340] Thus, in his treatise, Story strongly disagreed with earlier treatises supporting a constitutional right of secession written by scholars such as St George Tucker[341] and William Rawle.[342]

Webster's speech in 1830 was part of a concerted strategy on his part to, as Robert Pierce Forbes puts it, "piec[e] together a new national mythology,"[343] pursuant to which the past claims to nullification and secession would be set aside in favor of a national consensus in which northern non-slave states would recognize the legitimacy of slavery and the provisions in the Constitution that preserved and protected it and southern slave states would, in return, maintain their loyalty to the Union. It was with this in mind that, in his speech, Webster said:

> The domestic slavery of the Southern States I leave where I find it,—in the hands of their own Governments. It is their affair, not mine. . . . . The Union itself is too full of benefit to be hazarded in propositions for

changing its original basis. I go for the Constitution as it is, and for the *Union as it is* (emphasis added).[344]

Webster's arguments against the existence of any constitutional right of secession were warmly greeted by his political opponent, President Andrew Jackson, a slaveholder who, in his proclamation on 10 December 1832, adopted the position that because the United States was a perpetual union, secession was treasonous,[345] thereby becoming "the first and only statesman of the early national period to deny publicly the right of secession."[346] Webster's speech as well as Jackson's ringing endorsement of the perpetual nature of the Union remained principal sources for the nationalist theory of the Constitution and significantly influenced Abraham Lincoln's arguments against secession in 1860–1861. However, they were never accepted as expressions of the true nature of the Constitution by the political elites in the southern slave states who remained loyal the basic tenets of the compact theory of the Constitution.

THE 1850 COMPROMISE

With the passing of the tariff crisis of the 1830s, sectionalism and the threats of secession lay dormant until further territorial expansion took place in the 1840s. The first instance of this territorial expansion was the Union's annexation of Texas as a slave state in December 1845. Texas had previously gained its independence from Mexico in 1836. Its annexation was prompted by fears that British influence in the Lone Star Republic might lead to the abolition of slavery there.[347] However, the annexation was bitterly opposed by many in the northern non-slave states.[348] For example, former president John Quincy Adams viewed the annexation as "a signal triumph of the slave-representation in the Constitution of the United States."[349]

Following the accession of Oregon Territory pursuant to a negotiated settlement with Great Britain in 1846,[350] the Union's westward expansion across the North American continent was completed with territory gained at Mexico's expense following the Mexican-American War of 1846–1848. In 1853, a further 29,670 square miles of territory was obtained from Mexico pursuant to the Gadsden Purchase.[351] The purchase of this territory was engineered by Jefferson Davis, then secretary of war, to ensure that a proposed transcontinental railroad would take a southerly route and therefore most benefit the South.[352]

The Union's territorial aggrandizement at Mexico's expense was the key factor in the reemergence of sectional tensions that was ignited in 1846, a few months after the outbreak of the Mexican-American War, when Representative David Wilmot from Pennsylvania introduced a proposal which, had it been adopted by Congress, would have excluded slavery from any territory gained as a result of the Mexican-American War. In introducing this proposal, Wilmot was not, as he conceded, motivated by any "morbid sympathy for the slave." Rather, as he said, it was proposed for "the cause and rights of the white freeman" so as to "preserve to free white labor a fair country, a rich inheritance, where the sons of toil, of my own race and own color, can live without the disgrace which association with negro slavery brings upon free labor."[353]

The issue of slavery in the territories that were ceded to the Union by Mexico by the terms of the 1848 Treaty of Guadalupe[354] coincided with increased sectional tensions over the issue of the rendition of fugitive slaves. In 1793, Congress had enacted the Fugitive Slave Act, which regulated the procedures for the capture and return of runaway slaves.[355] This legislation, in denying any due process rights to slaves who had escaped captivity, led to a number of northern states enacting so-called personal liberty laws, which effectively sought to undermine the 1793 Act. Although in 1842 the Supreme Court in *Prigg v. Pennsylvania*[356] upheld the constitutionality of the 1793 Act and declared Pennsylvania's personal liberty law unconstitutional, southern slave states nevertheless began to demand a strengthening of the 1793 legislation, which many in these states had from the outset seen as inadequate.

It was in this context that a number of calls for the dissolution of the Union were voiced. From the North, on 31 May 1848, New Hampshire's John P. Hale, who had been expelled from the Democratic Party in 1845 on account of his fierce antislavery stance,[357] demanded of his Senate colleagues that "if this Union, with all its advantages, has no other cement than the blood of human slavery, let it perish!"[358] Echoing this sentiment was William Lloyd Garrison, who had since the mid-1840s been publicly calling for "NO UNION WITH SLAVEHOLDERS."[359] This sentiment led the New-England Anti-Slavery Society, which was led by Garrison, resolving that it was the "first duty for [abolitionists] to agitate for the dissolution of the Union."[360] And in a speech that he delivered on 5 March 1858, he said: "We shall be told that this [disunion] is equivalent to a dissolution of the Union. Be it so! Give us Disunion with liberty and a good conscience, rather than Union with slavery and moral degradation."[361] However, Garrison's disunionism was one presented as a choice between "Repeal [the Union] *or* Abolition," which meant, as Henry Mayer points out, that "he was not so much threatening political secession as he was pointing out the inevitable collapse of a society built upon the great contradiction of slavery."[362]

However, the most significant call for dissolution came from the Mississippi legislature,[363] which, at John C. Calhoun's suggestion,[364] in March 1850 issued a call for a convention of southern states to meet in Nashville, Tennessee in June 1850 "to counsel together for their common safety."[365] Calhoun's views on the need for the Convention were expressed in April 1849 in private correspondence, where he wrote:

> I am of the impression that the time is near at hand, when the South will have to choose between disunion, and submission. I think so, because I see little prospect of arresting the aggression of the North. . . . . [A] Convention of the South is an indispensible means to discharge a great duty we owe to our partners in the Union; that is to warn [the North] in the most solemn manner that if they do not desist from aggressions & cease to disregard our rights & the stipulations of the Constitution, the duty we owe to ourselves & posterity, would compel us to dissolve forever the partnership with them.[366]

The Nashville Convention was held against the backdrop of negotiations that, in September 1850, led to Congress passing of a series of acts, proposed by Henry Clay—then a senator from Kentucky—known as the 1850 Compromise. When Clay contracted tuberculosis, the key figure in the passage of this legislation through the Senate was Senator Stephen A. Douglas from Illinois.[367] The trigger for the 1850 Compromise was a request in December 1849 from the territory of California to be admitted to the Union as a non-slave state. This bought to the fore the unresolved question of the extension of slavery into the territories acquired as a result of the Mexican-American War. The 1850 Compromise legislation resulted in (1) California being admitted as a free state;[368] (2) resolution of the Texan border;[369] (3) the creation of the territories of New Mexico[370] and Utah,[371] in which the issue of slavery was left to be decided by their inhabitants pursuant to the principle of popular sovereignty; (4) the abolition of the slave trade, but not slavery, in the District of Columbia;[372] and (5) amendments to the Fugitive Slave Act of 1793, strengthening the rights of slaveholders to recover runaway slaves.[373]

While the 1850 Compromise legislation was being debated, the Nashville Convention met in early June 1850 and passed resolutions that (1) called for the right of slaveholders to settle in the territories with their slaves; (2) affirmed the right to recapture runaway slaves; (3) asserted that slavery was "recognized, by the Constitution as a three-fold aspect, first as property, second, as a domestic relation of service or labor under the law of a State, and lastly as a basis for political power;" and (4) as a measure for compromise, suggested extending the Missouri Compromise line to the Pacific Ocean as a means of preserving "the stability of our institutions [i.e., slavery]."[374]

TOWARDS DISUNION IN THE 1850S

Although the 1850 Compromise served to preserve the Union, in a memorandum of his conversation with Calhoun in March 1850, James M. Mason noted Calhoun's prediction that a "catastrophe" awaited the Union within twelve years, with the "probability that it [would] explode in a Presidential election."[375]

The first major step towards the realization of Calhoun's fears occurred when Congress passed the Kansas-Nebraska Act in 1854.[376] This legislation dealt with the organization of the territories of Kansas and Nebraska. These territories, forming part of the territory acquired by the Louisiana Purchase, were north of latitude 36 degrees 30 minutes north as set out in the Missouri Compromise legislation. The Kansas-Nebraska Act was the outcome of a political deal negotiated by Senator Stephen A. Douglas to ensure that a transcontinental railway would pass through his home state of Illinois. In order to get southern support for this railway route, the legislation included a provision that stipulated that the doctrine of popular sovereignty would determine the issue of slavery in any future states created out of these two territories. In so doing, it declared the Missouri Compromise provisions with respect to these two territories "inoperative and void,"[377] with the result that the "Union as it was" that Daniel Webster defended in 1830 no longer existed.[378]

The Kansas-Nebraska Act was a significant victory for the southern slave states. It opened up the possibility of redressing the consequences of the 1850 Compromise that saw the admission of California tipping the sectional balance in the Senate in favor of non-slave states by a score of sixteen to fifteen. However, the effect of the legislation was a bloody conflict between proslavery and antislavery forces over the issue of slavery in the proposed state of Kansas.[379] The failure to secure Kansas's admission as a slave state, combined with the admission of Minnesota in 1858 and Oregon in 1859 as non-slave states served only to further exacerbate the sectional imbalance in the Senate.[380] The Kansas-Nebraska Act and the "bleeding of Kansas" conflict that it spawned was also the major factor in the emergence of the Republican Party in 1854,[381] whose unwavering opposition to the expansion of slavery into any of the Union's territories was seen by both sides of the sectional divide, if implemented, as inexorably leading to the eventual extinction of slavery.[382]

On the other hand, a measure of solace for the slave states was that the territorial legislatures in Utah in 1851 and New Mexico in 1859 legalized slavery and adopted slave codes.[383] However, their future admission to the Union as slave states would be threatened if the Republican Party came to power following the 1860 elections.

The complete dismantling of the Missouri Compromise occurred in 1857 with the Supreme Court decision in *Dred Scott v. Sandford*.[384] This complex case involved a number of issues. Its critical facts revolved around whether Dred Scott, a slave from Missouri, had become a free person by virtue of having lived, for more than two years, in the non-slave state of Illinois and territory that had been declared as non-slave territory by the terms of the Missouri Compromise and would become, in 1858, the free state of Minnesota. The Supreme Court, by a seven to two majority, ruled against Scott.

Reflecting William Lloyd Garrison's claim that the Constitution was a "covenant with death" and "an agreement with hell,"[385] the opinion of the Court, delivered by Chief Justice Taney, contained two key rulings. In what Kermit Roosevelt persuasively argues was "the natural consequence of the pro-slavery tilt of the Founders' Constitution,"[386] the first ruling was that no African American, be they a slave or free person, could be a citizen of the United States, although, under the concept of dual citizenship, they could be a citizen of a state pursuant to that state's law. In making this ruling, Taney ignored the fact that free African Americans in seven States[387] had voted in the elections for delegates to the conventions for the ratification of the Constitution in 1787–1788 and that in five northern states, free blacks were at that time entitled to vote.[388]

The second ruling was that Congress did not have the power to regulate or prohibit slavery in federal territories.[389] This ruling rendered the Missouri Compromise unconstitutional and therefore void. Both of these rulings were underpinned by a finding that, as Taney put it, "the right of property in a slave is distinctly and expressly affirmed in the Constitution."[390] For Taney, this meant that, as inferior and degraded people, slaves (as well as free blacks) were neither able to bear the obligations, nor assume the benefits, of citizenship. Furthermore, because Congress had no power to restrict the rights of persons to take their property with them when entering the Union's territories, these persons were free to settle in those territories with their slaves. Although politically explosive, this ruling represented a major victory for the interests of slave states, not only because slavery was now a possibility in those parts of the Louisiana Purchase that had not yet been formed into states, but more importantly, because slave states could be created in the vast territory ceded to the Union as a result of its war with Mexico.

However, for slave states, the Republican Party represented a major threat to the victories gained as a result of *Dred Scott v. Sandford*. Because Article V of the Constitution required three-quarters of the states to ratify an amendment to the Constitution, the Republican Party's policy objective of not permitting slavery in any of the Union's territories could not be realistically achieved by a constitutional amendment. However, given that the Republicans made it clear that they were prepared to make rejection of *Dred Scott v. Sandford* a prerequisite to any new appointments to the Supreme Court, the more ominous possibility was achieving their policy objective through the courts.[391] The election of a Republican administration in November 1860 was seen by the southern slave states as the start of a new reality in which the expansion of slavery into the western territories would thereafter be impossible. This meant that "[a] West without slavery was a frightening prospect to individuals who believed the South needed fresh soils to survive."[392]

Running parallel to the issue of slavery in the territories was ongoing sectional tension over the rendition of runaway slaves, triggered by the strengthening of fugitive slave legislation as part of the 1850 Compromise. The importance to the slave states of the strengthened fugitive slave legislation was evidenced by a resolution in the qualified endorsement of the 1850 Compromise by Georgia's state convention that adopted the "Georgia Platform" in December 1850. The "Georgia Platform," having first declared that "the American Union [is] secondary in importance only to the rights and principles it was designed to perpetuate," went on to stipulate "that upon the faithful execution of the Fugitive Slave Bill by the proper authorities depends the preservation of our much loved Union."[393] However, this did not prevent a number of northern non-slave states adopting personal liberty laws during the 1850s aimed at undermining the strengthened federal fugitive slave legislation of 1850.

The fears within the slave states over the future enforcement of fugitive slave legislation, coupled with the Republican Party's firm opposition to permitting slavery in the Union's territories, notwithstanding the decision in *Dred Scott v. Sandford*, significantly increased secessionist sentiment in the southern slave states, especially in the Deep South. This sentiment was further strengthened when, on 16 October 1859, with just over twelve months to go before the 1860 presidential election, the radical abolitionist John Brown led a raid at Harpers Ferry in Virginia, hoping to incite an armed slave revolt. Brown's raid was a dismal failure and he was quickly captured, arrested, tried for treason and murder, and, finally, executed on 2 December 1859.[394] Although Brown's attempt to raise a slave insurrection was condemned not only by slaveholders but also by the Republican Party,[395] it nevertheless brought to the surface the extant fears of white southerners of what the end of slavery would entail, be it pursuant to a slave insurrection or emancipation.

Slavery and Secession

As foreseen by Calhoun in 1850, the "catastrophe" that awaited the Union did explode in the wake of Lincoln's victory in the November 1860 presidential election. South Carolina's secession a month later triggered secessions by six other Deep South slave states prior to Lincoln's inauguration in March 1861,[396] leading to what Leonardis W. Spratt, the editor of the *Charleston Mercury*, described as "the formation of a *Slave* Republic" that was "bound together" by "the three [great] relations of husband and wife, and parent and child, and master and slave."[397] Four more secessions took place after the first shot of the Civil War was fired at Fort Sumter in April 1861.[398] Of these eleven states, South Carolina had the highest proportion of slaves (57 percent) and Arkansas had the lowest (26 percent). The four slave states that did not secede had proportionately far fewer slaves than did the eleven states that did secede—Delaware (2 percent), Kentucky (19 percent), Maryland (13 percent),[399] and Missouri (10 percent).[400] The low percentage of slaves in these four Upper South slave states explains why secessionist sentiment in them was not enough to lead them to secede from the Union.

In their secession ordinances, ten of the seceding states, in various formulations, explicitly declared that they were thenceforth free and independent States. The eleventh state, South Carolina, did so implicitly, with its ordinance repealing the ordinance of 1788 by which it ratified the Constitution. Subsequently, all eleven states came together to form the Confederate States of America.

Notwithstanding Lost Cause assertions to the contrary, as the prosecessionist delegate to the South Carolina secession convention Lawrence Keitt put it, "[T]he question of slavery . . . is the great central point from which we are now seceding."[401] And as Alexander Stephens, the Confederacy's vice-president, put it on 21 March 1861, "African slavery as it exists among us—the proper *status* of the negro in our form of civilization . . . was the immediate cause of the late rupture and present revolution," and further, the Confederacy's "corner-stone rests, upon the great truth, that the negro is not equal to the white man; that slavery—subordination to the superior race—is his natural and moral condition."[402] Scholarly analyses[403] confirm what, as far back as 1937, the historian Percy Rainwater concluded when, in the case of Mississippi's secession, he wrote that it was viewed as "the best means to be employed for preserving slavery."[404] More recently, the historian Dwight Pitcaithley wrote that "[e]leven southern states seceded in 1860–1861, not in defense of states' rights but in defense of property rights."[405] This is amply confirmed by the formal declarations and statements issued by these states, an exemplar of which is South Carolina's "Declaration of the Immediate Causes Which Induce and Justify the Secession" (the Declaration). In justifying secession on the grounds of breaches by nonslave states of constitutional obligations pertaining to slavery, it said:

> The right of property in slaves was recognized [in the Constitution] by giving free persons distinct political rights, by giving them the right to represent, and burthening them with direct taxes for three-fifths of their

> slaves; by authorizing the importation of slaves for twenty years; and by stipulating the rendition of fugitives from labor. We affirm that these ends for which this Government was instituted have been defeated, and the Government itself has been made destructive of them by the action of the non-slaveholding States. Those States have assumed the right of deciding upon the propriety of our domestic institutions; and have denied the rights of property established in fifteen of the States and recognized by the Constitution; they have permitted the open establishment among them of societies, whose avowed object is to disturb the peace and to eloign the property of the citizens of other States. They have encouraged and assisted thousands of our slaves to leave their homes; and those who remain have been incited by emissaries, books and pictures to servile insurrection.[406]

Similarly, in detailing the "the immediate causes" of its secession, Mississippi noted that its position was "thoroughly identified with the institution of slavery."[407] Alabama, in the Preamble to its ordinance of secession, asserted that secession was justified on the ground that the newly elected Republican administration was "avowedly hostile to the domestic institutions and the peace and security of the people of the State of Alabama."[408] The reference in the ordinance to "domestic institutions" was code for slavery, as is evidenced by a statement by a delegate to Alabama's secession convention that the ordinance rested "in a great measure, upon our assertion of a right to enslave the African race, or, what amounts to the same thing, to hold them in slavery."[409] In Texas, secession was, as stated in its secession ordinance, grounded in the claim that northern states had engaged in actions that were "violative of the compact between the States and the guarantees of the Constitution."[410] In an accompanying declaration, Texas referred to the Union as one "established exclusively by the white race, for themselves and their posterity," in which African Americans were "rightfully held and regarded as an inferior and dependent race." Furthermore, the declaration made it clear that secession from the Union was justified because breaches of the Constitution's slavery provisions by northern states had undermined "the rights of slave-holding States in their domestic institution."[411] Underlying the fear that slavery was in peril was that most southern whites feared that such an eventuality would lead to a possible race war, racial equality between whites and African Americans, and the demise of white racial purity through racial amalgamation.

The centrality of the defense of slavery as the trigger for secession was also evidenced in the work of commissioners from five of the Deep South states who were tasked with promoting the secessionist cause across the slave states. Reflective of the causal reason for secession that these commissioners articulated are the words of Henry L. Benning, Georgia's commissioner to Virginia. In addressing Virginia's secession convention, he emphasized that "the reason that induced Georgia [to secede] . . . was a conviction, a deep conviction . . . on the part of Georgia, that a separation from the North was the only thing that could prevent the abolition of slavery. This conviction . . . was the main cause."[412] To similar effect, South Carolina's commissioner to Texas, John McQueen, enjoined the Texas secession convention to unite with the states that had by then already seceded to create "a Southern Confederacy, to perpetuate the institutions of our ancestry, who transmitted them to us, to have them but as usufruct, and transmit them, untarnished, to our posterity."[413] And George Williamson, Louisiana's commissioner to Texas, explained that Louisiana's objective in seceding from the Union was "the formation of a Southern confederacy to preserve the blessings of African slavery."[414]

The confederacy's vice-president, Alexander Stephens, neatly summed up the reason for secession in his diary entry for 5 June 1865, where he wrote:

> Slavery was without doubt the occasion of secession; out of it rose the breach of compact, for instance, on the part of several Northern States in refusing to comply with Constitutional obligations as to rendition of fugitives from service, a course betraying total disregard for all constitutional barriers.[415]

After the Civil War, and notwithstanding the emergence of the Lost Cause, from time to time defenders of the Confederacy conceded that its cause was the preservation of slavery. For example, in 1868, the Richmond, Virginia, journalist Edward A. Pollard wrote that "the true question" of the Civil War was "the supremacy of the white race, and along with it the preservation of the political traditions of the country" and that the result of the war was to "destroy [the] barrier [between the races] and throw upon the country the ultimate question of the Negro."[416] The same concession was made by Jubal A. Early, a prominent promoter of the Lost Cause who had served as general for the Confederacy, notwithstanding that, as a Unionist, he had voted against secession at Virginia's secession convention.[417] In 1915, in his posthumously published book, Early wrote that "[t]he struggle for independence made by the Southern States of the American Union, grew out of the questions of self-government arising mainly in regard to the institution of slavery as it existed in those states."[418]

In the histories of various Confederate military units, similar statements were made. For example, the history of the 3rd Louisiana regiment asserted that New England "fanaticism" had incited the Civil War, and that "[t]he first aim and object of this foul spirit was the eradication of slavery on this continent, an interference with the peculiar institutions of one section by the powerful arm of the opposing section."[419] And the history of the 6th Georgia regiment asserted that its soldiers went off to fight for "the safety, protection, and perpetuation of their political rights and institutions," a prominent one being "the Institution of Slavery."[420] Thus, it was hardly surprising that, in a well-received speech delivered in 1890, Captain Charles K. Maddox from Georgia asserted that the South fought the Civil War "for the supremacy of the white race in America; for civilization against abolition theories; the cause of truth against abolition prejudice; and the cause of common sense against the foulest errors that will ever astonish posterity."[421] And finally, in her 1909 book, *Historic Papers of the Causes of the Civil War*, the Kentuckian writer and member of the United Daughters of the Confederacy, Eugenia Dunlap Potts, was to the point when she wrote: "That the question of slavery lay at the root of the dissension cannot be doubted by any who are conversant with the political history of the United States."[422]

Although grievances related to the compact theory of the Constitution and federal tariff legislation were aired at the various secession conventions, neither of these were the reason why the eleven slave states seceded.

In relation to tariffs, the issue was, as Marc Egnal observes, "as much about defending slavery as it was about resisting an oppressive federal tax," in that it reflected "the determination of members of the planting class to resist steps that might lead to the end of their way of life."[423] That the issue of tariffs was inextricably linked to slavery was made clear by John C. Calhoun when, in the context of the tariff crisis of the early 1830s, he wrote:

> I consider the Tariff as the occasion, rather than the real cause of the present unhappy state of things. The truth can no longer be disguised, that the peculiar domestick institution of the Southern States, and the consequent direction, which that and her soil and climate have given to her industry, has placed them in regard to taxation and appropriations in opposite relation to the majority of the Union, against the danger of which, if there be no protective power in the reserved rights of the States, they must in the end be forced to rebel, or submit to have their paramount interests sacrificed [*sic*], their domestick institutions subordinated by Colonization and other schemes, and themselves & children reduced to wretchedness. Thus situated, the denial of the right of the State to interfere constitutionally in the last resort, more alarms the thinking, than all other causes.[424]

The North also understood that the issue of tariffs, of itself, was not South Carolina's real concern during this crisis. In his speech to the House of Representatives in January 1833, Nathan Appleton, a Massachusetts representative and textile magnate, noted that the South Carolinians were motivated by the "fear and apprehension of the South that the General Government may one day interfere with the right of property in slaves" and that this fear was "the bond which unites the South in a solid phalanx."[425] And in July 1833, Tilgham Howard, a lawyer and politician from Indiana whom President Jackson appointed as the Union's attorney for Indiana, wrote: "I believe the tariff was not the *cause* of [the South's] discontent, but only its *occasion*—the cause being more deeply seated. It is not to be supposed that they fear direct legislation, upon the question, but the *effect* of it, when legitimately exercised upon *other questions*."[426]

That the preservation of slavery was at the heart of the Confederate secessions was hardly surprising given that the nearly four million slaves in the slave states on the eve of the Civil War represented, as James Huston observes, "a mountain of wealth."[427] By 1860 slaves were, as Gerald Gunderson notes, "profitable investments for southern owners" which was "an attractive employment of capital and was expected to remain so."[428] This emphasis on wealth, based upon ownership of slaves, stood in stark contrast to wealth in the Northern states that was based in ownership of land.[429] By 1860, the wealth in slave ownership accounted for more than 30 percent of the annual income of free citizens in six Lower South states (Alabama, Florida, Georgia, Louisiana, Mississippi, and South Carolina) and more than 20 percent of the annual income in Texas and four border states (Arkansas, North Carolina, Tennessee, and Virginia).[430] Thus, it was unsurprising that, in October 1860, the *Charleston Mercury* proclaimed that "[s]lave property, is the foundation of all property in the South. When security in this is shaken, all other property partakes of instability."[431]

In relation to the compact theory of the Constitution and the states' rights that flowed from it, secessionists did not, as the lawyer and author, John Codman Hurd observed in 1881, "take up arms to carry out abstract ideas about anything, not even about government or about the possession of sovereignty."[432] Notwithstanding Lost Cause claims to the contrary after the Civil War, they did not in 1860–1861 claim that the defense of states' rights was the impulse for secession. Rather, as is evidenced by the ordinances of secession, the compact theory of the Constitution was relied upon as the legal basis for unilateral secession from the Union.

The secession ordinances of seven states dissolved what was explicitly referred to as the "compact between" them and other states.[433] The other four states used words that, properly construed, amounted to the same thing. Georgia and Virginia referred to the "union between" them and other states. Florida referred to "the confederacy of States," and Tennessee referred to the "federal relations between" it and other States. All states except Alabama repealed, rescinded, or annulled either their ratifications of the Constitution or agreements by which they entered the Union. Alabama merely declared that it had withdrawn from, and thereafter ceased to be, "one of the said United States." As a result of these stipulations, five states asserted that that they fully possessed and exercised all the rights of sovereignty appertaining to "free and independent States."[434] Four states asserted that they were, as a result, sovereign and independent states.[435] Alabama asserted that it "of right ought to be a Sovereign and Independent State." Only South Carolina's ordinance made no express claim to independent statehood, although this was implied given that it repealed its ratification of the Constitution and dissolved its union with the other states of the Union.

That the compact theory of the Constitution and the rights of states pursuant to it was not the impulse for secession is also made clear in the declarations justifying and explaining secession published by South Carolina,[436] Mississippi,[437] Georgia,[438] and Texas.[439] None of them made any reference to states' rights or the compact theory as the impulse for secession. Rather, they all were clear in asserting that the compact theory provided the legal basis for secession. For example, South Carolina's Declaration, after asserting that the Constitution was established "by compact between the States," stated:

> We maintain that in every compact between two or more parties, the obligation is mutual; that the failure of one of the contracting parties to perform a material part of the agreement, entirely releases the obligation of the other; and that where no arbiter is provided, each party is remitted to his own judgment to determine the fact of failure, with all its consequences. . . . . [T]he constitutional compact has been deliberately broken and disregarded by the non-slaveholding States, and the consequence follows that South Carolina is released from her obligation.[440]

Shearer Bowman correctly points out that in the antebellum period, "[t]he doctrine of states' rights, like that of federal supremacy [could] promote and protect any number of agendas or interests."[441] In invoking the compact theory of the Constitution during the great secession winter of 1860–1861, the Confederate states did so because it provided a legal basis for their unilateral secessions from the Union which was the means by which their interest in the institution of slavery was to be preserved and protected. And as David Blight points out, "[T]he significance of any exercise of a states' rights doctrine [was] in the issue for which it [was] employed."[442] Thus, as Lawrence Anderson notes, "Except for a few Southern fire-eaters, . . . adherence to states' rights was not ideological."[443]

Conclusion

If the Declaration of Independence of 1776 can be considered as the American Revolution's opening salvo, its final outcome was the "more perfect Union" ordained and formed by the Constitution that came into operation in March 1789. Four score and five years after the Declaration, Abraham Lincoln referred to it as "an 'apple of gold' . . . [and the] *Union*, and the *Constitution*, are the *picture* of *silver*, subsequently framed around it . . . not to *conceal*, or *destroy* the apple; but to *adorn*, and *preserve* it."[444] However, the Declaration's assertion that "all men are created equal" was anything but an "apple of gold" for the Union's millions of African Americans. Throughout the antebellum era, the overwhelming majority of them were enslaved, and the overwhelming majority of white Americans were content to keep them enslaved, although they grew increasingly divided over just where slavery could exist within the Union. However, this is not to deny that for many free African Americans in the northern states, the Declaration held out the hope that, one day, African Americans would be free and equal under the law with all other Americans. This is evident in the work of the free northern African Americans in developing an antislavery constitutionalism which entailed the obligation of equality under the law, reading into the Constitution such an obligation which they derived from the Declaration.[445]

In his Second Inaugural Address in March 1865, Lincoln, after referring to "the peculiar and powerful interest" that was slavery, asserted that "all knew that this interest was, somehow, the cause of the war."[446] He was right. Southern secessionists saw Lincoln's election victory in November 1860 and the armed conflict that ensued in the wake of his inauguration as president as simply the logical next stage of a war that he implicitly declared in his "House Divided" speech, delivered on 16 June 1858, in which he said:

> A House Divided against itself cannot stand. I believe this government cannot endure, perpetually half *slave* and half *free*. I do not expect the Union to be *dissolved*—I do not expect the house to *fall*—but I *do* expect it will cease to be divided. It will become *all* one thing, or *all* the other.[447]

Lincoln was determined that the Union would have to cease being a "House Divided" and that, in achieving that objective, the Union would not be dissolved and slavery would have to be abolished. In August 1855, in private correspondence, he recognized "that there is no peaceful extinction of slavery in prospect for us."[448] In December 1859, he made clear who would be the victor in any war over slavery when he said:

> If we shall constitutionally elect a President, it will be our duty to see that you submit. Old John Brown has just been executed for treason against a state..... [If] constitutionally we elect a President, and therefore you undertake to destroy the Union, it will be our duty to deal with you as old John Brown has been dealt with.[449]

As Otto Olsen points out, Lincoln's views "constituted a revolutionary development in national politics" because "[he] and his party were radically departing from the principles and practices that had governed the nation since the American Revolution."[450]

During the secession conventions of 1860–1861, various secessionists referenced Lincoln's "House Divided" speech. For example, Fulton Anderson, when addressing the Virginia convention, recognized that there was "indeed an irrepressible conflict," and that the time had come for slave states to "make it fruitful of good by ending forever the fatal struggle and placing our institutions beyond the reach of further hostility."[451] By the very act of declaring their independence from the Union, the eleven Confederate states implicitly affirmed their belief that they would win the war that Lincoln had implicitly declared in his "House Divided" speech. Indeed, a southern secessionist could well have delivered a "House Divided" speech in 1858 along the following hypothetical lines:

> A House Divided against itself cannot stand. I believe this government cannot endure, perpetually half *slave* and half *free*. I expect the Union to be *dissolved*—I expect the house to *fall*–I *do* expect it will be divided. One part will become *all* one thing, and one part will be *all* the other.

The ordinances of secession, the justifications for secession, the work of slave state commissioners, and the explicit statements of the Confederacy's leaders such as Alexander Stephens all amply confirm that concerns over the future of the South's peculiar institution ignited their departure from the Union and the ensuing armed conflict by which the Confederate states sought to preserve their part of the divided House. Southern economic grievances were not, of themselves, the basis for secession. Rather, they underpinned the constitutionally protected institution of slave-based property which secessionists were determined to preserve at all costs by forming a more perfect slaveholders' union. Or, as South Carolina put it in "The Address of the People of South Carolina Assembled in Convention, to the People of the Slaveholding States of the United States," to create "a great Slaveholding Confederacy, stretching its arms over a territory larger than any power in Europe possesses—with a population four times greater than that of the whole United States when they achieved their independence of the British Empire."[452]

In articulating their grievances surrounding slavery, secessionists in 1860–1861 viewed their cause in the same way that late-nineteenth-century American historian Moses Coit Tyler interpreted the secession of the thirteen colonies from Great Britain in the 1770s, that is, as being directed "not against tyranny inflicted, but only against tyranny anticipated."[453] Whether secession in pursuance of that cause was constitutionally permissible, as the seceding states claimed, depended upon a number of issues. The first of these, which is explored in the next chapter, was whether the Constitution allowed a state to unilaterally secede from the Union.

2

"An Indestructible Union?"

Nationalist and Compact Theories of the Constitution

This chapter deals with the pivotal question of whether the Constitution, as it stood in 1860–1861, allowed a state to unilaterally secede from the Union. There was no express provision in the Constitution on the issue of secession. Therefore, as Akhil Reed Amar points out, the legal answer to the "burning issues raised by . . . the secession crisis of 1860–1861 . . . reside[s] in the relevant legal materials of 1787–1788."[1] The antebellum debate on the issue of secession primarily revolved around the implications that could be drawn from the Constitution's Preamble, which stated that the Constitution was ordained and established by "the People of the United States, in Order to form a more perfect Union." Although the Constitution made no express reference to sovereignty, if it was "the People" who ordained and established the Constitution, it was clear that sovereignty vested in "the People." If it was "the People" in whom sovereignty was vested, it was generally agreed that the issue of secession was one to be determined by "the People." As will be discussed below, much of the argument over a state's right of secession revolved around competing meanings of the phrase "We the People" in the Preamble.

That sovereignty vested in "the People" was not a matter in dispute. The location of sovereignty in "the People" is evident from the Declaration of Independence's assertion that in order to secure man's "unalienable Rights . . . Governments are instituted among Men, deriving their just powers from the consent of the governed." Thus, as Gordon Wood aptly observes, this theory of sovereignty "pervaded the arguments of the whole Revolutionary generation from the moment in the 1760s when it was first raised through to the adoption of the federal Constitution in

1787."[2] For that generation, the location of sovereignty was never in dispute—it derived from, was vested in, and was retained by "the People."[3] As Edmund Morgan observes, "By the eighteenth century [in America], the sovereignty of the people was taken for granted."[4]

The sovereignty of the people was confirmed in the constitutions that were proclaimed by a number of States in the wake of the Declaration of Independence. Article I of North Carolina's 1776 constitution declared that "all political power is vested in and derived from the people."[5] The Preamble to Pennsylvania's 1776 constitution stated that all government is "derived from the authority of the people."[6] Provisions to the same effect were included in the constitutions of Maryland (1776),[7] Virginia (1776),[8] Georgia (1777),[9] Massachusetts (1780),[10] and New Hampshire (1784).[11]

During the debates over the ratification of the Constitution, the location of sovereignty in the people was confirmed by two future justices of the Supreme Court. At the North Carolina convention, James Iredell said: "[O]ur governments have been clearly created by the people themselves."[12] At the Pennsylvania convention, James Wilson said: "The truth is, that, in our governments, the supreme, absolute, and uncontrollable power *remains* in the people . . . and they never part with it."[13] The Union's first president, George Washington, made the same point in discarded and undelivered fragments of his First Inaugural Address which stated that the "Constitution, is really in its formation a government of the people; that is to say, a government in which all power is derived from, and at stated period reverts to them."[14] In 1793, this sentiment was explicitly confirmed by Supreme Court Chief Justice John Jay, in *Chisholm v. Georgia*, when he said that the consequence of the Declaration of Independence was that "sovereignty . . . passed to the people."[15]

It was thus unsurprising that the Constitution's Preamble, in its relevant parts, stipulated as follows: "We the People of the United States . . . do ordain and establish this Constitution for the United States of America." What the Preamble's "People" meant was aptly described by Chief Justice Roger Taney when, in delivering the opinion of the Supreme Court in 1857 in *Dred Scott v. Sandford*, he referred to them as "the political body who . . . form the sovereignty, and who hold the power and conduct the Government through their representatives."[16]

A consequence of the Constitution being anchored in the sovereignty of the people was that the right of secession from the Union logically also vested in them. This was made clear, again by both Iredell and Wilson during the ratification debates. Iredell, having said that the people created the Constitution, went on to say: "The same authority that created can destroy" and that "when the principles of the constitution are violated, the constitution itself is dissolved, or may be dissolved at the pleasure of the parties to it."[17] Wilson made the same point when he said: "[T]he people possess, over our constitutions, control in act, as well as in right [with the] consequence that the people may change their constitutions whenever and however they please."[18] He also said that, given that it was the people who ordained and established the Constitution, "[t]hose who ordain and establish have the power, if they think proper, to repeal and annul."[19]

Grammatically, the word "people" can be either singular or plural. Given this, as Edward Larson states, "indeterminate" nature of the phrase "We the People of the United States,"[20] if a right of secession was vested in the sovereignty of "the People" of the Preamble, ascertaining who were "the People" is of pivotal importance. In this respect, as Forrest McDonald points out, "it is interesting to note that in the instances in the body of the Constitution in which construction requires a decision in a matter as to singularity versus plurality, the document opts for the latter."[21] Thus, in each of Article I, Section 9 and Article III, Sections 2 and 3 of the Constitution, the reference to "the United States" is in the plural "them" or "their," rather than in the singular "it."[22] Furthermore, when, in 1798, in *Calder v. Bull*, Justice Samuel Chase wrote that "the people of the *United States* erected their Constitutions, or forms of government, to establish justice, to promote the general welfare, to secure the blessings of liberty; and to protect their *persons* and *property* from violence,"[23] the use of the plural "Constitutions" clearly means that he was referring to the peoples of the individual states of the United States rather than a single people of the United States.

As noted in Chapter 1, in the 1830s a debate emerged between two rival schools of thought over the who constituted "the People." This debate, often passionate and heated, reflected the essential truth of Justice Joseph Story's observation in *Martin v. Hunter's Lessee* that the Constitution's "language is essentially defective in precision."[24] Thus, the critical question in this debate was whether the Preamble's "People" was to be construed as referring to a single people or a number of peoples. In other words, did the Preamble refer to a single people of the United States or to a number of peoples of the United States?

The first school of thought argued that the Preamble's reference to "the People" referred to a single American people and that, therefore, the Constitution and the Union that it created was ordained and established by this single American people. This interpretation of "the People" formed the bedrock of the nationalist theory of the Constitution. A consequence of this theory was, as George Wythe observed at Virginia's ratification convention, that the Constitution gave rise to a "firm indissoluble Union of the States."[25] From such a union, as Amar points out, unilateral secession was constitutionally impossible, because a state could only secede from the Union with the consent of this American people.[26]

The second school of thought argued that the Preamble's reference to "the People" referred to a number of different peoples, and that, therefore, the Constitution and the Union that it created was ordained and established by the peoples of each of the States that ratified the Constitution, who, as stated by John Rutledge at the Philadelphia Convention, thereby became "parties to the Union."[27] This interpretation of "the People" formed the bedrock of the compact theory of the Constitution which held that the Constitution was, as Thomas Jefferson asserted, "a compact of independent nations."[28] As Harry Jaffa, a fervent defender of the nationalist theory, nevertheless concedes, the consequence of the compact theory was that if a state or states breached the constitutional compact, a non-breaching state had a constitutional right to unilaterally secede from the Union.[29]

As detailed in this chapter, an analysis of the merits of the arguments put forth by exponents of the rival theories leads to the conclusion that the compact theory is the better argument. The consequence of this conclusion is that sovereignty vested in the peoples of each of the states of the Union, and that, in appropriate circumstances, a state had a constitutional right to unilaterally secede from the Union. The validity of this conclusion is dependent upon an affirmative answer to each of the following three propositions:

1. the Constitution was ordained and established by the sovereign peoples of each of the States that ratified it, rather than by a single sovereign American people; and
2. the sovereignty of the peoples of each of the States of the Union was indivisible; and
3. the sovereignty of the peoples of each of the States of the Union entailed a right of unilateral secession from the Union.

Although the issue of sovereignty was the focal point of debate on the issue of secession, exponents of the nationalist theory also raised arguments against any right of unilateral secession based upon several articles of the Constitution. These arguments asserted that states were perpetually bound to the Union in the sense that unilateral secession from it was legally impossible.

In setting out the analysis in relation to the competing theories of the Constitution, this chapter first deals with the arguments against secession referred to in the preceding paragraph. This will be followed by the analysis of the arguments surrounding each of the three propositions that underpin the compact theory's claim that "the People" of the Preamble meant the peoples of each of the states of the Union rather than a single American people.

The Perpetuity Argument

In 1833, in his treatise on constitutional law, Justice Joseph Story described the Constitution as "a constitution of government, framed for the general good, and designed for perpetuity."[30] In the same year, his friend and fellow nationalist Daniel Webster asserted that the Union created by the Constitution was "perpetual and immortal" and that it "shall last through all time."[31] This claim, the consequence of which was that a state could not secede, at least not unilaterally, from the Union was based on several grounds. The first was that the Constitution implied that states were bound to the Union in perpetuity. The second was that the "more perfect Union" referred to in the Constitution's Preamble meant that states were perpetually bound to remain part of the Union. The third ground was anchored in the resolutions by which the Constitution was ratified, the argument being that ratification meant that States joined the Union on a forever basis and that, therefore, they could not unilaterally secede from it. Finally, the legal scholar Akhil Reed Amar has articulated a perpetuity argument grounded in Queen Anne's speech at the time of the Union of England and Scotland in 1707.

IMPLIED PERPETUITY

In his argument, articulated in 1861, against the legality of the secessions of the Confederate states, President Abraham Lincoln argued that the Union was "perpetual," by which he meant that a state was forever bound to remain within it, with the consequence that "no State, upon its own mere motion, could lawfully get out of the Union."[32] To allow such a secession would, according to Lincoln, "destroy" the Union.[33] This perpetuity based argument was made even though the word "perpetual" does not appear in the text of the Constitution.

One ground upon which Lincoln based his perpetuity argument was that, even though the Constitution did not expressly declare that the Union was perpetual, nevertheless, it was so because "[p]erpetuity is implied . . . in the fundamental law of all national governments," with the consequence that it was legally or constitutionally "impossible to destroy [the Union]" by means of unilateral secession from it.[34] For Lincoln, the implication that the Union was perpetual was buttressed by the fact that the union created by the Articles of Confederation was expressly stated to be perpetual and this was "most conclusive"[35] that the Constitution's Union was also perpetual.

Lincoln's argument here is difficult to sustain. Had, as Justice Story asserted and Lincoln believed, the framers of the Constitution created a Constitution, and therefore the Union, that was "designed for perpetuity"[36] and which possessed "a permanent form of government, where the powers, once given, are irrevocable, and cannot be resumed or withdrawn at pleasure,"[37] it is reasonable to assume that explicit words to that effect would have been included in the Constitution, especially so given that the union created by the Articles of Confederation was, as previously noted, expressly declared to be perpetual. However, as Amar observes, there was a "good reason" for the absence of the word "perpetual" in the Constitution, namely: "Why borrow a word from the Articles of Confederation that did not quite mean what it said in that document, a word that was being thrust aside by the very act of constitution itself?"[38] And, as Sanford Levinson aptly observes, given the presence of the word "perpetual" in the Articles of Confederation, its absence in the Constitution cannot be dismissed as being of no relevance.[39]

When the Constitution was being drafted, it was clear that the union of the Articles of Confederation was not perpetual. Delegates to the Philadelphia Convention, such as Nathaniel Gorham,[40] James Madison,[41] Oliver Ellsworth,[42] James Wilson,[43] and Alexander Hamilton[44] readily accepted that this was so. Indeed, it was the circumstance that the Confederation was on the verge of disintegration that the Convention met with the assigned task of drafting amendments to the Articles of

Confederation.[45] However, the Convention recommended the proposed Constitution instead, which, when ratified, rendered both the Articles of Confederation and the Confederation that they created no longer operative. Against this background, it is difficult to sustain an argument, in the absence of any express statement in the Constitution that the Union was to be perpetual, that a State's ratification of the Constitution implied its perpetual membership of the Union.

THE PREAMBLE'S "MORE PERFECT UNION" AND PERPETUITY

Lincoln had a second basis upon which he grounded his perpetuity argument, namely, the Preamble's phrase "to form a more perfect Union." For Lincoln, although the Constitution did not expressly stipulate that the Union was perpetual, it did so implicitly by its reference to it forming a "more perfect Union." This meant that a state's unilateral secession from the Union was legally impossible because if it was "lawfully possible, the Union is *less* perfect than before the Constitution, having lost the vital element of perpetuity." Thus, for Lincoln, it logically followed "that no State, upon its own mere motion, can lawfully get out of the Union."[46] Lincoln's perpetuity argument replicated that of his immediate predecessor, James Buchanan, who in his Fourth Annual Message to Congress on 3 December 1860, after referring to the Preamble's "more perfect Union" phrase, asserted that "the union was designed to be perpetual" and that the Constitution's "framers never intended to implant in [the Union's] bosom the seeds of its own destruction, nor were they at its creation guilty of the absurdity of providing for its own dissolution."[47] On 8 January 1861, in his special message to Congress, Buchanan wrote that his Fourth Annual Message to Congress expressed his "conviction . . . that no State has a right by its own act to secede from the Union."[48] However, Buchanan, relying upon the views of James Madison,[49] differed from Lincoln in that he believed that states could not be forcibly coerced to remain within the Union.[50]

The major problem with Lincoln's perpetuity argument here is that the words "perfect" and "perpetual" are not synonyms. Rather, as Mark Brandon suggests, a proper construction of the Preamble's "to form a more perfect Union" phrase is that it meant that an old and imperfect form of association—the Confederation—was abandoned in favor of a new and better one—the Union, rather than making the latter perpetual in the way Lincoln construed the Preamble.[51] More importantly, the historical record clearly suggests that the Philadelphia Convention did not have excluding a right of secession on its mind when it included the words "more perfect Union" in the Preamble. There is no evidence pointing to this phrase implicitly referring to, let alone precluding, secession, an issue that, as Max Farrand points out, was not raised, let alone debated, at the Convention.[52] It must be recalled that the Constitution was drafted in response to dissatisfaction with the terms of the Articles of Confederation and the dysfunctional Confederation that it created. In particular, the requirement that nine States had to approve any major legislation, especially in relation to raising of revenue, rendered the Confederation weak and ineffective to meet both domestic problems as well as the threat of intervention by external powers. In addressing this problem, the Constitution created a federal legislature that, pursuant to Article I, Section 8, possessed significantly greater legislative competence than its predecessor, the Confederation Congress. What antifederalists, in opposing the ratification of the Constitution, feared was that this expanded legislative power of the federal government in the Constitution's "more perfect Union" would, in time, lead to a "perfect Union" in which all legislative power was vested in the federal government. As Robert Yates, the prominent antifederalist, writing under the pseudonym Brutus, observed: "To make a union of this kind perfect, it is necessary to abolish all inferior governments, and to give the general one compleat legislative, executive and judicial powers to every purpose."[53] Thus, the Preamble's "more perfect Union" phrase referred to establishing a viably functioning or improved union, rather than making it perpetual in the sense that Lincoln construed the word "perfect."

Two further points can be made in refutation of Lincoln's perpetuity argument based upon his construction of the Preamble's "more perfect Union" phrase. The first is that he was mistaken in asserting that unilateral secession would "destroy" the Union. Rather, it would merely reduce its geographic scope. As Mark Brandon explains: "[S]ecession accomplishes merely the withdrawal of a geographic part of the nation and leaves the old national government intact over the rest."[54] This point was recognized at the time by the nationalist lawyer and historian Sidney George Fisher, who in 1862 argued against any constitutional right of unilateral secession, but nevertheless conceded that, if the Confederate states were lost to the Union, the Union would "remain a great and powerful nation . . . [which,] if wisely governed might be expected to endure for many years."[55] Indeed, Lincoln himself implicitly conceded that secession would merely truncate, rather than destroy, the Union. In his Message to Congress in Special Session, delivered on 4 July 1861, he conceded that a state could lawfully "withdraw from the Union" if it had the "consent of the Union."[56] In so conceding, he said nothing about such a secession destroying the Union. Indeed, he implicitly recognized that the Union, albeit smaller in its geographic scope, would continue to exist. The same would apply following a state's unilateral secession from the Union.

The second point is that Lincoln's argument is undermined by his claim, analyzed below, that the Union was formed, not by the ratification of the Constitution, but in 1776. If so, then in March 1789, when the Constitution came into operation, the Union consisted of only eleven of the Confederation's thirteen States. At that date, North Carolina and Rhode Island had not ratified the Constitution. Prior to the Constitution being ratified by North Carolina on 21 November 1789,[57] and Rhode Island, on 29 May 1790,[58] there remained what Lincoln referred to in his First Inaugural Address as an "impassable wall"[59] between these two States and the Union that was then constituted by eleven of the former States of the Confederation. Prior to their ratifications, North Carolina and Rhode Island were treated as foreign States vis-à-vis the Union. This is evidenced by the fact that, following Rhode Island's ratification of the Constitution, Congress enacted legislation that extended to North Carolina and Rhode Island the operation of various laws previously enacted by Congress dealing with matters that included tariffs, customs collection, and the Judiciary Act of 1789.[60] Clearly, for Lincoln, the ratification and coming into effect of the Constitution did not destroy the union that he argued had existed since 1776. However, it did mean that North Carolina and Rhode Island ceased to be part of it between the time the Constitution came into operation in March 1789 and when these two States joined the Union by their ratifications of the Constitution in 1789 and 1790 respectively. In substance, Lincoln's argument that the Union was formed in 1776 leads to the absurd conclusion that, due to the "impassable wall" that arose after the Constitution came into operation in March 1789 between North Carolina and Rhode Island, on the one hand, and the Union on the other, the former, by their failure to ratify the Constitution by that date, had, in effect, seceded from the union that Lincoln claimed arose in 1776. However, the reality was, as Amar points out, that the other eleven States had seceded from the Confederation and agreed "to form a new, more perfect union."[61] On 8 June 1789, during the debate in the House of Representatives over proposed amendments to the Constitution, James Madison said: "It is a desirable thing, on our part as well as theirs [i.e., North Carolina and Rhode Island], that a *re-union* should take place as soon as possible" (emphasis added).[62] This "re-union" occurred when the Constitution was subsequently ratified by North Carolina and Rhode Island.

PERPETUITY AND THE RATIFICATION RESOLUTIONS

Although Lincoln's perpetuity argument, grounded in the Preamble's "more perfect Union" phrase, should be viewed as a flawed attempt to, as Mark Neely puts it, "smuggle perpetuity into the text of the Constitution,"[63] it has been argued that there is another basis, independent of the Preamble, upon which it can be supported. The argument here is that ratification of the Constitution committed the ratifying States to membership of the Union forever. A corollary of this argument is that a State could not reserve a right to withdraw from the Union by conditionally ratifying the Constitution.

This argument is rooted in a letter written in July 1788 by James Madison to Alexander Hamilton on the terms of a State's resolution that ratified the Constitution. In his letter, Madison opined that "a reservation of a right to withdraw" from the Union was "a *conditional* ratification" and that such a ratification "must vitiate ratification."[64] For Madison, this was the logical consequence of his claim that "[t]he Constitution requires adoption *in toto*, and *for ever*." However, Madison went on to say that, in the case of a conditional ratification, he was not sure "what the new Congress by virtue of the power to admit new states, may be *able* & disposed to do in such a case."[65] In effect, Madison recognised that his opinion would be rendered wrong if states that conditionally ratified the Constitution were admitted to the Union without objection.

Notwithstanding Madison's doubts as to whether such a conditional ratification would be effective, at New York's ratification convention, Alexander Hamilton relied upon Madison's letter to assert that a "conditional ratification would not be received by Congress."[66] Hamilton made this comment in response to a proposal by John Lansing that New York's ratification resolution should reserve "a right to recede and withdraw itself as one of the members of the said government" unless certain amendments to the Constitution were, within an unspecified number of years, "submitted to a general convention." This proposal was rejected by New York's ratification convention by a slim margin of thirty-one to twenty-eight.[67]

Akhil Reed Amar argues that the supporters of Lansing's proposal put it up for a vote because there was no belief in, or acceptance of, the view that the Constitution permitted unilateral secession. Amar then argues that, because this proposal was rejected, the Constitution did not allow a state to unilaterally secede from the Union.[68] However, Amar's argument is flawed for two reasons. First, his conclusion that the convention's rejection of Lansing's proposal meant that the Constitution did not allow unilateral secession is not the logical consequence of the rejection of Lansing's proposal. All that the convention's rejection meant was that New York would not assert a right of unilateral secession in the event that its proposed constitutional amendments were not adopted. It had to nothing to say about whether such a right existed. Second, even if one could sustain Amar's interpretation of the resolution rejecting Lansing's proposal, it is inconsistent with and negated by the terms of New York's ratification resolution that, as is detailed below, reserved the right of unilateral secession.

Forty-five years later, in his *Commentaries on the Constitution*, Joseph Story echoed Madison's opinion that ratification was on a forever basis, when he wrote that the Constitution was "a permanent form of government, where the powers, once given, are irrevocable, and cannot be resumed or withdrawn at pleasure.[69] And, Madison's opinion was relied upon in December 1860 by Senator Andrew Johnson from Tennessee as a basis for arguing that the southern slave states had no constitutional right to unilaterally secede from the Union.[70] Waitman T. Willey, a unionist and delegate to Virginia's secession convention, also relied on Madison's letter to argue against Virginia seceding from the Union.[71]

The problem with Madison's opinion that ratification was on a forever basis is that he subsequently rejected it and conceded that secession from the Union could occur. Although, as he made clear in private correspondence, the prospect of secession was "more painful than words can express,"[72] Madison nevertheless recognised that it was legally possible. He made this clear when he wrote that a state could secede if it was "released [from the Constitution] by consent"[73] or had the "consent of the others."[74] Given his view that the Constitution was "established . . . by . . . the sovereign people of the several States who were parties to it,"[75] that consent would have to come from the states of the Union.

More significantly, Madison also recognised that a state could *unilaterally* secede from the Union. In 1832, he wrote that a state would be "absolved [from the Constitution] by an intolerable abuse of power."[76] In a letter, in 1833, he wrote that "[a] rightful secession" could occur as the result of "the abuse of the compact absolving the seceding party from the obligations imposed by it."[77] When read in the light of his statement during the debate in the House of Representatives on 8 June 1789 over proposed amendments that "the people have an indubitable, unalienable, and indefeasible right to reform or change their Government, whenever it be found adverse or inadequate to the purposes of its institutions,"[78] his later statements may be merely referring to a revolutionary right of secession. If so, it could be argued, as does Daniel Farber, that Madison's 1833 letter is a "significant piece of direct evidence" against the Confederate states having had any constitutional right to unilaterally secede from the Union.[79] However, the letter is more consistent with recognising a constitutional right to unilaterally secede from the Union. The reference in the 1832 statement to the "abuse of the compact" can only mean breaches by a state or states of the Constitution. References to a state being "absolved" or "absolving" a state from further membership of the Union implies an agreed right to be released from such membership in the event of breaches of the Constitution, rather than recognising a revolutionary right, which, by its very nature, requires no formal acknowledgment of its existence. Revolutionary rights exist dehors any formal or legal document. Describing secession in these circumstances as "rightful," underscores the idea that Madison is referring to a legal, rather than the revolutionary, right of secession.

Furthermore, the argument against any right of secession based upon Madison's letter to Hamilton has to be considered in the light of conditional ratifications of the Constitution by three States that were admitted to the Union. On 26 June 1788, in Virginia's documentation ratifying the Constitution, "the Delegates of the People of Virginia . . . in the name and in behalf of the People of Virginia" declared that Virginia's ratification of the Constitution was subject to the condition "that the powers granted under the Constitution, being derived from the People of the

United States, may be resumed by them, whensoever the same shall be perverted to their injury or oppression."[80] On 26 July 1788, in New York's documentation ratifying the Constitution, "the Delegates of the People of the State of New York" declared that New York's ratification of the Constitution was subject to the condition "[t]hat the Powers of Government may be reassumed by the People, whensoever it shall become necessary to their Happiness."[81] The ratification resolution of the Rhode Island convention of 29 May 1790 was in identical terms to New York's resolution.[82]

In New York, the conditional nature of its ratification was reinforced with its declaration that "*until a Convention shall be called and convened* for proposing Amendments" (emphasis added),[83] Congress would be limited in exercising it powers in relation to New York on a variety of matters including its state militia, federal elections, excises, and direct taxes. Furthermore, in writing to other State governors on the day after New York ratified the Constitution, Governor George Clinton effectively restated that New York's ratification was conditional upon the Constitution being amended, when he wrote:

> We, the Members of the Convention of this State, have deliberately and maturely considered the Constitution proposed for the United States. Several articles in it appear so exceptionable to a Majority of us, that *nothing but the fullest confidence, of obtaining a Revision of them*, by a General Convention, and the invincible reluctance of separating from our Sister States, *could have prevailed upon a sufficient Number to ratify it, without stipulating for previous Amendments.*—We all unite in opinion that *such a Revision will be necessary* to recommend it to the approbation and support of a numerous body of our constituents (emphasis added).[84]

It is important to note that Virginia, New York, and Rhode Island were admitted to the Union. The conditions attached to their ratification resolutions were not rejected. Nor was the efficacy of the ratifications queried or doubted. Thus, Madison's doubts about the veracity of his opinion were proven to be well founded when these three States were admitted to the Union without objection to the conditional nature of their ratification resolutions. In such circumstances, it must be presumed that the expressly claimed right to resume the powers that they had granted to the federal government was recognised by the other states of the Union. Furthermore, on the basis of the principle of equality of the states, all the other states of the Union must be taken to have possessed the same right. In this respect, it can be noted that, of the twenty states admitted to the Union after the thirteen States of the Confederation had ratified the Constitution and prior to South Carolina's secession from the Union, the legislation, resolutions and/or proclamations admitting seventeen of them expressly stated that admission to the Union was on the "equal [or same] footing . . . in all respects" as the "original states."[85] Such terminology was not necessary in the case of Tennessee, in 1796, because it was treated as if it was an "original state." The legislation admitting Tennessee to the Union stipulated that Tennessee was admitted to the Union "as if [it] had been originally one of the United States."[86] And, because Vermont in 1791 and Kentucky in 1792 were carved out of parts of states that were "original states," such terminology was also unnecessary when they were both admitted as "a new and entire member" of the Union.[87] The equality of these states with the thirteen "original states" was confirmed by the Supreme Court in 1845, in *Pollard's Lessee v. Hagan*, where the Court ruled that the admission of a new state to the Union meant that it possessed "the same rights, sovereignty, and jurisdiction . . . as the original states."[88] In so ruling, the Court gave legal effect to an understanding of the Philadelphia Convention that the Union's thirteen original states should not be treated more favorably than states subsequently admitted to the Union. This understanding is evidenced by James Madison's statement, in 1819, that a proposition "to discriminate between the old and new States, by an Article in the Constitution declaring that the aggregate number of representatives from the States thereafter to be admitted, should never exceed that of the States originally adopting the Constitution" was "happily . . . rejected" by the Convention.[89]

The question in relation to the right to resume the powers granted under the Constitution is whether it amounted to the right of a state to unilaterally secede from the Union. That it did is clear. The right to resume the powers of the government referred to in the three conditional ratifications resolutions refer to powers granted to the federal government by the Constitution. If these powers were resumed by a state, that can only have meant that that state had seceded from the Union.[90]

It could be argued that the right of secession derived from the conditional ratifications of the Constitution by these three States merely referred to the accepted revolutionary right of secession, and not to a constitutional right of secession. This argument should be rejected. This stems from the fact that the conditional ratifications clearly indicate that the right to secession arises only in appropriate circumstances. As was detailed in the Introduction, invoking a revolutionary right does not require satisfying some preexisting moral or other criterion and that revolution succeeds as a matter of fact. The fact that the conditional ratifications did impose the precondition of appropriate circumstances is thus inconsistent with them referring to the revolutionary right of secession. Furthermore, as previously noted, revolutionary rights, by their very nature, require no formal acknowledgment of their existence. Given that the conditional ratifications were acts by which Virginia, New York, and Rhode Island legally joined the Union, their express reservations of a right to leave that Union in appropriate circumstances implies a constitutionally legal, rather than a revolutionary, right of secession.

The more critical question here is whether these conditional ratifications enabled a state, by resuming the powers granted to the federal government, to *unilaterally* secede from the Union. The ratifications resolutions of New York and Rhode Island clearly suggest an affirmative answer to that question. These resolutions were made by "the people of New York" and "the people of Rhode Island" respectively. Both stipulated that the powers of government could be resumed by "the people." Thus, these resolutions can only be taken to mean that the peoples who adopted the ratification resolution, that is, the peoples of New York and Rhode Island respectively, were the peoples who could resume the powers their States granted to the federal government, and thereby effect the unilateral secessions of their states from the Union.

On the other hand, Virginia's ratification resolution, although adopted by the "people of Virginia," stated that the resumption of the powers of the federal government required the approval of "the people of the United States." A literal construction of this resolution, drafted by a committee of five Federalists, which included James Madison, John Marshall, and Edmund Randolph,[91] suggests that no state could unilaterally secede from the Union. Indeed, in reliance upon the literal construction of Virginia's ratification resolution, Joseph Story argued that there was "no reservation on the part of any state, to dissolve its connexion, or to abrogate its assent, or to suspend the operation of the constitution, as to itself."[92] However, perhaps because, as Bauer suggests, Story "came to his work with his mind already made up, and perhaps, closed,"[93] he neglected to note that, as already explained, the ratification resolutions of New York and Rhode Island did reserve such a right to a state.[94] Story's argument against unilateral secession was followed at that time by Daniel Webster,[95] and repeated at the time of the Confederate secessions by nationalists such as John Northrop Motley[96] and Edward Everett,[97] and subsequently by scholars such as Akhil Reed Amar.[98]

However, a literal construction of Virginia's ratification resolution should be rejected in favor of a construction that means "that the powers granted under the Constitution being derived from the *peoples* of the United States, may be resumed by them." Construed in this way, Virginia's ratification resolution would mean that Virginia recognised that any state, including itself, had a right to unilaterally secede from the Union. Support for this construction of Virginia's ratification resolution can be found in several statements made at its ratification convention by supporters of ratification. These statements supported the view that Virginia could unilaterally resume the powers granted to the federal government. Edmund Randolph referred to the resolution by which "*Virginia adopted* [the Constitution]," which contained the right of "*the people*" to resume the powers granted to the federal government, as having the consequence that "*we* should be at liberty to consider as a violation of the Constitution, every exercise of a power not expressly delegated therein" (emphasis added).[99] The reasonable interpretation of Randolph's reference to "we" and "the people" is that these expressions refer to the people of Virginia given that it was by their decision that "Virginia adopted [the Constitution]."

A few days after Randolph's statement, during the brief debate on the text of the ratification resolution, there were only scant references to this part of the resolution. George Nicholas referred to "the people," not "the people of the United States," as having the right to resume the powers of government.[100] And so too did James Madison, who said that Randolph's earlier observations on this issue "correspond precisely with my opinion," which he restated when he said that "the powers granted by the proposed Constitution, are the gift of the people, and may be resumed by them when perverted to their oppression, and every power not granted thereby, remains with the people, and at their will."[101] In effect, this statement confirmed his earlier statement that if Virginia was "dissatisfied with the national Government" it could "choose to renounce it."[102]

In support of this construction of Virginia's ratification resolution, it must be kept in mind that its ratification resolution, and therefore the delegation of certain powers to the federal government, was achieved by a slim majority vote of eighty-nine to seventy-nine.[103] It is difficult to conceive that Virginians would have readily agreed to leave the decision to resume those powers to anybody but themselves. As Charles Francis Adams wrote of the Virginians of 1788:

> [I]n a vague way, the Virginians never proposed to cease be Virginians, or to permit Virginia to become other than a Sovereign State. It was so with the others.[104]

Thus, it was unsurprising that at the Virginia secession convention, its ratification resolution was specifically referred to by delegate Henry A. Wise,[105] Virginia's governor from 1856 to 1860, as accurately reflecting a resolution that the convention adopted by a vote of seventy-nine for and forty-one against[106] which stated that Virginia could "resume the powers granted by her under the Constitution of the United States, and to throw herself upon her reserved rights."[107] The same point was made by his fellow convention delegates Benjamin F. Wysor[108] and Robert L. Montague.[109] Florida also made reference to the conditional ratification resolutions of New York, Virginia, and Rhode Island as supporting its rights of secession in 1861.[110]

What can thus be concluded from the ratification resolutions adopted by Virginia, New York, and Rhode Island is that, rather than supporting the argument that the Union was perpetual in the sense that unilateral secession from it was constitutionally impossible, they supported the existence of a right of a state to unilaterally secede from the Union in some circumstances. Jefferson Davis summed up this conclusion when, in relation to the ratification resolutions of these three states, he wrote:

> These expressions are not mere obiter dicta, thrown out incidentally, and entitled only to be regarded as an expression of opinion by their authors. Even if only such, they would carry great weight as the deliberately expressed judgment of enlightened contemporaries, but they are more: they are parts of the very acts or ordinances by which these States ratified the Constitution an acceded to the Union, and cannot be detached from them. If they are invalid, the ratification itself was invalid, for they are inseparable. By inserting these declarations in their ordinances, Virginia, New York, and Rhode Island, formally, officially, and permanently declared

> their interpretation of the Constitution as recognizing the right of secession by redemption of their grants. By accepting the ratifications with this declaration incorporated, the other States as formally accepted the principle which it asserted.[111]

AMAR'S PERPETUITY ARGUMENT

Akhil Reed Amar has articulated an alternative basis of support for the substance of Lincoln's perpetuity argument, namely that, "[a]lthough states would enter the Constitution as true sovereigns, they would not remain so after ratification." This stemmed from the fact that, according to Amar, "[t]he formation of a 'more perfect Union' would itself end each state's sovereign status and would prohibit future unilateral secession, in plain contrast to the decidedly less-than-perfect union under the Articles."[112] Amar's argument is grounded in Queen Anne's speech at the time of the 1707 Act of Union between Scotland and England. In that speech, Queen Anne referred to that Act as creating an "entire and perfect Union." Amar argues that the 1707 Act was understood as precluding the unilateral secession of Scotland and that in *Federalist 5*,[113] John Jay, when quoting Queen Anne's reference to an "entire and perfect Union," did so in support of the proposition that unilateral secession from the Union was illegal.[114]

Amar's argument may have merit in the British context, but not in relation to the Constitution. This is because Article I of the 1707 Act stipulated that England and Scotland would be united as from 1 May 1707 "and forever after."[115] However, there is no such stipulation in the Constitution. Furthermore, Queen Anne's use of the "entire and perfect Union" phrase was, as she said, to provide "a solid foundation of lasting peace . . . [and amongst other things] remove . . . the jealousies and differences betwixt our two kingdoms . . . [so that] this Union will be enabled to resist all its enemies." That Jay quoted these words in arguing for "a more perfect Union" was not surprising, given that he went on to argue that should the States "divide themselves into three of four nations . . . they would always be envolved in disputes and war, or live in the constant apprehension of them."[116] It is to the avoidance of such consequences, rather than a prohibition of unilateral secession, that Jay referenced Queen Anne's speech. Thus, Queen Anne's speech does not support for Amar's perpetuity argument.

However, it could be that Amar's argument here is merited in relation to Vermont's admission to the Union on 4 March 1791. Vermont, constituted by territories claimed by New York and New Hampshire, had declared that it was "a free and independent jurisdiction, or state" on 15 January 1777,[117] but had not then been recognised as an independent State by either the Confederation or the Union.[118] On 10 January 1791, a convention of delegates of "*the people of the State Vermont*" resolved that admission to the Union would be "binding on [them], and the people of the state of Vermont, *forever*" (emphasis added).[119] Arguably, Vermont's express commitment to perpetual membership of the Union may have been, and may still be, binding upon it. However, of the thirty-three states that constituted the Union at the end of 1860, only Vermont had expressly pledged that its membership of the Union was on a forever basis. Any argument that Vermont's express commitment to perpetual membership of the Union also applied to the other thirty-two states must be rejected, if only because, as argued above, the ratification resolutions adopted by Virginia, New York, and Rhode Island rejected the proposition that any state was bound to perpetual membership of the Union. Furthermore, it is unreasonable to hold that Vermont should be perpetually bound to remain part of the Union. The argument here is that, although the people of Vermont in 1791 ratified the Constitution on a forever basis, that cannot bind subsequent generations of the people of Vermont.[120] Nor can it be argued that periodic participation in the institutions of the Union by the people of Vermont in the form of voting is enough to clearly establish a continuation of the original ratification or consent to be bound to remain in the Union.[121] Thus, in appropriate circumstances, Vermont would have been in a position to unilaterally secede from the Union in 1861.

The Supremacy Clause

Nationalists, such as Justice Story, Edward Everett,[122] and John Lothrop Motley,[123] argued that unilateral secession from the Union was precluded by the terms of the Constitution's supremacy clause. This clause, set out in Article VI, Clause 2, of the Constitution, stipulates that the "Constitution, and the Laws of the United States . . . shall be the supreme Law of the Land; and the Judges in every State shall be bound thereby, any thing in the Constitution or Laws of any State to the Contrary notwithstanding."

In his *Commentaries on the Constitution*, after citing the supremacy clause, Story posed the following rhetorical question: "If [the Constitution] is the supreme law, how can the people of any state, either by any form of its own constitution, or laws, or other proceedings, repeal, or abrogate, or suspend it?"[124] However, the problem with Story's argument is that it does not make clear why the supremacy clause has anything to do with secession. The purpose of the supremacy clause was to render unconstitutional any state law or action by state officials that conflicted with any law of the federal government that was validly enacted within the limited powers granted to it by the Constitution. This meant, as Chief Justice John Marshall put it in *McCulloch v. Maryland*, that "the government of the Union, though limited in its powers, is supreme within its sphere of action."[125] Nothing in the powers granted to the federal government has anything to do with whether or not a state may secede from the Union. Thus, given that there was nothing in the Constitution that explicitly prohibited secession and, further, that the Congress had no power granted to it to pass any law dealing with secession, the actions by the Confederate states in unilaterally seceding from the Union did not invoke the operation of the supremacy clause.

Amar also argues that the supremacy clause "clearly resolves the secession question, though without using the word 'secession.'"[126] He bases his argument on two grounds. The first is the claim that a unilateral declaration of independence constitutes an act by a state that violates the Constitution because it would constitute an amendment to the Constitution without meeting the requirements for amending the Constitution set out in Article V. Thus, Amar argues, the effect of the supremacy clause is that whenever the Constitution conflicts with the act of a state, the Constitution always prevails.[127] Amar's second ground is the claim that the supremacy clause is "logically inconsistent with the sovereignty of the people of each state."[128] For Amar, this means that the supremacy clause supports the proposition that the Preamble's "We the People" phrase should be understood to refer to a single American people. If either of these two grounds are correct, Amar's argument against a right of unilateral secession would be correct. However, that cannot be said of either ground.

In relation to the first ground, a state's unilateral declaration of independence is not an act seeking to amend the Constitution. Rather it is an act by which that state has resolved no longer to be bound it. A state's secession from the Union in no way amends the Constitution. Although secession reduces the geographic scope of the Union, the Union's Constitution remains unchanged. The supremacy clause governs the acts of a state or state officials done in the context of that state continuing to be a part of the Union. It says nothing about and has no relevance to the issue of whether a state can secede from the Union.

Amar's second ground against secession based upon the supremacy clause cannot be sustained because the basis upon which it is built is flawed, if only because Amar does not explain why the supremacy of a federal law over an inconsistent state law is inconsistent with the sovereignty of the people of each state within their sphere of legitimate action. Indeed, if anything, the supremacy clause is consistent with the sovereignty of the peoples of each state because it presupposes the sovereignty of the peoples of each of the states. This is so because the legislative powers delegated by the Constitution to the federal government were powers that would otherwise have been exercisable by state legislatures as expressions of the sovereignty of their respective peoples. The purpose of the supremacy clause was to ensure that federal legislation that fell within the parameters of legislative powers delegated to Congress prevailed over any inconsistent action by state officials or legislation enacted by a state legislature as the representative of the people of that state and that would have otherwise been valid, but for the fact that certain legislative powers had been delegated to Congress. In a federal system of government where legislative capacity was, in effect, apportioned between state and federal legislatures, the supremacy clause served the necessary purpose of resolving situations where state legislation impinged upon the domain of federal legislative capacity, but nothing more than that.

The reality is that the supremacy clause had nothing to do, one way or the other, with whether or not a state could unilaterally secede from the Union. Its relevance was confined to precluding a state from legislating or acting in a manner inconsistent with the Constitution while it was a part of the Union.[129] This was recognised by James Madison when, in 1833, he wrote that "*whilst a State remains within the Union* it cannot withdraw its citizens from the operation of the Constitution & laws of the Union" (emphasis added).[130]

In assessing the argument that the supremacy clause precluded unilateral secession as "not worth the sadly perishable paper on which it was printed," David Currie writes:

> Yes, [the supremacy clause] made the Constitution, federal statutes, and treaties the "law of the land" throughout the United States, but to say that it forbade secession was to reason in a circle. For the question at issue was whether states that attempted to secede were still part of the "land" in which those laws were supreme; the Constitution gave them primacy nowhere else.[131]

The Guarantee Clause

The Constitution's guarantee clause was also relied upon to argue that unilateral secession from the Union was precluded. Set out in Article V, Section 4, it stipulates:

> The United States shall guarantee to every State *in this Union* a Republican Form of Government, and shall protect each of them against Invasion; and on the Application of the Legislature or Executive (when the Legislature cannot be convened) against domestic violence [emphasis added].

In *Federalist 39*, Madison defined a republican form of government as one "which derives all its powers directly or indirectly from the great body of the people, and is administered by persons holding their offices during pleasure, for a limited period, or during good behaviour."[132] In *Federalist 43*, he stated that the only obligation that the guarantee clause imposed upon states while in the Union was that they could "not exchange republican for antirepublican Constitutions."[133]

In his Message to Congress in Special Secession, Abraham Lincoln argued that if a state could secede, it could lead to that state discarding its republican form of government. For Lincoln, the only way in which a republican form of government could be guaranteed was by a state remaining within the Union.[134] Lincoln further argued that, with the possible exception of South Carolina, the secession ordinances of the seceding states departed from the requirements of a republican form of government. In this respect, Lincoln said:

> It may well be questioned whether there is, to-day, a majority of the legally qualified voters of any State, except perhaps, South Carolina, in favor of disunion. There is much reason to believe that the Union men are the majority in many, if not in every other one, of the so-called seceded States.

Lincoln went on to dispute the legitimacy of any referenda that affirmed secession when he said: "[T]he result of an election, held in military camps, where the bayonets are all on one side of the question voted upon, can scarcely be considered as demonstrating popular sentiment. At such an election, all that large class who are, at once *for* the Union, and *against* coercion would be coerced to vote against the Union."[135] Therefore, for Lincoln, unilateral secession was constitutionally impermissible, and the use of force to prevent the Confederate states from seceding, which he had by then authorised, was justified.

From the perspective of legal principle, Lincoln's argument has two flaws. The first is that, like the supremacy clause, the guarantee clause is only applicable, as the clause itself says, while the state is "in this Union." Of itself, it says nothing as to whether a state can or cannot leave the Union. The second flaw stems from Lincoln's concession that there can be a consensual secession from the Union. However, if the Union is to guarantee each state a republican form of government, a consensual secession of a state could not be permitted because that state could, just like a state that unilaterally seceded from the Union, discard the republican form of government.

In relation to Lincoln's claim that the Confederate states, with the possible exception of South Carolina, had departed from the requirements of a republican form of government, the evidence refutes more than supports that claim. Ten of the eleven Confederate states processed their secession ordinances in the same way that the Constitution was ratified, namely, through conventions of elected delegates called for that purpose. Texas and Virginia subsequently held referenda which endorsed secession. In Texas, pro-secessionists received 77.3 percent of the vote. In Virginia, they received 86.1 percent of the vote.[136] Only Tennessee did not call for a secession convention. However, its legislature passed legislation for a referendum on secession,[137] which was supported by 69.0 percent[138] of those who voted. Thus, the processes by which the secession ordinances were adopted were in accordance with what would be expected of states with a "Republican Form of Government." Although the referenda in Texas, Virginia, and Tennessee were carried by strong majorities, there were nevertheless significant numbers that voted against secession, which strains the credibility of Lincoln's assertion that the pro-secession votes were the product any systematic or widespread coercion.

Scholars generally agree that there was popular support for secession within the Confederate states. In relation to the Lower South states,

James McPherson, arguably the pre-eminent scholar of the Civil War, states that "[i]n Texas the voters endorsed secession by a margin of three to one; there is little reason to believe that the result would have been different in the other six states."[139] To similar effect, Sean Wilentz concludes that "only a minority of southern whites . . . denied as a matter of principle the basic right of individual states to secede" and that "the idea that secession was some sort of coup d'etat by fire-eaters, who undemocratically pulled an unwilling white citizenry out of the Union, does not stand up to serious scrutiny."[140] Thus, Lincoln's claim that the processes by which the Confederate states adopted their secession ordinances was in any way inconsistent with what would be required of a state with a "Republican Form of Government" cannot be sustained. As Amar states, on this basis "the Republican Guarantee Clause fades away."[141] In light of these circumstances, the guarantee clause was not, as Lincoln argued, a basis upon which force could be used to prevent these states from seceding from the Union.

Of course, the popular support for secession ignored the views of the overwhelmingly enslaved African American population, because slaves could not vote or in any way participate in the processes leading to secession. The same can be said about popular support for the earlier ratification of the Constitution. In the case of secession, it is reasonable to assume that slaves would have overwhelmingly opposed secession. The same can be reasonably assumed in relation to free African Americans in both the slave states and in all but five non-slave states, because, in all of those states, they were denied the right to vote.

The Presidential Oath of Office Clause

A final constitutional provision that was alleged to preclude a state's unilateral secession from the Union was the presidential oath of office clause. Set out in Article II, Section 1, it required a president to "preserve, protect and defend the Constitution." In his First Inaugural Address, Lincoln construed this clause to mean that it constituted a "solemn" obligation upon a president to preserve, protect and defend "the government"[142] and, furthermore, that imposed upon him a "duty . . . to transmit it, unimpaired . . . to his successor", which precluded him from "fix[ing] the terms of separation of the States."[143]

However, Lincoln's construction of Article II, Section 1 must be rejected for the following two reasons. The first, and obvious, reason, as Noah Feldman notes, is that "[h]is oath of office was to 'preserve, protect, and defend' the Constitution, not the government."[144] In the context of secession, this would mean that if the Constitution recognized any right of secession, the president would be required to "preserve, protect and defend" that right, rather than view it as illegal.

Second, even if one accepts Lincoln's view that Article II, Section 1 imposes a duty upon the president to transmit an unimpaired government to his successor, a secession from the Union does not result in a breach of that duty. Lincoln implicitly accepted this, given that, as detailed above, he conceded that a state could secede from the Union by consent. If a consensual secession was constitutionally possible, presumably for Lincoln such a secession would not constitute breach of a president's duty to transmit an unimpaired government to his successor. If so, the same would apply if the Constitution permitted unilateral secession from the Union. In both cases, the government that existed before secession remains the government after secession, albeit of a Union reduced in size, but also one that continues to exist.

The Preamble's "We the People" and Sovereignty

Of the provisions of the Constitution analyzed in this chapter to this point that were claimed to preclude the existence of a legal right to unilaterally secede from the Union in 1860–1861, none of them revolved around or were dependent upon resolving the issue of whether, for the purposes of the Union's constitutional law, sovereignty vested in a single American people or the peoples of each of the states of the Union.

However, this issue was of pivotal importance because, as outlined in the introduction to this chapter, if sovereignty vested in the people of each of the states of the Union, then, according to the compact theory of the Constitution, in 1860–1861 a state could, in appropriate circumstances, unilaterally secede from the Union. This theory was dependent upon construing the word "People" in the Preamble's "We the People of the United States" as a plural noun, rather than a singular noun. This argument was rooted in the proposition that the Declaration of Independence of 1776—"the first formal secession proclamation in world history"[145]—led to the creation of free, sovereign, and independent States and that it was the peoples of each of these States in whom sovereignty was vested and that, through conventions of delegates whom they elected, they ordained and established the Constitution and the Union that it formed. The Constitution so ordained and established constituted a compact or contract between the peoples of the States of the Confederation that ratified it. Pursuant to the already noted principle of equality of the states that was confirmed by the Supreme Court, in 1845, in *Pollard's Lessee v. Hagan*,[146] the states, and consequently their peoples, subsequently admitted to the Union pursuant to Article IV, Section 3 of the Constitution became parties to that compact on an equal footing in all respects with the thirteen original states and their peoples. The consequence of the compact theory was that, in appropriate circumstances, the Constitution allowed any state to unilaterally secede from the Union.

The argument of the nationalist theory of the Constitution against unilateral secession from the Union was primarily based upon interpreting the Preamble's "We the People" phrase to mean that sovereignty vested in a single American people and that it was this American people that ordained and established the Constitution and the Union that it formed. This construction of the Preamble's words was forcefully enunciated in 1816 in *Martin v. Hunter's Lessee*, where, in delivering the opinion of the Supreme Court, Justice Story asserted that "[t]he constitution of the United States was ordained and established, not by the states in their sovereign capacities, but emphatically, as the preamble of constitution declares, by 'the people of the United States.'"[147] Secession from the Union could be achieved, as Abraham Lincoln recognized, by this American people "themselves . . . if they chose."[148] And, as was conceded by John C. Calhoun, the compact theory's leading exponent during the antebellum era, if sovereignty vested in a single American people, unilateral secession was "an absurdity."[149]

The issue of which of these competing theories is to be preferred is best approached by an interrogation of the various bases upon which the nationalist theory is anchored. The first anchor is the Preamble's "We the People" phrase, which, it is argued refers to a single American people that predated the Constitution, having emerged with the Declaration of Independence in 1776. The second anchor is the ratification of the Constitution, which, it is argued, transformed the peoples of each of the States that ratified it into a single "We the People" referred to in the Preamble. As will be demonstrated, an analysis of these arguments shows that neither supports the nationalist theory, but rather supports the compact theory of the Constitution. This conclusion is further supported by an analysis of the Constitution's articles dealing with elections, citizenship, treason, and amendment of the Constitution, together with the 1791 constitutional amendments. Although these articles and amendments say nothing about secession itself, they amply demonstrate the pivotal role of the states in the Union and thereby reflect a reality that the Constitution was a compact between the states of the Union rather than the creation of an American people, or as Mark Brandon puts it, "that the founding was an act of sovereign states, or, if popular, the *people* of those states."[150]

THE EXISTENCE OF AN AMERICAN PEOPLE BEFORE THE CONSTITUTION

The first basis upon which the nationalist theory of the Constitution was anchored, was in the proposition that "the People" referred to in the Preamble was a single American people that emerged as a result of the Declaration of Independence in 1776 and subsequently ordained and established the Constitution.

During the drafting and ratification of the Constitution, James Wilson was arguably the most prominent exponent of this argument. At the Philadelphia Convention, he claimed that "[w]e are now one nation of brethren,"[151] and that the free and independent States that emerged as a result of the Declaration of Independence "were independent, not *Individually* but *Unitedly*."[152] For Wilson, the Constitution was, as stated in the Preamble, "an ordinance and establishment of the people."[153] This meant that the Constitution did not have "the least trace of compact" in it because "[t]here can be no compact unless there are more parties than one."[154]

Similar assertions were made by each of the three contributors to the *The Federalist*—John Jay in *Federalist 2*,[155] James Madison in *Federalist 46*,[156] and Alexander Hamilton in *Federalist 22*[157] and *Federalist 85*.[158] In 1793, Jay reiterated this view when, as chief justice of the Supreme Court, in *Chisholm v. Georgia*, he said that, following the Declaration of Independence, although "thirteen sovereignties were considered as emerged from the principles of the Revolution . . . the people nevertheless continued to consider themselves, in a national point of view, as one people" and that subsequently "the people, in their collective and national capacity, established the present Constitution."[159] During the antebellum era, various individuals, such as Nathan Dane;[160] Justice

Story,[161] in his well-known *Commentaries on the Constitution of the United States*;[162] Daniel Webster;[163] John Quincy Adams;[164] and Andrew Jackson[165] all argued that this American people predated the ratification of the Constitution and therefore was "the People" referred to in the Preamble. These writings and speeches, particularly those of Webster[166] and Jackson,[167] were influential in developing Abraham Lincoln's thinking in arguably the most famous and influential articulation of the "single American people" argument that he expressed in two speeches delivered in 1861.

In his First Inaugural Address, Lincoln said:

> The Union is much older than the Constitution. It was formed in fact, by the Articles of Association in 1774. It was matured and continued by the Declaration of Independence in 1776. It was further matured and the faith of all the then thirteen States expressly plighted and engaged that it should be perpetual, by the Articles of Confederation in 1778. And finally, in 1787, one of the declared objects for ordaining and establishing the Constitution was "*to form a more perfect Union*."[168]

Four months later, in his Message to Congress in Special Secession, Lincoln elaborated upon the creation and role of the Union's states. Lincoln argued that the "object" of the Declaration of Independence "was not to declare [the colonies'] independence of *one another*, or of the *Union*" and, furthermore, that they had "never been States, either in substance, or in name, *outside* of the Union." Indeed, for Lincoln, "[n]ot one of them ever had a state constitution, independent of the Union" because "[t]he Union [was] older than any of the States; and, in fact, it created them."[169]

Before evaluating the merits of Lincoln's argument, it must be pointed out that Lincoln subsequently changed the date of the formation of the Union from 1774 to 1776, the year of the Declaration of Independence.[170] This change reflected the centrality that the Declaration had, by 1861, come to occupy in his thinking.[171] Thus, he declared that he "never had a feeling politically that did not spring from the sentiments embodied in the Declaration of Independence,"[172] which, according to Lincoln, had announced a struggle "for national independence by a single people."[173] He reiterated this sentiment in his Gettysburg Address in 1863, where he opined that "[f]our score and seven years ago [i.e., 1776] our fathers brought forth on this continent, a new nation."[174] These statements make it clear that, for Lincoln, 1776 saw a "single people" emerge as "a new nation" within a political union. In his First Inaugural Address, he referred to this "new nation" as the "American People" who, pursuant to the Union's "national Constitution," imposed upon him as president a constitutional obligation to prevent "the destruction of [the Union's] national fabric."[175] This obligation stemmed from the fact that this "new nation" or "American people," as he asserted in his Message to Congress in Special Session, "calling itself 'We the People,'" was "that power which made the Constitution."[176]

The Declaration of Independence

Lincoln's claim that that a "new nation" and the Union emerged in 1776 is one whose merits need to be evaluated against the historical record of events leading up to the ratification of the Constitution. As will be demonstrated, the historical record does not support Lincoln's claim. However, before recounting the historical record, it can be noted that Lincoln's argument flies in the face of the Preamble's assertion that the Constitution was designed to "*form* a more perfect Union" (emphasis added). As Akhil Reed Amar points out, "the Preamble spoke precisely of its purpose to "*form*" a new—more perfect—union rather than simply "continue" or "improve" the old union."[177] This is confirmed by Article VI, Clause 2 of the Constitution, which stipulates that "[a]ll debts contracted and Engagements entered into, before the Adoption of this Constitution, shall be valid against the United States under this Constitution, *as under the Confederation*" (emphasis added). In stipulating the continued validity of these debts, it is significant that Article VI, Clause 2 refers to their previous validity "as under the Confederation" rather pursuant to the Articles of Confederation. Had the clause stipulated the Confederation's debts "shall be valid against the United States under this Constitution, as under the Article of Confederation," it could be maintained that the "more perfect Union" formed by the Constitution was a continuation of the union known as the Confederation. However, as drafted, Article VI, Clause 2 can only be construed as stating that "the United States under this Constitution" was a successor to, rather than a continuation of, "the Confederation." Thus, the reality was that when, on 21 June 1788, New Hampshire became the ninth State to ratify the Constitution, the union created by Articles of Confederation was destroyed and replaced by a new union created by the Constitution, which came into operation in March 1789, by which time two further States had ratified the Constitution. As William Whatley Pierson points out:

> The Union of the Constitution was not the union of the Confederation; the one destroyed the other absolutely. . . . . Despite the fact that the congress of the Confederation acquiesced in the call for the constitutional convention, the framing, adoption, and ratification of the Constitution were revolutionary. The old union existed, it is true, while the means of its destruction were being forged, but it ceased to exist so far as public law is concerned at the moment the ninth State ratified the Constitution.[178]

This reality was evidenced on 15 July 1788 when, after Virginia became the tenth State to ratify the Constitution, the *New York Packet* correctly asserted: "*Now* there is in fact a secession of Ten States from the old Union, whereby the others are left to shift for themselves."[179] With New York ratifying the Constitution eleven days later, this meant that after March 1789, Rhode Island and North Carolina were the two States that were "left to shift for themselves" until they eventually ratified the Constitution and thereby joined the Union. Madison described this situation in *Federalist 43* as one in which "no political relation can subsist between the assenting and dissenting States."[180] That the Constitution led to the creation of a new union, rather than, as Lincoln asserted, the maturing of an existing one, was confirmed by the Supreme Court in *Dred Scott v. Sandford*, where Chief Justice Taney said that the States, in ratifying the Constitution, were "about to *dissolve*" the Confederation[181] and that the Union was "the political community *formed and brought into existence* by the Constitution of the United States" (emphasis added).[182]

That the Union came into existence with the ratification of the Constitution is also confirmed by the historical record. That record shows that, although the independence of the thirteen British colonies is commonly thought to have been formally declared by the Declaration of Independence on 4 July 1776, this is not so. On 10 May 1776, seventy-seven days before the adoption of the Declaration, the Continental Congress, passed a resolution that "recommended" that "the respective assemblies and conventions of the United Colonies . . . adopt such government as shall, in the opinion of the representatives of the people, best conduce to the happiness and safety of their constituents in particular, and America in general."[183]

This resolution could be seen as supporting Lincoln's assertion in his

Message to Congress in Special Session that "[t]he Union [was] older than any of the States; and, in fact, it created them." However, this argument cannot be sustained for two reasons. First, the 10 May 1776 resolution did not mandate that the colonies adopt permanent forms of government—it merely recommended that they do so. Second, three colonies had adopted constitutions as independent States prior to Congress's resolution of 10 May 1776—New Hampshire, on 5 January 1776,[184] South Carolina, on 26 March 1776,[185] and Virginia, on 6 May 1776.[186] Furthermore, two of the colonies had already begun that process by asserting their independence before the resolution of 10 May 1776. Thus, on 12 April 1776, North Carolina, adopted a declaration in which it sought its "Independency . . . reserving to this colony the sole and exclusive right of forming a Constitution and Laws for this Colony."[187] And, On 4 May 1776, Rhode Island repealed legislation that secured its allegiance to Great Britain and "authorized and empowered" its delegates to Congress to promote a "confederation between the . . . United Colonies, for exerting their whole strength and force to annoy the common enemy, and to secure their rights and liberties" and "to secure to this colony, in the strongest and most perfect manner, its present established form, and all the powers of government, so far as they relate to its internal police and conduct of our own affairs, civil and religious."[188]

Six other colonies quickly followed the lead of these five colonies by declaring their independence prior to the proclamation of the Declaration of Independence on 4 July 1776. The first was Pennsylvania, which, on 8 June 1776, authorized its delegates to Congress "to concur with the Delegates in Congress in forming such further compacts between the United Colonies . . . for promoting the liberty, safety, and interests of America; reserving to the people of this colony the sole and exclusive right of regulating the internal government and police of the same."[189] On 24 June 1776, Pennsylvania formally declared its independence when it adopted a "Declaration on the subject of the Independence of this Colony of the Crown of *Great Britain*" which went on to announce its "willingness to concur in a vote of the Congress declaring the United Colonies free and independent States."[190]

In Connecticut, on 14 June 1775, the Connecticut Assembly resolved that its delegates propose to Congress to declare "the United *American* colonies free and independent States, absolved from all allegiance to the King of *Great Britain*."[191]

On 14 June 1776, the Delaware Assembly passed a resolution stating that is was "necessary" that the "authority" of the British Crown be "suppressed, and [that] all the powers of government [be] exerted under the authority of the people of the Colonies, for the preservation of internal peace, virtue and good order, as well as for the defence of their lives, liberties and properties."[192] On the following day Delaware's delegates to Congress were instructed to "concur" in the formation of "such further compacts between the United Colonies" in order to achieve these objectives, on the basis of "reserving to the people of [Delaware], the sole and exclusive right of regulating the internal government and police of the same."[193]

On 15 June 1776, New Hampshire adopted a declaration that urged Congress to declare "the thirteen United Colonies a free and independent State" for the purpose of ensuring "the present safety of future advantage of these *American* colonies."[194]

On 22 June 1776, New Jersey resolved to empower its delegates to Congress to join with the other colonies in "declaring the United Colonies independent of *Great Britain*" and to enter with them "into a Confederacy for union and common defence," provided that "whatever plan of Confederacy' was entered into "the internal police of this Province is to be reserved to the Colony Legislature."[195]

On 28 June 1776, Maryland "authorized and empowered" its delegates to the Continental Congress "to concur with the other United Colonies, or a majority of them, in declaring the United Colonies free and independent States . . . *Provided*, The sole and exclusive right of regulating the internal Government and Police of this colony be reserved to the people thereof."[196] On 6 July 1776, this resolution was reiterated and stated to be for the purpose of establishing a "Confederation" between the "United Colonies" for the purpose of the "defence of our common rights, and in the maintenance of the freedom of [Maryland] and her sister colonies."[197]

The declarations and resolutions of these nine colonies were, as Pauline Maier describes, "carefully crafted, formal statements [that] proclaimed a state's commitment to nationhood."[198] What they all sought was a declaration by Congress that they were free and independent States and a public statement of the reasons for independence. The colonies all saw themselves as on the way towards independent statehood. It must be kept in mind that statehood at this time meant possessing the attributes of a State in international law. The use of the word "state" to describe a federal or sub-national unit of a State would only emerge later with the ratification of the Constitution and the federal system of government that it established.

In the wake of what Maier aptly refers to as these "other 'declarations of independence,'"[199] on 2 July 1776, Congress did what it was requested it to do when the colonies voted unanimously to adopt the Resolution for Independence, which Richard Henry Lee had proposed on 7 June 1776.[200] The Resolution declared:

> That these United Colonies are, and, of right, ought to be, Free and Independent States; that they are absolved from all allegiance to the British crown, and that all political connexion between them and the state of Great Britain, is, and ought to be, totally dissolved.[201]

Having declared their independence on 2 July 1776, two days later, on 4 July 1776, Congress adopted what is now commonly referred to as the "Declaration of Independence," but which, on 18 July 1776, Congress formally named "The unanimous declaration of the thirteen United States of America."[202] In providing "a formal justification of an act already accomplished,"[203] the Declaration proclaimed to the world at large the independence of these thirteen "free and independent States." This was, as Thomas Jefferson stated at the time, "the whole object" of what he labelled "the present controversy."[204]

In the Declaration, "the Representatives of the united States of America, in General Congress, Assembled . . . in the Name, and by Authority of the good People of [the] Colonies" did "publish and declare" precisely what the Resolution for Independence declared, namely, that the former British colonies were now "Free and Independent States," the consequence of which was that "they [had] full Power to levy War, conclude Peace, contract Alliances, establish Commerce, and to do all other Acts and Things which Independent States may of right do." These thirteen former British colonies were effectively recognized as such by France pursuant to a treaty, in February 1778, which stated that it was entered into between "[t]he Most Christian King [of France] and the United States of North America: to wit; New-Hampshire, Massachusetts-bay, Rhode-Island, Connecticut, New-York, New-Jersey, Pennsylvania, Delaware, Maryland, Virginia, North-Carolina, South-Carolina and Georgia."[205]

The Resolution for Independence of 2 July 1776 and the Declaration of Independence that followed two days later are important documents against which to assess Lincoln's argument that the Declaration gave birth of what he referred to as an "American People" or "new nation." A plain reading of both the Resolution and Declaration indicates that they did no such thing. Both documents unambiguously referred to the former colonies becoming "free and independent states," and not a single, unified State. Furthermore, the Declaration was a declaration made, as its formal title clearly spells out, by "the thirteen United States of America," which consistently referred to the "States" in the plural as "these States," or as "these Colonies," or as "these united Colonies," or as "them," or as "they."[206] The adjectival[207] use of the word "united" in the both the title and text of the Declaration reflected a unity of purpose against a common foe, rather than the creation of a single political entity or union. This is evidenced by the resolution of the Continental Congress on 30 June 1777 that affirmed that it was "composed of delegates chosen by, and representing the communities respectively inhabiting the territories" of the thirteen States formed "for the purposes of securing and defending . . . [themselves] against the usurpations, oppressions, and hostile invasions of Great Britain."[208]

In achieving these purposes, on 7 June 1776, Congress had, in anticipation of the Declaration of Independence, resolved that "a plan of confederation be prepared and transmitted to the respective Colonies for their consideration and approbation."[209] If any form of union of the former colonies was created in 1776, there would have been no need for a resolution calling for the preparation of a plan of confederation for the individual colonies to consider. However, given that the colonies had been established at different times, had their own histories, and were governed in accordance with the own charters or constitutions, no such union existed at that time. Fisher Ames, a staunch Federalist and representative from Massachusetts, recognized this reality when, in 1792, he wrote: "Instead of feeling as a Nation, a State is our country. We look with indifference, often with hatred, fear, and aversion, to the other States."[210] It was thus unsurprising that the revolutionary leaders focused their energies on writing the constitutions of their respective States rather than giving much attention to the form and structure of the proposed plan of confederation that eventually emerged in the form of the Articles of Association.[211]

Following the Resolution for Independence and Declaration of Independence, the self-declared "free and independent States" proceeded to act upon Congress's recommendation of 10 May 1776 that they "adopt such government as shall . . . best conduce to the happiness and safety of their constituents."[212] This they did by adopting their own constitutions, which explicitly or implicitly reaffirmed their status as free and/or independent States with their own governmental structures and institutions.

The constitutions of six States did so explicitly. The constitutions of Massachusetts, in 1780 (Part I, Article IV)[213] and New Hampshire, in 1784 (Part I, Article VII)[214] both stipulated that "[t]he people of this Commonwealth have the sole and exclusive right of governing themselves as a free, sovereign, and independent state." In their Preambles, the constitutions of Pennsylvania in 1776,[215] Maryland in 1776,[216] New York in 1777,[217] and South Carolina in 1778[218] all contained express provisions declaring themselves to be free and/or independent States.

The constitutions of five States implicitly referred to their new status as free and independent States by reference to various resolutions of the Continental Congress that referred to the former colonies as free and independent States. In North Carolina, the Preamble to its Constitution of 1776[219] stipulated that the constitution of "the State" of North Carolina, sourced in "the authority of the people" of North Carolina, was a necessary consequence of the fact that the Declaration of Independence led to the colonies becoming "forever . . . free and independent States." In New Jersey, the Preamble to its Constitution of 1776, as amended in 1777, referred to New Jersey as a "a State" whose Constitution was enacted pursuant to various resolutions of the Continental Congress from May 1776 to the Resolution for Independence of 2 July 1776.[220] In Virginia, the Preamble to its Constitution of 1776 declared that it was enacted "in compliance with a recommendation of the General Congress."[221] In Georgia, the Preamble to its Constitution of 1777 referred to both the 10 May 1776 resolution and the Declaration of Independence as the basis for its constitutional provisions for "the future government of *this State*" (emphasis added).[222] In Delaware, although its Constitution of 1776 made no reference to the Declaration of Independence, Article I implicitly declared Delaware to be a free and independent State with its declaration that Delaware had been transformed from a colonial entity into "The Delaware State."[223]

Of the remaining two former colonies, in Connecticut, independence was asserted in 1776 by means of a resolution of its assembly, which, after approving the Declaration of Independence, resolved "that *this Colony* is and of right ought to be *a* free and independent *State*."[224] Rhode Island was the only former colony not to in some way reaffirm its independence.

In light of these the reaffirmations of independent statehood by twelve of the thirteen former colonies, Lincoln's assertions in his Message to Congress in Special Session that these States never had a State constitution, were never independent of the Union, and were, supposedly, created by the Union that was formed by the Constitution, cannot be sustained. That the states were not so created is also evidenced by the fact that, at the Philadelphia Convention, Alexander Hamilton, in arguing that "the general power . . . must swallow up the State powers" because "[t]wo sovereignties can not co-exist within the same limits," effectively argued that the States should be abolished as such and "be divided into election districts."[225] What is clear from Hamilton's proposal is that, not only did the states exist prior to the Constitution and were not created by the Union that the Constitution formed, but that their sovereignty and continued existence was seen by Hamilton as a major stumbling block to any new union that retained them. Even the avowed nationalist James Wilson rejected Hamilton's proposal. He argued in favor of retaining the states in any new union so that "they might (not) only subsist but subsist on friendly terms with [the national government]."[226] As Lincoln's admiring biographer Michael Burlingame recognizes, Lincoln's argument here is based upon "questionable logic."[227]

In relation to Lincoln's assertion that the Declaration of Independence marked the creation of what he referred to as an "American people" or a "new nation," a literal reading of the Declaration's statement that it was made "in the Name, and by Authority of the good People of [the] Colonies," could be interpreted to lend support to this claim. However, such a reading is difficult to sustain because it is inconsistent with the reality, that, as John Harvie, a delegate to the Continental Congress from Virginia, assured Jefferson in 1777, "our Confederacy is not founded on Brotherly Love."[228] This meant, as Maryland's attorney general, Luther Martin, said at the Philadelphia Convention, that in 1776, Americans "preferred the Establishment of themselves into thirteen separate sovereignties instead of incorporating themselves into one."[229] Thus, at the conclusion of the Convention, on 17 September 1787, in his covering letter to at the Confederation Congress, George Washington observed that the Convention's principal difficulty that it had to overcome in drafting the proposed Constitution was the "Difference among the several States as to their Situation Extent Habits and particular Interests."[230] And in 1818, John Adams recalled that the "colonies had grown up under constitutions of government so different, there was so great a variety of religions, they were composed of so many different nations, their customs, manners, and habits had so little resemblance, and their intercourse so rare, and their knowledge of each other so imperfect, that to unite them in the same principles in theory and the same system of action, was certainly a very difficult enterprise . . . [and] perhaps a singular example in the history of mankind." In further writing that "[t]hirteen clocks were made to strike together" and that this represented "a perfection of mechanism which no artist had ever before effected,"[231] Adams was marveling at the fact that they were able to come together for the common purpose of defeating the British, and not that they transformed themselves into a single American nation.

As Gordon Wood points out, these States, "inherited not only their [colonial] geographic boundaries but also the affections and loyalties of the people."[232] The colonists were, as Alan Taylor notes, "[d]iverse and fractious" and "lacked common bonds as Americans."[233] Thus, as David Hendrickson points out, if the signatories to the Declaration sought to create "one people . . . that possessed national sovereignty, it would seem rather strange that they should employ language so unambiguously affirming that the American states were now possessed of the rights that all states had in a state of nature."[234] This assessment is supported by the way in which the signatures to the Declaration were affixed to the document. As Bernadette Meyler points out, they were "grouped by state, even if not explicitly so labeled,"[235] indicating that the Declaration was signed by the representatives of separate colonies and their respective peoples rather than representatives of a single American people.

It is also clear that this understanding of the Declaration was the understanding of the generation involved in the American Revolution. Thus, in 1796, in the Supreme Court decision in *Ware v. Hylton*, Justice Samuel Chase, a signatory to the Declaration of Independence on behalf of Maryland, said:

> I consider this as a declaration, not that the United Colonies *jointly*, in a *collective* capacity, were independent states, &c. but that *each* of them was

> a sovereign and independent state, that is, that *each* of them had a right to govern itself by its own authority, and its own laws, without any control from any other power upon earth. . . . . From the 4th of *July*, 1776, the *American* states were *de facto*, as well as *de jure*, in the possession and actual exercise of *all* the *rights* of independent governments. . . . . [A]ll laws made by the legislatures of the several states after the declaration of independence were the laws of sovereign and independent governments.[236]

Similar sentiments were expressed in 1808 in *McIlvaine v. Coxe's Lessee*, by Justice William Cushing, who had, prior to his appointment to the Supreme Court in 1789, served first as a justice and then as chief justice of Massachusetts' Superior Court. In delivering the Supreme Court's opinion, Cushing said:

> This opinion is predicated upon a principle which is believed to be undeniable, that the several states which composed this union, so far at least as regarded their municipal regulations became entitled, from the time when they declared themselves independent, to all the rights and powers of sovereign states, and that they did no derive them from concessions made by the British King. The treaty of peace contains a recognition of their independence, not a grant of it. From hence it results, that the laws of the several state governments were the laws of sovereign states, and as such were obligatory upon the people of such state, from the time they were enacted.[237]

Cushing's chief justice in this case, John Marshall, who served in the Continental Army during the American Revolution and was a delegate to Virginia's convention that ratified the Constitution, reiterated this sentiment, in 1819, in *Sturges v. Crowninshield*, when, in delivering the opinion of the Court, he said that "previous to the formation of the [Constitution], we were divided into independent States, united for some purposes, but, in most respects, sovereign."[238] And finally, in 1822, President James Monroe, a veteran of the American Revolution, in a message to the House of Representatives, said that "[t]he Declaration of Independence . . . announced to the world new States, possessing and exercising complete sovereignty, which they resolved to maintain."[239]

This continued to be the view of the Supreme Court through to the outbreak of the Civil War. Writing extrajudicially in 1837, Justice Henry Baldwin, in his study on the origin and nature of the Constitution, was emphatic in stating that the thirteen former British colonies became free and independent States in which sovereignty vested in their respective peoples.[240] He restated this view when, in the following year, in *State of Rhode Island and Providence Plantations v. Commonwealth of Massachusetts*, in delivering the opinion of the Supreme Court, he said that the effect of the American Revolution was that it "devolved on each state the prerogative of the king as he had held it in the Colonies."[241] To similar effect, in 1850, in *Wheeler v. Smith*, Justice John McLean, speaking for a unanimous Supreme Court, said: "When this country achieved its independence, the prerogatives of the Crown devolved upon the peoples of the States."[242] And, Marshall's successor as Chief Justice, Roger Taney, in delivering the opinion of the Court, in 1857, in *Dred Scott v. Sandford*, said that when "the thirteen colonies . . . separated from Great Britain [they] formed new sovereignties, and took their places in the family of independent nations."[243] Finally, in 1861, ten days after Lincoln took his oath of office as president, in *Kentucky v. Dennison*, Taney noted that by the time the thirteen former British colonies formed the Confederation in March 1781, they had, "by the Declaration of Independence, become separate and independent sovereignties, against which treason might be committed."[244]

The Articles of Confederation

Following the adoption of the Declaration of Independence, the thirteen self-declared "free and independent States" were, until 1 March 1781, "in a state of nature with reference to each other except in their informal relations in the Congress as a mere place of meeting and of concerting policy as independent nations."[245] It was, as Alan Taylor states, "[o]nly the pressures of war against the British superpower"[246] that corralled these self-declared "free and independent States" to come together on 1 March 1781 to create what Alison LaCroix accurately describes as "the leanest possible union,"[247] in the form of the Confederation, by ratifying the Articles of Confederation which had been approved by the Continental Congress in 1777.[248] As even the committed nationalist Joseph Story conceded, the Confederation "possessed no one solid attribute of power" and "[i]n truth, . . . possessed only the power of recommendation" because "[i]t depended altogether upon the good will of the states, whether a measure should be carried into effect or not."[249]

The Articles of Confederation clearly reaffirmed that each of its members was, and remained, a free and independent state. Article II stipulated that "[e]ach state retains its sovereignty, freedom, and independence and every power, jurisdiction, and right" other than those "expressly delegated" to the Confederation Congress.[250] This Article was included to make clear that the Continental Congress was not the representative body of a single American people as had been suggested by a minority of its delegates such as James Wilson, Benjamin Rush, and John Adams.[251] Furthermore, the word "retain" in Article II made it clear that these States had been sovereign from their creation as free and independent States by virtue of the Resolution for Independence on 2 July 1776.

Article III implicitly set out the limited purposes of the Confederation by stipulating that its member States agreed that they had entered "into a firm league of friendship with each other, for their common defence, the security of their liberties, and their mutual and general welfare, binding themselves to assist each other, against all force offered to, or attacks made upon them, or any of them, on account of religion, sovereignty, trade, or any other pretence whatever."[252] The fact that these States negotiated separate trade agreements with other powers and imposed their own levies on imports[253] is consistent with their status as free and independent States.

Finally, Article XIII stipulated that "the union shall be perpetual" and that any amendment of the Articles had to be agreed to by the Confederation Congress "and be afterwards confirmed by the legislatures of every State."[254] The understanding of sovereignty at that time, as Akhil Reed Amar points out, meant that "the mere fact that each of the thirteen states agreed to what the Articles called a 'perpetual' 'union' in no way negated each state's continuing sovereign status."[255]

The Articles of Confederation were a treaty between sovereign and independent States,[256] which, as Alan Taylor notes, "built an alliance of states rather than a cohesive nation."[257] These States, as Gordon Wood notes, "jealously guarded their independence and sovereignty" and "assumed the powers of a sovereign state . . . even in violation of the Articles . . . [by] making war, providing armies, laying embargoes, [and] . . . in some cases carrying on separate diplomatic correspondence and negotiations abroad."[258] That this was so was unsurprising because, as Jack Rakove points out, local and state, and not national, issues were what Americans had in mind and it was to "[t]hese. . . . . levels of governance whose decisions affected their daily lives and which had to cope with the aftermath of a prolonged revolutionary struggle that had placed so enormous a strain on American society."[259]

The independence and sovereignty of the Confederation's thirteen States was further confirmed in 1783 by the terms of the Treaty of Paris, which formally ended the American Revolutionary War. By the terms of its Article I, Great Britain recognized its thirteen former colonies "to be free, sovereign and independent States" and that it would treat "*them* as such," and in Article VII stipulated that there would be "a firm and perpetual peace between his Britannic Majesty and the said States" (emphasis added).[260] As stated by Justice Cushing in 1808, in *McIlvaine v. Coxe's Lessee*, the Treaty constituted "a recognition of their independence, not a grant of it."[261] This recognition meant that the thirteen States "secured the complete array of sovereign rights and powers recognized by the law of nations."[262]

That contemporaries saw it this way is clear. In April 1787, James Madison, then a delegate to the Confederation Congress from Virginia, described the Confederation as "nothing more than a treaty of amity of commerce and of alliance, between independent and Sovereign States" whose decisions required the "unanimous and punctual obedience of 13 independent bodies."[263] During the Virginia ratification debates, he noted that the Confederation's "component States retained their sovereignty."[264] John Adams, a seconder to the Resolution for Independence of 2 July 1776 and signatory to the Declaration of Independence, said of the Confederation Congress that it "is not a legislative assembly, nor a representative assembly, but only a diplomatic assembly." Of its delegates, he said that they were "responsible to the states; their authority is clearly ascertained; and the states, in their separate capacities, are the checks" who were "able . . . at all times to control their delegates."[265] And, Henry Knox, who served as the Confederation's secretary of war, wrote that "[e]very State considers its representative in Congress not so much the Legislator of the whole Union, as its own immediate Agent or Ambassador."[266] This meant, as Alexander Hamilton noted, that "the concurrence of thirteen distinct sovereign wills" was necessary for any important decision of the Confederation.[267] Thus, Amar describes the Confederation Congress as "not so much a national 'legislature' . . . as an international assembly of ambassadors."[268]

At the Philadelphia Convention, of the delegates who addressed the issue, the majority sentiment was that the Confederation's States were independent and sovereign States, as is evidenced in statements to that effect made by Charles Pinckney, David Brearley, William Paterson, Roger Sherman, Luther Martin, Oliver Ellsworth, Jonathan Dayton, and Gunning Bedford.[269] In contrast, a minority of delegates claimed they were not. Rufus King argued they were not independent and sovereign States because they had no power to declare war, make peace, or enter into alliances or treaties.[270] James Wilson and Alexander Hamilton argued that the Declaration of Independence meant that the States were "independent, not Individually but Unitedly."[271] Finally, Elbridge Gerry, although asserting that the States were not independent, recognized and "lamented" that they acted as if they were.[272] However, these arguments cannot be sustained in the face of the explicit assertions of independent statehood in the Articles of Confederation. That the States of the Confederation were free and independent States was confirmed by Chief Justice Marshall in 1824, in *Gibbons v. Ogden*, when, in delivering the opinion of the Supreme Court, he said that, in relation to the States in the union created by the Articles of Confederation, "they were sovereign, were completely independent, and were connected with each other only by a league."[273] In 1851, shortly before being appointed as a justice of the Supreme Court, Benjamin Curtis stated that if, in the mid-1780s, "Massachusetts was an independent, sovereign state, possessing . . . all the powers over its own citizens in reference to foreign states which constitute and arise from sovereignty," one of which was "the power to make binding compacts with other states,"[274] so too were the twelve other States of the Confederation. Similar views were expressed by Chief Justice Taney in *Dred Scott v. Sandford*[275] and *Kentucky v. Dennison*.[276] In the former case, in adding that the Confederation itself "had none of the attributes of sovereignty in legislative, executive, or judicial power,"[277] Taney clearly implied that this sovereignty vested in the States of the Confederation. And it was delegates of these sovereign States that met at the Philadelphia Convention to draft a Constitution in which, as will be detailed below, they delegated some of their sovereign powers to the federal government, but, nevertheless, retained their sovereignty. This is clear from George Washington's covering letter to the Confederation Congress on 17 September 1787, in which he said that it was "obviously impracticable in the foederal Government Of these States, *to secure all Rights of independent Sovereignty to each* and yet provide for the Interest and Safety of all" (emphasis added).[278] What is clear from this statement is that that the delegates of sovereign States drafted the Constitution in which their sovereignty was retained, albeit that some of their sovereign powers had to be delegated, as Washington said, so as to "provide for the interests and safety of all."

The Constitution's Preamble

Given that, as has already been noted, grammatically, the word "people" can be either singular or plural, much of the debate over the existence of a constitutional right of a state to, in appropriate circumstances, unilaterally secede from the Union revolved around the meaning of the Constitution's Preamble with its assertion that it was "the People of the United States" that ordained and established the Constitution. Did this phrase refer to a single American people, as argued by exponents of the nationalist theory, or did it refer to the peoples of each of the States of the Union, as argued by their compact-theory opponents?

An interpretation of the Preamble's "We the People" as referring to a single American people that ratified the Constitution is difficult to sustain. As Akhil Reed Amar points out:

> [W]e must resist the temptation to place exclusive reliance on the Preamble's opening phrase. Any argument based solely on these words proves too much. The Declaration of Independence was made "in the Name, and by the Authority of *the* good People (not Peoples) of these colonies," and the Articles of Confederation spoke of "*the* people (again singular) of the different states in the union." Yet, . . . neither of these documents, taken as a whole, is best understood as proclaiming that Americans were one sovereign People.[279]

An examination of the drafting and ratification of the Constitution gives credence to Amar's caution and support for the Preamble's "We the People" being construed to refer to the peoples of the individual States of the Confederation as the "People of the United States" who ordained and established the Constitution.

When the first draft of the Constitution was presented to the Philadelphia Convention on 6 August 1787, it was then understood that it would create a compact between the States that ratified it. This was reflected in the draft Preamble that was unanimously accepted by the Convention's Committee of the Whole on the following day[280] and which commenced with the words "We the people of the States of . . ." and then proceeded to list the then thirteen sovereign and independent States that would "ordain, declare, and establish" the Constitution.[281]

Subsequently, on 31 August 1787, when the Convention resolved that only nine States needed to ratify the Constitution for it to come into effect,[282] it became necessary for the Convention's Committee of Style and Arrangement to "revise the stile of and arrange the articles which had been agreed to."[283] Because it was not known how many States would ratify the Constitution, it was impossible to list the States by name in the Preamble. This difficulty was, as Max Farrand observes, "cleverly avoided"[284] by redrafting the Preamble to commence with the words "We the People of the United States."[285] On the basis that the Committee had been authorized only to revise the style and order of the proposed Constitution's provisions and not to substantively alter them, it is reasonable to assume that, when the revised wording of the Preamble was added without any debate during the final few days of the Convention, it was considered to retain the essential meaning of the originally approved Preamble, namely that it was the people of each of the States and not a single American people, who would, in due course, ratify the Constitution.

That the Preamble's "We the People" should be interpreted in this way was recognized at that time by key members of the Philadelphia Convention. Thus, Gouverneur Morris, who, as James Madison confirmed, had played the pivotal role in the "finish given to the style and arrangement of the Constitution,"[286] informed the Convention that

> [h]e came [to the Convention] to *form a compact* for the good of America. He was *ready to do so with all the States*: He hoped & believed that all would enter into *such a compact*. If they would not he was ready *to join with any States* that would (emphasis added).[287]

Morris re-iterated this view in a letter, written in 1803, in which he said:

> [T]he Constitution was a compact, not between solitary individuals, but between political societies, the people not of America but of the United States, each enjoying sovereign power, and of course equal rights.[288]

At the Philadelphia Convention, in a debate over whether the federal government could use force against a delinquent state, Madison referred to the proposed Constitution as "A Union of States."[289] This is also clearly implied from his statement in *Federalist 43* that "no political relation can subsist between assenting and dissenting states."[290] This "Union of States" flowed from the fact, as he detailed in *Federalist 39*, that "the Constitution is to be founded on the assent and ratification . . . to be given by the people, not as individuals composing one entire nation; but as composing the distinct and independent States to which they respectively belong."[291] Madison went on to write that this meant that "[e]ach State in ratifying the Constitution, is considered as a sovereign body independent of all others, and only to be bound by its own voluntary act."[292] On the other hand, in *Federalist 46*, Madison directly contradicted these statements when he wrote of sovereignty vesting in "the great body of citizens of the United States."[293]

However, in the light of his subsequent statements, Madison's views in *Federalist 39*, rather than *Federalist 46*, should be taken to represent his considered thought on the issue as it is the view he consistently espoused. At the Virginia ratification convention, he said that the Constitution was to be formed by "[t]he people—but not the people as composing one great body—but the people as composing thirteen sovereignties."[294] Subsequently, in 1821, he wrote that "[o]ur Our Governmental System is established by a compact . . . between the States as sovereign communities."[295] In 1829, he wrote that "the real parties to the constl. compact of the US are the States—that is, the people thereof respectively in their sovereign character, and they alone."[296] In 1830, in describing what he called the "the true character of the Constitution," after stating that the Constitution was not "formed by the majority of the people of the US as a single community," he wrote:

> It was formed by the States—that is by the people in each of the States, acting in their highest sovereign capacity; and formed, consequently by the same authority which formed the State Constitutions.[297]

In 1833, in a letter to Daniel Webster, Madison wrote:

> [T]he undisputed fact is, that the Constitution was made by the people, but as embodied into the several States, who were parties to it; and, therefore, made by the States in their highest authoritative capacity. . . . . The Constitution of the United States [was] established by a Competent Authority, by that of the sovereign people of the several States who were the parties to it."[298]

And, in 1835, he wrote that the "competent authority" that formed the United States was "the people of the several States in their highest sovereign authority."[299]

The Constitution's Ratification Clause

The compact theory's construction of the word "People" in the Preamble's "We the People of the United States" as a plural noun, rather than a singular noun, is also reflected in the Constitution's ratification clause set out in Article VII. At the Philadelphia Convention, in the first draft of the Constitution, the ratification clause stipulated that "[t]he ratifications of the Conventions of [blank space] States shall be sufficient for organizing this Constitution."[300] When it was subsequently agreed that only nine States were needed to ratify the Constitution, it became necessary to amend the ratification clause because, as Rufus King put it, "otherwise . . . the Constitution . . . will operate on the whole though ratified by a part only."[301] Nine States were chosen as the required number because, as George Mason noted, that number "had been required in all great cases under the Confederation & that number was on that account preferable."[302] The Convention then resolved to add the words "between the said States" to the clause, so as to, in King's words, "confine the operation of the Govt. to the States ratifying it."[303] Thus, what became Article VII of the Constitution was amended to read: "The ratification of the conventions of nine States, shall be sufficient for the establishment of this constitution between the States so ratifying the same."[304]

There was a sound legal reason why Article VII mandated ratification by the individual States of the Confederation. That reason lay in the fact that ratification of the Constitution involved amending the existing constitutions of these States, which could only be done by the respective States. This could be achieved through conventions of the States, which is why ratification of the Constitution had to be processed through such conventions. Given that ratification by means of conventions in each of the States was required, Article VII is entirely consistent with the compact theory of the Constitution because, as Forrest McDonald points out, this manner of ratifying the Constitution "unmistakably implied that the source of sovereignty was the people of the states,"[305] rather than a single American people.

In relation to the meaning of Article VII's reference to the "States," it is clear that it meant the peoples of the States. This was also the view, in 1795, of Justice Iredell in *Penhallow v. Doane*, where he said that he was "not capable of comprehending" any distinction "between *a State and the people of the State*" and noted that by "the State" he meant *"all the citizens who compose the State, and are . . . integral parts of it; all together forming a body politic."*[306] Thus, ratification resulted in the "establishment" of the Constitution, as Clause VII expressly states, "between" the peoples of each of the States that ratified it. The words "*between* the States" (emphasis added) in Article VII clearly point to the Constitution as a compact to which the States were the parties. At the Virginia ratification convention, James Madison was correct when he analogized the ratification of the Constitution to "mak[ing] a contract."[307]

A further critical aspect of Article VII was, as it clearly stipulates, that it was to be ratified by a supermajority of the thirteen States. This was to be done through conventions elected by the peoples of each of the States. These States were, as the Declaration of Independence proclaimed and the Articles of Confederation affirmed, "free and independent states." It was the peoples of these States, rather than an American people, that ratified the Constitution. If so, it makes sense to regard these peoples, rather than a single American people, as the entities that did "ordain and establish" the Constitution.

In the light of the ratification of the Constitution by the peoples of each of the States, it was hardly surprising that the compact theory of the Constitution was invoked by Madison and Thomas Jefferson in reaction to the federal Alien and Sedition Acts passed by Congress in 1798. Resolutions adopted by Virginia and Kentucky in response to this legislation expounded the view that the Constitution was a compact or contract between the states of the Union.

The Virginia Resolutions, authored by Madison, stated:

> That this Assembly doth explicitly and peremptorily declare, that it views the powers of the federal government, as resulting from the compact to which the states are parties; as limited by the plain sense and intention of the instrument constituting that compact.[308]

The Resolutions asserted that the Alien and Sedition Acts were unconstitutional because they relied upon a federal legislative power that was "not delegated by the constitution," and indeed, "was expressly and positively" forbidden by the Constitution's Tenth Amendment,[309] which stipulated that "[t]he powers not delegated to the United States by the Constitution, nor prohibited by it to the States, are reserved to the States respectively, or to the people." The Resolutions then went on to seek the support of other states "in maintaining unimpaired the authorities, rights, and liberties, reserved to the States respectively, or to the people."[310] In adopting the Resolutions, in an address to the people of Virginia, its General Assembly referred to the Constitution as being a "federal compact."[311]

In 1800, in his Report on the Resolutions, Madison wrote that although "the term 'States' is sometimes used in a vague sense," in the Resolutions it meant "the people composing those political societies, in their highest sovereign capacities." It was "in that sense, the Constitution was submitted to the 'States': In that sense the 'States' ratified it; and in that sense of the term 'States,' they are consequently parties to the compact from which the powers of the Federal Government result."[312] This meant, according to Madison, that "[t]he constitution of the United States was formed by the sanction of the states, given by each in its sovereign capacity."[313] Pursuant to the Constitution, Madison concluded, the federal government was "composed of powers specifically granted, with a reservation of all others to the states or to the people."[314] That "all powers" not granted to the federal government were "reserved," was seen by the Philadelphia Convention to be "a fundamental and characteristic principle of the constitution."[315]

In the Kentucky Resolutions, authored by Jefferson, the first resolution stated:

> Resolved, that the several states composing the United States of America, are not united on the principle of unlimited submission to their General Government; but that, by compact under the style and title of a Constitution for the United States and of amendments thereto, they constituted a General Government for special purposes, delegated to that Government certain definite powers, reserving each state to itself, the residuary mass of right to their own self Government; and that whensoever the General Government assumes undelegated powers, its acts are unauthoritative, void, and of no force: That to this compact each state acceded as a state, and is an integral party, its co-states forming as to itself, the other party.[316]

The critical difference between the resolutions authored by Madison and Jefferson was that for Madison, a state, as a party to the constitutional compact, could go no further than declare a federal law to be unconstitutional and seek constitutional change by taking action to render federal law unenforceable in practice within the boundaries of a state (interposition), whereas Jefferson maintained that a state could go further and declare such a law to be void and of no effect (nullification).[317] For Madison, interposition meant the right of states to act in concert with each other to seek "redress against . . . acts of usurped power" which could be rightfully invoked when a state invited other states "to concur in declaring [such] acts to be unconstitutional, and to co-operate by the necessary and proper means in maintaining unimpaired the authorities rights & liberties reserved to the State respectively & to the people."[318]

On the other hand, Madison rejected the validity of nullification, as espoused by Jefferson. He regarded Jefferson's nullification argument as a "preposterous & anarchical pretension" that had "not a shadow of countenance in the Constitution."[319] For Madison, nullification entailed a "more formidable" consequence than interposition, in that "[i]t asked whether a State, by resuming the sovereign form in which it entered the Union, might not of right withdraw from it at will."[320] In his detailed analysis of nullification, Madison made the same point when he described it as "a deadly poison"[321] that possessed a "hideous aspect & fatal tendency."[322] Madison's suggestion that unilateral secession of a state from the Union was, in effect, a logical extension of nullification is one that has since been accepted by various scholars.[323] However, although the compact theory of the Constitution is the basis of both the right of states to nullify federal laws and to unilaterally secede from the Union, the latter was not the logical extension of the former. Given that, on the basis of the Constitution's supremacy clause, which rendered valid federal legislation impervious to being made inoperative by a state enacting legislation nullifying it, nullification was clearly unconstitutional. As Chief Justice Marshall pointed out in *Fletcher v. Peck*, a state of the Union "is a member of the American union; and that union has a constitution the supremacy of which all acknowledge, and which imposes limits to the legislatures of the several states, which none claim a right to pass."[324] Thus, while a state remains a member of the Union it was bound to comply with constitutionally valid federal legislation. However, this had nothing to do with the issue of unilateral secession. Limitations placed upon a state while a part of the Union were of no relevance as to whether a state was entitled to unilaterally secede from it.

This point was argued by then-Senator Jefferson Davis from Mississippi, in his speech to the Senate on 21 January 1861, in which he pointed out that nullification and unilateral secession were "often confounded," but were nevertheless "antagonistic principles." Unilateral secession was, for Davis, "an essential attribute of State sovereignty," whereas nullification amounted to "the right of a State to remain in the Union, and to disregard its constitutional obligations."[325] Davis went on and said that, whatever right there was to "execute the [federal] laws" against a state within the Union, to maintain that the same applied to a state that had seceded from the Union was a "perversion of terms." Davis concluded that this put secession, which stemmed from "the inalienable rights of the people of the States" by which a sovereign state was able to "reclaim the grants which it has made to any agent whomsoever," in "a different class of remedies" to that of nullification.[326] Thus, Mark Brandon writes the following on the issue of the relationship between nullification and unilateral secession:

> [T]hey are almost mutually exclusive in that each tends to ameliorate the impulse that generates the necessity of the other. Under almost all conceivable circumstances, nullification would have provided sufficient security for local self-determination that the need for an exit from the Union would have been practically nil. Especially in Calhoun's hands, nullification was an attempt to reconstruct the notion of a national majority so as to render secession unnecessary and to defuse it as an explosive constitutional issue.[327]

As to the response of the other sixteen states of the Union to the Virginia and Kentucky Resolutions, in his detailed study of them, Wendell Bird concludes that "only half of the sixteen states responded negatively" and that "[t]he other half . . . supported or did not oppose" them.[328] Significantly, as Bird points out, of the states responding negatively, none "expressly objected to the resolutions' claim that there were delegated federal powers and reserved state powers," although Massachusetts may have implicitly done so.[329] In fact, as Bird concludes, the underlying constitutional theories outlined by Madison and Jefferson were "widely accepted."[330] Indeed, they were relied upon by New England states when they threatened secession during the later presidencies of both Jefferson and Madison. For example, in the wake of the Embargo Act of 1807,[331] which imposed an embargo on foreign trade in an attempt to secure diplomatic neutrality during the Napoleonic Wars (1803–1815) between the French and British which had devastated the Union's economy, Rhode Island's legislature adopted a resolution condemning it in which it was said:

> [T]he people of this State, as one of the parties to the Federal compact, have a right to express their sense of any violation of its provisions and that it is the duty of this General Assembly as the organ of their sentiments and the depository of their authority, to interpose for the purpose of protecting them from the ruinous inflictions of usurped and unconstitutional power.[332]

During the antebellum era, the Virginia and Kentucky Resolutions were a significant influence on John C. Calhoun, the leading apostle of the compact theory of the Constitution during the antebellum era.[333] In *A Discourse on the Constitution and Government of the United States*, published in 1850, he wrote:

> [T]he government is a federal, in contradistinction to a national government;—a government formed by the States; ordained and established by the States, and for the States—without any participation or agency whatever, on the part of the people, regarded in the aggregate as forming a nation. . . . . In all its parts . . . [our system of government] emanated from the same source,—the people of the several States. The whole, taken together, form a federal community—a community composed of States united by a political compact;—and not a nation composed of individuals united by, what is called, a social compact.[334]

Calhoun's conception of the Constitution as a compact between the states is reflected in a number of resolutions that he proposed and which, following two weeks of debate, were adopted by the Senate on 12 January 1838 by a vote of thirty-five to nine.[335] The first resolution stated:

> [I]n the adoption of the Federal Constitution, the States adopting the same acted, severally, as free, independent, and sovereign States; and that each, *for itself*, by its own voluntary assent, entered the Union with a view to its increased security against all dangers (emphasis added).[336]

The third resolution stated that the federal government "was instituted and adopted by the several States of this Union as a common agent, in order to carry into effect those powers which they had delegated by the Constitution."[337]

Alison LaCroix, in her detailed study of the ideological origins of American federalism, comes to much the same conclusion as Calhoun as to what was meant by federalism in 1789. LaCroix writes:

> To the delegates at Philadelphia and their contemporaries, a federal union meant the same thing that it had to [the Scottish nationalist] James Hodges in 1703: an association "whereby Distinct, Free, and Independent Kingdoms, Dominions or States, do unite their separate Interests into one common Interest, for the mutual benefit of both, so far as relates to certain Conditions and Articles agreed upon betwixt them, *retaining in the meantime their several Independencies, National Distinctions, and the different Laws, Customs, and Government of each*." . . . This was Pufendorf's vision as well: the "system of states" in which "several States are, by some special Band, so closely united, as that they seem to compose one body, and *yet retain each of them the sovereign Command in their respective Dominions*" (emphasis added).[338]

The Resolutions Ratifying the Constitution

The understanding that the Constitution was, pursuant to its Article VII, ratified by the peoples of each of the States, rather than a single American people, is further supported by the Philadelphia Convention's resolutions concerning the ratification of the Constitution, the Confederation Congress's resolution dealing with ratification, and the ratification resolutions of the conventions of the thirteen free and independent States called for that purpose.

On 17 September 1787, notwithstanding that not all the delegates to the Philadelphia Convention agreed to sign the proposed Constitution, in words proposed by Gouverneur Morris,[339] the signed proposed Constitution stated that it had been approved "by the Unanimous Consent of the States present" at the Convention.[340] In his diary on the same date, in his only substantive diary comment about the Convention, George Washington wrote that "the Constitution received the Unanimous assent of 11 States and Colo. Hamilton's from New York (the only delegate from thence in Convention)."[341] This reflected, and was a consequence of, the fact that at the Philadelphia Convention each state had one vote and that therefore the vote on any issue was determined by a majority of States rather than a majority of delegates.[342] Thus, it was entirely to be expected that Connecticut's Roger Sherman would, in private correspondence in December 1787 setting out his support for the ratification of the Constitution, note that there was "unanimity of the convention . . . in favour of the constitution" and that "all the States present concurred in it."[343] If the Constitution was, as the nationalist theory argued, the product of a single American people, one would have thought the proposed Constitution would have been approved by the delegates on behalf of that people rather than on behalf of the States represented at the Convention. The same can be said of the resolution adopted on the same day that, in the name of the twelve States represented at the Convention, recommended that the proposed Constitution be presented to the Confederation's Congress for it to submitted to "a Convention of Delegates, *chosen in each State by the People thereof*." The resolution went on to state that upon "*each Convention assenting to, and ratifying the Same*," it "should give Notice thereof to the United States in Congress assembled" (emphasis added).[344] That the Convention's delegates signed the proposed Constitution document on behalf of the States is further confirmed by the circumstances surrounding North Carolina's William Blount's signature. Blount initially refused to sign it because he was not entirely satisfied with it. However, he relented on the basis, as it was explained to him, that by signing it he was merely confirming that the proposed Constitution "was the unanimous act of the States in Convention."[345]

On the basis of the Convention's recommendation, on 28 September 1787 the Confederation Congress unanimously resolved to forward the proposed Constitution to the Confederation's thirteen States for each of them to submit it for ratification by "a convention of delegates *chosen in each state by the people thereof* in conformity to the resolves of the Convention made and provided in that case" (emphasis added).[346] These resolutions clearly point to the existence of there being separate peoples in each of the States, rather than an American people, who, through conventions elected by each of these peoples, rather than an American people, were tasked with ratifying the Constitution.

In relation to the ratification resolutions of these thirteen States, all of them explicitly stated that the ratification resolution was made by and on behalf of the people of the relevant State. As Edward Larson points out, "[n]one of these state conventions represented the American people as a whole; they represented states."[347] In Delaware, it was the "Deputies of the People of the Delaware State" that ratified the Constitution "for and in behalf of ourselves and our Constituents."[348] In Pennsylvania, it was "Delegates of the People of the Commonwealth of Pennsylvania . . . in the Name and by the authority of the Same People, and for ourselves" that ratified the Constitution.[349] In New Jersey, it was "the Delegates of the State of New-Jersey chosen by the People thereof" that ratified the Constitution "for and on the behalf of the People of the said State of New-Jersey."[350] In Georgia, it was the "Delegates of the People of the State of Georgia" who by "virtue of the powers and authority to Us given by the People of the said State" ratified the Constitution "for, and in behalf of ourselves and our Constituents."[351] In Connecticut, it was the "Delegates of the people of the [the State of Connecticut]" that ratified the Constitution "[i]n the Name of the People of the State of Connecticut."[352] In Massachusetts, it was "the delegates of the People of the Commonwealth of Massachusetts" that, "in the name & in behalf of the People of the Commonwealth of Massachusetts," ratified the Constitution.[353] In Maryland, it was "the Delegates of the People of the State of Maryland" that ratified the Constitution "for ourselves and in the Name and on behalf of the people of this State."[354] In South Carolina, it was a "Convention of the people of South Carolina by their Representatives" that ratified the Constitution "in the name and behalf of the people of this State."[355] In New Hampshire, it was a "Convention of Delegates of the People of the State of New-Hampshire" that ratified the Constitution "in the Name & behalf of the People of the State of New-Hampshire."[356] In Virginia, it was "the Delegates of the People of Virginia" that ratified the Constitution "in the name and in behalf of the People of Virginia."[357] In New York, it was "the Delegates of the People of the State of New York" that ratified the Constitution "in the Name and in the behalf of the People of the State of New York."[358] In North Carolina, the ratification convention ratified the Constitution "in behalf of the freemen, citizens and inhabitants of the State of North Carolina."[359] In Rhode Island, it was "the Delegates of the People of the State of Rhode-Island, and Providence Plantations" that ratified the Constitution "in the name, and in the behalf of the People of the State of Rhode-Island, and Providence-Plantations."[360]

What is clear from these resolutions is that the States of the

Confederation, through their respective peoples, played the central role in ratifying the Constitution. John C. Calhoun summed up this reality when, in 1832, he wrote that the peoples of the individual States

> met in convention as States, acted and voted, as States; and the Constitution, when formed, was submitted for ratification to the people of the several States; it was ratified by them as States, each State for itself; each by its ratification binding its own citizens; the parts, thus separately binding themselves, and not the whole, the parts; to which, if it be added, that it is declared in the preamble to the Constitution to be ordained by the people of *the United States*, and in the article of ratification, when ratified, it is declared "*to be binding between the States so ratifying*," the conclusion is inevitable, that the Constitution is the work of the people of the States, considered, as separate and independent communities—that they are its authors—their power created it—their voice clothed it with and authority—that the Government it formed is in reality their agent—and that the Union, of which it is the bond, is an Union of States, and not of individuals.[361]

The counterargument offered, in 1861, by nationalists, such as Francis Lieber, was that Article VII represented "[t]he mere *modus*"[362] by which a single American people ratified the Constitution. A recent defender of this proposition is Samuel Beer. He initially deals with the question of why the Constitution was not ratified by what he refers to as a "general convention, chosen by the voters of a nationwide constituency and acting for the whole country by a majority or greater vote of its delegates."[363] He concedes that, given that a national election for members of the House of Representatives pursuant to Article I of the Constitution was held soon after its ratification, a national election for delegates to a national ratification convention could readily have been organized.[364] That a national convention was not chosen as the means by which the Constitution was to be ratified was, he argues, because it had two significant drawbacks. However, his arguments here are threadbare and should be rejected.

The first drawback Beer cites is that holding a national ratification convention was not desirable because it would simply repeat and reveal the divisions that were evident at the Philadelphia Convention.[365] However, these divisions over the provisions in the Constitution and whether it should be ratified were always going to occur, as is amply evidenced by the heated debates over these matters at a number of the State ratification conventions and the fact that neither North Carolina nor Rhode Island chose to ratify the Constitution prior to it coming into operation in March 1789.

The second drawback Beer cites is that even if the Constitution was ratified at a national convention, it would still have had to be ratified by State ratification conventions pursuant to the ratification clause in Article VII.[366] However, if the ratification clause was a "mere *modus*" by which a single American people ratified the Constitution, it would have been logical for Article VII to go on and stipulate that the ratification would have resulted in the establishment of the Constitution for the American people, rather than, at it states, "between the States" that ratified it. In making his argument in support of the "mere *modus*" proposition, Beer fails to confront the implications of the actual text of Article VII for his argument. In adopting Article VII, the Philadelphia Convention clearly envisaged ratification by the peoples of each of the States rather than a single American people. Had the Convention envisaged ratification by a single American people it would have adopted a proposal moved by Gouverneur Morris that ratification be submitted to a single national convention[367] and then drafted an Article VII that was consistent with that proposal. In that case there would have been no need for the national convention's ratification of the Constitution to be endorsed by later State ratification conventions. Instead, the Convention rejected Morris's proposal without any debate for want of a seconder.[368] Had it been adopted, a stronger case could be made for the view that the Constitution was ratified by a single American people.

In his defense of the "the mere *modus*" argument advanced by nationalists such as Lieber, Beer also argues that Article VII's nine-State ratification formula was sufficient because such a ratification reflected the will of the majority of the single American people,[369] which Beer, like Lincoln, claims existed prior to the ratification of the Constitution.[370] Beer's argument is based on the fact that, if all States ratified the Constitution, the Union's first House of Representatives would have had a total of sixty-five representatives. If only nine States ratified the Constitution, the first House would have at least thirty-three representatives, irrespective of which States constituted the group of nine. For Beer, because thirty-three representatives represented a majority of the possible sixty-five representatives that could have been elected to the first House of Representatives if all States ratified the Constitution, ratification by any nine States meant that the Constitution would reflect ratification by a majority of the single American people.

Beer's argument has superficial appeal, but closer examination of it reveals it to be flawed. His argument ultimately stands for the proposition that a nine-State ratification of the Constitution would reflect the will of the majority of the single American people spread across the thirteen States of the, by then, rapidly disintegrating Confederation. The argument could be sustained if such a ratification bound all thirteen of these States. However, that is not what Article VII stipulated. Article VII made it clear that a nine-State ratification bound only those nine states. If the Constitution was ratified by only nine States, the question arises as to how Beer would regard the peoples of the other four States. They certainly could not be part of the "We the People" that ordained and established the Constitution which was not binding on them, because their States had not ratified it. If, as Beer claims, they were up to that point part of an American people, their failure to ratify the Constitution presumably transformed them into being the peoples of their respective States. Indeed, that is what supposedly happened in the case of North Carolina and Rhode Island who were not part of the Union when the Constitution came into operation in March 1789. The logical consequence of Beer's argument is that the people of, for example, Rhode Island, were Americans from 1776 to March 1789, were then transformed into Rhode Islanders until May 1790, when, by ratifying the Constitution, they were transformed back to being Americans.

To maintain such transformations stretches credulity beyond reasonable bounds. History and common sense suggest an obvious and reasonable alternative proposition, namely, that the people of Rhode Island were Rhode Islanders in 1776, in March 1789, and in May 1790. That they were Rhode Islanders at the time they ratified the Constitution is undeniably true, given that their ratification resolution explicitly states that it was adopted by delegates of "the People of the State of Rhode-Island, and Providence Plantations."[371] Had they considered themselves part of an American people, their ratification resolution would surely have said so, but it did not. Thus, during this stretch of time the people of Rhode Island were Rhode Islanders and not part of a single American people. And the same can be said of the people of the other twelve States of the Confederation.

Thus, Article VII did not provide for "the mere *modus*" by which a single American people ratified the Constitution. Rather the text of Article VII is entirely consistent with and confirms the proposition that, for the Constitution to be ratified, the peoples of at least nine of the Confederation's States had to ratify it, and that the ratifying resolutions of those States created a binding commitment between them, and concomitantly their respective peoples, to be bound by the provisions set out in the Constitution.

THE TRANSFORMATION OF PEOPLES INTO A PEOPLE

The second ground upon which it is argued that "the People" referred to in the Preamble was an American people is that the Constitution transformed the peoples of each of the States that ratified it into a single American people. A major exponent of this argument is Akhil Reed Amar.

As previously noted, Amar cautioned against construing the Preamble's "We the People" to mean that the Constitution was ratified by a single American people. This stemmed from his rejection of Lincoln's claim that a single American people existed before the Constitution was drafted and ratified,[372] and led him to the conclusion that "[t]he very process by which Americans in thirteen distinct states ordained the Constitution in the late 1780s and early 1790s confirmed that they were not a single indissolubly united people prior to the act of ordainment."[373]

Although Amar accepts that prior to the ratification of the Constitution, "the People of each state were indeed sovereign," he argues that, by their acts of ratification, "previously separate state Peoples agreed to 'consolidate' themselves into a single continental People." This "transcendent consequence," as he describes it, was achieved by the ratifying conventions acting as "meta-legal" bodies by which "formerly distinct sovereign Peoples, each acting in convention, agreed to reconstitute themselves into one common sovereignty."[374]

Amar argues that ratification transformed "previously separate state peoples into one continental people—Americans!"[375] on two grounds. The first is by drawing upon a corporate law analogy as follows:

> [C]ompany A and company B agree to merge, with the merger approved by lawful majorities of each company's shareholders; but after the merger, we look to the lawful majority of shareholders of the newly formed company, United A&B.[376]

However, this is a false analogy. It overlooks the fact that the formation of "United A&B" leads to the extinction of companies A and B, whereas, given that a state's ratification of the Constitution led to the "the establishment of [the] constitution *between the States* so ratifying [it]," the states nevertheless, continued to exist after ratification and, as will be detailed below, were central to the operation of the Constitution's institutions.

Amar's second ground draws upon the Constitution's Tenth Amendment. It stipulates that "powers not delegated to the United States by the Constitution, nor prohibited by it to the states, are reserved to the states respectively, or to the people." Amar argues that the juxtaposition of the plural reference to "the states respectively" and the singular reference to "the people" in the Tenth Amendment "underscores the unity of the American People and strongly confirms that the Preamble means exactly what it seems to mean at first glance."[377]

However, the problem with this argument stems from the Amendment's stipulation that non-delegated powers are reserved "to the states respectively, *or* to the people" (emphasis added). This clearly means that all these non-delegated powers would be reserved to either the states or the people. If it were intended that all these powers be reserved to the states, then the inclusion of the words "or to the people" in the Amendment are rendered unnecessary and meaningless. And, if it were intended that all these powers be reserved to "the people," then the inclusion of the words "to the states respectively, or" are rendered unnecessary and meaningless. Furthermore, if this were the intended meaning of the Amendment, and its reference to "the people" is to a single American people, it then needs to be determined as to how these powers are to be exercised by that people. The logical answer is they would be exercised by the federal government, as the representative of the single American people. If so, this creates the absurd situation in which powers that are not delegated to the federal government are reserved to the federal government.

If, as it is argued here, the non-delegated powers are not reserved exclusively to either the states or the people, the Tenth Amendment logically envisages some of these powers being reserved to the states and some to the people. If so, the Amendment's "the people" cannot not be construed to mean a single American people. This is because if some of the non-delegated powers are reserved to a single American people, it gives rise to the already noted absurdity that arises if all non-delegated powers are reserved to a single American people. However, there is meaning in the Tenth Amendment if it is construed to mean that non-delegated powers would be reserved to the states respectively or their respective peoples. Some of these non-delegated powers would be properly exercised by state governments and some by the peoples of the states in the same manner in which the Constitution was ratified in 1787–1788, namely by a convention of elected delegates by the people of the state, or by a state referendum. The convention was the manner in which states amended or replaced existing constitutions during the antebellum era. It was also the manner by which ten of the Confederate states passed their secession ordinances. The eleventh, Tennessee, did so pursuant to a referendum.

A further argument that points to the Tenth Amendment's reference to "the people" as being directed to the peoples of each of the states, stems from the other 1791 constitutional amendments that were ratified at the same time as was the Tenth Amendment. These amendments were, as stated by Chief Justice Marshall, in 1833, in *Barron v. Mayor and City Council of Baltimore*, ratified so as "to guard against the abuse of power . . . [and as] security against the apprehended encroachments of the general government."[378] The "apprehended encroachments" to which Marshall was referring were of the federal government against the states. This would imply that the Tenth Amendment's reference to "the people" should be understood to mean the peoples of the individual states.

The reality is that wording of the Tenth Amendment stands as testimony to Justice Story's observation in *Martin v. Hunter's Lessee* that the Constitution's "language is essentially defective in precision."[379] Its author's lack of precision in drafting the Amendment was not replicated by those who, in March 1861, included the essence of the Tenth Amendment in the Constitution of the Confederate States of America, which in Article VI, Section 6 stipulated that "[t]he powers not delegated to the Confederate States by the Constitution, nor prohibited by it to the States, are reserved to the States, respectively, or to the people thereof."

Finally, one further point can be raised that undercuts Amar's transformation argument. It concerns a principle which Amar accepts as being correct[380] and which will be further detailed later in this chapter, namely, that sovereignty is inalienable. If the peoples of each of the States were sovereign prior to the ratification of the Constitution, as Amar concedes, he does not explain—because it cannot be explained—how these peoples alienated their inalienable sovereignty to a single American people. Even if it could be so alienated, Amar offers no evidence of it being alienated. Furthermore, there is nothing in the ratification resolutions of the thirteen States that eventually ratified the Constitution to support a claim that they alienated their sovereignty.

Notwithstanding the problems with Amar's proffered bases of support for his transformation argument, support for it is arguably to be found in the Supreme Court decision, in 1819, in *McCulloch v. Maryland*.[381] This case dealt with the constitutional validity of Maryland's legislation that imposed a tax on the Second Bank of the United States, on the grounds that the bank was not incorporated pursuant to an act of the Maryland legislature. However, this issue was dependent upon determining whether the federal legislation that established that bank in 1816 was authorized by the Constitution. Only if the federal government had legislative competence to establish the bank would the issue of the constitutional validity of Maryland's taxing legislation arise. Whether the federal legislation was constitutionally valid was, pursuant to Section 25 of the federal Judiciary Act of 1789,[382] a matter for the Supreme Court to determine.

In delivering the opinion of the Court, Chief Justice Marshall ruled that, although there was no express constitutional power to create a central bank, the Constitution nevertheless granted Congress an "implied" authority "of selecting the means for executing the enumerated powers."[383] He then went on to rule that, because the legislation establishing the bank was "legitimate" and "within the scope of the constitution . . . [it was] not prohibited, but consist[ent] with the letter and spirit of the constitution."[384] Thus, Maryland's taxing legislation was unconstitutional on the basis of the Constitution's supremacy clause set out in Article VI, Clause 2, which rendered unconstitutional any state legislation that was inconsistent with a valid federal law.

In the course of delivering the opinion of the Court, Marshall argued that prior to the ratification of the Constitution, "[n]o political dreamer was ever wild enough to think of breaking down the lines which separate the States, and of compounding the American people into one common mass."[385] Nevertheless, he went on to say that the "government of the Union" is "emphatically and truly, a government of the people" and that "[i]n form, and in substance, it emanates from them. Its powers are granted by them, and are to be exercised directly on them, and for their benefit."[386] This language can be read to indicate that formerly separate peoples of the States were transformed into a single national people as a result of ratifying the Constitution. Indeed, Daniel Farber suggests that Marshall's opinion in *McCulloch v. Maryland* stands for the proposition that the Constitution amounted to "the agreement of the peoples of various states to transform the existing league into a nation, in the process transforming themselves from thirteen separate peoples into 'We the People of the United States.'"[387]

However, the problem with Farber's suggestion is that Marshall's opinion in *McCulloch v. Maryland* is not altogether clear on who is "the People" referred to in the Preamble. Indeed, based upon his subsequent comments about the decision, it can be argued that Marshall saw *McCulloch v. Maryland* as a decision consistent with the compact theory of the Constitution. These comments appeared in a series of nine articles, published between 30 June 1819 and 15 July 1819, under the pseudonym of "A Friend of the Constitution." In these articles, Marshall sought to defend his opinion against attacks by its opponents that, in Marshall's opinion, demonstrated a "desire to strip the [federal] government of those effective powers, which enable it to accomplish the objects for which it was created."[388]

Some of Marshall's articles contain passages that argue that what he said in *McCulloch v. Maryland* was indeed consistent with the compact theory of the Constitution. In the sixth article, he referred to specific passages in *McCulloch v. Maryland*, including his description of Maryland as "a sovereign state."[389] This, he asserted, demonstrated that his opinion in *McCulloch v. Maryland* did not ascribe to "the doctrine that the government of the United States is a consolidated one."[390] He then went on to say:

> The counsel for the state of Maryland . . . contended that the constitution was the act of sovereign states, as contradistinguished from the people. In opposition to this proposition, the court maintained that the constitution is not the act of the state governments, but of the people of the states. In

> the course of this argument, the term—*the people*—without any annexation, is frequently used; but never in a sense excluding the idea that the people were divided into distinct societies, or indicating the non-existence of the states.[391]

In response to his critics' assertion that "the constitution was adopted by the several states acting in separate conventions," in his seventh article, Marshall wrote that "[t]his is what the court had previously said."[392] He then referred to a Confederation Congress resolution of 1787 that stipulated that the proposed Constitution "be submitted to a convention of delegates, chosen by the people thereof . . . for their assent and ratification." In relation to this resolution Marshall said that "[l]anguage, I think, cannot be more explicit than this; nor more entirely repugnant to the idea that the people acted in one body, and not by states."[393] Finally, he rejected the notion that the "We the People of the United States" phrase in the Constitution's Preamble meant a national populace. In this respect he said:

> The opinion [in *McCulloch v. Maryland*] cannot be inspected without perceiving that these words are not quoted, as "importing" in the constitution, "the people of America in exclusion of those of the *several* states," but as importing the people, in exclusion of their governments. The court then has not denied, but has affirmed, that the constitution was adopted by the people acting as states.[394]

On the other hand, in his eighth article, Marshall made the following statement: "Our constitution is not a compact. It is the act of a single party. It is the act of the people of the United States, assembling in their respective states, and adopting a government for the whole of the nation."[395] This passage is clearly at odds with the content of what Marshall wrote in his previous two articles. Some scholars have focused on this article, to the exclusion of the other two, to affirm that Marshall's opinion in *McCulloch v. Maryland* was fully in accordance with the nationalist theory of the Constitution.[396] However, Martin Flaherty, in the most thorough analysis of Marshall's anonymous writings, states:

> [I]f the "single party" [passage in the eighth article] cannot in the end be squared with everything else, the choice then becomes to privilege a single sentence over page upon page of clear and close analysis. Failing that, "We the Peoples" should prevail after all.[397]

Flaherty then goes on to conclude that in his articles, "Marshall had been at pains to point out, [that] "the people of the United States" is properly understood to mean the peoples of the several states in their highest capacity, assembled conventions."[398]

Whatever the merits of the competing views of Marshall's opinion in *McCulloch v. Maryland* on the issue of the meaning of the Preamble's "We the People," that was not the central issue before the court in that case. Nor was it the critical bone of contention in the subsequent debate over the decision between Marshall and his critics. What was central to both was the extent of the legislative powers granted to the federal government by the Constitution.

What concerned opponents of Marshall's opinion was its ruling granting the federal government an implied legislative power in relation to implementing its enumerated powers set out in the Constitution. It was the possibility that the concept of implied legislative powers would lead to an expansion of federal legislative competence to the extent that Congress could prohibit slavery that sparked the attacks on Marshall's opinion and his defense of it.[399] For example, Thomas Jefferson[400] feared that the implied powers dimension of the opinion, handed down just three weeks after Congress began debating the admission of Missouri to the Union as a slave state, could be used by Congress to preclude slavery from new states created out of territories held by the Union.[401] These concerns were shared at the time by James Madison, who also was of the view that had Marshall's interpretation of the scope of federal legislative competence been known when the proposed Constitution was forwarded to the states for ratification, that could well have "prevented its ratification."[402]

In the end, and as argued above, none of the arguments in support of the transformation argument are satisfactory. Nor are they sustainable in the face of the history of the American Revolution, whose final outcome was the Constitution. As Beer writes, in critiquing Amar's transformation argument:

> [It] requires us to believe that the great body of citizens who took part in that process and theretofore remained dispersed in thirteen separate political communities during their agitation against British rule, their declaration of independence, their long war effort, and their years of self-government after victory, but now in a brief period of a few months in

1787–88 transformed themselves into "the American people." One can conceive this, but one cannot imagine it.[403]

CONSTITUTIONAL PROVISIONS CONSISTENT WITH THE COMPACT THEORY

In drafting the Constitution at the Philadelphia Convention, it is clear that, in relation to the institutional structure of the proposed Union, the focus of Convention delegates was on the preservation and protection of the States that appointed them as their delegates to the Convention.[404] Critical provisions in the Constitution to this effect were those that protected the states from invasion (Article IV, Section 4), guaranteed them rights of free commerce (Article I, Section 9), guaranteed them a republican form of government (Article IV, Section 4), protected them from domestic violence (Article IV, Section 4), and guaranteed them degree of equality in the form of equal representation in the Senate (Article I, Section 3). As Roosevelt sums up, these provisions demonstrated that it was the "rights and existence" of the states that were "protected and harmonized" by the Constitution.[405] Given its focus on the centrality of the states, viewing the Constitution as a compact between the states of the Union that it formed is logical and understandable. This is further reflected in the Constitution's provisions dealing with elections, citizenship, treason, and constitutional amendment; and in the 1791 constitutional amendments. The argument here is that none of these provisions would have been drafted in the form that they were if the Constitution had been ordained and established by a single American people. On the contrary, their wording is quite consistent with the Constitution being ordained and established by the peoples of each of the States that ratified it as well as being reflective of the centrality of the States to the nature of the Union created by the Constitution.

Elections

At the Philadelphia Convention, James Wilson and George Mason favored the idea that Congress and president should be elected "by the people."[406] Such a proposal implied the existence of a single American people and was logical if the Constitution was ordained and established by a single American people. It would have meant that the right to vote in the election of federal officials would have been determined by federal law. However, given the disparate laws on voter eligibility in the various states, "the right of suffrage," as Oliver Ellsworth observed, "was a tender point, and strongly guarded" by the States, and best left to them to judge "the circumstances and temper of their own people."[407] For Ellsworth, the Union's states were entitled to retain their individual rules as to the right to vote because it would be "improper to have either uniform or fixed qualifications."[408] Therefore, the Convention left voter eligibility to the states because, as Wilson noted, it "was difficult to form any uniform rule of qualifications for all the States."[409] Thus, what James Madison referred to as "one of the fundamental articles of republican Government,"[410] the regulation of the right to vote, at both state and national elections, was left to the states to regulate.

In relation to the election of members to the House of Representatives, Article I, Section 2 stipulated that representatives were to be elected "by the People of the several States" in elections governed by state laws. In relation to the Senate, Article I, Section 3 stipulated that senators were to be chosen by each state's legislature, which in turn was elected according to each state's law governing the right to vote. During the ratification debates in Massachusetts[411] and North Carolina,[412] several delegates noted that this reflected the sovereignty of the states. It was thus unsurprising that, at Virginia's ratification convention, Edmund Pendleton, an ardent supporter of the Constitution, said that the federal government was, on various grounds, including the election of senators, "absolutely dependent on the State Governments."[413] Pendleton's observation was further underpinned by Article II, Section 2, which gave a special role to the Senate by requiring its "Advice and Consent" to treaties and to the appointment of federal judges and executive branch officials.

At the Philadelphia Convention, Wilson proposed that the choice of president be by "an election by the people."[414] Similarly, George Mason argued that the president should be "elected by the people at large, by the freeholders of the Country."[415] Only Pennsylvania voted for this proposal.[416] James Madison opposed this idea on the ground that it would negate the influence of southern slave states because, he argued, "[t]he right of suffrage was more diffusive in the Northern than the Southern States; and the latter could have no influence in the election [of the President] on the score of the Negroes."[417] This "problem" was overcome by the terms of Article II, Section 1, which stipulated that the president was to be chosen by electors appointed by the states. Each state was entitled to appoint a number of electors to an Electoral College that equated to the total number of its representatives in both houses of Congress. As to the appointment of electors, this was to be determined by the legislature of each state. For some time, a number of states legislatures did this without holding popular elections, the last state to do so being South Carolina in 1836.[418] Thereafter, the uniform practice was to appoint electors that reflected the popular vote in each state, where the election was governed by state law.

The system of electing federal government officials was viewed by nationalists such as Daniel Webster as being a "popular government, erected by the people," the people being a single American people.[419] The fact that state laws played a pivotal role in the process of electing these officials "[did] not affect the proposition, that this whole government, President, Senate, and House of Representatives, is a popular government."[420] This view is difficult to sustain. In *Federalist 45*, Madison was much closer to the mark when, in reference to the role of the states in the election of federal officials, he wrote:

> The State governments may be regarded as constituent and essential parts of the federal government; whilst the latter is nowise essential to the operation or organization of the former. . . . . [E]ach of the principal branches of the federal government will owe its existence more or less to the favor of the State governments, and must consequently feel a dependence, which is much more likely to beget a disposition too obsequious than too overbearing towards them.[421]

In relation to the Electoral College system of choosing the president, in outlining the results of the Philadelphia Convention, Madison, in a letter to Jefferson written five weeks after the Convention ended, after noting that "[i]n the American Constitution the general authority will be derived entirely from the subordinate authorities," wrote that "[t]he President . . . derives his appointment from the States, and is periodically accountable to them."[422] Although Madison did not explain just how the president was to be accountable to the states, his statement demonstrates that the states were central to the Union created by the Constitution.

The only scope for federal legislation in relation to federal elections was pursuant to Article I, Section 4 and Article II, Section 1 of the Constitution. The former empowered Congress to determine the time, place, and manner of the election of members of the House of Representative and the time and manner of electing senators. The latter empowered Congress to determine the dates electors to the Electoral College were appointed and voted. This Congress did in 1792[423] and 1845.[424] This limited role confirmed that the Constitution's provisions relating to elections of federal officials reflected the central place of the states to the Union established by the Constitution. This was recognized by, for example, William Davie, a delegate to the Philadelphia Convention from North Carolina and a supporter of its ratification when, at his state's ratification convention, he said:

> [T]he state governments are the pillars upon which this government is extended over such an immense territory, and are essential to its existence. The House of Representatives are immediately elected by the people. The senators represent the sovereignty of the states; they are directly chosen by the state legislatures, and no legislative act can be done without their concurrence. The election of the executive is in some measure under the control of the legislatures of the states, the electors being appointed under their direction.[425]

The practical effect of these electoral provisions, as Henry Paul Monaghan points out, has been that for "over 200 years under the Constitution, that Constitution has never seen a national 'We the People' vote on anything. For constitutional purposes, voting on every issue, from presidential elections down, has always been state by state."[426]

Citizenship

The Constitution recognizes that a citizen of the United States is also a citizen of that person's home state. State-based citizenship is highlighted in a number of the Constitution's articles. Thus, Article III, Section 2, in dealing with judicial power of the United States, states that this federal judicial power includes dealing with cases in which the parties were "Citizens of different States." Furthermore, Article IV, Section 2 stipulates that "[t]he Citizens of each State shall be entitled to all the Privileges and Immunities of Citizens in the several States." In recognizing state-based citizenship, these provisions denote the states as bodies politic to which allegiance is owed, and, again, emphasizes the centrality of the states and, by implication, their respective peoples, to the nature of the Union created by the Constitution.

Treason

On 24 June 1776, ten days before issuing the Declaration of Independence, the Continental Congress "recommended" that the each of the colonies "pass laws for punishing" various acts of treason.[427] All the colonies except Georgia enacted laws punishing treason.[428] At the Philadelphia Convention, delegates such as Gouverneur Morris, Rufus King, and John Dickinson argued that treason could only be committed against the United States and not against any of its states.[429] On the other hand, delegates such as Oliver Ellsworth and Roger Sherman argued that because the states were sovereign, treason could be committed against them.[430] By a slim majority of six States to five, the Convention rejected a proposal from Rufus King that the states would have no power "to declare the punishment of Treason."[431] The sentiment underpinning this resolution is reflected in the Constitution's Article III, Section 3, which stipulates that "[t]reason against the United States, shall consist only in levying War against *them*, or in adhering to *their* Enemies, giving *them* Aid and Comfort" (emphasis added). In referring to treason as levying war against "them," or adhering to "their" enemies, Section 3 can only be referring to the states of the Union. Furthermore, Article II, Section 2 stipulates that trials for treason "shall be held in the State where [treason] shall have been committed." It was on the basis of these provisions that, of the thirty-four states of the Union at the outbreak of the Civil War, only Michigan and Oregon had not, either in their state constitutions or by legislation, adopted provisions that defined and punished treason against their state.[432] During the antebellum period there were two cases in which prosecutions for treason against a state were completed. The first was in Rhode Island in 1844 against Thomas Dorr. The second was in Virginia in 1859 against John Brown. In both cases the courts upheld the constitutional validity of the state provisions on treason.[433] What can be concluded from this account of the Constitution's treason clauses is that they reflect the centrality of states in the Union's constitutional structure and that they are entirely consistent with, and reflect, the notion that the Constitution was a compact between sovereign States. Otherwise, they would be meaningless and otiose.

Amendment of the Constitution

The Constitution's amendment procedure, set out in Article V, highlights the central role of the states with the requirement that amendments be ratified by either the legislatures or conventions of three-quarters of the Union's states. As Andrew Kilberg notes, this process "is focused on the states as bodies politic, not the national population."[434]

In the light of the ratification clause in Article VII, the Article V amendment procedure makes perfect sense. If, as has been discussed, for the Constitution to be ordained and established, it had to be ratified by at least nine of the Confederation's thirteen States and upon ratification it became operative between those States, it was entirely logical and consistent that amendments to the Constitution had to be approved by a similar supermajority of the states of the Union, either through their legislatures or state conventions. Furthermore, that Article V also stipulates that no amendment can deprive a state "of its equal Suffrage in the Senate" without that state's consent, reinforces the centrality of states and the argument that the Constitution was a compact between the states that ratified it.

If the Constitution had been ordained and established by a single American people, constitutional amendment would logically have been achieved by that single American people without any necessary involvement of the states. In such a case, instead of requiring three-quarters of the states to approve an amendment, Article V would, arguably, have required three-quarters of that single American people to approve an amendment.

The 1791 Constitutional Amendments

Following ratification of the Constitution, the centrality of the states was further underpinned by the first eight of the ten amendments to the Constitution that were ratified in 1791.[435] These amendments were formulated from proposed amendments proffered by seven of the last eight states to ratify the Constitution.[436] At their ratification conventions it was clear that the primary purpose of these requested amendments was to protect the states of the Union from federal government encroachment that many delegates saw as the likely effect of a broad interpretation of Article I, Section 8, Clause 18, which delegated to the federal government power "[t]o make all Laws which shall be necessary and proper for carrying into Execution" the express powers granted to it.

It is clear, as was noted by Elbridge Gerry during the debate in the Union's First Congress dealing with the proposed amendments, that "[t]he ratification of the Constitution in several States would never have taken place, had they not been assured that the objections would have been duly attended to by Congress."[437] This echoed the views of James Madison, who had written that the Constitution "would have been *certainly* rejected, had no assurances been given by its advocates that such provisions would be pursued."[438] It is also clear that, had they not been adopted, some states would have seceded from the Union. Indeed, five states indicated that they were prepared to secede over the issue.[439]

As is evident in the fact that the 1791 constitutional amendments bound only the federal government and not the states, at that time the states were seen as protectors of individual liberties and the purpose of the amendments was to prevent federal government enacting legislation that would diminish individual liberty.[440] Thus, in 1833, in *Barron v. Mayor and City Council of Baltimore*, in delivering the unanimous opinion of the Supreme Court, Chief Justice Marshall said the purpose of the 1791 constitutional amendments was "to guard against the abuse of power . . . [and as] security against the apprehended encroachments of the general government."[441] The First Amendment did so expressly by prohibiting Congress from passing any law "respecting an establishment of religion, or prohibiting the free exercise thereof; or abridging the freedom of speech, or of the press; of the right of the people peaceably to assemble, and to petition the Government for a redress of grievances." The Second Amendment also did this expressly by stipulating that "A well regulated Militia, being necessary to the security of a *free State*, the right of the people to keep and bear Arms, shall not be infringed" (emphasis added). In *Federalist 46*, James Madison pointed out that, in the event that the armed forces of a tyrannical federal government oppressed the people, "the State Governments with the people on their side would be able to repel the danger."[442] The Second Amendment was an affirmation of Madison's statement.

What can be concluded from the analysis of these two constitutional amendments is that they, along with the provisions dealing with elections, citizenship, treason, and constitutional amendment, all point towards a construction of the Constitution consistent with the compact theory of the Constitution. In stipulating the particular matters dealt with in these constitutional amendments, their substance and/or drafting are all consistent with construing the Constitution's "We the people of the United States" phrase in the Preamble to be referring to the Constitution being ordained and established by the individual peoples of each ratifying State, rather than a single American people. The same can be said of the provisions dealing with elections, citizenship, treason, and constitutional amendment because they all revolve around the states. If the Constitution was truly ordained and established by a single American people, the substance of these provisions could, and arguably would, have been dealt without the involvement or recognition of the states. That the states were central to all of them is telling. That this was so is hardly surprising given that, as John Ferling points out, "the overwhelming majority of delegates [to the Philadelphia Convention] attended with the scarcely hidden expectation of defending the interests of their states."[443]

The Indivisibility of Sovereignty

To this point, this chapter has demonstrated that, in the absence of any express provision in the Constitution dealing with secession, arguments against the right of a state to secede from the Union based upon the reference to a "more perfect Union" in the Preamble, and the supremacy, guarantee, and presidential oath of office clauses cannot be sustained. Furthermore, it has been argued that the Constitution was ordained and established, not by a sovereign American people, but rather by the sovereign peoples of each of the States that ratified the Constitution and that the peoples of the states that were subsequently admitted to the Union had the same sovereign rights as those of the thirteen States of the Confederation that ratified the Constitution.

A critical conceptual question underpinning the issue of whether a state could unilaterally secede from the Union was whether or not the sovereignty of the peoples of each of the states was divisible. The issue of the divisibility of sovereignty stemmed from the provisions in the Constitution that allocated certain legislative powers to Congress and raised the question of whether these provisions divided sovereignty between the states and Congress. This involved determining whether the Constitution's conferral of powers upon the federal government, by virtue of its Article I, Section 8, involved a surrender or delegation of sovereignty rights by the states to the federal government. In answering this question, the precise meaning of the verbs "surrender" and "delegate" is important. According to Noah Webster's 1828 dictionary, to "delegate" meant "[t]o entrust; to commit; to deliver to anothers [*sic*] care and exercise; as, to *delegate* authority or power to an envoy, representative or judge."[444] On the other hand, according to the dictionary's definition of to "surrender," it meant "[t]o yield; to give up."[445] Thus, if sovereignty rights could be, and were, surrendered, sovereignty was divisible and sovereignty rights, once surrendered by the state, could not be reclaimed. However, if sovereignty rights were only delegated, sovereignty was indivisible and, as such, a delegation could always be revoked.

However, George Ticknor Curtis, who conceded that the normal meaning of to "delegate" entailed the right to reclaim what had been delegated, argues that, in the context of the Constitution, to "delegate" meant to "surrender." Although he does not use the word "surrender," he uses synonyms for it when he argues that, although people such as Alexander Hamilton repeatedly used the word "delegate," they "made use of the term "*delegated* powers" in the sense of *granted*, *ceded*, *conveyed*, and *alienated*; and that they never supposed it to imply a revocation or withdrawal, as a principal may revoke or withdraw the powers of an agent."[446] Curtis's argument should be dismissed because it is, in fact, not an argument at all. It is simply an assertion for which no evidence is tendered.

Therefore, if some sovereignty rights were surrendered to the federal government, then, according to what is referred to as the dual sovereignty theory, the consent of both the federal government and the states was required for a state to legally secede from the Union. Thus, a state could not unilaterally secede from the Union. However, if sovereignty rights were only delegated to the federal government, that delegation could be revoked. Whether this entailed a right of a state to unilaterally secede from the Union by a state will be analyzed later in this chapter.

THE SURRENDER ARGUMENT

Support for the notion that Article I, Section 8 involved a surrender of sovereignty rights to the federal government is found in Alexander Hamilton's statement to the New York ratification convention. He said that the notion "that two supreme powers cannot exist together, is false" and that "[t]hey are inconsistent only when they are aimed at each other, or at one indivisible object.[447] At the Massachusetts ratification convention, James Bowdoin observed that ratification of the Constitution would mean only that each State would be "*giving up* a portion of its sovereignty, and thereby better . . . secur[ing] the remainder of it" (emphasis added).[448]

The most significant adherent to dual sovereignty was James Madison, who was of the view, as Akhil Reed Amar puts it, that "[n]either the people of each state nor the people of the nation were wholly sovereign" because sovereignty was divided between them.[449] Madison's adherence to dual sovereignty is reflected in *Federalist 39*, where he wrote that the Constitution was "neither a national nor a federal Constitution; but a composition of both."[450] This stemmed from the fact that the delegation of powers to the federal government meant that the Constitution, "leaves to the several States a residuary and inviolable sovereignty over all other objects."[451] As to the extent of these "other objects," in *Federalist 45*, he wrote that "in the ordinary course of affairs, [they concern] the lives, liberties and properties of the people; and the internal order, improvement, and prosperity of the State."[452] Madison subsequently, and repeatedly, reiterated his adherence to dual sovereignty. For example, in 1835, he wrote that he viewed the Constitution as "dividing sovereignty between the Union and the States" and "that sovereignty was partly in the Union, partly in the States."[453]

An early judicial statement consistent with dual sovereignty theory is found in the judgment of Justice Iredell, in 1783, in *Chisholm v. Georgia*, where he said:

> Every State in the *Union* in every instance where its sovereignty has not been delegated to the *United States*, I consider to be as compleatly sovereign, as the *United States* are in respect to the powers surrendered. The *United States* are sovereign as to all the powers of Government actually surrendered: Each State in the *Union* is sovereign as to all the powers reserved. It must necessarily be so, because the *United States have* no claim to any authority but such *as the States have surrendered to them*: Of course the part not surrendered must remain as it did before.[454]

Prior to the outbreak of the Civil War, the most notable judicial exponent of dual sovereignty was Chief Justice Taney, who, in *Ableman v. Booth*, referred to the existence of two "separate and distinct sovereignties acting separately and independently of each other, within their respective spheres."[455] In 1869, in *Texas v. White*, Taney's successor, Chief Justice Chase, also espoused dual sovereignty. In that case, Chase referred to the provisions of the Constitution's Tenth Amendment as the basis for the "distinct and individual existence . . . [and] right of self-government by the States" which meant that "the preservation of the States, and the maintenance of their governments, are as much within the design and care of the Constitution as the preservation of the Union and the maintenance of the National government."[456]

THE DELEGATION ARGUMENT

The most notable adherent of the argument that sovereignty was indivisible was John C. Calhoun. In *A Discourse on the Constitution and Government of the United States*, he rejected the notion that the powers delegated to the federal government were "absolutely surrendered and irretrievably transferred" on the basis that such a view gave rise to "inexplicable difficulties." For him, delegation of powers to the federal government was, in effect, the states, acting as principal, delegating to the federal government, as agent. For Calhoun, this stemmed from the fact that "[s]overeignty [was] an entire thing;—to divide, is—to destroy it."[457] This meant, as he stated in a speech to the Senate in 1833, that it was "a gross error to confound the *exercise* of sovereign powers with *sovereignty* itself, or the *delegation* of such powers with the *surrender* of them."[458]

The contemporary evidence in support of Calhoun's argument is considerable. The notion that the states only delegated sovereignty powers rather than surrendered them was accepted prior to the drafting and ratification of the Constitution. This is illustrated by provisions in two state constitutions then in force. Part 1, Article IV of Massachusetts' 1780 Constitution[459] and Part 1, Article VII of New Hampshire's 1784 constitution[460] both stipulated that the people of these "free, sovereign, and independent" States would "forever hereafter . . . exercise and enjoy every power, jurisdiction, and right" which was not then or thereafter "by them expressly delegated to the [Confederation], in Congress assembled."

During the campaign to ratify the Constitution, Charles Cotesworth Pinckney referred to the Constitution as "delegating express powers."[461] His cousin, Charles Pinckney, in a speech in the House of Representatives on 14 February 1820, referred to the Constitution as "consisting wholly of delegated powers, all power not expressly delegated, being reserved to the people or the States."[462] In January 1788, Connecticut's delegate to the Philadelphia Convention, Roger Sherman, writing under the pseudonym of "A Citizen of New Haven," wrote that "[t]he powers vested in the federal government are particularly defined, so that each state retains its sovereignty in what concerns its own internal government and a right to exercise every power of a sovereign state not particularly delegated to the government of the United States."[463] At Pennsylvania's ratification convention, James Wilson said that although "supreme power" is "vested in the people" and is "inalienable in its nature,"[464] the people "can delegate it in such proportions, to such bodies, on such terms, and under such limitations as they think proper."[465] However, Wilson also made clear that "sovereignty never goes from the people,"[466] a point he made earlier at the convention when he said that "sovereignty resides in the people; *they have not parted with it*; they have only dispensed such portions of power as were conceived necessary for the public welfare" (emphasis added).[467] He reiterated this point when, as a justice of the Supreme Court, in 1796, in *Ware v. Hylton*, he said that, "in relation to the present Constitution, [Virginia] still retains her sovereignty and independence as a State, except in instances of express delegation to the Federal Government."[468] At the Virginia ratification convention, John Marshall referred to the powers of the federal government as "delegated powers,"[469] a point he reiterated as chief justice, in 1819, in *McCulloch v. Maryland*.[470] Other Supreme Court cases also referred to the powers of the federal government being delegated.[471]

It can also be noted that in fourteen of the papers in *The Federalist*, the words "delegate" or "delegated" are used to describe the means by which the federal government gained its powers.[472] That the powers of the federal government were only delegated to it is, in effect, confirmed in *The Federalist's* only use of the word "surrender" in this context when, in *Federalist 84*, Alexander Hamilton noted that "the people surrender nothing; and they retain every thing."[473]

The most important evidence that the legislative powers of the federal government were merely delegated to it is the Constitution's Tenth Amendment. The Tenth Amendment arose from concerns, expressed in three different ways in the ratification resolutions of seven States, over the extent of federal legislative powers. The first, and most strongly stated, amounted to virtual conditional ratifications of the Constitution by South Carolina and New York. South Carolina's ratification resolution, having stated that South Carolina ratified the Constitution, went on to assert that nothing in the Constitution "warrants a Construction that the states do not retain every power not expressly relinquished by them and vested in the General Government of the Union."[474] In a similar way, New York's resolution asserted that "every Power, Jurisdiction and right" which was not "clear delegated" to federal government institutions "remains to the People of the several States, or to their respective State Governments to whom they have granted the same."[475] Three States requested a constitutional amendment that stated that powers not "expressly delegated" to the federal government be reserved to the states.[476] Two States requested a constitutional amendment that stated that powers not "delegated" to the federal government be reserved to the states,[477] and this proved to be the model for the Tenth Amendment, which stated: "The powers not delegated to the United States by the Constitution, nor prohibited by it to the states, are reserved to the states respectively, or to the people."

The meaning and effect of the Tenth Amendment was articulated by Samuel Adams when, in addressing Massachusetts' proposal for such an amendment, he said: "[This proposal] is consonant with the second article in the [Articles of] Confederation, that each state retains its sovereignty, freedom, and independence, and every power, jurisdiction, and right, which is not, by this Confederation, expressly delegated to the United States in Congress assembled."[478]

The omission of the word "expressly" from the Tenth Amendment, spearheaded by Madison,[479] was significant. Madison's objection to its inclusion stemmed from views he stated in *Federalist 44*, where he wrote: "No axiom is more clearly established in law, or in reason, than that wherever the end is required, the means are authorised; wherever a general power to do a thing is given, every particular power necessary for doing it is included."[480] For Madison, the inclusion of the word "expressly" would have rendered nugatory the power of the federal government pursuant to the necessary and proper clause set out in Article I, Section 8 of the Constitution. This was of major significance in terms of the extent of federal legislative competence, given that, as Madison noted in *Federalist 45*, the express powers delegated to the federal government were "few and defined."[481] What Madison was keen to avoid was the situation that had arisen under the Articles of Confederation where the Confederation Congress could not exercise even perfunctory powers such as issuing passports because such a power was not expressly granted to it. This point was confirmed by Chief Justice Marshall, in 1819, in *McCulloch v. Maryland*, where he noted that "expressly" was excluded from the Tenth Amendment because "[t]he men who drew and adopted this amendment had experienced the embarrassments resulting from the insertion of this word in the Articles of Confederation, and probably omitted it to avoid those embarrassments."[482]

Whatever the effect the Tenth Amendment had on the scope of federal legislative power, nothing in Article 1, Section 8 of the Constitution, either expressly or by implication, conferred power on the federal government in relation to secession. On the basis that the peoples of each of the States retained their sovereignty after ratification of the Constitution, the exercise of any right to secede from the Union must have been one of the powers reserved to the peoples of each of the states by virtue of the Tenth Amendment. This may seem strange, given that the practice of reserving powers to a particular authority is generally associated with maintaining existing political structures, rather than their breakup. However, there is nothing in the wording of the Tenth Amendment to preclude the reservation of a power to the peoples of each of the sovereign states that, if exercised, would lead to secession from the Union.

The preferable conclusion to be reached on the question of the divisibility of sovereignty is that because the federal government's powers were merely delegated to it, rather than surrendered to it, sovereignty was indivisible and ultimately inhered in the peoples of the several states. This conclusion is consistent with the view of the overwhelming majority of opinion at the time the Constitution was ratified.[483] For example, in summing up the Constitution in December 1787, Roger Sherman wrote that because the powers of the federal government were "particularly defined . . . each State retains its sovereignty . . . and a right to exercise every power of a sovereign State not delegated to the united States."[484] Accordingly, the dual sovereignty theory, together with its claim that a state had no constitutional right to unilaterally secede from the Union, cannot be sustained. If a state's sovereignty was indivisible, this raised the question, which now needs to be considered, of whether that sovereignty included the right of the state to unilaterally secede from the Union.

Indivisible State Sovereignty and Secession

Apart from adherents to dual sovereignty theory, there was no dispute between adherents of the nationalist and compact theories of the Constitution that, in the words of James Wilson, sovereignty was not only "inalienable in its nature," it was also "indefinite in its extent."[485] This "uncontrollable power," Wilson went on to say, vested in "the people." It thus followed that the question of secession was one to be determined by "the people."[486] Of course, for Wilson, "the people" meant the single American people, which meant that a state could only secede with the consent of that people. Abraham Lincoln, in his two major speeches during 1861,[487] and Chief Justice Chase, in 1869, in *Texas v. White*,[488] both agreed that the Constitution did not preclude the consensual secession of a state from the Union. Just how that would be achieved was, and arguably still is, unclear. However, what is clear is that for Wilson and, indeed, all who subscribed to the nationalist theory of the Constitution, it meant that a state could not *unilaterally* secede from the Union.

However, if, as has been argued above, pursuant to the compact theory of the Constitution, indivisible sovereignty vested in the people of each of the states of the Union, then unilateral secession from the Union was constitutionally possible. Although Joseph Story argued that the compact theory had "no foundation in the words of the constitution" and was "altogether a gratuitous assumption,"[489] he nevertheless conceded that, if the theory was accepted, "each [state] retains the power to withdraw from the confederacy."[490] This is precisely the point John C. Calhoun made in *A Discourse on the Constitution and Government of the United States*, where he wrote:

> That a State, as a party to the constitutional compact, has a right to secede,—acting in the same capacity in which it ratified the constitution—cannot, with any show of reason, be denied by any one who regards the constitution as a compact—if a power should be inserted by the amending power, which would radically change the character of the constitution, or the nature of the system; or if the former should fail to fulfil the ends for which it was established. This results, necessarily, from the nature of a compact—where the parties to it are sovereign; and, of course, have no higher authority to which to appeal.[491]

For Calhoun, secession was a dreaded prospect and one which he described as a "knife of separation through a body politic . . . which has been so long bound together by so many ties, political, social, and commercial."[492] He wrote that one could not "*resort to or even to look to that extreme remedy, until all others have failed.*"[493] For Calhoun, this right of unilateral secession could only be exercised in limited circumstances, such as, if powers under the Constitution were exercised in a manner that was "inconsistent with the character of the constitution and the ends for which it was established."[494] In November 1860, Justice John Archibald Campbell of the Supreme Court expressed a similar view when, writing extrajudicially, he said that a state was entitled to secede following "*deliberate, plain, and palpable* violations of the Constitution—violations showing enormity of mischief and where no other form of redress exists."[495]

In his First Inaugural Address, Lincoln argued against the substance of Calhoun's claim when he said that even if one accepted the compact theory of the Constitution, unilateral secession was nevertheless prohibited. In accepting the compact theory for the purposes of his argument, Lincoln questioned whether the compact, "as a contract" could "be peaceably unmade, by less than all the parties who made it." Lincoln then went on and said: "One party to a contract may violate it—break it, so to speak; but does it not require all to lawfully rescind it?"[496] The unstated answer to this rhetorical question was that, in the event of a breach of the Constitution by a state, all states had to agree to allow an affected state to secede from the Union. According to Amar, Lincoln here "hoisted the compact theorists on their own petard."[497]

However, Lincoln's argument here did no such thing. To use the contract analogy to which Lincoln refers, the agreement of all the parties to a contract to bring it to an end is only necessary where there has been no previous terminating breach or repudiation of the contract. If one party commits such a breach or repudiation, the other party can, by service of a notice of termination, terminate the contract. Thereafter, both parties are discharged from any further performance of the contract. This point was made by James Madison at the Constitutional Convention when, albeit in discussing the union as constituted by the Articles of Confederation, he said: "If we consider the federal union as analogous . . . to the conventions among individual States . . . a breach of any one article, by any one party, leaves the other parties at liberty, to consider the whole convention as dissolved, unless they choose to compel the delinquent party to repair the breach."[498] Thus, if a state is affected by the constitutional equivalent of a terminating breach or repudiation of a contract, it would be entitled to unilaterally secede from the Union. It was on this basis that, for example, South Carolina asserted that it was entitled to unilaterally secede. In its "Declaration of the Immediate Causes Which

Induce and Justify the Secession of South Carolina" of 24 December 1860, South Carolina asserted the following:

We maintain that in every compact between two or more parties, the obligation is mutual; that the failure of one of the contracting parties to perform a material part of the agreement, entirely releases the obligation of the other; and that where no arbiter is provided, each party is entitled to his own judgment to determine the fact of failure, with all its consequences.[499]

Conclusion

In light of the absence of any express provision in the Constitution dealing with secession, Amar argues that the fact that, during the period in which it was being ratified, "[n]o leading Federalist ever publicly sought to win over states' rightists by conceding that a state could unilaterally . . . secede in the event it later became dissatisfied"[500] indicated that it was agreed by all that such a right did not exist.

However, the absence of any significant debate or discussion about secession during the drafting and ratification of the Constitution meant, at the very least, that the Constitution did not forbid secession[501] and arguably that, at that time, nobody doubted the existence of such a right. In his observations concerning the Americans of the 1830s, de Tocqueville wrote that for them "the existing Union is advantageous to all the states, but it is not indispensable to any one of them" and that the relevant task to be addressed was "not to inquire whether the states of the existing Union are capable of separating, but whether they will choose to remain united."[502] The historical evidence outlined in Chapter 1 and this chapter's analysis of the competing theories of the Constitution indicate that his observations applied with equal, or greater, force in 1787, with respect to the Union that was formed by the ratification of the Constitution. Equally clear is J. P. Gordy's observation, written in 1895, in his history of political parties in the United States, when he said:

> If the Constitution . . . had said that to adopt it was to acknowledge the sovereignty of the one American people, no part of which could sever its connections without the consent of the whole, it would probably have been rejected by every state in the union.[503]

Indeed, given the federal nature of the Constitution's Union, as Sanford Levinson observes, one of the many possible meanings of federalism is that "the original entity that chose to enter into the union retains an option to exit."[504] Liah Greenfeld makes the same point when she writes that "[t]he separatist impulse was inherent in the very conception of the Union . . . and its legitimacy was . . . explicit."[505] That the exit option was not one that any state contemplated exercising at the time during which the Constitution was being ratified is reflected in James Wilson's statement at the Pennsylvania ratification convention when he said that the "bonds of our Union *ought* therefore to be indissolubly strong" (emphasis added).[506] In suggesting that the Union "ought . . . to be" indissoluble, Wilson was not saying that ratification of the Constitution would mean that the Union would be or was indissoluble. Yet that is precisely what Amar claims Wilson said. In quoting Wilson, Amar breaks up the quoted Wilson passage so as to be able to delete Wilson's "ought . . . to be" and replace it with his "would be." Thus, Amar writes that Wilson viewed the proposed Constitution as one "in which 'the bonds of our union' would be 'indissolubly strong.'"[507]

Words matter. They mattered to Lincoln, who described them as "the great invention of the world."[508] In construing the words of key documents—most importantly the Constitution—to determine their meaning, this chapter has argued that, of the competing theories of the nature of the Constitution, the compact theory is the better one. If so, then, in appropriate circumstances there existed the right of a state to unilaterally secede from the Union.

This chapter's argument is based upon two pillars. The first pillar is that the nationalist theory's arguments against such a right are flawed. In this context the principal nationalist argument was that a single sovereign American people ordained and established the Constitution, a consequence of which was that secession required the consent of that sovereign people. The consequence of this argument was that the people of a state of the Union, as part of that single American people, could not unilaterally secede from the Union. The second pillar was that although the Constitution did not expressly deal with the existence of a right of unilateral secession, it contained provisions that implied such a right. On the other hand, the compact theory argument was that the Constitution was ordained and established, not by a sovereign single American people, but by the sovereign peoples of the individual states that ratified the Constitution.

In relation to the nationalist theory's arguments against the existence of a right of unilateral secession from the Union, many of them were articulated, in 1861, by Abraham Lincoln in his First Inaugural Address and his subsequent Message to Congress in Special Session. His argument that the Constitution was ordained and established by a single sovereign American people was based upon the claim that the Union and its single American people emerged in 1776 and that the Articles of Confederation and Constitution were merely instruments that, as he put it, "matured"[509] that union. Although Vasan Kesavan and Michael Stokes Paulsen regard Lincoln's First Inaugural Address as "a masterpiece of constitutional analysis" and "a classic of carefully reasoned legal analysis of the text, structure, and internal logic of the Constitution,"[510] other scholars have pointed out that Lincoln's recounting of history, as this chapter has demonstrated, is essentially flawed.[511] For example, Pauline Maier bluntly concludes that Lincoln's "version of what the founders meant was full of wishful suppositions."[512] Mark Neely assesses Lincoln's historical argument as "weak" and argues that it led him "to invent a mythical national past for Americans."[513] Indeed, Lincoln's own words suggest that he would have agreed with Neely's assessment. In his First Inaugural Address, Lincoln appealed to "[t]he mystic chords of memory, stretching from every battle-field, and patriot grave, to every living heart and hearthstone, all over this broad land."[514] Lincoln's "mystic chords of memory" constituted what Alan Taylor aptly calls "a useful fiction"[515] which amounted to an exemplar of Ernest Renan's observation that "[f]orgetting, and . . . historical error are an essential factor in the creation of a nation."[516]

Furthermore, in the wake of Jefferson Davis's flight from Richmond at the end of the Civil War, Lincoln reportedly told General William T. Sherman: "I am bound to oppose the escape of Jeff Davis, but if you could manage to have him slip out unbeknownst-like, I guess it wouldn't hurt me much!"[517] This statement, although made jokingly, nevertheless indicates that Lincoln recognized that proving that unilateral secession was constitutionally illegal in order to convict Davis of treason would, at best, be difficult, and, at worst, impossible. Finally, shortly after this statement to Sherman, in April 1865, Lincoln, in his last public address, argued in favor of the readmission of the Confederate states to the Union "without deciding, or even considering, whether these states have been out of the Union, than with it."[518] Undoubtedly this statement was made with a view to restoring the Union as quickly as possible. However, although Lincoln had no doubts himself that unilateral secession from the

Union was constitutionally prohibited, his April 1865 statement is consistent with the view that he recognized that he may have been proven wrong if Jefferson was not convicted of treason.

If Lincoln had avoided what Renan referred to as "historical error," he would have recognized that, prior to the American Revolution, colonists identified themselves as being British. With the separation from their imperial masters, their identities, not surprisingly, became associated with their State or region, given that each of the colonies had had some form of identity for at least ninety years prior to the outbreak of the American Revolution. As Jack Greene observes, although the American Revolution provided the colonists with "an instant common past," it did not make them identify as Americans, because "each of [the] colonies had its own peculiar constitution, institutions, laws, history, and identity to which its inhabitants were, for the most part, both well-socialized and strongly attached."[519] In America at that time there was no "new nation" as Lincoln referred to it in his Gettysburg Address or "people" in the romantic nationalism sense popularized, in particular, by Johan Gottfried von Herder. This was because, as James Madison said, in *Federalist 46*, it was "beyond doubt that the first and most natural attachment of the people will be to the governments of their respective States."[520] Thus, Jennifer Ratner-Rosenhagen concludes:

> America did not have a *Volk* nurtured by a common *Kultur*, which was expressive of a singular *Geist*. And it certainly was no *Fatherland*—it was nothing other than a contractual arrangement. America was populated with peoples, but not a people, who, with the exception of the Indians, were all transplants from different parts of Europe, each with their own mother tongues, faith traditions, and cultural sensibilities. In fact, there was no substantive "American" anything.[521]

Lincoln's other major argument was that the Union was perpetual in the sense that secession from it was legally impossible. Mark Brandon fairly, but caustically, ridicules this argument when he writes that "the idea that perpetuity is a necessary adjunct to perfection would seem silly except that so many intelligent people have cited it" and that it needed "[a]t the very least, . . . more than simple assertion to support it."[522] Indeed, as is demonstrated in this chapter, several the State resolutions ratifying the Constitution clearly point to the Union not being perpetual in that, contrary to assertions by people such as James Madison, ratification was not on a forever basis and that states had a legal right to exit the Union in appropriate circumstances. The perpetuity argument in this context was, as Kenneth Stampp observes, an argument for which "the logic behind it was far from perfect."[523] To similar effect, G. Edward White notes that arguments against the compact theory of the Constitution "were primarily couched in terms of practical necessities rather than constitutional logic."[524]

On the other hand, the compact theory's argument that the Constitution was ordained and established by the sovereign peoples of the States that ratified it stems from the fact that their free and independent status as States emerged in 1776 and that it was the sovereign peoples of these States who ratified the Constitution. Given that, grammatically, the word "people" can be either singular or plural, the Preamble's "We the People of the United States" is capable of being construed as referring to the single American people or the individual peoples of the States that ordained and established the Constitution. However, the relevant documents, especially the Constitution's Tenth Amendment, and historical context in which they were created all point to it being the latter construction. Furthermore, ratification did not transform the sovereign peoples of the states into a single sovereign American people. The sovereignty of these peoples remained, was indivisible, and entailed sovereign powers that had not been delegated to the federal government. Included within the scope of these retained sovereign powers was the right of the individual peoples of the states, in appropriate circumstances, to ordain that their states unilaterally secede from the Union.

Whether appropriate circumstances existed in late 1860 to justify the eleven Confederate states exercising a constitutional right to unilaterally secede from the Union is a matter explored in the ensuing two chapters.

3

"A Slaveholders' Union?"
The Constitution and Slavery

In Chapter 2, it was argued that, in the words of John C. Calhoun, a state could unilaterally secede from the Union "if the [Constitution] should fail to fulfil the ends for which it was established."[1] As was detailed in Chapter 1, it was the issue of slavery that led the Confederate states to proclaim their ordinances of secession. For these states, the Constitution had failed to meet the "ends" for which it was established in relation to slavery. In practical terms, this failure consisted of breaches of the Constitution's provisions that dealt with slavery. Whether these provisions fell within the ambit of Calhoun's "ends" for which the Constitution was established involves an assessment of their importance or significance in relation to the objective of establishing and ordaining the Constitution that formed the Union. This chapter argues that the Constitution's slavery provisions were essential to that objective, in the sense that without them, that objective would almost certainly not have been achieved and that, therefore, they fell within the ambit of the "ends" for which the Constitution was established. At the Philadelphia Convention, Gouverneur Morris articulated this view when, having referred to slavery as a "nefarious institution," he vented "that Domestic slavery is the most prominent feature in the aristocratic countenance of the proposed Constitution."[2] From a practical perspective, breaches related to any of those provisions grounded an affected state's right to unilaterally secede from the Union. Whether such breaches occurred will be discussed in the next chapter.

Although the Constitution contained various provisions that either expressly or impliedly dealt with slavery, none of them explicitly dealt with the question of whether slavery should or should not exist. It was recognised by all that this was a matter for individual states to determine for themselves. Rather, the "end" to which the Constitution's slavery provisions was directed, was the protection and preservation of the institution of slavery in states where it existed at the time, or would exist in states subsequently admitted to the Union. There were four major provisions in the Constitution that were directly targeted at achieving this "end." In order of their appearance in the Constitution, they were the three-fifths clause (Article I, Section 2, Clause 3), the slave importation clause (Article I, Section 9, Clause 1), the fugitive slave clause (Article IV, Section 2, Clause 3), and the admission of new states and territories clauses (Article IV, Section 3). The first three expressly dealt with slavery. The fourth, as will be detailed below, did so implicitly.

These provisions were agreed to by the Philadelphia Convention, of whose fifty-five delegates, eight[3] had signed a document—the Declaration of Independence—that declared that "all Men are created equal," and thirty had seen active military service[4] in defence of the thirteen "Free and Independent States" that it proclaimed. Furthermore, twenty-five of the Convention's delegates were slaveholders.[5] These slaveholders included such influential men as George Washington, James Madison, George Mason, Edmund Randolph, Robert Morris, William Paterson, Luther Martin, Charles Pinckney, Charles Cotesworth Pinckney, John Rutledge, and Pierce Butler.[6] Indeed, Washington (one of the largest slave owners in Virginia, who then owned more than one hundred slaves and controlled almost two hundred more that were inherited as dower slaves by his wife),[7] Madison, and Mason brought slaves with them to Philadelphia.[8] For these men, as Mason stated, slaves were a "peculiar species of property, over and above other species of property common to all the States,"[9] or as Henry Clay, another slaveholder, put it, in 1818, "a certain species of property" which he considered "as inviolable as any other."[10] It was thus unsurprising that Benjamin Franklin decided not to present to the Convention a petition from the Pennsylvania Society for the Abolition of Slavery, of which he was president, on the basis that, in his words, he "thought it advisable to let them lie over for the present."[11]

Not all delegates at the Philadelphia Convention were so enmeshed with slavery. Indeed, as Madison stated, the "important truth" about the Convention was the fact that "the States were divided into different interests not by their difference of size, . . . but principally from . . . their having or not having slaves."[12] To similar effect, he observed that "[i]t seemed now to be pretty well understood that the real difference of interests lay, not between the large & small but between the N. & Southn. States" and that "[t]he institution of slavery & its consequences formed the line of discrimination."[13] Other delegates expressed similar sentiments.[14] That this was so was unsurprising, as will be detailed below, given that a sectional division between the States had already emerged over the Confederation's dispute with Spain over navigation rights on the Mississippi River and the issue of slavery in the territory acquired from the British pursuant to the Treaty of Paris in 1783. Indeed, such was the extent of this sectional division that William Blount, a delegate to the Confederation Congress and the Philadelphia Convention from North Carolina, wrote, in private correspondence on 19 July 1787: "[F]or as I have before said, I still think we shall ultimately and not many Years hence be separated and distinct Governments perfectly independent of each other."[15]

This sectional division reflected the existence of slavery in the Confederation's states. The number of slaves in the South far outnumbered the number in the North. Using the 1790 census as a guide, approximately 93 percent of the slave population lived in the South, whereas only approximately 6 percent lived in the North.[16] This disparity in numbers led to the creation of what Ira Berlin refers to as "slave societies" in the South and "societies with slaves" in the North. Berlin describes the former as ones in which "slavery stood at the center of economic production," whereas in the latter, "slaves were marginal to the central productive processes" and "slavery was just one form of labor among many." This meant that in slave societies, "the master-slave relationship provided the model for all social relationships"[17] because, as Edward Rugemer points out, "[s]laveholders' wealth, identities, prestige, and future prosperity all depended on the permanence of their right to own black Americans as slaves."[18] On the other hand, in societies with slaves, "no one presumed the master-slave relationship to be the social exemplar."[19]

Although various delegates, such as Madison[20] and Mason,[21] recognised slavery as being a moral evil, as the records of the Philadelphia Convention demonstrate, they had no reservations about using the words such as "slaves," and to a lesser extent "blacks" and "Negroes."[22] However, the use of the words "slave" and "slavery" in the Constitution was assiduously avoided when referring to what, from the 1830s onwards, was often referred to as the southern slave states' "peculiar institution." At the Convention, Madison attributed this to the fact that delegates "had scruples against admitting the terms "Slaves" into the Instrument."[23] Delaware's John Dickinson made the same point when he said that, by omitting the word "slavery," it would "be regarded as an Endeavour to conceal a principle of which we are ashamed."[24] To similar effect, at North Carolina's ratification convention, James Iredell commented that the word "slave" was omitted from the Constitution due to the "particular scruples on the subject of slavery" on the part of delegates from the northern States.[25] And, during Maryland's ratification of the Constitution, Luther Martin caustically observed that the Convention was anxious "to avoid the admission of expressions which might be odious in the ears of Americans, although they were very willing to admit into their system those *things* which the *expressions* signified."[26] However, as William Lloyd Garrison later noted, "Though no such words are contained in the instrument," the delegates used "other words . . . intelligently and specifically, to meet the necessities of slavery."[27] Thus, as the nationalist lawyer and historian Sidney George Fisher conceded in 1862, "sugar-coated" euphemisms for slaves or slavery were employed in the three-fifths clause, the fugitive slave clause, and the slave importation clause, as the founders of the Constitution "proclaimed to the world that they approved of slavery and the slave trade."[28]

In the context of the secessions of the Confederate states, it was argued that breaches related to the Constitution's admission of new states and territories clauses and the fugitive slave clause gave rise to the right of an affected state to unilaterally secede from the Union. For this reason, these clauses are the focus of this chapter. However, the four provisions that expressly or impliedly dealt with slavery were interrelated and can be viewed as components of a package of provisions that together protected and preserved the institution of slavery. For this reason alone, the three-fifths clause and slave importation clauses warrant a briefer analysis. This will be followed by the detailed analyses of admission of new states and territories clauses and the fugitive slave clause.

The Three-Fifths Clause

The relevant parts of the Constitution's three-fifths clause, set out in Article I, Section 2, Clause 3 of the Constitution, stipulated that "Representatives and direct Taxes" were to "be apportioned among the several

States . . . according to their respective Numbers." These numbers were to be "determined by adding to the whole Number of free Persons . . . three fifths of all other Persons." At the Massachusetts ratification convention, Rufus King confirmed that the "other Persons" were "*slaves*."[29]

The three-fifths clause was the second of the Philadelphia Convention's two major compromises. The first, which was the makeup of Congress, led to representation in the Senate being the same for all states irrespective their populations, whereas representation in the House of Representatives was determined by the population of each state. In determining what persons counted as part of a state's population, delegates from northern states such as Alexander Hamilton,[30] William Paterson,[31] and Elbridge Gerry[32] proposed that it be confined to the number of its free persons. However, delegates from southern slave states, such as Pierce Butler,[33] Charles Cotesworth Pinckney,[34] and Charles Pinckney,[35] proposed that slaves be counted as part of a state's population.[36] The practical ramification of these divergent proposals was that, given that the population, including slaves, of the five most southern slave states was then roughly equal to the total population of the eight northern states, these five slave states, forty percent of whose population were slaves, would have significantly less representation in the House of Representatives on the first proposal than on the second.[37]

Such was the importance to slave States of slaves being counted for the purposes of representation in the House of Representatives that Gouverneur Morris suggested that, rather than remaining united, the slave and non-slave States should "at once take a friendly leave of each other."[38] This was not to be, because delegates such as Rufus King and Edmund Randolph recognised the need to provide some form of "security"[39] for the interests of slaveholders. This led to the necessity of compromise in the form of the three-fifths clause that was first raised by James Wilson.[40] Slave states' delegates, such as North Carolina's William Davie, made it clear that their states would "never confederate on any terms that did not rate them [i.e. slaves] at least as [three-fifths of a person]."[41] That this was so was conceded by Alexander Hamilton, who, at New York's ratification convention, said that the three-fifths clause was "one result of the spirit of accommodation, which governed the [Philadelphia] Convention; and without this indulgence, no union could possibly have been formed."[42] Hamilton's fellow convention delegate Melancton Smith, although regarding the three-fifths clause as "founded on unjust principles," said that it was a necessary "accommodation" that could not be avoided "if we mean to be in union with the southern states."[43] Similarly, Rufus King, an ardent antislavery delegate from Massachusetts, when speaking in the Senate, probably in 1819, as a senator from New York, acknowledged that the three-fifths clause's "inequality in the appointment of representatives was not misunderstood at the adoption of the constitution" and that this concession "was made to secure the adoption of the constitution."[44] This "indulgence" that Hamilton referred to was agreed to notwithstanding that, as Luther Martin pointed out, "it was inconsistent with the principles of the revolution and dishonourable to the American character to have such a feature in the Constitution."[45]

The "indulgence" that Hamilton referred to was also a tacit recognition that slaves were seen as property. Delegates from both the South and North believed that wealth should be reflected in political representation. Thus, South Carolina's John Rutledge observed that "[p]roperty was certainly the principal object of Society; and that in fixing a ratio this ought not to be excluded."[46] And Rufus King, notwithstanding his opposition to slavery, argued that, because "property was the primary object of Society,"[47] it ought to be a factor in determining political representation and that, therefore, he always expected that, "as the Southern States are the richest," they would not agree with the North to any constitution unless "some respect were paid to their superior wealth."[48] This "respect" came in the form of the three-fifths clause.

In summing up the practical impact of the three-fifths clause, in *Federalist 54* James Madison wrote that the Constitution regarded slaves as "inhabitants" that were "debased by servitude below the equal level of free inhabitants, which regards the *slave* as divested of two fifths of the *man*."[49] However, as the historian Imani Perry points out, it "is not the case . . . that the clause was a term of art meaning that the Black people counted for three-fifths of a person. They did not count at all. Rather slaveholders were made larger people by virtue of holding others as slaves."[50] It was thus hardly surprising that, in his Farewell Address to the Senate on 21 February 1861, Jefferson Davis spoke of the racist nature of the Constitution's slavery provisions when he said that, in relation to slaves, the three-fifths "provision made for that very class of persons as property" and that "[slaves] were not put upon the footing of equality with white men—not even upon that of paupers and convicts; but, so far as representation was concerned, were discriminated against as a lower caste, only to be represented in the numerical proportion of three fifths."[51]

It should also be noted that the three-fifths clause was a significant factor in the Convention's decision to create the Electoral College as the system by which the Union's president was to be elected. The Electoral College system was agreed upon after the Convention had rejected proposals by Gouverneur Morris[52] and James Wilson[53] that the president be elected directly by the people. What prompted the Convention's decision to adopt the Electoral College system was the need to increase the influence of southern slave states in the outcome of a presidential election by recognising the existence of slaves as part the population but at the same time denying them the right to vote.[54] As James Madison pointed out, although "the people at large" were "the fittest" to choose the president, there was "one difficulty . . . of a serious nature" with such a proposal. This difficulty arose because "[t]he right of suffrage was much more diffuse in the Northern than the Southern States; and the latter could have no influence in the election on the score of the Negroes."[55] This was because, as North Carolina's Hugh Williamson bluntly pointed out, in a popular vote for the presidency, "slaves will have no suffrage."[56] For Madison, the three-fifths clause, by increasing the number of electors to the Electoral College from slave states, "obviated this difficulty."[57]

The Slave Importation Clause

The slave importation clause, set out in Article I, Section 9, Clause 1 of the Constitution, stipulated that the "Migration or Importation of such Persons as any of the States now existing shall think proper to admit" could not be "prohibited by the Congress prior to the Year one thousand eight hundred and eight." The phrase "Persons as any of the States now existing shall think proper to admit" was, as James Madison conceded, a euphemism for Africans who were to be imported into the Union as slaves.[58] In 1807, Congress enacted legislation that, as from the start of 1808, prohibited the importation into the Union for sale as a slave of "any negro, mulatto, or person of color."[59]

The roots of the slave importation clause can be traced back to Article 2 of the Articles of Association, adopted by the First Continental Congress on 20 October 1774, by which the colonies agreed to "wholly discontinue the slave trade."[60] Congress reaffirmed this provision, on 6 April 1776, by adopting a resolution that stipulated that "no slaves shall be imported into any of the thirteen United Colonies."[61] These measures were not expressions reflecting an anti-slavery sentiment. Rather, concern over the importation of slaves was, as Virginia pointed out in April 1772, driven by the reality that this trade "greatly retards the settlement of the colonies with more useful inhabitants and may in time have the most destructive influence."[62] This lack of "more useful inhabitants" was, as Virginia's governor, Lord Dunmore, pointedly observed, due to the fact that there was then a preponderance of African Americans in Virginia, which had given rise to a "just cause to apprehend the most dangerous consequences therefrom," and that any increase in their number would be "sufficient to alarm not only [Virginia] but all the colonies of America."[63] Thus, when Virginia did ban the further importation of slaves in 1778, it was, as Kenneth Morgan points out, "far from being a humanitarian gesture, [and] was designed to protect Virginia from an oversupply of new slaves in a context where demographic growth among creole slaves in Virginia was flourishing."[64]

Although most States adopted measures to reduce the importation of slaves, it nevertheless continued. As Thomas Jefferson acidly pointed out, in July 1776, "South Carolina & Georgia . . . had never attempted to restrain the importation of slaves and . . . on the contrary still wish to continue it," while in the northern colonies, "their people have very few slaves themselves yet they have been pretty considerable carriers of them to others."[65]

At the Philadelphia Convention, it was understood that, under the proposed Constitution, the Union's Congress would have the power to ban the importation of slaves. The Convention's debate centered on whether the Constitution should include a provision preventing Congress doing so immediately. Most northern State delegates wished to see the immediate end of the importation of slaves because, according to Gouverneur Morris, its continuation would result in increases in the slave population and, therefore, the augmentation of slave state representation in Congress by virtue of the three-fifths clause.[66] Many in the southern slave States were also willing to see an end to the importation of slave because they, as Paul Finkelman writes, "believed that slavery was an inherent threat to society, and continuing to import African slaves would only exacerbate an already dangerous situation. Having just fought a revolution for their own liberty, many Americans worried that slaves might follow the model of their masters."[67] And in Virginia and Maryland, slaveholders supported this approach for economic reasons. In these States, there was a significant natural increase in the number of slaves, making them net exporters of slaves to other States. For them, as Connecticut's Oliver Ellsworth observed, "it was cheaper to raise than import them."[68] As South Carolina's Charles Pinckney pointed out, "Virginia . . . will gain by stopping the importations" because "[h]er slaves will rise in value, & she has more than she wants."[69] In his opposition to the continued importation of slaves, George Mason, a slaveholder from Virginia, said that the "evil" of slavery led to "the most pernicious effect on manners," and that more slaves would "prevent the immigration of Whites, who really enrich & strengthen a Country."[70] And at the Virginia ratification convention, he added that the inclusion of the slave importation clause meant that the proposed Constitution had "not secured us the property of the slaves we already have."[71]

However, the slave States of South Carolina, North Carolina, and Georgia were, as James Madison observed at the time, "inflexible" in their opposition to banning the importation of slaves.[72] Two interrelated factors explained this inflexibility. The first was the importance of slavery to their agricultural economies that were based upon slave labor. As South Carolina's John Rutledge said in his "strenuous" opposition at the Convention to an immediate ban on the importation of slaves, these States would not agree to the proposed Constitution "unless their right to import slaves be untouched . . . [because the] people of those States will never be such fools to give up so important an interest."[73] As Jonathan Mercantini observes, this "rhetorical commitment to slavery was not mere bluster but rather a true reflection of . . . [a] mentality regarding the central importance of slavery."[74] The second factor stemmed from the significant loss of their slave populations due to death, desertion, or confiscation by the British during the course of the American Revolution.[75] Kenneth Morgan writes that Georgia lost two-thirds of its slave population (approximately 10,000 slaves) and that South Carolina lost approximately 20,000 of its slaves during the American Revolution.[76] The importation of slaves would redress this problem and help sustain slavery, an institution that was, in the view of many, such as

Charles Pinckney, "justified by the example of all the world."[77] And Richard Dobbs Spaight, a delegate to the Convention from North Carolina, said, at his State's ratification convention, that "South Carolina and Georgia insisted on [the slave importation] clause, as they were now in want of hands to cultivate their lands; that in the course of twenty years they would be fully supplied; [and] that the trade would be abolished then."[78] He was proven correct, given that, in the two decades prior to 1808, just over 200,000 slaves were imported into North Carolina, South Carolina, and Georgia.[79]

The compromise between these two divergent positions was to prevent Congress from prohibiting the importation of slaves before the end of 1807. A significant factor in southern States accepting this limited time period to legally import slaves from Africa was the reality that the healthy growth in slave numbers through natural increase meant that an eventual ban in the importation of slaves posed no long-term threat to slavery.[80] This, combined with two other factors, facilitated the passage of federal legislation banning the further importation of slaves in 1807. The first was the fear, generated by the slave revolt in Saint-Domingue in the 1790s, that new slaves from Africa were more prone to attempt a revolt.[81] The second was that enforcement of the ban, which had a relatively short term of imprisonment of between two and four years if breached, was left to the states and not the federal government.[82]

Northern States agreed to the Constitution's slave importation clause in order to ensure that slave States, especially South Carolina and Georgia, would ratify the Constitution.[83] To this effect, Oliver Ellsworth argued that it would be "unjust" to South Carolina and Georgia to immediately ban the importation of slaves.[84] As with the three-fifths clause, the Constitution would not have been ratified by all thirteen States of the Confederation without this compromise on the importation of slaves. Ellsworth made this point when he said that without the slave importation clause, the States of the Confederation would "most probably [divide] into several confederations and not without bloodshed."[85] Roger Sherman made the same point when he justified the inclusion of the slave importation clause on the basis that "it was expedient to have as few objections as possible to the proposed scheme of government" and that "it was better to let the S. States import slaves than to part with them, if they made that a sine qua non."[86] And, at Virginia's ratification convention, James Madison, who had previously, in *Federalist 42*, conceded the "barbarism" of the trafficking in slaves,[87] nevertheless, claimed that "[t]he Southern States would not have entered into the Union of America, without the temporary permission of that trade."[88] Madison's claim was justified given that, at the Philadelphia Convention, John Rutledge was unequivocal in his assertion that the fate of the importation of slaves raised "[t]he true question . . . [of] whether the Southn. States shall or shall not be parties to the Union."[89] That Rutledge subsequently successfully insisted that the Constitution's amendment clause (Article V) contain a proviso that there could be no amendment to the slave importation clause prior to 1808[90] reinforced the *sine qua non* nature of the slave importation clause to South Carolina and Georgia.

The combined effect of the federal legislation banning the importation of slaves and the healthy number of slaves in states such as Virginia and Maryland led to a change in the nature of the trafficking of slaves. Up to that point, the trade had been centered on the importation of slaves into the Union. However, as Madison noted, the slave importation clause left unaffected the "removal, voluntary or involuntary, of Slaves . . . from one to another part of the U. States."[91] Thereafter, the slave trade was dominated by a domestic trade in which, between 1820 and 1860, an estimated 875,000 slaves were transferred from the Upper South to the Lower South.[92] A consequence of the dramatic upsurge in the intra-Union slave trade after 1808, was the deleterious effect it had on the lives of slaves due to the breaking up of families by the sale of a spouse or young children. This was especially so in the case of female slaves, who were no longer seen as valuable for their ability to perform work, but rather, pursuant to the American adaptation of the legal doctrine of *partus sequitur ventrem*,[93] as breeders of future slaves.[94]

In relation to this intra-Union slave trade, the question that arose was whether Congress could regulate it pursuant to the Constitution's commerce clause set out in Article I, Section 8, Clause 3 of the Constitution. This clause stipulated that Congress had the power to "regulate Commerce with foreign Nations, and among the several States, and with the Indian Tribes." In his analysis of the antebellum Supreme Court decisions on the commerce clause, David Lightner observes that not a single justice stated a belief that Congress had the power to abolish the interstate slave trade, whereas eight justices, either explicitly or implicitly, were of the view that Congress had no such power.[95] The most notable case in this respect was the decision, in 1841, in *Groves v. Slaughter*.[96]

In *obiter dicta*, six of the seven justices in that case confirmed that the regulation of the intra-state trade in slaves was a matter for the individual states.[97] Furthermore, and notwithstanding that the commerce clause appeared to grant Congress the right to regulate the interstate trade in slaves, three of the justices expressed the view, for different reasons, that it did not.[98]

The Admission of New States and Territories Clauses

By the terms of Article II of the Treaty of Paris of 1783,[99] as was confirmed by the Supreme Court in 1827, in *Harcourt v. Gaillard*,[100] Great Britain ceded to its former colonies a vast swathe of territory west of the Appalachian Mountains stretching south of the Great Lakes to what is today the northern border of Florida, referred to here after as "the western territory." None of this territory belonged to the Confederation as a result of the cession.[101] A number of the Confederation's States claimed parts of the western territory, usually being parts adjacent to the claimant State. In due course, some of these States ceded their parts of the western territory to the Confederation. After the Constitution came into operation in March 1789, those parts of the western territory that had not, by then, been ceded to the Confederation, were, in due course, ceded to the Union.

In relation to the western territory, Article IV, Section 3 of the Constitution contained two clauses. Clause 1 stipulated that "New States may be admitted by Congress" into the Union. Clause 2 stipulated: "The Congress shall have the Power to dispose of and make all needful Rules and Regulations respecting the Territory or other Property belonging to the United States." In the years preceding the ratification of the Constitution, as increasing numbers of settlers began moving into the western territory, the most important issue confronting the Confederation was gaining control over its administration and future development. The Confederation's most significant achievement in this respect was the adoption of "An Ordinance for the Government of the Territory of the United States Northwest of the River Ohio" (the Northwest Ordinance) on 13 July 1787.[102] When the Union came into operation in March 1789, one of the first acts of Congress was to re-enact the Northwest Ordinance as federal legislation.[103] This meant that, pursuant to the

Constitution's two clauses in Article IV, Section 3, it was left to Congress to pass legislation dealing deal with the question of slavery in the western territory and ultimately the admission of new states that were carved out of it.[104] Pursuant to the Supreme Court's ruling in 1803, in *Marbury v. Madison*,[105] the constitutional validity of any such legislation would be determined by the Supreme Court. That the Philadelphia Convention chose this way of dealing with the issue of slavery in the western territory and the states to be carved out of it, did not mean that it regarded this as an unimportant matter. In fact, the Convention was acutely aware of the importance of the future development of the western territory. For example, James Madison recognized that the western territory was "a mine of vast wealth" which would "soon become a national stock."[106] This meant, as he noted, that the admission of new states and territories clauses granted Congress "a power of very great importance."[107]

Why the Convention left it to Congress to deal with the question of slavery in the western territory and ultimately the admission of new states that were carved out of it can be explained by understanding the background and context in which the admission of new states and territories clauses were drafted. This involves detailing two matters. The first matter is the course and resolution of the dispute between the Confederation and Spain over navigation rights on the Mississippi River that were of particular importance to the settlers, mainly from Virginia, in the southern part of the western territory and the states in the South from where they came.[108] According to Eli Merritt, this dispute spawned a sectional debate "which threatened the dissolution of the Confederation" and which many Congressional delegates "fear[ed] that [its] outcome . . . would determine the success of reform and ultimately, the fate of the Union."[109] This is important because it demonstrates both the urgency of the Confederation's efforts to gain control over the administration and future development of the western territory, as well as the emergence of what Jack Rakove aptly describes as the "stark sectional division"[110] between the Confederation's northern non-slave States and its southern slave States.[111] The second matter is the debate in the Confederation's Congress over slavery in the western territory that eventually culminated in the Northwest Ordinance, the provisions of which, as noted, were quickly re-enacted by the Union's Congress once the Union formed by the Constitution came into operation.

THE COURSE AND RESOLUTION OF THE MISSISSIPPI RIVER DISPUTE

In addition to Article II's cession of the western territory to the Confederation, by Article VIII of the Treaty of Paris, Great Britain granted to "the citizens of the United States" navigation rights on the Mississippi River "from its source to the ocean . . . for ever."[112] However, the Americans' claim to these rights was disputed by Spain. Spain claimed that although it granted Great Britain navigation rights on the Mississippi River in 1763 following the conclusion of the Seven Years War, that grant was nullified by its declaration of war against Great Britain in 1778, with the consequence that the British had nothing to grant to "the citizens of the United States" in 1783. The matter was further complicated by the fact that a separate treaty between Great Britain and Spain in 1783, by which the British ceded to Spain East Florida and West Florida (the Old Southwest), made no mention of navigation rights on the Mississippi River.[113]

For "the citizens of the United States," the dispute between the Confederation and Spain became critical in July 1784, when Spain issued a proclamation that closed off access by "the citizens of the United States" to the Mississippi River south of the latitude thirty-two degrees north. Spain's proclamation was prompted by fears that the increasing spread of American settlers moving into the southern part of the western territory posed a threat to its hold on the Old Southwest. On the other hand, the proclamation dramatically affected these settlers and the southern States of the Confederation from where the great majority of them came from. These settlers, numbering approximately 75,000 people (including slaves), included slaveholders who brought with them their slaves to work the plantations that they established. Their futures and the economic viability of their plantations were severely threatened by the Spanish proclamation because it closed off the only way that they could get their products to market, namely via the Mississippi River to the sea.[114] The result of the Spanish proclamation was an escalation of intensity in the existing negotiations between the Confederation and Spain for a treaty to settle their differences. Such was the importance of these negotiations to the Confederation that, in a letter to Marquis de Lafayette in March 1785, James Madison, then a delegate to the Confederation Congress, after referring to "[t]he repugnance of Spain to an amicable regulation of the use of the Mississippi," asked his friend to do what he could do to obtain French support for the Confederation in relation to its negotiations with Spain.[115]

The Confederation's position on navigation rights on the Mississippi River was formulated on 3 June 1784, when its Congress instructed its negotiators with foreign powers "not to relinquish or cede, in any event whatsoever, the rights of the citizens of these United States to the free navigation of the river Mississippi from its source to the ocean, as established in their treaties with Great Britain."[116] The Confederation's negotiations with the Spanish were led by its secretary for foreign affairs, John Jay. In the wake of the arrival in America of Spain's chargé d'affaires, Diego de Gardoqui, to further conduct negotiations with the Americans, on 15 August 1785 Congress confirmed its approach to the negotiations when is resolved that any treaty with the Spanish must ensure that the "the citizens of the United States" would have free navigation rights on the Mississippi River south of latitude thirty-two degrees north through to the sea.[117] For Madison, such a stance was imperative, as he made clear in a letter to James Monroe on 21 June 1786, in which he expressed his "amazement that a thought should be entertained *surrendering* the *Mississippi* and . . . *guarantying* the *possessions in Spain in America*" and questioned whether there could be "a more shortsighted or dishonorable policy."[118] However, northern States, especially in New England, were less concerned about the navigation rights on the Mississippi River than about securing from Spain most-favored-nation status for the Confederation and the lucrative prospects for commercial interests in the northern States that would flow from such a treaty. In the words of Henry Lee, a delegate to Congress from Virginia: "The eastern states consider a commercial connextion with Spain, as the only remedy for the distresses which oppress their citizens, most of which they say flow from the decay of commerce."[119] Jay was receptive to the views of the northern States and, on 3 August 1786, he presented his reasons to Congress in support of a proposed treaty that he had negotiated with de Gardoqui.[120] The proposed treaty's key terms were that, for a period of twenty-five or thirty years, "all Commercial regulations affecting each other shall be founded in perfect reciprocity" and that the Confederation's States would have full and free access to Spanish ports for their goods and Spain would enjoy the same access rights to the ports of the Confederation's States for their goods, especially fish and naval timber (this was of considerable benefit to northern States), but excluding tobacco (this negatively affected southern States).[121] However, the proposed treaty would be dependent upon the Confederation agreeing, for the same period, to "forbear to use the Navigation of the River below their territories to the Ocean."[122]

Jay's proposed treaty ignited a bitter debate that led to a sectional conflict, evidenced by a letter, on 12 August 1786, by James Monroe, then a delegate to the Confederation Congress from Virginia, to his State's governor, Patrick Henry. In this letter Monroe said that Jay's treaty proposal was "one of the most extraordinary transactions" that he had witnessed and was the result of "a minister negotiating expressly for the purpose of defeating the object of his instructions, and by a long train of intrigue & management seducing the representatives of the States to concur in it."[123] This sentiment was echoed by de Gardoqui when, on 20 August 1786, he wrote that "[n]ever in Congress has there been a controversy more combatted than that of our Mississippi."[124] As Edward Beach points out, in this sectional conflict "northern states wanted to secure a treaty with Spain that allocated benefits to the northern majority—in the form of a commercial boon for northern fisheries—while imposing costs on the southern minority by limiting access to the Mississippi River and hindering western expansion."[125] This sectional conflict between southern States, which were "slave societies," and northern States, which were "societies with slaves," was one which, as George Van Cleve points out, threatened "the viability of the Confederation."[126]

Jay's proposed treaty was welcomed by most delegates from the northern States.[127] For example, Rufus King saw it as being of "vast importance to the Atlantic states" because "the Fish, Flour and other products of the U.S. [would] acquire . . . a manifest superiority in Spain over other similar commodities of any other country."[128] The proposed treaty was necessary, according to King, because of "the distressed state of the Eastern States . . . [who] had an ungrateful soil & no staple but what they drew from the sea." As to the temporary loss of navigation rights on the Mississippi, it was just that, giving "time to the U.S. to acquire strength, arrange their affairs, & strengthen the Union, so that at the end of the term they may be prepared to assert their right."[129]

On the other hand, Jay's proposed treaty was implacably opposed by most delegates from the southern States.[130] The concern of the southern States was most forcefully articulated by South Carolina's Charles

Pinckney, when he said that a surrender of navigation rights on the Mississippi River would "at once deprive the Citizens of the Atlantic states from navigating it, or from having intercourse with the settlements on its banks" and would "immediately destroy all Connexion between them and the inhabitants of the Western Country," thereby rendering the latter "dependant on Spain." For Pinckney, any treaty that did not secure navigation rights on the Mississippi represented a policy which was "calculated to acquire benefits for one part of the Confederacy at the expense of the other."[131] And William Grayson from Virginia complained that the proposed treaty would lead to "the occlusion of the river [which] would destroy the hopes of the principal men in the S. States in establishing the future fortunes of their families—that it would render the western country of no value & thereby deprive the US of the fund on which they depend to discharge the domestic debt—that it would separate the interest of the western Inhabitants from that of the rest of the Union & render them hostile to it—that it would weaken if not destroy the union by disaffecting the S States when they saw their dearest interests sacrificed & given to obtain a trivial commercial advantage for their brethren in the East."[132] Thus, as representatives of the southern States made clear to the French chargé d'affaires to the Confederation, Louis Guillaume Otto, "the navigation of the Mississippi is the most important object for the United States."[133]

Notwithstanding the strong opposition of the southern States to Jay's proposed treaty with Spain, on 29 August 1786, the Confederation Congress adopted a resolution repealing the August 1785 instructions to Jay concerning the matter of navigation rights on the Mississippi River. The Congress was split along sectional lines on this issue, with seven northern states (Connecticut, Massachusetts, New Jersey, New Hampshire, New York, Pennsylvania, and Rhode Island) voting for the repeal and five southern States (Georgia, Maryland, North Carolina, South Carolina, and Virginia) voting against it.[134] Two days later, the same voting blocs rejected a proposed resolution to reinstate the August 1785 instructions.[135] A similar proposal was again rejected by the same voting blocs on 28 September 1786.[136] However, this constituted only a pyrrhic victory for the northern states because, as stipulated in Article IX of the Articles of Confederation, any treaty with Spain required the support of nine of the Confederation's states for it to be ratified.

A byproduct of Jay's proposed treaty was the transformation of separatist sentiment in the western territory. Prior to then, the Tennessee region, claimed by North Carolina, and the Kentucky region, claimed by Virginia, had sought to be admitted as States of the Confederation.[137] However, Jay's proposed treaty had many settlers in those regions arguing for secession from the Confederation as their best course because it would enable them to negotiate with Spain to secure their desperately needed navigation rights on the Mississippi River.[138] Negotiations with de Gardoqui with this objective in mind were undertaken by James White from North Carolina in relation to the Tennessee region and James Wilkinson from the Kentucky region and lingered on until after the Constitution was ratified.[139] Although they proved to be unsuccessful, attempts by Spain to lure these regions away from the United States continued through to, and beyond, the drafting and ratification of the Constitution.[140] On the other hand, there was secessionist sentiment in the northern States, if Jay's treaty proposal was not adopted by Congress.[141] For example, Theodore Sedgwick, a delegate to Congress from Massachusetts, wrote that "[i]t well becomes the eastern and middle States, who are in interest one, seriously to consider what advantages result from them from their connection with the Southern States."[142]

The heightened sectional conflict over negotiations with Spain on the Mississippi River issue and the secessionist threats that it produced came at a time when plans were afoot for the Confederation's States to address the weaknesses of the Confederation. For Madison, as he explained in a letter to Thomas Jefferson on 12 August 1786, the sectional conflict threatened to be "fatal to an augmentation of federal authority" which he believed was required by "the necessity of making the Union respectable."[143] Madison reiterated these concerns through to the period leading up to the Philadelphia Convention.[144] For example, in a letter to George Washington on 7 December 1786, he admitted that he was "entirely convinced . . . that unless the project of Congs. [for ceding to Spain the Mississippi for twenty-five years] can be reversed, the hopes of carrying [Virginia] into a proper federal system will be demolished."[145] Similar concerns were expressed by Jefferson to Madison on 30 January 1787 when he expressed his "uneasiness" at "the possibility that the navigation of the Mississippi may be abandoned to Spain," fearing that such an act would constitute "an act of separation between the Eastern and Western country."[146] Madison's fears reflected the concerns of his home state, Virginia, whose House of Delegates had, in late November

1786, resolved that the sacrifice of navigation rights on the Mississippi River "would be a flagrant violation of Justice, a direct contravention of an end for which the foederal Government was instituted, and an alarming innovation of the System of Union" and directed its delegates to Congress "to oppose any attempt . . . to barter or surrender to any Nation whatever the right of the United States to the free and common use of the River Mississippi."[147] And North Carolina's delegate to the Confederation Congress, Benjamin Hawkins, in a letter to Jefferson on 8 March 1787, said that if there was a suspension of navigation rights on the Mississippi River, "[o]ur Western citizens will feel much alarmed for their situation" and that they would have "less confidence in the justice of Congress and be disposed to carve for themselves."[148]

In an effort to defuse the sectional tensions exposed by the Mississippi River issue, on 13 March 1787, Madison met with de Gardoqui with the aim of countering Jay's approach to the treaty negotiations.[149] As is clear from his notes on the meeting, he was unceremoniously rebuffed. In them he recorded that de Gardoqui emphasized that, in relation to the "right to the navigation of the Mississippi by the U.S. . . . Spain would never give up this point," that "Spain would act according to her own ideas," that "[s]he would not be governed by other people's ideas of her interest," and that the Americans "remember what he had said as to the inflexibility of Spain on the point of the Mississippi and the consequences to America of her adherence to her present pretentions."[150]

Spain's position on the matter remained unchanged through to the start of the Philadelphia Convention, as is made clear by Jay's report to Congress on 11 April 1787, in which he stated that de Gardoqui remained "decided in refusing to admit us to navigate the river below our limits on any terms or conditions."[151] Thus, on 15 April 1787, in writing to Edmund Randolph, Madison expressed "little confidence" in resolving the treaty issue.[152] On the following day, in a letter to George Washington, he wrote that "[t]he business with Spain is becoming extremely delicate, and the information from the Western settlements truly alarming."[153] Three days later, Jay advised Congress that he had agreed with de Gardoqui to include a provision in a treaty with Spain for the suspension of navigation rights on the Mississippi River.[154] This prompted Madison, in his letter to Jefferson on the following day, to label Jay's proposal as "the sacrifice of the Mississippi," with consequences "likely to be very serious" and which would "foment distrusts among the Atlantic States" at a time when "harmony and confidence ought to have been studiously cherished."[155] Although, in the same letter, Madison suggested that the negotiations over the matter had been "arrested,"[156] the issue continued to raise his concerns, as illustrated by his letter to Jefferson on 23 April 1787, where he wrote that the "Spanish negociation is in a very ticklish situation" and referred to support for what he called the "obnoxious project" of "ceding the Mississippi."[157] However, on the same day Jay agreed "that it was expedient to retract the step taken for ceding the Mississpi,"[158] and on 9 May 1787, five days before the start of the Philadelphia Convention,[159] he sought instructions on what approach to take in relation to negotiations with de Gardoqui.[160]

With the start of the Philadelphia Convention approaching, both parties stepped back from any further efforts to negotiate a treaty, leaving matters to lie pending the outcome of the Convention.[161] However, as Alexander Hamilton noted, one of the reasons that led to the holding of the Convention was the failure of the Confederation to resolve the issue of whether Americans were "entitled by nature and compact to a free participation in the navigation of the Mississippi."[162] Thus, it was unsurprising that, at the Convention, on 18 June 1787, Hamilton argued that, if the Convention failed in its objective of creating a stronger union, "foreign nations would not respect our rights or grant us reciprocity" which would reduce the Confederation to a "passive Commerce" with the loss of the rights to the rights of fisheries, the Great Lakes, and the "Navigation . . . of the Mississippi fleet."[163] At North Carolina's ratification convention, William Davie, a delegate to the Convention, also criticized the Confederation, when he stated that one of its failures was that it could not "secure to us the enjoyment or our territories, or even the navigation of our own rivers."[164] Thus, as Eli Merritt writes, the Philadelphia Convention "was called and conducted against the backdrop of a spreading separatist sentiment among settlers in the West inflamed by the Mississippi question" and the dispute with Spain over this issue was "one of the most significant issues that led to and shaped the Philadelphia Convention."[165] It was with this situation in mind that, on the fifth day of the Convention, Virginia's Edmund Randolph stated that one of the reasons why the Convention needed to reach agreement on a new form of government was to secure the future Union "against dissentions between members of the Union, or seditions in particular states."[166] However, the records of the Convention debates contain only scant references to the Mississippi River issue.[167] The only time it was raised in the debates over the Constitution's slavery provisions was when Gouverneur Morris predicted that the three-fifths clause would lead to slave states gaining power at the national level and that the growth of slavery would "inevitably bring on a war with Spain for the Mississippi."[168] On the other hand, the significance of Mississippi River at that time is attested to by the fact that William Blount, a delegate to the Convention from North Carolina, felt compelled to temporarily leave Philadelphia and travel to New York to attend the Confederation Congress, of which he was also a delegate, in order, as his biographer puts it, "to continue the fight for an untrammeled navigation of the Mississippi, for which struggle the Southern delegations in Congress were now dangerously few."[169]

The Mississippi River issue was, however, more extensively featured in the debates over the ratification of the Constitution, especially in Virginia and North Carolina.[170] These two States feared that a new federal government established pursuant to the Constitution would accede to Spain's demands in relation to navigation rights on the Mississippi River, which, in turn, would increase the risk that what became the future states of Kentucky (carved out of western territory claimed by Virginia) and Tennessee (carved out of western territory claimed by North Carolina), would secede from the Union.[171] This fear had been voiced by Madison in his letter to Jefferson on 23 August 1788, in which he wrote that he feared that Spain would capitalise on separatist sentiment in Kentucky "to seduce them from the union, holding out an object which will never be obtained by them as part of the union."[172] However, unlike his opponents to the ratification of the Constitution, Madison was convinced, as he argued at the Virginia ratification convention, that "the establishment of the new Government will be the best possible means of securing our rights as well in the western parts as elsewhere."[173]

The ratification of the Constitution with its Article IV, Section 3, Clause 1, dealing with the admission of new states and Article II, Section 2, Clause 2, dealing with treaties, provided a means by which the sectional conflict over the issue of navigation rights on the Mississippi River was resolved.

In relation to the admission of new states, any treaty with Spain that would finally resolve the dispute over navigation rights on the Mississippi River was of significance in terms of the balance of power in the sectional conflict between the northern and southern States that had been exposed by the treaty negotiations with Spain. On this issue, delegates to the Philadelphia Convention from northern States were acutely aware of the likelihood that settlement of the southern part of the western territory would result in new slaves states being admitted to the Union that would be aligned with the existing southern slave states, and would therefore diminish the power and influence of the Union's northern states.[174] For this reason alone, as Madison pointed out at the Convention, "[t]he prospect of many new States to the Westward was another consideration of importance."[175] At the time of the Convention, nearly all the settlement in the western territory was in that part south of the Ohio River, with only very little settlement north of the Ohio River.[176] For northern States, such an eventuality would be minimized if the treaty with Spain was based upon that proposed by Jay in August 1786. However, for the southern States, Jay's proposed treaty would leave them at the mercy of the then majority northern States. For them, gaining navigation rights on the Mississippi was an absolute requirement in any treaty with Spain. As was pointed out by William Grayson, a delegate to both the Confederation Congress and the Virginia ratification convention, "If the Mississippi be shut up, emigrants will be stopped entirely. There will be no new States formed on the Western Waters. This will be a government of seven [northern] States," Thus, as Grayson went on to point out, "This contest of the Mississippi involves this great national contest—That is, whether one part of the Continent will govern the other. The Northern States have the majority, and will endeavor to retain it. This is therefore a contest for dominion—for empire."[177] This was clear to foreign observers as well. Thus, when reporting back to his superiors in France, Louis Guillaume Otto observed that "the true motive of [the] vigorous opposition" from northern States to the requirement that a treaty with Spain ensure navigation rights on the Mississippi was to be found "in the great preponderance of the northern states, eager to incline the balance toward their side." Otherwise, he went on to write, the flow of settlers into the southern part of the western territory would lead to the formation of new States that would "augment greatly the mass of the southern states."[178]

Given that there was this "great national contest" over admission of states from the western territory into a future Union, there was a heated debate at the Convention over both the clause dealing with the admission of new states and the treaties clause.

In relation to the admission of new states clause, in the original draft of that clause, it was stipulated that "new States shall be admitted on the same terms with the original States."[179] In the debates concerning the representation of states in Congress, Gouverneur Morris voiced his fear that the new states that would emerge from the western territory would, in due course, "outnumber the Atlantic states" and expressed his wish "to put it in the power of the latter to keep the majority of votes in their own hands."[180] He thus proposed that the Constitution should contain a "[p]rovision . . . to prevent the maritime States from being hereafter outvoted by [new states]."[181] Morris's argument that the Constitution should "secure the Atlantic States a prevalence in the National Councils" was anchored in his belief that "new States [would] know less of the public interest" and "[would] have an interest in many respects different" to that of the thirteen States of the Confederation.[182] Furthermore, he said, because the new states "would not be able to furnish men equally enlightened to share in the administration of our common interests," if they achieved power, "they [would] ruin the Atlantic interests."[183] Elbridge Gerry from Massachusetts also had concerns about the possible power of new states carved out of the western territory, because they "[would] oppress commerce, and drain our wealth into the Western Country." To preclude this, he proposed that it was "necessary to limit the number of new States to be admitted into the Union, in such a manner, that they should never be able to outnumber the Atlantic States."[184] Gerry's proposal was seconded by Rufus King,[185] a man whom the historian Richard Morris describes as a "vigilant observer and critic of Southern expansionist aspirations."[186]

In opposition to these suggestions, Virginia's George Mason argued that new states from the western territory "must . . . be treated as equals, and subjected to no degrading discriminations," because otherwise, they will "either not unite with or will speedily revolt from the Union" and that, in relation to navigation rights on the Mississippi River, "though Spain might for a time deprive them of the natural outlet for their productions, yet she will, because she must, finally yield to their demands."[187]

With the concerns of the potential power of new states in mind, Gouverneur Morris moved that the equality of new states stipulation in the initial draft of the admission of new states clause be deleted because, as he said, he "did not wish to throw the power" into the hands of new states that would emerge from the western territory.[188] New Hampshire's John Langdon also supported removal of the stipulation because he believed that circumstances "might arise which would render it inconvenient to admit new states on terms of equality."[189] Although Morris's motion to remove equality of new states stipulation was approved by a vote of nine States to two,[190] this victory for Morris did not prevent the admission of new states on terms of equality with existing states. They were so admitted, and in 1845, in *Pollard's Lessee v. Hagan*, the Supreme Court confirmed that the admission of a new state to the Union meant that it possessed "the same rights, sovereignty, and jurisdiction . . . as the original states."[191]

In relation to the treaties clause, the uncertainty around the issue of navigation rights on the Mississippi River was pivotal to the requirement in Article II, Section 2, Clause 2 of the Constitution that any treaty negotiated by the president required the concurrence of "two thirds of Senators present." As Hugh Williamson, a delegate to the Convention from North Carolina, confirmed, in a letter to Madison on 2 June 1788, this proviso was agreed upon so "that the Navigation of the Mississippi after what had already happened in [the Confederation] Congress was not to be risqued in the Hands of a meer majority."[192] The existing "meer majority" of northern States feared the emergence of a new majority of states that would negotiate a treaty that was detrimental to their interests. The feared new majority was that of the existing southern States combining with new states created out of the western territory. Indeed, two new states, namely Kentucky and Tennessee, were in the process of seeking statehood and were admitted to the Union in 1792 and 1796 respectively. On the other hand, southern States feared that the existing "meer majority" of northern States would quickly negotiate a treaty with Spain that compromised the navigation rights granted to "the citizens of the United States" by Great Britain in 1783. For example, at the North Carolina ratification convention, William Porter said that he feared that the president and northern states would be able to pass a treaty "which will be of great advantage to the Northern States, and equal injury to the Southern States" and that they "might give up the rivers and territory of the South States."[193] Thus, it was in the interests of both sides of this sectional dispute to agree to the supermajority requirement in the treaties clause.[194] Indeed, one of the grounds for opposition to the ratification of the Constitution at the Virginia and North Carolina ratification conventions was that the treaties clause did not go far enough in that it should have required a supermajority vote of all senators, rather than merely senators present at the time of the vote.[195] As Charles Warren aptly notes: "The argument [here] was far-fetched, but in the excited condition of the debates, it carried weight."[196] That it was these two States that raised opposition to ratification on the basis of the treaties clause as drafted was no coincidence. This was so because it was from parts of the western territory claimed by them that claims to statehood were then being made, and it was feared that if the navigation rights on the Mississippi River were not secured for "the citizens of the United States," these emerging states would seek to align themselves with Spain and secede from the Union. The reality of such a prospect is evidenced in the letter from John Brown, a delegate to the Confederation Congress, to Jefferson in August 1788, in which he wrote that "the ill advised attempt to cede the navigation of that River has laid the foundation for dismemberment of the American Empire by destroying the confidence of the people in the Western Country in the future of the Union & by inducing them to dispair of obtaining possession of that Right by means of any other exertions than their own."[197]

It was thus not surprising that the ratification resolutions of both Virginia and North Carolina contained requests (duly rejected by the Union's first Congress[198]) for the following amendments to the Constitution: (i) that commercial treaties require the concurrence of two-thirds of all the members of the Senate, rather than two-thirds of the members present at the particular time, as set out in the Constitution, notwithstanding that the Philadelphia Convention had rejected a similar provision by a vote of eight States to three;[199] (ii) that, except in cases of extreme or urgent necessity, any treaty ceding, contracting, or restraining the navigation of rivers require the concurrence of three-quarters of the all members of both houses of Congress; and (iii) any federal navigation law require the consent of two-thirds of members present of both houses of Congress.[200] The grounds for the opposition to the treaty clause as it stood and for the proposed amendments to the Constitution was the fear that northern states would be able to approve a treaty that would, as Warren points out, "disastrously interfere with the interest of the South, not only as to their territorial rights but as to their slave trade and their commercial interests."[201]

The process of resolving the Mississippi River dispute effectively began with on 16 September 1788. On that day, in light of the reality that eleven of the Confederation's States had ratified the Constitution, in a secret session of the Confederation's Congress, after declaring "that the free navigation of the River Mississippi is a clear and essential right of the United States," Congress resolved to terminate further negotiations with Spain, leaving the matter to be further negotiated by the new "federal government which is to assemble in March [1789]."[202] The Union's prospects of resolving the dispute with Spain improved when, in 1788, faced with the reality that its proclamation of 1784 had failed to retard settlement and development of the southern part of the western territory, Spain allowed American traders to navigate the Mississippi River to New Orleans, and therefore to the ocean. As Michael Allen points out, by this switch in policy Spain "hoped to win the western Americans' loyalty, create a buffer state in the Old Southwest, and halt further encroachments from the United States of America." However, this was a forlorn hope because "[m]ost Westerners were . . . unwilling to exchange American rule for that of an autocratic Spanish regime."[203] In the wake of this Spanish failure, the issue of navigations rights on the Mississippi River was finally resolved by a treaty between Spain and the United States in 1795, which, in Article IV, confirmed for Americans the right of free navigation on the Mississippi River that they had first demanded back in 1785 and, in Article XXII, granted them duty-free transport for a period of three years through the port of New Orleans, then under Spanish control.[204] These rights were incontrovertibly secured in 1819 when, pursuant to the Treaty of Adams-Onis, Spain ceded its Old Southwest territory to the United States.[205]

THE NORTHWEST ORDINANCE AND SLAVERY

The Confederation's dispute with Spain over navigation rights on the Mississippi River was one of the two issues concerning the western territory that highlighted the need for the Confederation to assert control over the administration and future development of the western territory. The other was what, in 1787, Alexander Hamilton referred to as concerns over the "valuable territories and important posts in the possession of foreign powers [i.e. Great Britain], which by express stipulations ought to long since have been surrendered," which he listed as one of the failures of the Confederation that led to the holding of the Philadelphia Convention.[206] Hovering around these two matters was the continued violence flowing from the dispossession by incoming settlers of Native American peoples from their traditional homelands. As Susan Gaunt Stearns points out, for both the incoming settlers and Native Americans, "violence and potential violence remained central facts of everyday life."[207] Against this background, Richard Morris writes that the critical question confronting the Confederation was: "Could the West, cut off from the thirteen states by a mountain range, be effectively governed and permanently united with the original states?"[208]

In seeking to accomplish this goal, the Confederation was handicapped by the fact that, under the Articles of Confederation, it lacked clear jurisdiction over the western territory. Thus, given the reality that, following the Treaty of Paris of 1783, individual States of the Confederation claimed jurisdiction over various individual parts of the western territory, the Confederation's first objective was to assert jurisdiction over the western territory for itself. This was, in part, achieved when various parts of the western territory north of the Ohio River (the Northwest Territory) were, by the end of 1786, ceded to the Confederation by New York,[209] Virginia (the claimant of the largest part of it),[210] Massachusetts,[211] and Connecticut.[212] However, jurisdiction over parts of territory south of the Ohio River was divided between Virginia, North Carolina, and Georgia.[213]

The Confederation's adoption of the Ordinance of 1784 represented its first effort in establishing a system of government over the western territory. However, its adoption was accompanied by the same sectional division evident in relation to the Confederation's negotiations with Spain over navigation rights on the Mississippi River, this time over the issue of the existence of slavery in the western territory.

The Ordinance of 1784, although never implemented, was intended to provide for a general framework for the government of "the territory ceded or to be ceded by individual states to the [Confederation]."[214] The driving force behind it, and its principal draftsman, was Thomas Jefferson. A key part of Jefferson's initial proposal for the Ordinance was that "after the year 1800 of the Christian era, there shall be neither slavery nor involuntary servitude in any of the . . . States" carved out of the western territory.[215] Although in Jefferson's mind, his proposal "would have prevented this abominable crime from spreading itself over the new country,"[216] William Cohen is probably closer to the mark when he writes that under his proposal "bondage would have been legal in the area for sixteen years; and it seems likely that, if the institution of slavery had been allowed to get a foothold in the territory, the prohibition would have been repealed."[217]

However, on 19 April 1784, at the behest of delegates from North

Carolina and South Carolina, a vote was taken on whether this part of Jefferson's proposal should be included in the Ordinance. Only six northern States (one short of the required majority) voted in the affirmative,[218] and it was, therefore, omitted from the Ordinance when it was adopted four days later.

The division over slavery in the western territory continued to divide Congress. Opposition to slavery being allowed to spread into the western territory was raised by Rufus King from Massachusetts on 16 March 1785, when he proposed that a committee of Congress be appointed to consider the immediate abolition of slavery in the western territory. Although the motion was adopted by eight States, it was opposed by delegates from the four southern slave States of Virginia, North Carolina, South Carolina, and Georgia.[219] On 6 April 1785, the appointed committee submitted a resolution that replicated Jefferson's 1784 proposal that slavery be abolished in the western territory as of 1800, but with an added provision that allowed for the recovery of fugitive slaves who escaped from any of the thirteen States of the Confederation. This additional provision was not enough to attract sufficient support from slave States to support the resolution, with the result that Congress did not adopt it.[220] Thus, when an ordinance "for ascertaining the mode of disposing the lands of the western territory" was adopted on 20 May 1785, it contained no provision excluding slavery from that territory.[221]

The issue of slavery in the western territory was finally resolved, on 13 July 1787, with the passage of the Northwest Ordinance, which superseded and formally repealed the 1784 Ordinance. The debate leading up to the Northwest Ordinance commenced in September 1786.[222] On 10 May 1787, the Congress proceeded with the third reading of an ordinance "for the government of the Western Territory," but which, again, did not contain any provision concerning slavery.[223] Following a period during which Congress failed to attract a quorum, on 11 July 1787, a new proposed ordinance was read for the first time. Although this proposed ordinance also did not have any provisions relating to slavery, it differed in one very significant way from the proposed ordinance of 10 May 1787, in that it was to be confined to "the territory of the United States North West of the river Ohio." Following its second reading on the following day,[224] on 13 July 1787, Congress voted unanimously[225] to adopt the Northwest Ordinance, Article VI of which stipulated that "[t]here shall be neither slavery nor involuntary servitude" in the Northwest Territory.[226] Significantly, five of the six southern slave States voted for the Ordinance. The sixth, Maryland, was not present at the meeting. The three northern States that were represented in Congress and voted for the Ordinance were Massachusetts, New York, and New Jersey. When the Union came into operation in March 1789, one of the first acts of the Union's Congress was the re-enactment of the Northwest Ordinance as federal legislation.[227]

Thus, in the space of two days, with the knowledge of the acrimonious debate over the three-fifths clause taking place at the Philadelphia Convention at that same time, the Confederation's Congress resolved a deadlock over the issue of slavery in the western territory that had bedeviled the Confederation for the previous three years. In fact, the Northwest Ordinance was the product of a deal between the northern States and the southern slave states which Douglas Egerton describes as "a quiet compromise" in which "[n]orthern congressmen surreptitiously permitted slavery to expand into America's southwestern regions in exchange for restriction in northwestern portions, lands that few southerners coveted in any case."[228] In practical terms, it meant that each part of the sectional divide over slavery in the western territory would be able to exploit, each in its own way, the "mine of vast wealth" that, as noted above, Madison believed would "soon become a national stock."

For southern States and for the slaveholders that had settled in the southern part of the western territory, the bargain over the existence of slavery in the western territory was of particular importance, in that their livelihoods were not threatened, as they would have been if slavery was prohibited in all of the western territory. With this in mind, it was also less likely that the slaveholders in the southern part of the western territory would seek to reach an accommodation with Spain and possible secession from the Confederation in the context of the still unresolved dispute over navigation rights on the Mississippi River.

Northern states accepted this bargain, as Nathan Dane stated in 1830, because they saw the Northwest Territory as being "prepar[ed] . . . principally, for New England settlers," and were therefore willing to let territory south of the Ohio River to be settled with slaves "because slavery had taken root in it, and it was then probable, it would be settled, principally, by slave owners."[229] James Madison made the same point when he wrote in 1819 that "[w]hen the existence of slavery in that territory was precluded, the importation of slaves was rapidly going on, and the only mode of checking it was by narrowing the space open to them."[230]

Dane's 1830 statement discloses two of the major factors that explain why the Northwest Ordinance received the unanimous support of the eight States that constituted the Congress on 13 July 1787. The first was that the Northwest Territory was envisaged as being principally settled by settlers from New England. The second was that territory south of the Ohio River, which contained the great majority of settlers into the western territory to that point of time, was principally settled by slaveholders, and would continue to be settled by slaveholders. Each of these two factors needs to be further detailed.

Dane's statement that the Northwest Territory was going to be settled principally for settlers from the New England States was a reference to the sale of western territory to property speculators who would develop the land for these anticipated settlers.[231] A particular sale of land in the Ohio Valley was in the offing at the time of the passage of the Ordinance. The prospective purchaser was the Ohio Company of Associates (Ohio Company), which had been formed in Massachusetts in 1786. One of the major investors in the Ohio Company was Manasseh Cutler, a Congregational minister, lawyer, and, much like his close friend, Benjamin Franklin, a keen student of various scientific disciplines.[232] The concern for Cutler, and other potential speculators in western territory land, was the lack of control by Congress over its manner of development and settlement. Having been dispatched by the Ohio Company to represent its interest to Congress, Cutler impressed upon various of its delegates of the need for Congress to assert control over the western territory and, as he wrote, in return the Ohio Company would, "leav[e] no vacant lands exposed to be seized by such lawless banditti as usually infest the frontiers of countries distant from the seat of government."[233] The concerns over the Congress's lack of jurisdiction over the western territory had previously been voiced by the Confederation's secretary of war, Henry Knox, in a letter to the president of Congress on 16 April 1787, in which he referred to the existing settlers in the western territory as "intruders" and went on to assert that "the usurpation of the public lands by a body of armed men highly deserves the attention of Congress" because "[i]f such audacious defiance of the power of the United States be suffered with impunity a precedent will be established, to wrest all the immense property of the western territory out of the hands of the public."[234] Three days later, in his report to the secretary of Congress, Knox warned that unless "immediate measures" were undertaken to assert control over the western territory, "the great national advantages resulting from the wise administration of the western territory" would likely be lost.[235]

That the Northwest Ordinance addressed the concerns of the Ohio Company by creating optimal conditions for speculators to acquire land is evidenced by a letter to George Washington from Richard Henry Lee, a delegate to Congress from Virginia, written two days after the Ordinance's passage. In his letter, after first stating that the Ordinance was "passed in Congress for establishing a temporary government beyond the Ohio, as a measure preparatory to the sale of the Lands," Lee went to emphasize that the Ordinance was "necessary, for the security of property among uninformed, and perhaps licentious people, as the greater part of those who go there are, that a strong toned government should exist, and the rights of property be clearly defined." Finally, Lee went on to note that Congress's "next object" was the sale of western territory land, which was "an object of much consequence," namely that it would help extinguish "part of the public debt."[236] That such a sale would take place was beyond doubt. On 9 May 1787, on the day of the second reading of the proposed ordinance for the whole of the western territory, a Memorial for the purchase of the Ohio Valley land was presented on behalf of the Ohio Company by its director and agent, Samuel Holden Parsons. The Memorial was referred to a committee of Congress which included two delegates to the Philadelphia Convention, namely James Madison and Rufus King.[237] On 10 July 1787, three days before the passage of the Northwest Ordinance, the Committee recommended that the Confederation's Treasury Board be authorized to negotiate a sale of the land to the Ohio Company.[238] A slightly amended version of the Committee's recommendation was tabled before Congress on 23 July 1789.[239] The Contract for the purchase of the Ohio Valley was signed on 27 October 1789.[240] Against this background, and given that the northern States had relatively fewer slaves than did the southern States and that the antislavery movement that had emerged during the Revolutionary period was mainly present in these States, it was entirely understandable they would insist that settlement of the Northwest Territory be on the basis that slavery would be prohibited there.

As to why the southern slave states agreed to the Ordinance's Article VI with its prohibition of slavery in the Northwest territory, the minimal extant evidence provides no clear answer.[241] However, there are three reasons, either of which, or together, provides a reasonable explanation of why they did so. First, prior to 1787, nearly all of the development in the western territory had been in that part of the territory south of the Northwest Territory, where the population already included over 15,000 slaves[242] and, in the later words of John Quincy Adams, slavery was "a condition of existence."[243] Given the reality that, as Richard Morris notes, "[t]he South was not ready to abolish slavery in future territories south of the Ohio,"[244] the southern States reasonably assumed that, by agreeing to prohibit slavery in the Northwest Territory, it was implied that it would not be prohibited south of it, and that slaveholders from adjoining slave States would be free to settle in that part of the western territory.[245]

Subsequent events support this implication, as can be seen from the terms of the cession agreements that the Confederation entered into with South Carolina and Georgia in relation to territory south of the Northwest Territory claimed by these two States. The agreement with South Carolina,[246] entered into a mere twenty-seven days after the adoption of the Northwest Ordinance, did not include any provision precluding the Confederation from prohibiting slavery in the ceded territory. However, the circumstances in which the agreement was entered into are indicative of the existence of a tacit understanding that the Confederation would not seek to do so. It must be kept in mind that South Carolina's cession took place at a time when the Philadelphia Convention was coming towards the end of its deliberations, during which South Carolina had fought hard to ensure the inclusion into the proposed Constitution of explicit protections for the institution of slavery. If South Carolina had any concerns about the future of slavery in the territory it was about to cede to the Confederation, it is hard to believe that it would not also have insisted upon an express stipulation permitting slavery in that territory. In relation to the agreement with Georgia, it related to only a very small part of the territory south of the Northwest Territory that Georgia claimed. This agreement, entered into six months after the South Carolina cession agreement, was on the same terms as South Carolina's.[247]

In relation to remaining parts of the territory south of the Northwest Territory, two cession agreements took place after the ratification of the Constitution.[248] The first of those was with North Carolina. On

22 December 1789, one month after it ratified the Constitution, North Carolina passed legislation authorizing the cession to the Union of that part of the western territory that it had claimed. This legislation stipulated the terms of the proposed cession, one of which stated that "no regulations made or to be made by Congress shall tend to emancipate slaves."[249] North Carolina formalized the cession on these terms by a deed which was executed on 25 February 1790.[250] On 2 April 1790, Congress enacted legislation accepting the cession on the terms set out in the deed.[251] The government for this territory, established by Congress on 26 March 1790,[252] was constituted on the basis that Congress could not legislate to abolish slavery in the territory.[253] The second cession agreement relating to territory south of the Northwest Territory was with Georgia, in 1802. This agreement dealt with the great bulk of territory that Georgia had claimed following the Treaty of Paris of 1783. On 24 April 1802, Georgia ceded this territory to the Union on the basis that the provisions of the Northwest Ordinance applied to it with one exception, namely that slavery was not forbidden in the ceded territory.[254] The cession was communicated to Congress two days later.[255]

Why cession agreements with the Union expressly confirmed that slavery would not be prohibited in the territories ceded to the Union as opposed to the absence of express terms to that effect in the cession agreements with the Confederation can be explained by the different ways in which the Confederation and the Union passed legislation. Under the Confederation, the Northwest Ordinance's implication that the Confederation could not prohibit slavery in territory south of the Northwest Territory was sufficient because the number of slave States was always going to be sufficient to block any attempt to prohibit slavery in territory south of the Northwest Territory. However, under the Constitution, with its system of legislation being voted upon by the two houses of Congress, the capacity of slave states to block such legislation was less certain. Therefore, express terms that precluded Congress from abolishing slavery in the ceded territories were necessary.

The second reason for slave States accepting Article VI's prohibition of slavery in the Northwest Territory was, according to Virginia's William Grayson, "for the purpose of preventing Tobacco & Indigo from being made on the N.W. side of the Ohio, as well as for sevl. other political reasons,"[256] thereby eliminating competition against southern plantation owners engaged in these industries. These industries were major sources of wealth and prosperity in the southern slave States at that time. Given that slaves were the basic source of labor for the profitable production of these crops, this objective would be achieved by banning the further entry of slaves into the Northwest Territory.[257] It is likely that this was one of the reasons why later requests, from slaveholders in the Northwest Territory,[258] to suspend the operation Article VI of the Ordinance in the Northwest Territory, were, as Hugh A. Garland wrote in 1851, "always opposed and defeated by Southern men."[259] For example, in 1802, in response to a request from William Henry Harrison, the then governor of the Indiana Territory, that the operation of Article VI be suspended for a period of ten years so that slave labor could be employed in that territory, South Carolina's John Randolph, a fervent defender of the interests of slaveholders, wrote, in opposition to that request, "that the labor of slaves is not necessary to promote the growth and settlement of Colonies in that region" and that it would be "highly dangerous and inexpedient to impair a provision wisely calculated to promote the happiness and prosperity of the Northwestern Country."[260]

The third reason for slave States accepting Article VI's prohibition of slavery in the Northwest Territory stemmed from the dispute with Spain over navigation rights on the Mississippi. George Van Cleve argues that the southern States "proffered their support for the Northwest Ordinance . . . in return for the abandonment of the treaty [with Spain] by the Northern states (in the event that the Constitution was ratified), in effect compensating the Northern states for their loss."[261] Van Cleve bases his argument on a letter written three days before the Ordinance was adopted, from Benjamin Hawkins, a delegate to the Confederation Congress from North Carolina, to his State's governor, Richard Caswell, in which he wrote of the pressing concern of "Western citizens of the southern States" in relation to Mississippi River, but went on to refer to recent decisions of Congress that the proposed treaty had, "at length, from a variety of circumstances unnecessary as well perhaps improper to relate, been put in a better situation than heretofore." Having earlier in his letter referred to the need for "securing and preserving . . . the free and common use of the navigation of the Mississipi" for the "Western Citizens," in concluding the letter he wrote that it was "indispensably necessary for the well-being of the Southern States, that they should keep up respectable representations in Congress until their *rights* are *perfectly* secured."[262] Hawkins's concerns were shared by William Grayson, who was the (temporary) chairman of Congress when it debated and voted upon the Northwest Ordinance in July 1787. A foremost concern of Grayson's was, according to his biographer, the matter of navigation rights on the Mississippi River, because Grayson "viewed the whole [western] land matter as subordinate to an issue he believed the keystone of American and especially Southern interests—Mississippi River navigation rights."[263]

Thus, for southern States and for the slaveholders that had settled in the southern part of the western territory, the practical consequence of the Northwest Ordinance's bargain over the existence of slavery in the western territory was that their livelihoods were not as threatened as they would have been if slavery was prohibited in all of the western territory. And, with this in mind, it was also less likely that the slaveholders in the southern part of the western territory would seek to reach an accommodation with Spain and possible secession from the Confederation in the context of the still unresolved dispute over navigation rights on the Mississippi River.

In terms of the Northwest Ordinance's longer-term impact and effect, Richard Morris states that it "proved hospitable to the opening up of the West" in that it "served as a model for the admission of new states in other parts of the Union, and did so at a crucial moment, since the federal Constitution then being drafted managed to avoid any mention of territories."[264] To similar effect, Van Cleve argues that it constituted "an informal sectional bargain on economic development that began the process of dividing the west."[265] This bargain was maintained without any controversy or objection in relation to the territory gained by the terms of the Treaty of Paris of 1783. This is evidenced by the almost unanimous approval from Congress in organizing the territorial administrations in that part of the western territory south of the Ohio River.[266] It was only with the later acquisition of the Louisiana Purchase territory in 1803 that the issue of slavery in the territories emerged as a contested political issue. However, with respect to the Louisiana Purchase territory, the Northwest Ordinance's "informal sectional bargain" served as a basis for Congressional legislation in 1820[267] that, as Edward Coles pointedly observed in 1856, excluded slavery from the northern part of that territory in language that was virtually identical to that used in Article VI of the Northwest Ordinance.[268]

However, this sectional bargain collapsed with the passage of the

Kansas-Nebraska Act in 1854. This legislation created the territories of Kansas and Nebraska out of territory originally acquired as part of the Louisiana Purchase. Although these two territories were, by the terms of the Missouri Compromise legislation, to be free of slavery, the Kansas-Nebraska Act stipulated that these terms were "inoperative and void" and that the people of the two territories or any states to emerge from them were "free to form and regulate their domestic institutions in their own way."[269]

The ensuing violence and political conflict over whether Kansas would be admitted to the Union as a slave or non-slave state brought into sharp focus the meaning of the admission of new states and territories clauses. This issue was resolved by the Supreme Court in 1857, in *Dred Scott v. Sandford*. The decision in this case was made against the background of important rulings from two earlier Supreme Court cases. The first was the 1845 decision in *Permoli v. Municipality No 1 of the City of New Orleans*, where the court ruled that provisions in federal legislation with respect to territories ceased to have any effect on any territory once it was admitted as a state of the Union.[270] This ruling was reinforced in *Strader v. Graham* in 1851, where the court ruled that nothing in the Constitution detracted from the right of states "to determine the *status*, or domestic and social condition, of the persons domiciled within its territory."[271] The combined effect of these two cases was that any territory, regardless of whether or not slavery had been prohibited there by federal legislation, could, upon becoming a state, choose to become a slave state.

In delivering the opinion of the court in *Dred Scott v. Sandford*, Chief Justice Roger Taney ruled that the Constitution's territories clause was "confined, and was intended to be confined, to the territory which at the time [i.e., 1787] belonged to, or was claimed by, the United States . . . and can have no influence upon a territory afterwards acquired."[272] Taney went on to note that although the territories clause did not enable Congress to legislate with respect to slavery in the Louisiana Purchase territory, it had the power to do so pursuant to the admission of new states clause.[273] More specifically, Taney ruled that the new states clause enabled Congress to prohibit slavery in any territory acquired by the Union after the Constitution's ratification, unless other Constitutional provisions precluded it from doing so.[274] Having so stated, Taney ruled that the Constitution's Fifth Amendment, fugitive slave clause, and importation of slaves clause were such provisions.

In relation to the Fifth Amendment, Taney ruled that its stipulation that "no person shall . . . be deprived of life liberty or property, without due process of law" meant that legislation that banned slavery in the territories was unconstitutional because such legislation "could hardly be dignified with the name of due process of law."[275] For Taney, this ruling was a reflection of the fact that even though the Constitution "distinctly and expressly affirmed" that slaves were "articles of merchandise,"[276] they had an elevated status over and above other forms of property. This elevated status stemmed from the Constitution's fugitive slave and importation of slaves clauses which, according to Taney, demonstrated that "the right of property in a slave [was] distinctly and expressly affirmed in the Constitution."[277] Furthermore, this property right of slaveholders was one that Congress had "the power coupled with the duty of guarding and protecting."[278] Although Congress could ban other forms of property from the territories, the elevated status accorded to slave property meant, on this ground alone, that any legislation that sought to ban slavery in the territories "was not warranted by the Constitution, and [was] therefore void."[279]

The consequence of Taney's opinion was that the Missouri Compromise legislation banning slavery in the Louisiana Purchase territory north of latitude thirty-six degrees thirty minutes north was unconstitutional.[280] Furthermore, it meant that Congress could not prohibit slavery in any of the Union's territories, leaving it open for any state carved out of them being admitted as a slave state. In effect, the *Dred Scott v. Sandford* decision implemented the essence of a resolution proposed by John C. Calhoun in the Senate on 19 February 1847. The resolution, which was not voted upon by the Senate, asserted that any Congressional legislation that deprived anyone from any state "from emigrating with their property into any of the territories of the United States . . . would be a violation of the Constitution."[281]

The *Dred Scott v. Sandford* decision was subsequently hotly debated, no more so than by Abraham Lincoln and Stephen Douglas during the 1858 Illinois senatorial election campaign.[282] Its correctness was vigorously rejected by antislavery activists in the northern non-slave states.[283] However, whatever view one took of the decision, it rendered any Congressional legislation that prohibited slavery in the Union's territories unconstitutional. This was a reality recognized by all, including those who opposed any extension of slavery into these territories. Thus, Abraham Lincoln, in his First Inaugural Address, while clearly hoping that its "evil effect" would one day be overruled by a later Supreme Court decision, recognized that it was, until then, "binding . . . upon the parties to the suit . . . [and] entitled to very high respect and consideration, in all parallel cases, by all other departments of the government."[284]

THE ESSENTIAL IMPORTANCE OF THE ADMISSION OF NEW STATES AND TERRITORIES CLAUSES

The essential nature and importance of the Constitution's admission of new states and territories provisions was inextricably linked to the Confederation Congress's adoption of the Northwest Ordinance. Its adoption in July 1787 contributed significantly to the resolution of two pressing matters, both fundamentally concerned with the institution of slavery, that were of huge significance for the western territory acquired from the British in 1783. In so doing, the Ordinance impacted directly on the question of whether the Constitution should explicitly stipulate whether or not slavery was permitted in the Union's territories and the new states that would, in due course, be carved out of them, or whether these matters were to be left to the Union's Congress to determine. In the light of the sectional differences between the Convention's delegates over, in particular, the Constitution's three-fifths and slave importation clauses, as well as the debates in the Confederation Congress over the two pressing matters that led to the adoption of the Northwest Ordinance, it was clear that the Convention would not secure enough support for provisions in the Constitution to either prohibit or permit slavery in the territories and the new states to be carved out of them. Rather, the compromise on the issue of slavery in the territories that was formalized by the adoption of the Northwest Ordinance provided the Convention with the solution on this fundamentally important matter, namely, leaving it to be determined in the future by the enactment of legislation by the Union's Congress, which is precisely what its First Congress did when in August 1789, the Union's First Congress, by one of its very first legislative enactments, passed the necessary legislation in order that the Northwest Ordinance "may *continue* to have full effect" (emphasis added).[285]

As detailed above, the first of the two pressing matters that the Confederation was confronted with was that of securing the interests of settlers in the southern part of the western territory and maintaining their loyalty to the Confederation in the wake of secessionist threats in the

Tennessee and Kentucky regions that surfaced in the context of the unresolved dispute with Spain over navigation rights on the Mississippi River. The second matter was securing control of the Northwest Territory in the face of the continued presence there of the British after the Treaty of Paris in 1783, so as to enable the future development of this largely unpopulated, by whites, vast tract of territory. On both of these matters the debates revealed deep sectional divisions over the existence of slavery in the western territory, with the States in the South insisting that "slave societies" be permitted to emerge there, while the States in the North, where slaves were far fewer in number and where growing anti-slavery sentiment was moving towards banning slavery, desired the exclusion of slavery from all of the western territory. The passage of the Northwest Ordinance largely resolved these two matters, and by so doing, impacted significantly on the on the final form of the Constitution's admission of new states and territories clauses. In this respect, the Northwest Ordinance was, as George Anastaplo, writes, "the most critical American provision with respect to slavery in 1787–1788."[286]

The debates in the Confederation's Congress over the matter of slavery in the western territory clearly shows that northern States were generally against its spread into the western territory and, by extension, would have opposed its extension into any further territory that the Union might subsequently obtain. It is also clear that, if there had been proposals at the Philadelphia Convention that the Constitution's admission of new states and territories clauses prohibit slavery in the new states and territories, they would have met with the same resistance and fate as did the proposal to immediately ban the importation of slaves. It is in this context that the bargain struck in relation to the inclusion of Article VI into the Northwest Ordinance explains the essential nature of the Constitution's admission of new states and territories clauses.

The inclusion of Article VI in the Northwest Ordinance constituted a compromise on the issue of slavery in the western territory. The compromise effectively amounted to an agreement not to include virtually unamendable provisions in the Constitution on the issue of slavery in the Union's territories and new states carved out of these territories, but rather to leave these issues to be negotiated by Congress.[287] At the Philadelphia Convention there was extensive debate over clauses dealing with the admission of new states and territories. What this debate clearly indicates is the importance of these clauses for the future of the western territory. However, the matter of slavery in the territories did not feature in debates over these clauses. That this was so is, however, unsurprising given that the issue of slavery in the western territory was being debated at the Confederation and was ultimately resolved by the passage of the Northwest Ordinance. The Philadelphia Convention was well aware of the proceedings of the Confederation's Congress, given that thirteen of the its delegates were, at that time, also delegates to the Confederation Congress,[288] and eight had served as delegates to it at times during the period between the signing of the Treaty of Paris in 1983 and the start of the Convention in May 1787.[289] Indeed, three delegates, William Blount, William Few, and William Pierce, travelled to New York during the Convention to ensure that there was a quorum present on the vote for the Northwest Ordinance.[290] Furthermore, there was regular correspondence between delegates to the Confederation's Congress in New York and the Convention's delegates in Philadelphia. Such correspondence was able be delivered on the next day, given that overnight communication covering the ninety-one miles between New York and Philadelphia had been established before the American Revolution.[291] Thus, on 10 September 1787, almost two months after the adoption of the Northwest Ordinance, when the Convention submitted its final draft of the Constitution to the Committee of Style and Arrangement, which had been appointed two days earlier "to revise the stile of and arrange the articles which had been agreed to,"[292] there was no mention of slavery in the draft's Article XVII, which dealt with the admission of new states and territories.[293] It was also hardly surprising that, as noted, the Union's First Congress promptly enacted a law for the continued application of the Northwest Ordinance.

In effect, the Northwest Ordinance was, as George Van Cleve points out, a "side bargain" of the Philadelphia Convention.[294] And it was Article VI of this "side bargain" that pointed to the essential nature of the Constitution's admission of new states and territories clauses. They were essential provisions of the Constitution, not because of words that were included in them, but precisely because they said nothing about slavery in the territories and future new states. And, as Van Cleve goes on to say, the expansion of slavery into the southern part of the western territory, which the Northwest Ordinance, and by extension the Constitution, permitted, was, along with the Constitution's other major protections for slavery, "essential" to its "drafting and ratification."[295]

In leaving the issue of slavery in the territories (apart from the Northwest Territory) and the new states that would emerge from them to be dealt with by the future Union's Congress, Article VI of the Northwest Ordinance became an informal precedent on how the issue might be dealt with by Congress in the future. There was little doubt that, as was anticipated in the Articles of Confederation in the context of the Confederation, the Union would acquire further territories in the future to which this precedent was intended to apply. And so it was with the Missouri Compromise of 1820, which substantively reflected the approach of Article VI in relation to slavery in the Louisiana Purchase territory.[296]

However, in *Dred Scott v. Sandford*, the Supreme Court overturned this consensus to the advantage of the Union's slave states with its ruling that Congress could not ban slavery in any of the Union's territories acquired after the Constitution was ratified. In 1860, William H. Seward, then a senator from New York and soon to be the Union's secretary of state, stated the reality that the Court's decision laid bare the fact that the Constitution "[was] not a constitution of liberty, but that it [was] a constitution of human bondage" and "that slavery [was] the normal condition of the American people on each acre of the domain of the United States not organized into states."[297]

The Fugitive Slave Clause

The second of the two grounds upon which the Confederate states claimed the right to unilaterally secede from the Union stemmed from alleged breaches of legislation enacted pursuant to the Constitution's fugitive slave clause. This provision, set out in Article IV, Section 2, Clause 3, stipulated: "No Person held to Service or Labour in one State, under the Laws thereof, escaping into another, shall, in Consequence of any Law or Regulation therein, be discharged from such Service or Labour, but shall be delivered up on Claim of the Party to whom such Service or Labour may be due." It can be noted that there is no record of any specific debate or vote on this wording of Article IV, Section 2, Clause 3. What the extant records reveal is that this wording of the fugitive slave clause was put to the Convention when the final form of the Constitution was presented and voted upon on 15 September 1787. What the records also show is that on that day, "[o]n the question to agree to the Constitution, as amended," all the States present voted "ay."[298] One of the said amendments was to an earlier version of the fugitive slave clause that had been unanimously approved by the eleven States present at the Convention on 29 August 1787.[299] Article IV, Section 2, Clause 3 was the result of stylistic amendments to that clause made by the five-member Committee of Style and Arrangement.

The purpose of the fugitive slave clause was, as stated by Edmund Randolph at Virginia's ratification convention, to give authority "to owners of slaves to vindicate their property,"[300] because, in the words of Bruce Ragsdale, for slaveholders, such as George Washington, "the most serious betrayal of the presumed duty of an enslaved laborer was the act of running away."[301] Washington had made this clear when, six months prior to the Philadelphia Convention, in relation to a prospective purchase of six healthy male slaves, he wrote that he wanted to be sure that "none of them [are] addicted to running away." Of slave flight he said, for emphasis: "I abominate [it]."[302]

Initially it can be noted that the fugitive slave clause is distinguished in its wording from the clause immediately preceding it (Article IV, Section 2, Clause 2), which related to the extradition of persons "flee[ing] from Justice" in relation to charges of treason, felony, or other crimes. As George Anastaplo suggests, the implication to be drawn from this is that runaway slaves were not regarded as fugitives fleeing "from Justice."[303] Rather, the fugitive slave clause was, as Chief Justice Taney wrote in *Dred Scott v. Sandford*, a provision by which "the States pledge[d] themselves to each other to maintain the right of property of the master, by delivering up to him any slave who may have escaped from his service, and be found within their respective territories."[304]

ORIGINS OF THE FUGITIVE SLAVE CLAUSE

At the time of the Philadelphia Convention, "the interstate rendition of fugitive slaves among American states was a well-established constitutional tradition."[305] During colonial times, many runaway slaves sought and obtained refuge with Native American tribes which, in the latter part of the eighteenth century, saw colonies such as Maryland and Virginia offering them rewards if they returned runaway slaves.[306]

In the colonial era, the first significant fugitive slave provision was Article 8 of the Articles of Confederation of the United Colonies of New England of 1643, which stipulated:

> If any servant run away from his master into any of these Confederated Jurisdictions, that in such case, upon the certificate of one magistrate in the jurisdiction out of which the servant had fled or upon other due proof, the said servant shall be delivered either to his master or to any other that pursues and brings such certificate or proof.[307]

In dispensing with any requirement of a trial and deeming a certificate as sufficient, Article 8 served as a prototype for later fugitive slave provisions. In the mid-1780s, the Confederation entered into treaties with various Native American tribes, some of which included fugitive slave clauses. For example, the treaties with the Cherokee, Choctaw, and Chickshaw tribes all mandated that they return "all the Negroes, and all other property . . . to such person, and at such time and place" as determined by the Confederation's officials.[308]

During the Philadelphia Convention, as previously noted, three of its delegates who were also members of the Confederation Congress travelled to New York in order that there be a quorum for a meeting of the Confederation Congress that, on Friday 13 July 1787, adopted the Northwest Ordinance. The Ordinance's Article VI, after prohibiting slavery in the Northwest Territory, further stipulated that, in relation to any slave who escaped into the Northwest Territory, "such fugitive may be lawfully re-claimed and conveyed to the person claiming his or her labor or service aforesaid."[309] As discussed above, southern slave States voted for the prohibition of slavery in the Northwest Territory for a number of reasons, including that they recognized that slavery would not take root in the Northwest Territory and because of a tacit understanding that slavery was to be permitted in territory south of the Ohio River.[310]

As to the Constitution's fugitive slave clause, support for it from the northern States was really a continuation of existing policy on this matter. They had previously supported the fugitive slave provisions in the treaties with Native American tribes and in the Northwest Ordinance. Furthermore, States such as Pennsylvania, Connecticut, Massachusetts, New Jersey, New York, Pennsylvania, and Rhode Island all enacted their own legislation for the return of fugitive slaves.[311] For these States, fugitive slave clauses were important for various reasons. First, they knew that, in their States, "powerful merchants, who profited from carrying slave-produced agricultural commodities from the southern States to foreign markets,"[312] had a vested interest in protecting the interests of Southern slaveholders by means of fugitive slave provisions. Furthermore, these provisions "prevented an influx of runaway slaves whose presence white taxpayer majorities often objected to on racist grounds or believed would result in unwanted social costs such as increased poor-relief taxes and discouragement of white immigration."[313]

For the southern slave States, according to North Carolina's delegation to the Philadelphia Convention, the important consequence of the Constitution's fugitive slave clause was that it gave "Southern States . . . a much better Security for the Return of Slaves who might endeavour to escape than they had under the Original Confederation."[314] To similar effect, Charles Cotesworth Pinckney, in addressing his fellow South Carolinians, argued that it gave slaveholders "a right to recover [their] slaves in whatever part of America they may take refuge, which is a right [they] had not before."[315]

This greater security stemmed from the fact that the fugitive slave clause effectively reversed the principle that emerged from the English decision in *Somerset v. Stewart*,[316] which ruled that a slave who found his or her way to England, could not be transported back to his or her master's jurisdiction against his or her wishes. If applied to the American context, this suggested that a slave would become a free person if he or she escaped to a non-slave State. Thus, the status of an escaped slave would be determined by the law of the State to which the slave escaped, rather than the law of the State of the slave's origin.[317] However, as James Madison argued at Virginia's ratification convention, the fugitive slave clause reversed this position:

> [The fugitive slave] clause secures us that property which we now possess. At present, if any slave elopes to any of those States where slaves are free, he becomes emancipated by their laws. For the laws of the States are uncharitable to one another in this respect. But in this Constitution, . . . [the fugitive slave] clause was expressly inserted to enable owners of slaves to reclaim them. This is a better security than any that now exists. No power is given to the General Government to interpose with respect to the property in slaves now held by the States.[318]

Madison's argument was proven to be correct when, in 1842, in delivering the Supreme Court's opinion in *Prigg v. Pennsylvania*, Justice

Joseph Story wrote that the fugitive slave clause's grant of the right to slaveholders to the return of their slaves was a "positive, unqualified right . . . which no state law or regulation can in any way qualify, regulate or control, or restrain."[319] That the fugitive slave clause rejected the principle laid down in *Somerset v. Stewart* was confirmed by the Supreme Court, in 1847, in *Jones v. Van Zandt*, where Justice Levi Woodbury, in delivering the court's opinion, said that the fugitive slave clause recognized "the clear right of every man at common law to make fresh suits and recover his own property" and had the effect of overcoming a doctrine, described as "too harsh," by which a slave could gain his or her freedom by "merely crossing the line of an adjoining State."[320]

CONGRESSIONAL FUGITIVE SLAVE LEGISLATION

Although the fugitive slave clause had, as clearly stated by Story in *Prigg v. Pennsylvania*, the "well known . . . object of . . . secur[ing] to the citizens of slaveholding states the complete right and title to ownership of their slaves, as property, in every state in the Union into which they might escape,"[321] it left it to Congress to determine just how, in the words of the clause, the "Person held to Service or labour" was to "be delivered up on Claim of the party to whom such Service or labour may be due."

Congress carried out this task in 1793 when, with the overwhelming support of the House of Representatives and the unanimous support of Senate,[322] it enacted the Fugitive Slave Act (FSA 1793).[323] Section 3 of the act stipulated that a master or his agent could reclaim a runaway slave—referred to as "a person held to labor"—from anywhere in the Union and take him or her before a judge. Upon being satisfied of the master's right of ownership of the slave, the judge had a "duty" to issue a certificate which authorized the slave's removal from the place to which he or she had fled. Section 4 provided for a fine of $500 against any person who obstructed the recovery or return of a runaway slave.[324] The overall effect of these two sections was that an alleged fugitive slave was not entitled to any due process hearing or trial, apart from the summary proceeding to establish that he or she was a runaway slave. The significance of the FSA 1793 to the slave states stemmed from slaves being their most valuable form of personal property. This was reflected in the fact that these states imposed stiff penalties against those who stole, or assisted in the theft of, slaves. In some states, the theft of slaves attracted the death penalty, while fines, often totaling the value of a slave, attached to persons assisting in the theft of a slave.[325]

An issue relating to the FSA 1793 stemmed from the congressional legislation, in 1789, that incorporated into federal law the provisions of the Northwest Ordinance adopted by the Confederation Congress in 1787. The Ordinance's fugitive slave clause, set out in its Article VI, referred to the return of slaves from "one of the original states." This would suggest that the FSA 1793 would *not* apply to two categories of runaway slaves. The first category was slaves in any of the new states admitted into the Union after the Constitution had been ratified by the thirteen States of the Confederation. The second category was slaves in any of the Union's territories. In relation to the first category, in *Jones v. Van Zandt*, the Supreme Court ruled that the FSA 1793 applied to all states, and was not confined to the thirteen former States of the Confederation.[326] In relation to the limitation in the second category, it must also be noted that the Constitution's fugitive slave clause referred only to slaves in a state who ran away. It said nothing about slaves in the Union's territories. Although Section 1 of the FSA 1793 explicitly referred to slaves in states or territories who ran away, in none of the Supreme Court cases dealing with the constitutionality of Congressional fugitive slave legislation was its constitutional validity with respect to slaves in the territories questioned or ruled upon. Thus, the legislation remained in force with respect to runaway slaves in the territories throughout the antebellum era.

The constitutional validity of the FSA 1793 was challenged before the Supreme Court in *Prigg v. Pennsylvania*. Taking a strict and narrow interpretation of the Constitution's fugitive slave clause, counsel for Pennsylvania argued that nothing in the fugitive slave clause or elsewhere in the Constitution granted Congress the power to pass any laws concerning slavery.[327] In rejecting this argument, Justice Story ruled that, given that the purpose of the fugitive slave clause was to give slaveholders an absolute right to the return of runaway slaves, a slaveholder was "clothed with the entire authority, in every state of the Union, to seize and recapture his slave, whenever he can do it without any breach of the peace, or any illegal violence."[328] Story then concluded that, on the basis of the words of the fugitive slave clause that an escaped slave "shall be delivered up on Claim of the Party to whom such Service or Labour may be due," the FSA 1793 was constitutionally valid. This was so because it was necessary to invoke "the aid of legislation to protect the right, to enforce the delivery, and to secure the subsequent possession of the slave." This conclusion stemmed from the principle that if "the Constitution guarantees the right, and it requires the delivery upon a claim of the owner, . . . the natural inference certainly is, that the national government is clothed with the appropriate authority and functions to enforce it."[329] In upholding the constitutional validity of the FSA 1793, Story effectively overruled the unreported, and largely unknown at the time, decision, in 1836, in *State v. The Sheriff of Burlington*, where the New Jersey Chief Justice, Joseph C. Hornblower, although not declaring the FSA 1793 void, nevertheless did suggest that it was unconstitutional.[330]

In relation to state legislation dealing with the rendition of fugitive slaves, Story ruled that it could "never be permitted to interfere with or to obstruct the just rights of the owner to reclaim his slave . . . or with the remedies prescribed by Congress to aid and enforce the same."[331] However, this did not mean that state legislation had no role to play in assisting in the recovery of fugitive slaves. It could, for example, facilitate the arrest and removal of runaway slaves from their borders. It was on the basis of this ruling that the Supreme Court, in 1852, in *Moore v. Illinois*, upheld the validity of legislation in Illinois that criminalized the harboring of runaway slaves.[332]

A final matter dealt with in *Prigg v. Pennsylvania* concerned the issue of enforcement of the FSA 1793 by state officials. On this matter, Story held that, because the Constitution's fugitive slave clause "[did] not point out any state functionaries, or any state action, to carry its provisions into effect . . . the states, cannot, therefore, be compelled to enforce [the provisions of the FSA 1793]."[333] However, Story went on to hold that, nevertheless, state magistrates "may, if they choose, exercise that authority, unless prohibited by state legislation."[334] On the basis of this ruling, and much to the chagrin of the slave states, Massachusetts (1843), Vermont (1843), Connecticut (1844), New Hampshire (1846), Pennsylvania (1847), and Rhode Island (1848) enacted laws prohibiting state officials from enforcing the FSA 1793 and denying the use of jails and prison facilities to slave catchers.[335] Although the constitutional validity of these state laws was not tested, in unambiguous language in extrajudicial comments, two justices of the Supreme Court—Robert Grier, in 1850, and Samuel Nelson in 1851—said that they were unconstitutional.[336] The exclusion of state officials from enforcement of the FSA 1793 that flowed from this state legislation, combined with the paucity of federal judges to enforce the FSA 1793, were factors that led to slave states demanding stronger fugitive slave legislation. These demands were met with the passage of amendments to the FSA 1793.[337] These amendments, commonly referred to as the Fugitive Slave Act 1850 (FSA 1850), formed part of the package of measures that constituted the 1850 Compromise, and, in the words of Thomas Morris, were "scarcely a compromise" because "[e]very guarantee, every security in the new law was for the 'rights' of slave owners."[338]

Section 4 of the FSA 1850 authorized federal district judges to appoint commissioners who were vested with the "authority to take and remove such fugitives from service or labor . . . to the State or Territory from which such persons may have escaped or fled." Section 5 stipulated that any marshal who failed "to serve such warrant, or other process, when tendered, or to use all proper means diligently to execute the same" was liable to a penalty of $1,000. Furthermore, if a fugitive slave escaped from the custody of a marshal, the marshal was liable for "the full value of the service or labor of said fugitive in the State, Territory or District whence he escaped." On the other hand, Section 8 gave marshals an incentive to comply with the legislation by providing for payment for each slave they arrested. In effect, this section turned the recovery of runaway slaves into a form of federally authorized bounty hunting.

Section 5 also empowered commissioners to call upon any persons in the community to assist in the recapture of fugitive slaves. Section 6 retained the right of reclamation of fugitive slaves by stipulating that runaway slaves could be pursued and reclaimed, either pursuant to a court-approved warrant or by seizing the runaway slave and bringing him or her before a court. In the latter situation, upon proof of that person being a runaway slave, the court had the "duty" to issue a certificate of removal which authorized the release of the runaway slave to the slaveholder. The certificate of removal was "conclusive of the right" of the slaveholder to remove the fugitive slave to the place from where he or she had escaped and protected the slaveholder from "all molestation . . . by any process issued by any court, judge, magistrate, or other person whomsoever." In addition to denying the alleged runaway slave the right to testify, the legislation also denied him or her legal rights, such as the right to a trial by jury and the right to *habeas corpus*.

Section 7 stipulated that persons who knowingly obstructed the arrest and return of fugitive slaves or harbored or concealed them were liable to a fine of $1,000 and imprisonment for up to six months, as well as being liable for damages to a slaveholder in the sum of $1,000 for each slave lost as a result of such conduct.

During the 1850s, in circuit court decisions, four Supreme Court justices from northern states—John McLean,[339] Robert Grier,[340] Samuel Nelson,[341] and Benjamin Curtis[342]—all upheld the constitutional validity of the FSA 1850. These views were endorsed by the full Supreme Court, in 1859, in *Ableman v. Booth*, where, in part of a single sentence at the end of the court's unanimous opinion, Chief Justice Taney ruled that the FSA 1850 was "in all of its provisions, fully authorized by the Constitution of the United States."[343]

From the perspective of southern slave states, the FSA 1850 was critical. Although the number of runaway slaves was not high in proportion of their total number, they were overwhelmingly able-bodied, prime-age males.[344] Because it was easier to escape to a non-slave state from the border states of Maryland, Virginia, Kentucky, and Missouri than from Deep South states, the majority of runaway slaves came from these border states. According to a study by Stanley Campbell, of the 191 cases that were litigated through the federal courts between 1850 and 1860, 82.2 percent resulted in the slaves being returned to their claimants.[345] However, for slaveholders this was of little comfort given the significant numbers of slaves that sought to escape bondage. Scholars have estimated that each year during the 1850s, as many as 50,000 slaves attempted to escape to freedom.[346] A strong motivating factor for a slave seeking to escape was that he or she had been sold or was likely to be sold and therefore separated from family.[347] Most attempts to escape were unsuccessful, and the number who actually reached their promised land is unknown.[348] However, the fact that many slaves attempted to escape remained a matter of concern to southern slaveholders.

THE ESSENTIAL NATURE OF THE FUGITIVE SLAVE CLAUSE

Because there was little debate about the fugitive slave clause at the Philadelphia Convention or during the various State conventions that ratified the Constitution, evidence that the Constitution's founders recognized its essentiality to the establishment of the Constitution must be sourced elsewhere.

The first source is the fact that that, when it came to the issue of the fugitive slave clause, the existence of slavery and its continuation had already been acknowledged by the terms of the three-fifths clause and then confirmed following the heated debate over the slave importation clause, which granted slaveholders the right, albeit temporarily, to import slaves. Given that these clauses had already been agreed to, there was no necessity to debate and bargain over a fugitive slave clause, which, as a critical component of the Northwest Ordinance, had already been agreed upon by the Confederation Congress during the time that the Philadelphia Convention was in progress. In such circumstances, the lack of debate at the Philadelphia Convention over the fugitive slave clause does not detract from its essentiality to the establishment of the Constitution.

The second source is the Confederation's Northwest Ordinance, which stated that Article VI's fugitive slave provision was to be "forever unalterable unless by common consent."[349] This effectively insurmountable hurdle to any proposal to amend or repeal Article VI reflected its essential nature. The absence of a "common consent" phrase in the Constitution's fugitive slave clause is readily explained by the effect of the amendment clause in Article V of the Constitution, because it achieved the same purpose and effect as did the Ordinance's "common consent" phrase. In requiring the approval of three-quarters of the Union's states for any proposal to amend or repeal a provision of the Constitution, Article V effectively represented an insurmountable hurdle to any proposal to amend or repeal the Constitution's fugitive slave clause.

The third source of evidence concerns the circumstances that led to the adoption of Article VI of the Northwest Ordinance, at the time when the Philadelphia Convention was underway. As already noted, Article VI, in addition to including a fugitive slave clause, also prohibited slavery in the Northwest Territory. It was the inclusion of this prohibition that provides a key to establishing the essential nature of the Constitution's fugitive slave clause. In 1856, Edward Coles published his account of the history of the Northwest Ordinance. In that account, he wrote of a conversation he had had with then president, James Madison, for whom he served as private secretary from 1810 to 1815. In that conversation, Madison told Coles that southern slave States agreed to Article VI's prohibition of slavery in the Northwest Territory in return for northern States not only agreeing to include the fugitive slave clause in the Northwest Ordinance, but also giving an assurance that the same clause would be included in the Constitution.[350]

As to existence of such an agreement, it should be noted that Madison was a delegate to the Philadelphia Convention as well as a member of the Confederation Congress and had concerns about the sectional conflict that had arisen as result of the dispute with Spain over navigation rights on the Mississippi River and whether or not slavery should be permitted in the western territory. These concerns were undoubtedly on his mind when he left the Congress in mid-May 1787 to be present at the start of the Convention.[351] Given his intimate involvement in the proceedings of the Convention, it is inconceivable that he would not have known of such a deal, even if he was not involved in its making. Given that Coles, who happened to be a cousin of Madison's wife,[352] was Madison's private secretary, there is likely to have been a trusting relationship between the two men. It is thus reasonable to infer that there is no reason to doubt that Madison told Coles about the bargain and that Coles accurately recalled and recorded the details of his conversation with Madison. It can also be noted that this bargain was reached at a time when the absence of any fugitive slave provisions had, in the words of Joseph Story, been "felt as a grievous inconvenience, by the slave-holding states."[353]

Although Coles's account of his conversation with Madison is the only documentary evidence of such an agreement, circumstantial evidence corroborates it. First, Article VI significantly changed the scope and nature of a proposed ordinance that was originally intended to deal with all the Confederation's territories. Thus, Article VI's inclusion converted the original proposed ordinance from being one intended to deal with all the Confederation's territories, to dealing only with the Northwest Territory. Furthermore, as already discussed above, the Confederation Congress had not previously agreed to any provision prohibiting slavery in any of its territories, And as to runaway slaves there was barely a mention of it in Congress's debates over proposed ordinances for the western territory. A rare exception to this was a proposal, submitted to Congress on 6 April 1785, to include a clause that was essentially identical to Article VI in such an ordinance, which was immediately rejected.[354] Article VI, and the profound changes it had for the original proposed ordinance that morphed into the Northwest Ordinance, was suddenly and with only minimal notice put to the Congress on the very eve of the vote to adopt it and was quickly adopted without debate.[355]

The suddenness and speed with which Congress adopted an article that contained provisions that it had previously clearly been rejected can be readily explained as the result of the agreement referred to by Coles being reached between persons negotiating on behalf of the Confederation and the Philadelphia Convention.

The second piece of circumstantial evidence that supports Coles's account of his conversation with Madison is that it was on 28 August 1787, six weeks after the Northwest Ordinance was adopted, that there was a proposal put to the Philadelphia Convention to include a fugitive slave clause in the proposed Constitution.[356] More significantly, the Convention unanimously adopted it the next day.[357] The existence of the agreement referred to by Coles is a reasonable explanation of why the Convention adopted the fugitive slave clause without debate, so far as is apparent from the extant records, unanimously, and so swiftly. That Convention delegates were aware of the agreement referred to be Coles can be readily inferred from the fact that, as previously noted, three members of the Confederation who participated in the Congress's adoption of the Ordinance were also Convention delegates. Indeed, one of them, North Carolina's William Blount, having arrived in Philadelphia, was summoned by the Confederation Congress's secretary, Charles Thomson, to attend the Congress to help constitute a quorum "for the great purpose of the Union." When he left Philadelphia in order to participate in Congress's proceedings leading up to the Northwest Ordinance, he was accompanied by Benjamin Hawkins, his fellow delegate to Congress from North Carolina, who happened to be in Philadelphia at that time.[358] Georgia's William Few and William Pierce, also left Philadelphia for the same reason. All four of these men voted in favor of adopting the Ordinance.[359] After voting for the Ordinance, Few and Blount returned to Philadelphia in the first week of August 1787[360] and participated in the Convention's unanimous vote in favor of the fugitive slave clause and its inclusion in the Constitution. It is inconceivable that Few and Blount did not inform fellow delegates at Philadelphia about the circumstances surrounding the adoption of the Article VI of the Northwest Ordinance. Furthermore, Rufus King, who had been an active participant in Congress's debates on both the dispute with Spain over navigation rights on the Mississippi River and the existence of slavery in the territories, although choosing to remain in Philadelphia, was informed of the debates and proceedings of the Confederation Congress through regular correspondence with his fellow delegate to the Confederation from Massachusetts, Nathan Dane, who informed him by letter dated 16 July 1787, that the States present and voting, had unanimously adopted the Ordinance's Article VI.[361]

The third item of circumstantial evidence that supports Coles's account of his conversation with Madison is the use of essentially identical expressions in the two fugitive slave clauses when referring to a "person" that is "held in labor or service" (a slave), "labor or service" (slavery), and "person claiming" or "Claim of the Person" (the slave's owner).

A fourth, and final, source evidencing that the Constitution's founders recognized the essential nature of the fugitive slave clause is the actions they took in relation to the rendition of fugitive slaves prior to and soon after the Constitution came into operation in March 1789. One such action was the enactment of the FSA 1793 that gave operational effect to the Constitution's fugitive slave clause.

Although not enacted in the immediate wake of the Constitution coming into operation, in the circumstances in which the federal government found itself with respect to the issue of fugitive slaves in 1789, the enactment of the FSA 1793 four years later can be considered as evidence of a tacit recognition of the essential nature of the Constitution's fugitive slave clause. The particular circumstance that impeded the speedier enactment of fugitive slave legislation was the then ongoing and more pressing efforts to resolve the issue of the rendition of fugitive slaves who had escaped to places outside the territorial scope of the Confederation and subsequently the Union. It was these places that were, and remained up to the end of the eighteenth century, the primary destinations to which fugitive slaves sought to escape to in search of their freedom.[362] The first of these efforts related to a very live issue at the time of the Philadelphia Convention. It concerned the return of slaves who had escaped to the British forces during the American Revolution. Pursuant to Article VII of the Treaty of Paris, in 1783,[363] the British were precluded from "carrying away any negroes or other property of the American inhabitants." This provision, which was inserted into the Treaty at the insistence of the American treaty negotiators,[364] led to concerted efforts for the return of the many thousands of these slaves. However, these efforts were rebuffed by the British, who had, since Dunmore's Proclamation in 1775, treated escaped slaves as free African Americans[365] and therefore not covered by Article VII. The British facilitated safe haven for these escaped slaves in places such as England, Nova Scotia, and Sierra Leone, a colony established on the west African coast.[366] The determination to seek the rendition of slaves who had escaped to places outside the Union was also evident in relation to slaves who had, at that time, escaped to the Old Southwest and been provided sanctuary by Spanish authorities.[367] In his October 1787 letter to Thomas Jefferson reporting on the Philadelphia Convention, Madison noted Georgian complaints to the effect that "their fugitive slaves are encouraged by East Florida."[368] This eventually led, in 1792, to Charles Pinckney, at the request of Thomas Jefferson, then secretary of state, negotiating an agreement with Spain for the rendition of fugitive slaves in return for the Union agreeing to reimburse Spanish authorities for expenses incurred in apprehending and maintaining the runaways.[369] When considered in the light of the immediate needs to deal with Great Britain and Spain in relation to the rendition of fugitive slaves, the delay of four years in enacting the FSA 1793 can be seen as relatively prompt action by Congress on the issue of fugitive slaves and therefore a tacit recognition of the essential nature of the Constitution's fugitive slave clause.

The understanding by the founding generation of the essential nature of the Constitution's fugitive slave clause, evidenced by these efforts, was subsequently recognized and articulated in a series of judicial decisions, principally by the Supreme Court, but also lower courts. Thus, in 1842, in *Prigg v. Pennsylvania*, Justice Story, after stating that "it cannot be doubted that *it* [ie the fugitive slave clause] *constituted a fundamental article, without the adoption of which the Union could not have been formed* [emphasis added],"[370] went on to say:

> [I]f the Constitution had not contained this clause . . . [it] would have created the most bitter animosities, and engendered perpetual strife between the different states. The clause was, therefore, of the last importance to the safety and security of the southern states; and could not have been surrendered by them without endangering their whole property in slaves. The clause was accordingly adopted into the Constitution by the unanimous consent of the framers of it; a proof at once of its intrinsic and practical necessity.[371]

Story's observation about the "fundamental" nature of the Constitution's fugitive slave clause echoed earlier decisions of state courts, especially those of William Tilghman, chief justice of the Pennsylvania Supreme Court,[372] which were endorsed by the United States Supreme Court, in 1847, in *Jones v. Van Zandt*, where Justice Woodbury described the fugitive slave clause as "one of [the Constitution's] sacred compromises."[373] Furthermore, in a speech, in 1850, then future justice of the Supreme Court, Benjamin Curtis, said that "it was . . . certain, that the Union could not have been formed, and the Constitution adopted, without this article."[374] And, in 1853, in *Miller v. McQuerry*, Justice John McLean affirmed that "without a provision on the subject [of fugitive slaves] no constitution could have been adopted."[375]

Some scholars have contested Story's assertion that the fugitive slave clause was "a fundamental article" in relation to the adoption of the Constitution.[376] For example, Paul Finkelman suggests that, because there was little debate over the fugitive slave clause at either the Philadelphia Convention or during the debates over the ratification of the Constitution, Story's assertion should be rejected.[377] However, that the Convention unanimously agreed to the fugitive slave clause was no surprise, given that the Confederation Congress, of which several Convention delegates were members and voted at, had unanimously agreed to a fugitive slave clause in the Northwest Ordinance that was adopted six weeks before the fugitive slave clause was first proposed at the Convention. And, as Finkelman recognizes, the Northwest Ordinance's fugitive slave clause "was an important victory for slavery."[378] Furthermore, Finkelman's argument really relates to whether the fugitive slave clause was a controversial issue at that time. Whether the clause was a fundamental or essential part of the Constitution is a different question to that of whether it was a subject of controversy at the time. It was not controversial, as indicated by its unanimous acceptance. But it was essential because both sides of the sectional conflict over slavery needed it. Northerners, for the reasons stated above, needed the fugitive slave clause in order keep fugitive slaves out of their States. Southerners needed it to keep their slaves within their States. In the words of George Van Cleve, unanimity over the fugitive slave clause was achieved because "controlling fugitive slavery . . . served the congruent sociopolitical interests of the various states."[379] This reality meant that both pro- and antislavery delegates clearly understood, as Andrew Delbanco writes, "that if there had been no provision for recovering fugitive slaves, there would have been no nation."[380]

Conclusion

In evaluating the significance of the Constitution's provisions dealing with slavery, an institution that most of the founding generation regarded as immoral, the mere presence of several provisions preserving and protecting slavery that were, as Joseph Fishkin and William Forbath state, "deeply embedded into the architecture of the Constitution"[381] would indicate its central importance to the Constitution and the Union that it created. In relation to the critical provisions for the purposes of this book's argument, namely, the admission of new states and territories clauses and the fugitive slave clause, their centrality was made quite clear at the time the Constitution was being drafted and subsequently ratified. When these provisions are considered together with the three-fifths clause and the slave importation clause, it is true, as Georgia's William Pierce Jr. put it at the Philadelphia Convention, that "the dissonant interests of the different parts of the Union, made it impossible to give [the proposed Constitution] any other shape or form."[382] The reason for this was bluntly stated by his fellow delegate from South Carolina, Pierce Butler, when he said that the southern slave States needed "[t]he security . . . that their negroes would not be taken from them which some [people] . . . have a very good mind to do."[383]

The Constitution, with its slavery provisions, was, as Mark Graber argues, a document in which the founders were shown to be incapable of realizing or living up to the principles of equality proclaimed in the opening paragraphs of the Declaration of Independence.[384] Gary Nash makes the same point when he writes that "[t]he revolutionary generation's problem was not in its conception of universal rights, as expressed in the [Declaration of Independence], but rather its inability to honor them."[385] This constituted what Graber refers to as a "constitutional evil" and was committed notwithstanding that the overwhelming majority of the founders, both slaveholders and non-slaveholders, knew that slavery was immoral. As late as 1860, Sidney George Fisher, the nationalist lawyer and anti-secessionist, wrote, approvingly, that the Constitution "was not made for [slaves.] . . . [T]hey are not part of our people, they are not even men, they are property," with the consequence that "[they] cannot participate in our liberty [or] in our constitution."[386] The radical secessionist, William L. Yancey, made the same point at the Alabama secession convention when, in summing up the revolutionary period that led to the ratification of the Constitution, he said:

> The Declaration of Independence brought Freedom, with its guaranties of self-government, and of the writ of habeas corpus, and trial by jury to the white race alone. The Articles of Confederation were based upon this order of things; and the Federal Constitution, designed as a "more perfect Union," but perfected and perpetuated the great distinction. It was made by our ancestors, in their own expressive language, "to secure the blessings of liberty to ourselves and our posterity." In was founded on the inseparable and divinely instituted relation of freedom to the white man and slavery to the black man, of a political, civil and moral distinction, between the destinies of the children of Ham and of the descendants of Shem and Japheth.[387]

That the founding generation was prepared to adopt such a Constitution was because they believed that, by constitutionally entrenching slavery, it would, as Graber writes, "prevent irreconcilable sectional differences from disrupting national union, their most valued constitutional commitment."[388] This was what Abraham Lincoln was referring to when he said that, although slavery was "morally wrong,"[389] the slavery provisions in the Constitution were included because its framers "were obliged to bow to necessity."[390] Thus, the protection and preservation of slavery was an "end" for which the Constitution was established. The admission of new states and territories clauses contributed to this "end" by enabling slavery's expansion into the Union's territories and, eventually, the states that they spawned. The fugitive slave clause, in dealing with what Joseph Story, writing extrajudicially, referred to a "a subject so delicate to Southern interests,"[391] contributed to this "end" by, as he said in *Prigg v. Pennsylvania*, "secur[ing] to the citizens of slaveholding states the complete right and title to ownership of their slaves, as property, in every state in the Union into which they might escape."[392] Reflecting on the decision twelve months later, the antislavery former president John Quincy Adams in substance made the same point when he wrote that the court's decision confirmed "the transcendent omnipotence of slavery in these United States, riveted by [the fugitive slave clause]."[393] As Jack Rakove concludes, in his detailed account of the drafting and ratification of the Constitution, the Constitution's euphemisms for slavery "could never disguise its accommodation of slavery as a fundamental element in the structure of American politics and law."[394]

It is thus understandable that the Confederation's slave States, when ratifying the Constitution, were satisfied that it adequately secured and protected slavery. For example, in January 1788, in his speech to the South Carolina House of Representatives, Charles Cotesworth Pinckney said:

> We have a security that the general government can never emancipate them [i.e. slaves], for no such authority is granted; . . . We have obtained a right to recover our slaves in whatever part of America they may take refuge, which is a right we had not before. In short, considering all circumstances, we have made the best terms for the security of this species of property it was in our power to make. We would have made better if we could; but, on the whole, I do not think them bad.[395]

Similarly, in February 1788, in the leadup to the Virginia ratification convention, in reference to "the property we have in slaves," George Nicholas, a delegate to the convention, wrote that "we can venture to say that the new government will be the best security that we can have for retaining that property."[396]

In a circuit court opinion in 1833, Justice Henry Baldwin of the Supreme Court stated that "although [slavery's] existence is abhorrent to all our ideas of natural right and justice," the Constitution created a system by which "the foundations of government are laid, and rest upon the rights of property in slaves."[397] That such a Constitution could be fairly described as a proslavery document was something that slaveholders and many, but not all, abolitionists both agreed upon. This was confirmed, in 1844, by the publication of *The Constitution, A Pro-Slavery Compact*, a pamphlet complied by Wendell Phillips, a radical abolitionist and colleague of William Lloyd Garrison. This pamphlet extracted relevant parts of the proceedings of the Philadelphia Convention dealing with slavery as recorded in James Madison's notes that were published in 1840. There was little that proslavery advocates could object to in Phillips' pamphlet. Thus, in November 1847, in a letter to John C. Calhoun, John A. Campbell, the proslavery Alabama politician and future justice of the Supreme Court, wrote:

> Garrison & Phillips say that the Constitution . . . is a pro-slavery contract—containing powerful & stringent securities for the slaveholder. Phillips has written quite an able pamphlet to prove this—a pamphlet we might circulate to great advantage excluding a few paragraphs.[398]

It was thus not surprising that, in 1850, Frederick Douglass, pithily commented that "Garrison sees in the Constitution precisely what John C. Calhoun sees there."[399]

According to George Van Cleve, the proslavery spirit at the Constitutional Convention produced a "slaveholders' union" in which the "Constitution's formal and informal protections for slavery resembled a broad and well-built canal through which the growing river of slave labor could flow unimpeded."[400] Michael and Luke Paulsen make the same point when they write that "[t]he Constitution's protections of slavery, when combined, were worse than the sum of their parts. Together . . . [they] tended to reinforce each other and make the institution of slavery stronger and stronger."[401] The Constitution was designed to ensure that Southern slave States would join the new Union formed by the ratification of the Constitution. So successful was the Constitution in this respect that, by 1860, it was, as Van Cleve notes, "an obstacle to ending black slavery in America."[402] It was thus hardly surprising that in the winter of 1860–1861, during the targeted efforts at keeping the southern slave states within the Union, northern non-slave states were willing to maintain "a slaveholder's union." This is most convincingly demonstrated by the proposed Corwin amendment to the Constitution[403] that was ratified by Kentucky, Ohio, Rhode Island, Maryland, Illinois, and the legislature of the emerging state of West Virginia.[404] By its terms, this proposed amendment would have expressly guaranteed the perpetuation of slavery in the states where it already existed.[405] Amongst the various proposals to resolve the secession crisis, this was the only one that was approved by Congress—a Congress that no longer contained members from a number of slave states that had by then declared their independence from the Union. It was also endorsed at the time by Abraham Lincoln, in his First Inaugural Address,[406] and William H. Seward.[407] Whether it was simply too late, given that seven states had declared their independence by then, or, as is suggested by Raymond Diamond, it was "intransigence"[408] on the part of the pro-secessionists in the South that led to this proposal falling by the wayside is a matter that can be debated. However, whatever view one may take on this issue, the fact remains that the eleven slave states that declared their independence from the "more perfect Union" formed in 1788 did so with the intent of establishing a more perfect slaveholders' union in 1861. These eleven slave states argued that, because there had been breaches of some of the

Constitution's essential slavery provisions detailed in this chapter, on the basis of the compact theory of the Constitution, they were entitled to unilaterally secede from the Union. Whether such breaches did take place is explored in the next chapter.

4

"Towards a More Perfect Slaveholders' Union?"

Breaches of the Constitution's Slavery Provisions

On 7 February 1861, Senator Robert Ward Johnson, a dominant player in Arkansas politics, asserted that the right of secession claimed by the Confederate states was "amply justified by the systematic violation of the Constitution by the Northern States."[1] This sentiment was echoed, fourteen days later, when Jefferson Davis, in his Farewell Address to the Senate, said: "It has been a conviction of pressing necessity, it has been a belief that we are to be deprived in the Union of the rights which our fathers bequeathed to us, which has brought Mississippi into her present position."[2]

In Chapter 2, it was argued that the preferred view as to the nature of the Constitution was that, pursuant to the compact theory of the Constitution, a state had a constitutional right to unilaterally secede if, in the words of John C. Calhoun, "the [Constitution] should fail to fulfil the ends for which it was established."[3] In Chapter 3, it was argued that various Constitutional provisions relating to slavery served the "end" of protecting and preserving slavery. In a letter to the people of Georgia written on 6 December 1860—two days before he resigned as secretary of the treasury in the administration of President James Buchanan—Howell Cobb set out the two provisions of the Constitution that had been breached and therefore justified the unilateral secessions of the Confederate states. They were the Constitution's admission of new states and territories clauses, by which citizens had "the right to go with their slave property into the common territories of the Union" and the fugitive slave clause, by which "the owner of a slave is entitled to reclaim his property in any State into which the slave may escape."[4]

If there were breaches of the Constitution stemming from either, or both, of the admission of new states and territories clauses or the fugitive slave clause, then affected slave states could unilaterally secede from the Union and thereby no longer be bound by the Constitution. Although nationalists rejected the compact theory of the Constitution, they did, nevertheless, concede that, if it was correct, breaches of the Constitution did, in principle, give rise to the right of a state to unilaterally secede from the Union.

This chapter argues that breaches stemming from both the Constitution's admission of new states and territories clauses and its fugitive slave clause did occur.

An important preliminary issue that needs to be analyzed relates to who were the parties that committed these breaches. As detailed in Chapter 2, the compact theory of the Constitution held that the parties to the constitutional compact were the states of the Union. Thus, if a state breached the Constitution, any state affected by that breach was entitled to unilaterally secede from the Union. Given that breaches stemming from the Constitution's fugitive slave clause were alleged to have been committed by several northern non-slave states, such breaches would have entitled affected states to unilaterally secede from the Union.

However, the breach stemming from the admission of new states and territories clauses was alleged to have been committed not by a state, but rather by the incoming Republican administration following the 1860 elections. This administration, or federal government, was not a party to the constitutional compact, but a creation of it. The question that this raised was whether a breach by an entity that was not a party to the constitutional compact entitled affected states to unilaterally secede from the Union. It could be argued that because the breach was not committed by a party to the constitutional compact, it could not give rise to a right of a state to unilaterally secede from the Union. However, it is argued below that there are bases upon which affected states could unilaterally secede even though a breach was committed by the federal government, rather than one or more states.

The remainder of this chapter will demonstrate that the Confederate states based their right of unilateral secession on alleged breaches of the Constitution, more specifically those related to slavery in the territories and new states and fugitive slaves. In dealing with the breach related to the admission of new states and territories clauses, a particular issue relevant to it will also be covered, namely the fact that seven states from the Deep South seceded from the Union before the Republican administration took office on 4 March 1861. The conclusion that is reached is that, pursuant to the compact theory of the Constitution, both the breach stemming from the Constitution's admission of new states and territories clauses as well as the breaches stemming from its fugitive slave clause gave rise to a constitutional right of affected slave states to unilaterally secede from the Union. This they did by declaring their independence from the Union in the secession winter of 1860–1861.

The Entities Committing the Breaches

As detailed in Chapter 2, the compact theory of the Constitution held that the Constitution was a compact or contract between the states. The compact theory's recognition of a right of a state to unilaterally secede from the Union was based upon an application by analogy of common law rules concerning contracts. This analogy is appropriate. At the Virginia ratification convention, James Madison said that the Constitution was to be formed by "the people as composing thirteen sovereignties,"[5] and analogized the ratification of the Constitution to "mak[ing] a contract."[6] If the principles of contract law are analogized to the making of the Constitution, they can also be analogized to the rights of the Constitution's "sovereignties" in relation to breaches of the Constitution.

The important contract law rule that applied by analogy to the right to unilaterally secede from the Union in the event of breaches of the Constitution was set out by Theophilus Parsons, the Dane Professor of Law at Harvard University from 1848 to 1870, in his treatise on contract law, first published in 1853. The rule relates to actual breaches of contract, and, as set out by Parsons, stipulates that "a breach of a condition [of the contract] is a breach of the whole contract, which gives to the other party the right of avoiding or rescinding it altogether."[7] Joseph Story made the same point when he wrote that, in the private law of contract, "each party . . . has an equal right to judge of its terms, to enforce its obligations, and to insist upon redress for any violation of them."[8] Story accepted that if the compact theory of the Constitution was correct, the contract rule applied by analogy to the Constitution, with the consequence that breaches of the constitutional compact meant that "each [state] retain[ed] the power to withdraw from the confederacy."[9] In applying contract law by analogy, it must be kept in mind that a breach of contract may be an actual breach of one of its conditions, or it may be a repudiation or renunciation of one's obligation under the contract.

Applying contract law by analogy to the Constitution, the relevant breaches are breaches of any of the Constitution's slavery provisions. This is so because, as provisions that were included in the Constitution to fulfil the "end" of protecting and preserving the institution of slavery, they are analogous to conditions, or what is also referred to as the essential terms of a contract. The right of "avoiding or rescinding [the contract] altogether" is the equivalent of a state unilaterally seceding from the Union. The application of contract law to the right of Confederate states to unilaterally secede from the Union was expressly asserted by South Carolina in its "Declaration of the Immediate Causes Which Induce and Justify the Secession of South Carolina," which stated:

> [W]e hold . . . that the mode of [the Constitution's] formation subjects it to a . . . fundamental principle, namely: the law of compact. We maintain that in every compact between two or more parties, the obligation is mutual; that the failure of one of the contracting parties to perform a material part of the agreement, entirely releases the obligation of the other.[10]

The Declaration went on to state that, because "the ends for which this Government was instituted have been defeated, and the Government itself has been made destructive of them by the action of the non-slaveholding States,"[11] the affected slave states had the right to exercise their right to rescind the constitutional compact by seceding from the Union.

In relation to breaches stemming from the Constitution's fugitive slave clause, it is clear that the breaches were alleged to have been committed by a number of the Union's non-slaveholding states. Such breaches constituted an application by analogy of actual breaches of a contract. If such breaches were established, they were committed by parties to the constitutional compact, and therefore entitled the affected slave states to unilaterally secede from the Union. Thus, in a speech in 1851, Daniel Webster said:

> How absurd is it to suppose that when different parties enter into a compact for certain purposes, either can disregard any one provision, and nevertheless expect the other to observe the rest! . . . [I]f the Northern

> States refuse, wilfully and deliberately, to carry into effect that part of the Constitution which respects the restoration of fugitive slaves, and Congress provide no remedy, the South would no longer be bound to observe the compact. A bargain cannot be broken by one side and still bind the other side.[12]

However, the breach of the Constitution stemming from the admission of new states and territories clauses was not alleged to have been committed by a state or states, but rather by the incoming Lincoln administration following the 1860 elections. Initially, it can be noted that such a breach is not analogous to an actual breach of contract, as in the case of breaches of the Constitution's fugitive slave clause, but to a repudiation or renunciation of the contract.

Given that the breach associated with the new states and territories clauses was allegedly committed by the federal government and not a state or states, such a breach was not committed by a party to the constitutional compact, with the consequence, it was argued, that such a breach did not trigger the right of an affected state to unilaterally secede from the Union. This argument was articulated by Joseph Story, amongst others.[13] Story, accepting, for the purpose of the argument, that the compact theory of the Constitution was correct, rejected the claim that a state could unilaterally secede from the Union in the event of any breach of the Constitution by the federal government. In relation to such a claim, he wrote:

> The difficulty of maintaining it, however, seems absolutely insuperable. The federal government is the result of the constitution, or (if the phrase is deemed by any person more appropriate) the creature of the compact. How, then, can it be a party to that compact, to which it owes its existence? How can it be said, that it has entered into a contract, when at the time it had no capacity to contract; and was not even *in esse*? If any provision was made for a general government's becoming a party, and entering into a compact, after it was brought into existence, where is that provision to be found? It is not to be found in the constitution itself. Are we at liberty to *imply* such a provision, attaching to no power given in the constitution? This would push the doctrine of implication to an extent truly alarming; to draw inferences, not from what is, but from what is not, stated in the instrument. But, if any such implication could exist, when did

> the general government signify its assent to become such a party? When did the people authorize it to do so, without the express authority of the people?[14]

However, the argument mounted by Story and others against the existence of such a right in these circumstances is, for the following reasons, flawed, and should be rejected.

First, as Abel Parker Upshur argued in response to Story, the federal government, as a creation of the constitutional compact, was in fact the creation of the states as parties to that compact. Upshur wrote that the federal government was "the creature of [the] agreement which was made by the States as parties [to the Constitution]," which meant that it was "a mere agent, entrusted with limited powers for certain specified objects."[15] Upshur argued that a breach of the constitutional compact by the federal government meant, on agency principles, that there was a breach by the states, who were parties to the constitutional compact. Subsequently, this argument was detailed by John C. Calhoun when he wrote that secession of a state is allowed "where the intention of the association, or Union, *has failed*, either by an abuse of power on the part of its members, or other causes."[16] The "other causes" referred to by Calhoun arose when the federal government, acting as an agent in relation to powers delegated to it by the Constitution, exercised a power in a manner "such as *to defeat the object of the association or union.*" Such an exercise of power "would then become an abuse of power on the part of the principals [i.e., the states]; and thus present a case where secession would apply; but in no other, could it be justified."[17] That the federal government was an agent for the states is supported by the resolution of the Senate in 1838, which stated that the federal government "was instituted and adopted by the Several States of this Union as a common agent, in order to carry into effect those powers which they had delegated by the Constitution."[18]

A second argument upon which breaches by the federal government could give rise to the right of a state to unilaterally secede stems from the possibility of there being, as Story conceded, an implied term in the Constitution to that effect. Thus, Story recognized that, just as terms may be implied into a contract,[19] obligations or rights may be implied into the Constitution. Story correctly dismissed the proposition that there is an implied term to the effect that the federal government is a party to the constitutional compact. However, in contract law there is nothing that prevents the implication of a term that gives a contracting party the right to terminate the contract term in circumstances that arise but are not caused by either party to the contract. Applying that contract law rule by analogy, a breach of the Constitution by the federal government could, by implication, give rise to a right of an affected state to unilaterally secede from the Union, especially so given that the federal government was a creation of the state parties to the constitutional compact. Such a right can, on the basis of necessity, be implied in relation to breaches of the Constitution by the federal government. The argument here stems from the fact that, although both state and federal governments exercise legislative powers, in each case the extent of this legislative competence is circumscribed. Story conceded that under the compact theory of the Constitution, if a state exceeded its legislative powers, affected states had a right to unilaterally secede from the Union.[20] If so, then the same right must necessarily be implied in relation to instances of the federal government exceeding its legislative powers. The necessity of the implication can be illustrated by reference to the alleged breaches stemming from the Constitution's fugitive slave clause and its admission of new states and territories clauses. These were essential to the Constitution as they served the "end" of protecting and preserving the institution of slavery. If a breach stemming from the Constitution's fugitive slave clause gave rise to the right of a state to unilaterally secede from the Union, it would be incongruous if a breach stemming from the Constitution's admission of new states and territories clauses did not, simply on account of the fact that it was committed by the federal government rather than a state. In order to overcome this incongruity, it is necessary to imply a right into the Constitution that gives rise to the right of a state to unilaterally secede from the Union in circumstances where the breach is one committed by the federal government.

Secession Based upon Alleged Breaches Stemming from the Constitution's Essential Slavery Provisions

Although secessionists asserted various, and at times numerous, violations of their rights, the Confederate states' claim to a legal right of secession pursuant to the compact theory of the Constitution could only be based upon establishing at least one of two specified breaches of the

Constitution's essential provisions associated with slavery. The first concerned *actual* breach by various non-slave states of the Constitution's fugitive slave clause. The second concerned the *repudiation* by the federal government that came to power in the wake of the 1860 elections of the constitutional limitation that Congress could not legislate to prohibit slavery in the Union's territories. The secession ordinances of the eleven seceding slave states were brief and generally confined to declaring their independence from the Union. Only three made specific references to these two alleged breaches. Of the eleven seceding slave states, all except Tennessee held conventions of elected delegates to determine whether or not their state should secede. With the exception of Louisiana and North Carolina, these conventions adopted reports or issued statements that explicitly or implicitly referred to these two breaches as justifications for secession. Some of these states also did the same in the form of legislation or resolutions of their state legislatures. That Louisiana, North Carolina, and Tennessee justified secession on the same legal basis is evidenced from a variety of other sources.

It should also be noted that other sources such as speeches made or documents presented at the conventions, speeches made and pamphlets published by a variety of persons at the time, and newspaper editorials and commentaries, corroborate the claims that secession was justified upon the same alleged breaches of the Constitution.[21]

SOUTH CAROLINA

The opening two paragraphs of "Address to the People of Carolina," which was authorised for public distribution by South Carolina's secession convention, referred to the "unconstitutional wrongs, perpetrated by the people of the North on the people of the South" which caused "the overthrow of the Constitution of the United States" and justified South Carolina "dissolv[ing] her connexion with the States, constituting the United States."[22] The Address went on to reiterate this point when it asserted that, with the election of Lincoln to the presidency, the "experiment" that was the Constitution had "failed"[23] due to the actions of the North in "violat[ing] the express provisions of the Constitution."[24]

The critical breaches of the Constitution referred to in this document were clearly articulated in "Declaration of the Immediate Causes Which Induce and Justify the Secession of South Carolina," also approved by the South Carolina secession convention for public distribution. After first asserting that "fourteen of the States have deliberately refused for years past to fulfil their constitutional obligations,"[25] the Declaration referred to the Constitution's fugitive slave clause as being "so material to the compact, that without it that compact would not have been made," and then asserted that personal liberty legislation by non-slave states "led to a disregard of their obligations, and the laws of the General Government have ceased to effect the objects of the Constitution" in that they "either nullify the Acts of Congress or render useless any attempt to execute them." This meant that "the constitutional compact has been deliberately broken and disregarded by the non-slaveholding States."[26] On the incoming Republican government's policy of excluding slavery from the territories, the Declaration asserted that this meant that "[t]he Guaranties of the Constitution will then no longer exist; the equal rights of the States will be lost."[27]

MISSISSIPPI

On 29 November 1860, Mississippi's legislature passed legislation for the election of delegates to a convention "to adopt such measures for vindicating the sovereignty of [Mississippi], and the protection of its institutions."[28] On the following day, it adopted a resolution which highlighted the recognition of slavery in the Constitution and asserted that any action by "Congress, or any of the free States" to "impair its value or lessen its duration" would constitute "a violation of the compact of Union, and is destructive of the ends for which it was ordained." One such violation related to runaway slaves, where it was alleged that the "free States" had "by State intervention, obstructed and prevented their rendition under the fugitive slave law." Another was that these states "claim the right, and demand its execution by Congress, to exclude slavery from the Territories . . . and declare . . . their unutterable determination to exclude from admittance into the Union of any new State that tolerates slavery in its Constitution." The resolution concluded by asserting that the "secession of each aggrieved State is the proper remedy for these injuries."[29]

Following its secession, Mississippi's "Declaration of the Immediate Causes Which Induce and Justify the Secession of Mississippi" included amongst its "prominent reasons," all to do with slavery, the claim that the "dissolution of the Union" was justified on the ground that the non-slave states had "utterly broken the compact which our fathers pledged their faith to maintain." One such reason was the non-slave state laws that "nullified the Fugitive Slave Law in almost every free State in the Union." Another was the Republican Party policy that "refuses the admission of new slave states into the Union, and seeks to extinguish [slavery] by confining it within its present limits."[30]

FLORIDA

On 7 January 1861, Florida's secession convention adopted a resolution that asserted that, given that the "anti-slavery sentiment" in non-slave states threatened "the safety and honor of the slaveholding States," Florida had a right to unilaterally secede from the Union.[31] Two days later, the convention adopted a report which justified secession on the ground that Florida's people were no longer secure in relation to "the rights of life, liberty and property, and the pursuit of happiness, which were promised her on her admission to the Union," with the consequence that "[t]he contract is therefore wilfully and materially broken."[32] Given that it was "anti-slavery sentiment" that threatened "the safety and honor of the slaveholding States," it is clear that the words "liberty and property" in this report implicitly referred to constitutional provisions associated with fugitive slaves and slavery in the territories. Given, furthermore, that the this led to the Constitution being "wilfully and materially broken," the convention adopted its secession ordinance on the following day.[33]

ALABAMA

On 24 February 1860, Alabama's legislature foreshadowed possible secession when it adopted a resolution requiring the calling of a convention of delegates to consider Alabama's future in the event that the Republican Party won that year's presidential election. This course of action was deemed necessary because

> anti-slavery agitation persistently continued in the non-slaveholding States of the Union . . . marked at every stage . . . by contempt for the obligations of law and the sanctity of compacts, evincing a deadly hostility to the rights and institutions of the Southern people, and a settled purpose to effect their overthrow even by the subversion of the Constitution.[34]

On 7 January 1861, the opening day of Alabama's secession convention, Alabama's delegates unanimously adopted a resolution which, in its Preamble, asserted that the Union's "Constitution has been *violated*, both by the Government of the United States, and by a majority of the Northern States, in their separate legislative action, *denying* the people of the Southern States their Constitutional rights."[35]

A report by the convention's Committee of Thirteen recommending that Alabama join the confederacy of southern slave states referred to violations of the Constitution by "Northern States" in relation to runaway slaves which had the effect of "setting at naught one of the plainest provisions of the Federal Compact" together with "other dangerous misinterpretations of that instrument."[36] Finally, in the preamble to its secession ordinance, Alabama asserted that secession was justified on the ground that the newly elected Republican administration was "avowedly hostile to the domestic institutions [i.e. slavery] and the peace and security of the people of the State of Alabama" which had been preceded by "many and dangerous infractions of the constitution of the United States by many of the States and people of the Northern section."[37]

GEORGIA

In Georgia, a "Report," adopted by its secession convention, justified secession by reference to the actions of "non-slaveholding" states who, on "the subject of African slavery," had "persistently refused to comply with their express constitutional obligations to [the slave states] in reference to that property."[38] After referring to the personal liberty laws of non-slave states as being "in conflict with the clearest provisions of the Constitution," the "Report" asserted that they had the effect of rendering federal fugitive slave legislation "a dead letter, for all practicable purposes, in every non-slaveholding State in the Union."[39] In his letter to the people of Georgia, Howell Cobb claimed that the aim of these personal liberty laws was "to defeat the fugitive slave act of Congress and annul a plain provision of the Constitution of the United States."[40] Furthermore, the Report referred to, as an "insulting and unconstitutional demand," the assertion of non-slave states to a "right to exclude slavery" from what it had earlier described as "the common Territories of the Republic."[41] Cobb reiterated this claim when he asserted that the newly elected Republican administration would violate the Constitution by acting on its belief that it was "the duty of the Congress by law to prevent any Southern man from going into the common territories of the Union with his slave property."[42]

LOUISIANA

On 24 December 1860, Louisiana's governor, Thomas A. Moore, issued a proclamation convening his state's legislature for the purpose of enacting legislation for the election of delegates to that state's secession convention. In it, he referred to "a sectional and aggressive anti-slavery party, whose hostility to the people and institutions of the South has been evidenced by repeated and long continued violations of the Constitution."[43] On the first day of the convention, Moore referred to Abraham Lincoln's election victory as constituting "the threatened destruction of essential rights and most vital interests of the slaveholding States under the forms of a perverted Constitution."[44] A similar sentiment was expressed by Alcibiade DeBlanc, a convention delegate, who alleged that Republican Party members had "announced their determination to disregard the Constitution, laws, obligations, and judgments of the Courts of the Republic."[45] Other delegates indicated precisely what these constitutional violations were. Thus, Joseph R. Rozier asserted that the Republican Party had "proclaimed that slavery shall be prohibited . . . in the Territories" and that non-slave states had "passed laws with the design and effect of . . . preventing the operation of that clause in the Constitution and the laws of Congress, . . . in regard to the reclaiming of slaves, thus trampling one of the clearest and valued rights secured to the South by the Constitution and laws."[46] And William R. Miles asserted that non-slave states had "violated the Constitution . . . by enacting personal liberty laws, or laws nullifying or impeding the execution of the fugitive slave law."[47]

TEXAS

The Texas secession ordinance referred to the actions of the northern non-slave states as "violative of the compact between the States and the guarantees of the Constitution."[48] This assertion was reiterated in the "Declaration of the Causes which Impel the State of Texas to Secede," which asserted "that the federal constitution has been violated and virtually abrogated by the [northern] States."[49] One such violation was the personal liberty laws of northern states which were described as "legislative enactments, [which] have deliberately, directly or indirectly violated" the Constitution's fugitive slave clause and the federal legislation enacted pursuant to it, "thereby annulling a material provision of the [Constitution]."[50] In relation to the territories, the Declaration asserted that the Republican Party's policy was aimed at excluding "the citizens of the Southern States, unless under odious and unconstitutional restrictions, from the immense territory owned in common by all the States" which had the aim of "destroying the institutions [i.e., slavery] of Texas and her sister slaveholding States."[51]

VIRGINIA

Virginia's secession ordinance asserted that the "powers granted under the . . . Constitution" had been "perverted" by the "Federal Government . . . not only to the injury of the people of Virginia, but to the oppression of the Southern slaveholding States."[52]

In the light of the extensive debate at Virginia's secession convention, there is no doubt that the perversions of the Constitution included those related to the Constitution's fugitive slave clause and the issue of slavery in the territories. Thus, in relation to the right of slaveholders to the rendition of their runaway slaves, Henry L. Benning, Georgia's commissioner to Virginia, alleged that the northern states' "personal liberty bills were unconstitutional; they were deliberate infractions of the Constitution."[53] Commissioner John S. Preston, from South Carolina, asserted that northern states had "refused to carry out . . . provisions of the Constitution" relating to fugitive slaves by enacting "stringent laws to prevent the execution of those provisions."[54] Convention delegate George Baylor referred to northern non-slave states that had "passed [personal liberty] laws to obstruct the execution of the Fugitive Slave Law."[55] His fellow delegates Thomas F. Goode[56] and Henry A. Wise[57] both asserted that these personal liberty laws had "nullified" federal fugitive slave legislation.

In relation to the issue of slavery in the territories and new states, convention delegate George W. Richardson referred to "a wanton exercise of power on the part of [the] Northern majority to exclude Southern people from an equal right to carry their property into the Territories."[58] And Fulton Anderson, Mississippi's commissioner to Virginia, alleged that the Republican Party would seek, "by the exertion of bare-faced power, to exclude slavery from the public Territory, the common property of all the States."[59]

In relation to both the right of slaveholders to the rendition of their runaway slaves and the issue of slavery in the territories and new states, convention delegate Benjamin F. Wysor claimed that "[a] majority of [non-slave] States have persistently refused to comply with the provisions of the Federal Constitution for the rendition of fugitive slaves" and "denied [Virginia] and other slaveholding States an equal participation in the common territory of the United States, with the avowed object of confining slavery within its present limits," with the result that "the Constitution [had] been perverted."[60] His fellow delegate John R. Chambliss asserted that, as a result of a "spirit of pharisaical fanaticism," northern states had passed "laws to obstruct a law of Congress passed in pursuance of a plain provision of the Constitution" and "shown . . . their openly avowed determination to circumscribe the institution of slavery within the Territory of the States now recognizing it."[61]

ARKANSAS

Arkansas's secession ordinance referred to "well-founded causes of complaint" detailed in a resolution of its secession convention on 11 March 1861 as the basis for secession.[62] This resolution included, as "just causes of complaint," assertions that the northern states had "denied to the people of the southern states the right to equal participation in the benefits of the common territories of the Union . . . by declaring that no more slave states shall be admitted into the Union" as well as having, "in disregard of their constitutional obligations, obstructed the faithful execution of fugitive slave laws by enactments of their state legislatures."[63]

NORTH CAROLINA

On 20 December 1860, Alabama's commissioners to North Carolina, R. H. Smith and Isham V. Garrott, in a letter addressed to the North Carolina General Assembly, "the tone and sentiment of [which] met with approbation," asserted that non-slave states had committed "violations of their obligations [under the Constitution]." Smith and Garrott asserted that "the plain letter of the Constitution, providing for the rendition of fugitive slaves, has . . . been annulled by the non-slaveholding states" and that the Lincoln administration had a settled policy of "exclusion of the people of the South from the common Territories of the country."[64] And Samuel L. Hall, Georgia's commissioner to North Carolina, in addressing North Carolina's secession convention, referred to the fugitive slave legislation as having been "trampled under foot by Northern mobs, and nullified by Northern courts,"[65] and observed that non-slave states had "rendered the fugitive slave law . . . worse than a dead letter."[66]

TENNESSEE

Although Tennessee's ordinance of secession ordinance expressly "waive[d] any expression of opinion on the abstract doctrine of secession,"[67] allegations of breaches of the Constitution were nevertheless made in the leadup to secession. Unlike the other ten Confederate states, where the debate over secession took place in specially constituted conventions, in Tennessee the debate took place in its General Assembly.

On 7 January 1861, in a speech to the General Assembly urging support for a February 1861 referendum on the issue of whether a convention should be called to consider secession, Governor Isham G. Harris asserted that non-slave states had, by their "systematic, wanton, and long continued agitation of the slavery question," committed "actual and threatened aggressions . . . upon . . . well-defined constitutional rights," and then proceeded to list twenty-two specific wrongs or constitutional violations, all related to slavery, allegedly perpetrated by non-slave states. These aggressions included "deliberate Legislative enactments" which "openly and flagrantly nullified" federal legislation enacted pursuant to the Constitution's fugitive slave clause, as well as seeking "to appropriate to itself, and to exclude the slaveholder from the territory acquired by the common blood and treasure of all the States."[68] In relation to the latter, on 31 January 1861, in the House of Representatives, Representative William T. Avery referred to Republican Party policy which was adopted "in defiance of the Supreme Court" and which had the effect that Tennesseans "cannot carry [their] property into [the] common territory."[69] Although the referendum failed to carry, following the outbreak of armed conflict in April 1861, Harris called the General Assembly into session and urged his state to secede. On 6 May 1861, legislation was enacted to submit an ordinance of secession "to a vote of qualified voters . . . for their ratification or rejection."[70] On 8 June 1861, 69 percent of those who voted, voted to ratify the ordinance of secession.[71]

Breach Stemming from the Constitution's New States and Territories Clauses

Although the Supreme Court had in 1857, in *Dred Scott v. Sandford*,[72] ruled that the Constitution's new states and territories clauses did not allow Congress to prohibit slavery in the Union's territories, the

Republican Party's major policy going into the 1860 elections, which the Lincoln administration was committed to implementing, was to prevent slavery in the territories.

If a breach, stemming from the admission of new states and territories clauses, was committed by the Union's federal government, rather than a state, such a breach, as was argued above, nevertheless, gave affected states a right to secede from the Union. If so, this gives rise to two questions. The first is whether the Republican administration that took office, on 4 March 1861, committed such a breach. The second, is, even if it did, whether the breach served as a ground justifying the secession of the seven states from the Deep South that seceded *before* the Republican administration took office on 4 March 1861.

In relation to the first question, it is clear that prior to the secession of any of the Confederate states, the Republican administration did not commit an actual breach of the admission of new states and territories clauses. However, it is equally clear that, upon taking office on 4 March 1861, the administration would not abide by the ruling in *Dred Scott v. Sandford*, in that it would not allow slavery to expand into the Union's territories. As such, this constituted a breach of the Constitution by way of a repudiation of its new states and territories clauses. Indeed, before, during, and after the 1860 elections, both Lincoln and the Republican party were firmly committed to such a repudiation.

For the 1856 elections, the then fledgling Republican Party declared, in its platform, that it was "both the right and the imperative duty of Congress to prohibit in the Territories those twin relics of barbarism—Polygamy, and Slavery."[73] In his failed bid to be elected as a senator from Illinois, in 1858, Abraham Lincoln echoed this policy when he said that it was his "belief in the *right* and *duty* of Congress to prohibit slavery in all the United States Territories."[74] This was, and remained, as Lucas Morel states, "the raison d'être of the Republican Party."[75] In the 1860 election, the Republican Party's policy platform stipulated that, because "the normal condition of all the territory of the United States is that of freedom," a Republican Party administration would not give "legal existence to slavery in any territory of the United States," and that, as a consequence, Kansas should be "immediately admitted" to the Union as a non-slave state.[76]

During the frantic negotiations to resolve the secession crisis following the 1860 elections, Lincoln, as president-elect, repeatedly insisted that there could be no compromise agreement that permitted the spread of slavery into the territories.[77] Thus, on 10 December 1860, when Congress was considering the so-called Crittenden Compromise, in a letter to Senator Lyman Trumbull, Lincoln said: "Let there be no compromise on the question of *extending* slavery."[78] On the following day, in a letter to William Kellogg, he wrote: "Entertain no proposition for a compromise in regard to the *extension* of slavery."[79] When, on 13 December 1860, he urged Representative Elihu B. Washburne to "hold firm, as with a chain of steel," Lincoln made it clear that his objective was to sabotage the Crittenden Compromise because it involved allowing slavery into the territories above the line of latitude thirty-six degrees thirty minutes north as established by the Missouri Compromise.[80]

As a result of the Republican Party's policy against the expansion of slavery into the territories, slave states feared that Lincoln's administration would simply ignore the Supreme Court's ruling in *Dred Scott v. Sandford*. This fear was given credence by Lincoln himself when, in his First Inaugural Address, he said:

> I do not forget the position assumed by some, that constitutional questions are to be decided by the Supreme Court; nor do I deny that such decisions must be binding in any case, upon the parties to a suit, as to the object of that suit..... At the same time the candid citizen must confess that if the policy of the Government, upon vital questions, affecting the whole people, is to be irrevocably fixed by decisions of the Supreme Court, the instant they are made, in ordinary litigation between parties, in personal actions, the people will have ceased, to be their own rulers, having, to that extent, practically resigned their Government, into the hands of that eminent tribunal.[81]

Although Lincoln maintained that he had no plan "directly or indirectly, to interfere with the institution of slavery in the States where it exists" and furthermore, that he had "no lawful right to do so,"[82] there is no doubt that his party's policy against expansion of slavery into the territories was perceived as the first step towards the complete extinction of slavery in the Union. That Lincoln so thought is evident from his "House Divided" speech on 16 June 1858 when he said:

> I believe . . . [e]ither the *opponents* of slavery, will arrest the further spread of it, and place it where the public mind shall rest in the belief that it is

> in course of ultimate extinction; or its *advocates* will push forward, till it shall become alike lawful in *all* the States, *old* as well as *new—North* as well as *South*.[83]

Scholars have reached the same conclusion. For example, in his analysis of 175 speeches that Lincoln gave between 1854 and 1860, Waldo Braden concludes that Lincoln was essentially a "one-issue man" whose "central message" was the need to prevent slavery spreading into the territories as the first step to putting an end to slavery altogether.[84]

Slave state secessionists also believed that prohibiting slavery in the territories would inevitably lead to the demise of slavery everywhere in the Union. Thus, South Carolina's "Address to the People of Carolina" expressed this sentiment with the rhetorical question: "If it is right, to preclude or abolish slavery in a Territory—why should it be allowed to remain in the States?" It went on to assert that any submission by slave states to the incoming Republican administration would, "directly or indirectly," lead to "the emancipation of the slaves of the South."[85] South Carolina's "Declaration of the Immediate Causes Which Induce and Justify the Secession of South Carolina" similarly asserted that the installation of a new Republican Party administration would mean "that Slavery is in the course of ultimate extinction."[86] Georgia's "Report" asserted that the non-slave North's policy with respect to the territories was the "fixed purpose to limit, retrain and finally to abolish slavery in the States where it exists."[87] And Texas's "Declaration of the Causes which Impel the State of Texas to Secede" asserted that "the non-slaveholding States . . . demand the abolition of negro slavery throughout the confederacy."[88]

That the slave states had good reason to believe that the incoming Republican administration and Lincoln would do precisely what they said they would do was confirmed by their subsequent actions. Thus, during the secession winter of 1860–1861, on 29 January 1861, Kansas, governed by a constitution adopted in 1859, which banned slavery,[89] was admitted into the Union as a non-slave state.[90] In April 1862, Congress passed legislation that abolished slavery in the District of Columbia.[91] Two months later, in defiance of the decision in *Dred Scott v. Sandford*, Congress passed legislation that prohibited slavery in all of the Union's territories.[92]

In relation to the fact that seven Deep South states seceded before the

Republican administration formally assumed office on 4 March 1861, the question that arises is whether it can be said that they could claim that their secessions were legally justified on the basis of a breach committed by an administration that had not yet taken office. The argument here against legal justification of secession in relation to the admission of new states and territories clauses, can be sustained to a point, in that secession of any of these states prior to the elections on 6 November 1860 could not be based upon an alleged breach of the new states and territories clauses. However, following the elections of Lincoln and a new Congress on that date, the circumstances changed dramatically. Their elections rendered both the incumbent president, James Buchanan, and the then Congress, lame ducks. The stance and intentions on the issue of slavery in the territories that Lincoln and a Republican Party administration would adopt as of 4 March 1861 if it successfully contested the 1860 elections were well known and understood on polling day, and consistently restated by both Lincoln and members of the Republican administration-in-waiting after the election and through to taking office on 4 March 1861. In these circumstances, to argue that the seven Deep South states that seceded between polling day and 4 March 1861 could not base their legal argument for a right to secede based upon a breach of the Constitution's admission of new states and territories clauses, would be to give effect to form over substance, and should, therefore, be rejected.

Breaches Stemming from the Constitution's Fugitive Slave Clause

The allegations of breaches stemming from the Constitution's fugitive slave clause centered on the personal liberty laws enacted by non-slave states. These state laws were enacted in response to federal fugitive slave legislation in 1793 that was substantially strengthened in 1850. This federal legislation deprived runaway slaves of basic due process rights in the course of their rendition after capture. The state personal liberty laws sought to provide a modicum of due process rights to these slaves and thereby prevent free African Americans from being kidnapped and then sold into slavery.

Slave states objected to these personal liberty laws, claiming that they were unconstitutional. In this, they had respectable legal opinion on their side. An example of such opinion was provided by Senator Daniel

Webster, who had appeared as counsel before the Supreme Court in some of the major constitutional cases of the antebellum era and was regarded as one of the Union's preeminent constitutional lawyers. In a speech to the Senate, in March 1850, dealing with what he referred to as "the complaints of the South" in relation to personal liberty laws, Webster said that they had a "just foundation" and that "the North" had no right "in their legislative capacity . . . to endeavor to get round [the] Constitution, or to embarrass the free exercise of the rights secured by the Constitution to the persons whose slaves escape from them."[93] Webster went on to say that slave states had "a right to complain" and that the northern non-slave states had "been too careless of what . . . the Constitution peremptorily and emphatically enjoins upon [them] as a duty."[94] In the wake of this speech, Webster observed that "several of the States have enacted laws to hinder, obstruct, and defeat the [Fugitive Slave Act of 1793], to the utmost of their power,"[95] and described the personal liberty law enacted by Massachusetts in 1843 as "a penal act," by which "the Constitution and the law of Congress both become a dead letter" in Massachusetts.[96] To similar effect is a statement by President James Buchanan, whose status as an eminent lawyer is attested to by the fact that, earlier in his career, he was offered, but declined to accept, an appointment as a justice of the Supreme Court.[97] In December 1860, in his Annual Message to Congress, he made the point that "[t]he most palpable violations of constitutional duty which have yet been committed consist in the acts of different State legislatures to defeat the execution of the fugitive-slave law."[98] Finally, it can be noted that on 1 March 1860, the Senate adopted a resolution that stipulated that "all acts of individuals or of State Legislatures to defeat the purpose or nullify the requirements of the [Constitution's fugitive slave clause], and the laws made in pursuance of it, are hostile in character, subversive of the Constitution, and revolutionary in their effect."[99]

PRIGG V. PENNSYLVANIA

The views of these eminent lawyers were completely in accord with the Supreme Court's decision, in 1842, in *Prigg v. Pennsylvania*. In that case the Supreme Court upheld the constitutional validity of the Fugitive Slave Act of 1793 (FSA 1793). However, the court also had to consider the constitutional validity of Pennsylvania's personal liberty law of 1826. Section I of this law stipulated that any person who, by force, removed from Pennsylvania any "negro or mulatto" would be guilty of kidnapping punished by means of a fine and imprisonment. Section II imposed similar penalties on any person who sold or purchased "any negro or mulatto." The remainder of the law stipulated procedures for the legal removal of alleged runaway slaves. Section VI required a claimant of an alleged runaway slave to obtain from a Pennsylvania court a certificate of removal before the runaway slave could be taken out of Pennsylvania. To obtain such a certificate, the claimant had to establish that the alleged runaway slave was a slave that he or she owned. Evidence from the claimant was not admissible on this matter.[100]

The facts of *Prigg v. Pennsylvania* concerned the slave Margaret Morgan, who had moved from Maryland to Pennsylvania and who was alleged to belong to Margaret Ashmore. Edward Prigg and Nathan Bemis were engaged by Ashmore to bring Morgan back to Maryland. Prigg and Bemis made an unsuccessful application to the Pennsylvania court for a certificate of removal. Nevertheless, they forcibly removed Morgan from Pennsylvania and returned her to Maryland. Prigg and Bemis were convicted of breaching the Pennsylvania personal liberty law. On appeal to the Supreme Court, their convictions were overturned.

Justice Joseph Story, in delivering the opinion of the court, ruled that Pennsylvania's personal liberty law was "unconstitutional and void"[101] on the ground that the Constitution provided that "the power of legislation on [fugitive slaves] to be exclusive in Congress."[102] States could not enact legislation that, as Story put it, "interrupts, limits, delays, or postpones the right of the owner to the immediate possession of the slave."[103] Story described the rights of the slaveowner in this context as follows:

> [T]he owner must . . . have the right to seize and repossess the slave, which the local laws of his own state confer upon him as property; and we all know that this right of seizure and recaption is universally acknowledged in all the slaveholding states. Indeed, this is no more than a mere affirmance of the principles of the common law applicable to this very subject. . . . . [U]nder and in virtue of the Constitution, the owner of a slave is clothed with entire authority, in every state in the Union, to seize and recapture his slave, whenever he can do it without any breach of the peace, or any illegal violence.[104]

Pennsylvania's response to the decision in *Prigg v. Pennsylvania* came in the form of personal liberty legislation in 1847. This legislation

(1) made it a criminal offence to remove free blacks from the state with the intention enslaving them (Sections 1 and 2); (2) withdrew Pennsylvania's cooperation in enforcing the FSA 1793 (Section 3); (3) granted a modicum of protection to fugitive slaves by fining a person who breached the peace by unlawfully seizing an alleged fugitive slave (Section 4); (4) reaffirmed a court's power to issue a writ of habeas corpus (Section 5); (5) removed the prohibition on slaves being able to testify in court (Section 7); and (6) denied the use of state prisons to hold suspected fugitive slaves (Section 6),[105] although this section of the legislation was repealed in 1852.[106]

Following the passage of the Fugitive Slave Act 1850 (FSA 1850), antislavery sentiment in northern states markedly increased. A contributing factor to this increase was the legislation's requirement that, when called upon, citizens were to participate in the rendition of fugitive slaves. By 1860, in addition to the Pennsylvania legislation of 1847, Connecticut (1844, 1848, and 1854), Maine (1855 and 1857), Massachusetts (1843, 1855, 1858, and 1859), Michigan (1855), New Hampshire (1846 and 1857), New Jersey (1846), Ohio (1847 and 1857), Rhode Island (1848 and 1854), Wisconsin (1857), and Vermont (1843, 1850, 1854, and 1858) enacted personal liberty legislation in response to either the decision in *Prigg v. Pennsylvania* or the FSA 1850.[107] As Larry Gara observes, "[o]n the surface [these] laws provided legal protection for Free negroes but they were designed to impede the enforcement of the federal statute."[108] Andrew Delbanco, after noting that these laws were "greeted in the South with something between exasperation and outrage," summarizes their aims as follows:

> They prohibited state officers from assisting, and state facilities from being used, in the capture of fugitives under federal law. They included provisions intended to protect free blacks from kidnapping and, in direct conflict with the law of 1850, to prevent the return of runaways without due process (by which was meant jury trial) in the state of capture.[109]

Vermont's personal liberty laws are a good illustration of this summary. In November 1850, its Habeas Corpus Law stipulated that: (1) Vermont's attorneys had a duty to "protect, defend, and procure to be discharged" any person in Vermont "arrested or claimed as a fugitive slave" (Section 2); (2) Vermont's attorneys could obtain a writ of habeas corpus for any person "arrested, claimed, or imprisoned as a fugitive slave" (Section 3); and (3) Vermont's judicial and executive officers had a duty to notify a state's attorney if they had reason to believe that any person in Vermont was "about to be arrested or claimed as a fugitive slave" (Section 4). In commenting on this legislation, Vermont's governor asserted that Vermont considered a fugitive slave as a "citizen."[110] In 1858, Vermont passed further legislation which stated, inter alia, that (1) no person within Vermont could be "considered as property" (Section 1); (2) persons claimed to be fugitive slaves had a right to trial by jury (Section 3); (3) persons attempting to recover fugitive slaves, other than in accordance with the provisions of this legislation, would be fined between $500 and $2000 or be imprisoned for a period of up to ten years (Section 4); (4) fugitive slaves that arrived in Vermont would be freed (Section 6); and (5) any person who held or attempted to hold a person in the state of slavery would be imprisoned for a period of one to ten years and fined a maximum of $2000.[111] The personal liberty laws in other states also had significant penalties attached to persons attempting to reclaim fugitive slaves, with fines ranging from $1000 to $5000 and imprisonment from between three months to fourteen years.[112]

ABLEMAN V. BOOTH

The 1850s also witnessed a series of highly publicized slave escapes and rescues of slaves from captivity that were assisted by existing vigilance and safety committees in the northern non-slave states.[113] The decade also saw much of the free African American abolitionist movement abandon its erstwhile nonviolent resistance to slavery in favor of a more militant approach that countenanced the use of force.[114] The climactic legal event of the decade was the Supreme Court decision, in 1859, in *Ableman v. Booth*.[115]

The essential facts of this complex case concerned the federal prosecution of Sherman Booth, a fiery abolitionist and newspaper editor, for his role in the rescue from jail and escape to Ontario of the fugitive slave Joshua Glover in March 1854. Following his conviction for violating the FSA 1850, Booth sought his freedom by applying to a state court in Wisconsin for a writ of habeas corpus. When the writ was granted, Stephen Ableman, the responsible US marshal appointed pursuant to the FSA 1850, appealed to the Wisconsin Supreme Court, which ordered Booth's release from federal custody. Furthermore, in a decision which Jeffery Schmitt describes as one in which "[t]he Wisconsin court used legal theory to effectively advance an ongoing social movement,"[116] by a two-to-one majority, the court ruled that the FSA 1850 was unconstitutional.[117] Ableman then turned to the federal legal structure, and a federal grand jury indicted Booth, who was again arrested and imprisoned. Following his conviction for aiding and abetting Glover's escape, Booth again successfully applied to the Wisconsin Supreme Court for a writ of habeas corpus.[118] In effect, the Wisconsin Supreme Court annulled the judgment of a federal court, in a decision that David Potter describes as an act of "nullification in a form that even John C. Calhoun had not advocated."[119] In *Ableman v. Booth*, the Supreme Court unanimously overturned the decision of the Wisconsin Supreme Court.

In delivering the opinion of the Supreme Court, Chief Justice Taney, after upholding the constitutional validity of the FSA 1850, reversed the Wisconsin Supreme Court decision, thereby upholding Booth's conviction. In due course, Booth was imprisoned, but was pardoned by President Buchanan on 3 March 1861, the day before Abraham Lincoln was inaugurated as president.[120]

In relation to the decision of the federal court to convict and imprison Booth for breaches of the FSA 1850, Taney ruled that the commissioner, who issued the warrant for Booth's arrest in relation to his involvement with Glover's escape, "had lawful authority to issue the warrant and commit [Booth] and that [the commissioner's] proceedings were regular and comformable to law."[121] In coming to that conclusion, Taney held that the federal courts had exclusive jurisdiction in relation to matters concerning federal government laws and that state courts had no jurisdiction in relation to the enforcement of such laws. Taney made it clear that when a petitioner was in the custody of a federal officer pursuant to federal law, a state court judge could not issue a writ of habeas corpus. In this respect, Taney said:

> We do not question the authority of State court, or judge, who is authorized by the laws of the State to issue the writ of *habeas corpus*, to issue it in any case where the party is imprisoned within its territorial limits, provided it does not appear, when the application is made, that the person imprisoned is in custody under the authority of the United States. The court or judge has a right to inquire, in this mode of proceeding, for what cause and by what authority the prisoner is confined within the territorial limits of the State sovereignty. . . . . But, . . . [once] the State judge or court

> [is] judicially apprized that the party is in custody under the authority of the United States, they can proceed no further. They then know that the prisoner is within the dominion and jurisdiction of another Government, and that neither the writ of *habeas corpus,* nor any other process issued under State authority, can pass over the line of division between the two sovereignties. He is then within the dominion and exclusive jurisdiction of the United States. If he has committed an offence against their laws, their tribunals alone can punish him. If he is wrongfully imprisoned, their judicial tribunals can release him and afford him redress.[122]

Taney went on to say that if there was any interference by state courts in the enforcement of a federal statute such as the FSA 1850, federal officials were duty-bound to resist such interference. In this respect, Taney said:

> [I]f the authority of a State, in the form of judicial process or otherwise, should attempt to control the marshal or other authorized officer or agent of the United States, in any respect, in the custody of his prisoner, it would be his duty to resist it, and to call to his aid any force that might be necessary to maintain the authority of law against illegal interference. No judicial process, whatever form it may assume, can have any lawful authority outside of the limits of the jurisdiction of the court or judge by whom it is issued; and an attempt to enforce it beyond these boundaries is nothing less than lawless violence.[123]

The decision in *Ableman v. Booth* effectively overruled existing and long-standing practice to the effect that a writ of habeas corpus could be issued by a state court judge in relation to a person held in the custody of a federal government official pursuant to a federal law, in this case the FSA 1850.[124]

The response of Wisconsin to the Supreme Court decision is significant in that it indicated that Wisconsin, and perhaps other northern non-slave states, would continue with their policy of nullifying the FSA 1850. On 19 March 1859, twelve days after the Supreme Court handed down its decision, the Wisconsin legislature passed a series of resolutions nullifying the effect of the Supreme Court decision. One of the resolutions, drawing directly on the wording of the Kentucky Resolution of 1798,[125] read as follows:

> That the principle and construction . . . that the general government is the exclusive judge of the extent of the powers delegated to it, is nothing short

> of despotism; . . . that the several states which formed the instrument being sovereign and independent, have the unquestionable right to judge of its infractions; and that a *positive defiance* of these sovereignties, of all unauthorized acts done under color of that instrument, is the rightful remedy.[126]

Furthermore, Governor Alexander W. Randall indicated that, in direct opposition to the Supreme Court decision, he would use the power of the state to enforce the earlier decisions of the Wisconsin Supreme Court.[127] The extent of popular support for the actions of the state of Wisconsin is attested to by the campaign, in the immediate wake of the Supreme Court decision in *Ableman v. Booth*, for the election of a judge to the Wisconsin Supreme Court. One of the candidates was Byron Paine, who, in 1854, as one of Booth's lawyers, had contended that in the North the Constitution was a "Charter of Freedom," while, in the South it was viewed as a "Charter of Slavery."[128] A notable speech in support of Paine's candidacy was delivered by the former German revolutionary turned antislavery activist and lawyer, Carl Schurz. Under the banner of "States Rights and Byron Paine," Schurz invoked the Virginia and Kentucky Resolution of 1798 in what his biographer describes as a "ringing speech . . . in defence of states' rights," in which Schurz "announced that centralization and liberty were incompatible" and that "[t]rue freedom could be preserved only by the states."[129] In this speech Schurz referred to John C. Calhoun as "a high democratic authority," before denouncing the Constitution as "not worth the paper on which it is printed, if the authority to construe it, is exclusively and absolutely vested in the central government."[130] In an election that had Wisconsin's highest voter turnout for an election for state office, Paine's comfortable victory was, as H. Robert Baker notes, "attributable, at least in part" to the electorate's rejection of the decision in *Ableman v. Booth*.[131]

Wisconsin's reaction to the decision in *Ableman v. Booth* reflected a continuing attitude of denying the constitutional validity of federal fugitive slave legislation. It mirrored the actions of many non-slave states to persist in enacting personal liberty laws following the *Prigg v. Pennsylvania* decision and the FSA 1850. Massachusetts proffered a justification for this approach when, on 6 April 1855, its legislature passed a resolution claiming that the federal government had no constitutional authority to enact fugitive slave legislation and that the FSA 1850 was a direct violation of the Constitution's Tenth Amendment.[132] Thus, it was hardly surprising that Wisconsin's reaction to *Ableman v. Booth* was, as Jeffrey Schmitt points out, cited by slave state secessionists as "a primary example of northern constitutional violations."[133]

However, with the increased likelihood of a victory of an antislavery Republican Party in the 1860 presidential election, support for states' rights in Wisconsin dissipated. As Schmitt points out, with the "Republicans expected to gain control of the national government in the 1860 election . . . a political theory that vested supreme political power in the states was no longer in their interests."[134] In the wake of Lincoln's electoral triumph, efforts were made to persuade non-slave states to repeal their personal liberty laws as a means of preserving the Union. Thus, in mid-December 1860, forty-two prominent persons from Massachusetts, headed by that state's former chief justice, Lemuel Shaw, called upon John A. Andrew, the incoming governor of Massachusetts, to push his state's legislature to repeal its personal liberty law as a means of supporting southern unionists and thereby preventing further secessions of southern slave states.[135] Although this call generated a vigorous debate over the validity of personal liberty laws, Andrew remained staunch in his support for retaining Massachusetts' existing personal liberty laws.[136] In his Annual Message to Congress, in December 1860, President Buchanan urged non-slave states to "repeal [their] unconstitutional and obnoxious enactments" which "[t]he Southern States, standing on the basis of the Constitution, have a right to demand [as an] act of justice from the States of the North."[137] Similarly, William H. Seward, soon to be Lincoln's secretary of state, in a speech to the Senate on 12 January 1861, recognized that personal liberty laws were unconstitutional, and said that they "ought to be repealed."[138] All these pleas were ignored, and as Thomas Morris notes, the "[personal liberty] laws passed through the secession crisis generally unscathed."[139] For example, in Vermont, a bill to repeal that state's personal liberty law was defeated by a two-thirds majority.[140]

Lincoln's electoral triumph engendered fear in slave states that non-slave state opposition to federal fugitive slave legislation would be accommodated by the new administration simply not enforcing it. In early January 1861, David Clopton, Alabama's commissioner to Delaware, gave voice to this fear when he said that "[l]aws passed . . . for the security and protection of property in slaves will avail nothing where their execution depends upon Republican appointees of a Republican President."[141] Salmon P. Chase, Lincoln's soon-to-be secretary of the treasury, gave credence to this belief a month later when, at the Peace Conference in Washington, he said:

> The people of the free States . . . who believe that slaveholding is wrong, cannot and will not aid in the reclamation [of fugitive slaves], and the [fugitive slave legislation] becomes therefore a dead letter.[142]

In his First Inaugural Address, Lincoln, in essence, reiterated Chase's statement when, first, he declined to "specify particular acts of Congress to be enforced," indicating only that he would "conform to, and abide by, all those acts which stand unrepealed"[143] and later went on to indicate the FSA 1850 could only be "as well enforced . . . as any law can ever be in a community where the moral sense of the people imperfectly supports the law itself."[144] It was thus hardly surprising that the secessionist slave states would claim[145] that the Lincoln administration would not be vigilant in enforcing federal fugitive slave legislation because, as Earl Maltz points out, "[t]he election of Lincoln in 1860 made it clear that [strong] support would not be forthcoming on issues relating to slavery."[146]

Conclusion

The declarations and deliberations of the Confederate states at the times of their secessions demonstrate that they asserted that essential constitutional provisions associated with slavery were breached, namely those associated with the new states and territories clauses and the fugitive slave clause. Pursuant to the compact theory of the Constitution, breaches of these provisions gave rise to a constitutional right of affected slave states to unilaterally secede from the Union.

The breach stemming from the Constitution's admission of new states and territories clauses was constituted by the Lincoln administration's declared policy of not permitting slavery in the Union's territories. On this issue, Lincoln was, as he said, "inflexible."[147] This policy was an unambiguous rejection of the Supreme Court's construction of the Constitution's admission of new states and territories clauses in *Dred Scott v. Sandford* and a repudiation of the limits that the Constitution placed on the powers of the federal government.

The breaches stemming from the Constitution's fugitive slave clause were the enactment of personal liberty laws by northern non-slave states. Adherents to the compact theory of the Constitution did not assert that an isolated breach of such legislation would trigger the right of an affected state to unilaterally secede. As Thomas Jefferson pointed out in 1799: "[W]e should never think of separation but for repeated and enormous violations" of the Constitution,[148] which is what was the case with the enactment of personal liberty laws on a multitude of occasions and, following the Supreme Court ruling in *Prigg v. Pennsylvania*, in the full knowledge that such legislation was unconstitutional. In relation to Wisconsin's defiance of the Constitution that culminated in the Supreme Court decision in *Ableman v. Booth*, James Read and Neal Allen aptly conclude that "nullification as practiced in the 1850s—whereby . . . Wisconsin's legislature nullified the US Supreme Court's ruling . . . was not a sustainable constitutional practice."[149] Wisconsin's defiance of the Supreme Court decision itself and the refusal by northern states to repeal their personal liberty laws in the wake of the Supreme Court decision, escalated the breach of the fugitive slave legislation well beyond the isolated act of a single state. The actions of the northern non-slave states in this context constituted breaches of the Constitution that triggered the right of unilateral secession.

Given that, as G. Edward White aptly notes, "the conditions of slavery and slaveholding were foundations of American Law" and that "[t]he Union of American states was a union with slavery at its foundation,"[150] these breaches gave rise to the right of affected states to unilaterally secede from the Union. As the breaches stemming from the Constitution's fugitive slave clause were committed by states that were parties to the constitutional compact, the Confederate states were entitled to unilaterally secede from the Union. This chapter has argued that, although the breach stemming from the Constitution's new states and territories clauses was committed by the federal government, rather than a state party to the constitutional compact, it nevertheless gave rise to the right of the Confederate states to unilaterally secede from the Union. However, even if it did not, the breaches stemming from the Constitution's fugitive slave clause were enough to trigger the right of the Confederate states to unilaterally secede from the Union.

5

The Final Word

As noted in the opening paragraph of the introduction to this book, 9 April 1865 effectively marked the end of the Civil War. It was also the death knell of the quest by the eleven southern slave states which had unilaterally seceded from the Union in 1860–1861 to form a more perfect slaveholders' union. Although the Union's military victory over the Confederacy preserved the territorial integrity of the Union, it left open the question of whether the secessions of the Confederate states were constitutionally lawful.

In 1869, in the case of *Texas v. White*, the Supreme Court ruled that Texas, and therefore also the other ten seceding states, had no legal right to unilaterally secede from the Union. Because it was, in the opinion of Chief Justice Chase, "needless to discuss at length" whether Texas's secession from the Union was "consistent with the Constitution of the United States,"[1] in delivering the opinion of the Supreme Court, he did so in only 452 words, the most famous of which were that "[t]he Constitution, in all its provisions, looks to an indestructible union, composed of indestructible states."[2]

This book's analysis of the Union's constitutional law as it stood at the time of the Confederate secessions questions the validity of Chase's ruling. In doing so, in assessing whether the Confederate states were entitled to unilaterally secede from the Union, the first critical question examined was whether, pursuant to the state of the Union's constitutional law as of 1860–1861, a state had, in particular circumstances, a constitutional right to unilaterally secede from the Union. If such a right did exist, the question that then arose was whether it was validly exercised by the Confederate states.

As detailed in Chapter 2, the question of whether a constitutional right of unilateral secession from the Union existed revolved around the relative merits of the nationalist and compact theories of the Constitution. Exponents of the nationalist theory relied upon a number of provisions in the Constitution to support their claim that a state had no such right. The most significant of these was the Preamble's statement that it was "the People of the United States" who ordained and established the Constitution. This they construed to mean that a single American people, formed during the American Revolution, was the sovereign power that established the Constitution. The consequence of this was that any secession from the Union had to be approved by that people.[3] A close examination of the historical record leading up to the ratification of the Constitution, as well as the Constitution's ratification clause and the resolutions of the conventions of the States that ratified the Constitution, reveals that this construction of the Preamble is not warranted. Rather, in accordance with the compact theory of the Constitution, it was the peoples of each of the Confederation's sovereign, free, and independent States that ratified the Constitution. The consequence of this is that, in appropriate circumstances, a right of unilateral secession from the Union did exist. Other arguments raised by exponents of the nationalist theory were also examined and found to be wanting. They were that the states were bound to the Union in perpetuity on the basis of the "more perfect Union" phrase in the Preamble, as well as the Constitution's supremacy, guarantee, and presidential oath of office clauses.

On the basis that the preferred theory of the Constitution was the compact theory, the question of whether the right to unilaterally secede from the Union in accordance with that theory was validly exercised was examined in the following two chapters. Supporters of the compact theory recognized that a state had to have a valid reason before this right could be exercised. In the words of John C. Calhoun, a valid reason would arise "if the [Constitution] should fail to fulfil the ends for which it was established."[4] For the Confederate states, the relevant "end" was the preservation and protection of slavery. As detailed in Chapter 3, the relevant provisions in the Constitution in this respect were those dealing with, firstly, the extent to which the federal government could regulate slavery pursuant to its powers relating to the Union's territories and the admission of new states into the Union and, secondly, the rendition of fugitive slaves. These provisions formed part of a suite of provisions dealing with slavery that proved to be, as Akhil Reed Amar notes, the Constitution's "Achilles' heel."[5] In relation to the issue of slavery in the territories and new states, the concern of slave states was the threat posed by the federal administration elected in 1860 towards preventing slavery expanding into the territories and, by extension, to the states to be carved out of those territories. In relation to the rendition of fugitive slaves, the concern of slave states stemmed from federal legislation enacted to give effect to the Constitution's fugitive slave clause. This legislation regulated the rights of slaveholders to the return of their runaway slaves. Because this legislation, which was upheld as constitutional by the Supreme Court in *Prigg v. Pennsylvania*,[6] denied alleged fugitive slaves any meaningful due process rights, most northern non-slave states enacted personal liberty laws that sought to give runaway slaves basic due process rights in proceedings related to their recapture and return to their owners. These personal liberty laws negatively impacted upon the rights of slaveholders under the federal fugitive slave legislation. It was breaches of constitutional obligations stemming from these provisions that triggered the secessions of the eleven Confederate states.

In Chapter 4, the breaches relating to the Constitution's provisions concerning slavery in the territories and fugitive slave clause were examined. In relation to the former, the breach was the declared plan of the incoming Lincoln administration to implement its policy against the spread of slavery into the Union's territories, in violation of the Supreme Court's ruling in *Dred Scott v. Sandford*.[7] In relation to the latter, the breach was the repeated enactment by northern non-slave states of personal liberty laws, which the Supreme Court had declared unconstitutional, particularly in the case of *Prigg v. Pennsylvania*.[8] Pursuant to the compact theory, which James Madison had analogised to "mak[ing] a contract,"[9] these breaches gave affected slave states a right to unilaterally secede from the Union, much like a contracting party is entitled to terminate a contract for breach or repudiation of a contract's essential terms. All the Confederate states except Tennessee did this by withdrawing from the Union using the same means by which the Constitution was ratified, that is, by means of a popularly elected convention of delegates. In Tennessee, its General Assembly passed secession legislation which was then approved at a referendum.

As is clear from this recapitulation of this book's argument, the pivotal issue in the arguments for or against a constitutional right of unilateral secession was the question of whether such a right existed. There was little disagreement between exponents of both the national and compact theories of the Constitution of the consequences that flowed from each of these theories. Nationalist theory exponents conceded that unilateral secession could take place if the compact theory was correct, and compact theory exponents conceded that it could not take place if the nationalist theory was correct.

Because the decision in *Texas v. White* reflected the nationalist theory, it was understandable that Chief Justice Chase dealt only with the issue of whether a right of secession existed under the Constitution. If the Confederate states did have a constitutional right to unilaterally secede from the Union and therefore, *Texas v. White* was wrongly decided, a critical analysis of this case is warranted.

The litigation in *Texas v. White* commenced in February 1867 when the Reconstruction administration in Texas initiated proceedings for the recovery of bonds that were issued, during the Civil War, to George White and John Chiles, on the ground that the bond issue was illegal. The bond issue was authorized by legislation passed by the secessionist Texan legislature in January 1862 that was aimed at raising funds for military purposes. For Texas to succeed, it had to establish that the Supreme Court had jurisdiction to hear the dispute. Pursuant to Article III, Section 2, Clause 1 of the Constitution, the Court only had jurisdiction if the case was one "between a State and Citizens of another State." This then raised the question of whether Texas was a state of the Union at the time the case was initiated and heard. If it was not, the Court was bound to dismiss the case for lack of jurisdiction.[10]

In a statement which Charles Fairman states has since become "a national motto,"[11] Chief Justice Chase asserted that, following its admission to the Union in 1845, Texas became part of "an indestructible Union, composed of indestructible States."[12] As a consequence, "the union between Texas and the other States was as complete, as perpetual, and as indissoluble as the union between the original States."[13] This meant that Texas's secession ordinance had no legal effect and that "Texas continued to be a State, and a State of the Union."[14] However, this did not mean that Texas's rights with respect to the Union remained unaltered during the time it was controlled by its secessionist government. Being hostile to the government of the Union meant that, at that time, Texas was not entitled to representation in Congress. Nor was Texas entitled, at that time, to bring an action before the Supreme Court. According to Chase, such "rights of the State [of Texas] as a member [of the Union], and of her people as citizens of the State, were suspended."[15]

However, the case before the Court was one in which the proceedings were initiated and prosecuted by the Reconstruction government of Texas. According to Chase, following the collapse of the secessionist government in Texas in 1865, it was the "duty of the United States to provide for the restoration of . . . a government [in Texas]."[16] The authority to do this stemmed from Article IV, Section 4 of the Constitution, which stipulates that "[t]he United States shall guarantee to every State in this Union a Republican Form of Government." Chase ruled that a Presidential Proclamation of 1865 and the Congressional Reconstruction legislation of 1867–1868 were the means by which Article IV, Section 4 was implemented in relation to Texas. Chase ruled that, in exercising power during the period of Reconstruction, Texas's governors "exercised executive functions and actually represented the State in the executive department."[17] This was sufficient to render Texas a legitimate state for the purposes of the Constitution even though, at the time of the proceedings, it was not represented in Congress. Therefore, according to Chase, Texas's "suit was instituted and prosecuted by competent authority."

Having resolved the jurisdictional issue in favor of Texas, Chase then considered the effect of legislation passed by the secessionist administration in Texas. He noted that any such legislation that addressed issues relating to the "peace and good order among citizens" was valid. This included legislation relating to matters such as marriage, conveyancing and property transfer, and remedies for the victims of personal injuries. However, legislation whose purpose was to provide for, and support, the war effort against the Union was invalid.[18] The 1862 Texan legislation fell into this category. This meant that "the title of the State [to the bonds] was not divested by the act of the insurgent government in entering into [the] contract [with White and Chiles]."[19] Thus, Texas was entitled to the recovery of the bonds.

The critical part of Chase's opinion for the purposes of this book's argument was his ruling that the *unilateral* secession of a state "for any cause, regarded by herself as sufficient," was unconstitutional. In coming to this conclusion, in a passage described by one scholar as "the most eloquent passage in the opinion" and "an adornment to legal literature"[20] and by another as "a constitutional and political tour de force,"[21] Chase said:

> The Union of the States never was a purely artificial and arbitrary relation. It began among the Colonies, and grew out of common origin, mutual sympathies, kindred principles, similar interests, and geographical relations. It was confirmed and strengthened by the necessities of war, and received definite form, and character, and sanction from the Articles of Confederation. By these the Union was solemnly declared to "be perpetual." And when these Articles were found to be inadequate to the exigencies of the country, the Constitution was ordained "to form a more perfect Union." It is difficult to convey the idea of indissoluble unity more clearly than by these words. What can be indissoluble if a perpetual Union, made more perfect, is not?[22]

Chase then went on to say:

> The Constitution, in all its provisions, looks to an indestructible Union, composed of indestructible States. When, therefore, Texas became one of the United States, she entered into an indissoluble relation. All the obligations of perpetual union, and all the guaranties of republican government in the Union, attached at once to the State. The act which consummated her admission into the Union was something more than a compact; it was the incorporation of a new member into the political body. And it was final. The union between Texas and the other States was as complete, as perpetual, and as indissoluble as the union between the original States. There was no place for reconsideration, or revocation, except through revolution, or through the consent of the States.[23]

The essence of Chase's opinion on the issue of secession is set out in his claim that "[t]he Constitution, in all its provisions, looks to an indestructible Union, composed of indestructible States."[24] However, there are a number of problems with Chase's reasoning that call into question the correctness of his opinion.

The first problem with Chase's opinion is that, in the 452 words that he devotes to the issue of secession, in reasoning that unilateral secession from the Union was constitutionally impossible, he essentially parroted the historical argument against such a right that Lincoln expounded in his First Inaugural Address and Message to Congress in Special Session. Like Lincoln, Chase did not refer to, or rely upon, any specific provisions in the Constitution's articles in support of his ruling that the Constitution prohibited secession. And as the legal historian G. Edward White observes, although "the Framers anticipated a permanent Union," that is "not the same thing as showing that they had refused to allow states to withdraw from it."[25] In Chapter 2, the flawed nature of Lincoln's argument is laid out. For the same reasons, Chase's is similarly flawed. Thus, if, as Akhil Reed Amar recognizes, Lincoln's argument here was "hard to swallow,"[26] the same can be said of Chase's reasoning in *Texas v. White*. Moreover, as Amar also concedes, there existed an "alternative narrative" to that propounded by Lincoln and Chase which he admits is "compelling, and with good reason."[27] This "compelling" alternative argument, the substance of which is also detailed in Chapter 2, was the subject of detailed submissions to the Court by Albert Pike, counsel for John Chiles.[28] In his submissions on behalf of Texas, George W. Paschal did not present any substantive counterargument, but simply dismissed Pike's submissions as the "quaint rhetoric" of its "misguided author."[29] In an act of abnegation of judicial responsibility, Chase went one step further and simply failed to mention, let alone address, Pike's submissions. Had he not done so, the "compelling" argument presented by Pike would have required Chase to confront the issue of slavery, which was, as outlined in Chapter 3, a core feature of the Constitution, and then address the proposition that what the Confederate states sought was, as Mark Brandon aptly puts it "hardly a radical alteration of existing relations" and that their aim was "to preserve what many saw as the extant order."[30] This order was founded on what James Madison referred to as America's "original sin."[31] The legal and practical consequences of Amar's "compelling" alternative narrative were that the Confederate states had a right to unilaterally secede from the Union and that their peoples could continue to exercise their constitutional right to sin unhindered.

The second problem with Chase's reasoning stems from his assertion that both the Union and its states were "indestructible." In relation to the Union, the "indestructible" nature of the Union meant for Chase that a state could not secede from it. However, if one accepts, for the purposes of the argument, that the Union was "indestructible," it is clear that a state was not "indestructible," in the sense that part of a state could not depart from that state and become a new state of the Union. Indeed, the Constitution explicitly allowed for this to occur. Article IV, Section 3 of the Constitution permitted the formation of a new state from "within the jurisdiction of any other State" provided there was consent for such a formation from the said state and Congress. During the antebellum era, it was pursuant to Article IV, Section 3 that part of New York was admitted to the Union as the state of Vermont in 1791, part of Virginia was admitted to the Union as Kentucky in 1792, and, as part of the Missouri Compromise, part of Massachusetts was admitted to the Union as the state of Maine in 1820.[32]

The third problem that emerges from Chase's opinion is also one that is of practical relevance to this day. In his opinion, Chase qualified his claim that the Constitution created "an indestructible Union" by conceding that a constitutionally valid secession was possible, after all, if achieved "through [the] consent of the States."[33] Thus, Chase's opinion against the constitutional validity of secession is confined to unilateral secession. For him the Confederate unilateral secessions were unconstitutional, as Herman Belz puts it, "because [their] proponents wrongly claimed for individual states a power rightly possessed by the states in union or collectively."[34] For Chase, as an adherent to the dual sovereignty theory of the Constitution, the consent of the states was necessary because they too were "indestructible," this attribute stemming from the Constitution's Tenth Amendment, which, in reserving to the states all powers not delegated to the federal government, led to the "distinct and individual existence . . . [and] right of self-government by the States."[35] Thus, the indestructibility of the states stemmed from their sovereignty pursuant to the Tenth Amendment. As the states were sovereign entities that divided sovereignty between themselves and the federal government, their consent was needed for any constitutional secession from the purportedly "indestructible Union." In relation to this statement, in the most detailed scholarly analysis of *Texas v. White*, William Pierson writes:

> There was in this [statement] a curious inconsistency of reasoning which destroyed the logical finality of the conclusions which Chief Justice Chase had drawn from the preambles of the Articles of Confederation and the Constitution respecting the perpetuity and indissolubility of the Union. There was after all a way by which the Union could be broken up.[36]

The "curious inconsistency" that Pierson refers to was also evident in Lincoln's argument against secession in his First Inaugural Address and his Message to Congress in Special Session. In his First Inaugural Address, Lincoln referred to the right of secession that vested in "the people" who could thereby "exercise their *constitutional* right of amending [the Constitution]."[37] He then went on and said that, although as president he had no authority "to fix the terms of separation of the States . . . [t]he people themselves can do this . . . if they choose."[38] In his Message to Congress in Special Session, he referred to, but rejected, the Confederate states' argument that a state could "withdraw from the Union, without the consent of the Union or of any other State."[39] Later he questioned whether a state could "go off without leave" or "without consent."[40] In opposing secession without consent, Lincoln clearly implied that secession could legally occur with the leave or consent of the Union.

What can be said about these statements by Chase and Lincoln is that, in recognizing that a consensual secession from the Union was possible, they do not differ from the compact theory of the Constitution, by which the state parties to the Constitution could agree to the secession of a state from the Union. However, what is not addressed in their statements is who are the parties to negotiate such a secession or, as Mark Brandon puts it, "how their will might be represented."[41] One way by which this could be legally done according to Chase, in *Texas v. White*, and Lincoln, in his First Inaugural Address, is that all states would need to agree to the secession of a state. Indeed, in private correspondence in December 1860, Lincoln expressed his opinion that "no state can, in any way lawfully, get out of the Union, without the consent of the others."[42] This view was also shared by some Republicans in the immediate wake of the secessions of the Confederate states.[43] An argument against this view is, as Brandon points out, that it is "more stringent than a fair reading of [the Constitution's ratification Article]."[44]

On the other hand, in Lincoln's two speeches there are indicators of other possible means for achieving a consensual secession. In his First Inaugural Address, Lincoln clearly contemplates a constitutional amendment pursuant to Article VII of the Constitution, when he said, as previously noted, that "[w]henever [the people] shall grow weary of the existing government, they can exercise their constitutional right of amending it."[45] This statement echoed his views as recorded by his secretary, John G. Nicolay, who, in a memorandum, dated 13 December 1860, summarized Lincoln's views on secession as follows:

> As a matter of theoretical speculation it is probably true that if the people, (with whom the whole question rests) should become tired of the present government they may change it in the manner prescribed by the Constitution.[46]

However, before such an amendment could even be proposed, there is a necessary precondition to be met, namely, that the people of the state wishing to secede have to demonstrate their desire to secede. Lincoln made this point clear in his Message to Congress in Special Session when he questioned whether the people any of the Confederate states, except South Carolina, had given their consent to secession. In this respect, he said:

> It may well be questioned whether there is, to-day, a majority of the legally-qualified voters of any State, except perhaps South Carolina, in favor of disunion. There is much reason to believe that the Union men are the majority in many, if not every other one, of the so-called seceded States.[47]

If this precondition is met, then Article V can be invoked. Article V contains a two-step procedure to be followed. The first is generating a valid proposal for a constitutional amendment. The second is the ratification of the proposed amendment.

As to the first step, Article V stipulates that a constitutional amendment can be proposed by a resolution passed by each of the two houses of Congress by a two thirds majority of members present, or by a convention that is called for by the legislatures of at least two thirds of the states. In relation to the second step, Congress must stipulate that the proposed amendment be adopted either by the legislatures of at least three fourths of the states or by conventions in at least three fourths of the states.[48]

The argument propounded here by Lincoln resonates with modern constitutional law theory, as articulated by the Canadian Supreme Court in 1988, in the context of a possible secession of Quebec from Canada. In *Reference re: Secession of Quebec*, the court held that there were "four fundamental and organizing principles"[49] of Canada's Constitution that underpinned the right of a Canadian province to secede from Canada by means of a constitutional amendment if certain preconditions were satisfied. The four principles were "federalism; democracy; constitutionalism and the rule of law; and respect for minorities."[50] These principles mandated that, following a referendum in a Canadian province in which there was a "clear expression by the people of the province of their will to secede from Canada,"[51] the federal government and other provinces were obliged to enter into negotiations with that province, the purpose of which would be to seek an agreement on a constitutional amendment to facilitate its secession from Canada.[52] The reason why such negotiations are required is that such a referendum represents a "clear repudiation by the people of [the province] of the existing constitutional order [such that] would confer legitimacy on the demands for secession."[53] However, the failure to reach an agreement for an appropriate constitutional amendment would mean that secession was legally impossible.[54] On the other hand, the Court conceded that an illegal unilateral secession by a province might be recognized by the international community of States.[55]

In his Message to Congress in Special Session, Lincoln suggested a somewhat different way by which a consensual secession could be achieved. Although the meaning of Lincoln's reference there to the illegality of any secession that does not have "the consent of the Union or of any other State" is not altogether clear, Douglas Sanders argues that Lincoln meant that, for a secession of a state to be legal, the consent of "a majority of the populace" as well as "a majority of the states" was required.[56] In this context, Akhil Reed Amar has argued that the consent of the majority of the populace alone, in the form of a national referendum that endorsed a state's desire to secede, would have been accepted by Lincoln. Amar argues that, given Lincoln's commitment to principles of democratic majoritarianism, "in a regime based upon the people's ultimate sovereignty," such a referendum would have carried "great moral weight with those government actors . . . ordinarily involved in the amendment process."[57] Indeed, support for Amar's argument comes from Lincoln himself. As noted above, in his First Inaugural Address Lincoln stated that "the terms of separation of the States" could be facilitated by "[t]he people themselves . . . if they [so] choose."[58] Further support for Amar's argument comes from the Constitution's Preamble and its assertion that "We the People of the United States . . . do ordain and establish this Constitution." As "the People"—a single American people pursuant to the nationalist theory—are the supreme authority in the United States, then logically they could, through a national referendum, consent to the secession of a state of the Union.

If, as was conceded by both Chase and Lincoln, a consensual secession from the Union was possible, the possible mechanisms, outlined above, by which the requisite consent could be obtained would have likely presented insurmountable hurdles for the consensual secession of any of the Confederate states in 1860–1861. And it is improbable that any of these mechanisms could be met to enable a state to secede at the start of the third decade of the twenty-first century, notwithstanding the existence of a relatively significant level of popular support for the right of a state to secede from the Union.[59]

The final problem with Chase's opinion relates to the issue of whether the Court had jurisdiction to hear the claim brought by Texas. When Texas was admitted to the Union in 1845, in accordance with the principle affirmed by the Supreme Court in *Pollard's Lessee v. Hagan*, it possessed "the same rights, sovereignty, and jurisdiction . . . as the original states."[60] Whether Texas possessed these attributes at the time that its provisional government initiated its claim was disputed by opposing counsel acting for White and Chiles. In submitting that the court had jurisdiction to hear the case, and thus that the provisional government had standing to pursue the claim, George W. Paschal anchored his argument on the assertion that "[t]he State [of Texas] as a State, could not and did not rebel against the United States."[61] This meant that the Union was indissoluble and that "[Texas's] secession ordinance was void; the attempted dissolution of the Union was void; the relations of the new confederacy were void; all legislation in contravention of the Constitution, treaties, and laws of the United States, and in aid of the rebellion, was void and, therefore, the body politic no more ceased to be a State of the Union than was the vast domain geographically elided from the boundaries of the United States."[62] In effect, Paschal's argument was that, as William Whatley Pierson notes, "[t]hrough all the manifold changes undergone, the status of Texas as a State of the Union remained the same; and alterations were of no effect, because they had no standing in law."[63] However, the counterargument to this submission was that the provisional government that initiated the claim did so on behalf of what Congress had defined to be a "rebel" state that was "in all respects subject to the paramount authority of the United States at any time to abolish, modify, control, or supersede the same."[64] A consequence of this status was that, at that time, Texas was denied representation in both house of Congress. In light of these circumstances, in arguing that Texas's provisional government had no standing to bring the claim in this case, Albert Pike said that "[t]here can be union only among equal States," with the consequence that "[i]t cannot be [that Texas is] a state for the purpose of suing here, and not a State for the purpose of taking part in the legislation of the country."[65] It is telling that Chase neither mentioned the fact that Texas was not represented in Congress nor addressed Pike's arguments. Rather, in a further abnegation of judicial responsibility, Chase simply, as Walter Lee Brown puts it, "adopted Paschal's argument almost verbatim."[66]

On the other hand, Justice Grier did acknowledge the "very astute arguments" that had been presented by Paschal and Pike, but felt no need to rely upon them in delivering his dissenting opinion in *Texas v. White*.[67] However, in ruling that the Court lacked jurisdiction to hear the case, his reasoning was largely consistent with Pike's submissions. For Grier, the status of Texas was in substance no different to that of one of the Union's territories. For him, Texas could not, as a matter of fact, be a state because, pursuant to the Congressional Reconstruction legislation, Congress had ruled that she was not a state of the Union.[68] As he put it, the question of whether Texas was a state was "to be decided as *a political fact*, not a *legal fiction*."[69]

Given the paucity of Chase's reasoning, Cynthia Nicoletti describes his opinion in *Texas v. White* as a "half-hearted effort to settle the secession question" and says that "Chase was doing what was necessary to ensure that the law as made by the courts fit with the ruling already issued on the battlefield."[70] This came as no surprise to Pike, who was, as his biographer notes, "well aware that it was inevitable that the results of the Federal triumph in the Civil War should be upheld by the Supreme Court," but also "always bitter over the inconsistency of the [court's] decision."[71] It was also unsurprising that in the immediate wake of the decision being handed down, the *New Orleans Times-Piayune* newspaper asserted that his ruling meant that the law on secession had been "stated as a dogma—for which no argument is thought to be necessary."[72] That *Texas v. White* has been subsequently viewed in this way is confirmed by the acceptance of its authority without question by the Supreme Court.[73] Nor, given the paucity of its reasoning, is it surprising that *Texas v. White* is, at best, only mentioned, and rarely extracted,[74] in the leading casebooks used by students of American constitutional law. Notwithstanding the fundamental importance of the issue dealt with by the case, it appears that the fraternity of law teachers in the United States has followed the approach of Thomas M. Cooley in the last decade of the nineteenth century when dealing with the issue of secession. Cooley accepted that the United States was "an indestructible Union" simply because the Supreme Court said so in *Texas v. White*.[75] This neglect in evaluating the reasoning in *Texas v. White* is, perhaps, the inevitable consequence of the fact that, as Nicoletti points out, Chase's opinion was "a form of legal wallpaper that camouflaged the Court's extraordinary efforts to reconcile the war with the law."[76] In essence, Chase's opinion reflected the truth of Oliver Wendell Holmes's general observation that "[t]he substance of the law at any given time pretty nearly corresponds . . . with what is then understood to be convenient."[77] It is thus unsurprising that in the scholarly literature, *Texas v. White* is sometimes simply referred to in a footnote, which is exactly where Cass Sunstein cites it as authority for his assertion that "no serious scholar or politician now argues that a right to secede exists under American constitutional law."[78]

Although secessionist movements have existed in many states since the Civil War, to date, none have had any realistic prospect of attracting sufficient support for secession to be seriously threatened. And as noted in the Introduction, in response to petitions from people within the fifty states seeking permission to secede from the United States, the White House, during the administration of President Barack Obama, responded by asserting that, because *Texas v. White* had ruled that the Union was perpetual, secession from it was impossible.[79] For this reason, the possibility of secession has not attracted serious debate in what can be referred to as "mainstream literature," at least not until recently. In the context of the so-called "red-blue divide" in which the United States now finds itself, thoughtful studies on the possibility of secession in the United States have made their way into "mainstream literature."[80] Although these studies generally concede that the possibility of secession today remains low, that does not mean that courts will not be confronted with cases that squarely raise the issue of secession. Indeed, secession was the issue which Alaska's Supreme Court had to grapple with 137 years after the Supreme Court handed down its decision in *Texas v. White*.

The Alaskan case had its origins in a resolution adopted by the Alaskan Independence Party (AIP) in 2003 to seek, as required by Alaskan state law, approval for a referendum to be held in Alaska on whether Alaska should secede from the United States. However, Alaska's state law precludes the holding of a referendum on a proposal that is unconstitutional. It was on this basis that, in 2006, in *Kohlhaas v. Alaska*, Alaska's Supreme Court ruled that a popular referendum on the question proposed by the AIP could not proceed. In coming to its decision, the Court relied on the decision in *Texas v. White*, which it viewed as authority for the proposition that in the United States, "secession is clearly unconstitutional."[81]

The fact that Alaska's Supreme Court relied on the flawed decision in *Texas v. White* is not the major problem with its ruling in *Kohlhaas v. Alaska*. Rather, it is the fact that *Texas v. White* does not stand for the proposition that "secession is clearly unconstitutional." As is noted above, *Texas v. White* only rules that *unilateral* secession is illegal and leaves it open for a constitutionally legal secession of a state to be achieved with the consent of the states. However, the AIP's referendum proposal had nothing to do with unilateral secession. The proposed referendum question was whether or not Alaska should secede "if such independence is legally possible."[82] On the basis of the decision in *Texas v. White*, such a question does not deal with an issue that is, as Alaska's Supreme Court incorrectly asserted, "clearly unconstitutional."[83]

The above analysis of the Supreme Court's decision in *Texas v. White* demonstrates that this book's argument has significant implications for any future litigation in the United States on the issue of secession. Its argument that on the issue of the constitutional validity of the Confederate secessions, the better view is that the Confederate states exercised a constitutional right to unilaterally secede, calls into question Sunstein's assertion that *Texas v. White* provides a sound basis for his assertion that "no serious scholar or politician now argues that a right of secession exists under American constitutional law."[84]

Although *Texas v. White* provides no basis for Sunstein's assertion, Sections 1 and 3 of the Fourteenth Amendment of the Constitution, which was ratified in 1868, provide separate bases upon which his assertion may be sustained. Firstly, Daniel Farber has argued that two clauses in Section 1 provide a basis upon which Sunstein's assertion may be sustained. The first clause, referred to here as "the Citizenship Clause," stipulates that "[a]ll persons born or naturalized in the United States, and subject to the jurisdiction thereof, are citizens of the United States and of the State wherein they reside." The second clause, referred to here as "the Privileges or Immunities Clause," stipulates that "[n]o State shall make or enforce any law which shall abridge the privileges or immunities of citizens of the United States." Farber argues that, whereas in the antebellum era, citizenship of the United States was derived from citizenship in a state, the Fourteenth Amendment's Citizenship Clause reversed this order of things. Thus, a citizen's primary loyalty was no longer to his or her state, but to the United States. Secession of a state would sever the bond, created by the Citizenship Clause, between a citizen and the United States, thereby, Farber argues, violating the Privileges or Immunities Clause, which prevents a state from interfering with the rights attached to citizenship. Section 5 of the Fourteenth Amendment reinforces this position by giving Congress the power, by appropriate legislation, to enforce the provisions set out in Section 1.[85] As to the merits of Farber's argument, if, as is argued in Chapter 2, the Constitution's supremacy and guarantee clauses do not provide a basis for denying any right of unilateral secession from the Union because they only apply while a state is part of the Union and, of themselves, say nothing about whether or not a state can or cannot leave the Union, then the same can said of Farber's argument based upon the Fourteenth Amendment.

The second basis upon which Sunstein's assertion may be supported is Section 3 of the Fourteenth Amendment, which stipulates the following:

> No person shall be a Senator or Representative in Congress, or elector of President and Vice-President, or hold any office, civil or military, under the United States, or under any State, who, having previously taken an oath, as a member of Congress, or as an officer of the United States, or as a member of any State legislature, or as an executive or judicial officer of any State, to support the Constitution of the United States, shall have engaged in insurrection or rebellion against the same, or given aid or comfort to the enemies thereof. But Congress may by a vote of two-thirds of each House, remove such disability.

As Senator Waitman T. Willey from West Virginia made clear in his speech to the Senate on 31 May 1866, Section 3 was directed against those "who, while acting under the obligation of the oath to support the Constitution of the United States . . . betrayed their country and betrayed their trust."[86] In stipulating that this betrayal was constituted by being "engaged in insurrection or rebellion" against the Union, Section 3 implies that the Confederate secessions were unconstitutional and that any future unilateral secessions would also be unconstitutional. Willey's speech, which was representative of Republican Party sentiment in relation to Section 3, also reflects this sentiment. After stating that the purpose of Section 3 was "not to punish the men who engaged in the rebellion for the crime which they have committed," Willey went on to say:

> It is designed to prevent a repetition of the treason by these men, and being a permanent provision of the Constitution, it is intended to operate as a preventive of treason hereafter by holding out to the people of the United States that such will be the penalty of the offence if they dare to commit it. It is therefore not a measure of punishment, but a measure of self-defence.[87]

However, a possible problem construing Section 3 as a provision rendering unilateral secession unconstitutional is that there is no solid evidence to suggest that this was its intended purpose. If that had been the intention, a constitutional amendment expressly stating so would have been the way to achieve that objective. It is reasonable to believe that such an amendment would have been ratified, given that in 1867, Congressional legislation required, as a precondition to admission to the Union, all the Confederate states except Tennessee[88] to insert such provisions into their state constitutions, which they all did. Against this background it is reasonable to assume that, as required by Article V of the Constitution, three-quarters of the states would have ratified such an amendment to the Constitution. The absence of evidence pointing to the intended purpose of Section 3 being to prohibit a state from unilaterally seceding front the United States stands in contrast to the extant evidence that reveals, as Mark Graber argues, that Section 3 was part of the Republican Party strategy to ensure "to the extent feasible that persons who remained loyal to the Union during the Civil War would control the meaning of the post–Civil War Constitution."[89] By excluding from public office those former federal and state officials that served with the Confederacy, the Republican Party was able to prevent them from holding offices during Reconstruction and thereby preserve their hold on power at the federal level, in stark contrast to the hold on power by southern Democrats in the decade prior to the outbreak of the Civil War. Nevertheless, the implication in Section 3 against any constitutional right for a state to unilaterally secede from the United States is an argument in support of Sunstein's assertion. However, what is striking about this Section 3 argument is that it has not been relied upon by the courts, scholars, or politicians in asserting that, since 1868, a state has no constitutional right to unilaterally secede from the United States.[90]

In addition to the implications for any state that may, in the future, seek to secede from the United States, this book also brings into sharp focus the hypocrisy of the Philadelphia Convention's fifty-five white men, drawn from the ranks of "the well-bred, the well-fed, the well-read, and the well-wed,"[91] twenty-five of whom were slaveholders, in producing a Constitution with slavery at its core.[92] By doing so, what Edward Larson refers to as a "compromised convention"[93] disregarded the Declaration of Independence's assertion that "all Men are created equal," viewing it, in the words of Joseph Ellis, as nothing more than "a rhetorical overture of minimal significance."[94]

It is clear that delegates from the southern slave State would have resisted moves to take steps towards abolish slavery, given the slave societies from where they came. However, in the northern states where slavery was far less prevalent and where antislavery sentiment was the strongest, their delegates were reluctant to take steps towards the abolition of slavery. As W. E. B. Du Bois, the renowned African American sociologist, historian, and civil rights activist, put it, the North "was not abolitionist. It was overwhelmingly in favor of Negro slavery, so long as this did not interfere with Northern moneymaking."[95] Furthermore, there existed, as a Massachusetts Federalist put it in early 1788, a fear that a "[g]reat numbers of slaves becoming citizens, might be burdensome and dangerous to the Public."[96] Thus, writing in 1795, John Adams said that "[j]ustice to the Negroes would require that they should not be abandoned by their Masters and turned loose upon a World" at that time, and that nothing should be done "untill the increasing Population of the Country shall have multiplied the whites to such a Superiority of Numbers, that the Blacks may be liberated by Degrees, with the Consent both of Master and Servant."[97] Thus, the Constitution prepared by the Philadelphia Convention, as Noah Feldman points out, "was not a moral ideal,"[98] but rather a document based upon "a compromise that was understood from the start to be amoral or even immoral: namely, the preservation and perpetuation of slavery."[99] Indeed, the fact that so many of the founding generation were slaveholders provided invaluable ammunition for pro-slavery arguments during the antebellum era. As Jonathan Crider observes, George Washington's "Virginia origins and his status as a slave owner provided one of the most effective arguments for the legitimacy of the pro-slavery position. Thomas Jefferson as author of the Declaration of Independence also served to bolster the claim that not only was slavery accepted by the most of the founding generation but also woven into the principles of the nation through law."[100]

During the antebellum era it was abolitionists who publicly proclaimed this truth. Thus, in the 1840s, William Lloyd Garrison wrote that the Constitution "was formed at the expense of human liberty, by a profligate surrender of principle, and . . . [was] cemented with human blood." Garrison went on to refer to the argument that the recognition and entrenchment of slavery by the Constitution was a "necessary evil" in order to create the Union as the "confession of sin, but the denial of any guilt in its perpetration."[101] Thus, it was entirely logical that Jefferson Davis could, in the words of his biographer, assert that "the Confederacy [was] the true descendant of the American Revolution and the Constitution . . . [because] since the American Revolution . . . [w]hite liberty and black slavery were inextricably intertwined."[102]

Although slavery was the root cause of the Civil War, in 1860–1861 it was only the abolitionists, still only a small, but noisy, fringe group, that wanted to exorcise this evil from the Constitution. Of the rest of the American population, one section did not view slavery as a moral wrong, but rather as a "positive good." Another section was quite prepared to live with slavery where it existed, but was not concerned with abolishing it. Where the two sections were divided was over the issue of whether slave states should continue to practice this evil within the confines of the states of the Union or were free to continue to do so outside the confines of the Union by departing from it. That, in December 1865, slavery was abolished pursuant to the ratification of the Thirteenth Amendment to the Constitution, does not detract from the reality that this was a by-product of a Civil War entered into and fought over the issue of whether, in appropriate circumstances, a state had a constitutional right to unilaterally secede from the Union.

In ruling that the Confederate states had no constitutional right to unilaterally secede from the Union, the Court in *Texas v. White*, and subsequently the American public, was able to avoid dealing with the root cause of the Confederate secessions, namely the reality that the Constitution's founders created a document that preserved and protected race-based slavery. Dealing with this issue would only have arisen if the Confederate states had, in appropriate circumstances, a constitutional right, to unilaterally secede from the Union. If they did possess such a right, this would have compelled a recognition, in the words of "The Real Federalist," an opponent of the Constitution's ratification, that slavery had "blackened half the plains of America with a race of wretches, made so cruel by our policy and, which appears to me to be clearly repugnant to every principle of humanity, morality, religion and good policy" and that the Constitution was a document that "departed widely from the principles and political faith of [17]76."[103] The consequences of so departing were presciently stated, in 1785, when, in the wake of the Confederation Congress's rejection of Thomas Jefferson's proposal that slavery be abolished in the Union's territories after 1800, the Congress's secretary, Charles Thomson, wrote to Jefferson as follows:

> [Slavery] is a cancer that we must get rid of. It is a blot in our character that must be wiped out. If it cannot be done by religion, reason and philosophy, confident I am that it will one day be by blood.[104]

The fulfilment of Thomson's prediction was presaged by Abraham Lincoln's Emancipation Proclamation, issued on 1 January 1863.[105] By this executive order, Lincoln declared free all slaves in most of the Confederate states. Excluded from the Proclamation were slaves in Tennessee, parts of Louisiana, and that part of Virginia that would constitute the state of West Virginia,[106] which was to be admitted into the Union on 20 June 1863,[107] as well as the slaves from the four slave states[108] that did not secede from the Union.

In a speech in January 1864, Frederick Douglass envisaged that the Emancipation Proclamation would inevitably lead to the abolition of slavery, which indeed occurred with ratification of the Thirteenth Amendment in December 1865. However, for Douglass this was not enough. For him, in a United States without slavery, the primary task to be pursued was to "invest the black man[109] everywhere with the right to vote and to be voted for, and remove all discriminations against his rights on account of his color, whether as a citizen or as a soldier."[110]

The passage of two further amendments to the Constitution seemingly guaranteed that this objective had been met. The Fourteenth Amendment, ratified in July 1868, granted citizenship to all persons "born or naturalized in the United States," including former slaves, and precluded a state from enacting any law that would "deprive any person of life, liberty or property, without due process of law" or "deny to any person within its jurisdiction the equal protection of the laws." The Fifteenth Amendment, ratified in February 1870, prohibited states from disenfranchising voters "on account of race, color, or previous condition of servitude." These amendments transformed the Constitution of the antebellum era, with its slavery provisions, into what Noah Feldman calls, at least in a formal sense, "the moral Constitution."[111] Indeed, the three post–Civil War amendments have been viewed by some scholars as the Civil War's crowning achievement and as constituting the Second American Revolution.[112] In so doing, these scholars implicitly recognize the reality, and indeed shortcomings, of the Constitution, the final outcome of the "first" American Revolution, and that Thomas Paine was mistaken when, in reference to the cause that underpinned the American Revolution, he wrote that "[t]he sun never shined on a cause of greater worth."[113] In his 1864 speech, Frederick Douglass expressed the hope that the post–Civil War constitutional order would result in all Americans living in a country which would "not brand the Declaration of Independence as a lie."[114] However, although the Confederacy's slaveholders' union was short-lived and the constitutional evil that was slavery was abolished upon its demise, Douglass's hope was not, and remains, unfulfilled. The racist legacy of the Constitution drafted at Philadelphia in the summer of 1787, as Paul Finkelman notes, "continues to haunt American society and American law more than two centuries after the Founding period."[115] To the same effect, in the wake of what he described as the "senseless and brutal killing" of George Floyd in May 2020, a month later, General Mark Milley, chairman of the Joint Chiefs of Staff, said: "What we are seeing is the long shadow of our original sin in Jamestown 401 years ago, liberated by the Civil War, but not equal in the eyes of the law until 100 years later in 1965. We are still struggling with racism, and we have much work to do."[116]

NOTES

ABBREVIATIONS

Ames	Ames, Herman V., ed. *State Documents on Federal Relations: The States and the United States*. Philadelphia: University of Pennsylvania, 1911.
AC	*Annals of Congress: Debates and Proceedings, 1789–1824*. Library of Congress Online.
Carter	Carter, Clarence Edwin, ed. *The Territorial Papers of the United States*, vols. 2, 4 and 5. Washington: Government Printing Office, 1934–1936.
CG	*Congressional Globe: Debates and Proceedings, 1833–1873*. Library of Congress Online.
CWAL	Basler, Roy P., ed. *The Collected Works of Abraham Lincoln*, vols. 1–8. New Brunswick, NJ: Rutgers University Press, 1953.
DHCUSA	*Documentary History of the Constitution of the United States of America, 1787–1870*, vol. 2. Washington: Department of State, 1894.
DHRC	Jensen, Merrill, et al., eds. *The Documentary History of the Ratification of the Constitution: The Ratification of the Constitution by the States*, vols. 2, 5, 8–10 and 22–23. Madison, WI: State Historical Society of Wisconsin, 1976–2009.
Elliot	Elliot, Jonathan, ed. *The Debates in the Several State Conventions on the Adoption of the Federal Constitution as Recommended by the General Convention at Philadelphia in 1787*, vols. 1–4. Washington: Published Under the Sanction of Congress, 1836.
Federalist	Ball, Terence, ed. *Hamilton, Madison, and Jay: The Federalist with Letters of "Brutus."* Cambridge, UK: Cambridge University Press, 2003.
Force	Force, Peter, ed. *American Archives: Fourth Series*, vols. 5–6. Washington: M. St. Clair Clarke and Peter Force, 1844–1846.
JCC	*Journals of the Continental Congress 1774–1789*, vols. 1, 4–5, 8, 26–29, and 32–34, Washington: Government Printing Office, 1904–1937.
JSCAL	Smith, William R., ed. *The History and Debates of the Convention of the People of Alabama*. Tuscaloosa, AL: White, Pfister & Co., 1861.
JSCAR	*Journal of Both Sessions of the Convention of the State of Arkansas Which were Begun and Held in the Capital, in the City of Little Rock*. Little Rock, AR: Johnson & Yerkes, State Printers, 1861.
JSCFL	*Journal of the Proceedings of the Convention of the People of Florida Begun and Held at the Capitol in the City of Tallahassee on Thursday, January 3, A.D. 1861*. Tallahassee, FL: Dyke & Carlisle, 1861.
JSCGA	*Journal of the Public and Secret Proceedings of the Convention of the People of Georgia Held in Milledgeville and Savannah in 1861, Together With the Ordinances Adopted*. Milledgeville, GA: Boughton, Nisbet & Barnes, 1861.

JSCLA *Official Journal of the Proceedings of the Convention of the State of Louisiana*. New Orleans, LA: J. O. Nixon, Printer to the State Convention, 1861.

JSCMS *Journal of the State Convention and Ordinances and Resolutions Adopted in January, 1861, With An Appendix*. Jackson, MS: E. Barkdale, State Printer, 1861.

JSCSC *Journal of the Convention of the People of South Carolina, Held in 1860, 1861 and 1862, Together With The Ordinances, Reports, Resolutions, etc.*, Columbia, SC: R. W. Gibbes, Printer to the Convention, 1862.

JSCTX Winkler, Ernest William, ed. *Journal of the Secession Convention of Texas 1861*. Austin, TX: Austin Printing Co, 1912.

LDC Smith, Paul H. ed. *Letters of Delegates to Congress, 1774–1789*, vols. 1, 4, and 22–25, Washington: Library of Congress, 1976- 1996.

LOWJM *Letters and Other Writings of James Madison, Fourth President of the United States*, vols. 3–4. Philadelphia: J. B. Lippincott & Co., 1865–1867.

Moore Moore, Frank, ed. *The Rebellion Record: A Diary of American Events, with Documents, Narratives, Illustrative Incidents, Poetry, etc*, vol. 1. New York: G. P. Putnam, 1861.

MJQA Adams, Charles Francis, ed. *Memoirs of John Quincy Adams, Comprising Portions of His Diary from 1795 to 1848*, vols. 5, 8–9, and 11–12. Philadelphia: J. B. Lippincott & Co., 1875–1877.

PDW Wiltse, Charles M., ed. *The Papers of Daniel Webster: Speeches and Formal Writings*, vols. 1–2, Hanover, NH: University Press of New England, 1986–1988.

PJCC Wilson, Clyde N. et.al. eds. *The Papers of John C Calhoun*, vols. 10–12, 14, and 24–27. Columbia, SC: University of South Carolina Press, 1977–2003.

PJM Hutchinson, William T., et al., eds. *The Papers of James Madison*, vols. 1, 8–12, and 17, Charlottesville, VA: University of Virginia Press, 1962–1991.

PJMRS Mattern, David B., et al., eds. *The Papers of James Madison: Retirement Series*, vols. 1–3. Charlottesville, VA: University of Virginia Press, 2009–2016.

PTJ Boyd, Julian P., et al., eds. *The Papers of Thomas Jefferson*, vols. 1–2, 6–7, 9–12, and 30–31. Princeton, NJ: Princeton University Press, 1950–2004.

PTJRS Looney, J. Jefferson, ed. *The Papers of Thomas Jefferson: Retirement Series*, vols. 7, and 15–16. Princeton, NJ: Princeton University Press, 2010–2019.

PVSC Reese, George H., ed. *Proceedings of the Virginia State Convention of 1861*, 4 vols. Richmond, VA: Virginia State Library, 1965.

RDC *Register of Debates: Debates and Proceedings, 1824–1837*. Library of Congress Online.

RFC Farrand, Max, ed. *The Records of the Federal Convention of 1787,*

	Revised Edition in Four Volumes, vols. 1–4. New Haven, CT: Yale University Press, 1966.
RFCS	Hutson, James H. ed. *Supplement to Max Farrand's The Records of the Federal Convention of 1787*. New Haven, CT: Yale University Press, 1987.
Story	Story, Joseph. *Commentaries on the Constitution of the United States With a Preliminary Review of the Constitutional History of the Colonies and States, Before the Adoption of the Constitution*, 3 vols. Boston: Hilliard, Gray, & Company, 1833.
WJM	Hunt, Gaillard, ed. *The Writings of James Madison*, vols. 2, 6, and 9. New York: G. P. Putnam's Sons, 1901–1910.
Tansill	Tansill, Charles C. ed. *Documents Illustrative of the Formation of the Union of the American States*. Washington: Government Printing Office, 1927.
Thorpe	Thorpe, Francis Newton, ed. *The Federal and State Constitutions, Colonial Charters, and Other Organic Laws of the States, Territories, and Colonies Now or Heretofore Forming the United States of America*, 7 vols. Washington: Government Printing Office, 1909.
USSL	*United States Statutes at Large*, 1850–1869, vols. 1–15. Library of Congress Online.

PROLOGUE

1. David Goldfield, *America Aflame: How the Civil War Created a Nation* (New York: Bloomsbury Press, 2011), 1.
2. Sanford Levinson, "'Perpetual Union,' 'Free Love,' and Secession: On the Limits of the 'Consent of the Governed,'" *Tulsa Law Review* 39, no. 3 (Spring 2004): 461–462.
3. *Texas v. White*, 74 U.S. 700, 724, 726 (1869).
4. Cass R. Sunstein, "Constitutionalism and Secession," *University of Chicago Law Review* 58, no. 2 (Spring 1991): 633. After citing Sunstein's statement, Brandon comments that "American scholars have had great difficulty talking coherently about the matter": Mark E. Brandon, "Secession, Constitutionalism, and American Experience," in *Secession and Self-Determination*, eds. Stephen Macedo and Allen Buchanan (New York: New York University Press, 2003), 273.
5. Akhil Reed Amar, *The Constitution Today: Timeless Lessons for the Issues of Our Era* (New York: Basic Books, 2016), 402. In 1850, Senator Daniel Webster, an ardent nationalist, expressed similar sentiments, but less caustically, when he described secessionists as "learned and eloquent" but said of their legal arguments that they were "a very insufficient plea in the law; they are bad on general demurrer for want of substance": Daniel Webster, "Speeches at Capon Springs, Va.," 28 June 1851, in *The Writings and Speeches of Daniel Webster*, vol. 13 (Boston: Little, Brown, & Company, 1903), 435. As a counter to this view, in February 1861, the pro-secessionist social theorist George Fitzhugh boasted that "[d]issolving the Union will be attended with little difficulty. It is a natural operation; the Union has served its purposes, and expires in gentle euthanasia.

The apple is ripe, and drops from its parent-stem": George Fitzhugh, "The Message, The Constitution, and the Times," *De Bow's Review* 30, no. 2 (February 1861): 165.

6. Robert Penn Warren, *The Legacy of the Civil War: Meditations on the Centennial* (New York: Random House, 1961), 3.
7. Kermit Roosevelt III, *The Nation That Never Was: Reconstructing America's Story* (Chicago: University of Chicago Press, 2022), 111.
8. Dumas Malone, *Jefferson and the Ordeal of Liberty* (Boston: Little, Brown & Co., 1962), 421.
9. Niels Eichhorn, *Liberty and Slavery: European Separatists, Southern Secession, and the American Civil War* (Baton Rouge, LA: Louisiana State University Press, 2019), 14–15.
10. James Crawford, *The Creation of States in International Law*, 2nd ed. (Oxford: Clarendon Press, 2006), 375.
11. Many scholars argue that States that emerge as a result of decolonization are not instances of secession. However, as Coggins points out, they should be so considered because, although "anti-colonial secessions and non-colonial secessions have different inherent characteristics and conflict dynamics, both types ultimately sought to separate from an existing state to create a new one": Bridget L. Coggins, "The History of Secession: An Overview," in *The Ashgate Research Companion to Secession*, eds. Aleksandar Pavković and Peter Radan (Farnham, UK: Ashgate Publishing Ltd., 2011), 26n7.
12. Alexis de Tocqueville, *Democracy in America,* vol. 1 (New York: Everyman's Library, 1994), 387–388.
13. Mark E. Brandon, *Free in the World: American Slavery and Constitutional Failure* (Princeton, NJ: Princeton University Press, 1998), 167. However, as Brandon also notes: "Had New England seceded, forming a slaveless commercial republic, or had the Garrisonians persuaded the North and the West to secede and establish a new republic of free citizens, we might now view secession as an institution of liberty and righteousness": Brandon, *Free in the World*, 198–199. Levinson makes the same point when he writes: "[W]ith regard to secession itself, we should ask what our response would be if the Abolitionists had become sufficiently strong to make their cry 'No Union With Slaveholders' the justification for secession by, say, New England, from a Union basically dominated by the Slaveocracy": Sanford Levinson, "The Ten Year War: What if Lincoln Had Not Exited After Four Years?" *Tulsa Law Review* 51, no. 2 (Winter 2016): 321.
14. G. Edward White, *Law in American History,* vol. 1: *From the Colonial Years Through the Civil War* (Oxford: Oxford University Press, 2012), 482.
15. Daniel Farber, *Lincoln's Constitution* (Chicago: University of Chicago Press, 2003), 79.
16. Levinson, "'Perpetual Union,'" 462.
17. Sanford Levinson, *Written in Stone: Public Monuments in Changing Societies,* twentieth anniversary edition (Durham, NC: Duke University Press, 2018), 50.
18. Levinson, *Written in Stone*, 195.
19. Levinson, "'Perpetual Union,'" 470.
20. Levinson, "'Perpetual Union,'" 470.

21. Linda Colley, *The Gun, The Ship and the Pen: Warfare, Constitutions and the Making of the Modern World* (London: Profile Books Ltd., 2021), 13.
22. Roman J. Hoyos, "Peaceful Revolution and Popular Sovereignty: Reassessing the Constitutionality of Southern Secession," in *Signposts: New Directions in Southern Legal History*, eds. Sally E. Hadden and Patricia Hagler Minter (Athens, GA: University of Georgia Press, 2013), 242.
23. Paul Finkelman, *Slavery and the Founders: Race and Liberty in the Age of Jefferson*, 2nd ed. (New York: M. E. Sharpe Inc., 2001), ix, x.
24. Paul Finkelman, "States' Rights, Southern Hypocrisy, and the Crisis of the Union," *Akron Law Review* 45, no. 2 (2012): 469–477. Finkelman suggests that, had the Framers of the Constitution taken a stronger stance against slavery, instead of the formation of the Union, there would have emerged "two separate nations, one based on slavery and one based on liberty," with the consequence that "there would have been no Civil War": Paul Finkelman, "The Founders and Slavery: Little Ventured, Little Gained," *Yale Journal of Law and the Humanities* 13, no. 2 (Summer 2001): 415.
25. George Ticknor Curtis, *Constitutional History of the United States from their Declaration of Independence to the Close of their Civil War*, vol. 2 (New York: Harper & Brothers, 1896), 293.
26. Cynthia Nicoletti, *Secession on Trial: The Treason Prosecution of Jefferson Davis* (New York: Cambridge University Press, 2018), 2.
27. Daniel Wait Howe, *Political History of Secession to the Beginning of the American Civil War* (New York: G. P. Putnam's Sons, 1914), 36. See also Edward Payson Powell, *Nullification and Secession in the United States* (New York: G. P. Putnam's Sons, 1897), 372; Charles Francis Adams, *Trans-Atlantic Historical Solidarity* (Oxford: Clarendon Press, 1913), 51; Andrew C. McLaughlin, *A Constitutional History of the United States* (New York: D. Appleton-Century, 1936), vii; James M. McPherson, "The Civil War and the Transformation of America," in *In the Cause of Liberty: How the Civil War Redefined American Ideals*, eds. William J. Cooper Jr. and John M. McCardell Jr. (Baton Rouge, LA: Louisiana State University Press, 2009), 4–5; William B. Hesseltine and Hazel C. Wolf, "Lincoln, the Governors, and States' Rights," *The Social Studies* 39, no. 8 (December 1948): 350, 355.
28. Laurence H. Tribe, *The Invisible Constitution* (New York: Oxford University Press, 2008), 29, 210. Elsewhere, Tribe makes the same claim: Laurence H. Tribe, *American Constitutional Law*, vol. 1, 3rd ed. (Mineola, TX: Foundation Press, 2000), 1246n48. See also David A. Strauss, "New Textualism in Constitutional Law," *George Washington Law Review* 66, nos. 5–6 (July-September 1998): 1155–1156; Michael Stokes Paulsen, "The Civil War as Constitutional Interpretation," *University of Chicago Law Review* 71, no. 2 (Spring 2004): 703; Mark A. Graber, *A New Introduction to American Constitutionalism* (New York: Oxford University Press, 2013), 155; Daniel W. Hamilton, "Still Too Close to Call?: Rethinking Stampp's 'The Concept of a Perpetual Union,'" in *Union and States' Rights: A History and Interpretation of Interposition, Nullification, and Secession 150 Years After Sumter*, ed. Neil H. Cogan (Akron, OH: University of Akron Press, 2014), 85; H. Jefferson Powell, "William Rawle and Secession: Legal Rights and Political Wrongs," in Cogan, *Union & States' Rights*, 111, 120;

Lee J. Strang, "Originalism's Limits: Interposition, Nullification, and Secession," in Cogan, *Union & States' Rights*, 221; Paul Finkelman, "How the Civil War Changed the Constitution," in *Disunion: A History of the Civil War*, ed. Ted Widmer (New York: Oxford University Press, 2016), 201; Robert Icenhauer-Ramirez, *Treason on Trial: The United States v. Jefferson Davis* (Baton Rouge, LA: Louisiana State University Press, 2019), 297–298.

29. *Walker v. Christian*, 62 Va. 291, 301 (1871).
30. Nicoletti, *Secession on Trial*, 5.
31. Mark E. Brandon, "Secession and Nullification in the Twenty-First Century," *Arkansas Law Review* 67, no. 1 (2014): 98–99. The Confederacy's vice-president, Alexander H. Stephens, made the same point soon after the Civil War when he wrote that the legality of secession "involves questions that cannot be settled by arms": Alexander H. Stephens, *A Constitutional View of the Late War Between the States: Its Causes, Character, Conduct and Results*, vol. 1 (Philadelphia: National Publishing Company, 1885), 658. See also John C. Hurd, *The Theory of Our National Existence, As Shown by the Action of the Government of the United States Since 1861* (Boston: Little, Brown, & Company, 1881), 3–4; Brandon, *Free in the World*, 206; Levinson, "'Perpetual Union,'" 461; Jack N. Rakove, "'A Real Nondescript,' James Madison's Thoughts on States' Rights and Federalism," in Cogan, *Union & States' Rights*, 15; Sanford Levinson, "The Twenty-First Century Rediscovery of Nullification and Secession in American Political Rhetoric: Frivolousness Incarnate, or Serious Arguments to Be Wrestled With?" in *Nullification and Secession in Modern Constitutional Thought*, ed. Sanford Levinson (Lawrence, KS: University Press of Kansas, 2016,) 39.
32. Akhil Reed Amar, *America's Unwritten Constitution: The Precedents and Principles We Live By* (New York: Basic Books, 2012), 85.
33. Abraham Lincoln, "First Inaugural Address," 4 March 1861, CWAL 4:262–271.
34. Abraham Lincoln, "Message to Congress in Special Session," CWAL 4:421–441.
35. Akhil Reed Amar, *The Law of the Land: A Grand Tour of Our Constitutional Republic* (New York: Basic Books, 2015), 3.
36. Amar, *Law of the Land*, 4–25. Amar's supportive view of Lincoln's arguments mirrors the views of prominent lawyers and historians of Lincoln's time such as Sidney George Fisher and John Lothrop Motley: Michael Burlingame, *Abraham Lincoln: A Life*, vol. 2 (Baltimore, MD: Johns Hopkins University Press, 2008), 171–172.
37. Akhil Reed Amar, *America's Constitution: A Biography*, (New York: Random House, 2005), 38–39.
38. Herman Belz, "Lincoln, Secession, and Revolution: The Civil War Challenge to the Founding," in *Constitutionalism in the Approach and Aftermath of the Civil War*, eds. Paul D. Moreno and Jonathan O'Neill (New York: Fordham University Press, 2013), 108.
39. Tribe, *American Constitutional Law*, 32n3. See also Frederick Trevor Hill, *Lincoln the Lawyer* (New York: Century Co., 1906), 295–298; Farber, *Lincoln's Constitution*, 3, 90; Daniel A. Farber, "Completing the Work of the Framers: Lincoln's Constitutional Legacy," *Journal of the Abraham Lincoln Association* 27, no. 1 (Winter 2006): 2–6; Thomas L. Krannawitter, *Vindicating Lincoln: Defending the Politics of Our Greatest President* (Lanham, MD: Rowman

& Littlefield Publishers Inc., 2008), 145–198; Arthur T. Downey, *Civil War Lawyers: Constitutional Questions, Courtroom Dramas, and the Men Behind Them* (Chicago: ABA Publishing, 2010), 117–119; David Brian Robertson, *The Original Compromise: What the Constitution's Framers Were Really Thinking* (New York: Oxford University Press, 2013), 228; Graber, *A New Introduction to American Constitutionalism*, 154–155; Michael Stokes Paulsen and Luke Paulsen, *The Constitution: An Introduction* (New York: Basic Books, 2015), 168–169; Amar, *The Constitution Today*, 401.

40. Peter Lindsay and Christopher Heath Wellman, "Lincoln on Secession," *Social Theory and Practice* 29, no. 1 (January 2003): 132. See also Christopher Heath Wellman, *A Theory of Secession: The Case for Political Self-Determination* (New York: Cambridge University Press, 2005), 86.
41. William Whatley Pierson Jr., *Texas versus White: A Study in Legal History*, (Durham, NC: The Seeman Printery, 1916), 40; Walter Stahr, *Salmon P. Chase: Lincoln's Vital Rival* (New York: Simon and Schuster, 2021), 607.
42. J. T. M., "State Governments—Reorganization After the Rebellion—Alienation of State Property During the War," *American Law Register* 17, no. 6 (June 1869): 371–376; Anon., "Summary of Events: United States," *American Law Review* 3, no. 4 (July 1869): 765; Anon., "Summary of Events: United States," *American Law Review* 4, no. 1 (October 1869): 172.
43. Harold M. Hyman, *The Reconstruction of Justice Salmon P. Chase: In Re Turner and Texas v. White* (Lawrence, KS: University Press of Kansas, 1997), 9.
44. Charles Fairman, *Reconstruction and Reunion, 1864–1888,* part 1 (New York: Macmillan Company, 1971), 641.
45. Herman Belz, "Deep-conviction Jurisprudence and *Texas v. White*: A Comment on G. Edward White's Historicist Interpretation of Chief Justice Chase," *Northern Kentucky Law Review* 21, no 1 (Fall 1993): 130.
46. Thomas M. Cooley, *A Treatise on the Constitutional Limitations Which Rest Upon Legislative Power of the States of the American Union*, 4th ed. (Boston: Little, Brown, & Company, 1878), 10. See also Thomas M. Cooley, *The General Principles of Constitutional Law in the United States of America* (Boston: Little, Brown, & Company, 1880), 28–29.
47. Cooley, *Treatise on the Constitutional Limitations*, 10.
48. T. M. Cooley, "Sovereignty in the United States," *Michigan Law Journal* 1, no. 3 (April 1892): 89.
49. John W. Burgess, "The American Commonwealth: Changes in Relation to the Nation," *Political Science Quarterly* 1, no. 1 (March 1886): 10–11; Cass R. Sunstein, "Constitutionalism and Secession," *University of Chicago Law Review* 58, no. 2 (Spring 1991): 633; Louise Weinberg, "Fear and Federalism," *Ohio Northern University Law Review* 23, no. 4 (1997): 1309; Timothy S. Huebner, *Liberty and Union: The Civil War Era and American Constitutionalism* (Lawrence, KS: University Press of Kansas, 2016), 389; Jonathan O'Neill, "The South and American Constitutionalism after the Civil War," in *The Political Thought of the Civil War*, eds. Alan Levine, Thomas W. Merrill and James R. Stoner Jr. (Lawrence, KS: University Press of Kansas, 2018), 381; Timothy William Waters, *Boxing Pandora: Rethinking Borders, States, and Secession in a Democratic World* (New Haven, CT: Yale University Press, 2020), 20, 204;

Anthony J. Bellia Jr. and Bradford R. Clark, "The International Law Origins of American Federalism," *Columbia Law Review* 120, no. 4 (May 2020): 880n209.

50. Robert Bruce Murray, *Legal Cases of the Civil War* (Mechanicsburg, PA: Stackpole Books, 2003), 149–159; Randy E. Barnett, "From Antislavery Lawyer to Chief Justice: The Remarkable Career of Salmon P. Chase," *Case Western Reserve Law Review* 63, no. 3 (Spring 2013): 679–683; Erin Ryan, "Secession and Federalism in the United States: Tools for Managing Regional Conflict in a Pluralist Society," *Oregon Law Review* 96, no. 1 (2017): 147–149.
51. Brandon, *Free in the World*, 179.
52. Donald W. Livingston, "The Secession Tradition in America," *Secession, State and Liberty*, ed. David Gordon (New Brunswick, NJ: Transaction Publishers, 1998), 1–33; Clyde N. Wilson, "Secession: The Last, Best Bulwark of Our Liberties," in Gordon, *Secession, State and Liberty*, 89–98; James Ostrowski, "Was the Union Army's Invasion of the Confederate States a Lawful Act? An Analysis of President Lincoln's Legal Arguments Against Secession," in Gordon, *Secession, State and Liberty*, 159–178; Thomas J. DiLorenzo, *The Real Lincoln: A New Look at Abraham Lincoln, His Agenda, and an Unnecessary War* (Roseville, CA: Forum, 2002), 110–122. A rare exception here is Morse, who says nothing about the reasons the Confederate states seceded, but simply argues that they had a constitutional right to do so: H. Newcomb Morse, "The Foundations and Meaning of Secession," *Stetson Law Review* 15, no. 2 (Spring 1986): 419–436.
53. The term "Lost Cause" was derived from the title of Edward A. Pollard's book *The Lost Cause: A New Southern History of the War of the Confederates* (New York: E. B. Treat and Co., 1866). For an account of the book's content and Pollard's other writings in defense of the South, see Brook Thomas, "Complicating the Myth of the Myth of the Lost Cause: The Calhoun Monument, Reconstruction and Reconciliation," in *Reading Confederate Monuments*, ed. Maria Seger (Jackson, MS: University Press of Mississippi, 2022), 23–27. Recent examples of Lost Cause literature include: Charles Adams, *When in the Course of Human Events: Arguing the Case for Southern Secession* (Lanham, MD: Rowman & Littlefield Publishers, Inc., 2000); John Remington Graham, *A Constitutional History of Secession* (Gretna, LA: Pelican Publishing Company, 2002); Robert F. Hawes Jr., *One Nation, Indivisible: A Study of Secession and the Constitution* (Palo Alto, CA: Fultus Books, 2006); Gene Kizer Jr., *Slavery Was Not the Cause of the War Between the States: The Irrefutable Argument* (Charleston, SC: Charleston Athenaeum Press, 2014); Walter Kirk Wood, *Beyond Slavery: The Northern Romantic Nationalist Origins of America's Civil War* (Columbia, SC: Shotwell Publishing, 2018); Samuel W. Mitcham Jr., *It Wasn't About Slavery: Exposing the Great Lie of the Civil War* (Washington: Regnery History, 2020.
54. Jefferson Davis, *The Rise and Fall of the Confederate Government*, vol. 1 (New York: D. Appleton and Company, 1881), 80. Alexander H. Stephens, in his account of the Civil War, concurred with his president's views: Stephens, *A Constitutional View of the Late War Between the States*, 10. In *Texas v. White*, Albert Pike, in arguing the case that Texas had a right to secede from the Union, claimed that when "[t]he southern States withdrew from the Union . . . [t]hey

fought for a great principle, for the rights of the States, as they understood them": *The State of Texas v. White & Chiles*, 25 Texas Reports (Supplement) 465, 533 (1869).

55. Cooley, "Sovereignty in the United States," 83.
56. Daniel Farber, *Lincoln's Constitution* (Chicago: University of Chicago Press, 2003), 26–69, 77–91.
57. Stephen C. Neff, "Secession and Breach of Compact: The Law of Nature Meets the US Constitution," in Cogan, *Union & States' Rights*, 96–106.
58. Kris Manjapra, *Black Ghost of Empire: The Long Death of Slavery and the Failure of Emancipation* (London: Allen Lane, 2022), 1.
59. RFC 1:135.
60. Harriet Martineau, *Society in America,* vol. 1, (London: Saunders and Otley, 1837), 64.
61. RFC 2:221–222.
62. MJQA 5:4, 11.
63. *Jones v. Van Zandt*, 46 U.S. 215, 231 (1847).
64. Manisha Sinha, *The Slave's Cause: A History of Abolition* (New Haven, CT: Yale University Press, 2016), 77.
65. William M. Wiecek, "'The Blessings of Liberty': Slavery in the American Constitutional Order," in *Slavery and Its Consequences: The Constitution, Equality, and Race*, eds. Robert A. Goldwin and Art Kaufman (Washington: American Enterprise Institute for Public Policy Research, 1988), 24.
66. James T. Kloppenberg, *Toward Democracy: The Struggle for Self-Rule in European and American Thought* (New York: Oxford University Press, 2016), 407–408. Amar makes the same point when he writes that "the universal right to be free . . . found little support in the federal Constitution as actually implemented in antebellum America": Amar, *America's Unwritten Constitution*, 261. Brandon writes that, pursuant to the Constitution, slaves were "constitutionally choiceless and voiceless": Brandon, *Free in the World*, 32. Brandon also notes that the situation with free blacks was much the same because "black participation in the formal constitution of the Republic was so rare as to render blacks almost invisible, as most public forms of participation were foreclosed to most blacks, slave or free, North and South."
67. Douglas R. Egerton, "Slavery and the Union, 1789–1833," in *A Companion to the Civil War and Reconstruction*, ed. Lacy K. Ford (Chichester, UK: Wiley-Blackwell, 2011), 26. For Kateb this entrenchment of slavery meant that "we cannot say merely that oppression was a bad spot on an otherwise morally admirable constitution. We must say that the US Constitution was unworthy of obedience, even though it was prudent to obey it. . . . . From a moral point of view, and hence as defined by its worst major feature, it was a constitution of slavery:" George Kateb, *Lincoln's Political Thought* (Cambridge, MA: Harvard University Press, 2015), 106.
68. George Washington, "To Lafayette," 18 September 1787, in *The Papers of George Washington: Confederation Series,* vol. 5, *1 February 1787—31 December 1787*, ed. W. W. Abbott (Charlottesville, VA: University of Virginia Press, 1987), 334.
69. Noah Feldman, *The Broken Constitution: Lincoln, Slavery, and the Founding of America* (New York: Farrar, Straus and Giroux, 2021), 8.

70. James Madison, "To Robert Walsh Jr.," 27 November 1819, PJMRS 1:553.
71. For Morris, slavery was a "was a nefarious institution—It was a curse of heaven on the States where it prevailed" and, further, the international trade in slaves was a practice conducted "in defiance of the most sacred laws of humanity [which] tears away his fellow creatures from their dearest connections & dam(n)s them to the most cruel bondages": RFC 2:221–222.
72. For Rufus King, although necessity required concessions to be made to the slaveholding States over the issue of slavery, nevertheless, as he made clear in a speech to the Senate, probably in 1819, "all laws and compacts imposing [slavery] upon any human being are absolutely void, because [they are] contrary to the law of nature, which is the law of God": quoted in *The Life and Correspondence of Rufus King*, vol. 6, *1816–1827*, ed. Charles R. King (New York: G. P. Putnam's Sons, 1900), 276. On King's anti-slavery stance, see Joseph L. Arbena, "Politics or Principle? Rufus King and the Opposition to Slavery, 1785–1825," *Essex Institute Historical Collections* 101, no. 1 (January 1965): 56–77.
73. Luther Martin regarded slavery as "*inconsistent* with the *genius* of *republicanism*, and has a tendency to *destroy* those *principles* on which it is *supported*, as it *lessens* the *sense* of the *equal rights* of *mankind*, and habituates us to *tyranny* and *oppression*": Luther Martin, "Genuine Information," 29 November 1787, RFC 3:212.
74. At the Convention, Virginia's George Mason referred to "the evil of having slaves": RFC 2:370. However, as Beeman points out, "Mason's rhetorical aversion to slavery would remain a constant throughout his life, yet he never moved beyond rhetoric. He made no attempt to halt the expansion westward of slavery in his own colony, nor did he free his own slaves. The same man who spoke of every slave owner being born a petty tyrant showed little discomfort with his own role as master of his own self-contained world supported by the three hundred slaves in his possession": Richard Beeman, *Plain, Honest Men: The Making of the American Constitution* (New York: Random House, 2009), 323. In assessing Mason's approach to slavery, Peter Wallenstein concludes: "Whatever his occasional rhetoric, George Mason was . . . proslavery, not antislavery. He acted on behalf of Virginia slaveholders, not Virginia slaves, when he supported restrictions against further slave immigration": Peter Wallenstein, "Flawed Keepers of the Flame: The Interpreters of George Mason," *The Virginia Magazine of History and Biography* 102, no. 2 (April 1994): 253.
75. Martin, "Genuine Information," 211.
76. Elliot 2:204.
77. "Garrison's First Anti-slavery Address in Boston," 4 July 1829, https://www.loc.gov/resource/gdcmassbookdig.firstantislavery00garr/?sp=5&st=image, 6.
78. Noah Feldman, *The Three Lives of James Madison: Genius, Partisan, President* (New York: Random House, 2017), 164.
79. Gordon S. Wood, *The Idea of America: Reflections on the Birth of the United States* (New York: Penguin Press, 2011), 206.
80. CG, 36th Congress, 2nd Session, 74.
81. Frederick Douglass, "The Mission of the War," 13 January 1864, in *Frederick Douglass: Selected Speeches and Writings*, ed. Philip S. Foner (Chicago: Lawrence Hill Books, 1999), 627. By the same token, from the outset, Douglass

argued that the Civil War was a war over whether or not slavery would continue to exist in the United States: Eric Foner, *Forever Free: The Story of Emancipation and Reconstruction* (New York: Alfred A. Knopf, 2005), 47.

82. Imani Perry, *South to America: A Journey Below the Mason-Dixon to Understand the Soul of a Nation* (New York: Echo, 2022), xvii.
83. Gerald Horne, *The Counter-Revolution of 1776: Slave Resistance and the Origins of the United States of America* (New York: New York University Press, 2014), x–xi.
84. Edward J. Larson, *American Inheritance: Liberty and Slavery in the Birth of a Nation, 1765-1795* (New York: W. W. Norton & Company, 2023), 202.
85. Mark A. Graber, *Dred Scott and the Problem of Constitutional Evil*, (New York: Cambridge University Press, 2006), 245.
86. David W. Blight, "Traced in Blood: African Americans and the Legacies of the Civil War," in Cooper and McCardell, *In the Cause of Liberty*, 137. See also Roosevelt, *The Nation That Never Was*, 143–145.

INTRODUCTION

1. J. David Hacker, "A Census-Based Count of the Civil War Dead," *Civil War History* 57, no. 4 (December 2011): 311. While the surrender of the Confederacy at Appomattox marks the end of the armed conflict between its two sides, it has been argued that, from a legal perspective, the Civil War only came to an end when Georgia, the last Confederate state to be readmitted to the Union on 15 July 1870, had all its congressmen and senators admitted to their seats in Congress in February 1871: Gregory P. Downs, *After Appomattox: Military Occupation and the Ends of War* (Cambridge, MA: Harvard University Press, 2015), 236.
2. Henry Adams, "The Great Secession Winter of 1860–61," *Proceedings of the Massachusetts Historical Society, Third Series* 43 (1909): 686.
3. Arthur Bestor, "The American Civil War as a Constitutional Crisis," *The American Historical Review* 69, no. 2 (January 1964): 328–329. Pitcaithley states that the sectional crisis leading up to the Civil War was "fundamentally a constitutional crisis": Dwight T. Pitcaithley, *The US Constitution and Secession: A Documentary Anthology of Slavery and Supremacy* (Lawrence, KS: University Press of Kansas, 2018), 4. Conlin writes that "[t]he crisis of 1860–1861 was a constitutional crisis": Michael F. Conlin, *The Constitutional Origins of the American Civil War* (Cambridge, UK: Cambridge University Press, 2019), 220. Belz writes that "the deepest meaning of the Civil War lay in the extent to which northern and southern constitutional provisions affirmed, or challenged and broke faith with, the principles of the founding": Herman Belz, "Lincoln, Secession, and Revolution," in *Constitutionalism in the Approach and Aftermath of the Civil War*, eds. Paul D. Moreno and Jonathan O'Neill (New York: Fordham University Press, 2013), 97.
4. Timothy B. Smith, *The Mississippi Secession Convention: Delegates and Deliberations in Politics and War, 1861–1865* (Jackson, MS: University Press of Mississippi, 2015), 5.
5. Edward Mayes, ed., *Lucius Q C Lamar: His Life, Times, and Speeches, 1825–1893* (Nashville, TN: Methodist Episcopal Church, South, 1896), 468.

6. Akhil Reed Amar, "An Open Letter to Professors Paulsen and Powell," *Yale Law Journal* 115, no. 8 (June 2006): 2105.
7. Max Farrand, *The Framing of the Constitution of the United States* (New Haven, CT: Yale University Press, 1913), 206.
8. Farrand, 206.
9. Mark E. Brandon, *Free in the World: American Slavery and Constitutional Failure* (Princeton, NJ: Princeton University Press, 1998), 182–183.
10. Andrew Delbanco, *The War Before the War: Fugitive Slaves and the Struggle for America's Soul from the Revolution to the Civil War* (New York: Penguin Press, 2018), 220.
11. Kenneth M. Stampp, "The Concept of a Perpetual Union," *Journal of American History* 65, no. 1 (June 1978): 6. The issue of the legality of the Confederate secessions was implicitly raised on 14 March 1861 during the Senate debate concerning the status of senators from the seven slave states that had withdrawn from the Senate after their states had, by then, seceded from the Union. The resolution that was voted upon referred to the seats of the departing senators as being "vacant." It was clear from the tone of the debate that a vote in favor of the resolution implied that the secessions of the seven states were unconstitutional and that a "nay" vote implied that they were constitutional. The resolution was carried by a vote of twenty-four to ten, with the ten "nay" votes overwhelmingly cast by senators from the remaining eight slave states: CG, 37th Congress, 4th Session, 1456. In a Senate vote on the same issue on 11 July 1861, by which time a further four slave states had seceded, the resolution declared that departing senators had been "expelled" from the Senate. In moving that resolution, Senator Daniel Clark from New Hampshire stated that its intent was "to deny, on the floor of the Senate, the right of any State to secede": CG, 37th Congress, 1st Session, 63. The resolution was passed by a vote of thirty-two to ten, with the bare majority of "nay" votes cast by senators from the four slave states that had not seceded: CG, 37th Congress, 1st Session, 64. It is reasonable to assume that the overwhelming majority of senators who had withdrawn from the Senate at the times these resolutions were voted upon were of a like mind to senators who opposed the two resolutions. If so, that would indicate that, in 1861, the senators elected to the 37th Congress were deeply divided over the issue of the constitutionality of the Confederate state secessions.
12. Tennessee was excluded from this process because it had already been readmitted to the Union on 24 July 1866, following its ratification of the Thirteenth and Fourteenth Amendments to the Constitution, on 7 April 1865 and 18 July 1866 respectively: Timothy S. Huebner, *Liberty and Union: The Civil War Era and American Constitutionalism* (Lawrence, KS: University Press of Kansas, 2016), 361, 370.
13. "An Act to provide for the more efficient Government of the Rebel States," 2 March 1867, USSL 14:429.
14. "Constitution of Alabama, 1867," Article 1, Section 37, Thorpe 1:135; "Constitution of Arkansas, 1868," Article 1, Section 1, Thorpe 1:307; "Constitution of Florida, 1868," Article 1, Section 3, Thorpe 2:705; "Constitution of Georgia, 1868," Article 1, Section 33, Thorpe 2:824; "Constitution of Louisiana,1868," Articles 2 and 148, Thorpe 3:1449, 1467; "Constitution of Mississippi, 1868," Article 1, Section 20, Thorpe 4:2070; "Constitution of North Carolina, 1868,"

Article 1, Section 4, Thorpe 5:2801; "Constitution of South Carolina, 1868," Article 1, Section 5, Thorpe 6:3281–3282; "Constitution of Texas, 1868," Preamble, Thorpe 6:3591; "Constitution of Virginia, 1870," Article 1, Section 2, Thorpe 7:3873. These ten states were readmitted to the Union on the following dates: Arkansas on 22 June 1868, Florida on 25 June 1868, North Carolina on 4 July 1868, Louisiana and South Carolina on 9 July 1868, Alabama on 13 July 1868, Virginia on 26 January 1870, Mississippi on 23 February 1870, Texas on 30 March 1870, and Georgia on 15 July 1870.

15. Morse puts the argument in stronger language when he writes that the requirement upon the Confederate states to expressly exclude the right of secession in their state constitutions meant that "the United States government had implicitly admitted that those states originally *had the right*" to unilaterally secede from the Union: H. Newcomb Morse, "The Foundations and Meaning of Secession," *Stetson Law Review* 15, no. 2 (Spring 1986): 433.
16. Quoted from the indictment in David K. Watson, "The Trial of Jefferson Davis: An Interesting Constitutional Question," *Yale Law Journal* 24, no. 8 (1914–1915): 671.
17. Quoted in Cynthia Nicoletti, *Secession on Trial: The Treason Prosecution of Jefferson Davis* (New York: Cambridge University Press, 2018), 221.
18. William J. Cooper Jr., *Jefferson Davis: American* (New York: Vintage Books, 2000), 606.
19. "By the President of the United States of America: A Proclamation," 25 December 1868, USSL 15:712.
20. Robert Icenhauer-Ramirez, *Treason on Trial: The United States v. Jefferson Davis* (Baton Rouge, LA: Louisiana State University Press, 2019), 291–292.
21. *Texas v. White*, 74 U.S. 700, 724, 726 (1869). Previously, Chase, sitting as a circuit court judge in North Carolina, ruled that North Carolina's declaration of independence "did not effect, even for a moment, the separation of North Carolina from the Union": *Shortridge v. Macon*, 22 Fed. Cas. 20, 21 (1867). Furthermore, in June 1868, a majority of the Supreme Court of Georgia ruled that Georgia's secession was unconstitutional. The reasoning of the majority was in part based on reasoning similar to that of Chase in *Texas v. White*, but also on the basis of the Constitution's supremacy clause: *Central Railroad and Banking Company v. Ward*, 37 Ga. 515, 542–543 (1868).
22. Sanford Levinson, "The 21st Century Rediscovery of Nullification and Secession in American Political Rhetoric: Frivolousness Incarnate, or Serious Arguments to Be Wrestled With?" in *Nullification and Secession in Modern Constitutional Thought*, ed. Sanford Levinson (Lawrence, KS: University Press of Kansas, 2016), 37–38.
23. *Kohlhaas v. State of Alaska*, 223 P. 3d. 105, 110 (2010).
24. Ames, 274.
25. Mark A. Graber, *Dred Scott and the Problem of Constitutional Evil* (New York: Cambridge University Press, 2006), 1.
26. Sidney George Fisher, *The Trial of the Constitution* (Philadelphia: J. B. Lippincott & Co., 1862), 269–270.
27. Akhil Reed Amar, *America's Constitution: A Biography* (New York: Random House, 2005), 20.

28. Paul Starr, *Entrenchment: Wealth, Power, and the Constitution of Democratic Societies* (New Haven, CT: Yale University Press, 2019), 99. It was against this background that, in 1849, Frederick Douglass declared that he would "continue to denounce the Constitution and government of the United States as a most foul and bloody conspiracy against the rights of three millions of enslaved and imbruted men": Frederick Douglass, "Comments on Gerrit Smith's Address," *The North Star*, 30 March 1849, in *Frederick Douglass: Selected Speeches and Writings*, ed. Philip S. Foner (Chicago: Lawrence Hill Books, 1999), 140. Although, by 1851, Douglass had abandoned his adherence to the Garrisonian view of the Constitution as a "covenant with death," this statement's description on the condition of slavery was one that he continued to propound. Thus, on 5 July 1852, in a speech marking the 76th anniversary of the Declaration of Independence, in which he referred to the Constitution as a "glorious liberty document," he also said: "My subject, then fellow-citizens, is American slavery. I shall see this day and its popular characteristics, from the slave's point of view. Standing, there, identified with the American bondman, making his wrongs mine, I do not hesitate to declare, with all my soul, that the character and conduct of this nation never looked blacker to me than on this 4th of July! Whether we turn to the declarations of the past, or to the professions of the present, the conduct of the nation seems equally hideous and revolting. America is false to the past, false to the present, and solemnly binds herself to be false to the future": Frederick Douglass, "The Meaning of the July Fourth for the Negro," 5 July 1852, in Foner, *Frederick Douglass*, 195, 204. It was for this reason that, prior to the Civil War, free African Americans in the northern non-slave states did not celebrate 4 July. Rather, they celebrated Emancipation Day on 1 August, being the date when, in 1838, slaves in the British West Indies finally became free in accordance with the British Slavery Abolition Act of 1833: Adam Hochschild, *Bury the Chains: The British Struggle to Abolish Slavery* (London: Macmillan, 2005), 358.
29. James Buchanan, "Remarks," 9 March 1836, in *The Works of James Buchanan*, vol. 3, *1836-1838*, ed. John Bassett Moore (Philadelphia: J. B. Lippincott Company, 1908), 26.
30. Graber, *Dred Scott*, 245.
31. George William Van Cleve, *A Slaveholders' Union: Slavery, Politics, and the Constitution in the Early American Republic* (Chicago: University of Chicago Press, 2010), 179.
32. *The Antelope*, 23 U.S. 66, 114 (1825).
33. Paul Finkelman, *Supreme Injustice: Slavery in the Nation's Highest Court* (Cambridge, MA: Harvard University Press, 2018), 36.
34. Jefferson Davis, "Inaugural Address," 22 February 1862, in *Jefferson Davis, Constitutionalist: His Letters, Papers and Speeches*, vol. 5, ed. Dunbar Rowland (Jackson, MS: Mississippi Department of Archives and History, 1923), 200.
35. Unlike many of the founding generation, Marshall did not inherit slaves, but acquired them during the course of his life. One such acquisition took place in 1787, on the eleventh anniversary of the signing of the Declaration of Independence, at a time when the Philadelphia Convention was drafting the Constitution: Finkelman, *Supreme Injustice*, 2018, 38. In June 1788, Marshall played

an important role in getting a majority of delegates at Virginia's ratification convention to ratify the Constitution: Joel Richmond Paul, *Without Precedent: John Marshall and His Times* (New York: Riverhead Books, 2018), 43–44.

36. See, for example, Jefferson Davis, "Inaugural Address of the President of the Provisional Government," 18 February 1861, in Rowland, *Jefferson Davis*, 50; Henry M. Rector, "Governor's Message [to Arkansas Secession Convention]," 2 March 1861, JSCAR, 43.
37. William W. Freehling, "Reviving State Rights," in *A Political Nation: New Directions in Mid-Nineteenth-Century American Political History*, eds. Gary W. Gallagher and Rachel A. Shelden (Charlottesville, VA: University of Virginia Press, 2012), 118.
38. James H. Read, "From Calhoun to Secession," in *The Political Thought of the Civil War*, eds. Alan Levine, Thomas W. Merrill, and James R. Stoner Jr. (Lawrence, KS: University Press of Kansas, 2018), 160.
39. Abraham Lincoln, "Speech in the United States House of Representatives: The War with Mexico," 12 January 1848, CWAL 1:438; "Resolutions on Behalf of Hungarian Freedom," 9 January 1852, CWAL 2:115.
40. Abraham Lincoln, "First Inaugural Address," CWAL 4:267. Lincoln here echoes the view of Andrew Jackson, who in 1832 expressed the view that "secession . . . may be morally justified by the extremity of oppression": Andrew Jackson, "Proclamation on Nullification," 10 December 1832, in *The Papers of Andrew Jackson*, vol. 10, ed. Daniel Feller (Knoxville, TN: University of Tennessee Press, 2016), 702.
41. Lincoln, "First Inaugural Address," 267.
42. Abraham Lincoln, "Message to Congress in Special Session," CWAL 4:426, 434n83.
43. Abraham Lincoln, "Speech at Edwardsville, Illinois," 11 September 1858, CWAL 3:92.
44. Indeed, as Foner points out: "For nearly two years after the war began . . . the Lincoln administration insisted that the preservation of the Union, not the abolition of slavery, was the war's goal": Eric Foner, *Forever Free: The Story of Emancipation and Reconstruction* (New York: Alfred A. Knopf, 2005), 42.
45. "Resolutions Drawn up for Republican Members of Senate Committee of Thirteen," 20 December 1860, CWAL 4:157. At the time, Henry Adams wrote that Congressional approval for the amendment would not have been obtained without Lincoln lobbying for it on the eve of his inauguration on 4 March 1861: Adams, "The Great Secession Winter of 1860–61," 683. Burlingame states that "Lincoln may have gone to the Capitol and lobbied for the measure without knowing its precise details": Michael Burlingame, *Abraham Lincoln: A Life,* vol. 2 (Baltimore, MD: Johns Hopkins University Press, 2008), 47.
46. Lincoln, "First Inaugural Address," 270. The Corwin Amendment was also supported by William H. Seward, Lincoln's soon-to-be Secretary of State: William H. Seward, "The State of the Union," 12 January 1861, in *The Works of William H Seward*, vol. 4, ed. George E. Baker (Boston: Houghton, Mifflin and Company, 1884), 667.
47. Lincoln's reluctant endorsement of the proposed Corwin Amendment was antithetical to his distaste for, and opposition to, slavery. That he publicly

expressed it in his First Inaugural Address was explained by the reality that this speech was, for him, a conciliatory one that he believed would strengthen the position of Unionists in the Union's fifteen slave states, and usher in a retraction of the secession ordinances of those that had, by then, seceded and prevent the secession of those that had not: Daniel W. Crofts, *Lincoln and the Politics of Slavery: The Other Thirteenth Amendment and the Struggle to Save the Union* (Chapel Hill, NC: University of North Carolina Press, 2016), 236–237; Leonard L. Richards, *Who Freed the Slaves? The Fight Over the Thirteenth Amendment* (Chicago: University of Chicago Press, 2015), 23. For the mixed reception to the First Inaugural Address, see Burlingame, *Abraham Lincoln*, 62–68. Given that Lincoln's speech did not achieve his goal of peaceably maintaining the territorial integrity of the Union, his Message to Congress in Special Session, delivered four months later, was more aggressive in its tone towards the eleven states that had seceded and formed the Confederacy. Aimed principally at a northern state audience, it was received with widespread, but not universal, approval: Burlingame, 170–173.

48. It can be noted that at the start of the Civil War, Lincoln did not, as he conceded three years later, "anticipate that domestic slavery would be much affected by the war": Abraham Lincoln, "Address at Sanitary Fair, Baltimore, Maryland," 18 April 1864, CWAL 7:301.
49. "Legislative Address to the People of Tennessee," 9 May 1861, in *Senate Journal of the Second Extra Session of the Thirty-Third General Assembly of the State of Tennessee Which Convened at Nashville on Thursday, the 25th Day of April, A.D. 1861* (Nashville TN: J. O. Griffith and Company, Public Printers, 1861), 88.
50. Sanford Levinson, *Written in Stone: Public Monuments in Changing Societies, Twentieth Anniversary Edition* (Durham, NC: Duke University Press, 2018), 99. See also Daniel Farber, *Lincoln's Constitution* (Chicago: University of Chicago Press, 2003), 101–105; John Rawls, *The Law of Peoples* (Cambridge, MA: Harvard University Press, 1999), 38; Belz, "Lincoln, Secession, and Revolution," 86, 96, 109.
51. Harriet Martineau, *Society in America,* vol. 1, (London: Saunders and Otley, 1837), 390.
52. Crofts, *Lincoln and the Politics of Slavery*, 238.
53. "Joint Resolution to amend the Constitution of the United States," 2 March 1861, USSL 12:251.
54. Crofts, *Lincoln and the Politics of Slavery*, 245–254.
55. William W. Freehling, *The Road to Disunion,* vol. 2: *Secessionists Triumphant, 1854–1861* (New York: Oxford University Press, 2007), 470.
56. *Calder v. Bull*, 3 U.S. 386, 393 (1798).
57. *Williams v. Bruffy*, 96 U.S. 176, 186 (1877). In his opinion, Field cited with approval the circuit court decision of *Shortridge v. Macon*, 22 Fed. Cas. 20, 23 (1867), where Chief Justice Chase said: "Those who engage in rebellion must consider the consequences. If they succeed, rebellion becomes revolution, and the new government will justify its founders. If they fail, all their acts hostile to the rightful government are violations of law, and originate no rights which can be recognized by the courts of the nation whose authority and existence

have been alike assailed." Joel Parker and Sidney George Fisher, both of whom denied the existence of a constitutional right of secession and supported Lincoln's military campaign against the Confederacy, recognized that the morality or otherwise of any secession was irrelevant: Joel Parker, *The Right of Secession: A Review* (Cambridge, MA: Welch, Bigelow, and Company, 1861), 13; Fisher, *The Trial of the Constitution*, 165–166. This approach is also reflected in contemporary views on secession as evidenced in the decision of the Supreme Court of Canada in 1998 in *Reference re: Secession of Quebec* [1998] 2 S.C.R. 217, 272–275, 289, 296.

58. Howard Jones, *Union in Peril: The Crisis Over British Intervention in the Civil War* (Lincoln, NE: University of Nebraska Press, 1992), 2–3; John M. Taylor, *William Henry Seward: Lincoln's Right Hand* (New York: HarperCollins Publishers, 1991), 177–179.
59. *Gibbons v. Ogden*, 22 U.S. 1, 188 (1824).
60. *Prigg v. Pennsylvania*, 41 U.S. 539, 621 (1842).
61. *Dred Scott v. Sandford*, 60 U.S. 393, 410 (1857).
62. *Dred Scott v. Sandford*, 60 U.S. 393, 405 (1857).
63. RFC 2:666.
64. DHRC 2:496.
65. James Madison, "To N. P. Trist," 2 March 1827, LOWJM 3:565. See also "The Federalist No. 37 (Madison)," Federalist, 172.
66. James Madison, "To Thomas Grimke," 15 January 1828, LOWJM 3:611. See also James Madison, "To Spencer Roane," 2 September 1819, PJMRS 1:502.
67. *McCulloch v. Maryland*, 17 U.S. 316, 414 (1819).
68. *Martin v. Hunter's Lessee*, 14 U.S. 304, 374 (1816).
69. Richard Beeman, *Plain, Honest Men: The Making of the American Constitution* (New York: Random House, 2009), 407. According to De Pauw, the essays were singularly unsuccessful in converting any opponent into a supporter of ratification at New York's ratification convention: Linda Grant DePauw, *The Eleventh Pillar: New York State and the Federal Constitution* (Ithaca, NY: Cornell University Press, 1966), 106–117. Johnson argues that the essays were "of marginal value" in relation to influencing the outcome of the ratification conventions: Calvin H. Johnson, *Righteous Anger at Wicked States: The Meaning of the Founders' Constitution* (Cambridge, UK: Cambridge University Press, 2005), 138.
70. James Madison, "To Edward Livingston," 17 April 1824, PJMRS 3:265–266.

CHAPTER 1. "AN IRREPRESSIBLE CONFLICT"

1. Paine's book, *Common Sense*, published in 1776, "was a sensation, selling 150,000 copies in three months, the modern equivalent of 50 million copies, placing it at or near the all-time best-seller list for non-fiction": Joseph J. Ellis, *The Cause: The American Revolution and its Discontents, 1773–1783* (New York: Liveright Publishing Corporation, 2021), 67.
2. Thomas Paine, *Rights of Man—Common Sense* (New York: Alfred A. Knopf, 1994), 249. Writing in 1805, John Adams, who loathed Paine and regarded him as "a mongrel between pig and puppy, begotten by a wild boar on a bitch wolf," nevertheless, conceded that "I know not whether any man in the world has had

more influence on its inhabitants or affairs for the last thirty years than Tom Paine:" quoted in Gary B. Nash, *The Unknown American Revolution: The Unruly Birth of Democracy and the Struggle to Create America* (London: Jonathan Cape, 2006), 425.

3. "Declaration of Independence," 4 July 1776, Tansill, 25.
4. "Definitive Treaty of Peace Between the United States of America and his Britannic Majesty," 3 September 1783, USSL 8:81.
5. "Articles of Confederation," 1 March 1781, Tansill, 27.
6. "The Federalist No. 14 (Madison)," Federalist, 59.
7. Gordon S. Wood, *Power and Liberty: Constitutionalism in the American Revolution* (New York: Oxford University Press, 2021), 64–65.
8. Henry Knox, "To Rufus King," 15 July 1787, in *Life and Correspondence of Henry Knox*, ed. Francis S. Drake (Boston: Samuel G. Drake, 1873), 96.
9. *Owings v. Speed*, 18 U.S. 420, 422 (1920), but see Gary Lawson and Guy Seidman, "When Did the Constitution Become Law?" *Notre Dame Law Review* 77, no. 1 (November 2001): 1–38; Vasan Kesavan, "When Did the Articles of Confederation Cease to be Law?" *Notre Dame Law Review* 78, no. 1 (December 2002): 35–82.
10. Kenneth Morgan, *Slavery and Servitude in Colonial North America: A Short History* (New York: New York University Press, 2001), 29.
11. James Madison, "To Lafayette," 25 November 1820, PJMRS 2:159. At New Hampshire's convention, called to debate ratification of the Constitution, Joshua Atherton opposed ratification because it would make supporters of ratification "*consenters to*, and *partakers in*, the sin of this abominable traffic": Elliot 2: 203.
12. Thomas D. Morris, *Southern Slavery and the Law, 1619–1860* (Chapel Hill, NC: University of North Carolina Press, 1996), 38–39.
13. Edward S. Morgan, *American Slavery, American Freedom: The Ordeal of Colonial Virginia* (New York: W. W. Norton & Company, Inc., 1975), 297.
14. George William Van Cleve, *A Slaveholders' Union: Slavery, Politics, and the Constitution in the Early American Republic* (Chicago: University of Chicago Press, Chicago, 2010), 22–23.
15. Van Cleve, *Slaveholders' Union*, 41.
16. Gavin Wright, *Slavery and American Economic Development* (Baton Rouge, LA: Louisiana State University Press, 2006), 30. See also Anne Farrow, Joel Long and Jennifer Frank, *Complicity: How the North Promoted, Prolonged and Profited from Slavery* (New York: Ballantine Books, 2006), 48–49; Eric Kimball, "'What Have We to Do with Slavery?' New Englanders and the Slave Economies of the West Indies," in *Slavery's Capitalism: A New History of American Economic Development*, eds. Sven Beckert and Seth Rockman (Philadelphia: University of Pennsylvania Press, 2016), 185–190.
17. Jay Coughtry, *The Notorious Triangle: Rhode Island and the African Slave Trade 1700–1807* (Philadelphia: Temple University Press, 1981), 5–42; James A. Rawley with Stephen D. Behrendt, *The Transatlantic Slave Trade: A History*, rev. ed. (Lincoln, NE: University of Nebraska Press, 2005), 305–330; Kimball, "'What Have We to Do with Slavery?'" 184–185.

18. Wendy Warren, *New England Bound: Slavery and Colonization in Early America* (New York: Liveright Publishing Corporation, 2016), 43–44.
19. Christy Clark-Pujara, *Dark Work: The Business of Slavery in Rhode Island* (New York: New York University Press, 2016), 154.
20. Alan J. Singer, *New York and Slavery: Time to Teach the Truth* (Albany, NY: State University Press of New York, 2008), 57–58. On the slave trade and New England in the seventeenth century, see Warren, *New England Bound*, 49–81.
21. Steven Deyle, "'By Far the Most Profitable Trade': Slave Trading in British Colonial North America," *Slavery and Abolition* 10, no. 2 (1989): 119.
22. Paul Finkelman, "The First Civil Rights Movement: Black Rights in the Age of the Revolution and Chief Justice Taney's Originalism in *Dred Scott*," *University of Pennsylvania Journal of Constitutional Law* 24, no. 3 (June 2022): 691–694.
23. Rawley with Behrendt, *The Transatlantic Slave Trade*, 266. See also Morgan, *American Slavery, American Freedom*, 327-337.
24. Elizabeth R. Varon, *Disunion! The Coming of the American Civil War, 1789–1859* (Chapel Hill, NC: University of North Carolina Press, 2008), 41–42.
25. Thomas Jefferson, "To Lafayette," 26 December 1820, PTJRS 16:494; Steven Deyle, *Carry Me Back: The Domestic Slave Trade in American Life* (Oxford: Oxford University Press, 2005), 26.
26. Thomas Jefferson, "To Albert Gallatin," 26 December 1820, PTJRS 16:489. James Madison was also an adherent to diffusion theory. In 1820, in a letter to James Monroe, he wrote that "an uncontrouled dispersion of the slaves, now within the U. S., was not only best for the nation, but most favorable for the slaves also, both as to their prospects of emancipation, and as to their condition in the mean time": James Madison, "To James Monroe," 23 February 1820, PJMRS 2:17. The devastating rejoinder to diffusion was provided by Jefferson's friend and interlocutor the Marquis de Lafayette, who wrote to Jefferson: "I would have thought that By spreading the prejudices, Habits, and Calculations of planters over a larger Surface You Rather Encrease the difficulties of final liberation": "Lafayette to Jefferson," 1 July 1821, in *The Letters of Lafayette and Jefferson*, ed. Gilbert Chinard (Baltimore, MD: The Johns Hopkins Press, 1929), 407.
27. Dennis C. Rasmussen, *Fears of a Setting Sun: The Disillusionment of America's Founders* (Princeton, NJ: Princeton University Press, 2021), 166. See also William Cohen, "Thomas Jefferson and the Problem of Slavery," *Journal of American History* 56, no. 3 (December 1969): 503–526; Paul Finkelman, "Jefferson and Slavery: 'Treason Against the Hopes of the World,'" in *Jeffersonian Legacies*, ed. Peter S. Onuf (Charlottesville, VA: University Press of Virginia, 1993), 181–221.
28. Robert Pierce Forbes, "Introduction," in *Notes on the State of Virginia: An Annotated Edition*, ed. Robert Pierce Forbes (New Haven, CT: Yale University Press, 2022), xix-lx, xix. Jefferson's fellow Virginian and slaveholder James Madison confirmed the racist nature of American slavery in his discussions with the English social theorist Harriet Martineau during her visit to the United States in 1834–1835. Of her encounter with Madison, Martineau wrote: "Mr.

Madison told me, that if he could work a miracle, he knew what it should be. He would make all the blacks white; and then he could do away with slavery in twenty-four hours": Harriet Martineau, *Society in America*, vol. 1, (London: Saunders and Otley, 1837), 382.

29. Forbes, *Notes on the State of Virginia*, 212–215, 218. Jefferson's views on African Americans reflected the thinking of various European intellectuals, including David Hume and François Marie Arouet Voltaire: Henry Louis Gates Jr. and Andrew S. Curran, "The 1741 Contest on the 'Degeneration' of Black Skin and Hair,'" in *Who's Black and Why? A Hidden Chapter from the Eighteenth-Century Invention of Race*, eds. Henry Louis Gates Jr. and Andrew S. Curran (Cambridge, MA: Belknap Press, 2022), 20–21, 41–43.
30. Jennifer Ratner-Rosenhagen, *The Ideas That Made America: A Brief History* (New York: Oxford University Press, 2019), 41. See also Forbes, "Introduction," xix-lx, lviii-lix.
31. "Memorial," 13 December 1831, in *The Papers of John Marshall*, vol. 12, ed. Charles F. Hobson (Chapel Hill, NC: University of North Carolina Press, 2006), 127–131, 130. Marshall's views here echoed those of Jefferson, who, in a letter in 1814 to Edward Coles, in voicing his opposition to emancipation, wrote: "[T]the idea of emancipating the whole at once, the old as well as the young, and retaining them here, is of those only who have not the guide of either knolege or experience of the subject. for, men, probably of any colour, but of this color we know, brought up from their infancy without necessity for thought or forecast, are by their habits rendered as incapable as children of taking care of themselves, and are extinguished promptly wherever industry is necessary for raising the young. in the mean time they are pests in society by their idleness, and the depredations to which this leads them. their amalgamation with the other colour produces a degradation to which no lover of his country, no lover of excellence in the human character can innocently consent": Thomas Jefferson, "To Edward Coles," 25 August 1814, PTJRS 7:604.
32. John C. Calhoun, "A Disquisition on Government," in *Union and Liberty: The Political Philosophy of John C. Calhoun*, ed. Ross M. Lence (Indianapolis, IN: Liberty Fund, 1992), 44.
33. *Somerset v. Stewart* (1772) 98 E.R. 499.
34. Steven M. Wise, *Though the Heavens May Fall: The Landmark Trial That Led to the End of Human Slavery* (Cambridge, MA: Da Capo Press, 2005), 129.
35. On Sharp's antislavery activism, see Kris Manjapra, *Black Ghost of Empire: The Long Death of Slavery and the Failure of Emancipation* (London: Allen Lane, 2022), 77–82. Larson describes Sharp as "the acknowledged mastermind for the *Somerset* lawsuit:" Edward J. Larson, *American Inheritance: Liberty and Slavery in the Birth of a Nation, 1765-1795* (New York: W. W. Norton & Company, 2023), 157.
36. *Somerset v. Stewart* (1772) 98 E.R. 499, 510.
37. Manjapra, *Black Ghost of Empire*, 98.
38. William M. Wiecek, "*Somerset*: Lord Mansfield and the Legitimacy of Slavery in the Anglo-American World," *University of Chicago Law Review* 42, no 1 (Autumn 1974): 87.
39. *Somerset v. Stewart* (1772) 98 E.R. 499, 510.

40. Quoted in Wise, *Though the Heavens May Fall*, 201.
41. Wiecek, "*Somerset*," 113–115.
42. Aziz Rana, *The Two Faces of American Freedom* (Cambridge, MA: Harvard University Press, 2010), 85–87.
43. Slave revolts in the colonial era first took place took place in the late seventeenth century but only took the form of more ominous threats to the interests of slaveholders in the early decades of the eighteenth century: Morgan, *Slavery and Servitude*, 87–92; Herbert Aptheker, "American Negro Slave Revolts," *Science and Society* 1, no. 4 (Summer 1937): 513–518.
44. Gary J. Kornblith, *Slavery and Sectional Strife in the Early American Republic, 1776–1871* (Lanham, MD: Rowman & Littlefield Publishers, Inc., 2010), 25; Alan Gilbert, *Fighting for Emancipation in the War for Independence* (Chicago: University of Chicago Press, 2012), 9.
45. James Madison, "To William Bradford," 26 November 1774, PJM 1:130.
46. Gerald Horne, *The Counter-Revolution of 1776: Slave Resistance and the Origins of the United States of America* (New York: New York University Press, 2014), 211.
47. Scholars have not compiled a list of the Declaration's signatories who owned slaves at that time. Based upon research undertaken by *Politifact* of the Poynter Institute and internet searches, the following thirty-eight signatories were slaveholders: Josiah Bartlett, Carter Braxton, Charles Carroll, Samuel Chase, Abraham Clark, William Floyd, Benjamin Franklin, Button Gwinnett, Lyman Hall, John Hancock, Benjamin Harrison, Joseph Hewes, Thomas Heyward Jr, William Hooper, Stephen Hopkins, Francis Hopkinson, Thomas Jefferson, Francis Lightfoot Lee, Richard Henry Lee, Francis Lewis, Robert R. Livingston, Thomas Lynch, Arthur Middleton, Lewis Morris, Robert Morris, Thomas Nelson Jr, William Paca, John Penn, George Read, Caesar Rodney, Benjamin Rush, Edward Rutledge, Richard Stockton, Thomas Stone, William Whipple, John Witherspoon, Oliver Wolcott, George Wythe. The remaining eighteen signatories did not own slaves: Samuel Adams, George Clymer, William Ellery, Elbridge Gerry, John Hart, Samuel Huntington, Thomas McKean, John Morton, Robert Treat Paine, George Ross, Roger Sherman, John Smith, George Taylor, Martin Thornton, George Walton, William Williams and James Wilson: Signers of the Declaration of Independence, https://www.archives.gov/founding-docs/signers-factsheet; Politifact Spreadsheet, https://docs.google.com/spreadsheets/d/1Tq3u2XkluveKhJXAFJNfPq8uaxMnJ3ylM1cXecYrB-Q/edit#gid=0; Tom Kertscher, "Thirty-four of the Forty-seven Men Depicted in the Famous "Declaration of Independence" Painting were Slaveholders," Politifact, 10 September 2019, https://www.politifact.com/factchecks/2019/sep/10/arlen-parsa/evidence-shows-most-47-men-famous-declaration-inde/.
48. In 1769, Jefferson offered a reward for a runaway slave named Sunny, whom he described as "greatly addicted to drink, and when drunk is insolent and disorderly, in his conversation he swears much, and his behaviour is artful and knavish": "Advertisement for a Runaway Slave," 7 September 1769, PTJ 1:33. In the year that he drafted the Declaration of Independence, in a census on the "Number of souls in my family," Jefferson stated that there were 117, of which eighty-three were slaves: Lucia Stanton, *"Those Who Labor for My Happiness":*

Slavery at Thomas Jefferson's Monticello (Charlottesville, VA: University of Virginia Press, 2012), 4. And as Roosevelt points out, "Jefferson wrote the Declaration of Independence with the enslaved Robert Hemings—the Black son of Jefferson's father-in-law—waiting on him": Kermit Roosevelt III, *The Nation That Never Was: Reconstructing America's Story* (Chicago: University of Chicago Press, 2022), 131.

49. Declaration of the Rights of Man, https://avalon.law.yale.edu/18th_century/rightsof.asp.
50. Jeff Broadwater, *Jefferson, Madison, and the Making of the Constitution* (Chapel Hill, NC: University of North Carolina Press, 2019), 50, 53.
51. Robert G. Parkinson, *Thirteen Clocks: How Race United the Colonies and Made the Declaration of Independence* (Chapel Hill, NC: University of North Carolina Press, 2021), 156.
52. Pauline Maier, *American Scripture: Making the Declaration of Independence* (New York: Alfred A. Knopf, 1997), 118, 121.
53. George Anastaplo, *Reflections on Slavery and the Constitution* (Lanham, MD: Lexington Books, 2012), 49.
54. Parkinson, *Thirteen Clocks*, 94.
55. Robert G. Parkinson, *The Common Cause: Creating Race and Nation in the American Revolution* (Chapel Hill, NC: University of North Carolina Press, 2016), 253.
56. This grievance was reiterated in Thomas Paine's influential publication, *Common Sense*, published in January 1776, where Paine wrote that there were "tens of thousands [of Americans], who would think it glorious to expel from the continent, that barbarous and hellish power, which hath stirred up the Indians and Negroes to destroy us": Paine, *Rights of Man—Common Sense*, 280.
57. Ovid Demaris, *America the Violent* (New York: Cowles Book Company, Inc., 1970), 64–65.
58. Horne, *The Counter-Revolution of 1776*, 112.
59. George Washington, "To the General Court of Massachusetts Bay," 11 July 1776, in *Papers of George Washington: Revolutionary War Series:* vol. 5, *16 June 1776—12 August 1996*, ed. W. W. Abbott (Charlottesville, VA: University of Virginia Press, 1993), 271.
60. Quoted in Noel Rae, *The Great Stain: Witnessing American Slavery* (New York: The Overlook Press, 2018), 204–205.
61. "Constitution of South Carolina -1776," Thorpe 6:3242.
62. "Constitution of Virginia -1776," Thorpe 7:3815.
63. The omission of the word "slavery" in the Declaration of Independence was deliberate. This stemmed from its appropriated and repeated used by the American rebels during the American Revolution to describe what awaited white colonials if the revolt against the British failed. For example, an appeal to the people of Great Britain, approved by the Continental Congress on 21 October 1774, spoke of "a plan [by the British] for enslaving your fellow subjects in America": JCC 1:84. And, in a letter to George Washington in January 1776, John Hancock, the President of the Continental Congress, wrote that the aim of the rebellion was "rescue from slavery" and that the British objective was "to conquer and enslave" the American colonies: "From John Hancock," 6

January 1776, in *The Papers of George Washington: Revolutionary War Series*, vol. 3, *1 January 1776—31 March 1776*, ed. W. W. Abbott (Charlottesville, VA: University Press of Virginia, 1988), 42, 43. In generating support from the broader white population, colonial political and military elites repeatedly asserted that theirs was a struggle for independence and liberty against slavery at the hands of the British: Parkinson, *Thirteen Clocks*, 52. African Americans, enslaved or free, were not intended to be the beneficiaries of the liberty to be obtained if the British were defeated. As Perry points out, "The Declaration of Independence . . . said nothing about Whiteness but very clearly *meant* Whiteness": Imani Perry, *South to America: A Journey Below the Mason-Dixon to Understand the Soul of a Nation* (New York: Echo, 2022), 36. It was for this reason that the rebels initially maintained white-only armed forces, and it was only under the pressure of military necessity that African Americans, free and slave, were eventually allowed to join the rebels' armed forces. George Washington, a wealthy slaveholder himself, provides an example of how colonial military and political elites used the word "slavery," while simultaneously revealing how slavery was practiced in the colonies, when, in 1774, he fretted that the British wanted to "make us as tame, & abject Slaves, as the Blacks we Rule over with such arbitrary Sway": George Washington, "To Bryan Fairfax," 24 August 1774, in *The Papers of George Washington: Colonial Series*, vol. 10, *21 March 1774—15 June 1775*, ed. W. W. Abbott (Charlottesville, VA: University Press of Virginia, 1995), 155. Throughout the revolutionary period, slaves were, as Taylor writes, "depicted as too passive to qualify for freedom," with the consequence that, in the wake of victory over the British, "whites especially cherished their freedom because they denied it to the enslaved": Alan Taylor, *American Revolutions: A Continental History, 1750–1804* (New York: W. W. Norton & Company, 2016), 464–465.

64. Ellis, *The Cause*, 317.
65. Roosevelt, *The Nation That Never Was*, 134. On the clash between the ideals of the Declaration of Independence and the existence of slavery, Fishkin and Forbath write that "the only defense that seemed to allow American slavery to coexist with American democracy, was a racial one: Black racial inferiority justified slavery, and justified applying the principles of the Declaration only to whites": Joseph Fishkin and William E. Forbath, *The Anti-Oligarchy Constitution: Reconstructing the Economic Foundations of American Democracy* (Cambridge, MA: Harvard University Press, 2022), 90.
66. "Report of the New Haven Convention," 30 January 1778, in *The Public Records of the State of Connecticut*, vol. 1, ed. Charles J. Hoadley (Hartford, CT: Press of the Case, Lockwood and Brainard Company, 1894), 613.
67. Abraham Lincoln, "Address Delivered at the Dedication of the Cemetery at Gettysburg," 19 November 1863, CWAL 7:22–23, 22. Roosevelt, in his analysis of the Declaration of Independence, concludes that "[t]he core principle of Jefferson's Declaration has nothing to do with equality: it is independence, the right of the people to define itself and to separate from a larger political order": Roosevelt, *The Nation That Never Was*, 166.
68. Abraham Lincoln, "Speech at Springfield, Illinois," 26 June 1857, CWAL 2:406. Lincoln repeated his view of the Declaration in his seventh debate with Stephen

Douglas in October 1858: Abraham Lincoln, "Seventh and Last Debate with Stephen A. Douglas at Alton, Illinois," 15 October 1858, CWAL 3:301.

69. Abraham Lincoln, "Eulogy on Henry Clay," 5 July 1852, CWAL 2:130. In relation to the words in the opening paragraphs of the Declaration of Independence that foreshadowed conditions of freedom and equality, in his Farewell Address to the Senate in February 1861, Jefferson Davis said that, because those words were "to be construed by the circumstances and purposes for which it was made," they had "no reference to the slave; else, how happened it that among the items of arraignment made against George III was that he endeavored to do just what the North has been endeavoring of late to do—to stir up insurrection among our slaves?" CG, 36th Congress, 2nd Session, 487.
70. Thorpe 1:562 (Delaware, 1776); Thorpe 2:777 (Georgia, 1777); Thorpe 3:1691 (Maryland, 1776); Thorpe 5:2789 (North Carolina, 1776); Thorpe 5:3082 (Pennsylvania, 1776); Thorpe 6:3248 (South Carolina, 1778).
71. Quoted in Micah Alpaugh, *Friends of Freedom: The Rise of Social Movements in the Age of Atlantic Revolutions* (Cambridge, UK: Cambridge University Press, 2022), 178.
72. Quoted in Don E. Fehrenbacher, *The Slaveholding Republic: An Account of the United States Government's Relations to Slavery* (New York: Oxford University Press, 200), 16.
73. "Abigail Adams to John Adams," 22 September 1774, in *My Dearest Friend: Letters of Abigail and John Adams*, eds. Margaret A. Hogan and C. James Taylor (Cambridge, MA: Harvard University Press, 2007), 47–48. See also Larson, *American Inheritance*, 8-9.
74. Parkinson, *The Common Cause*, 664.
75. James Madison, "To William Bradford," 19 June 1775, PJM 1:154.
76. James Iredell, "Causes of the American Revolution," June 1776, in *The Papers of James Iredell*, vol. 1, *1767–1777*, ed. Don Higginbotham (Raleigh, NC: North Carolina Division of Archives and History, 1976), 409.
77. "Declaration of the Causes and Necessity of Taking Up Arms," 6 July 1775, Tansill, 15.
78. "Benjamin Franklin to Jonathan Shipley," 7 July 1775, LDC 1:606–607. Franklin reiterated these sentiments a year later when he wrote of British acts of "wanton Barbarity and Cruelty" that included that they had "excited . . . our slaves to Murder their Masters": "Benjamin Franklin to Lord Howe," 20 July 1776, LDC 4:499. In September 1775, John Houston and Archibald Bullock, delegates to the Continental Congress from Georgia, expressed to John Adams, their fears that if the British landed in Georgia, they would "proclaim Freedom to all the Negroes who would join [the British]" and that "20,000 Negroes would join . . . in a fortnight": in *Diary and Autobiography of John Adams*, vol. 2, *Diary 1771–1781*, ed. L. H. Butterfield (Cambridge, MA: Belknap Press, 1961), 182–183.
79. On the activities of slaves in Virginia to exploit the emerging conflict between the British and white colonials in the years preceding Dunmore's Proclamation, see Woody Holton, *Forced Founders: Indians, Debtors, Slaves, and the Making of the American Revolution in Virginia* (Chapel Hill, NC: University of North Carolina Press, 1999), 137–143, 160. On Dunmore's actions in the lead-up to

his proclamation, see Horne, *The Counter-Revolution of 1776*, 219–222; Gilbert, *Fighting for Emancipation*, 17–22.

80. "Lord Dunmore's Proclamation," 7 November 1775, in *The American Revolution: Writings from the War of Independence*, ed. John Rhodehamel (New York: Library of America, 2001), 82. Dunmore's Proclamation was foreshadowed on 1 May 1775 when he warned that, unless colonial unrest ceased, "I shall be forced and it is my fixed purpose to arm all my own Negroes and receive all others that will come to me whom I shall declare free": "Governor Earl of Dunmore to Earl of Dartmouth," 1 May 1775, in K. G. Davies, *Documents of the American Revolution 1770–1783,* vol. 9, *Transcripts 1775, January to June* (Dublin: Irish University Press, 1975), 109. News of Dunmore's warning "startled the insurgents": "Lieut.-General Thomas Gage to Earl of Dartmouth," 15 May 1775, in Davies, 132. Dunmore recognized that his warning "stirred up fears in them" but justified such a course of action on the grounds that he "had full right to make use of any means" as a "defence against a furious people": "Governor Earl of Dunmore to Earl of Dartmouth," 25–27 June 1775, in Davies, 204.

81. Cassandra Pybus, "Jefferson's Faulty Math: The Question of Slave Defections in the American Revolution," *The William and Mary Quarterly* 62, no. 2 (April 2005): 261.

82. Gary B. Nash, *The Forgotten Fifth: African Americans in the Age of Revolution* (Cambridge, MA: Harvard University Press, 2006), 5. Thomas Jefferson estimated that 70,000 slaves fled to the British: Andrew Delbanco, *The War Before the War: Fugitive Slaves and the Struggle for America's Soul from the Revolution to the Civil War* (New York: Penguin Press, 2018), 74. Morgan and Nicholls estimate that six thousand slaves (approximately 3 percent—one of the lowest percentage rates in the colonies) of Virginia's slaves escaped during the American Revolution: Philip D. Morgan and Michael L. Nicholls, "Slave Flight: Mount Vernon, Virginia, and the Wider Atlantic World," in *George Washington's South*, eds. Tamara Harvey and Greg O'Brien (Gainesville, FL: University Press of Florida, 2004), 206–209.

83. Nash, *The Unknown American Revolution*, 426.

84. "Council of War," 8 October 1775, in *The Papers of George Washington: Revolutionary War Series,* vol. 2, *16 September 1775—31 December 1775*, ed. W. W. Abbott (Charlottesville, VA: University Press of Virginia, 1987), 125.

85. "Minutes of Conference," 18–24 October 1775, in Abbott, *The Papers of George Washington: Revolutionary War Series,* vol. 2, 199.

86. George Washington, "To Richard Henry Lee, 26 December 1775, in Abbott *The Papers of George Washington: Revolutionary War Series,* vol. 2, 611.

87. "Direction by the Virginia Convention, on Lord Dunmore's Proclamation, offering freedom to such able-bodied Slaves willing to join him," 14 December 1775, https://digital.lib.niu.edu/islandora/object/niu-amarch:100939.

88. Pete Maslowski, "National Policy toward the Use of Black Troops in the Revolution," *The South Carolina Historical Magazine* 73, no. 1 (January 1972): 5; Bruce A. Ragsdale, *Washington at the Plow: The Founding Farmer and the Question of Slavery* (Cambridge, MA: The Belknap Press, 2021), 91.

89. JCC 4:60.

90. Gilbert, *Fighting for Emancipation*, 98–105.
91. Fritz Hirschfeld, *George Washington and Slavery: A Documentary Portrayal*, (Columbia, MO: University of Missouri Press, 1997), 148–152; Larson, *American Inheritance*, 113–116.
92. Alexander Hamilton, "To John Jay," 14 March 1779, in *The Papers of Alexander Hamilton*, vol. 2, *1779–1781*, ed. Harold C. Syrett, (New York: Columbia University Press, 1961), 17–18.
93. Manisha Sinha, *The Slave's Cause: A History of Abolition* (New Haven, CT: Yale University Press, 2016), 49–50. See also Finkelman, "The First Civil Rights Movement," 703–706.
94. Larson, *American Inheritance*, 130.
95. Thomas Jefferson, "To John Randolph," 29 November 1775, PTJ 1:269.
96. Richard Henry Lee to Catherine Macaulay, 29 November 1775, http://leefamilyarchive.org/papers/letters/transcripts-gw%20delegates/DIV0248.html.
97. Gilbert, *Fighting for Emancipation*, 37; Larson, *American Inheritance*, 98.
98. Horne, *The Counter-Revolution of 1776*, 234.
99. Horne, 233. In his assessment of the extent to which slavery was a factor leading to the Declaration of Independence, Roosevelt concludes that "a fair look at the evidence suggests that a concern to protect slavery probably deserves some place among the reasons for the revolution": Roosevelt, *The Nation That Never Was*, 58.
100. Van Cleve, *A Slaveholders' Union*, 54.
101. Van Cleve, *A Slaveholders' Union*, 53–54.
102. Benjamin Quarles, *The Negro in the American Revolution* (Chapel Hill, NC: University of North Carolina Press, 1996), 191–193; Kornblith, *Slavery and Sectional Strife in the Early American Republic*, 12–13; Sinha, *The Slave's Cause*, 37–41; Alpaugh, *Friends of Freedom*, 172–174.
103. James Otis, *The Rights of the British Colonies Asserted and Proved*, 3rd ed. (London: J. Williams & J. Almond, 1766), 56, 99.
104. Kornblith, *Slavery and Sectional Strife in the Early American Republic*, 13–16.
105. Christopher Leslie Brown, "The Problems of Slavery," in *The Oxford Handbook of the American Revolution*, eds. Edward G. Gray and Jane Kamensky (Oxford: Oxford University Press, 2013), 437. On the economic aspects of Northern antislavery sentiment, see James L. Huston, *Calculating the Value of the Union: Slavery, Property Rights, and the Economic Origins of the Civil War* (Chapel Hill, NC: University of North Carolina Press, 2003), 69–103; Eric Foner, *Free Soil, Free Labor, Free Men: The Ideology of the Republican Party Before the Civil War* (New York: Oxford University Press, 1970.
106. James Oakes, "'The Compromising Expedient:' Justifying a Proslavery Constitution," *Cardozo Law Review* 17, no. 6 (May 1996): 2027. Larson writes that this and the freedom of slaves in the wake of Dunmore's proclamation meant that "[o]ne way or another, the American Revolution resulted in the first great emancipation of enslaved Blacks in the New World:" Larson, *American Inheritance*, ix.
107. "From John Adams to Jeremy Belknap," 21 March 1795, https://founders.archives.gov/documents/Adams/99-02-02-1659. In this letter, Adams went

on to say: "The *common* white People, or rather the labouring People, were the Cause of rendering Negroes unprofitable servants. Their Scoffs & Insults, their continual Informations, filled the Negros with Discontent, made them lazy idle, proud, vicious, and at length wholly Useless to their Masters: to such a Degree that the Abolition of Slavery became a measure of œconomy."

108. Finkelman, "The First Civil Rights Movement," 701–703.
109. Oakes, "The Compromising Expedient," 2027–2028; Taylor, *American Revolutions*, 466–468.
110. Based on figures for the 1790 Census in *Return of the Whole Number of Persons Within the Several Districts of the United States* (Philadelphia: n.p., 1793), 4.
111. Manjapra, *Black Ghost of Empire*, 17, 21.
112. Manjapra, *Black Ghost of Empire*, 18.
113. Quarles, *The Negro in the American Revolution*, 40.
114. JCC 1:77.
115. Oakes, "The Compromising Expedient," 2029.
116. Leonardo Marques, "Slave Trading in a New World: The Strategies of North American Slave Traders in the Age of Abolition," *Journal of the Early Republic* 32, no. 2 (Summer 2012): 240–241.
117. Oakes, "The Compromising Expedient," 2028–2029.
118. Oakes, "The Compromising Expedient," 2029.
119. Daniel Wait Howe, *Political History of Secession to the Beginning of the American Civil War* (New York: G. P. Putnam's Sons, 1914), 13.
120. Paul Finkelman, "Slavery and Bondage in the 'Empire of Liberty'" in *The Northwest Ordinance: Essays on Its Formation, Provisions, and Legacy*, ed. Frederick D. Williams (East Lansing, MI: Michigan State University Press, 1988), 80. On the persistence of slavery in the Northwest Territory after the passage of the Northwest Ordinance, see Paul Finkelman, "Evading the Ordinance: The Persistence of Bondage in Indiana and Illinois," *Journal of the Early Republic* 9, no. 1 (Spring 1989) 21–51.
121. Thorpe 2:980–981.
122. Thorpe 2:1008.
123. Thorpe 2:1002.
124. Article XIV also required its legislature to enact laws that would, in effect, be a form of support for the Constitution's fugitive slave clause. The article stipulated that the legislation had to "prevent the owners of slaves from bringing them into [Illinois] for the purposes of setting them free": Thorpe 2:1009. This provision was complemented by a provision in Illinois' Criminal Code that criminalized the harboring of runaway slaves. The constitutional validity of this provision was upheld by the Supreme Court in *Moore v. Illinois*, 55 U.S. 13, 21 (1852).
125. MJQA 9:349.
126. Samantha Seeley, *Race, Removal, and the Right to Remain: Migration and the Making of the United States* (Williamsburg, VA: Omohundro Institute of Early American History and Culture, 2021), 235–236.
127. Kate Masur, *Until Justice Be Done: America's First Civil Rights Movement, from Revolution to Reconstruction* (New York: W. W. Norton & Company, 2021), 241–244. On the policies discriminating against African Americans in

the states that emerged from the Northwest Territory, see Jon K. Lauck, *The Good Country: A History of the American Midwest, 1800–1900* (Norman, OK: University of Oklahoma Press, 2022), 122–130.

128. Alabama, Florida, Kentucky, Louisiana, Maryland, North Carolina, South Carolina, Tennessee, Texas, Virginia. Louisiana in 1852 and Tennessee in 1854 went one step further and required emancipated slaves to leave the United States: Benjamin Joseph Klebaner, "American Manumission Laws and the Responsibility for Supporting Slaves," *Virginia Magazine of History and Biography* 63, no. 4 (October 1955): 448–449.

129. Alexis de Tocqueville, *Democracy in America*, vol. 1 (New York: Everyman's Library, 1994), 360. However, with the increased likelihood of secession in the late 1850s, Louisiana in 1857, Arkansas in 1859, Alabama in 1860, and Maryland in 1860 all passed laws imposing a total ban on manumission: Klebaner, "American Manumission Laws and the Responsibility for Supporting Slaves," 443.

130. Calvin H. Johnson, *Righteous Anger at Wicked States: The Meaning of the Founders' Constitution* (Cambridge, UK: Cambridge University Press, 2005), 213–222; George William Van Cleve, *We Have Not a Government: The Articles of Confederation and the Road to the Constitution* (Chicago: University of Chicago Press, 2017), 214–242, 275–276.

131. On the flaws in the Articles of Confederation that led to the Constitutional Convention see Michael J. Klarman, *The Framers' Coup: The Making of the United States Constitution* (New York: Oxford University Press, 2016), 11–125.

132. RFCS, 93. William Pierce, from Georgia, described the Confederation as being "like a ship bearing under the weight of a tempest; it is trembling, and just on the point of sinking": "Extract of a letter from Hon. William Pierce, Esq., to St. George Tucker, Esq.," 28 September 1787, in Anon., "Notes of Major William Pierce on the Federal Convention of 1787," *The American Historical Review* 3, no. 2 (January 1898): 314. For James Madison, the Confederation had "*mortal* diseases": James Madison, "To James Madison, Sr.," 1 April 1787, PJM 9:359.

133. Thomas Jefferson, "To John Adams," 30 August 1787, PTJ 12:69. France's chargé d'affaires, Louis Guillaume Otto, was equally effusive in describing the fifty-five chosen delegates, writing that "[i]f all the delegates named for this Convention at Philadelphia are present, we will never have seen, even in Europe, an assembly more respectable for the talents, knowledge, disinterestedness, and patriotism of those who compose it": quoted in Richard B. Morris, *The Forging of the Union, 1781-1789* (New York: Harper and Row, Publishers, 1987), 269. Georgia's Convention delegate, William Pierce, described the Convention as "the wisest Council in the World": Anon., "Notes of Major William Pierce," 334. Notwithstanding that many of his proposals were rejected by the Philadelphia Convention, in 1835, James Madison wrote of its delegates "that there never was an assembly of men, charged with a great and arduous trust, who were more pure in their motives, or more exclusively or anxiously devoted to the object committed to them, than were the members of the Federal Convention of 1787": James Madison, "A Sketch Never Finished Nor Applied," circa 1835, WJM 2:411.

134. David C. Hendrickson, *Peace Pact: The Lost World of the American Founding*, (Lawrence, KS: University of Kansas Press), 2003, 259.
135. At the Philadelphia Convention, Madison conceded that there had been "numerous & notorious" violations of the Articles of Confederation and stated that "a breach of any one article, by any of the parties, absolved the other parties from (the whole) obligation": RFC 1:122–123, 315. He repeated this sentiment in *Federalist 43*, where he wrote that in "a compact between independent sovereigns . . . all the articles are mutually conditions of each other . . . and that a breach, committed by either of the parties, absolves the others; and authorizes them, if they please, to pronounce . . . [it] violated and void": "The Federalist No 43. (Madison)," Federalist, 216.
136. Charles F. Hobson, "The Negative on State Laws: James Madison, the Constitution, and the Crisis of Republican Government," *The William and Mary Quarterly* 36, no. 2 (April 1979): 215; Ralph Ketcham, *James Madison: A Biography* (New York: The Macmillan Company, 1971), 229; John R. Vile, *The Constitutional Convention: A Comprehensive Encyclopedia of America's Founding*, vol. 1, rev. second ed. (Clark, NJ: Talbot Publishing, 2016), 473; Michael Stokes Paulsen and Luke Paulsen, *The Constitution: An Introduction* (New York: Basic Books, 2015), 11.
137. Forrest McDonald asserts that the epithet is a "myth": Forrest McDonald, *Novus Ordo Seclorum: The Intellectual Origins of the Constitution* (Lawrence, KS: University Press of Kansas, 1985), 205–209. Bilder's analysis of Madison's role in the Constitutional Convention leads her to conclude that "Madison was not the intellectual father of the Constitution": Mary Sarah Bilder, *Madison's Hand: Revising the Constitutional Convention* (Cambridge, MA: Harvard University Press, 2015), 7. One contender for that epithet is James Wilson: Stephen B. Presser, *Law Professors: Three Centuries of Shaping American Law* (St. Paul, MN: West Academic Publishing, 2017), 35–37. Another is George Washington: Akhil Reed Amar, "Founding Myths," in *Myth America: Historians Take on the Biggest Legends and Lies About Our Past*, eds. Kevin M. Kruse and Julian E Zelizer (New York: Basic Books, 2022), 26–30.
138. "The Federalist No. 41 (Madison)," Federalist, 195.
139. Robert E. Bonner, *Mastering America: Southern Slaveholders and the Crisis of American Nationhood* (New York: Cambridge University Press, 2009), 6. From the Confederacy's perspective, this is exactly what happened to it when Lincoln issued the Emancipation Proclamation on 1 January 1861.
140. AC, 16th Congress, 1st Session, 1313.
141. George Washington, "From George Washington to Henry Lee, Jr.," 22 September 1788, in *The Papers of George Washington: Confederation Series,* vol. 6, *1 January 1788—23 September 1788*, ed. W. W. Abbot (Charlottesville, VA: University of Virginia Press, 1997), 529.
142. Luther Martin, "Genuine Information," 29 November 1787, RFC 3:210, 212.
143. JSCAL, 244.
144. "The Federalist No. 54 (Madison)," Federalist, 265.
145. James Madison, "To Robert J Evans," 15 June 1819, PJMRS 2:470.
146. Paul Finkelman, "The Founders and Slavery: Little Ventured, Little Gained," *Yale Journal of Law and the Humanities* 13, no. 2 (Summer 2001): 414.

147. For Abraham Lincoln, these provisions gave rise to "constitutional relations between the slave and free States, which are degrading to the latter": Abraham Lincoln, "Speech at Peoria, Illinois," 16 October 1854, CWAL 2:268.
148. Alpaugh, *Friends of Freedom*, 193.
149. Roosevelt, *The Nation That Never Was*, 46.
150. "The Declaration of Independence: The Jefferson Draft With Congress's Editorial Changes," in Maier, *American Scripture*, 239.
151. Richard D. Brown, *Self-Evident Truths: Contesting Equal Rights from the Revolution to the Civil War* (New Haven, CT: Yale University Press, 2017), 112.
152. John Jay, "Jay to English Anti-Slavery Society," June [?] 1788, in *The Correspondence and Public Papers of John Jay, 1782–1793,* vol. 3, ed. Henry P. Johnston (New York: G. P. Putnam's Sons, 1891), 341–342. In 1839, following the publication of James Madison's notes on the proceedings at the Philadelphia Convention, which revealed the debates on the Constitution's slavery provisions, Jay's son, William Jay, wrote that "[o]ur Fathers, in forming the Federal Constitution, entered into a guilty compromise on the subject of Slavery, and heavily is their sin now visited upon their children": William Jay, *A View of the Action of the Federal Government in Behalf of Slavery*, 2nd. ed. (New York: The American Anti-Slavery Society, 1839), 21.
153. *Dred Scott v. Sandford*, 60 U.S. 393, 411 (1857). Forbes sees Taney's ruling as "[w]ithout question . . . the fruit of [Jefferson's] *Notes* [*on the State of Virginia*]": Forbes, "Introduction," xix-lx, lix. Taney's ruling on this point reflected views he held while serving as attorney general (1831–1833) during the administration of Andrew Jackson: Noah Feldman, *The Broken Constitution: Lincoln, Slavery, and the Founding of America* (New York: Farrar, Straus and Giroux, 2021), 105. However, his ruling is somewhat incongruous with his statement in 1819 in legal proceedings on behalf of an abolitionist, in which he described slavery as "a blot in our national character" and asserted that "every real lover of freedom hopes that it will be effectually, though it must be gradually, wiped away" and his action in the following year of emancipating all but two of his slaves—the two retained being too old to provide for themselves: Timothy S. Huebner, "Roger B. Taney and the Slavery Issue: Looking beyond—and before *Dred Scott*," *Journal of American History* 97, no. 1 (June 2010): 17, 20.
154. Sidney George Fisher, *The Trial of the Constitution* (Philadelphia: J. B. Lippincott & Co., 1862), 293.
155. Parkinson, *Thirteen Clocks*, 184.
156. William Lloyd Garrison, "The United States Constitution," in *Selections from the Writings and Speeches of William Lloyd Garrison* (Boston: R. F. Wallcut, 1852), 310–311.
157. RFC 2: 370. It is ironic that the single bloodiest day of the Civil War, the Battle of Antietam, took place on 17 September 1862, the seventy-fifth anniversary of the signing of the draft Constitution at the Philadelphia Convention.
158. Quoted in James T. Kloppenberg, *Toward Democracy: The Struggle for Self-Rule in European and American Thought* (New York: Oxford University Press, 2016), 574.
159. Rawley with Behrendt, *The Transatlantic Slave Trade*, 264–265.

160. Fisher, *The Trial of the Constitution*, 273; Mark A. Graber, *Dred Scott and the Problem of Constitutional Evil* (New York: Cambridge University Press, 2006), 107–110; Gordon S. Wood, "The Revolutionary Origins of the Civil War," *Northwestern University Law Review* 114, no. 2 (2019): 546–549.
161. RFC 2:371. See also Benjamin Franklin, "An Address to the Public From the Pennsylvania Society for Promoting the Abolition of Slavery, and the Relief of Free Negroes Unlawfully Held in Bondage," 9 November 1789, in *The Works of Benjamin Franklin*, vol. 8, ed. John Bigelowed (New York: G. P. Putnam's Sons, 1904), 157–158.
162. Gordon S. Wood, *The Idea of America: Reflections on the Birth of the United States* (New York: The Penguin Press, 2011), 268.
163. Finkelman, "The Founders and Slavery," 419.
164. George Washington, "To Thomas Jefferson," 13 February 1789, in *The Papers of George Washington: Presidential Series,* vol. 1, *24 September 1788—31 March 1789*, ed. Dorothy Twohig (Charlottesville, VA: University of Virginia Press, 1987), 300.
165. Sven Beckert, *Empire of Cotton: A New History of Global Capitalism* (London: Penguin Books, 2015), 102.
166. Beckert, *Empire of Cotton*, 104.
167. Alan Greenspan and Adrian Wooldridge, *Capitalism in America: A History* (New York: Penguin Press, 2018), 33–34. During a Continental Congress debate in 1776, South Carolina's Thomas Lynch made this point when he said: "Freeman cannot be got to work in our Colonies; it is not in the ability or inclination of freemen to do the work that the negroes do": JCC 6:1080.
168. Thorpe 3:1287.
169. Thorpe 2:801.
170. AC, 1st Congress, 2nd Session, 1198.
171. Based upon official census figures set out in Mason I. Lowance Jr, *A House Divided: The Antebellum Slavery Debates in America, 1776–1865* (Princeton, NJ: Princeton University Press, 2003), 6.
172. Estimates as to the number of slaves imported prior to 1808 range from approximately 113,000 to around 290,000: Van Cleve, *A Slaveholders' Union*, 327; Adam Rothman, *Slave Country: American Expansion and the Origins of the Deep South* Cambridge, MA: Harvard University Press, 2005, 19. Estimates of the number of slaves illegally imported from 1808 to 1861 range from 50,000 to 250,000: Rawley with Behrendt, *The Transatlantic Slave Trade*, 284; David Eltis, "The US Transatlantic Slave Trade, 1644–1867: An Assessment," *Civil War History* 54, no. 4 (December 2008): 353; Andrew Wender Cohen, *Contraband: Smuggling and the Birth of the American Century* (New York: W. W. Norton & Company, New York, 2015), 65.
173. Richard Young and Jeffrey Meiser, "Race and the Dual State in the Early American Republic," in *Race and American Political Development*, eds. Joseph, Julie Novkov, and Dorian Warren (New York: Routledge, 2008), 45.
174. Beckert, *Empire of Cotton*, 105–106.
175. Rothman, *Slave Country*, 46.
176. Beckert, *Empire of Cotton*, 119; Greenspan and Wooldridge, *Capitalism in America*, 74.

177. Brian Schoen, *The Fragile Fabric of Union: Cotton, Federal Politics, and the Global Origins of the Civil War* (Baltimore, MD: Johns Hopkins University Press, 2009), 264–266. Whether slavery was inefficient, unproductive, cruel, and, by 1860, dying; or productive, profitable, mildly humane, and viable into the future, has been a topic of intense debate amongst scholars ever since the publication, in 1974, of Robert William Fogel and Stanley L. Engerman's book, *Time on the Cross: The Economics of Negro Slavery* (Boston: Little, Brown & Company, 1974). For an assessment of that debate, see Eric Hilt, "Revisiting *Time on the Cross* After 45 Years: The Slavery Debates and the New Economic History," *Capitalism: A Journal of History and Economics* 1, no. 2 (Spring 2020): 456–483.
178. CG, 35th Congress, 1st Session, 961.
179. CG, 36th Congress, 2nd Session, 73. North Carolina's Senator Thomas J. Clingman expressed the same sentiment on 4 December 1860 when he declared that southerners "have no fears of the future, if driven to rely on themselves" and that if one took into consideration the "position, climate and fertility" of the southern states "there [was] not upon earth a body of territory superior to it": CG, 36th Congress, 2nd Session, 4. Not all southerners shared the bravado of Hammond, Wigfall, and Clingman. John H. Wood, an anti-secessionist from Mississippi, argued that their sentiments amounted to a "delusion" and that "England and France . . . would not take part in the conflict . . . because of the prejudices of the . . . people against slavery. . . . The sympathies, not only of France and England, but of the civilized world will be against us": quoted in Roger G. Kennedy, *Cotton and Conquest: How the Plantation System Acquired Texas* (Norman, OK: University of Oklahoma Press, 2013), 17. On the commercial future that the Confederacy expected, see Adrian Brettle, *Colossal Ambitions: Confederate Planning for a Post-Civil War World* (Charlottesville, VA: University of Virginia Press, 2020), 11–41.
180. John Darwin, *Unlocking the World: Port Cities and Globalization in the Age of Steam, 1830–1930* (London: Allen Lane, 2000), 177.
181. In order: South Carolina, Mississippi, Louisiana, Georgia, Connecticut, Alabama, Florida, Texas, Rhode Island, and Virginia: Huston, *Calculating the Value of the Union*, 30. It was no coincidence that the first seven Confederate states in this list were also the seven states that seceded from the Union prior to the inauguration of Abraham Lincoln in March 1861.
182. Beckert, *Empire of Cotton*, 171.
183. Beckert, 140.
184. Darwin, *Unlocking the World*, 202–203.
185. Michael Lind, *Land of Promise: An Economic History of the United States* (New York: HarperCollins, 2012), 107.
186. Mark Thornton and Robert B. Ekelund Jr., *Tariffs, Blockades, and Inflation: The Economics of the Civil War* (Washington: Scholarly Resources Inc., 2004), 11–13.
187. Lind, *Land of Promise*, 35.
188. John Majewski, *Modernizing a Slave Economy: The Economic Vision of the Confederate Nation* (Chapel Hill, NC: University of North Carolina Press, 2009), 110.

189. Cohen, *Contraband*, 56.
190. David P. Currie, *The Constitution in Congress, 1829–1861: Democrats and Whigs* (Chicago: University of Chicago Press, 2005), 90; Lawrence M. Anderson, *Federalism, Secession and the American State: Divided, We Secede* (New York: Routledge, 2013), 29.
191. Majewski, *Modernizing a Slave Economy*, 112.
192. David O. Whitten, "Tariff and Profit in the Antebellum Louisiana Sugar Industry," *Business History Review* 44, no. 2 (Summer 1970): 227–229.
193. Bonner, *Mastering America*, 60.
194. Brown, *Self-Evident Truths*, 13.
195. Caitlin Rosenthal, *Accounting for Slavery: Masters and Management* (Cambridge, MA: Harvard University Press, 2018), 195.
196. Carl Lawrence Paulus, *The Slaveholding Crisis: Fear of Insurrection and the Coming of the Civil War* (Baton Rouge, LA: Louisiana State University Press, 2017), 3.
197. Adam Hochschild, *Bury the Chains: The British Struggle to Abolish Slavery* (London: Macmillan, 2005), 260. At 261, Hochschild notes that Saint-Domingue, which William Pitt the Younger had called "the Eden of the Western World," was a colony whose "annual production of sugar and other crops was roughly double that of all British West Indies islands put together. No colony anywhere made so large a profit for its mother country."
198. Timothy M. Matthewson, "George Washington's Policy Toward the Haitian Revolution," *Diplomatic History* 3, no. 3 (July 1979): 321–336.
199. Darwin, *Unlocking the World*, 168. On the slave system in Saint-Domingue, the slave revolution, and the subsequent imposition on Haiti for compensation payments to be made to France, see Manjapra, *Black Ghost of Empire*, 45–64.
200. Alfred N. Hunt, *Haiti's Influence on Antebellum America: Slumbering Volcano in the Caribbean* (Baton Rouge, LA: Louisiana State University Press, 1988), 2. See also Paulus, *The Slaveholding Crisis*, 13.
201. Paulus, *The Slaveholding Crisis*, 24–32.
202. Morgan, *Slavery and Servitude*, 92–94; Paulus, *The Slaveholding Crisis*, 42–45.
203. Rothman, *Slave Country*, 107–113; Paulus, *The Slaveholding Crisis*, 40–41.
204. Paulus, *The Slaveholding Crisis*, 62–71; Varon, *Disunion!*, 74–78.
205. "Report," JSCGA, 112.
206. "Declaration of the Immediate Causes Which Induce and Justify the Secession of Mississippi from the Federal Union," JSCMS, 87.
207. "Declaration of the Immediate Causes Which Induce and Justify the Secession of South Carolina From The Federal Union," JSCSC, 464, 465.
208. "A declaration of the causes which impel the State of Texas to secede from the Federal Union," JSCTX, 64.
209. de Tocqueville, *Democracy in America*, 359.
210. Paul Starr, *Entrenchment: Wealth, Power, and the Constitution of Democratic Societies* (New Haven, CT: Yale University Press, 2019), 97. Nat Turner's Revolt inspired Aleck, a slave owned by John C. Calhoun, to escape. However, he was recaptured the following day. Calhoun ordered that he be jailed for a week and given thirty lashes: Robert Elder, *Calhoun: American Heretic* (New York: Basic Books, 2021), 273–275.

211. Louis P. Masur, "Nat Turner and Sectional Crisis," in *Nat Turner: A Slave Rebellion in History and Memory*, ed. Kenneth S. Greenberg (Oxford: Oxford University Press, 2003), 149.
212. Edward B. Rugemer, "The Southern Response to British Abolitionism: The Maturation of Proslavery Apologetics," *Journal of Southern History* 70, no. 2 (May 2004): 223, 247. See also Joseph T. Murphy, "The British Example: West Indian Emancipation, The Freedom Principle, and the Rise of Antislavery Politics in the United States, 1833–1843," *The Journal of the Civil War Era* 8, no. 4 (December 2018): 621–646; Hochschild, *Bury the Chains*, 347. The emancipation of slaves by the British Slavery Abolition Act was on terms that mandated the payment of compensation to slaveowners—but not to their slaves—which was financed by the United Kingdom borrowing £20 million (finally repaid in 2015) and required the freed slaves to remain "apprenticed" to their former owners for a period of four years: Kris Manjapra, "The Scandal of the British Slavery Abolition Act Loan," *Social and Economic Studies* 68, nos. 3–4 (September–December 2019): 165–184.
213. "An Act to provide for an exchange of lands with the Indians residing in any of the states or territories, and for their removal west of the river Mississippi," 28 May 1830, USSL 4:411–412.
214. Linda K. Kerber, "The Abolitionist Perception of the Indian," *Journal of American History* 62, no. 2 (September 1975): 295.
215. Henry Mayer, *All on Fire: William Lloyd Garrison and the Abolition of Slavery* (New York: St. Martin's Press, 1998), 138; Gerard N. Magliocca, "Indians and Invaders: The Citizenship Clause and Illegal Aliens," *University of Pennsylvania Journal of Constitutional Law* 10, no. 3 (March 2008) 515–516.
216. Kerber, "The Abolitionist Perception of the Indian," 283–284.
217. Steven Waldman, *Sacred Liberty: America's Long, Bloody, and Ongoing Struggle for Religious Freedom* (New York: HarperOne, 2019), 60.
218. On the development of African American abolitionism and its contribution to the post–Civil War constitutional amendments, see James W. Fox Jr., "The Constitution of Black Abolitionism: Reframing the Second Founding," *University of Pennsylvania Journal of Constitutional Law* 23, no. 2 (April 2021): 267–350; Lauck, *The Good Country*, 130–138.
219. Matthew Karp, *This Vast Southern Empire: Slaveholders at the Helm of American Foreign Policy* (Cambridge, MA: Harvard University Press, 2016), 16.
220. "Resolutions of South Carolina," Ames, 218.
221. Graber, *Dred Scott*, 128–129.
222. PVSC 1:468–469.
223. Cotton Mather, *A Good Master Well Served: A Brief Discourse on the Necessary Properties & Practices of a Good Servant* (Boston: B. Green and J. Allen, 1696), 53.
224. MJQA 5:10. This was a widespread view amongst southerners and propagated by men such as Governor Henry A. Wise of Virginia and Thomas R. R. Cobb, a leading legal scholar from Georgia: George M. Fredrickson, *The Black Image in the White Mind: The Debate on Afro-American Character and Destiny, 1817–1914* (New York: Harper & Row, Publishers, 1971), 62.
225. MJQA 9:284.

226. John C. Calhoun, "Speech on the War with Mexico," 4 January 1848, PJCC 25:64.
227. Elder, *Calhoun*, 337, 339.
228. John C. Calhoun, "Remarks on Receiving Abolition Petitions (First Report)," 6 February 1837, PJCC 13:395–396. Calhoun restated this belief in a speech to the Senate in 1848, when he said: "With us, the two great divisions of society are not the rich and poor, but white and blacks; and all the former, the poor as well as the rich, belong to the upper class, and are respected and treated as equals, if honest and industrious, and hence have a position and pride of character of which neither poverty not misfortune can deprive them": John C. Calhoun, "Speech On the Oregon Bill," 27 June 1848, PJCC 25:533. To similar effect, in his influential *Memoir on Slavery*, William Harper, the prominent politician, jurist, and social and political theorist from South Carolina, wrote that slavery was the "sole cause" of civilization and that without what he referred to as the "coercion of Slavery . . . there can be no accumulation of property, no providence for the future, no taste for comforts or elegancies, which are the characteristics and essentials of civilization. He who has obtained the command of another's labour, first begins to accumulate and provide for the future, and the foundations of civilization are laid. . . . . Since the existence of man upon earth . . . every society which has attained civilization, has advanced through this process." Harper went on to state that, although the enslavement of African Americans was appropriate because "the negro race, from their temperament and capacity, are peculiarly suited to the situation which they occupy . . .": William Harper, *Memoir on Slavery* (James S. Burges, Charleston SC, 1838), 4–5, 21. Finally, in a speech in March 1851, then-Senator Jefferson Davis stated his belief that the distinction between a white worker and a slave kept the former on the same level as his employer because in slave states the distinction between the classes was a distinction based upon color, rather than on wealth or property, with the consequence that all whites were equal in the sense that the poor white was not a degraded person as was the African American slave. An end to slavery would degrade the poor white to that of the colored African American: Jefferson Davis, "Speech of Jefferson Davis at Aberdeen, Mississippi," 26 May 1851, in *Jefferson Davis, Constitutionalist: His Letters, Papers and Speeches*, vol. 2, ed. Dunbar Rowland (Jackson, MS: Mississippi Department of Archives and History, 1923), 73–74.
229. Martineau, *Society in America*, 375.
230. In asserting the superiority of slave labor over free labor, Fitzhugh wrote: "The negro slaves of the South are the happiest and, in some sense, the freest people in the world. The children and the aged and infirm work not at all, and yet have all the comforts and necessaries of life provided for them. They enjoy liberty, because they are oppressed neither by care nor labor. The women do little hard work, and are protected from the despotism of their husbands by their masters. The negro men and stout boys work, on the average, in good weather, not more than nine hours a day. The balance of their time is spent in perfect abandon. Besides they have their Sabbaths and holidays. . . . . The free laborer must work or starve. He is more of a slave than the negro, because he works longer and harder for less allowance than the slave, and has no holiday,

because the cares of life with him begin when its labors end. He has no liberty, and not a single right. . . . . Under the delusive name of liberty, you [the capitalist] work him [the free laborer], 'from morn to dewy ever'—from infancy to old age—then turn him out to starve. You treat your horses and hounds better. Capital is a cruel master": George Fitzhugh, *Cannibals All! or, Slaves Without Masters* (Richmond, VA: A. Morris Publisher, 1857), 26–32. That slavery was far from being a "positive good" is evidenced in Harriet Martineau's observations of slavery, witnessed during her travels through the southern slave states in the mid-1830s. In her account of her travels she wrote: "The word 'hatred' is not too strong for the feeling of a large proportion of slave-holders towards particular slaves; or as they would call them (the word 'slave' never being heard in the south,) their 'force,' their 'hands,' their 'negroes,' their 'people.' I was frequently told of the 'endearing relation' subsisting between master and slaves; but, at the best, it appeared to me the same 'endearing relation' which subsists between a man and his horse, between a lady and her dog. As long as the slave remains ignorant, docile, and contented, he is taken good care of, humoured, and spoken of with a contemptuous kindness. But, from the moment he exhibits the attributes of a rational being,—from the moment his intellect seems likely to come into the most distant competition with that of whites, the most deadly hatred springs up;—not in the black, but in his oppressors": Martineau, *Society in America*, 381–382.

231. Fredrickson, *The Black Image in the White Mind*, 44–46, 53; Varon, *Disunion!*, 82–84. See also Edward A. Pollard, *Black Diamonds Gathered in the Darkey Homes of the South* (New York: Pudney & Russell, Publishers, 1859), 81–83.
232. John F. Kvach, *De Bow's Review: The Antebellum Vision of a New South* (Lexington, KY: University Press of Kentucky, 2013), 81–83. Established in 1846, *De Bow's Review* "quickly became the most widely circulated periodical in the South and even outperformed many similar publications in the more literate and densely populated northern states:" Jonathan B. Crider, "De Bow's Revolution: The Memory of the American Revolution on the Politics of the Sectional Crisis, 1850-1861," *American Nineteenth Century History* 10, no. 3 (September 2009): 319.
233. Quoted in Darwin, *Unlocking the World*, 178.
234. CG, 35th Congress, 1st Session, 962.
235. Fredrickson, *The Black Image in the White Mind*, 61.
236. Examples of similar views expressed in the leadup to, and during, the secession crisis of 1860–1861 can be seen in Edward Mayes, ed., *Lucius Q. C. Lamar: His Life, Times, and Speeches, 1825–1893* (Nashville, TN: Methodist Episcopal Church, South, 1896), 629–639; John Townsend, *The Doom of Slavery in the Union: Its Safety Out of It* (Charleston, SC: Evans and Cogswell, 1860), 23–24; JSCAL, 201 (delegate Mr Smith), 235 (delegate Mr Stone); *Senate Journal of the Extra Session of the Thirty-Third General Assembly of the State of Tennessee Which Convened at Nashville, on the First Monday in January A.D. 1861* (Nashville, TN: J. O. Griffith & Company, Public Printers, 1861), 141 (Hon. George W. Jones, of Tennessee). The view of slavery as a positive good was reflected in the Confederacy's Constitution, in which the words "slave(s)" or "slavery"

appeared eleven times, in contrast to the use of euphemisms for slavery in the Union's Constitution.

237. "Letter of Gov. Call of Florida, to J. S. Littell, of Pennsylvania," 12 February, 1861, Moore 1:417–421.
238. James Oakes, *The Scorpion's Sting: Antislavery and the Coming of the Civil War* (New York: W. W. Norton & Company, 2014), 81–82; Alan Taylor, *American Republics: A Continental History of the United States*, 1783–1850 (New York: W. W. Norton & Company, 2021), 156–157.
239. Taylor, *American Revolutions*, 468.
240. Thorpe 2:1009 (Article XIV).
241. Thorp 2:1095 (Article XIII).
242. Thorpe 5:3017 (Article XVII, Section 4). Oregon's provision against immigration by free African Americans saw significant opposition from some Republican Party congressmen opposing its admission as a state: Masur, *Until Justice Be Done*, 265–266.
243. Masur, 16–17.
244. Donald Yacovone, *Teaching White Supremacy: America's Democratic Ordeal and the Forging of Our National Identity* (New York: Pantheon Books, 2022), 7.
245. Ira Berlin, *Many Thousands Gone: The First Two Centuries of Slavery in North America* (Cambridge MA, Belknap Press, 1998), 239.
246. Maine, Massachusetts, New Hampshire, Rhode Island, and Vermont. See Allan J. Lichtman, *The Embattled Vote in American: From the Founding to the Present* (Cambridge, MA: Harvard University Press, 2018), 37, 45–63; Christopher Malone, "Race Formation, Voting Rights, and Democratization in the Antebellum North," *New Political Science* 27, no. 2 (June 2005): 177–198; Alexander Keyssar, *The Right to Vote: The Contested History of Democracy in the United States*, rev. ed. (New York: Basic Books, 2000), 44–47.
247. Sidney George Fisher, *The Laws of Race, As Connected with Slavery* (Philadelphia: Willis P. Hazard, 1860), 10–11. Fisher's racist views were repeated in Fisher, *The Trial of the Constitution*, 181–182, 269, 273–274, 292–294, 305, 309.
248. Fisher, *The Trial of the Constitution*, 291. In his *The Laws of Race*, Fisher approvingly wrote that the free African American "has no civil or political power whatever, by which to protect himself, and he may not lay a finger on one of those three wonderful boxes, the ballot box, the jury box and cartridge box, which contain the instruments and weapons by which freemen defend their rights. They are for the white race only": Fisher, *The Laws of Race*, 22. Fisher restated these sentiments in his diaries that he kept during the Civil War: Jonathan W. White, ed., *A Philadelphia Perspective: The Civil War Diaries of Sidney George Fisher* (New York: Fordham University Press, 2007), 198 (8 July 1863), 246 (9 November 1864), 250 (11 April 1865).
249. James Madison, "To Jedidiah Morse," 28 March 1823, PJMRS 3:24.
250. Yacovone, *Teaching White Supremacy*, 5–6. Brown writes that in the North, the development of American democracy at that time, "meant enfranchising poor white men while denying suffrage to poor black men": Brown, *Self-Evident Truths*, 21.

251. CG, 33rd Congress, 1st Session, Appendix, 214. Pettit's speech gained a degree of notoriety after being referenced by Abraham Lincoln in a speech he gave in October 1854: Lincoln, "Speech at Peoria, Illinois," 275.
252. "Address of Hon. W. L. Harris, Commissioner from the State of Mississippi, Delivered Before the General Assembly of the State of Georgia, on Monday, Dec. 17th, 1860," in Charles B. Dew, *Apostles of Disunion: Southern Secession Commissioners and the Causes of the Civil War* (Charlottesville, VA: University Press of Virginia, 2001), 83–89, 85.
253. Leon F. Litwack, *North of Slavery: The Negro in the Free States, 1790–1860* (Chicago: University of Chicago Press, 1961), 75.
254. *Hobbs v. Fogg*, 6 Watts. 553 (1837).
255. de Tocqueville, *Democracy in America*, 289n1. This sentiment led many in the northern non-slave states to also defend slavery. For an outline of white supremacist views of prominent intellectuals in northern non-slave states, such as Ralph Waldo Emerson, Walt Whitman, and Henry Adams, see Yacovone, *Teaching White Supremacy*, 15–23. On Emerson, see Peter S. Field, "The Strange Career of Emerson and Race," *American Nineteenth Century History* 2, no. 1 (Spring 2001): 1–32.
256. Feldman, *The Broken Constitution*, 61–75.
257. William Lloyd Garrison, "The American Union," 10 January 1845, in *William Lloyd Garrison and the Fight Against Slavery: Selections from The Liberator*, ed. William E. Cain (Boston: Bedford/St Martin's, 1995), 114. Garrison's abolitionism led him to call for the secession of northern non-slave states: Mayer, *All on Fire*, 313–316, 326, 341–342, 452–453, 469–470, 522–523.
258. Wendell Phillips, ed., *The Constitution, A Pro-Slavery Compact: or, Extracts from the Madison Papers etc*, 3rd ed. (New York: American Anti-Slavery Society, 1856), 6.
259. James Oakes, *The Crooked Path to Abolition: Abraham Lincoln and the Antislavery Constitution* (New York: W. W. Norton & Company, 2021), 38–41.
260. Feldman, *The Broken Constitution*, 68; David W. Blight, *Frederick Douglass: Prophet of Freedom* (New York: Simon & Schuster, 2018), 191, 207–208.
261. Gerrit Smith, *Constitutional Argument, Against American Slavery* (Utica, NY: Jackson and Chaplin, 1844), 3. In relation to the attitude of the northern non-slave states towards slavery, at the conclusion of his term in Congress, Smith wrote the following to Douglass: "[The North's] duty is to confess her shame and sorrow, that her political, ecclesiastical, and commercial influence has gone to uphold slavery, and to deceive the but-too-willing-to-be-deceived South into the belief, that slavery is right, or, at least, excusable": Gerrit Smith, "Letter to Frederick Douglass," 28 August 1854, in *Speeches of Gerrit Smith in Congress* (New York: Mason Brothers, 1855), 402.
262. On the background to the enactment of Ohio's legislation repealing laws that discriminated against its free African American population, see Masur, *Until Justice Be Done*, 185–223.
263. Masur, *Until Justice Be Done*, xiii-xiv.
264. Illustrative of the hostility to abolitionism in the northern-non-slave states was an incident that took place in Boston on 21 October 1835. On that day, Garrison, who was to deliver an anti-slavery lecture at an abolitionist meeting, was

dragged out by an anti-abolitionist mob and dragged through the streets of Boston, only to be rescued and, at the behest of the city's mayor, kept safe by spending the night in jail: Mayer, *All on Fire*, 200–206.

265. Graber, *Dred Scott*, 130; Fishkin and Forbath, *The Anti-Oligarchy Constitution*, 95.

266. Quoted in James A. Morone, *Republic of Wrath: How American Politics Turned Tribal, from George Washington to Donald Trump* (New York: Basic Books, 2020), 98.

267. Abraham Lincoln, "Speech at Peoria, Illinois," 268.

268. Lincoln, "Seventh and Last Debate with Stephen A Douglas at Alton, Illinois," 312. Jim Cullen writes: "Lincoln was not opposed to slavery because he cared very much about *slaves*. He was opposed because he cared very, very deeply about *whites* (and unlike some of his fellow Republicans, he cared about *all* whites). Slavery was bad for them. And it was bad because it contaminated and, if left unchecked, would eventually destroy the American Dream in which he so deeply believed": Jim Cullen, *The American Dream: A Short History of the Idea That Shaped a Nation* (New York: Oxford University Press, 2003), 84. To similar effect, Dirck writes that Lincoln's understanding of the Constitution was "rooted in an entrepreneurial ethic of free enterprise and individual pursuit of prosperity, values that were entirely incompatible with slavery's exploitation of labor, and what [he] and other Republicans saw as its suppression of American free enterprise spirit": Brian R. Dirck, *Lincoln and the Constitution* (Carbondale, IL: Southern Illinois University Press, 2012), 24. Finally, Carwardine notes that because Lincoln supported "a program designed to speed the transition from a subsistence to a market economy and encourage poor farmers and mechanics to aspire, though enterprise and self-discipline, to better themselves," this "dictated a social and moral order at odds with southern slavery," which he regarded as "the enemy of . . . economic meritocracy, [because it] stifled individual enterprise in both planters and slaves and sustained a fundamental inequality; depriving human beings of the just rewards of their labor": Richard Carwardine, "'A Party man who did not believe in any man who was not': Abraham Lincoln, the Republican Party, and the Union," in *In the Cause of Liberty: How the Civil War Redefined American Ideals*, eds. William J. Cooper Jr. and John M. McCardell Jr. (Baton Rouge, LA: Louisiana State University Press, 2009), 43. This view of Lincoln's opposition to slavery is one that was shared at the time by Frederick Douglass: Sean Wilentz, *The Politicians and the Egalitarians: The Hidden History of American Politics* (New York: W. W. Norton & Company, 2016), 190. On Lincoln and his attitude towards African Americans, slavery, and abolitionism, see Henry Louis Gates, Jr., "Abraham Lincoln on Race and Slavery," in *Lincoln on Race & Slavery*, ed. Henry Louis Gates Jr. (Princeton, NJ: Princeton University Press, 2009, xvii-lxxiii; Eric Foner, *The Fiery Trial: Abraham Lincoln and American Slavery* (New York: W. W. Norton & Company, 2010); Thomas L. Carson, *Lincoln's Ethics* (New York: Cambridge University Press, 2015), 335–401; George Kateb, *Lincoln's Political Thought* (Cambridge, MA: Harvard University Press, 2015), 87–104; Stanley Harrold, *Lincoln and the Abolitionists* (Carbondale, IL: Southern Illinois University Press, 2018).

269. Beckert, *Empire of Cotton*, 106.
270. Wright, *Slavery and American Economic Development*, 88–89.
271. McDonald, *Novus Ordo Seclorum*, 282.
272. The expression "manifest destiny" was coined on 27 December 1845 by John J. Sullivan, editor of the *Morning News*, in support of the annexation of Texas: Julius W. Pratt, "The Origin of 'Manifest Destiny,'" *The American Historical Review* 32, no. 4 (July 1927): 796; Lyon Rathburn, "The Debate over Annexing Texas and the Emergence of Manifest Destiny," *Rhetoric and Public Affairs* 4, no. 3 (Fall 2001): 486.
273. "Letter to Henry W. Livingston," 25 November 1803, in *The Diary and Letters of Gouverneur Morris*, vol. 2, ed. Anne Cary Morris (New York: Charles Scribner's Sons, 1888), 442. See also "Gouverneur Morris to Henry W. Livingston," 4 December 1803, RFC 3:404.
274. On the origins and course of antebellum territorial expansion see Robert Kagan, *Dangerous Nation: America's Foreign Policy from Its Earliest Days to the Dawn of the Twentieth Century* (New York: Alfred A. Knopf, 2006), 7–264; David C. Hendrickson, *Union, Nation, or Empire: The American Debate over International Relations, 1789–1941* (Lawrence, KS: University Press of Kansas, 2009), 25–226.
275. Stephen M. Chambers, *No God But Gain: The Untold Story of Cuban Slavery, the Monroe Doctrine, and the Making of the United States* (London: Verso, 2015); Karp, *This Vast Southern Empire*.
276. Majewski, *Modernizing a Slave Economy*, 16–17. See also John Majewski, "Why Did Northerners Oppose the Expansion of Slavery? Economic Development and Education in the Limestone South," in Beckert and Rockman, *Slavery's Capitalism*, 283–284.
277. John Stuart Mill, *The Contest in America* (Boston: Little, Brown and Company, Boston, 1862), 15–16.
278. Brettle, *Colossal Ambitions*, 65–67.
279. Eric Foner, *Gateway to Freedom: The Hidden History of the Underground Railroad* (New York: W. W. Norton & Company, 2015), 39–44. On the gradual nature of emancipation and how these laws enabled the continuation of slavery in New York until the 1850s and in New Jersey until 1865, see Manjapra, *Black Ghost of Empire*, 22–25.
280. Alexander Hamilton, "To Nathaniel Chipman," 22 July 1788, in *The Papers of Alexander Hamilton*, vol. 5, *June 1788—November 1789*, ed. Harold C. Syrett (New York: Columbia University Press, 1962), 186.
281. Alexander Hamilton, "To Nathaniel Chipman," in Syrett, *The Papers of Alexander Hamilton*, vol. 5, *June 1788—November 1789*, 219.
282. The non-slave states of Michigan, in 1837, and Wisconsin, in 1848, would also emerge from this territory.
283. "Treaty of Amity, Settlement, and Limits, Between the United States of America and his Catholic Majesty," 22 February 1819, USSL 8:200–206.
284. "Treaty Between the United States of America and the French Republic," 30 April 1803, USSL 8:254.
285. Henry Adams, *History of the United States of America During the Administrations of Thomas Jefferson* (New York: The Library of America, 1986), 334–335.

286. Hervey Putnam Prentiss, *Timothy Pickering as the Leader of New England Federalism, 1800–1815* (New York: De Capo Press, 1972), 24–35; Thomas J. Farnham, "The Federal-State Issue and the Louisiana Purchase," *Louisiana History* 6, no. 1 (Winter 1965): 11–12; Graber, *Dred Scott*, 118–119.
287. Quoted in Lynn W. Turner, *William Plumer of New Hampshire, 1759–1850* (Chapel Hill, NC: University of North Carolina Press, 1962), 137. Writing to John Quincy Adams in 1828, Plumer confirmed that he was, because of the Louisiana Purchase, "in favor of forming government in New England." However, he also noted that in later years he recanted his secessionism, having become "convinced that my opinion in favor of separation was the most erroneous that I ever formed upon political subjects": "William Plumer to John Quincy Adams," 20 December 1828, in William Plumer Jr., *Life of William Plumer* (Boston: Phillips, Sampson & Company, 1857), 292.
288. Quoted in Farnham, "The Federal-State Issue and the Louisiana Purchase," 21. Rufus King expressed similar concerns: "R. King probably to Col. Pickering," 4 November 1803, in *The Life and Correspondence of Rufus King, vol. 4, 1816–1827*, ed. Charles R. King (New York: G. P. Putnam's Sons, 1897), 324–325.
289. "T. Pickering to R. King," 4 March 1804, in King, 363–366. Pickering made similar comments to William Plumer later that year: Simeon E. Baldwin, "New England Secessionists," *The New Englander* 37, no. 3 (1878): 155.
290. "Roger Griswold to Oliver Wolcott," 11 March 1804, in *Documents Relating to New-England Federalism, 1800–1815*, ed. Henry Adams (Boston: Little, Brown, & Co., 1905), 356.
291. Kevin M. Gannon, "Escaping 'Mr Jefferson's Plan of Destruction': New England Federalists and the Idea of a Northern Confederacy, 1803–1804," *Journal of the Early Republic* 21, no. 3 (Fall 2001): 442.
292. Dinah Mayo-Bobee, *New England Federalists: Widening the Sectional Divide in Jeffersonian America* (Madison, NJ: Fairleigh Dickinson University Press, 2017), 10. On the views on slavery of these Federalists see Mayo-Bobee, 195–200; Matthew Mason, "Federalists, Abolitionists, and the Problem of Influence," *American Nineteenth Century History* 10, no. 1 (March 2009): 1–27.
293. Farnham, "The Federal-State Issue and the Louisiana Purchase," 17–24; Prentiss, *Timothy Pickering*, 21–22.
294. "The General Court of Massachusetts on the Embargo," 22 February 1814, Ames, 71–72.
295. Daniel Webster, "The Conscription Bill," 9 December 1814, PDW 1:30. In a letter to Ezekiel Webster in relation to a taxation bill on 22 December 1814, Daniel Webster wrote: "This bill . . . cannot be carried into effect, if the State Governments do not lend their aid to it. Of course it will be a dead letter in New England. . . . . The people must look for protection to the *State Govts.* This Govt. Cannot aid them—or will not—or both": Daniel Webster, "To Ezekiel Webster," 22 December 1814, in *The Papers of Daniel Webster: Correspondence*, vol. 1, *1798–1824*, ed. Charles M. Wiltse (Hanover, NH: University Press of New England, 1974), 178.
296. Keith E. Whittington, "The Political Constitution of Federalism in Antebellum America: The Nullification Debate as an Illustration of Informal Mechanisms

of Constitutional Change," *Publius: The Journal of Federalism* 26, no. 2 (Spring 1996): 5. For examples of state resolutions to this effect at this time, see James Rubin, "Documents Illustrating the Development of the Doctrine of Interposition: 1790–1832," *Journal of Public Law* 5, no. 1 (1956): 49–80; William J. Watkins Jr., *Reclaiming the American Revolution: The Kentucky and Virginia Resolutions and Their Legacy* (New York: Palgrave Macmillan, 2004), 83–96.

297. Quoted in James M. Banner Jr., *To the Hartford Convention: The Federalists and the Origins of Party Politics in Massachusetts, 1789–1815* (New York: Alfred A. Knopf, 1970), 313.

298. Donald R. Hickey, "New England's Defense Problem and the Genesis of the Hartford Convention," *The New England Quarterly* 50, no. 4 (December 1977): 587–604; Edward Payson Powell, *Nullification and Secession in the United States* (New York: G. P. Putnam's Sons, 1897), 220–227; Watkins, *Reclaiming the American Revolution*, 86–94; Hendrickson, *Union, Nation, or Empire*, 59–64.

299. Henry Adams, *History of the United States of America During the Administrations of James Madison* (New York: The Library of America, 1986), 1109.

300. Banner, *To the Hartford Convention*, 117–119; McDonald, *Novus Ordo Seclorum*, 281.

301. "Pickering to Edward Pennington," 12 July 1812, in Adams, *Documents Relating to New-England Federalism*, 389.

302. "Letter to Randolph Harrison," 22 January 1815, in Morris, *The Diary and Letters of Gouverneur Morris*, 582.

303. Jared Sparks, *The Life of Gouverneur Morris with Selections from His Correspondence and Miscellaneous Papers*, vol. 3, (Boston: Gray & Bowen, 1832), 326. See also Prentiss, *Timothy Pickering*, 110–117; Adams, *History of the United States of America During the Administrations of James Madison*, 1115–1117.

304. "Resolutions Adopted by The Hartford Convention," 4 January 1815, Ames, 84–85.

305. "Resolutions Adopted by The Hartford Convention," 4 January 1815, Ames, 85–86.

306. Daniel Webster, "To William Rowland," 11 January 1815, PDW 1:181. In 1830, Webster claimed he had "never read" the resolutions of the Hartford Convention and that, if it had, the purpose of "breaking up the Union" was "disloyal": Daniel Webster, "Second Reply to Hayne, January 26–27, 1830," PDW 1:299, 325.

307. "Treaty of Peace and Amity, Between his Britannic Majesty and the United States of America," 24 December 1814, USSL 8:218–223.

308. Banner, *To the Hartford Convention*, 347–348; Elder, *Calhoun*, 119–121.

309. John Quincy Adams said the following of the Hartford Convention: "The leaders of the party, by whom it had been devised, had been struggling seven years to organize such an assembly. And it was undoubtedly the measure indispensable for effecting the dissolution of the Union. The Hartford Convention was to the Northern Confederacy precisely what the Congress of 1774 was to the Declaration of Independence": John Quincy Adams, "To the Citizens of the United States," no date, in Adams, *Documents Relating to New-England Federalism*, 245.

310. Robert Pierce Forbes, *The Missouri Compromise and Its Aftermath: Slavery and the Meaning of America* (Chapel Hill, NC: University of North Carolina Press, 2007), 5.
311. AC, 15th Congress, 2nd Session, 1170.
312. Forbes, *The Missouri Compromise and Its Aftermath*, 50.
313. Graber, *Dred Scott*, 120–122.
314. Forbes, *The Missouri Compromise and Its Aftermath*, 45–47.
315. Forbes, *The Missouri Compromise and Its Aftermath*, 69–97.
316. "An Act for the admission of the state of Maine into the Union," 3 March 1820, USSL 3:544.
317. "An Act to authorize the people of the Missouri territory to form a constitution and state government; and for the admission of such state into the Union on an equal footing with the original states, and to prohibit slavery in certain territories," Section 1, 6 March 1820, USSL 3:545.
318. "An Act to authorize the people of the Missouri territory to form a constitution and state government; and for the admission of such state into the Union on an equal footing with the original states, and to prohibit slavery in certain territories," Section 8, 6 March 1820, USSL 3:548.
319. "Resolution providing for the admission of the state of Missouri into the Union, on a certain condition," 2 March 1821, USSL 3:645.
320. AC, 15th Congress, 2nd Session, 1204.
321. William Henry Trescot, *Oration Delivered Before the Beaufort Volunteer Artillery, on July 4th, 1850* Charleston, SC: Walker & James, 1850), 7.
322. MJQA 5:12. Adams reiterated this view in an October 1833 diary entry in which he wrote: "Slavery is, in all probability, the wedge which will ultimately split the Union": MJQA 9:23. Similarly, in the wake of the Missouri Compromise, Thomas Jefferson presciently wrote that he feared that, although it "hushed . . . for the moment" sectional tensions over slavery, it signaled the "knell of the Union": Thomas Jefferson, "To John Holmes," 22 April 1820, PTJRS 15:550. In addressing Virginia's secession convention in February 1861, Fulton Anderson said that it was during the Missouri Compromise crisis that "were heard the first sounds of that fatal strife which has raged, with occasional intermissions, down to this hour": "Fulton Anderson Address," 18 February 1861, PVSC 1:58.
323. "An Act in alteration of the several acts imposing duties on imports," 19 May 1828, USSL 4:270–275.
324. Ames, 152–157.
325. Ames, 158–163.
326. John Calhoun, "Rough Draft of What is Called the South Carolina Exposition," 25 November 1828, PJCC 10:444.
327. "An Act to alter and amend the several acts imposing duties on imports," 14 July 1832, USSL 4:583–594.
328. "Ordinance of Nullification of South Carolina," 24 November 1832, Ames, 171–173.
329. Andrew Jackson, "Proclamation on Nullification," 10 December 1832, in *The Papers of Andrew Jackson*, vol. 10, *1832*, ed. Daniel Feller (Knoxville, TN: University of Tennessee Press, 2016), 692, 710. One week after issuing

his proclamation, Jackson ordered his secretary of war, Lewis Cass, to have the military prepared and ready to, if necessary, "crush the monster [of nullification and secession] in its cradle before it matures to manhood": Andrew Jackson, "To Lewis Cass," 17 December 1832, in Feller, 730. See also Pekka Pohjankoski, "Federal Coercion and National Constitutional Identity in the United States 1776–1861," *American Journal of Legal History* 56, no. 3. (2016): 349–350. In relation to Jackson's response to the nullification crisis, Alexis de Tocqueville wrote: "I think . . . that the conduct of this President and the Federal government may be reckoned as one of the dangers that threatens [the Union's] continuance": de Tocqueville, *Democracy in America*, 413.

330. "An Act to modify the act of the fourteenth of July, one thousand eight hundred and thirty-two, and all other acts imposing duties on imports," 2 March 1833, USSL 4:629–631. See also Daniel Peart, *Lobbyists and the Making of US Tariff Policy, 1816–1861* (Baltimore, MD: Johns Hopkins University Press, 2018), 108–116.
331. "An Act further to provide for the collection of duties on imports," 2 March 1833, USSL 4:632–635. See also Currie, *The Constitution in Congress*, 115–116.
332. RDC, 22nd Congress, 2nd Session, 477–478.
333. Brian C. Neuman, *Bloody Flag of Anarchy: Unionism in South Carolina during the Nullification Crisis* (Baton Rouge, LA: Louisiana University Press, 2022), 89–90, 95–96.
334. Elder, *Calhoun*, 283–284.
335. "South Carolina's Final Action," 18 March 1833, Ames, 189; Neuman, *Bloody Flag of Anarchy*, 90. With the passing of the tariff crisis, Jackson privately boasted that "hereafter nullification and secession will never be heard of, except in holding up to scorn and detestation their advocates, and particularly their prime movers": Andrew Jackson, "To Robert Minns Burton," 20 March 1833, in *The Papers of Andrew Jackson,* vol. 11, *1833*, ed. Daniel Feller (Knoxville, TN: University of Tennessee Press, 2019), 176.
336. Henry Adams, *John Randolph* (Boston: Houghton, Mifflin & Company, 1882), 273. See also Kenneth M. Stampp, "The Concept of a Perpetual Union," *Journal of American History* 65, no. 1 (June 1978): 33.
337. Charles Francis Adams, *Trans-Atlantic Historical Solidarity* (Oxford: Clarendon Press, 1913), 45.
338. Forbes, *The Missouri Compromise and Its Aftermath*, 240.
339. Story. Similar views to those of Story were articulated in the ninth edition of Nathan Dane's *General Abridgement and Digest of American Law*, published in 1829: Elizabeth Kelley Bauer, *Commentaries on the Constitution, 1790–1860* (New York: Russell and Russell Inc., 1965), 276–280.
340. H. Jefferson Powell, "Joseph Story's Commentaries on the Constitution: A Belated Review," *Yale Law Journal* 94, no. 5 (April 1985): 1301.
341. St. George Tucker, *View of the Constitution of the United States, With Selected Writings* (Indianapolis, IN: Liberty Fund, Inc.,1999), 86.
342. William Rawle, *A View of the Constitution of the United States of America*, 2nd ed. (Philadelphia: Philip H. Nicklin, 1829), 296–297.
343. Forbes, *The Missouri Compromise and Its Aftermath*, 240.
344. Daniel Webster, "Second Reply to Hayne, January 26–27, 1830," PDW 1:296.

345. Jackson, "Proclamation on Nullification," 696, 709.
346. Robert V. Remini, *Andrew Jackson and the Course of American Democracy, 1833–1845* (New York: Harper & Row, 1984), 31.
347. Edward B. Rugemer, "Robert Monroe Harrison, British Abolition, Southern Anglophobia and Texas Annexation," *Slavery and Abolition* 28, no. 2 (2007): 169–181; Karp, *This Vast Southern Empire*, 82–100; Elder, *Calhoun*, 416–419.
348. Sinha, *The Slave's Cause*, 478–479.
349. MJQA 12:173.
350. "Treaty With Great Britain, In Regard to Limits Westward of the Rocky Mountains," 15 June 1846, USSL 9:869–670.
351. "By the President of the United States of America. A Proclamation," 30 December 1853, USSL 10:1031–1037.
352. William J, Cooper Jr., *Jefferson Davis: American* (New York: Vintage Books, 2000), 276.
353. CG, 29th Congress, 2nd Session, Appendix, 317.
354. "Treaty of Peace, Friendship, Limits, and Settlement With The Republic of Mexico," 2 February 1848, USSL 9:922–942.
355. "An act respecting fugitives from justice, and persons escaping from the service of their masters," 12 February 1793, USSL 1:302–305.
356. *Prigg v. Pennsylvania*, 41 U.S. 539 (1842).
357. Daniel Walker Howe, *What Hath God Wrought: The Transformation of America, 1815–1848* (New York: Oxford University Press, 2007), 652.
358. CG, 30th Congress, 1st Session, 805.
359. William Lloyd Garrison, "The American Union," 10 January 1845, in Cain, *William Lloyd Garrison and the Fight Against Slavery*, 115. At this time, Garrison's fellow abolitionist, Frederick Douglass, supported disunion as a means by which the North could achieve what he referred to as a "a separation from the slave power": Blight, *Frederick Douglass*, 185.
360. "No Union With Slaveholders!" 7 June 1844, in *Documents of Upheaval: Selections from William Lloyd Garrison's The Liberator, 1831–1865*, ed. Truman Nelson (New York: Hill & Wang, 1966), 206. Garrison also wrote: "Let us, who profess to abhor slavery, and who claim to be freemen indeed, dissolve the bands that connect us with the Slave Power, religiously and politically": William Lloyd Garrison, "The United States Constitution," in *Selections from the Writings and Speeches of William Lloyd Garrison*, 307. And, in a letter to his wife in July 1848, Garrison wrote that he stood for "the immediate dissolution of the Union": quoted in Wendell Phillips Garrison and Francis Jackson Garrison, *William Lloyd Garrison 1805–1879: The Story of His Life told by his Children*, vol. 3, *1841–1860* (New York: The Century Co., 1889), 231. On Garrison's disunionism, see Ronald Osborn, "William Lloyd Garrison and the United States Constitution: The Political Evolution of an American Radical," *Journal of Law and Religion* 24, no. 1 (2008–2009): 65–88. Abraham Lincoln's devotion to the Union led him to denounce views such as those of Garrison: Abraham Lincoln, "Eulogy on Henry Clay," 130.
361. Quoted in Lowance, *A House Divided*, 329.
362. Mayer, *All on Fire*, 313.
363. A state convention in Mississippi in October 1849 called upon the legislature

to issue the call for the Nashville Convention: "Report and Resolutions of the Mississippi Convention," 3 October 1849, PJCC 27:72.

364. Elder, *Calhoun*, 512.
365. "Mississippi Calls a Southern Convention," 6 March 1850, Ames, 257.
366. John C. Calhoun, "To J. H. Means," 13 April 1849, PJCC 26:374.
367. Peter B. Knupfer, *The Union As It Is: Constitutional Unionism and Sectional Compromise, 1787–1861* (Chapel Hill, NC: University of North Carolina Press, 1991), 181–195; David Potter, *The Impending Crisis, 1848–1861*, (New York: Harper and Row Publishers, 1976), 108–113.
368. "An Act for the Admission of the State of California into the Union," 9 September 1850, USSL 9:452–453.
369. "An Act proposing to the State of Texas the Establishment of her Northern and Western Boundaries, the Relinquishment by the said State of all Territory claimed by her exterior to said boundaries, and all her Claims upon the United States, and to establish a territorial Government for New Mexico," 9 September 1850, Section 1, UCCL 9:446–447.
370. "An Act proposing to the State of Texas the Establishment of her Northern and Western Boundaries, the Relinquishment by the said State of all Territory claimed by her exterior to said boundaries, and all her Claims upon the United States, and to establish a territorial Government for New Mexico, 9 September 1850," Sections 2–19, USSL 9:447–452.
371. "An Act to establish a Territorial Government for Utah," 9 September 1850, USSL 9:453–458.
372. "An Act to suppress the Slave Trade in the District of Columbia," 20 September 1850, USSL 9:467–468.
373. An Act to amend, and supplementary to, the Act entitled "An Act respecting Fugitives from Justice, and Persons escaping from the Service of their Masters,' approved February twelfth, one thousand seven hundred ninety-three," 18 September 1850, USSL 9:462–465.
374. "Resolves of the Southern Convention at Nashville," 10–11 June 1850, Ames, 263–269.
375. Virginia Mason, *The Public Life and Diplomatic Correspondence of James M Mason*, (Roanoke, VA: The Stone Printing & Manufacturing Company, 1903), 73. Similarly, in 1850, William Henry Trescot, a prominent lawyer, historian, and diplomat from South Carolina, suggested that "if the alternative placed before us be the abandonment of the institution of slavery or the dissolution of the Union . . . the dissolution of the Union is the next step in the path of our history": Trescot, *Oration*, 13.
376. "An Act to Organize the Territories of Nebraska and Kansas," 30 May 1854, Section 1 (Nebraska) and 19 (Kansas), USSL 10:277–278.
377. "An Act to Organize the Territories of Nebraska and Kansas," 30 May 1854, Section 14, USSL 10:283.
378. Forbes, *The Missouri Compromise and Its Aftermath*, 275.
379. Timothy S. Huebner, *Liberty and Union: The Civil War Era and American Constitutionalism* (Lawrence, KS: University Press of Kansas, 2016), 84–87.
380. Anderson, *Federalism, Secession and the American State*, 43–46.
381. Heather Cox Richardson, *To Make Men Free: A History of the Republican*

Party New York: Basic Books, 2014), 6–13. For detailed accounts of the Kansas-Nebraska Act and its consequences see William W. Freehling, *The Road to Disunion,* vol. 1: *Secessionists at Bay 1776–1854* (New York: Oxford University Press, 1990), 536–565; William W. Freehling, *The Road to Disunion,* vol. 2: *Secessionists Triumphant 1854–1861* Oxford: Oxford University Press, 2007), 123–144.

382. Oakes, *The Scorpion's Sting*, 22–50. Georgia's "Report," justifying its secession in 1861, stated that the Republican Party's opposition to the expansion of slavery into the Union's territories had the "fixed purpose to limit, restrain and finally abolish slavery in the States where it exists": "Report," JSCGA, 109. This was an accurate reflection of the Republican Party's hopes, as expressed by Senator Edward Baker from Oregon who said in the Senate on 3 January 1861: "We desire to circle the slave States with a cordon of free States, and thereby destroy the institution of slavery; to treat it like the scorpion girt by fire": CG, 36th Congress, 2nd Session, 240.

383. Dwight T. Pitcaithley, *The US Constitution and Secession: A Documentary Anthology of Slavery and Supremacy* (Lawrence, KS: University Press of Kansas, 2018), 27–28. A unionist delegate to the Virginia secession convention described the New Mexico code as being "as full, complete and perfect a codification of all acts necessary for the discipline, protection and safety of this population, as can be found in any one of the States of this Union": PVSC 1:554. On the New Mexico code see Mark J. Stegmaier, "A Law That Would Make Caligula Blush? New Mexico's Unique Slave Code, 1859–1861," *New Mexico Historical Review* 87, no. 2 (2012): 209–242; John P. Hays, "The Curious Case of New Mexico's Pre-Civil War Slave Code," *New Mexico Historical Review* 92, no. 3 (2017): 251–283.

384. *Dred Scott v. Sandford*, 60 U.S. 393 (1857).

385. William Lloyd Garrison, "The American Union," 10 January 1845, in Cain, *William Lloyd Garrison and the Fight Against Slavery*, 114.

386. Roosevelt, *The Nation That Never Was*, 118.

387. Connecticut, Massachusetts, New Hampshire, New Jersey, New York, North Carolina, and Pennsylvania.

388. Finkelman, "The First Civil Rights Movement," 679–685.

389. In his separate judgment, Justice Campbell also stated that Congress had no power to regulate or prohibit slavery in the territories: *Dred Scott v. Sandford*, 60 U.S. 393, 500–501 (1857). Campbell had been an influential delegate to the Nashville Convention in 1850, and his ruling here represented a repudiation of his earlier belief that Congress possessed such a power: Robert Saunders Jr., *John A. Campbell: Southern Moderate* (Tuscaloosa, AL: University of Alabama Press, 1997), 76–78, 87–92.

390. *Dred Scott v. Sandford*, 60 U.S. 393, 451 (1857).

391. Stephen Keogh, "Formal & Informal Constitutional Lawmaking in the United States in the Winter of 1860–1861," *The Journal of Legal History* 8, no. 3 (December 1987): 287.

392. Marc Egnal, *Clash of Extremes: The Economic Origins of the Civil War* (New York: Hill & Wang, 2009), 265.

393. "The Georgia Platform," 10 December 1850, 271–272. To similar effect, the

North Carolina Standard proclaimed that, if fugitive slave legislation was not properly enforced, "*we leave you!* Before God and man . . . if [the North] fails in this simple act of justice, *the bonds will be dissolved!*": quoted in Thomas D. Morris, *Free Men All: The Personal Liberty Law of the North 1780–1861* (Baltimore, MD: Johns Hopkins University Press, 1974), 147.

394. Potter, *The Impending Crisis*, 356–384.
395. In a speech delivered on the day after Brown's execution, Lincoln repudiated the raid at Harpers Ferry when he said: "Old John Brown has just been executed for treason against a state. We cannot object, even though he agreed with us in thinking slavery wrong. That cannot excuse violence, bloodshed, and treason": Abraham Lincoln, "Speech at Leavenworth, Kansas," 3 February 1859, CWAL 3:502. William Seward, in a speech in the Senate on 29 February 1860, said that Brown's raid was an "attempt to execute an unlawful purpose . . . [that] was an act of sedition and treason," that Brown was "of a class of men so misguided and so desperate to seek to enforce their peculiar principles by the sword," and that his execution was "necessary and just": William H. Seward, "The State of the Country," 29 February 1860, in *The Works of William H. Seward*, vol. 4, ed. George E. Baker (Boston: Houghton, Mifflin & Company, 1884), 637.
396. South Carolina (20 December 1860), Mississippi (9 January 1861), Florida (10 January 1861), Alabama (11 January 1861), Georgia (19 January 1861), Louisiana (26 January 1861), Texas (1 February 1861).
397. "A Letter from L. W. Spratt," 13 February 1861, Moore 2:358. On Spratt, see Dew, *Apostles of Disunion*, 42–45.
398. Virginia (17 April 1861), Arkansas (6 May 1861), North Carolina (20 May 1861), Tennessee (8 June 1861). Virginia's vote to secede reversed a decision of its secession convention on 4 April 1861, not to secede: PVSC 3:161–163.
399. Although Maryland did not secede, on 10 May 1861, its legislature passed a resolution imploring Lincoln to recognize the independence of the Confederacy and to cease the "unholy war" against the Confederacy which it regarded as "unconstitutional and repugnant to civilization, and will result in a bloody and shameful overthrow of our institutions": Moore 1:234.
400. Deyle, *Carry Me Back*, 61.
401. Quoted in Hans L. Trefousse, *The Radical Republicans: Lincoln's Vanguard for Racial Justice* (New York: Alfred A. Knopf, 1969), 166.
402. Alexander Stephens, "Speech Delivered on the 21st March 1861, In Savannah, Known as 'The Corner Stone Speech,' Reported in the Savannah Republican," in *Alexander H. Stephens in Public and Private with Letters and Speeches, Before, During, and Since the War*, ed. Henry Cleveland (Philadelphia: National Publishing Company, 1885), 721.
403. Dew, *Apostles of Disunion*; Huston, *Calculating the Value of the Union*, 65–66; Charles Edward Cauthen, *South Carolina Goes to War, 1860–1865* (Columbia, SC: University of South Carolina Press, 2005), 31–48; Sean Wilentz, "Why Did Southerners Secede?" in Cooper and McCardell, *In the Cause of Liberty*, 25–39; Paul Finkelman, "States' Rights, Southern Hypocrisy, and the Crisis of the Union," *Akron Law Review* 45, no. 2 (2012): 449–478; Anastaplo, *Reflections on Slavery and the Constitution*, 169–177; Roger C. Hartley, *Monuments:*

Reckoning with Jim Crow Era Confederate Monuments (Columbia, SC: University of South Carolina Press, 2021), 30–33.

404. Percy Lee Rainwater, *Mississippi: Storm Center of Secession, 1856–1861* (Baton Rouge, LA: Otto Claitor, 1938), 221. However, there were those that at the outbreak of the Civil War believed that secession would lead to the abolition of slavery. Indeed, as far back as November 1820, John Quincy Adams wrote in his diary: "If slavery be the destined sword of the hand of the destroying angel which is to sever the ties of this Union, the same sword will cut in sunder the bonds of slavery itself. A dissolution of the Union for the cause of slavery would be followed by a servile war in the slave-holding States, combined with a war between the two severed portions of the Union. It seems to me that its result might be the extirpation of slavery from this whole continent; and, calamitous and desolating as this course of events in its progress must be, so glorious would be its final issue, that, as God shall judge me, I dare not say that it is not to be desired": MJQA 5:210. Adams reiterated this sentiment in a November 1835 diary entry in which he wrote: "My opinion is, that the planters of the South will separate from the Union, in terror of the emancipation of slaves, and that then the slaves will emancipate themselves by servile war": MJQA 9:239. And, at the time of the Confederate secessions, George W. Bassett, an abolitionist from Illinois, argued that because the Union was "[i]n theory and in practice . . . the bulwark of chattel slavery—its impregnable fortress," the secessions of the slave states from the Union would necessarily "effect or hasten the termination of slavery": Geo W. Bassett, *A Northern Plea for the Right of Secession* (Ottawa, IL: Office of Free Trader, 1861), 23. Angelina Grimké, a South Carolina abolitionist and feminist, also predicted that the Confederate secessions would lead to the end of slavery when, on 12 December 1860, she wrote: "The South are dissolving the Union in order to prevent the abolition of Slavery and yet they are too blind to see that dissolution will only hasten instead or prevent its overthrow": quoted in Gerda Lerner, *The Grimké Sisters from South Carolina: Rebels Against Slavery* (Boston: Houghton Mifflin Company, 1967), 340. Six days later, Senator Andrew Johnson from Tennessee came to the same conclusion when, in a speech to the Senate, he said: "I believe a dissolution of the Union will . . . overthrow the institution of slavery": CG, 36th Congress, 2nd Session, 139. Similarly, in March 1861, former Governor of Tennessee, William B. Campbell, a self-described "pro-slavery man," opposed secession as being "unwise and impolitic, and tending to the ruin and overthrow of slavery. The rights of the slaveholder cannot be maintained out of the Union so well as in it, and I fear cannot be maintained at all outside of it": quoted in Daniel W. Crofts, *Reluctant Confederates: Upper South Unionists in the Secession Crisis* (Chapel Hill, NC: University of North Carolina Press, 1989), 109. For Frederick Douglass, it was the prospect of the abolition of slavery that led him to welcome the outbreak of the Civil War: Blight, *Frederick Douglass*, 336.
405. Pitcaithley, *The US Constitution and Secession*, 59.
406. "Declaration of the Immediate Causes Which Induce and Justify the Secession of South Carolina From the Federal Union," JSCSC, 464–465.

407. "Declaration of the Immediate Causes Which Induce and Justify the Secession of Mississippi from the Federal Union," JSCMS, 86. This sentiment is reflected in a speech to the Senate by Mississippi's Senator Albert Gallatin Brown on 27 December 1860 when he said: "Mr. President, it seems to me that northern Senators most pertinaciously overlook the main point at issue between the two sections of our Confederacy. We claim that there is property in slaves, and they deny it. Until we shall settle, upon some basis, that point of controversy, it is idle to talk of going any further": CG, 36th Congress, 2nd Session, 201.
408. "An Ordinance to dissolve the union between the State of Alabama and other States united under the compact styled The Constitution of the United States of America," 11 January 1861, JSCAL, 76.
409. JSCAL, 196.
410. "An Ordinance to Dissolve the Union between the State of Texas and the other States, united under the compact styled 'the Constitution of the United States of America,'" *The Constitution of the State of Texas, as Amended in 1861. The Constitution of the Confederate States of America. The Ordinances of the Texas Convention: and An Address to the People of Texas* (Austin, TX: Printed by Order of the Convention and Senate, Austin, 1861), 18.
411. "A declaration of the causes which impel the State of Texas to secede from the Federal Union," JSCTX, 63–64.
412. PVSC 1:62.
413. JSCTX, 51.
414. JSCTX, 122.
415. Myrta Lockett Avary, *Recollections of Alexander H. Stephens* (New York: Doubleday, Page and Company, 1910), 173. See also "Jefferson Davis to Confederate Congress," 29 April, 1861, in *Jefferson Davis, Constitutionalist: His Letters, Papers and Speeches*, vol. 5, ed. Dunbar Rowland (Jackson, MS: Mississippi Department of Archives and History, 1923), 70–72.
416. Edward A. Pollard, *The Lost Cause Regained* (New York: G. W. Carleton & Co., 1868), 13–14.
417. PVSC 4:144.
418. Jubal A. Early, *Heritage of the South: A History of the Introduction of Slavery, Its Establishment from Colonial Times and Final Effect Upon the Politics of the United States* (Lynchburg, VA: Brown-Morrison Co., 1915), 11.
419. Quoted in Caroline E. Janney, *Remembering the Civil War: Reunion and the Limits of Reconciliation* (Chapel Hill, NC: University of North Carolina Press, 2008), 145.
420. Quoted in Janney, *Remembering the Civil War: Reunion and the Limits of Reconciliation*, 145.
421. Quoted in Keith S. Bohannon, "'These Few Grey-Haired, Battle Scarred Veterans': Confederate Army Reunions in Georgia, 1885–95," in *The Myth of the Lost Cause and Civil War History*, eds. Gary W. Gallagher and Alan T. Nolan (Bloomington, IN: Indiana University Press, 2000), 89–110.
422. Eugenia Dunlap Potts, *Historic Papers on the Causes of the Civil War* (London: Forgotten Books, 2013), 11.
423. Egnal, *Clash of Extremes*, 84. See also Mark E. Brandon, *Free in the World: American Slavery and Constitutional Failure* (Princeton, NJ: Princeton

University Press, 1998), 49; Howe, *What Hath God Wrought*, 403; Lind, *Land of Promise*, 110.
424. John C. Calhoun, "To Virgil Maxcy," 11 September 1830, PJCC 11:229.
425. RDC, 22nd Congress, 2nd Session, 1206.
426. "From Tilgham Ashurst Howard," 27 July 1833, in Feller, *The Papers of Andrew Jackson*, vol. 11, 504.
427. Huston, *Calculating the Value of the Union*, 57.
428. Gerald Gunderson, "The Origin of the American Civil War," *Journal of Economic History* 34, no. 4 (December 1974): 916–917. See also Alfred H. Conrad and John R. Meyer, "The Economics of Slavery in the Ante Bellum South," *Journal of Political Economy* 66, no. 2 (April 1958): 95–130.
429. Wright, *Slavery and American Economic Development*, 60–61.
430. Gunderson "The Origin of the American Civil War," 922.
431. Quoted in Steven Deyle, "An 'Abominable' New Trade: The Closing of the African Slave Trade and the Changing Patterns of US Political Power, 1808–60," *The William and Mary Quarterly* 66, no. 4 (October 2009): 841.
432. John C. Hurd, *The Theory of Our National Existence, as Shown by the Action of the Government Since 1861* (Boston: Little, Brown, & Company, 1881), 533.
433. Alabama, Arkansas, Louisiana, Mississippi, North Carolina, South Carolina, and Texas.
434. Arkansas, Georgia, Louisiana, North Carolina, and Virginia.
435. Florida, Mississippi, Tennessee, and Texas.
436. "Declaration of the Immediate Causes Which Induce and Justify the Secession of South Carolina From The Federal Union; and the Ordinance of Secession," and "The Address of the People of South Carolina Assembled in Convention, to the People of the Slaveholding States of the United States," JSCSC, 461–476.
437. "Declaration of the Immediate Causes Which Induce and Justify the Secession of Mississippi from the Federal Union," 86–88.
438. "Report," JSCGA, 104–113.
439. "A declaration of the causes which impel the State of Texas to secede from the Federal Union," 61–66.
440. "Declaration of the Immediate Causes Which Induce and Justify the Secession of South Carolina From The Federal Union," 463–464.
441. Shearer Davis Bowman, *At the Precipice: Americans North and South During the Secession Crisis* (Chapel Hill, NC: University of North Carolina Press, 2010), 51.
442. David Blight, "Cup of Wrath and Fire," in *Disunion: A History of the Civil War*, ed. Ted Widmer (New York: Oxford University Press, 2016), 11.
443. Anderson, *Federalism, Secession and the American State*, 20.
444. Abraham Lincoln, "Fragment on the Constitution and the Union," c. Jan 1861, CWAL 4:169.
445. Simon J Gilhooley, *The Antebellum Origins of the Modern Constitution: Slavery and the Spirit of the American Founding* (Cambridge University Press, Cambridge UK, 2020, 43–56.
446. Abraham Lincoln, "Second Inaugural Address," 4 March 1865, CWAL 8:332.
447. Abraham Lincoln, "'A House Divided': Speech at Springfield, Illinois," 16 June 1858, CWAL 2:461. Lincoln reiterated this in September 1859: Abraham

Lincoln, "Speech at Columbus, Ohio," 16 September 1859, CWAL 3:407. Four months later, William H. Seward echoed this view in a speech at Rochester where he said that, given the existence of "an irrepressible conflict between opposing and enduring forces . . . the United States must and will, sooner or later, become either entirely a slaveholding nation, or entirely a free-labor nation": in Baker, *The Works of William H. Seward*, 56. In many ways Lincoln's House Divided speech echoed what John C. Calhoun said in his speech to the Senate in 1837 in which he claimed that "[a]bolition and the Union cannot co-exist," although he went on to say that the Union could survive if it was "not disturbed by the fell spirit of abolition": John C. Calhoun, "Remarks on Receiving Abolition Petitions (First Report)," 6 February 1837, PJCC 23:394–395.

448. Abraham Lincoln, "To George Robertson," 15 August 1855, CWAL 2:318.

449. Abraham Lincoln, "Speech at Leavenworth, Kansas," 3 December 1859, CWAL 3:502.

450. Otto H. Olsen, "Abraham Lincoln as Revolutionary," *Civil War History* 24, no. 3 (September 1978): 216.

451. "Fulton Anderson Address," 18 February 1861, PVSC 1:58. See also "Address [of Thomas J. Wharton]," JSCMS, 155–156; "Henry L. Benning Address," 18 February 1861, PVSC 1:63; Henry M. Rector, "Governor's Message [to Arkansas Secession Convention]," 2 March 1861, JSCAR, 44.

452. "The Address of the People of South Carolina Assembled in Convention, to the People of the Slaveholding States of the United States," 475.

453. Moses Coit Tyler, *The Literary History of the American Revolution, 1763–1783,* vol. 1, *1763–1776* (New York: G. P. Putnam's Sons, 1897), 8.

CHAPTER 2. "AN INDESTRUCTIBLE UNION?"

1. Akhil Reed Amar, *The Words That Made Us: America's Constitutional Conversation, 1760–1840* (New York: Basic Books, 2021), xi.
2. Gordon S. Wood, *The Creation of the American Republic, 1776–1787*, 1998 ed. (Chapel Hill, NC: University of North Carolina Press, 1998), 345.
3. Akhil Reed Amar, "The Consent of the Governed: Constitutional Amendment Outside Article V," *Columbia Law Review* 94, no. 2 (March 1994): 464; Alison L. LaCroix, *The Ideological Origins of American Federalism* (Cambridge, MA: Harvard University Press, 2010), 96.
4. Edmund S. Morgan, *Inventing the People: The Rise of Popular Sovereignty in England and America* (New York: W. W. Norton & Co., 1988), 143. It can be noted that only males formed the people. In 1776, John Adams explained that women were excluded from being part of the people because "Nature . . . made them fittest for domestic Cares" and therefore unfit for "the great Business of Life, and the hardy Enterprizes of War, as well as the arduous Cares of State." Furthermore, children, servants, and those without property were also excluded because they were "too little acquainted with public Affairs to form a Right Judgment, and too dependent upon other Men to have a Will of their own": "To James Sullivan," 26 May 1776, in *Papers of John Adams,* vol. 4, *February—August 1776*, ed. Robert J. Taylor (Cambridge, MA: Belknap Press, 1979), 210.
5. Thorpe 5:2787.

6. Thorpe 5:3081.
7. Thorpe 3:1686.
8. Thorpe 7:3812.
9. Thorpe 2:778.
10. Thorpe 3:1889.
11. Thorpe 4:2453.
12. Elliot 4:230.
13. DHRC 2:361–362.
14. George Washington, "Undelivered First Inaugural Address: Fragments," in *The Papers of George Washington: Presidential Series,* vol. 2, *1 April 1789–15 June 1789*, ed. Dorothy Twohig (Charlottesville, VA: University Press of Virginia, 1987), 164–165.
15. *Chisholm v. Georgia*, 2 U.S. 419, 470 (1793).
16. *Dred Scott v. Sandford*, 60 U.S. 393, 404 (1857).
17. Elliot 4:230.
18. DHRC 2:362.
19. DHRC 2:383.
20. Edward J. Larson, *American Inheritance: Liberty and Slavery in the Birth of a Nation, 1765–1795* (New York: W. W. Norton & Company, 2023), 200.
21. Forrest McDonald, *Novus Ordo Seclorum: The Intellectual Origins of the Constitution*, (Lawrence, KS: University of Kansas Press, 1985), 281n37.
22. Article I, Section 9, states: "No Title of Nobility shall be granted by the United States: And no Person holding and Office of Profit or Trust under *them*, shall, without the Consent of the Congress, accept of any present, Emolument, Office, or Title, of any kind whatever, from any King, Prince, or foreign State" (emphasis added). The relevant part of Article II, Section 2 states: "The Judicial Power shall extend to all Cases, in Law and Equity, arising under this Constitution, the Laws of the United States, and Treaties made, or which shall be made, under *their* Authority" (emphasis added). The relevant part of Article II, Section 3 states: "Treason against the United States, shall consist only in levying War against *them*, or in adhering to *their* Enemies, giving *them* Aid or Comfort" (emphasis added).
23. *Calder v. Bull*, 3 U.S. 386, 388 (1798).
24. *Martin v. Hunter's Lessee*, 14 U.S. 304, 374 (1816).
25. DHRC 10:1473.
26. Amar, "The Consent of the Governed," 506.
27. RFC 2:364.
28. Thomas Jefferson, "To Edward Everett," 8 April 1826, in *The Works of Thomas Jefferson,* vol. 12, ed. Paul Leicester Ford (New York: G. P. Putnam's Sons, 1905), 469.
29. Harry V. Jaffa, *A New Birth of Freedom: Abraham Lincoln and the Coming of the Civil War* (Lanham, MD: Rowman & Littlefield Publishers, Inc., 2000), 189.
30. Story 1:340.
31. Daniel Webster, "The Constitution not a Compact, February 16, 1833," PDW 1:597. Webster's speech was delivered during his Senate debate with John C. Calhoun in response to the Force Bill of 1833 passed by Congress as part of

the resolution of the 1830s tariff crisis and was aimed at refuting Calhoun's exposition of the compact theory of the Constitution. Although no friend of Calhoun's theorizing, John Quincy Adams was of the view that, in his speech, Webster had "hung his cause upon a broken hinge in maintaining that a Government is not a compact": MJQA 8:526.

32. Abraham Lincoln, "First Inaugural Address," 4 March 1861, CWAL 4:265.
33. Lincoln, "First Inaugural Address," 265.
34. Lincoln, "First Inaugural Address," 264–265.
35. Abraham Lincoln, "Message to Congress in Special Session," 4 July 1861, CWAL 4:434.
36. Story 1:340.
37. Story 1:319. Elsewhere in his *Commentaries*, Story states that the Constitution created "a solid and perpetual Union," "a perpetual bond of union," that it was founded with the object of "perpetual union," and that "the union of the states is permanent": Story 2:358–359, 406, 482.
38. Akhil Reed Amar, *America's Constitution: A Biography* (New York: Random House, 2005), 33.
39. Sanford Levinson, "'Perpetual Union,' 'Free Love,' and Secession: On the Limits of the 'Consent of the Governed'" *Tulsa Law Review* 39, no. 3 (Spring 2004): 465.
40. RFC 1:462.
41. RFC 1:466.
42. RFC 1:469.
43. DHRC 2:357–358.
44. "The Federalist No. 6 (Hamilton)," Federalist, 24.
45. That the Confederation was effectively at its end was recognized by delegates to the ratification conventions. Thus, at the South Carolina convention, Charles Cotesworth Pinckney said that the Confederation as "a compact that had been repeatedly broken," was "no longer binding": Elliot 4:308. At the North Carolina convention, James Iredell, after noting that there had been violations of the Articles of Confederation, said that they were "no longer binding": Elliot 4:230. And in his letter to William Cushing, Samuel H. Parsons, a jurist and general during the American Revolution, wrote that because the Articles of Confederation had been broken by all its member states, "that Covenant . . . [was] prostrate in the Dust": "Samuel Holden Parsons to William Cushing," 11 January 1788, in *The Debate on the Constitution: Federalist and Antifederalist Speeches, Articles, and Letters During the Struggle over Ratification*, part 1, ed. Bernard Bailyn (New York: Library of America, 1993), 753.
46. Lincoln, "First Inaugural Address," 264–265.
47. James Buchanan, "Fourth Annual Message," 3 December 1860, in *The Works of James Buchanan*, vol. 11, *1860–1868*, ed. John Bassett Moore (Philadelphia: J. B. Lippincott Company, 1910), 16.
48. James Buchanan, "To the Senate and House of Representatives," 8 January 1861, in Moore, *The Works of James Buchanan*, 95.
49. At the Philadelphia Convention, James Madison argued that "[t]he use of force agst. a State, would look more like a declaration of war, than an infliction

of a punishment, and would probably be considered by a party attached as a dissolution of all previous compacts by which it might be bound": RFC 1:54.

50. Buchanan, "Fourth Annual Message," 18–19. In his analysis of the Convention's debate on the issue of the use of force against a state, Pohjankoski concludes that, although the Convention declined to include an express federal power to coerce states, the issue was nonetheless not fully settled: Pekka Pohjankoski, "Federal Coercion and National Constitutional Identity in the United States 1776–1861," *American Journal of Legal History* 56, no. 3. (2016): 333–339. Feldman, in discussing Buchanan's position on this issue, argues that there was a strong constitutional argument in support of it: Noah Feldman, *The Broken Constitution: Lincoln, Slavery, and the Founding of America* (New York: Farrar, Straus & Giroux, 2021), 5, 135–136, 143–144, 156–159, 174. Furthermore, Buchanan's position had wide popular support: Michael F. Conlin, *The Constitutional Origins of the American Civil War* (Cambridge, UK: Cambridge University Press, 2019), 215.
51. Mark E. Brandon, *Free in the World: American Slavery and Constitutional Failure* (Princeton, NJ: Princeton University Press, 1998), 181.
52. Max Farrand, *The Framing of the Constitution of the United States* (New Haven, CT: Yale University Press, 1913), 206.
53. "Brutus XII," 7 February 1788, in *The Debate on the Constitution: Federalist and Antifederalist Speeches, Articles, and Letters During the Struggle over Ratification*, part 1, ed. Bernard Bailyn (New York: Library of America, 1993), 174.
54. Brandon, *Free in the World*, 180.
55. Sidney George Fisher, *The Trial of the Constitution* (Philadelphia: J. B. Lippincott & Co., 1862), 162–163.
56. Lincoln, "Message to Congress in Special Session," 433.
57. DHCUSA, 290.
58. DHCUSA, 310–320.
59. Lincoln, "First Inaugural Address," 269.
60. "An Act for giving effect to the several acts therein mentioned, in respect of the state of North Carolina, and other purposes," 8 February 1790, USSL 1:99–101; "An Act for giving effect to an Act entitled 'An Act to establish the Judicial Courts of the United States,' within the State of North Carolina," 4 June 1790: USSL 1:126; "An Act for the giving effect to the several Acts therein mentioned, in respect of the State of Rhode Island and Providence Plantations," 14 June 1790, USSL 1:126–128; "An Act for giving effect to an act intituled 'An act to establish the Judicial Courts of the United States,' within the State of Rhode Island and Providence Plantations," 23 June 1790:USSL 1, 128.
61. Amar, *The Words That Made Us*, 164. See also Sanford Levinson, Jack M. Balkin, Akhil Reed Amar, Reva B. Siegel, and Christina M. Rodriguez, eds., *Processes of Constitutional Decisionmaking: Cases and Materials*, 8th ed. (Frederick, MD: Aspen Publishing, 2022), 6.
62. AC, 1st Congress, 1st Session, 432.
63. Mark E. Neely, *Lincoln and the Triumph of the Nation: Constitutional Conflict*

in the American Civil War (Chapel Hill, NC: University of North Carolina Press, 2011), 53.

64. James Madison, "To Alexander Hamilton," 20 July 1788, PJM 11:189. See also Amar, *The Words That Made Us*, 261.
65. Madison, "To Alexander Hamilton," 189. A similar claim was independently made by James Iredell at the North Carolina ratification convention: Elliot 4:217.
66. DHRC 23:2297.
67. DHRC 23:2290, 2301. Melancton Smith had floated a similar proposal earlier during New York's convention: DHRC 22:2015; 23:2215. Smith's later decision to accept a ratification resolution that merely asked Congress to "use all reasonable means" to adopt various amendments to the Constitution was pivotal in the New York convention's thirty to twenty-seven vote in favor of ratification: Robin Brooks, "Alexander Hamilton, Melancton Smith, and the Ratification of the Constitution in New York," *The William and Mary Quarterly* 24, no. 3 (July 1967): 339–358.
68. Amar, *America's Constitution*, 38.
69. Story 1:319.
70. CG, 36th Congress, 2nd Session, 118.
71. PVSC 1:357–360.
72. James Madison, "To N. P. Trist," May 1832, WJM 9:480. Madison also wrote of the "awful consequences which a separation of the States portends": James Madison, "To Thomas Lehre," 2 August 1828, WJM 9:315. Elsewhere he referred to "[t]he disastrous consequences of disunion": James Madison, "To Henry Clay," 22 March 1832, WJM 9:478. When the possibility of secession was discussed in the context of the tariff crisis of the 1830s, Madison wrote that it would be "*madness* in the South, to look for greater safety in disunion. It would be worse than jumping out of the Frying-pan into the fire": James Madison, "To Henry Clay," June 1833, WJM 9:517.
73. James Madison, "To N. P. Trist," 23 December 1832, WJM 9:490.
74. James Madison," "To Alexander Rives," January 1833, WJM 9:495.
75. James Madison, "To Daniel Webster," 15 March 1833, LOWJM 4:293.
76. Madison, "To N. P. Trist," 23 December 1832:490.
77. Madison, "To Alexander Rives," 495.
78. AC, 1st Congress, 1st Session 434.
79. Daniel Farber, *Lincoln's Constitution* (Chicago: University of Chicago Press, 2003), 88.
80. DHCUSA, 145.
81. DHCUSA, 190–191.
82. DHCUSA, 311.
83. DHCUSA, 195.
84. "Circular Letter to the Executives of the States," 26 July 1788, DHRC 23:2335. Similar sentiments emanated from within Pennsylvania where, six months after its ratification convention, a circular letter argued that it would be "expedient" for a further constitutional convention to settle upon amendments which the convention thought were "essentially necessary" and that ratification was only

achieved in because it had "full confidence" that such amendment would be agreed to so as "to prevent the total defection of some members of the Union": "Proceedings of the Meeting at Harrisburg, in Pennsylvania," 3 September 1788, Elliott 2:543–544.

85. Ohio in 1803: USSL 2:173; Louisiana in 1812: USSL 2:703; Indiana in 1816: USSL 3:289; Mississippi in 1817: USSL 3:473; Illinois in 1818: USSL 3:429, 536; Alabama in 1819: USSL 3:490, 608; Maine in 1820: USSL 3:544; Missouri in 1821: USSL 3:545, 645, 797; Arkansas in 1836: USSL 5:50; Michigan in 1837, USSL 5:144; Florida in 1845: USSL 5:742; Texas in 1845: USSL 9:108; Iowa in 1846: USSL 9:117; Wisconsin in 1848: USSL 9:56, 179, 233; California in 1850: USSL 9:452; Minnesota in 1858: USSL 11:285; Oregon in 1859: USSL 11:383. The three states admitted to the Union after South Carolina's secession and prior to the end of the Civil War were admitted on exactly the same terms: Kansas in 1861: USSL 12:126; West Virginia in 1863: USSL 12:634; USSL 13:731; Nevada in 1864: USSL 13:30, 749.
86. USSL 1:492.
87. USSL 1:189 (Kentucky); 191 (Vermont).
88. *Pollard's Lessee v. Hagan*, 44 U.S. 212, 230 (1845) (see also 223–224).
89. James Madison, "To Robert Walsh Jr.," 27 November 1819, PJMRS 1:555.
90. In asserting that their ratifications were "permanent and irrevocable," Murphy incorrectly labels the reservations made by New York, Virginia and Rhode Islands as "understandings" and says that therefore "[n]o state convention *declared* any such power of resumption" (emphasis added): William P. Murphy, *The Triumph of Nationalism: State Sovereignty, The Founding Fathers, and the Making of the Constitution* (Chicago: Quadrangle Books, 1967), 405–406. However, the ratification resolutions by all three States expressly stated that their conventions did "declare and make known" their reservations. Although Krannawitter quotes the words of the New York and Rhode Island resolutions that state that the people could reassume the power granted to the federal government, he claims that they did not give rise to any implied right of a *state* to secede: Thomas L. Krannawitter, *Vindicating Lincoln: Defending the Politics of Our Greatest President* (Lanham, MD: Rowman & Littlefield Publishers Inc., 2008), 194. However, if "the people" are the people of a particular state, and that "people" resume the powers granted to the federal government, then that leads to the secession of the state.
91. DHRC 10:1513–1514.
92. Story 1:324.
93. Elizabeth Kelley Bauer, *Commentaries on the Constitution, 1790–1860* (New York: Russell and Russell Inc., 1965), 328. A similar observation can be made against Carpenter, Morse, Livingston, Haworth, and DiLorenzo, who all argue that the ratification resolutions of New York, Rhode Island, and Virginia reserved the right to secede, but fail to deal with the difference in wording between that of New York and Rhode Island, on the one hand, and Virginia, on the other: Jesse T. Carpenter, *The South as a Conscious Minority, 1789–1861: A Study in Political Thought* (New York: New York University Press, 1930), 212; Howard Newcomb Morse, "The Right of State Interposition," *Dickinson Law*

Review 51, no. 3 (March 1947): 179–180; H. Newcomb Morse, "The Foundations and Meaning of Secession," *Stetson Law Review* 15, no. 2 (Spring 1986): 428–429; Donald W. Livingston, "The Very Idea of Secession," *Society* 35, no. 5 (July-August 1998): 42; Peter Haworth, "The Con-Federal Constitution of the United States: A Review of 'John C. Calhoun and the Confederation Thesis'" *The Political Science Reviewer* 39, no. 1 (2010): 81–82; Thomas J. DiLorenzo, *The Problem With Lincoln* (Washington: Regnery History, 2020, 25), 41. The same can be said of the arguments made by Texas's Senator, Louis T. Wigfall, in a speech he made in September 1860: Louis T. Wigfall, *Speech of Hon Louis T. Wigfall on the Pending Political Issues, Delivered at Tyler, Smith County, Texas, September 3, 1860* (Washington: Lemuel Towers, 1860), 15.

94. Amar, *America's Constitution*, 37.
95. Webster, "The Constitution not a Compact, February 16, 1833," 595.
96. John Lothrop Motley, "Causes of the Civil War," Moore, 216.
97. Edward Everett, "The Questions of the Day," in *Orations and Speeches on Various Occasions by Edward Everett*, vol. 4 (Boston: Little, Brown, & Company, 1879) 365–366.
98. Amar, *America's Constitution*, 37.
99. DHRC 10:1456.
100. DHRC 10:1506.
101. DHRC 10:1501–1502.
102. DHRC 10:1303.
103. Pauline Maier, *Ratification: The People Debate the Constitution, 1787–1788* (New York: Simon and Schuster, 2010), 305.
104. Charles Francis Adams, *The Constitutional Ethics of Secession and "War is Hell"* (Boston: Houghton, Mifflin & Company, 1903), 10.
105. PVSC 3:405.
106. PVSC 3:434–435.
107. PVSC 1:527.
108. PVSC 1:490–491.
109. PVSC 3:20–21, 23.
110. JSCFL, 25.
111. Jefferson Davis, *The Rise and Fall of the Confederate Government*, vol. 1 (New York: D. Appleton and Company, 1881), 173.
112. Amar, *America's Constitution*, 33.
113. "The Federalist No. 5 (Jay)," Federalist, 16.
114. Amar, *America's Constitution*, 36; Akhil Reed Amar, *The Law of the Land: A Grand Tour of Our Constitutional Republic* (New York: Basic Books, 2015), 18–19. Edward Everett made the same argument in 1861: Everett, "The Questions of the Day," 364–365.
115. "Union With England Act, 1707," http://www.legislation.gov.uk/aosp/1707/7/.
116. "The Federalist No. 5 (Jay)," 17.
117. William Slade, ed., *Vermont State Papers; Being a Collection of Records and Documents, From the Year 1779 to 1786* (Middlebury, VT: J. W. Copeland, Printer, 1823), 69.
118. Peter S. Onuf, "State-Making in Revolutionary America: Independent Vermont

as a Case Study," *Journal of American History* 67, no. 4 (March 1981): 797–815. Although the independence of Vermont was not formally recognized, it was, as Alexander Hamilton conceded, "in fact *independent*": Alexander Hamilton, "New York Assembly. Remarks on an Act Acknowledging the Independence of Vermont," 14 March 1787, in *The Papers of Alexander Hamilton, vol. 4, January 1787—May 1788*, ed. Harold C. Syrett, (New York: Columbia University Press, 1962), 116.

119. Slade, *Vermont State Papers*, 194.
120. Peter Lindsay and Christopher Heath Wellman, "Lincoln on Secession," *Social Theory and Practice* 29, no. 1 (January 2003): 126–127; Christopher Heath Wellman, *A Theory of Secession: The Case for Political Self-Determination* (New York: Cambridge University Press, 2005), 80.
121. Brandon, *Free in the World*, 187–188.
122. Everett, "The Questions of the Day," 349.
123. Motley, "Causes of the Civil War," 213.
124. Story 1:322.
125. *McCulloch v. Maryland*, 17 U.S. 316, 405 (1819).
126. Akhil Reed Amar, "Abraham Lincoln and the American Union," 2001, no. 5 (2001): 1123.
127. Amar, "Abraham Lincoln and the American Union," 1123–1124.
128. Amar, "The Consent of the Governed," 507.
129. Stephen C. Neff, "Secession and Breach of Compact: The Law of Nature Meets the United States Constitution," in *Union and States' Rights: A History and Interpretation of Interposition, Nullification, and Secession 150 Years After Sumter*, ed. Neil H. Cogan (Akron, OH: University of Akron Press, 2014), 97.
130. James Madison, "To William Cabell Rives," 12 March 1833, WJM 9:513.
131. David P. Currie, "Prolegomena for a Sampler, Extrajudicial Interpretation of the Constitution, 1789–1861," in *Congress and the Constitution*, eds. Neal Devins and Keith E. Whittington (Durham, NC: Duke University Press, 2005), 28. See also Neff, "Secession and Breach of Compact," 97.
132. "The Federalist No. 39 (Madison)," Federalist, 182.
133. "The Federalist No. 43 (Madison)," Federalist, 212.
134. Lincoln, "Message to Congress in Special Session," 440.
135. Lincoln, "Message to Congress in Special Session," 437.
136. In Texas, the vote was 44,317 votes for and 13,020 votes against secession: Lawrence M. Anderson, *Federalism, Secession, and the American State: Divided, We Secede* (New York: Routledge, 2013), 116. In Virginia, the vote was 125,950 votes for and 20,373 votes against secession: Anderson, 120.
137. "An Act to Submit to a Vote of the People a Declaration of Independence, and for other purposes," 6 May 1861, Moore, 203–204.
138. In Tennessee, the vote was 104,913 votes for and 47,238 votes against secession: Anderson, *Federalism, Secession and the American State*, 123.
139. James M. McPherson, *Battle Cry of Freedom: The Civil War Era* (New York: Oxford University Press, 1988), 235. See also Ralph A. Wooster, "The Secession of the Lower South: An Examination of Changing Interpretations," *Civil War History* 7, no. 2 (June 1961): 124–127.
140. Sean Wilentz, "Why Did Southerners Secede?," in *In the Cause of Liberty:*

How the Civil War Redefined American Ideals, eds. William J. Cooper Jr. and John M. McCardell Jr. (Baton Rouge, LA: Louisiana State University Press, 2009), 28, 34. For a view that casts doubt on the extent of popular support for secession, see Mario L. Chacon and Jeffrey L. Jensen, "The Political and Economic Geography of Secession," *Journal of Economic History* 80, no. 2 (June 2020): 386–416. On anti-secession sentiment in the South, see Paul Quigley, *Shifting Grounds: Nationalism and the American South, 1848–1865* (Oxford: Oxford University Press, 2012), 114–125.

141. Amar, "Abraham Lincoln and the American Union," 1117.
142. Lincoln, "First Inaugural Address," 271.
143. Lincoln, "First Inaugural Address," 270. In a memorandum, dated 13 December 1860, Lincoln's secretary, John G. Nicolay, recorded Lincoln's views on the powers of a president in this context as follows: "It is the duty of a President to execute the laws, and maintain the existing government. He cannot entertain any proposition for dissolution or dismemberment. He was not elected for such a purpose": Michael Burlingame, ed., *With Lincoln in the White House: Letters, Memoranda, and Other Writings of John G Nicolay, 1860–1865*, (Carbondale and Edwardsville, IL: Southern Illinois University Press, 2000), 17.
144. Feldman, *The Broken Constitution*, 147.
145. David Armitage, "Secession and Civil War," in *Secession as an International Phenomenon: From America's Civil War to Contemporary Separatist Movements*, ed. Don H. Doyle (Athens, GA: University of Georgia Press, 2010), 48.
146. *Pollard's Lessee v. Hagan*, 44 U.S. 212, 230 (1845).
147. *Martin v. Hunter's Lessee*, 14 U.S. 304, 324 (1816).
148. Lincoln, "First Inaugural Address," 270.
149. John C. Calhoun, "To James Hamilton Jr.," 28 August 1832, PJCC 11:615.
150. Brandon, *Free in the World*, 192.
151. RFC 1:166.
152. RFC 1:324. Similar views were expressed by Rufus King, a delegate from Massachusetts: RFC 1:323.
153. DHRC 2:556.
154. DHRC 2:555.
155. "The Federalist No. 2 (Jay)," Federalist, 6. Lepore argues that the American Revolution "had little to do with the idea of an American nation," and that Jay's reference, in *Federalist 2*, to "one united people," was something that, in the context of a keenly contested ratification debate in New York, he and the Federalists "pretended already existed": Jill Lepore, *This America: The Case for the Nation* (New York: Liveright Publishing Corporation, 2019), 29, 32.
156. "The Federalist No. 46 (Madison)," Federalist, 228.
157. "The Federalist No. 22 (Hamilton)," Federalist, 106.
158. "The Federalist No. 85 (Hamilton)," Federalist, 431.
159. *Chisholm v. Georgia*, 2 U.S. 419, 470 (1793).
160. Nathan Dane, *A General Abridgment and Digest of American Law, With Occasional Notes and Comments*, vol. 9, (Boston: Hilliard, Gray, Little, & Wilkins, 1829), Appendix, 23, 25, 32–33. Dane was a delegate to the Hartford Convention: Henry Adams, *History of the United States of America During*

the Administrations of James Madison (New York: Library of America, 1986), 1111.

161. Story 1:197–203.
162. In his *Commentaries*, Story viewed adherents to the compact theory of the Constitution as men in search of "personal popularity . . . who have no eager desire for a wide spread of fame, or no acquirements to justify it" whereas as nationalists, such as himself, were "men of ardent ambition, comprehensive views, and powerful genius," and because the views of compact theorists, "as a matter of surprise," were "so extensively adopted, and so zealously propagated," he was led to writing this *Commentaries* to inspire "a profound reverence for the constitution and the Union": Story 1:265, 340, 759. Bauer, in her comprehensive analysis of antebellum writings on constitutional law, concludes that Story came to his work, written primarily to refute the doctrine of nullification, "with his mind already made up, and perhaps, closed": Bauer, *Commentaries on the Constitution*, 328.
163. "Mr Webster's Last Remarks," 26–27 January 1830, in *The Webster-Hayne Debate on the Nature of the Union: Selected Documents*, ed. Herman Belz (Indianapolis, IN: Liberty Fund, 2000), 153; Webster, "The Constitution not a Compact, February 16, 1833," 577–578.
164. John Quincy Adams, *An Oration Addressed to the Citizens of the Town of Quincy on the Fourth of July, 1831, The Fifty-Fifth Anniversary of the United States of America* (Boston: Richardson, Lord & Holbrook, 1831), 6–7, 17–18, 35–36.
165. Andrew Jackson, "Proclamation on Nullification," 10 December 1832, in *The Papers of Andrew Jackson, vol. 10, 1832*, ed. Daniel Feller (Knoxville, TN: University of Tennessee Press, 2016), 694–695.
166. Robert V. Remini, *Daniel Webster: The Man and His Life* (New York: W. W. Norton & Company, 1997), 331, 374. On Webster's nationalism, see Joel Richard Paul, *Indivisible: Daniel Webster and the Birth of American Nationalism* (New York: Riverhead Books, 2022).
167. Matthew S. Brogan, "Defending the Union: Andrew Jackson's Nullification Proclamation and American Federalism," *The Review of Politics* 73, no. 2 (Spring 2011): 269–273.
168. Lincoln, "First Inaugural Address," 265.
169. Lincoln, "Message to Congress in Special Session," 433–435.
170. Lincoln's reference to 1774 repeats Story's claim that one American people emerged in 1774: Story 1:186. However, it is difficult to sustain an argument that the Articles of Association saw the emergence of either a single or a political union of the colonies, given that the Articles referred to the colonists as "his majesty's most loyal subjects" and the "association" that they created was declared to last only until such time as the so-called "Intolerable Acts" of the British parliament to which the colonies objected were repealed: JCC 1:75, 79–80.
171. On the evolution of the Declaration in Lincoln thinking, see Robert L. Hatzenbuehler, "Abraham Lincoln's Evolving Appreciation of the Declaration of Independence," *American Nineteenth Century History* 21, no. 2 (2020): 171–186.

172. Abraham Lincoln, "Speech in Independence Hall, Philadelphia, Pennsylvania," 22 February 1861, CWAL 4:240. Lincoln's devotion to the Declaration of Independence is described by Adkins as follows: "The Declaration of Independence . . . represents the interpretive key to why he acted the way he did in particular circumstances. Above all Lincoln subordinated the particular provisions of the Constitution to its overall purpose of securing liberty and the true aims of republican government. . . . . The Constitution put into workable form the characteristics of democratic government that would allow the principles of the Declaration to flourish. . . . . [F]or Lincoln, the Constitution is the vehicle through which liberty and equality of opportunity for *all men* is advanced. The medium for that advancement is the Union itself. If the Union were to fail, the cause of liberty would fail as well. The Union, as sacred covenant of the people, is irrevocable. Thus, any act of secession would be unconstitutional, as undermining the purposes of both the Constitution, and the sacred text of the Declaration itself": Jason A. Adkins, "Lincoln's Constitution Revisited," *Northern Kentucky Law Review* 36, no. 2 (2009): 213, 224.
173. Abraham Lincoln, "To Henry L. Pierce and Others," 6 April 1859, CWAL 3:376.
174. Abraham Lincoln, "Address Delivered at the Dedication of the Cemetery at Gettysburg," 19 November 1863, CWAL 7:22.
175. Lincoln, "First Inaugural Address," 266.
176. Lincoln, "Message to Congress in Special Session," 437.
177. Amar, *America's Constitution*, 27; Kenneth M. Stampp, "The Concept of a Perpetual Union," *Journal of American History* 65, no. 1 (June 1978): 8.
178. William Whatley Pierson, Jr., *Texas versus White: A Study in Legal History* (Durham, NC: Seeman Printery, 1916), 51. See also Brandon, *Free in the World*, 180–181.
179. DHRC 22:2164.
180. "The Federalist No. 43 (Madison)," 216.
181. *Dred Scott v. Sandford*, 60 U.S. 393, 435 (1857).
182. *Dred Scott v. Sandford*, 60 U.S. 393, 403 (1857).
183. JCC 4:342.
184. Thorpe 4:2451–2453.
185. Thorpe 6:3241–3248.
186. Thorpe 7:3812–3819. It can be noted that five days after the Continental Congress adopted it on 10 May 1776, Virginia was unaware of it because on 15 May 1775, it adopted a resolution instructing its delegates to Congress "to propose to that respectable body, to declare the United Colonies, free and independent States": Force 6:1524.
187. Force 5:860.
188. John Russell Bartlett, ed., *Records of the Colony of Rhode Island and Plantation Provinces in New England*, vol. 7, (Providence, RI: A. A. Crawford Greene, State Printer, 1862), 522, 526.
189. Force 6:755.
190. Force 6:963–4.
191. Force 6:868.

192. George Herbert Ryden, ed. *Letters to and from Caser Rodney 1756–1784* (Philadelphia: University of Pennsylvania Press, 1933), 91.
193. Ryden, *Letters to and from Caser Rodney*, 92.
194. Force 6:1030.
195. Force 6:1628–1629.
196. Force 6:1491.
197. Force 6:1507.
198. Pauline Maier, *American Scripture: Making the Declaration of Independence* (New York: Alfred A. Knopf, 1997), 49.
199. Maier, *American Scripture*, 48.
200. JCC 5:425.
201. JCC 5:507. The significance of this resolution is attested to by John Adams who, in a letter to his wife, Abigail, on 3 July 1776, wrote: "The Second Day of July 1776, will be the most memorable Epoch, in the History of America. I am apt to believe that it will be celebrated, by succeeding Generations, as the great anniversary Festival. It ought to be commemorated, as the Day of Deliverance by solemn Acts of Devotion to God Almighty. It ought to be solemnized with Pomp and Parade, with Shews, Games, Sports, Guns, Bells, Bonfires and Illuminations from one End of this Continent to the other from this Time forward forever more": L. H. Butterfield, Marc Friedlaender and Mary-Jo Kline, eds., *The Book of Abigail and John: Selected Letters of the Adams Family, 1762–1784* (Cambridge, MA: Harvard University Press, 1975), 142. Wood suggests that the "real declaration of independence was 15 May 1776": Wood, *The Creation of the American Republic*, 132. This is based upon a resolution of the Continental Congress, passed on that day, which approved a Preamble that declared "that the exercise of every kind of authority under the . . . crown [of Great Britain] should be totally suppressed, and all the powers of government exerted, under the authority of the people of the colonies": JCC 4:358.
202. JCC 4:590–591.
203. Carl Lotus Becker, *The Declaration of Independence: A Study in the History of Political Ideas* (New York: Harcourt, Brace & Company, 1922), 5.
204. Thomas Jefferson, "To Thomas Nelson," 16 May 1776, PTJ 1:292.
205. "Treaty of Alliance Between the United States of America and His Most Christian Majesty," 6 February 1778, USSL 8:6.
206. "We, therefore, the Representatives of the united States of America, in General Congress, Assembled, appealing to the Supreme Judge of the world for the rectitude of our intentions, do, in the Name, and by Authority of the good People of these Colonies, solemnly publish and declare, That *these United Colonies* are, and of Right ought to be Free and Independent States; that *they* are Absolved from all Allegiance to the British Crown, and that all political connection between *them* and the State of Great Britain, is and ought to be totally dissolved; and that as Free and Independent States, *they* have full Power to levy War, conclude Peace, contract Alliances, establish Commerce, and to do all other Acts and Things which Independent States may of right do. And for the support of this Declaration, with a firm reliance on the protection of divine Providence, we mutually pledge to each other our Lives, our Fortunes and our

sacred Honor" (emphasis added): "Declaration of Independence," 4 July 1776, Tansill, 25.

207. An authenticated copy of the Declaration that was printed on the authority of Congress was headed "A DECLARATION By the REPRESENTATIVES of the UNITED STATES OF AMERICA": Dennis J. Mahoney, "The Declaration of Independence as a Constitutional Document," in *The Framing and Ratification of the Constitution*, eds. Leonard W. Levy and Dennis J. Mahoney (New York: Macmillan Publishing Company, 1987), 57. Hendrickson observes that, in the early years after the Declaration was adopted, correspondents used "united States" about as often as they used "United States," and concludes that "[i]n either case, the United States were invariably treated as a plural noun": David C. Hendrickson, *Peace Pact: The Lost World of the American Founding* (Lawrence, KS: University of Kansas Press, 2003), 261.
208. JCC 8:509.
209. JCC 5:425.
210. Seth Ames, ed., *Works of Fisher Ames, with a Selection From His Speeches and Correspondence*, vol. 1 (Boston: Little, Brown & Company, 1854), 113.
211. Jeff Broadwater, *Jefferson, Madison, and the Making of the Constitution* (Chapel Hill, NC: University of North Carolina Press, 2019), 54.
212. JCC 4:342.
213. Thorpe 3:1890.
214. Thorpe 4:2454. This provision was repeated in New Hampshire's Constitution of 1792: Thorpe 3:2472.
215. Thorpe 5:3081.
216. Thorpe 3:1686.
217. Thorpe 5:2628.
218. Thorpe 6:3248.
219. Thorpe 5:2789–2790.
220. Thorpe 5:2594.
221. Thorpe 7:3815.
222. Thorpe 2:777–778.
223. Thorpe 1:562.
224. Quoted in Amar, *America's Constitution*, 23.
225. RFC 1:287, 291.
226. RFC 1:322.
227. Michael Burlingame, *Abraham Lincoln: A Life*, vol. 1 (Baltimore, MD: Johns Hopkins University Press, 2008), 50.
228. "From John Harvie," 18 October 1777, PTJ 2:35.
229. RFC 1:340.
230. George Washington, "To President of Congress," 17 September 1787, in *The Papers of George Washington: Confederation Series*, vol. 5, *1 February 1787–31 December 1787*, ed. W. W. Abbott (Charlottesville, VA: University of Virginia Press, 1987), 330.
231. John Adams, "To H Niles," 13 February 1818, in *The Works of John Adams, Second President of the United States*, vol. 10, ed. Charles Francis Adams (Boston: Little, Brown & Company, 1856), 283.
232. Gordon S. Wood, *Power and Liberty: Constitutionalism in the American*

Revolution (New York: Oxford University Press, 2021), 33. See also John Ferling, *A Leap in the Dark: The Struggle to Create the American Republic* (Oxford: Oxford University Press, 2003), 178–179; Colin Woodard, *Union: The Struggle to Forge the Story of the United States Nationhood* (New York: Viking, 2020), 2–5.

233. Alan Taylor, *American Revolutions: A Continental History, 1750–1804* (New York: W. W. Norton & Company, 2016), 337.
234. Hendrickson, *Peace Pact*, 125. See also Taylor, *American Revolutions*, 39.
235. Bernadette Meyler, "Between the States and the Signers: The Politics of the Declaration of Independence Before the Civil War," *Southern California Law Review* 89, no. 3 (March 2016): 565.
236. *Ware v. Hylton*, 3 U.S. 199, 224–225 (1796).
237. *McIlvaine v. Coxe's Lessee*, 8 U.S. 209, 212 (1808).
238. *Sturges v. Crowninshield*, 17 U.S. 122, 192 (1819).
239. James Monroe, "Special Message to the House of Representatives Containing the Views of the President of the United States on the Subject of Internal Improvements," May 4, 1822, in *A Compilation of the Messages and Papers of the Presidents*, vol. 2, ed. James D. Richardson (New York: Bureau of National Literature, Inc., 1897), 714.
240. Henry Baldwin, *A General View of the Origin and Nature of the Constitution and Government of the United States* (Philadelphia: John C. Clark, 1837), 62–63.
241. *State of Rhode Island and Providence Plantations v. Commonwealth of Massachusetts*, 37 U.S. 657, 751 (1838).
242. *Wheeler v. Smith*, 50 U.S. 55, 78 (1850).
243. *Dred Scott v. Sandford*, 60 U.S. 393, 407 (1857). See also Justice John Campbell, at 502.
244. *Kentucky v. Dennison*, 65 U.S. 66, 101 (1861).
245. C. Perry Patterson, "State Sovereignty v. National Sovereignty Prior to 1789," *New York University Law Quarterly Review* 24, no. 3 (July 1949): 560.
246. Taylor, *American Revolutions*, 337.
247. LaCroix, *The Ideological Origins of American Federalism*, 127.
248. "Articles of Confederation," 1 March 1781, Tansill, 27–37.
249. Story 1:229.
250. "Articles of Confederation," Tansill, 27.
251. Aaron N. Coleman, *The American Revolution, State Sovereignty, and the American Constitutional Settlement, 1765–1800* (Lanham, MD: Lexington Books, 2016), 40–46.
252. "Articles of Confederation," 27–28. The centrality of the Confederation being a defensive alliance against foreign threats was confirmed at the Philadelphia Convention in statements made by Edmund Randolph ("Originally our confederation was founded on the weakness of each state to repel a foreign enemy") and Luther Martin ("The federal Govt. [was] formed, to defend the whole agst. foreign nations, in case of war, and to defend the lesser States agst. the ambition of the larger"): RFC 1:341.
253. Harlow Giles Unger, *"Mr President": George Washington and the Making of the Nation's Highest Office* (Boston: Da Capo Press, 2013), 21.

254. "Articles of Confederation," 35.
255. Amar, *America's Constitution*, 27.
256. Anthony J. Bellia Jr. and Bradford R. Clark, "The International Law Origins of American Federalism," *Columbia Law Review* 120, no. 4 (May 2020): 857; Wood, *Power and Liberty*, 6, 55–56; Joseph Fishkin and William E Forbath, *The Anti-Oligarchy Constitution: Reconstructing the Economic Foundations of American Democracy* (Cambridge, MA: Harvard University Press, 2022), 45.
257. Taylor, *American Revolutions*, 338.
258. Wood, *The Creation of the American Republic*, 356–357.
259. Jack N. Rakove, *Original Meanings: Politics and Ideas in the Making of the Constitution* (New York: Alfred A. Knopf, 1997), 29.
260. "Definitive Treaty of Peace Between the United States of America and his Britannic Majesty," USSL 8:81, 83.
261. *McIlvaine v. Coxe's Lessee*, 8 U.S. 209, 212 (1808).
262. Bellia and Clark, "The International Law Origins of American Federalism," 847.
263. James Madison, "Vices of the Political System of the United States," April 1787, PJM 9:351. See also Adam Tate, "James Madison and State Sovereignty, 1780–1781," *American Political Thought* (Fall 2013): 174–197.
264. DHRC 9:1029.
265. John Adams, *A Defence of the Constitutions of Government of the United States of America*, vol. 1 (London: C. Dilly, in the Poultry, 1787), 362–363.
266. "From Henry Knox," 31 January 1785, in *The Papers of George Washington: Confederation Series*, vol. 2, *18 July 1784–18 May 1785*, ed. W. W. Abbot (Charlottesville. VA: University Press of Virginia, 1992), 302. See also Raoul Berger, *Federalism: The Founder's Design* (Norman, OK: University of Oklahoma Press, 1987), 28–29; Maier, *Ratification*, 14.
267. "The Federalist No. 15 (Hamilton)," Federalist, 70.
268. Akhil Reed Amar, "Of Sovereignty and Federalism," *Yale Law Journal* 96, no. 7 (June 1987): 1446–1447.
269. RFC 1:16, 181, 182, 204, 340, 475, 499, 500.
270. RFC 1:323.
271. RFC 1:324.
272. RFC 1:467.
273. *Gibbons v. Ogden*, 22 U.S. 1, 187 (1824). Marshall made the same point when, in anonymously defending his opinion in *McCulloch v. Maryland*, he wrote that the States of the union created by the Articles of Confederation "were then truly sovereign, and were bound together only by a league": "A Friend of the Constitution No VII," 9 July 1819, in *The Papers of John Marshall*, vol. 7, ed. Charles F. Hobson (Chapel Hill, NC: University of North Carolina Press, 1995), 351.
274. Benjamin Robbins Curtis, "Speech in Faneuil Hall," 26 November 1850, in *A Memoir of Benjamin Robbins Curtis With Some of His Professional and Miscellaneous Writings*, vol.1, ed. Benjamin R. Curtis (Boston: Little, Brown, & Company, 1879), 129.
275. *Dred Scott v. Sandford*, 60 U.S. 393, 434 (1857).
276. *Kentucky v. Dennison*, 65 U.S. 66, 103 (1861).

277. *Dred Scott v. Sandford*, 60 U.S. 393, 434 (1857).
278. Washington, "To President of Congress," 330.
279. Amar, "Of Sovereignty and Federalism," 1450–1451.
280. RFC 2:193.
281. RFC 1:177.
282. RFC 2:477. In relation to the decision to require ratification by only nine states, James Madison, in *Federalist 43*, said: "To have required the unanimous ratification of the thirteen States, would have subjected the essential interests of the whole to the caprice or corruption of a single member. It would have marked a want of foresight in the Convention, which our own experience would have rendered inexcusable": "The Federalist No. 43 (Madison)," 215.
283. RFC 2:553. The members of the Committee were Alexander Hamilton, William Samuel Johnson, Rufus King, James Madison, and Gouverneur Morris. On the changes between the text of the Constitution as approved by the Convention and the final form of the Constitution produced by the Committee of Style, see William Michael Treanor, "The Case of the Dishonest Scrivener: Gouverneur Morris and the Creation of the Federalist Constitution," *Michigan Law Review* 120, no. 1 (October 2021): 46–104.
284. Farrand, *The Framing of the Constitution*, 191.
285. RFC 2:590.
286. James Madison, "To Jared Sparks," 8 April, 1831, WJM 9:448. See also "Ezra Stiles: Diary," 21 December, 1787, RFC 3:170; Adams, *Gouverneur Morris*, 162–164; Peter Charles Hoffer, *For Ourselves and Our Posterity: The Preamble to the Federal Constitution in American History* (New York: Oxford University Press, 2013), 69–71.
287. RFC 1:593.
288. Gouverneur Morris, "Letter to Lewis R. Morris, Springfield, Vermont," 10 December 1803, in Jared Sparks, *The Life of Gouverneur Morris with Selections from His Correspondence and Miscellaneous Papers*, vol, 3 (Boston: Gray and Bowen, 1832), 193.
289. RFC 1:54.
290. "The Federalist No. 43 (Madison)," 216.
291. "The Federalist No. 39 (Madison)," 184.
292. "The Federalist No. 39 (Madison)," 185.
293. "The Federalist No. 46 (Madison)," 228.
294. DHRC 9:995.
295. James Madison, "To Spencer Roane," 29 June 1821, PJMRS 2:347.
296. James Madison, "Outline," September 1829, WJM 9:352.
297. James Madison, "To Edward Everett," 28 August 1830, WJM 9:385–386. See also James Madison, "Outline," September 1829, WJM 9:352; James Madison, "To M. L. Hurlbert," May 1830, WJM 9:373.
298. "From James Madison," 15 March 1833, in *The Papers of Daniel Webster, Correspondence,* vol. 3, *1830–1834*, ed. Charles M. Wiltse (Hanover, NH: University Press of New England, 1977), 222. In the same year Madison referred to the states being "parties to the compact": Madison, "To Alexander Rives," 496.
299. James Madison, "On Nullification," 1835, LOWJM 4:422.
300. RFC 2:189.

301. RFC 2:469.
302. RFC 2:477.
303. RFC 2:475.
304. RFC 2:603.
305. McDonald, *Novus Ordo Seclorum*, 280.
306. *Penhallow v. Doane*, 3 U.S. 54, 93 (1795).
307. DHRC 10:1507.
308. House of Delegates, "Virginia Resolutions," 21 December 1798, PJM 17:189.
309. House of Delegates, "Virginia Resolutions," 189.
310. House of Delegates, "Virginia Resolutions," 190.
311. "Address of the General Assembly to the People of the Commonwealth of Virginia," 23 January 1799, WJM 6:333. Whether the "Address" was penned by Madison, as intimated by Gaillard Hunt in his edited collection of Madison's papers, is disputed by the editors of a later collection of Madison's papers: "Editorial Note," PJM 17:199–206.
312. James Madison, "The Report of 1800," 7 January 1800, PJM 17:308–309.
313. Madison, "Report of 1800," 309.
314. Madison, "Report of 1800," 326.
315. Madison, "Report of 1800," 339.
316. "Kentucky Resolutions Adopted by the Kentucky General Assembly," 10 November 1798, PTJ 30:550.
317. Jonathan Gienapp, "How to Maintain a Constitution: The Virginia and Kentucky Resolutions and James Madison's Struggle with the Problem of Constitutional Maintenance," in *Nullification and Secession in Modern Constitutional Thought*, ed. Sanford Levinson (Lawrence, KS: University Press of Kansas, 2016), 58–60.
318. Madison, "To Edward Everett," 402.
319. James Madison, "To N. P. Trist," December 1831, WJM 9:472.
320. James Madison, "To W. C. Rives," 12 March 1833, LOWJM 4:422, 290.
321. Madison, "On Nullification," 400.
322. James Madison, "To Henry Clay," 9 October 1830, WJM 9:411.
323. Arthur Bestor, "State Sovereignty and Slavery: A Reinterpretation of Proslavery Constitutional Doctrine," *Journal of the Illinois State Historical Society* 54, no. 2 (Summer 1961): 120–121; Daniel Walker Howe, *What Hath God Wrought: The Transformation of America, 1815–1848* (Oxford: Oxford University Press, 2007), 398; Harry L. Watson, *Building the American Republic: A Narrative History to 1877* (Chicago: University of Chicago Press, 2018), 406–407; Jill Lepore, *These Truths: A History of the United States* (New York: W. W. Norton & Co., 2018), 217–218.
324. *Fletcher v. Peck*, 10 U.S. 87, 136 (1810). Marshall's decision in this case built upon the earlier decision in *United States v Peters* where, in delivering the opinion of the Supreme Court, Marshall ruled that a state could not "annul the judgments of the courts of the United States": *United States v. Peters*, 9 U.S. 115, 136 (1809).
325. According to Brandon, by 1861, "nullification had been rejected so often for so long that it was widely considered politically untenable, as illustrated by Chief

Justice Taney's rejection of Wisconsin's claims in *Ableman*": Brandon, *Free in the World*, 176.
326. CG, 36th Congress, 2nd Session, 487.
327. Brandon, *Free in the World*, 175.
328. Wendell Bird, "Reassessing Responses to the Virginia and Kentucky Resolutions: New Evidence from the Tennessee and Georgia Resolutions and from Other States," *Journal of the Early Republic* 35, no. 2 (Winter 2015): 548. However, it can be noted that, during the nullification crisis of the early 1830s that was ignited by the Tariff of Abominations of 1828, Madison's home state of Virginia, in a resolution that specifically referenced its 1798 resolutions, after reaffirming "the doctrines of State Sovereignty and State Rights," rejected the doctrine of nullification: *State Papers on Nullification: Including the Public Acts of the Convention of the People of South Carolina*, (Boston: Dutton & Wentworth, Printers, 1834), 196–197.
329. Bird, "Reassessing," 526–527.
330. Bird, "Reassessing," 549.
331. "An Act laying an Embargo on all ships and vessels in the ports and harbors of the United States," 22 December 1807, USSL 2:451–453.
332. "Report and Resolutions of Rhode Island on the Embargo," 4 March 1809, Ames, 43. On the embargo which came into effect in 1808 and its eventual repeal, see Richard Mannix, "Gallatin, Jefferson, and the Embargo of 1808," *Diplomatic History* 3, no. 2 (April 1979): 151–172. On Rhode Island's reaction to the Embargo Act, see Harvey Strum, "Rhode Island and the Embargo of 1807," *Rhode Island History* 52, no. 2 (May 1994): 58–67.
333. John G. Grove, *John C. Calhoun's Theory of Republicanism* (Lawrence, KS: University Press of Kansas, 2016), 111–115.
334. John C. Calhoun, "A Discourse on the Constitution and Government of the United States," in *Union and Liberty: The Political Philosophy of John C. Calhoun*, ed. Ross M. Lence (Indianapolis, IN: Liberty Fund, 1992), 116. Calhoun had first publicly stated this view in 1831 in what is commonly referred to as his Fort Hill Address: John C. Calhoun, "To [Frederick W] Symmes," 26 July 1831, in PJCC 11:414–415. De Tocqueville saw the Union as did Calhoun when he wrote: "The Union was formed by the voluntary agreement of the states; and these, in uniting together, have not forfeited their sovereignty, nor have they been reduced to the condition of one and the same people": Alexis de Tocqueville, *Democracy in America*, vol. 1 (New York: Everyman's Library, 1994), 387.
335. Robert Elder, *Calhoun: American Heretic* (New York: Basic Books, 2021), 353–355.
336. CG, 25th Congress, 2nd Session, 98.
337. CG, 25th Congress, 2nd Session, 98.
338. LaCroix, *The Ideological Origins of American Federalism*, 130.
339. RFC 2:643.
340. RFC 2:663. Of the fifty-five delegates, only thirty-nine signed the proposed Constitution. Some delegates had already left the Convention, having other matters to attend to, or because they opposed the centralizing tendencies of the

Constitution, while three influential members (Elbridge Gerry, George Mason, and Edmund Randolph) refused to sign it on the last day of the Convention: Peter B. Knupfer, *The Union As It Is: Constitutional Unionism and Sectional Compromise, 1787–1861* (Chapel Hill, NC: University of North Carolina Press, 1991), 29–30.

341. Donald Jackson and Dorothy Twohig, eds., *The Papers of George Washington: Diaries*, vol. 5, *1 July 1776—31 December 1789* (Charlottesville, VA: University of Virginia Press, 1979), 185.
342. RFC 1:8.
343. RFCS, 287.
344. "Resolutions of the Convention Recommending the Procedures for the Ratification and for the Establishment of Government Under the Constitution by the Confederation Congress," 17 September 1787, DHRC 1:318.
345. RFC 2:646.
346. "Journals of Congress," 28 September 1787, DHRC 1:340.
347. Larson, *American Inheritance*, 205.
348. DHCUSA, 25.
349. DHCUSA, 44.
350. DHCUSA, 62.
351. DHCUSA, 83.
352. DHCUSA, 87.
353. DHCUSA, 93.
354. DHCUSA, 121.
355. DHCUSA, 138–139.
356. DHCUSA, 141.
357. DHCUSA, 145–146.
358. DHCUSA, 190, 195.
359. DHCUSA, 290.
360. DHCUSA, 310, 315.
361. John C. Calhoun, "To James Hamilton Jr.," 615–616.
362. Francis Lieber, *Two Lectures on the Constitution of the United States* (New York: Board of Trustees, 1861), 28.
363. Samuel H. Beer, *To Make a Nation: The Rediscovery of American Federalism* (Cambridge, MA: Belknap Press, 1993), 333.
364. Beer, *To Make a Nation*, 334.
365. Beer, *To Make a Nation*, 334.
366. Beer, *To Make a Nation*, 334.
367. RFC 2:93.
368. RFC 2:93.
369. Beer, *To Make a Nation*, 335–336.
370. Beer, *To Make a Nation*, 322.
371. DHCUSA, 310.
372. In 2001, Amar wrote that Lincoln's "historical narrative was problematic": Amar, "Abraham Lincoln and the American Union," 1125. By 2007, his view had matured to the point of writing that Lincoln had "mistakenly [read] later history back into an earlier period": Amar, *America's Constitution*, 27.
373. Amar, *America's Constitution*, 21.

374. Amar, "Of Sovereignty and Federalism," 1459–1460. In 1862, Sidney George Fisher presented an argument similar to that of Amar: Fisher, *The Trial of the Constitution*, 140–141, 147–148.
375. Amar, "The Consent of the Governed," 489.
376. Amar, "The Consent of the Governed," 489.
377. Amar, "Of Sovereignty and Federalism," 1456.
378. *Barron v. Mayor and City Council of Baltimore*, 32 U.S. 243, 250 (1833).
379. *Martin v. Hunter's Lessee*, 14 U.S. 304, 374 (1816).
380. Akhil Reed Amar, "Philadelphia Revisited: Amending the Constitution Outside Article V," *University of Chicago Law Review* 55, no. 4 (Autumn 1988): 1050.
381. Jean Edward Smith, *John Marshall: Definer of a Nation* (New York: Henry Holt and Company, 1996), 441.
382. The constitutional validity of Section 25 was upheld in *Martin v. Hunter's Lessee*, 14 U.S. 304, 337–352 (1816).
383. *McCulloch v. Maryland*, 17 U.S. 316, 412 (1819). Marshall did not rely on Article I, Section 8 of the Constitution which, after setting out the enumerated powers of Congress, stipulated that Congress had the power "[t]o make all Laws which shall be necessary and proper for carrying into Execution the foregoing Powers, and all other Powers vested by this Constitution in the Government of the United States, or in any Department or Officer thereof": Akhil Reed Amar, *America's Unwritten Constitution: The Precedents and Principles We Live By* (New York: Basic Books, 2012), 23–27.
384. *McCulloch v. Maryland*, 17 U.S. 316, 421 (1819).
385. *McCulloch v. Maryland*, 17 U.S. 316, 403 (1819).
386. *McCulloch v. Maryland*, 17 U.S. 316, 405 (1819).
387. Daniel A. Farber, "The Story of *McCulloch*: Banking on National Power," *Constitutional Commentary* 20, no. 3 (2003–2004): 714.
388. "A Friend of the Constitution No. 1," 30 June 1819, in *The Papers of John Marshall*, vol. 8, ed. Charles F. Hobson (Chapel Hill, NC: University of North Carolina Press, 1995): 318.
389. *McCulloch v. Maryland*, 17 U.S. 316, 400 (1819).
390. "A Friend of the Constitution No. 6," 6 July 1819, in Hobson, *The Papers of John Marshall*, vol. 8, 346.
391. "A Friend of the Constitution No. 6," 347.
392. "A Friend of the Constitution No. 7," 9 July 1819, in Hobson, *The Papers of John Marshall*, vol. 8, 349.
393. "A Friend of the Constitution No. 7," 349.
394. "A Friend of the Constitution No. 7," 350.
395. "A Friend of the Constitution No. 8," 14 July 1819, in Hobson, *The Papers of John Marshall*, vol. 8, 355.
396. Charles F. Hobson, *The Great Chief Justice: John Marshall and the Rule of Law* (Lawrence, KS: University Press of Kansas, 1996), 111–112; R. Kent Newmyer, "John Marshall, *McCulloch v. Maryland*, and the Southern States' Rights Tradition," *John Marshall Law Review* 33, no. 4 (Summer 2000): 897; Richard E. Ellis, *Aggressive Nationalism:* McCulloch v. Maryland *and the Foundation of Federal Authority in the Young Republic* (Oxford: Oxford University Press, 2007), 130; Hoffer, *For Ourselves and Our Posterity*, 112.

397. Martin S. Flaherty, "John Marshall, *McCulloch v. Maryland*, and 'We the People': Revisions in Need of Revising," *The William and Mary Law Review* 43, no. 4 (March 2002): 1379.
398. Flaherty, "John Marshall," 1389.
399. Howe, *What Hath God Wrought*, 221–222.
400. Thomas Jefferson, "To Albert Gallatin," 26 December 1820, PTJRS 16:489–490.
401. G. Edward White, *Law in American History,* vol. 1: *From the Colonial Years Through the Civil War* (Oxford: Oxford University Press, 2012), 236; Michael J. Klarman, "How Great Were The 'Great' Marshall Court Decisions?" *Virginia Law Review* 87, no. 6 (October 2001): 1140–1141; Paul, *Indivisible*, 65.
402. James Madison, "To Spencer Roane," 2 September 1819, PJMRS 1 502.
403. Beer, *To Make a Nation*, 321. Hurd is similarly critical when he writes of such a view as one rooted in "transcendental philosophy, instead of one of fact, to be settled by ordinary evidence": John C. Hurd, *The Theory of Our National Existence, as Shown by the Action of the Government of the United States Since 1861* (Boston: Little, Brown, & Company, 1881), 114.
404. De Tocqueville articulated this point when he wrote that the delegates to the Philadelphia Convention "were not appointed to constitute the government of a single people, but to regulate the association of several states." It was for this reason that he went on to state that "Americans have . . . much more to hope and to fear from the states than from the Union; and . . . are more likely to attach themselves strongly to the former than to the latter": de Tocqueville, *Democracy in America*, 382, 385.
405. Kermit Roosevelt III, *The Nation That Never Was: Reconstructing America's Story* (Chicago: University of Chicago Press, 2022), 70.
406. RFC 1:69.
407. RFC 2:201.
408. RFC 2:249.
409. RFC 2:201.
410. RFC 2:203.
411. Elliott 2:11, 18, 26, 46, 91, 145, 294.
412. Elliott 4:21, 123, 130, 133.
413. DHRC 9:948.
414. RFC 1:68.
415. RFC 2:29.
416. RFC 2:32.
417. RFC 2:57.
418. Alexander Keyssar, *Why Do We Still Have the Electoral College?* (Cambridge, MA: Harvard University Press, 2020), 32.
419. Daniel Webster, "Second Reply to Hayne, January 26–27, 1830," PDW 1:399.
420. Webster, "Second Reply," 400.
421. "The Federalist No. 45 (Madison)," Federalist, 225–226.
422. James Madison, "To Thomas Jefferson," 24 October 1787, PJM:10, 210–211.
423. "An Act relative to the Election of a President and Vice President of the United States, and declaring the Officer who shall act as President in case of Vacancies in the offices of both President and Vice President," USSL 1:239–241.

424. "An Act to establish a uniform time for holding elections of the President and Vice President in all States of the Union," USSL 5:721.
425. Elliott 4:21.
426. Henry Paul Monaghan, "We the People(s), Original Understanding, and Constitutional Amendment," *Columbia Law Review* 96, no. 1 (January 1996): 168.
427. JCC 5:475.
428. J. Taylor McConkie, "State Treason: The History and Validity of Treason Against Individual States," *Kentucky Law Journal* 101, no. 2 (2012–2013): 286.
429. RFC 2:345 (Morris), 349 (King), 350 (Dickinson).
430. RFC 2:349 (Ellsworth and Sherman).
431. RFC 2:348.
432. Based on data set out in McConkie, "State Treason," 291–293.
433. McConkie, "State Treason," 304, 308. See also Cynthia Nicoletti, *Secession on Trial: The Treason Prosecution of Jefferson Davis* (New York: Cambridge University Press, 2017), 138–141.
434. Andrew G. I. Kilberg, "We the People: The Original meaning of Popular Sovereignty," *Virginia Law Review* 100, no. 5 (September 2014): 1090.
435. Although invariably referred to today as the Bill of Rights Amendments, they were not known or referred to as such until the mid-1860s: Amar, *America's Unwritten Constitution*, 157–158.
436. Not all of the recommendations made by the seven states were incorporated in the joint resolution of the First Congress that, on 28 September 1789, resolved to put twelve amendments to the states for ratification. On 2 October 1789, President George Washington forwarded the twelve recommended amendments to the states for ratification. All of the proposed amendments, except what became the Fifth Amendment, were drawn from the recommendations made at the various ratification conventions. On 1 March 1792, Thomas Jefferson, in his capacity as secretary of state, certified that all but the first two of the proposed amendments had been ratified: Maier, *Ratification*, 452–454, 460; Leonard W. Levy, *Origins of the Bill of Rights* (New Haven, CT: Yale University Press, 1999), 32. Of the other amendments that had been recommended by the ratification resolutions, the proposal by Virginia, New York, and North Carolina that presidents could only serve for a maximum of two terms became the twenty-second amendment in 1951 in the wake of Franklin Delano Roosevelt's election in 1940 and 1944 to a third and fourth term respectively, in breach of what had been, until then, an accepted convention that presidents could only serve a maximum of two terms: Maier, *Ratification*, 466.
437. AC, 1st Congress, 1st Session 447.
438. James Madison, "To Richard Peters," 19 August 1789, PJM:12, 347.
439. Unger, *"Mr President,"* 104.
440. Roosevelt, *The Nation That Never Was*, 71–72.
441. *Barron v. Mayor and City Council of Baltimore*, 32 U.S. 243, 250 (1833).
442. "The Federalist No. 46 (Madison)," 232.
443. Ferling, *A Leap in the Dark*, 290.
444. American Dictionary of the English Language, http://webstersdictionary1828.com/Home?word=Delegate.

445. American Dictionary of the English Language, http://webstersdictionary1828.com/Home?word=surrender.
446. George Ticknor Curtis, *Constitutional History of the United States from their Declaration of Independence to the Close of their Civil War*, vol. 2 (New York: Harper & Brothers, 1896), 45.
447. DHRC 22:1960.
448. Elliott 2:129.
449. Amar, "The Consent of the Governed," 507.
450. "The Federalist No. 39 (Madison)," 187.
451. "The Federalist No. 39 (Madison)," 186.
452. "The Federalist No. 45 (Madison)," 227.
453. Madison, "On Nullification," 421. See also, James Madison, "To Spencer Roane," 347; James Madison, "To Joseph C Cabell," 22 March 1827, WJM 9:285; James Madison, "Sovereignty," December 1835, LOWJM 4:390, 391, 393, 395.
454. *Chisholm v. Georgia*, 2 U.S. 419, 435 (1793).
455. *Ableman v. Booth*, 62 U.S. 506, 516 (1859).
456. *Texas v. White*, 74 U.S. 700, 725 (1869). Chase's adherence to dual sovereignty was evident in the earlier case of *Lane County v. Oregon*, where, in delivering the opinion of a unanimous Supreme Court, he noted that the states existed before the Constitution and that within it, their "necessary existence . . . and . . . independent authority . . . is distinctly recognized": *Lane County v. Oregon*, 74 U.S. 71, 76 (1869).
457. Calhoun, "A Discourse on the Constitution and Government of the United States," 105.
458. John C. Calhoun, "Speech on the Force Bill," 15–16 February 1833, PJCC:12, 71.
459. Thorpe 3:1890.
460. Thorpe 4:2454.
461. Elliott 4:316.
462. AC, 16th Congress, 1st Session, 1316.
463. "Observations on the new Federal CONSTITUTION," *Connecticut Courant*, 7 January 1788, in *Collected Works of Roger Sherman*, ed. Mark David Hall (Indianapolis, IN: Liberty Fund, 2016), 492.
464. DHRC 2:348–349.
465. DHRC 2:472. For examples of references during the ratification conventions to powers being delegated to the federal government see, Elliott 1:322, 326, 327, 336; Elliott 2:34, 63, 64, 79, 85, 88, 89, 111, 131,151, 166.
466. DHRC 2:479.
467. DHRC 2:448.
468. *Ware v. Hylton*, 3 U.S. 199, 281 (1796).
469. DHRC 10:1431.
470. 17 U.S. 316, 405 (1819).
471. Justice Story in *Martin v. Hunter's Lease*, 14 U.S. 304, 338 (1816); Justice Mclean in *Groves v. Slaughter*, 40 U.S. 449, 504 (1841); Justices Story and Daniel in *Prigg v. Pennsylvania*, 41 U.S. 539, 618, 654 (1842); Justices Campbell and Curtis in *Dred Scott v. Sandford*, 60 U.S. 393, 509, 511, 513, 572 (1856).

472. Federalist, 67 (*Federalist 15*), 94 (*Federalist 21*), 106 (*Federalist 22*), 109 (*Federalist 23*), 123 (*Federalist 26*), 145 (*Federalist 32*), 220 (*Federalist 44*), 227 (*Federalist 45*), 244 (*Federalist 48*), 346 (*Federalist 70*), 364 (*Federalist 74*), 371 (*Federalist 76*), 379 (*Federalist 78*), 401 (*Federalist 82*).
473. "The Federalist No. 84 (Hamilton)," Federalist, 419.
474. DHCUSA, 140.
475. DHCUSA, 191.
476. DHCUSA, 93 (Massachusetts), 142 (New Hampshire), 316 (Rhode Island).
477. DHCUSA, 270 (North Carolina), 381 (Virginia).
478. Elliott 2:131.
479. Michael J. Klarman, *The Framers' Coup: The Making of the United States Constitution* (New York: Oxford University Press, 2016), 579.
480. "The Federalist No. 44 (Madison)," Federalist, 221.
481. "The Federalist No. 45 (Madison)," Federalist, 227.
482. *McCulloch v. Maryland*, 17 U.S. 316, 406–407 (1819).
483. Amar, "Of Sovereignty and Federalism," 1430–1436; Wood, *The Creation of the American Republic*, 345.
484. RFCS, 287.
485. DHRC 2:349.
486. DHRC 2:361–362. In *Federalist 78*, Alexander Hamilton made the same claim when he referred to "the right of the people to alter or abolish the established constitution whenever they find it inconsistent with their happiness": "The Federalist No. 78 (Hamilton)," Federalist, 381.
487. Lincoln, "First Inaugural Address," 269–270; Lincoln, "Message to Congress in Special Session," 433, 435.
488. *Texas v. White*,74 U.S. 700, 725–726 (1869).
489. Story 1:329.
490. Story 1:288.
491. Calhoun, "A Discourse on the Constitution and Government of the United States," 212.
492. John C. Calhoun, "To Anna Maria Calhoun Clemson," 25 January 1838, PJCC 14:107. See also Elder, *Calhoun*, 358–360.
493. John C. Calhoun, "To Percy Walker," 23 October 1847, PJCC 24:618. Although Calhoun advocated the doctrine of nullification, he went to great lengths to distinguish it from secession. He saw nullification, which he regarded as a logical extension of the Kentucky and Virginia Resolutions, as a means of preserving the Union and secession as a remedy of last resort if the Union could not be preserved: Elizabeth R. Varon, *Disunion! The Coming of the American Civil War, 1789–1859* (Chapel Hill, NC: University of North Carolina Press, 2008), 89.
494. Calhoun, "A Discourse on the Constitution and Government of the United States," 212.
495. Quoted in Robert Saunders Jr., *John A. Campbell: Southern Moderate* (Tuscaloosa, AL: University of Alabama Press, 1997), 138.
496. Lincoln, "First Inaugural Address," 265. Edward Everett also made the argument that one party to a contract cannot break it: Everett, "The Questions of the Day," 363.

497. Amar, "Abraham Lincoln and the American Union," 1113.
498. RFC 1:314. See also "The Federalist No. 43 (Madison)," 216. In his speech in the Senate on 31 December 1860, Louisiana's Senator Judah P. Benjamin made the same point when, in the context of defending South Carolina's act of secession, he said: "[A] bargain broken on one side is a bargain broken on all; and the compact is binding upon the generation of to-day only if the other parties to the compact have kept their faith": CG, 36th Congress, 2nd Session, 213.
499. "Declaration of the Immediate Causes Which Induce and Justify the Secession of South Carolina From The Federal Union," JSCSC, 463.
500. Amar, *America's Constitution*, 37. See also Akhil Reed Amar, *The Constitution Today: Timeless Lessons for the Issues of Our Era* (New York: Basic Books, 2016), 400; Amar, *The Words That Made Us*, 262.
501. Han Liu, "Three Arguments of "Right of Secession" in the Civil War: International Perspectives," *Hastings International and Comparative Law Review* 41, no. 1 (Winter 2018): 64–65.
502. De Tocqueville, *Democracy in America*, 388, 389.
503. J. P. Gordy, *A History of Political Parties in the United States in Three Volumes*, vol. 1 (Athens, OH: Ohio Publishing Co., 1895), 45–46.
504. Sanford Levinson, *An Argument Open to All: Reading* The Federalist *in the 21st Century* (New Haven, CT: Yale University Press, 2015), 144.
505. Liah Greenfeld, *Nationalism: Five Roads to Modernity* (Cambridge, MA: Harvard University Press, 1992), 431.
506. DHRC 2:478.
507. Amar, *America's Constitution*, 36–37. Alexander Hamilton echoed the sentiments of Wilson when, in urging New York to ratify the Constitution in order to protect American interests from foreign powers, he finished his argument in *Federalist 11* with a rallying cry urging the thirteen States of the Confederation to come together "in a strict and indissoluble union:" "The Federalist No. 11 (Hamilton)," Federalist, 52. This statement, read in context, cannot be construed to mean, as Amar asserts, that the Constitution created "a new plan . . . for a 'strict and indissoluble union'": Akhil Reed Amar, "Founding Myths," in *Myth America: Historians Take on the Biggest Legends and Lies About Our Past*, eds. Kevin M. Kruse and Julian E. Zelizer (New York: Basic Books, 2022), 34. Rather, like Wilson, Hamilton was expressing his hope that the Union would be indissoluble.
508. Abraham Lincoln, "Second Lecture on Discoveries and Inventions," 11 February 1859, CWAL 3:360.
509. Lincoln, "First Inaugural Address," 265.
510. Vasan Kesavan and Michael Stokes Paulsen, "Is West Virginia Unconstitutional," *California Law Review* 90, no. 2 (March 2002): 303.
511. Stampp, "The Concept of a Perpetual Union," 7; Brandon, *Free in the World*, 39; Levinson, "'Perpetual Union,'" 483; Amar, *America's Constitution*, 27; Daniel Farber, "The Fourteenth Amendment and the Unconstitutionality of Secession," *Akron Law Review* 45, no. 2 (2012): 486.
512. Maier, *American Scripture*, 206.
513. Neely, *Lincoln and the Triumph of the Nation*, 39–40.
514. Lincoln, "First Inaugural Address," 271.

515. Taylor, *American Revolutions*, 39.
516. Ernest Renan, "What is a Nation?" in *Nationalism in Europe, 1815 to the Present*, ed. Stuart Woolf (London: Routledge, 1996), 50.
517. Quoted in Nicoletti, *Secession on Trial*, 32–33.
518. Abraham Lincoln, "Last Public Address," 11 April 1865, CWAL 8:403.
519. Jack P. Greene, "The Background of the Articles of Confederation," *Publius: The Journal of Federalism* 12, no. 4 (Autumn 1982): 24.
520. "The Federalist No. 46 (Madison)," 229. Ellis writes that the "former colonists did not regard themselves as Americans, but rather as New Englanders, Virginians, or Pennsylvanians. No such thing as an American national identity yet existed": Joseph J. Ellis, *The Cause: The American Revolution and its Discontents, 1773–1783* (New York: Liveright Publishing Corporation, 2021), xi. Brandon writes that at that time the people "were the people of the states" and that "the United States was not yet a nation, as late as 1861": Brandon, *Free in the World*, 192.
521. Jennifer Ratner-Rosenhagen, *The Ideas That Made America: A Brief History* (New York: Oxford University Press, 2019), 56–57.
522. Brandon, *Free in the World*, 181.
523. Stampp, "The Concept of a Perpetual Union," 33.
524. White, *Law in American History*, 482.

CHAPTER 3. "A SLAVEHOLDERS' UNION?"

1. John C. Calhoun, "A Discourse on the Constitution and Government of the United States," in *Union and Liberty: The Political Philosophy of John C. Calhoun*, ed. Ross M. Lence (Indianapolis, IN): Liberty Fund, 1992), 212.
2. RFC 2:221–222.
3. George Clymer, Benjamin Franklin, Elbridge Gerry, Robert Morris, George Read, Roger Sherman, James Wilson, and George Wythe. Gerry refused to sign the proposed Constitution prepared by the Convention. Wythe did not sign it, having left the Convention before it had completed its work.
4. Linda Colley, *The Gun, the Ship and the Pen: Warfare, Constitutions and the Making of the Modern World* (London: Profile Books Ltd, 2021), 117.
5. Michael J. Klarman, *The Framers' Coup: The Making of the United States Constitution* (New York: Oxford University Press, 2016), 263.
6. John R. Vile, *The Constitutional Convention: A Comprehensive Encyclopedia of America's Founding*, vols. 1–2, rev. 2nd ed. (Clark, NJ: Talbot Publishing, 2016), 79–86, 325–334, 473–486, 494–500, 502–514, 633–648, 711–720, 762–769, 919–924; David Waldstreicher, *Runaway America: Benjamin Franklin, Slavery, and the American Revolution* (New York: Hill & Wang, 2004), 232–235; Marty D. Matthews, *Forgotten Founder: The Life and Times of Charles Pinckney* (Columbia, SC: University of South Carolina Press, 2004), 39–56; Marvin R. Zahniser, *Charles Cotesworth Pinckney: Founding Father* (Chapel Hill, NC: University of North Carolina Press, 1967), 87–96; Richard Beeman, *Plain, Honest Men: The Making of the American Constitution* (New York: Random House, 2009), 309–310.
7. Edward J. Larson, *The Return of George Washington, 1783–1789* (New York: William Morrow, 2014), 103. Hirschfeld notes that "[w]hatever Washington

may have thought of the slavery issue being debated and decided at the federal convention, the proslavery views that found their way into the Constitution were (coincidentally or not) those most compatible with Washington's own values and beliefs": Fritz Hirschfeld, *George Washington and Slavery: A Documentary Portrayal* (Columbia, MO: University of Missouri Press, 1997), 177. During the last six years of his presidency, while the capital of the Union was located in Philadelphia, Washington brought a number of slaves to service him and his wife in their official residence. Washington, acting on confidential advice from Attorney General Edmund Randolph, was vigilant in getting around Pennsylvania's legislation which stipulated that after six months continuous residence in that state, a slave became free, by having the slaves that he had with him in Philadelphia do a round trip to Virginia and back each six months: Mary V. Thompson, *"The Only Unavoidable Subject of Regret": George Washington, Slavery, and the Enslaved Community at Mount Vernon* (Charlottesville, VA: University of Virginia Press, 2019), 59–60. At the end of his term in office, Ona Judge, a slave who served as personal attendant for his wife escaped. Washington relentlessly, but unsuccessfully, sought her recapture up until his death in 1799: Erica Armstrong Dunbar, *Never Caught: The Washingtons' Relentless Pursuit of their Runaway Slave, Ona Judge* (New York: Atria Books, 2017); Edward J. Larson, *American Inheritance: Liberty and Slavery in the Birth of a Nation, 1765-1795* (New York: W. W. Norton & Company, 2023), 254-257. Judge was but one of at least forty-seven (approximately 7 percent) of the slaves that Washington or his wife owned that ran away between 1760 and his death in 1799: Philip D. Morgan and Michael L. Nicholls, "Slave Flight: Mount Vernon, Virginia, and the Wider Atlantic World," in *George Washington's South*, eds. Tamara Harvey and Greg O'Brien (Gainesville, FL: University Press of Florida, 2004), 197–204, 215. For a detailed study of Washington's use of slaves at his Mount Vernon estate, see Bruce A. Ragsdale, *Washington at the Plow: The Founding Farmer and the Question of Slavery* (Cambridge, MA: The Belknap Press, 2021).

8. Peter Charles Hoffer, *For Ourselves and Our Posterity: The Preamble to the Federal Constitution in American History* (New York: Oxford University Press, 2013), 60; Klarman, *The Framers' Coup*, 263–264; Noah Feldman, *The Three Lives of James Madison: Genius, Partisan, President* (New York: Random House, 2017), 156.
9. RFC 1:581. William Paterson referred to slaves as "property, & like other property entirely at the will of the Master": RFC 1:561. Elbridge Gerry observed that "blacks . . . were property in the South": RFC 1:201.
10. Henry Clay, "Motions and Speech at Meeting of American Colonization Society," 1 January 1818, in *The Papers of Henry Clay*, vol. 2, *The Rising Statesman, 1815–1820*, ed. James F. Hopkins (Lexington, KY: University of Kentucky Press, 1961), 420.
11. RFCS, 44.
12. RFC 1:486. At Virginia's ratification convention, Patrick Henry made the same point when he said: "There is a striking difference, and a great contrariety of interests, between the States. They are naturally divided into carrying and

productive states. This is an actual, existing distinction, which cannot be altered": DHRC 10:1221–1222.

13. RFC 2:9–10.
14. RFC 1:510 (Charles Pinckney), 566 (Rufus King), 605 (Pierce Butler); RFC 2:362 (George Mason).
15. Quoted in William H. Masterson, *William Blount* (Baton Rouge, LA: Louisiana State University Press, 1954), 126–127.
16. Census data is produced in Ira Berlin, *Many Thousands Gone: The First Two Centuries of Slavery in North America* (Cambridge, MA: Belknap Press, 1998), 369–370.
17. Berlin, *Many Thousands Gone*, 8.
18. Edward B. Rugemer, "The Southern Response to British Abolitionism: The Maturation of Proslavery Apologetics," *Journal of Southern History* 70, no. 2 (May 2004): 247.
19. Berlin, *Many Thousands Gone*, 8.
20. RFC 1:135.
21. RFC 2:370.
22. A scan of the first three volumes of Farrand's *The Records of the Federal Convention of 1787*, reveals that the words "slave" or slaves" or "slavery" or "enslaved" appear 301 times, the words "black" or "blacks" appear 41 times, and the words "Negro" or "Negroes" appear 38 times.
23. James Madison, "To Robert Walsh Jr.," 27 November 1819, PJMRS 1:553.
24. RFCS, 158. During the Convention's debate over representation, William Paterson pointed out that the Confederation's Congress "had been ashamed to use the term 'Slaves' & had substituted a description": RFC 1:561. Furthermore, in the debate over the importation of slaves, George Clymer agreed with Roger Sherman's statement that the use of the word "slave" was "not pleasing to some people": RFC 2:415. And George Mason, although unconcerned with the use of the word "slave," nevertheless recognized that its use might cause offence: RFC 2:415. In June 1798, New Jersey's Jonathan Dayton, then speaker of the House of Representatives, said that "sole reason" for avoiding the use of the word "slaves" in the context of the slave importation clause was so as "not to stain the Constitutional code with such as term": AC, 5th Congress, 2nd Session, 1993. This moral ambiguity towards slavery may explain the absence of any objection to the Convention's final form of the Constitution's fugitive slave clause, which was, in one way, significantly different to the version previously approved by the Convention, which referred to the return of slaves "to the person *justly* claiming their service or labor" (emphasis added): RFC 2:454. Gouverneur Morris, arguably the Convention's most vocal opponent of slavery, and the person to whom the Convention's Committee of Style and Arrangement delegated the task of drafting the final form of the Constitution, chose to omit the word "justly," thereby removing from the Constitution the implication that the Convention accepted that slavery was "just": William Michael Treanor, "The Case of the Dishonest Scrivener: Gouverneur Morris and the Creation of the Federalist Constitution," *Michigan Law Review* 120, no. 1 (October 2021): 43, 97–98. Wilentz rejects arguments that the exclusion of the

word "slaves" and "slavery" in the Constitution reflected shame or embarrassment by the delegates. He argues that it was deliberately excluded because their inclusion would have resulted in the Constitution legitimizing slavery rather than merely tolerating it: Sean Wilentz, *No Property in Man: Slavery and Antislavery at the Nation's Founding* (Cambridge, MA: Harvard University Press, 2018), 8–11.

25. Elliot 4:176. In 1799, Iredell stated that a euphemism for "slaves" was used in the slave importation clause "to accommodate different gentlemen, some of whom could not bear the name *slaves*, and others had no objection to it": James Iredell, "A Charge Delivered to the Grand Jury of the United States, for the District of Pennsylvania, in the Circuit Court of the United States for the said district," 11 April 1799, in *Life and Correspondence of James Iredell*, vol. 2, ed. Griffith J. McRee (New York: D. Appleton & Company, 1858), 558.
26. Luther Martin, "The Genuine Information," 29 November 1787, RFC 3:210.
27. William Lloyd Garrison, "The United States Constitution," in *Selections from the Writings and Speeches of William Lloyd Garrison* (Boston: R. F. Wallcut, 1852), 309.
28. Sidney George Fisher, *The Trial of the Constitution* (Philadelphia: J. B. Lippincott & Co., 1862), 272. The use of euphemisms for slaves was also evident in the drafting of the Articles of Confederation. On 12 1776, eight days after the Continental Congress declared that "that all men are created equal" and "endowed . . . with . . . [the] unalienable Rights . . . [of] Life, Liberty and the Pursuit of Happiness," a draft of the Articles of Confederation was considered by Congress. The draft's Article XI made a reference to "Inhabitants who are not slaves." During the debate on the draft Articles, the words "who are not slaves" were deleted and the word "white" was inserted before the word "Inhabitants": JCC 5:548. Thus, in the Articles as approved in 1781, in Article IX, which dealt with the substantive issue in draft Article XI, the aforementioned "Inhabitants who are not slaves" are referred to as "white inhabitants": "Articles of Confederation," 1 March 1781, Tansill, 33.
29. Elliot 2:36. Story, in his *Commentaries on the Constitution*, referred to the expression "other persons" as "the mild appellation" for slaves: Story 2:112.
30. RFC 1:31, 36.
31. RFC 1:561.
32. RFC 1:201, 208.
33. RFC 1:580–581, 592; RFCS, 150.
34. RFC 1:580.
35. RFC 1:542, 596.
36. The approach of these delegates from slave states meant that, at least for the purposes of taxation and representation, slaves, as persons, were, as the Declaration of Independence asserted, "created equal", whereas for these delegates from non-slave States, slaves did not come within the definition of "persons."
37. Klarman, *The Framers' Coup*, 266.
38. RFC 1:604.
39. RFC 1:566 (Rufus King), 594 (Edmund Randolph).
40. RFC 1:205; RFCS, 69.
41. RFC 1:593.

42. DHRC 22:1728.
43. DHRC 22:1715–1716. At North Carolina's ratification convention, William Davie, after referring to slaves as "an unhappy species of population" said that the three fifths clause was necessary because "we cannot at present alter their situation": Elliot 4:31.
44. Rufus King, "The Substance of Two Speeches on the Missouri Bill Delivered by Mr King in the Senate of the United States," March 1819, in *The Life and Correspondence of Rufus King*, vol. 6, *1816–1827*, ed. Charles R. King (New York: G. P. Putnam's Sons, 1900), 699. In private correspondence to Timothy Pickering in 1803, King regarded the three-fifths clause as "one of [the Constitution's] greatest blemishes": "R King probably to Col Pickering," 4 November 1803, in *The Life and Correspondence of Rufus King*, vol. 4, *1801–1806*, ed. Charles R. King (New York: G. P. Putnam's Sons, 1897), 324. In his *Commentaries on the Constitution*, Story wrote that the three-fifths clause "was a matter of compromise and concession, confessedly unequal in its operation, but a necessary sacrifice to the spirit of conciliation, which was indispensable to the union of states having a great diversity of interests, and physical condition, and political institution": Story 1:111.
45. RFC 2:364.
46. RFC 1:534. See also RFC 1:542 (Pierce Butler), 567 (Charles Cotesworth Pinckney), 581 (George Mason).
47. RFC 1:541. See also RFC 1:533 (Gouverneur Morris), 541 (Elbridge Gerry), 593 (William Samuel Johnson).
48. RFC 1:562.
49. "The Federalist No. 54 (Madison)," Federalist, 267.
50. Imani Perry, *South to America: A Journey Below the Mason-Dixon to Understand the Soul of a Nation* (New York: Echo, 2022), 36–37. To similar effect, Larson writes that the three-fifths clause "empowered slaveholders, not the enslaved": Larson, *American Inheritance*, 187.
51. CG, 36th Congress, 2nd Session, 487. The primary source on the question of whether the Constitution considered slaves as property or persons is its three provisions that explicitly deal with it. However, it is worth noting that even before the Constitution was drafted, the treatment of slaves as property was recognised by the terms of Article VII of the Treaty of Paris of 1783 which brought an end to the colonies' war with Great Britain. This provision, prohibiting British forces from removing "any Negroes or other property of the American inhabitants" from the territories of the former colonies, was inserted into the treaty at the insistence of the American treaty negotiators: Robert G. Parkinson, *The Common Cause: Creating Race and Nation in the American Revolution* (Chapel Hill, NC: University of North Carolina Press, 2016), 564. As George Van Cleve aptly notes, Article VII "classified 'Negroes' (slaves) as a form of property": George William Van Cleve, *A Slaveholders' Union: Slavery, Politics, and the Constitution in the Early American Republic* (Chicago: University of Chicago Press, 2010), 54.

    In relation to Constitution's provisions dealing with slavery, the slave importation clause, as is discussed below, prohibited Congress from banning the importation of slaves prior to 1808. The international slave trade involved the transfer of ownership of slaves from one person to another. The same applied to the domestic trade in slaves, which was not prohibited by the Constitution. The fact that a thing, including a living creature, such as a horse, is capable of being transferred, or to use the technical legal expression, "assigned," is the quintessential attribute of property. Thus, although the slave importation clause referred to slaves as "persons," the fact that it also referred to their "importation" suggests that they were property, which is how they were treated, given that they could be assigned, mortgaged, leased, and inherited.

In relation to the Constitution's fugitive slave clause, and the federal legislation enacted pursuant to it, its purpose was to protect a slaveowner's property interest. Notwithstanding that the fugitive slave clause referred to a slave as "a person held to service or labour," this was conceded by James Madison at the Virginia ratification convention when he said: "[The fugitive slave] clause secures us that property which we now possess. . . . . [I]n this Constitution, . . . [the fugitive slave] clause was expressly inserted to enable owners of slaves to reclaim them. This is a better security than any that now exists. No power is given to the General Government to interpose with respect to the property in slaves now held by the States": DHRC 10:1339. In *Prigg v. Pennsylvania*, 41 U.S. 539, 611 (1842), Justice Story referred to the purpose of the Constitution's fugitive slave clause as being "to secure to the citizens of slaveholding states the complete right and title of ownership in their slaves, as property." In *Jones v. Van Zandt*, 46 U.S. 215, 229 (1847), Justice Levi Woodbury referred to the fugitive slave clause as granting "the clear right of every man at common law to make fresh suits and recover his own property." And in *Dred Scott v. Sandford*, 60 U.S. 393, 411, 451 (1857), Chief Justice Taney held that the combined effect of fugitive slave and slave importation clause was that the Constitution "distinctly and expressly affirmed" that slaves were "articles of merchandise."

Although the Constitution's three-fifths clause also referred to slaves as "Persons," as Paul Finkelman pithily notes, they were "persons of a diminished capacity or value": Paul Finkelman, "Slavery in the United States: Persons or Property?" in *The Legal Understanding of Slavery: From the Historical to the Contemporary*, ed. Jean Allain (Oxford: Oxford University Press, 2012), 117. In his analysis of that debate over this clause, Larson pointedly observes that "no one could disguise" that the compromise that it led to was "merely a means to factor in the relative worth of southern property": Edward J. Larson, *George Washington, Nationalist* (Charlottesville, VA: University of Virginia Press, 2016), 157.

The overall effect of the Constitution's provisions that explicitly dealt with slaves was summed up by Justice Daniel in *Dred Scott v. Sandford*, 60 U.S. 393, 475–476, 490 (1856), when he said that "a slave . . . is strictly *property*, to be used in subserviency to the interests, the convenience, or the will, of the owner" and went on to say that their effect was that they "imposed . . . a direct obligation both on the States and the Federal Government to protect and *enforce*" what he described as "the only private property [that the Constitution] . . . *specifically recognized*," namely, "the property of the master in his slave."

That slaves were viewed as property was also explicitly confirmed by various delegates at the Philadelphia Convention. Thus, in relation to a proposal that property be the basis for determining representation in the House of Representatives, in one report of this debate, Elbridge Gerry opposed this proposed "rule of representation" because "[b]lacks are property, and are used to the southward as horses and cattle to the northward; and why should their representation be increased to the southward on account of the number of slaves, than horses and oxen to the north?" RFC 1:206. In another report of this debate, Gerry was of the view that "[i]f Negroes represented why not Horses and Cows—Slaves not to be taken in under any Idea of Representation": RFCS, 69. William Paterson referred to slaves as "property, & like other property entirely at the will of the Master": RFC 1:561. George Mason referred to slaves as a "peculiar species of property, over and above other species of property common to all the States": RFC 1:581.

It should also be noted that various Supreme Court cases during the antebellum era treated slaves as property. Apart from cases already mentioned, they included: *Hylton v. United States*, 3 U.S. 171, 177 (1796), which referred to a person who owned large numbers of slaves and extensive tracks of land; *Ware v. Hylton*, 3 U.S. 199, 201 (1796), which dealt with Virginia legislation which stated that property included "lands, slaves and other real estate."; *Wiscart v. Dauchy*, 3 U.S. 321, 321 (1796), which listed slaves together with goods, chattels, and land in the description of property in relation to whether these property items had been fraudulently conveyed; *Hamilton v. Russell*, 5 U.S. 309, 314–315(1803), which dealt with a bill of sale in relation to "a slave, and some other personal property."; *Spiers v. Willison*, 8 U.S. 398, 398 (1807) and *Ramsey v. Lee*, 8 U.S. 401, 401 (1807), both of which dealt with an action in detinue in relation to a slave; *The Antelope*, 23 U.S. 66 (1825), which dealt with the recovery of captured slaves; and *Lee v. Lee*, 41 US 539, 611 (1842), which concerned a contract for the hiring of slaves.

On the other hand, during the debate over the slave importation clause at the Philadelphia Convention, James Madison claimed that it would be "wrong to admit in the Constitution the idea that there could be property in man": RFC 2:417. Sean Wilentz is a contemporary proponent of the approach taken by Madison. He argues that the deliberate avoidance of the words "slaves" and "slavery" in the Constitution had "little or nothing to do with the prudent suppression of distasteful language," but had everything to do with "ensuring that the Constitution contained nothing that could be construed as acknowledging and thereby endorsing property in man": Wilentz, *No Property in Man*, 10–11. However, in the light of the above discussion, it is difficult to sustain Wilentz's view. Rather than viewing slaves as either persons or property, arguably they were regarded by the founding generation as both persons and property. It can be noted that the law does, on occasion, classify a particular thing differently for different purposes. For example, a mortgagor's right to set aside a fraudulent exercise of a mortgagee's power of sale is viewed as a proprietary interest in the context of succession, but as a non-proprietary personal right in the context of a priority dispute with another person's proprietary interest: *Latec Investments Ltd v Hotel Terrigal Pty Ltd* (1965) 113 C.L.R. 265, 291; John McGhee and Steven Elliott, *Snell's Equity*, 24th ed. (London: Sweet & Maxwell, 2020): 24-25. Thus, in *Federalist 54*, Madison wrote: "[W]e must deny the fact that slaves are considered merely as property, and in no respect whatever as persons. The true state of the case is, that they partake of both these qualities; being considered by our laws, in some respects, as persons, and in other respects as property. . . . . The Foederal Constitution therefore, decides with great propriety on the case of our slaves, when it views them in the mixt character of persons and of property. This is in fact their true character": "The Federalist No. 54 [Madison]," Federalist, 265. However, Amar regards Madison's writing of *Federalist 54* as "a shabby performance": Akhil Reed Amar, *The Words That Made Us: America's Constitutional Conversation, 1760–1840* (New York: Basic Books, 2010), 206.

52. RFC 2:29.
53. RFC 2:56.
54. Akhil Reed Amar, "Electoral College Reform, Lincoln-Style," *Northwestern University Law Review* 112, no. 1 (2017): 69–70.
55. RFC 2:56–57.
56. RFC 2:32.
57. RFC 2:57.
58. James Madison, "To Robert Walsh Jr.," 553.
59. "An Act to prohibit the importation of slaves into any port or place within the jurisdiction of the United States, from and after the first day of January, in the year of our Lord one thousand eight hundred and eight," 2 March 1807, USSL 2:426–430.
60. JCC 1:77. However, neither the First Continental Congress nor the Second Continental Congress did anything about the continued existence of slavery in the colonies: Larson, *American Inheritance*, 84, 91.
61. JCC 4:258.
62. "Address of House of Burgesses of Virginia to the King," 1 April 1772, in *Documents of the American Revolution, 1770–1783,* vol. 5, *Transcripts 1772*, ed. K. G. Davies (Dublin: Irish University Press, 1974), 57.
63. "Governor Earl of Dunmore to Earl of Hillsborough," 1 May 1772, in Davies, *Documents of the American Revolution*, 94.
64. Kenneth Morgan, *Slavery and Servitude in Colonial North America: A Short History* (New York: New York University Press, 2001), 108.
65. "Thomas Jefferson's Notes of Proceedings in Congress," 1–4 July 1776, LDC 4:359.
66. RFC 2:222–223.
67. Paul Finkelman, "The American Suppression of the African Slave Trade: Lessons on Legal Change, Social Policy and Legislation," *Akron Law Review* 42, no. 2 (2009): 442.
68. RFC 2:371.
69. RFC 2:371. In 1804, Virginia's governor, John Page, estimated that between 8,000 to 10,000 slaves were exported annually from Virginia to other states in the South: James A. Rawley with Stephen D. Behrendt, *The Transatlantic Slave Trade: A History*, rev. ed. (Lincoln, NE: University of Nebraska Press, 2005), 284.
70. RFC 2:370.
71. DHRC 10:1338.
72. James Madison, "To Thomas Jefferson," 24 October 1787, PJM 10:214. See also Madison, "To Robert Walsh Jr.," 553.

73. RFC 2:373.
74. Jonathan Mercantini, "'Most Contemptible in the Union': South Carolina, Slavery and the Constitution," in *Ambiguous Anniversary: The Bicentennial of the International Slave Trade Bans*, eds. David T. Gleeson and Simon Lewis (Columbia SC: University of South Carolina Press, 2012), 48.
75. Christopher Leslie Brown, "The Problems of Slavery," in *The Oxford Handbook of the American Revolution*, eds. Edward G. Gray and Jane Kamensky (Oxford: Oxford University Press, 2013), 429. Jonathan M. Bryant, *Dark Places of the Earth: The Voyage of the Slave Ship Antelope* (New York: Liveright Publishing Corporation, 2015), 156.
76. Morgan, *Slavery and Servitude in Colonial North America*, 107.
77. RFC 2:371.
78. Elliot 4:100. James Iredell, Spaight's fellow delegate to both the Philadelphia Convention and North Carolina's ratification convention, concurred with Spaight's assessment on this issue: Elliot 4:100–101.
79. Beeman, *Plain, Honest Men*, 333; Larson, *American Inheritance*, 196.
80. Alfred H. Conrad and John R. Meyer, "The Economics of Slavery in the Ante Bellum South," *Journal of Political Economy* 66. no. 2 (April 1958): 112.
81. Rawley with Behrendt, *The Transatlantic Slave Trade*, 361; Alan Taylor, *American Revolutions: A Continental History, 1750–1804* (New York: W. W. Norton & Company, 2016), 429.
82. Steven Deyle, *Carry Me Back: The Domestic Slave Trade in American Life* (Oxford: Oxford University Press, 2005), 20.
83. The only delegates to doubt that South Carolina and Georgia would not ratify the Constitution if the importation of slaves was immediately banned were James Wilson and John Dickinson: RFC 2:371-372.
84. RFC 2:371. The fact that banning the importation of slaves was only temporarily delayed led James Wilson, at the Pennsylvania ratification convention, to optimistically, but also unrealistically, view the slave importation clause "as laying the foundation for banishing slavery out of this country"; further that "in the mean time, the *new* states which are to be formed will be under *the control* of Congress in this particular, and slaves will never be introduced amongst them": Elliot 2:452.
85. RFC 2:375.
86. RFC 2:369, 374.
87. "The Federalist No. 42 (Madison)," Federalist, 204. However, Madison was dismissive of arguments for an immediate ban on the importation of slaves, writing that he would not answer them because "they deserve none": "The Federalist No. 42 (Madison)," 205.
88. DHRC 10:1338–1339. See also James Iredell, "Answer to Mr Mason's Objections to the New Constitution, recommended by the late Convention," January 1788, in *Pamphlets of the Constitution of the United States, Published During Its Discussion by the People 1787–1788*, ed. Paul Leicester Ford (Brooklyn, NY: n. p., 1888), 367; speech of General William Heath at the Massachusetts ratification convention: Elliot 2:115–116.
89. RFC 2:364.
90. RFC 2:559.

91. Madison, "To Robert Walsh Jr.," 554.
92. Deyle, *Carry Me Back*, 43, 283–289. At the same time there was the illegal sale of kidnapped free African Americans from northern non-slave states that were sold into slavery in the southern slave states: Kris Manjapra, *Black Ghost of Empire: The Long Death of Slavery and the Failure of Emancipation* (London: Allen Lane, 2022), 32–33.
93. Pursuant to this doctrine, in American law, this meant that a child born of a female slave was born a slave: Thomas D. Morris, *Southern Slavery and the Law, 1619–1860* (Chapel Hill, NC: University of North Carolina Press, 1996), 43. This doctrine, first enacted into law in Virginia in 1662, reversed the English common law rule that the status of the father determined the status of a child, and was, as Roosevelt states, "clearly designed to allow free men to enslave their children": Kermit Roosevelt III, *The Nation That Never Was: Reconstructing America's Story* (Chicago: University of Chicago Press, 2022), 45. The horrific consequences of this legal doctrine to female slaves was graphically described by Harriet Martineau in her account of her travels through the United States in the mid-1830s. Martineau wrote of meeting a runaway slave in Boston who once "was a slave, and was married to a slave, by whom she had two children. One day, her husband was sold away to a distance; and her master, whose object was to increase his stock as fast as possible, immediately required her to take another husband. She stoutly refused. Her master thought her so far worthy of being humoured, that he gave her his son,—forced him upon her. . . . . She had two more children, of much lighter complexion than the former. When the son left the estate, her master tried again to force a negro husband upon her. In desperation she fled, carrying one of her first children with her. She is now working to redeem the other, a girl; and she has not given up all hope of recovering her husband. She was asked whether she thought of doing anything for her two mulatto children. She replied, to be sure, they *were* her children; but that she did not think she ever *could* tell her husband that she had these two children": Harriet Martineau, *Society in America,* vol. 1 (London: Saunders & Otley, 1837), 384. However, slaveholders, such as Thomas Jefferson viewed the doctrine differently. In 1820, he wrote: "I consider a woman who brings a child every two years as more profitable than the best man of the farm. what she produces is an addition to the capital, while his labors disappear in mere consumption": Thomas Jefferson, "To John Wayles Eppes," 30 June 1820, PTJRS 16:67.
94. Steven Deyle, "An Ambiguous Legacy: The Closing of the African Slave Trade and America's Own Middle Passage," in Gleeson and Lewis, *Ambiguous Anniversary*, 141–144.
95. David L. Lightner, *Slavery and the Commerce Power: How the Struggle Against the Interstate Slave Trade Led to the Civil War* (New Haven, CT: Yale University Press, 2006), 88.
96. 40 U.S. 449 (1841).
97. *Groves v. Slaughter*, 40 U.S. 449, 507–508 (McLean J), 508 (Taney CJ), 510 (Story, Thompson, Wayne, and McKinley JJ) (1841).
98. *Groves v. Slaughter*, 40 U.S. 449, 507–508 (McLean J), 508 (Taney CJ), 512–516 (Baldwin J) (1841).

99. USSL 8:81–82.
100. 25 U.S. 523, 526 (1827).
101. James Brown Scott, *The United States of America: A Study in International Organization* (New York: Oxford University Press, 1920), 168.
102. Tansill, 47–54.
103. "An Act to provide for the Government of the Territory North-west of the Ohio River, 7 August 1789," USSL 1:50–53.
104. Van Cleve, *A Slaveholders' Union*, 167.
105. *Marbury v. Madison*, 5 U.S. 137 (1803). In this case, in delivering the opinion of the Court, at 177, Chief Justice Marshall said: "It is emphatically the province and duty of the judicial department to say what the law is. Those who apply the rule to particular cases, must of necessity expound and interpret that rule. If two laws conflict with each other, the courts must decide on the operation of each."
106. "The Federalist No. 38 (Madison)," Federalist, 180–181.
107. "The Federalist No. 43 (Madison)," Federalist, 211.
108. Jeffery Allen Zemler, *James Madison, the South, and the Trans-Appalachian West, 1783–180*, (Lanham, MD: Lexington Books, 2013), 54.
109. Eli Merritt, "Sectional Conflict and Secret Compromise: The Mississippi River Question and the United States Constitution," *American Journal of Legal History* 35, no. 2 (April 1991): 128. Van Cleve writes that the Mississippi River issue was the Confederation's "most intractable political stalemate": George William Van Cleve, *We Have Not a Government: The Articles of Confederation and the Road to the Constitution* (Chicago: University of Chicago Press, 2017), 185.
110. Jack N. Rakove, "Ambiguous Achievement: The Northwest Ordinance," in *The Northwest Ordinance: Essays on Its Formation, Provisions, and Legacy*, ed. Frederick D. Williams (East Lansing, MI: Michigan State University Press, 1988), 12.
111. In one of his notes in the multi-volume *Letters of Delegates to Congress* that he edited, Paul Smith states that "[p]art of the urgency in providing government for the western settlers" lay in a proposal, discussed later in this chapter, from the Ohio Company of Associates to purchase and develop land located in the Northwest Territory: LDC 24:355.
112. USSL 8:83.
113. Michael Allen, "The Mississippi River Debate, 1785–1787," *Tennessee Historical Quarterly* 36, no. 4 (Winter 1977): 450–451.
114. Van Cleve, *We Have Not a Government*, 162–163; Allen, "The Mississippi River Debate," 451–452; Merritt, "Sectional Conflict and Secret Compromise," 124–127. For detailed reasons set out in his letter to Jefferson, on 20 August 1784, Madison stated his belief, mistaken as it turned out to be, "that Spain will never be so mad as to persist in the doctrine She seems hitherto to have set up' in relation to the Mississippi River: James Madison, "To Thomas Jefferson," 20 August 1784, PJM 8:104.
115. James Madison, "To Lafayette," 20 March 1785, PJM 8:251; Ralph Ketcham, *James Madison: A Biography* (New York: The Macmillan Company, 1971), 176.
116. JCC 27:529–530.

117. JCC 31:236–244.
118. James Madison, "To James Monroe," 21 June 1786, PJM 9:82.
119. "Henry Lee to George Washington," 11 October 1786, LDC 23:591.
120. Klarman, *The Framers' Coup*, 57–58.
121. JCC 31:477.
122. JCC 31:480.
123. "James Monroe to Patrick Henry," 12 August 1786, LDC 23:464.
124. Quoted in Jon Kukla, *Patrick Henry: Champion of Liberty* (New York: Simon and Schuster, 2017), 303.
125. Edward C. Beach, Jr., "'The Good of Each of the Parts': A Collective Action Understanding of the Treaty Clause," *Duke Journal of Constitutional Law and Public Policy* 16 (2021): 288. See, for example, "Rufus King to Elbridge Gerry," 4 June 1786, 333–334; "Rufus King to Elbridge Gerry," LDC 23:470; "Charles Thomson's Notes of Debates," 16 August 1786, LDC 23, 485–486.
126. Van Cleve, *We Have Not a Government*, 172.
127. Klarman, *The Framers' Coup*, 61–62; Van Cleve, *We Have Not a Government*, 171–172.
128. "Rufus King to Elbridge Gerry," 4 June 1786, 332–333.
129. "Charles Thomson's Notes of Debates," 486.
130. Klarman, *The Framers' Coup*, 58–61; Van Cleve, *We Have Not a Government*, 170–171. A few delegates from the southern states supported Jay's treaty proposal for pragmatic reasons, arguing that for the settlers of the relatively unpopulated western territory, the loss of navigation rights on the Mississippi River was, according to Henry Lee from Virginia, of no consequence, and that when the "western country [became] more populous & capable, they will seize by force what may have be[en] yielded by treaty": "Henry Lee to George Washington," 7 August 1786, LDC 23:438.
131. "Charles Pinckney's Speech," 10 August 1786, LDC 23:454–455.
132. "Charles Thomson's Notes of Debates," 485. In his report to the North Carolina Assembly, Timothy Bloodworth saw Jay's proposed treaty as one in which "the Eastern States are to receive the benefits, by the sale of their fish & oile, which are consum'd in Spain, & the Southern States are to pay the purchase, by giving up the Missecippey": "Timothy Bloodworth to the North Carolina Assembly," 16 December 1786, LDC 24:51.
133. "Otto's letter for the comte de Vergennes," 23 August 1786, LDC 23:513.
134. JCC 31:574–596.
135. JCC 31:610–613.
136. JCC 31:694–697.
137. North Carolina's 1776 Constitution allowed for the creation of a new state with the consent of the North Carolina's government: "Constitution of North Carolina, 1776," Article XXV, Thorpe 5:2789. A bare majority of States at the Philadelphia Convention agreed to the inclusion of a similar provision in the Constitution's admission of new states clause (Article IV, Section 3, Clause 1): RFC 2:455.
138. Allen, "The Mississippi River Debate," 459; Richard B. Morris, *The Forging of the Union, 1781–1789* (New York: Harper & Row, Publishers, 1987), 223–226; Merritt, "Sectional Conflict and Secret Compromise," 134–136; Susan Gaunt

Stearns, "Federalism on the Frontier: Secession and Loyalty in the Trans-Appalachian West," in *From Independence to the U.S. Constitution: Reconsidering the Critical Period of American History*, eds. Douglas Bradburn and Christopher R Pearl (Charlottesville, VA: University of Virginia Press, 2022), 131–139.

139. Kevin T. Barksdale, "The Spanish Conspiracy on the Trans-Appalachian Borderlands, 1786–1789," *Journal of Appalachian Studies* 10, nos. 1–2 (Spring 2007): 96–123.

140. David Narrett, *Adventurism and Empire: The Struggle for Mastery in the Louisiana-Florida Borderlands, 1762–1803* (Chapel Hill, NC: University of North Carolina Press, 2015, 165–178.

141. Van Cleve, *We Have Not a Government*, 174–175.

142. "Theodore Sedgwick to Caleb Strong," 6 August 1786, LDC 23:436.

143. James Madison, "To Thomas Jefferson," 12 August 1786, PJM 9:97.

144. In a letter of 5 October 1786 to James Monroe, Madison expressed his frustration that the sectional conflict over the Mississippi River issue evidenced "an alarming proof of the predominance of temporary and partial interests over those just & extended maxims of policy . . . which can alone effectuate the durable prosperity of the Union": James Madison, "To James Monroe," 15 October 1786, PJM 9:140–141. In a letter of 1 November 1786 to his father, Madison wrote that the sectional conflict generated by the Mississippi River issue constituted "a great bar to the amendment of our Confederacy": James Madison, "To James Madison, Sr.," 1 November 1786, PJM 9:154.

145. James Madison, "To George Washington," 7 December 1786, PJM 9:200.

146. Thomas Jefferson, "To James Madison," 30 January 1787, PTJ 11:93.

147. "Resolutions Reaffirming American Rights to Navigate the Mississippi," 29 November 1786, PJM 9:182. According to Beach, for many Virginians, "the Jay-Gardoqui affair and the division it fomented became a substantial driving force behind the Constitutional Convention": Beach, "'The Good of Each of the Parts,'" 290.

148. "From Benjamin Hawkins," 8 March 1787, PTJ 11:202.

149. Van Cleve, *We Have Not a Government*, 182; Feldman, *The Three Lives of James Madison*, 90–91.

150. James Madison, "Notes on Debates," 13 March 1787, PJM 9:309–311. Madison's notes also recorded that "Spain would never accede to the claim of the U.S. to navigate the [Mississippi] river": James Madison, "Notes on Debates," 29 March 1787, PJM 9:338.

151. "Jay to the President of Congress," 11 April 1787, in *The Correspondence and Public Papers of John Jay*, vol. 3, *1782–1793*, ed. Henry P. Johnston (New York: G. P. Putnam's Sons, 1891), 240.

152. James Madison, "To Edmund Randolph," 15 April 1787, PJM 9:380.

153. James Madison, "To George Washington," 16 April 1787, PJM 9:386.

154. James Madison, "Notes on Debates," 18 April 1787, PJM 9:389.

155. James Madison, "To Thomas Jefferson," 19 March 1787, PJM 9:319–320. On 22 April 1787, in a letter to Edmund Pendleton, Madison noted that "[o]ur affair with Spain is on a very delicate footing": James Madison, "To Edmund Pendleton," 22 April 1787, PJM 9:396.

156. James Madison, "To Thomas Jefferson," 19 March 1787, 319.
157. James Madison, "To Thomas Jefferson," 23 April 1787, PJM 9:400.
158. James Madison, "Notes on Debates," 23 April 1787, PJM 9:402.
159. George Washington's diary entry for 14 May 1787 states that date as "being the day appointed for the Convention to meet": *The Papers of George Washington: Diaries*, vol. 5, *1 July 1776—31 December 1789*, eds. Donald Jackson and Dorothy Twohig (Charlottesville, VA: University of Virginia Press, 1979), 156. However, as his diary entry for 25 May 1787 records, it was only on 25 May 1787 that a sufficient number of delegates were present to constitute a quorum for the Convention to commence its deliberations: Jackson and Twohig, 162.
160. JCC 32:277.
161. In his letter to Madison of 31 August 1787, William Grayson noted that "[t]he Mississippi is in a State of absolute dormification": "From William Grayson," 31 August 1787, PJM 10:159.
162. "The Federalist No 15. (Hamilton)," Federalist, 65. The other issues mentioned by Hamilton included the failure to enforce national treaty obligations, the failure of states to pay off war debts, the refusal of the British to evacuate posts in the Northwest Territory, the disarray of national commerce, the disrespect of foreign nations, the low values of improved land, and the scarcity of private credit.
163. RFC 1:308. According to Robert Yates's notes on the Convention, on the same day, Hamilton spoke of the need for a strong federal government in order "to protects [Americans'] rights against . . . Spain in the South": RFC 1:297. And on 29 June 1787, Hamilton said that one of the "most serious" consequences "of a dissolution of the Union, and the establishment of partial confederacies" would be the formation of alliances with "different rival & hostile nations of Europes." Thus, he continued, it was a "critical moment" for forming a government of "sufficient stability and strength to make us respectable abroad": RFC 1:467. One of those "hostile nations" that he referred to was Spain. When writing as Publius, Hamilton argued that the issue of navigation rights on the Mississippi River was a right of "great moment" which "the interest of more powerful partners would hardly fail to solve to our disadvantage" if American unity was not maintained: "The Federalist No 11. (Hamilton)," Federalist, 50.
164. Elliot 4:19.
165. Merritt, "Sectional Conflict and Secret Compromise," 118–119, 121. Kukla notes that the consequence of the on-going Jay-de Gardoqui treaty negotiations over the Mississippi River issue was "inflamed regional jealousies in the debate over the new federal Constitution": Kukla, *Patrick Henry*, 304. And, Banning notes that, for Virginians, "no other episode . . . engendered such intense and uniform emotion and revulsion" or "suggested so convincingly how chronic differences between New England and Virginia could suddenly erupt in pressing dangers": Lance Banning, "Virginia: Sectionalism and the Common Good' in *Ratifying the Constitution: Ideas and Interests in the Several American States*, eds. Michael Allen Gillespie and Michael Lienesch (Lawrence, KS: University of Kansas Press, 1989), 267. See also Van Cleve, *A Slaveholders' Union*, 159–161.
166. RFC 1:18.
167. Merritt suggests that Madison, the main source of these records, is likely to have

deliberately excluded much of the discussion in his notes on the Convention because of the sensitivity of the issue. This sensitivity is evidenced by the fact that, in the private letters written on the issue in the many months prior to the Convention, those parts dealing with the Mississippi River issue were almost always written in code: Merritt, "Sectional Conflict and Secret Compromise," 120. The sensitivity that Merritt refers to is also evidenced in a report by North Carolina's delegates to the Confederation Congress to their State's Assembly on 15 December 1787, which stated that the issue of navigation rights on the Mississippi River was "so delicate a nature" that they could not commit details to paper, except to say that "it had been seriously agitated": "North Carolina Delegates to the North Carolina Assembly," 15 December 1787, LDC 24:586.

168. RFC 1:604.
169. Masterson, *William Blount*, 127.
170. According to Madison, at Virginia's ratification convention, the Mississippi River issue was one of "the principal topics of private discussion & intrigue, as well as of public declamation": James Madison, "To George Washington," 13 June 1788, PJM 11:134. The Virginia Convention spent two days, 12–13 June 1788, debating the issue.
171. R. Earl McClendon, "Origins of the Two-Thirds Rule in Senate Action upon Treaties," *The American Historical Review* 36, no. 4 (July 1931): 770–772.
172. James Madison, "To Thomas Jefferson," 23 August 1788, PJM 11:239.
173. DHRC 10:1208–1209. Ketcham notes that "the need to protect American access to the Mississippi revealed to Madison a vital connection between the effective conduct of Foreign affairs and a stronger Union": Ketcham, *James Madison*, 176.
174. Allen, "The Mississippi River Debate," 451–459.
175. RFC 1:322.
176. Charles Warren, "The Mississippi River and the Treaty Clause of the Constitution," *George Washington Law Review* 2, no. 3 (March 1934): 287–288.
177. DHRC 10:1259.
178. "Otto's letter for the comte de Vergennes," 10 September 1786, LDC 23:548.
179. RFC 2:188.
180. RFC 1:571.
181. RFC 1:533–534.
182. RFC 1:533.
183. RFC 1:583.
184. RFC 2:3.
185. RFC 2:3.
186. Morris, *The Forging of the Union*, 274.
187. RFC 1:578–579.
188. RFC 2:454.
189. RFC 2:454.
190. RFC 2:454.
191. 44 U.S. 212, 230 (1845) (see also 223–224).
192. "Hugh Williamson to James Madison," 2 June 1788, LDC 25:136.
193. Elliot 4:115.
194. On the Convention's debate on the treaty clause, see Warren, "The Mississippi

River and the Treaty Clause of the Constitution," 296, 293–296; Beach, "'The Good of Each of the Parts,'" 292–295.

195. For example, see Patrick Henry, William Grayson, and James Monroe at the Virginia convention, in DHRC 9:1051 (Henry); DHRC 10:1235 (Monroe), 1244 (Grayson), 1246 (Henry); William Porter at the North Carolina convention, in Elliot 4:115. Prior to Jay's August 1786 treaty proposal to the Confederation Congress, Henry was a supporter of the movement towards a stronger central government for the United States. However, thereafter, his attitude changed and he declined an appointment as a delegate to the Philadelphia Convention from Virginia and became a vocal and influential opponent of ratification of the Constitution: Kukla, *Patrick Henry*, 304–306.
196. Warren, "The Mississippi River and the Treaty Clause of the Constitution," 296.
197. "John Brown to Thomas Jefferson," 10 August 1788, LDC 25:283.
198. On 24 April 1789, the House of Representatives of the First Congress passed a resolution for the adoption of these amendments, as well as several others proposed by the various States at their ratification conventions. However, on 8 September 1789, the Senate rejected all of them: AC, 1st Congress, 1st Session, 75, 779.
199. RFC 2:549.
200. DHRC 2:271 (North Carolina), 382 (Virginia).
201. Warren, "The Mississippi River and the Treaty Clause of the Constitution," 299.
202. JCC 34:534–535.
203. Allen, "The Mississippi River Debate," 466. See also Ralph Lee Woodward, Jr., "Spanish Commercial Policy in Louisiana, 1763–1803," *Louisiana History* 44, no. 2 (Spring 2003): 153–154.
204. "Treaty of Friendship, Limits and Navigation, Between the United States of America, and the King of Spain," 27 October 1795, USSL 8:138–152.
205. "Treaty of Amity, Settlement, and Limits, Between the United States of America and his Catholic Majesty," 22 February 1819, USSL 8:200–206.
206. "The Federalist No 15. (Hamilton)," 65. At North Carolina's ratification convention, William Davie, who had been a delegate to the Philadelphia Convention, argued that a reason for ratifying the Constitution stemmed from the fact that the Confederation was "extremely defective' in terms of enforcing the 1783 Treaty of Paris because its "enemies, presuming on the weakness of our federal government, have refused to deliver up several important posts within the territories of the United States, and still hold them to our shame and disgrace": Elliot 4:18.
207. Stearns, "Federalism on the Frontier," 136.
208. Morris, *The Forging of the Union*, 220.
209. "New York: Cession of Western Land Claims," 1 March 1781, Carter, 2:3–5.
210. "Virginia: Cession of Western Land Claims," 1 March 1784, Carter 2:6–9.
211. "Massachusetts: Cession of Western Land Claims," 19 April 1785, Carter 2:10–12.
212. "Connecticut: Cession of Western Land Claims," 13 September 1786, Carter 2:22–24.
213. Morris, *The Forging of the Union*, 226–227.

214. "The Ordinance of 1784, By the United States in Congress, assembled," 23 April 1784, PTJ 6:613.
215. "Revised Report of the Committee," 22 March 1784, PTJ 6:608. The first draft of what eventually became Jefferson's proposal was prepared by Timothy Pickering, an antislavery activist from Massachusetts, who proposed the immediate prohibition of slavery in the western territory: Roger G. Kennedy, *Mr Jefferson's Lost Cause: Land, Farmers, Slavery, and the Louisiana Purchase* (Oxford: Oxford University Press, 2003), 76, 250. Jefferson's change of date infuriated Pickering: Douglas R. Egerton, *Death or Liberty: African Americans and Revolutionary America* (Oxford: Oxford University Press, 2009), 235.
216. "Jefferson's Observations on Démeunier's Manuscript," 22 June 1786, PTJ 10:58.
217. William Cohen, "Thomas Jefferson and the Problem of Slavery," *Journal of American History* 56, no. 3 (December 1969): 511. Similarly, Wiecek argues that Jefferson's proposal only had the appearance of being antislavery because it was "in effect, a permission to the western territories and states to establish slavery and retain it to the year 1800. Whether it would have been possible for the new states and territories to disestablish slavery once it gained a foothold is doubtful": William W. Wiecek, *The Sources of Antislavery Constitutionalism in America, 1760–1848* (Ithaca, NY: Cornell University Press, 1977), 60. And, as Finkelman points out, "[d]elaying abolition in the West until 1800 would have given slaveholders sixteen years . . . to lobby Congress for a change in the law": Paul Finkelman, "Jefferson and Slavery: '*Treason Against the Hopes of the World*,"' in *Jeffersonian Legacies*, ed. Peter S. Onuf (Charlottesville, VA: University Press of Virginia, 1930, 199.
218. JCC 26:246–247; Thomas Jefferson, "To James Madison," 25 April 1784, PTJ 7:118. Timothy Pickering was relieved that Congress did not adopt Jefferson's proposal for the eventual prohibition of slavery in the western territory. In March 1785, he wrote the following to his fellow delegate from Massachusetts, Rufus King: "I should indeed have objected to the period proposed (the year 1800) for the exclusion of slavery, for the admission of it for a day or an hour ought to have been forbidden. It will be infinitely easier to prevent the Evil at first, than to eradicate or check it at any future time": in *The Life and Correspondence of Rufus King*, vol. 1, *1755–1794*, ed. Charles R. King (New York: G. P. Putnam's Sons, 1894), 45.
219. JCC 28:164–165; King, *The Life and Correspondence of Rufus King*, vol. 1, 276–277; Van Cleve, *We Have Not a Government*, 145–146.
220. "Land Ordinance of 1785," 20 May 1785, Carter 2:12–18.
221. JCC 28:375–381.
222. King, *The Life and Correspondence of Rufus King*, vol. 1:286.
223. JCC 32:281.
224. JCC 32:333.
225. JCC 32:343. Writing to Rufus King three days after the vote, Nathan Dane advised that Article VI was "was agreed to without opposition": "Nathan Dane to Rufus King," 16 July 1787, LDC 24:358.
226. "An Ordinance for the Government of the Territory of the United States Northwest of the River Ohio," 13 July 1787, Tansill, 54.

227. "An Act to provide for the Government of the Territory North-west of the Ohio River," 7 August 1789, USSL 1:50–53.
228. Egerton, *Death or Liberty*, 237. To similar effect, see Staughton Lynd, "The Compromise of 1787," *Political Science Quarterly* 81, no. 2 (Summer 1966): 229–238; Beeman, *Plain, Honest Men*, 217; Klarman, *The Framers' Coup*, 296.
229. "From Nathan Dane [to Daniel Webster]," 26 March 1830, in *The Papers of Daniel Webster, Correspondence,* vol. 3, *1830–1834*, ed. Charles M. Wiltse (Hanover NH: University Press of New England, 1977), 47.
230. Madison, "To Robert Walsh Jr.," 556.
231. According to Cayton, it was important for government control to be exerted over the Northwest Territory, especially around Ohio, so as "to protect" what he refers to as "the immense property and prospects of the United States, and the elite's special interest in it, from the people on the frontier": Andrew R. L. Cayton, *The Frontier Republic: Ideology and Politics on the Ohio Valley Country, 1780–1825* (Kent, OH: Kent State University Press, 1986), 24.
232. Morris notes that Cutler was a "skillful lobbyist": Morris, *The Forging of the Union*, 228. Poole writes of Cutler: "Like Dr. Franklin, he took delight in the society of beautiful and accomplished women. His journal gives the minutest descriptions of the noted ladies he met in his travels, not omitting to describe their costumes, and the mode of dressing their hair": William Frederick Poole, "Dr. Cutler and the Ordinance of 1787," *The North American Review* 122, no. 251 (April 1876): 249.
233. Manasseh Cutler, *An Explanation of the Map* (Salem, MA: Dabney & Cushing, 1787), 14.
234. "The Secretary at War to the President of Congress," 16 February 1787, Carter 2:26.
235. "Report of the Secretary at War Relative to Intruders on Public Lands," 16 February 1787, Carter 2:27.
236. "Richard Henry Lee to George Washington," 15 July 1787, LDC 24:356.
237. JCC 32:276.
238. JCC 32:311–312.
239. JCC 32:399–401.
240. Charles S. Hall, *Life and Letters of Samuel Holden Parsons* (Binghamton, NY: Otseningo Publishing Co., 1905), 511.
241. Larson, *American Inheritance*, 175.
242. Van Cleve, *A Slaveholders' Union*, 153.
243. MJQA 5:69.
244. Morris, *The Forging of the Union*, 229.
245. Donald L. Robinson, *Slavery in American Politics, 1765–1820* (New York: Harcourt Brace Jovanovich Inc, 1971), 385; Paul Finkelman, *Slavery and the Founders: Race and Liberty in the Age of Jefferson*, 2nd ed. (Armonk NY: M. E. Sharpe, 2001), 42; Van Cleve, *A Slaveholders' Union*, 158.
246. JCC 33:475–477.
247. JCC 34:323–326.
248. That part of the territory south of the Northwest Territory known as Kentucky and which formed part of Virginia was not ceded to the Union. It can be noted that, following a number of applications to the Confederation for statehood, on

29 February 1788, Virginia's delegates to the Confederation Congress moved a motion that Kentucky be admitted as "a Separate and Independent Member of the federal Union": JCC 34:72. Congress resolved to refer the matter to a committee which, on 2 June 1788, recommended that "the district of Kentucky be erected into an independent state": "Continental Congress, Report on the Admission of Kentucky into the Union," 2 June 1788, in *The Papers of Alexander Hamilton,* vol. 5, *June 1788—November 1789*, ed. Harold C. Syrett (New York: Columbia University Press, 1962), 1. On the following day, Congress resolved that, because the admission of Kentucky to the Confederation "may be attended with dangerous consequences" and, furthermore, would "have no effect to make [Kentucky] a separate member of the federal Union formed by the adoption of the . . . constitution," it would be "manifestly inexpedient" for Kentucky to be admitted as a State of the Confederation. In these circumstances it was, the resolution went on to state, "expedient" that the matter of Kentucky's statehood be determined pursuant to the Congress established by the Constitution: JCC 34:289–290. Following the collapse of the Confederation and the Union coming into effect in early 1789, on 18 December 1789, the Virginia legislature passed legislation stipulating for a convention of delegates to be held in Kentucky to determine whether they that part of Virginia to "be erected into an independent state": "An act concerning the erection of the district of Kentuckey into an independent state," Section 4, 18 December, 1789, in *The Statutes at Large; Being a Collection of all the Law of Virginia from the First Session of the Legislature, in the year 1619*, vol. 8, ed. William Waller Hening (Philadelphia: Thomas Desilver, 1823), 18. On 28 July 1790, delegates to a convention in Danville voted 24–18 in favor of statehood for Kentucky: "From Kentucky Convention," 4 October 1790, in *The Papers of George Washington: Presidential Series,* vol. 6, *1 July 1790—20 November 1790*, ed. Mark A. Mastromarino (Charlottesville, VA: University Press of Virginia, 1996), 536n1. On 4 February 1791, Congress passed legislation that stipulated that "the State of Kentucky, shall be received and admitted into [the] Union, as a new and entire member of the United States of America" on 1 June 1792: An Act declaring the consent of Congress, that a State be formed within the jurisdiction of the Commonwealth of Virginia, and admitted into this Union, by the name of Kentucky," Section 2, 4 February 1791, USSL 1:189.

249. "North Carolina: Cession of Western Lands Claims," 22 December 1789, Carter 4:7. In April 1784, the North Carolina assembly passed legislation ceding to the Confederation part of the western territory that it claimed, on the condition that the Confederation Congress could not pass any regulations that "shall tend to emancipate slaves": "An Act Ceding to the Congress of the United States Certain Western Lands Therein Described, and Authorizing the Delegates from this State in Congress to Execute a Deed or Deeds for the Same," 19 April 1784, in *The State Records of North Carolina,* vol. 24, *Laws 1777–1788*, ed. Walter (Goldsboro, N.C: Nash Brothers, Book and Job Printers, 1905), 563. This legislation was, however, repealed in October 1784: "An Act to Repeal an Act of the Last General Assembly, Intituled, An Act Ceding to the Congress of the United States Certain Western Lands Therein Described, and Authorising the Delegates from This State in Congress to Execute a Deed

or Deeds for the Same," Article II, October 1784, in Clark, 679. See also Masterson, *William Blount*, 85–86, 91–94.

250. "North Carolina: Cession of Western Lands Claims," 22 December 1789, Carter 4:9–13.
251. "An Act to accept a cession of the claims of the state of North Carolina to a certain district of Western Territory," 2 April 1790, USSL 1:108.
252. "An Act for the Government of the Territory of the United States, south of the river Ohio," 26 May 1790, USSL 1:123.
253. Joshua D. Rothman, *The Ledger and the Chain: How Domestic Slave Traders Shaped America* (New York: Basic Books, 2021), 20. This territory was admitted to the Union as the state of Tennessee on 1 June 1796: "An Act for the Admission of the State of Tennessee into the Union," 1 June 1796, USSL 1:491–492. Article XI, Section 29 of Tennessee's state constitution of that year stipulated that "the free navigation rights of the Mississippi is one of the inherent rights" of Tennessee's citizens which could not be "conceded to any prince, potentate, power, person, or persons whatever": The Constitution of Tennessee, 1796, Thorpe 6:3424.
254. "Georgia: Cession of Western Lands Claims," 24 April 1802, Carter 5:145.
255. Carter 5:146. The territory ceded by Georgia became parts of the states of Mississippi, admitted to the Union on 10 December 1817, and Alabama, admitted to the Union on 14 December 1819. The convention that drafted Mississippi's constitution of 1817 passed an ordinance that stipulated that "the river Mississippi, and the navigable rivers and waters leading into the same, or into the gulf of Mexico, shall be common highways and forever free" to the citizens of Mississippi and other states of the Union: "Ordinance," 15 August 1817, Thorpe 4:2048.
256. "William Grayson to James Monroe," 8 August 1787, LDC 24:393.
257. Klarman, *The Framers' Coup*, 295.
258. Daniel Owen, "Circumvention of Article VI of the Ordinance of 1787," *Indiana Magazine of History* 36, no. 2 (June 1940): 110–116.
259. Hugh A. Garland, *The Life of John Randolph of Roanoke*, vol. 2 (Philadelphia: D. Appleton & Company, 1851), 125.
260. Quoted in William Cabell Bruce, *John Randolph of Roanoke, 1773–1833,* vol. 2 (New York: G. P. Putnam's Sons, 1922), 244–245. Similar requests to Harrison's emanated from Indiana in 1804, Virginia in 1806, and Indiana in 1807. All were refused: Edward Coles, *History of the Ordinance of 1787* (Philadelphia: Historical Society of Pennsylvania, 1856), 21–22. Although a defender of the interests of slaveholders, Randolph was no adherent to the "positive good" view of slavery. Rather, slavery was something that was an evil inherited from the British, but was a necessary evil in the sense that emancipation would have produced an unacceptable level of social disruption, miscegenation and race war: Nicholas Wood, "John Randolph of Roanoke and the Politics of Slavery in the Early Republic," *Virginia Magazine of History and Biography* 120, no. 2 (April 2012): 111–112.
261. Van Cleve, *A Slaveholders' Union*, 162. See also Beeman, *Plain, Honest Men*, 217.
262. "Benjamin Hawkins to Richard Caswell," 10 July 1787, LDC 24:351–352.

263. Quoted in Robert Alexander, *The Northwest Ordinance: Constitutional Politics and the Theft of Native Land* (Jefferson, NC: McFarland & Company, 2017), 90.
264. Morris, *The Forging of the Union*, 232.
265. Van Cleve, *A Slaveholders' Union*, 166.
266. Van Cleve, *A Slaveholders' Union*, 211–214.
267. "An Act to authorize the people of the Missouri territory to form a constitution and state government; and for the admission of such state into the Union on an equal footing with the original states, and to prohibit slavery in certain territories," Section 8, 6 March 1820, USSL 3:548.
268. Coles, *History of the Ordinance of 1787*, 30.
269. "An Act to Organize the Territories of Nebraska and Kansas," Sections 14, 32, 20, May 1854, USSL 10:283, 289.
270. *Permoli v. Municipality No 1 of the City of New Orleans*, 44 U.S. 589, 610 (1845).
271. *Strader v. Graham*, 51 U.S. 82, 93 (1851).
272. *Dred Scott v. Sandford*, 60 U.S. 393, 432 (1857).
273. *Dred Scott v. Sandford*, 60 U.S. 393, 447 (1857).
274. *Dred Scott v. Sandford*, 60 U.S. 393, 447 (1857).
275. *Dred Scott v. Sandford*, 60 U.S. 393, 450 (1857). Here, Taney was echoing Justice Samuel Chase in *Calder v. Bull*, who said that "[a]n ACT of the Legislature (for I cannot call it a law) contrary to the *great first principles* of the *social compact*, cannot be considered a *rightful exercise* of *legislative* authority": *Calder v. Bull*, 3 U.S. 386, 388 (1798).
276. *Dred Scott v. Sandford*, 60 U.S. 393, 411, 451 (1857). In this case Justice Daniel said that "the property of the master in his slave" was "the only private property which the Constitution . . . *specifically recognized*, and . . . imposed it as a direct obligation both on the States and the Federal Government to protect and *enforce*": *Dred Scott v. Sandford*, 60 U.S. 393, 490 (1857).
277. *Dred Scott v. Sandford*, 60 U.S. 393, 451 (1857).
278. *Dred Scott v. Sandford*, 60 U.S. 393, 452 (1857).
279. *Dred Scott v. Sandford*, 60 U.S. 393, 452 (1857).
280. Taney's ruling here reflected the view of James Madison, who, in 1819, wrote that Congress's power with respect to the territories "cannot well be extended beyond a power over the Territory as property, & a power to make the provisions really needful or necessary for the Govt of Settlers until ripe for admission as States into the Union. It may be inferred that Congress did not regard the interdict of slavery among the needful regulations contemplated by the constitution; since in none of the Territorial Governments created by them, is such an interdict found": Madison, "To Robert Walsh Jr.," 554–555.
281. CG, 29th, Congress, 2nd Session, 455. See also Robert Elder, *Calhoun: American Heretic*, (New York: Basic Books, 2021), 461–463.
282. For Lincoln, the *Dred Scott* decision did nothing more than determine that Dred Scott remained a slave, and not a free man. Thus, in relation to the issue of slavery in the territories, in a speech in June 1857, he claimed that the Supreme Court had "not . . . established a settled doctrine for the country": Abraham Lincoln, "Speech at Springfield, Illinois," 26 June 1857, CWAL 2:401.

283. For example, Thomas Hart Benton, *Historical and Legal Examination of that Part of the Decision of the Supreme Court of the United States in the Dred Scott Case Which Declares the Unconstitutionality of the Missouri Compromise Act, and the Self-extension of the Constitution to Territories, Carrying Slavery Along With It* (New York: D. Appleton & Company, 1860).
284. Abraham Lincoln, "First Inaugural Address," 4 March 1861, CWAL 4:268.
285. "An Act to provide for the Government of the Territory North-west of the river Ohio," 7 August 1789, USSL 1:51.
286. George Anastaplo, *Reflections on Slavery and the Constitution* (Lanham, MD: Lexington Books, 2012), 77.
287. Lynd argues that the Confederation's southern slave States accepted Article VI's prohibition of slavery in the Northwest Territory in return for northern States agreeing to include the three-fifths clause in the Constitution, rather than the fugitive slave clause: Lynd, "The Compromise of 1787," 243–250. Lynd slightly modified his argument and presented it in summary form in his "Introduction" to Alexander, *The Northwest Ordinance*, 10–12. Alexander's book agrees with Lynd's basic argument. Davis suggests that Lynd's argument "may well be right": David Brion Davis, "The Significance of Excluding Slavery from the Old Northwest in 1787," *Indiana Magazine of History* 84, no 1 (March 1988): 83. However, Hutson argues that the written evidence that Lynd bases his argument upon is "an unreliable source": James H. Hutson, "Riddles of the Federal Constitution," 44, no. 3 (July 1987): 417. Other scholars who reject Lynd's argument include Don E. Fehrenbacher, *The Dred Scott Case: Its Significance in American Law and Politics* (New York: Oxford University Press, 1978), 80–81; Paul Finkelman, "Slavery and Bondage in the 'Empire of Liberty,'" in *The Northwest Ordinance: Essays on Its Formation, Provisions, and Legacy*, ed. Frederick D. Williams (East Lansing, MI: Michigan State University Press, 1988), 70–71; Van Cleve, *A Slaveholders' Union*, 163; Beeman, *Plain, Honest Men*, 217.
288. Abraham Baldwin, William Blount, Jonathan Dayton, William Few, Nicholas Gilman, William Samuel Johnson, Rufus King, John Langdon, James Madison, Robert Morris, William Pierce, Charles Pinckney, and Hugh Williamson.
289. Gunning Bedford, Elbridge Gerry, William Churchill Houston, William Houstoun, James McHenry, Thomas Miflin, Roger Sherman, and Richard Dobbs Spaight.
290. JCC 32:343. See also "William Blount to Governor Caswell," 10 July 1787, RFC 3:57.
291. Alexander, *The Northwest Ordinance*, 18, 120–121.
292. RFC 2:553. The members of the Committee were Alexander Hamilton, William Samuel Johnson, Rufus King, James Madison, and Gouverneur Morris.
293. RFC 2:678.
294. Van Cleve, *A Slaveholders' Union*, 143. Duffey argues that the Ordinance, as well as the Declaration of Independence and the Federalist, are "constitutional documents," in that they are "authoritative foundational texts to which [Americans] look for guidance in trying to understand [their] national and political and legal traditions": Denis P. Duffey, "The Northwest Ordinance as a Constitutional Document," *Columbia Law Review* 95, no. 4 (May 1995): 933. Amar

describes the Ordinance as "a powerful counterpart of and precedent for the US Constitution itself": Amar, *The Words That Made Us*, 683.

295. Van Cleve, *A Slaveholders' Union*, 143.
296. In relation to the Missouri Compromise, in his 1851 biography of John Randolph of Roanoke, Garland wrote: "It seems to have grown up as a tacit, though well understood agreement, that North of a certain line involuntary servitude should not exist, and South of it slavery should be tolerated. The compromise Ordinance of 1787 originated in this feeling": Garland, *The Life of John Randolph of Roanoke*, 125.
297. William H. Seward, "The National Idea; Its Perils and Triumphs," 3 October 1860, in *The Works of William H. Seward*, vol. 4, ed. George E. Baker (Boston: Houghton, Mifflin & Company, 1884), 353.
298. RFC 2:633.
299. RFC 2:446. The wording of the clause as approved was: "If any Person bound to service or labor in any of the United States shall escape into another State, He or She shall not be discharged from such service or labor in consequence of any regulations subsisting in the State to which they escape; but shall be delivered up to the person justly claiming their service or labor."
300. DHRC 10:1484.
301. Ragsdale, *Washington at the Plow*, 156.
302. George Washington "To John Francis Mercer," 6 November 1786, in *The Papers of George Washington: Confederation Series*, vol. 4, *2 April 1786—31 January 1787*, ed. W. W. Abbot (Charlottesville, VA: University Press of Virginia, 1995), 336. During the Revolutionary War, a group of seventeen of Washington's slaves escaped in 1781, of which eight were eventually retrieved: Morgan and Nicholls, "Slave Flight," 200–201.
303. Anastaplo, *Reflections on Slavery and the Constitution*, 62.
304. *Dred Scott v. Sandford*, 60 U.S. 393, 411 (1857). In this case, Dred Scott was a slave who claimed he became a free man as a result of his residence for a period of time in a free state and then in free territory. The claim was denied by the Supreme Court. However, Scott ultimately got his freedom. In 1857 he was sold to Thomas Blow, who then promptly granted him his freedom: Fehrenbacher, *The Dred Scott Case*, 568.
305. Wiecek, *The Sources of Antislavery Constitutionalism in America*, 78.
306. C. W. A. David, "The Fugitive Slave Law of 1793 and its Antecedents," *Journal of Negro History* 9, no.1 (January 1924): 20.
307. "The Articles of Confederation of the United Colonies of New England—1643–1684," Thorpe 1:80.
308. "Treaty With The Cherokee, 1785; "Treaty With The Choctaw," 1786; "Treaty With The Chickshaw," 1786, in *Indian Affairs: Law and Treaties*, vol. 2, ed. Charles J. Kappler (Washington: Government Printing Office, 1904), 9, 12, 14.
309. "An Ordinance for the Government of the Territory of the United States Northwest of the River Ohio," 13 July 1787, Tansill, 54.
310. The fact that the Northwest Ordinance left territory south of the Ohio River open for slavery meant that its fugitive slave clause was important to influential slaveholders from Virginia such as Thomas Jefferson and James Monroe. As Kennedy points out, at that time, "Monroe owned or would soon own claims

upon more than a hundred thousand acres of potential plantation land in [the Kentucky territory immediately south of the Ohio River], where Jefferson and his immediate circle had even larger holdings," and which was, in 1792, "organized as a slave state on the Virginia model": Kennedy, *Mr Jefferson's Lost Cause*, 76–77.

311. Finkelman, *Slavery and the Founders*, 103; Van Cleve, *A Slaveholders' Union*, 91–93.
312. Rothman, *The Ledger and the Chain*, 6.
313. Van Cleve, *A Slaveholders' Union*, 172.
314. "North Carolina Delegates to Richard Caswell," 18 September 1787, LDC 24, 432.
315. Elliot 4:286.
316. *Somerset v. Stewart* (1772) 98 E.R. 499.
317. Harold Horowitz, "Choice of Law Decisions Involving Slavery: 'Interest Analysis' in the Early Nineteenth Century," *UCLA Law Review* 17, no. 3 (February 1970): 588.
318. DHRC 10:1339. Later at the convention Madison asserted that any attempt by the federal government to emancipate slaves would constitute a "usurpation of power": DHRC 10:1503.
319. *Prigg v. Pennsylvania*, 41 U.S. 539, 612 (1842).
320. *Jones v. Van Zandt* 46 U.S. 215, 229 (1847).
321. *Prigg v. Pennsylvania*, 41 U.S. 539, 611 (1842).
322. Van Cleve, *A Slaveholders' Union*, 204.
323. "An act respecting fugitives from justice, and persons escaping from the service of their masters," 12 February 1793, USSL 1:302–305.
324. Paul Finkelman, "The Kidnapping of John Davis and the Adoption of the Fugitive Slave Law of 1793," *Journal of Southern History* 56, no. 3 (August 1990): 419–420.
325. Jenny Bourne Wahl, *The Bondsman's Burden: An Economic Analysis of the Common Law of Southern Slavery* Cambridge, UK: Cambridge University Press, 1998), 132–133.
326. *Jones v. Van Zandt* 46 U.S. 215, 230–231 (1847).
327. Helen J. Knowles, "The Constitution and Slavery: A Special Relationship," *Slavery and Abolition* 28, no. 3 (2007): 314.
328. *Prigg v. Pennsylvania*, 41 U.S. 539, 613 (1842).
329. *Prigg v. Pennsylvania*, 41 U.S. 539, 615 (1842).
330. Paul Finkelman, "State Constitutional Protections of Liberty and the Antebellum New Jersey Supreme Court: Chief Justice Hornblower and the Fugitive Slave Law," *Rutgers Law Journal* 23, no. 4 (Summer 1992): 756.
331. *Prigg v. Pennsylvania*, 41 U.S. 539, 625 (1842).
332. *Moore v. Illinois*, 55 U.S. 13, 21 (1852).
333. *Prigg v. Pennsylvania*, 41 U.S. 539, 615 (1842).
334. *Prigg v. Pennsylvania*, 41 U.S. 539, 622 (1842).
335. Paul Finkelman, "*Prigg v. Pennsylvania* and Northern State Courts: Anti-Slavery Use of a Pro-Slavery Decision," *Civil War History* 25, no. 1 (March 1979): 21; David F. Ericson, *Slavery in the American Republic: Developing the Federal Government, 1791–1861* (Lawrence, KS: University of Kansas Press, 2011), 87.

336. Thomas D. Morris, *Free Men All: The Personal Liberty Law of the North 1780–1861* (Baltimore, MD: Johns Hopkins University Press, 1974), 152; Norman L. Rosenberg, "Personal Liberty Laws and Sectional Crisis: 1850–1861," *Civil War History* 17, no. 1 (March 1971): 28–29.
337. "An Act to amend, and supplementary to, the Act entitled 'An Act respecting Fugitives from Justice, and Persons escaping from the Service of their Masters,' approved February twelfth, one thousand seven hundred ninety-three," 18 September 1850, USSL 9:462–465. On Joseph Story's role and influence in the drafting of the FSA 1850, see Barbara Holden-Smith, "Lords of Lash, Loom, and Law: Justice Story, Slavery, and *Prigg v. Pennsylvania*," *Cornell Law Review* 78, no. 6 (1992–1993): 1137–1138.
338. Morris, *Free Men All*, 146–147.
339. *Miller v. McQuerry*, 17 F. Cas. 335, 337–341 (1853).
340. *United States v. Hanway*, 26 F. Cas. 105, 124 (1851).
341. *In re Charge to the Grand Jury—Fugitive Slave Law*, 30 F. Cas. 1007, 1010 (1851).
342. Stuart Streichler, *Justice Curtis in the Civil War Era: At the Crossroads of American Constitutionalism* (Charlottesville, VA: University of Virginia Press, 2005), 39, 54–65.
343. *Ableman v. Booth*, 62 U.S. 506, 526 (1859).
344. In relation to slaveholders that she met in 1834–1835 who granted permission for certain slaves to simply leave, Martineau wrote: "If this was meant to tell in favour of slavery, it failed of its effect. The argument was too shallow to impose upon a child. Of course, they were the least valuable slaves to whom this permission was given: and their declining to depart proved nothing so much as the utter degradation of human being who could prefer receiving food and shelter from the hand of an owner to the possession of themselves": Martineau, *Society in America,* 359. For an overview of Martineau's account on slavery as practiced in the United States, see Lisa Pace Vetter, "Harriet Martineau on the Theory and Practice of Democracy in America," *Political Theory* 36, no. 2 (April 2008): 437–440.
345. Stanley W. Campbell, *The Slave Catchers: Enforcement of the Fugitive Slave Law, 1850–1860* (Chapel Hill, NC: University of North Carolina Press, 1968), 207.
346. John Hope Franklin and Loren Schweninger, *Runaway Slaves: Rebels on the Plantation* (Oxford: Oxford University Press, 1999), 282; David Brion Davis, *The Problem of Slavery in the Age of Emancipation* (New York: Alfred A. Knopf, 2014), 235–236. Following her visit to the United States in 1834–1835, Harriet Martineau formed the view that "slaves do run away in much greater numbers than is supposed by any but those who lose them, and those who help them" and "that the loss by runaways, and the generally useless attempts to recover them, is a heavy item in the accounts of the cotton and sugar-growers of the south": Martineau, *Society in America,* 358–359. Such was the volume of advertisements offering rewards for fugitive slaves that historian Edward Baptist refers to them as "tweets of the master class": quoted in Andrew Delbanco, *The War Before the War: Fugitive Slaves and the Struggle for America's Soul from the Revolution to the Civil War* (New York: Penguin Press, 2018), 23.

347. Deyle, "An Ambiguous Legacy," 144–145.
348. Manisha Sinha, *The Slave's Cause: A History of Abolition* (New Haven CT: Yale University Press, 2016), 382. The escape of slaves was assisted by the activities of the so-called "Underground Railroad," constituted by antislavery advocates from the northern non-slave states: Henry Wilson, *History of the Rise and Fall of the Slave Power in America*, vol 2, (Boston: Houghton Mifflin Company, 1874), 62–73; Eric Foner, *Gateway to Freedom: The Hidden History of the Underground Railroad* (New York: W. W. Norton & Company, 2015), 18–21. The actions of persons involved in the Underground Railroad were often condemned by prominent politicians such as Henry Clay, with Daniel Webster referring to them as acts of treason: Robert J. Kaczorowski, "The Supreme Court and Congress's Power to Enforce Constitutional Rights: An Overlooked Moral Anomaly," *Fordham Law Review* 73, no. 1 (October 2004): 194.
349. "An Ordinance for the Government of the Territory of the United States Northwest of the River Ohio," 13 July 1787, Tansill, 51.
350. Coles, *History of the Ordinance of 1787*, 28–29.
351. Lynd, "The Compromise of 1787," 227.
352. Feldman, *The Three Lives of James Madison*, 447.
353. Story 3:677.
354. Van Cleve, *A Slaveholders' Union*, 154.
355. Scholars have generally accepted that Article VI of the Ordinance was proposed in Congress on the same day that it was voted upon, that is, 13 July 1787: Peter S. Onuf, *Statehood and Union: A History of the Northwest Ordinance* (Bloomington, IN: Indiana University Press, 1987), 110; Finkelman, *Slavery and the Founders*, 41. However, in a thorough examination of the documentary record, Alexander argues that the substance of Article VI was known by members of Congress on 11 July 1789: Alexander, *The Northwest Ordinance*, 108–121. Support for Alexander's argument is found in Paul Smith's notes in the multi-volume *Letters of Delegates to Congress* that he edited. Smith writes that when Congress reconvened on 8 July 1787, the of the draft Ordinance that had been read on 10 May 1787, was revised and that the revised ordinance, drafted largely by Nathan Dane, contained "far more structured conditions of admission to statehood." This revised ordinance was presented to Congress on 11 July 1787, whereupon it was "read successively through the 13th when it was adopted": LDC 24:355.
356. RFC 2:443.
357. RFC 2:446.
358. "William Blount to Governor Caswell," 57.
359. JCC 32:343.
360. RFC 3:587. For unknown reasons, Pierce did not return to Philadelphia. However, in relation to the Constitution as agreed to at Philadelphia, in a letter to St George Tucker on 28 September 1787, he wrote: "I approve of its principles, and would have signed it with all my heart, had I been present," "Notes of Major William Pierce on the Federal Convention of 1787," *The American Historical Review* 3, no. 2 (January 1898): 314.
361. "Nathan Dane to Rufus King," 16 July 1787, LDC 24:358.

362. Sinha, *The Slave's Cause*, 381.
363. USSL 8:83.
364. Parkinson, *The Common Cause*, 564.
365. Larson, *American Inheritance*, 131-132.
366. Alan Gilbert, *Fighting for Emancipation in the War for Independence* (Chicago: University of Chicago Press, 2012), 207–236; Benjamin Quarles, *The Negro in the American Revolution* (Chapel Hill, NC: University of North Carolina Press, 1996), 199–200; Adam Hochschild, *Bury the Chains: The British Struggle to Abolish Slavery* (London: Macmillan, 2005), 105–105, 174–178, 199–212; James Oakes, *The Scorpion's Sting: Antislavery and the Coming of the Civil War* (New York: W. W. Norton & Company, 2014), 108–118. A preliminary agreement in late 1792 between the British and Americans provided for the return of "Negroes or other property", which the British failed to carry out. In his letter to Guy Carleton on 6 May 1783 George Washington complained that, in providing safe haven to escaped slaves, the British were acting in a manner "totally different from the letter and spirit of the treaty" and demanded that the British agree to "measures, which may be deemed expedient, to prevent the future carrying away of any negroes or other Property of the American Inhabitants": George Washington, "To Guy Carleton," 6 May 1783, in *The Writings of George Washington*, vol. 9, *1782–1785,* ed. Washington Chauncey Ford (New York: G. P. Putnam's Sons, 1891), 247. Carleton responded that it was "utterly impracticable" to return escaped slaves who were regarded by the British as free and that, therefore, he could not "prevent their going to any part of the world they thought proper": "To George Washington from Guy Carleton," 12 May 1783, https://founders.archives.gov/documents/Washington/99–01–02–11252. For accounts of the negotiations between Carleton and Washington, see Hochschild, *Bury the Chains*, 101–105; Larson, *American Inheritance*, 153-155. With the signing of a treaty in November 1794 to resolve various outstanding issues between the United States and Great Britain in November 1794, efforts by the United States to obtain compensation in lieu of the return of escaped slaves were also abandoned: Daniel C. Littlefield, "John Jay, the Revolutionary, and Slavery," *New York History* 81, no. 1 (January 2000): 108–111; Sean Wilentz, *The Rise of American Democracy: Jefferson to Lincoln* (New York: W. W. Norton and Company, 2005), 67–68. In the debate over the treaty in the House of Representatives on 15 April 1796, James Madison complained that its result was that Great Britain was "wholly absolved from the obligation to fulfil one of the articles [of the Treaty of Paris of 1783], viz: that relating to the negroes." He also complained about the "very extraordinary abandonment of the compensation due for the negroes." For Madison, these matters meant that the treaty was "frequently wanting in both justice and reciprocity": AC, 4th Congress, 1st Session, 977–978.
367. Jane Landers, "Spanish Sanctuary: Fugitives in Florida, 1687–1790," *The Florida Historical Quarterly* 62, no. 3 (January 1984): 296–313.
368. James Madison, "To Thomas Jefferson," 24 October 1787, 219.
369. Matthews, *Forgotten Founder*, 79.
370. *Prigg v. Pennsylvania*, 41 U.S. 539, 611 (1842).
371. *Prigg v. Pennsylvania*, 41 U.S. 539, 612 (1842). In the year following the

decision in *Prigg v. Pennsylvania*, Story addressed the significance of the Constitution's fugitive slave clause, and therefore of the fugitive slave legislation that it spawned, in a lecture to students at Harvard University, one of whom was future President Rutherford B. Hayes. According to Hayes, Story said the following in relation to the Constitution's fugitive slave clause: "This clause, some people wish to evade, or are willing wholly to disregard. If one part of the country may disregard one part of the Constitution, another section may refuse to obey that part which seems to bear hard upon its interests, and thus the Union will become a mere 'rope of sand,' and the Constitution (worse than a dead letter), an apple of discord in our midst, a fruitful source of reproach, bitterness, and hatred, and in the end, discord and civil war; till exhausted, wasted and embittered, and deadly foes have severed this Union": ed., Charles Richard Williams, *Diary and Letters of Rutherford Birchard Hayes, Nineteenth President of the United States*, vol. 1, *1834–1860* (Columbus, OH: Ohio State Archaeological and Historical Society, 1922), 131.

372. *Commonwealth, Ex rel Negro Lewis v. Holloway*, 6 Binney. 213, 218 (Pa., 1814); *Commonwealth ex rel Wright v. Deacon*, 5 Serg. & Rawle 62, 62–63 (Pa., 1819).
373. *Jones v. Van Zandt*, 46 U.S. 215, 231 (1847).
374. Benjamin Robbins Curtis, "Speech in Faneuil Hall," 26 November 1850, in *A Memoir of Benjamin Robbins Curtis With Some of His Professional and Miscellaneous Writings*, vol. 1, ed. Benjamin R. Curtis (Boston: Little, Brown, & Company, 1879), 131.
375. *Miller v. McQuerry*, 17 F. Cas. 335, 338 (1853).
376. Paul Finkelman, "Story Telling on the Supreme Court: Prigg v. Pennsylvania and Justice Story's Judicial Nationalism," *Supreme Court Review1994* (1994): 247–294; Eric W. Plaag, "'Let the Constitution Perish'": *Prigg v. Pennsylvania*, Joseph Story, and the Flawed Doctrine of Historical Necessity," *Slavery and Abolition* 25, no. 3 (2004): 76–101; Klarman, *The Framers' Coup*, 293–294.
377. Finkelman, "Story Telling on the Supreme Court," 256–263. Holden-Smith, who argues that Story's opinion in *Prigg* "illustrates that Story cared far more about the protection of property rights and the expansion of federal power than he did about injustices being done to black people by the fugitive slave law," also agrees with Finkelman that there is no supporting evidence that the fugitive slave clause was vital for establishing the Union: Holden-Smith, "Lords of Lash, Loom, and Law Holden-Smith, "Lords of Lash, Loom, and Law," 1091, 1129–1130.
378. Finkelman, *Slavery and the Founders*, 38.
379. Van Cleve, *A Slaveholders' Union*, 168.
380. Delbanco, *The War Before the War*, 84.
381. Joseph Fishkin and William E. Forbath, *The Anti-Oligarchy Constitution: Reconstructing the Economic Foundations of American Democracy* (Cambridge, MA: Harvard University Press, 2022), 57.
382. "William Pierce to St. George Tucker," 28 September 1787, RFC 3:101.
383. RFC 1:605.
384. Mark A. Graber, *Dred Scott and the Problem of Constitutional Evil* (New York:

Cambridge University Press, 2006), 245. To similar effect, Anastaplo writes that "[t]he most glaring departure from the principle of equality proclaimed in the Declaration of Independence is, of course, the recognition in the Constitution of slavery": Anastaplo, *Reflections on Slavery and the Constitution*, 61.

385. Gary B. Nash, *The Unknown American Revolution: The Unruly Birth of Democracy and the Struggle to Create America* (London: Jonathan Cape, 2006), 212.
386. Sidney George Fisher, *The Laws of Race, As Connected with Slavery*, (Philadelphia: Willis P. Hazard, 1860), 13–14.
387. JSCAL, 244.
388. Graber, *Dred Scott and the Problem of Constitutional Evil*, 106.
389. Abraham Lincoln, "Speech at Harford Connecticut," 5 March 1860, CWAL 4:3, 9.
390. Abraham Lincoln, Speech at Springfield, Illinois," 17 July 1858, CWAL 2:520. In a speech, in 1854, Lincoln stated that "necessity drove" the framers of the Constitution to include the Constitution's clause that expressly dealt with slavery: Abraham Lincoln, "Speech at Peoria, Illinois," 16 October 1854, CWAL 2:274. In a speech, in 1858, Lincoln also noted that, because of the "necessity" of allowing slavery to remain, "we could not get our constitution": Abraham Lincoln, "Speech at Chicago, Illinois," 10 July 1858, CWAL 2:501. Three months later, in identical language, he made the same point: Abraham Lincoln, "Seventh and Last Debate with Stephen A Douglas at Alton, Illinois," 15 October 1858, CWAL 3:300. In a speech, in 1858, Lincoln said that the framers of the Constitution "made the perpetuation of the institution of slavery a necessity in this country": Abraham Lincoln, "Sixth Debate with Stephen A Douglas, at Quincy, Illinois' 13 October 1858, CWAL 3:276. In private correspondence, in 1858, Lincoln wrote that he believed that the Constitution was drafted as it was "because of the *necessity* springing from the actual presence of slavery, when it was framed": Abraham Lincoln, "To James N Brown," 18 October 1858, CWAL 3:327.
391. Joseph Story, *A Familiar Exposition of the Constitution of the United States* (Boston: Thomas H. Webb and Co., 1842), 243.
392. *Prigg v. Pennsylvania*, 41 U.S. 539, 611 (1842).
393. MJQA 11:336.
394. Jack N. Rakove, *Original Meanings: Politics and Ideas in the Making of the Constitution* (New York: Alfred A. Knopf, 1997), 93. Boonshoft reaches a similar conclusion when he writes that the delegates to the Philadelphia Convention and the state ratification debates "understood that the Constitution was pro-slavery to its core": Mark Boonshoft, "Doughfaces at the Founding: Federalists, Anti-Federalists, Slavery, and the Ratification of the Constitution in New York," *New York History* 93, no. 3 (Summer 2012): 191. Although Wilentz rejects the view that the Constitution was a proslavery document, he nevertheless recognizes that without its slavery provisions, "the slaveholding states . . . would never have ratified [the] Constitution": Wilentz, *No Property in Man*, 14.
395. Elliot 4:286. In his detailed study of the Philadelphia Convention, Klarmen

writes: "In South Carolina and Georgia, which were states most strongly committed to the indefinite perpetuation of slavery, very few voices criticized the Constitution as insufficiently protective of the institution. Georgia's convention unanimously ratified the Constitution, which would have been inconceivable had serious doubts existed about whether the safeguards for slavery were adequate. In South Carolina, nobody challenged [Charles Cotesworth] Pinckney's statement that the southern delegates in Philadelphia had secured a good deal for slave owners. Opponents of ratification in South Carolina, of whom there were a great many, rarely argued that the Constitution inadequately protected slavery": Klarman, *The Framers' Coup*, 302-303.

396. DHRC 8:369.

397. *Johnson v. Tompkins*, 13 Fed. Cas. 840, 843, 852 (1833).

398. "From John A. Campbell," 20 November 1847, PJCC 14:669. On Campbell's views on slavery, see Justine S. Mann, "The Political Thought of John Archibald Campbell: The Formative Years, 1847–1851," *Alabama Law Review* 22, no. 2 (Spring 1970): 289–295. Following the secession of his home state, Campbell resigned from the Supreme Court. Although he opposed secession, he served as assistant secretary for war in the Confederacy's government. Following the assassination of Abraham Lincoln in April 1865, Campbell was arrested, but not charged, on suspicion of being involved in the assassination plot. He was released from custody following intervention on his behalf by Justice Benjamin Curtis: Robert Saunders Jr., *John A. Campbell: Southern Moderate* (Tuscaloosa, AL: University of Alabama Press, 1997), 136–144, 185–189.

399. Quoted in Wilentz, *No Property in Man*, 274 (n. 21).

400. Van Cleve, *A Slaveholders' Union*, 179.

401. Michael Stokes Paulsen and Luke Paulsen, *The Constitution: An Introduction* (New York: Basic Books, 2015), 83.

402. Van Cleve, *A Slaveholders' Union*, 270. McCurry describes the Constitution of this more perfect slaveholders' union as "a document that defined slaves explicitly as property, put slaves definitively outside the boundaries of the political community, prohibited the incorporation of any new state that did not sanction slavery, and put beyond the power of [the Confederacy's] federal government to limit, revoke, or otherwise interfere with the legality of slave property or rights of slaveholders": Stephanie McCurry, *Confederate Reckoning: Power and Politics in the Civil War South* (Cambridge, MA: Harvard University Press, 2010), 221.

403. "Joint Resolution to amend the Constitution of the United States," 2 March 1861, USSL 12:251. The House of Representatives passed the resolution by a vote of 133 to 65 and the Senate by a vote of 24 to 12: CG, 36th Congress, 2nd Session, 1285, 1403.

404. Daniel W. Crofts, *Lincoln and the Politics of Slavery: The Other Thirteenth Amendment and the Struggle to Save the Union* (Chapel Hill, NC: University of North Carolina Press, 2016), 245–254. Amar argues that the ratification in Illinois was irregular: Amar, *America's Constitution*, 457. Hindsight would suggest that the Confederate states should have reversed course and ratified the Corwin Amendment. Such a step would have demonstrated the wisdom of

the words of Mick Jagger and Keith Richards: "You can't always get what you want, But if you try sometime you'll find, You get what you need": from the song "You Can't Always Get What You Want" on the Rolling Stones' album *Let it Bleed* (1969).

405. For the most comprehensive account of this proposed amendment, see Crofts, *Lincoln and the Politics of Slavery*, 2016. Other accounts include, R. Alton Lee, "The Corwin Amendment in the Secession Crisis," *Ohio Historical Quarterly* 70, no. 1 (January 1961): 1–26; A Christopher Bryant, "Stopping Time: The Pro-Slavery and 'Irrevocable' Thirteenth Amendment," *Harvard Journal of Law and Public Policy* 26, no. 2 (Spring 2003): 501–549.

406. Abraham Lincoln, "First Inaugural Address," 270. Lincoln's endorsement of the proposed amendment was tepid and motivated by political expediency. He believed that it was unlikely to be ratified, but may have allayed the fears of slaveholders in the border slave states that still had not decided whether to secede from the Union. On the other hand, had the proposed amendment been ratified there is little doubt that Lincoln would have abided by it, albeit grudgingly, given that such ratification would have complied with the Constitution and would have reflected the will of the people: Michael Burlingame, *Abraham Lincoln: A Life*, vol. 2 (Baltimore, MD: Johns Hopkins University Press, 2008), 48; Christian G. Samito, *Lincoln and the Thirteenth Amendment* (Carbondale, IL: Southern Illinois University Press, 2015), 25–26.

407. William H. Seward, "The State of the Union," 12 January 1861, in Baker, *The Works of William H. Seward*, vol. 4, 667.

408. Raymond T. Diamond, "No Call to Glory: Thurgood Marshall's Thesis On the Intent of a Pro-Slavery Constitution," *Vanderbilt Law Review* 42, no. 1 (November 1989): 129.

CHAPTER 4. "TOWARDS A MORE PERFECT SLAVEHOLDERS' UNION?"

1. "Address of Robert Ward Johnson," 7 February 1861, in *Slavery and Secession in Arkansas: A Documentary History*, ed. James J. Gigantino II (Fayettville, AR: University of Arkansas Press, 2015), 114.
2. CG, 36th Congress, 2nd Session, 487.
3. John C. Calhoun, "A Discourse on the Constitution and Government of the United States," in *Union and Liberty: The Political Philosophy of John C. Calhoun*, ed. Ross M. Lence (Indianapolis, IN: Liberty Fund, 1992), 212.
4. "Howell Cobb to the People of Georgia," 6 December 1860, in *The Correspondence of Robert Toombs, Alexander H. Stephens, and Howell Cobb*, ed. Ulrich Bonnell Phillips (Washington: American Historical Association, 1913), 509–510.
5. DHRC 9:995.
6. DHRC 10:507.
7. Theophilus Parsons, *The Law of Contracts*, vol. 2, 4th ed., (Boston: Little, Brown & Company, 1860), 40. Parsons' treatise has been referred to as "one of the most important contract treatises of the [nineteenth] century": James W. Fox Jr., "The Law of Many Faces: Antebellum Contract Law Background of Reconstruction-Era Freedom of Contract," *American Journal of Legal History* 49, no. 1 (January 2007): 80.

8. Story 1:292.
9. Story 1:288.
10. "Declaration of the Immediate Causes Which Induce and Justify the Secession of South Carolina From The Federal Union," JSCSC, 463.
11. "Declaration of the Immediate Causes," 465.
12. Daniel Webster, "Speeches at Capon Springs, Va.," 28 June 1851, in *The Writings and Speeches of Daniel Webster*, vol. 13 (Boston: Little, Brown, & Company, 1903), 438–439. At the Virginia secession convention, Henry L. Benning, Georgia's commissioner to Virginia, referred to Webster's speech as confirmation that breaches of the Constitution's fugitive slave laws by northern non-slave states gave slave states the right to unilaterally secede from the Union: PVSC 1:68–69.
13. For example, "Mr Webster's Last Remarks," 26–27 January 1830, in *The Webster-Hayne Debate on the Nature of the Union, Selected Documents*, ed. Herman Belz (Indianapolis, IN: Liberty Fund, 2000), 151.
14. Story 1:339.
15. Abel Parker Upshur, *A Brief Enquiry into the True Nature and Character of our Federal Government: Being a Review of Judge Story's Commentaries on the Constitution of the United States* (Petersburg, VA: Edmund and Julian C. Ruffin, 1840), 85.
16. John C. Calhoun, "To James Hamilton Jr.," 28 August 1832, PJCC 11:631.
17. Calhoun, "To James Hamilton Jr.," 632.
18. CG, 25th Congress, 2nd Session, 98.
19. William W. Story, *A Treatise on the Law of Contracts*, vol. 1 (Boston: Little, Brown & Company, 1856), 4–6.
20. Story 1:288.
21. See, for example, (1) convention statements in PVSC 1:45–46, 54, 68, 81, 272, 328–329, 343, 389, 490, 495, 535; JSCAL, 14–15, 27, 115, 376–381, 394–395, 403, 413, 434–435, 449; JSCMS, 151–152, 187–188, 204–205; JSCSC, 4, 31; JSCGA, 16, 335, 347, 355; Gigantino, *Slavery and Secession in Arkansas*, 165; (2) speeches and pamphlets such as Albert Pike, *State or Province? Bond or Free?*, (Little Rock, AR: n.p., 1861), 25, 28–29; "Thomas R. R. Cobb's Secessionist Speech, Monday Evening, November 12," in *Secession Debated, Georgia's Showdown in 1860*, eds. William W. Freehling and Craig M. Simpson (New York: Oxford University Press, 1992), 7–8 "Robert Toombs's Secessionist Speech, Tuesday Evening, November 13," in Freehling and Simpson, *Secession Debated*, 46–47; "Henry L. Benning's Secessionist Speech, Monday Evening, November 19," in Freehling and Simpson, *Secession Debated*, 123–125; Rev. James Henley Thornwell, "The State of the Country," January 1861, in *Southern Pamphlets on Secession, November 1860-April 1861*, ed. Jon L. Wakelyn (Chapel Hill, NC: University of North Carolina Press, 1996), 162; Isham G. Harris, "First Message of Governor Isham Harris to the Tennessee Assembly," 7 January 1861, in *Senate Journal of the Extra Session of the Thirty-Third General Assembly of the State of Tennessee Which Convened at Nashville, on the First Monday in January A.D. 186*, (Nashville, TN: J. O. Griffith & Company, Public Printers, 1861), 6–19; *Union—Slavery—Secession: Letter from Governor R. K. Call*

of Florida, to John S. Littell, of Germantown, Pennsylvania, (Philadelphia: C. Sherman and Son, Printers, 1861), 14, 22–23; (3) newspaper editorials and commentaries: Python, "The Secession of the South," *De Bow's Review*, 28, no. 4 (April 1860) 369–370; *Wilmington Journal* (North Carolina) in Joseph Carlyle Sitterson, *The Secession Movement in North Carolina* (Chapel Hill, NC: University of North Carolina Press, 1939), 179; *Fayettville Arkansian* (Arkansas) in Gigantino, *Slavery and Secession in Arkansas*, 37.

22. "The Address of the People of South Carolina Assembled in Convention, to the People of the Slaveholding States of the United States," JSCSC, 467.
23. "The Address of the People of South Carolina," 471.
24. "The Address of the People of South Carolina," 475.
25. "Declaration of the Immediate Causes," 463.
26. "Declaration of the Immediate Causes," 463–464.
27. "Declaration of the Immediate Causes," 465.
28. "An Act to Provide for a Convention of the people of the State of Mississippi," JSCGA, 313.
29. "Resolution Of the State of Mississippi, declaring secession to be the proper remedy for the Southern States," JSCGA, 315–316.
30. "Declaration of the Immediate Causes Which Induce and Justify the Secession of Mississippi from the Federal Union," JSCMS, 86–87.
31. JSCFL, 18.
32. JSCFL, 26.
33. JSCFL, 31.
34. JSCAL, 9.
35. JSCAL, 24, 30.
36. JSCAL, 131.
37. "An Ordinance to dissolve the union between the State of Alabama and other States united under the compact styled The Constitution of the United States of America," 11 January 1861, JSCAL, 76.
38. "Report," JSCGA, 104–105.
39. "Report," 111–112.
40. "Howell Cobb to the People of Georgia," 507.
41. "Report," 105, 108. Georgia's complaint about non-slave state complicity in failing to comply with federal fugitive slave legislation reflected a resolution its legislature adopted during the course of negotiations leading to the 1850 Compromise, which asserted that "the refusal of the part of the non-slaveholding States to deliver up fugitive slaves who have escaped to the said States . . . is a plain and palpable violation of the letter of the Constitution": "Resolutions of Georgia," 8 February 1850, Ames, 260.
42. "Howell Cobb to the People of Georgia," 509.
43. Quoted in Willie Malvin Caskey, *Secession and Restoration of Louisiana* (Baton Rouge, LA: Louisiana State University Press, 1938), 19.
44. "Message from the Governor," 24 January 1861, JSCLA, 13.
45. JSCLA, 9.
46. JSCLA, 10.
47. JSCLA, 43.

48. "The Texas Ordinance of Secession," 1 February 1861, Moore, 27.
49. "A Declaration of the Causes which Impel the State of Texas to Secede from the Federal Union," JSCTX, 65.
50. "A Declaration of the Causes which Impel the State of Texas to Secede," 63.
51. "A Declaration of the Causes which Impel the State of Texas to Secede," 62.
52. "Virginia's Ordinance of Secession," 17 April 1861, Moore, 70.
53. PVSC 1:68.
54. PVSC 1:81.
55. PVSC 1:272.
56. PVSC 1:328.
57. PVSC 1:535.
58. PVSC 3:104.
59. PVSC 1:54.
60. PVSC 1:490.
61. PVSC 1: 342–343.
62. "An Ordinance to dissolve the Union," 6 May 1861, JSCAR, 121.
63. "Resolutions," 11 March 1861, JSCAR, 52.
64. JSCAL, 430, 433–434.
65. JSCGA, 355.
66. JSCGA, 347.
67. "Tennessee Ordinance of Secession," 8 June 1861, Moore, 203.
68. Isham G. Harris, "First Message of Governor Isham Harris to the Tennessee Assembly," 7 January 1861, in *Senate Journal of the Extra Session of the Thirty-Third General Assembly of the State of Tennessee*, 6–11. On the issue of slavery in the territories, in his speech to the Senate on 24 December 1860, Tennessee's Senator Alfred O. P. Nicholson, after quoting the Republican Party's policy against allowing slavery in the territories, referred to it as an issue between the North and South which was "wholly irreconcilable" and one which aimed "to extinguish the institution of slavery": CG, 36th Congress, 2nd Session, 187.
69. CG, 36th Congress, 2nd Session, 123.
70. "An Act to Submit to a Vote of the People a Declaration of Independence, and for other purposes," 6 May 1861, Moore, 203.
71. 104,913 votes for and 47,238 votes against secession: Lawrence M. Anderson, *Federalism, Secession, and the American State: Divided We Secede* (New York: Routledge, 2013), 123; Charles L. Lufkin, "Secession and Coercion in Tennessee, the Spring of 1861," *Tennessee Historical Quarterly* 50, no. 2 (Summer 1991): 104.
72. *Dred Scott v. Sandford*, 60 U.S. 393, 452 (1857).
73. Republican Party Platform, June 18, 1856, https://www.presidency.ucsb.edu/documents/republican-party-platform-1856.
74. Abraham Lincoln, "Second Debate with Stephen A. Douglas at Freeport, Illinois," 27 August 1858, CWAL 4:40.
75. Lucas E. Morel, *Lincoln and the American Founding* (Carbondale, IL: Southern Illinois University Press, 2020), 101. Lincoln's position on slavery in the territories in 1860 represented a reversal of his position in 1854 when, in a speech delivered on 16 October 1854, in setting out his views of slavery he said that he would "not . . . resist the admission of Utah and New Mexico, even should they

ask to come in as slave States": Abraham Lincoln, "Speech at Peoria, Illinois," 16 October 1854, CWAL 2:260.

76. National Republican Platform Adopted by the National Republican Convention, May 17, 1860, https://www.loc.gov/resource/lprbscsm.scsm0716/.
77. Doris Kearns Goodwin, *Team of Rivals: The Political Genius of Abraham Lincoln* (New York: Simon and Schuster, 2005), 296–297.
78. Abraham Lincoln, "Letter to Trumbull," 10 December 1860, CWAL 4:149. Lincoln reiterated his views to Trumbull in a second letter on 17 December 1860: Abraham Lincoln, "Letter to Trumbull," CWAL 4:152.
79. Abraham Lincoln, "Letter to William Kellogg," 11 December 1860, CWAL 4:150. See also Abraham Lincoln, "Letter to William H. Seward," 1 February 1861, CWAL 4:183.
80. Abraham Lincoln, "To Elihu B. Washburne," CWAL 4:151. Although these statements were in private communications, they were made known to the public through press reports: Michael Burlingame, *Abraham Lincoln: A Life*, vol.1 (Baltimore, MD: Johns Hopkins University Press, 2008), 709.
81. Abraham Lincoln, "First Inaugural Address," 4 March 1861, CWAL 4:268.
82. Lincoln, "First Inaugural Address," 263.
83. Abraham Lincoln, "'A House Divided': Speech at Springfield, Illinois," 16 June 1858, CWAL 2:461–462.
84. Waldo W. Braden, *Abraham Lincoln: Public Speaker* (Baton Rouge, LA: Louisiana State University Press, 1993), 35–36.
85. "The Address of the People of South Carolina," 473–474.
86. "Declaration of the Immediate Causes," 465.
87. "Report," 109.
88. "A Declaration of the Causes which Impel the State of Texas to Secede," 63.
89. "Constitution of Kansas, Bill of Rights," Section 6, 29 July 1859, Thorpe 2:1242.
90. "An Act for the Admission of Kansas into the Union," 29 January 1861, USSL 12:126–128.
91. "An Act for the Release of Certain Persons held to Service or Labor in the District of Columbia," USSL 12:376–378.
92. "An Act to secure Freedom to all persons within the Territories of the United States," 19 June 1862, USSL 12:432. This legislation effectively repealed the legalization of slavery by the territorial legislatures of Utah in 1851 and New Mexico in 1859. In March 1861, two days before the inauguration of Abraham Lincoln, Congress created the Territory of Nevada out of the western half of the Territory of Utah: "An Act to Organize the Territory of Nevada," 2 March 1861, USSL 12:209–214. In March 1864 Congress legislated that the Territory of Nevada could seek admission to the Union as a state, provided that it adopted a constitution whose terms were "not repugnant to the constitution of the United States, and the principles of the Declaration of Independence" and which expressly prohibited slavery: "An Act to enable the People of Nevada to form a Constitution and State Government, and for the Admission of such State into the Union on an equal Footing with the original States," Section 4, 21 March 1864, USSL 13:31. Article 1, Section 17, of Nevada's Constitution of 1864, adopted at a convention on 4 July 1861 and approved at a referendum on 1 September 1864, expressly prohibited slavery: Thorpe 4:2403. On 31 October

1864, Nevada was admitted "into the Union on an equal footing with the original states": "Proclamation by the President of the United States of America," 31 October 1864, USSL 13:749.

93. Daniel Webster, "The Constitution and the Union, March 7, 1850," PDW 2:540–541.
94. Webster, "The Constitution and the Union, March 7, 1850," 541. The speech, although widely seen as having saved the Union, was also heavily criticized, especially in his home state of Massachusetts: Robert V. Remini, *Daniel Webster: The Man and His Life* (New York: W. W. Norton & Company, 1997), 675–678; Joel Richard Paul, *Indivisible: Daniel Webster and the Birth of American Nationalism* (New York: Riverhead Books, 2022), 405-407. Although the speech diminished his stature towards the end of his political career, on 12 March 1959, on the recommendation of a Special Senate Committee, chaired by then Senator John F. Kennedy, Webster was inducted into a senatorial "Hall of Fame" as one of the five outstanding senators in the history of the United States to that point of time. His contemporaries Henry Clay and John C. Calhoun were also inducted. The other two were Robert Taft and Robert La Follette. In 2004, Arthur Vandenberg and Robert Wagner joined this exclusive club: John T. Shaw, *JFK in the Senate: Pathway to the Presidency* (New York: Palgrave Macmillan, 2013), 141–165.
95. Daniel Webster, "Letter to Edward Sprague et. al," 15 May 1850, in *The Papers of Daniel Webster, Correspondence*, vol. 7, *1850–1852*, eds. Charles M. Wiltse and Michael J. Birkner (Hanover, NH: University Press of New England, 1986), 90.
96. Daniel Webster, "Letter to [George Ticknor]," 1 June 1850, Wiltse and Birkner, *The Papers of Daniel Webster, Correspondence*, 105.
97. Jean H. Baker, *James Buchanan* (New York: Times Books, 2004), 38–39.
98. James Buchanan, "Fourth Annual Message," 3 December 1860, in *The Works of James Buchanan*, vol. 11, *1860–1868*, ed. John Bassett Moore (Philadelphia: J. B. Lippincott Company, 1910), 11.
99. CG, Appendix, 36th Congress, 1st Session, 935.
100. "An act to give effect to the provisions of the constitution of the United States, relative to fugitives from labor, for the protection of free people of color, and to prevent kidnapping," 25 March 1826, reprinted in *Prigg v. Pennsylvania*, 41 U.S. 539, 550–556 (1842).
101. *Prigg v. Pennsylvania*, 41 U.S. 539, 625–626 (1842).
102. *Prigg v. Pennsylvania*, 41 U.S. 539, 625 (1842).
103. *Prigg v. Pennsylvania*, 41 U.S. 539, 612 (1842).
104. *Prigg v. Pennsylvania*, 41 U.S. 539, 613 (1842).
105. "An Act To prevent kidnapping, preserve public peace, prohibit the exercise of certain powers heretofore exercised by judges, justices of the peace, aldermen and jailors of this commonwealth, and to repeal certain slave laws," 3 March 1847, in *Laws of the General Assembly of the Commonwealth of Pennsylvania Passed at the Session of 1847 in the Seventy-First Year of Independence* (Harrisburg, PA: J. M. G. Lescure, Printer of the State, 1847), 206–209.
106. Thomas D. Morris, *Free Men All: The Personal Liberty Law of the North 1780–1861* (Baltimore, MD: Johns Hopkins University Press, 1974), 156.

107. Morris, *Free Men All*, 219–222.
108. Larry Gara, "The Fugitive Slave Law: A Double Paradox," *Civil War History* 10, no. 3 (September 1964), 236.
109. Andrew Delbanco, *The War Before the War: Fugitive Slaves and the Struggle for America's Soul from the Revolution to the Civil War* (New York: Penguin Press, 2018), 345.
110. Horace K. Houston Jr., "Another Nullification Crisis: Vermont's 1850 Habeas Corpus Law," *The New England Quarterly* 77, no. 2 (June 2004): 260–261.
111. "An Act to Secure Freedom to All Persons Within this State," 25 November 1858, in *The Acts and Resolves Passed by the General Assembly of the State of Vermont, at the October Session, 1858* (Bradford, VT: Joseph D. Clark, Printer, 1858), 42–44.
112. Clarence Phillips Denman, *The Secession Movement in Alabama* (Montgomery, AL: Alabama State Department of Archives and History, 1933), 67.
113. Manisha Sinha, *The Slave's Cause: A History of Abolition* (New Haven, CT: Yale University Press, 2016), 527–542; Eric Foner, *Gateway to Freedom: The Hidden History of the Underground Railroad* (New York: W. W. Norton & Company, 2015), 63–215; R. J. M. Blackett, *The Captive's Quest for Freedom: Fugitive Slaves, the 1850 Fugitive Slave Law, and the Politics of Slavery* (New York: Cambridge University Press, 2018, 137–440.
114. Elizabeth R. Varon, *Disunion! The Coming of the American Civil War, 1789–1859* (Chapel Hill, NC: University of North Carolina Press, 2008), 236–240
115. *Ableman v. Booth*, 62 U.S. 509 (1859).
116. Jeffrey Schmitt, "Rethinking *Ableman v. Booth* and States' Rights in Wisconsin," *Virginia Law Review* 95, no. 5 (September 2007): 1353.
117. *In re Sherman M. Booth*, 3 Wis. 1 (1854).
118. *In re Booth and Rycraft*, 3 Wis. 157 (1854).
119. David M. Potter, *The Impending Crisis, 1848–1861* (New York: Harper & Row Publishers, 1976), 295. Hagan offers a similar assessment of the approach of authorities in Wisconsin to the *Ableman v. Booth* case, when he writes of it as the "most glaring example of nullification in [American] history": Horace M. Hagan, "Ableman vs Booth," *American Bar Association Journal* 17, no. 1 (January 1931): 19.
120. H. Robert Baker, *The Rescue of Joshua Glover: A Fugitive Slave, The Constitution, and the Coming of the Civil War* (Athens, OH: Ohio University Press, 2006), 168.
121. *Ableman v. Booth*, 62 U.S. 506, 526 (1859).
122. *Ableman v. Booth*, 62 U.S. 506, 523 (1859).
123. *Ableman v. Booth*, 62 U.S. 506, 524 (1859).
124. Dallin H. Oaks, "Habeas Corpus in the States—1776–1865," *University of Chicago Law Review* 32, no. 2 (Winter 1965): 274–275.
125. Baker, *The Rescue of Joshua Glover*, 155–156.
126. "Wisconsin Defies the Federal Court," 19 March 1859, Ames, 305.
127. Schmitt, "Rethinking *Ableman v. Booth*," 1345.
128. Quoted in Michael F. Conlin, *The Constitutional Origins of the American Civil War* (Cambridge, UK: Cambridge University Press, 2019), 203.

129. Hans L. Trefousse, *Carl Schurz: A Biography* (Knoxville. TN: University of Tennessee Press, 1982), 75.
130. Carl Schurz, "State Rights and Byron Paine" Speech delivered at Albany Hall, Milwaukee, 23 March 1859, https://en.wikisource.org/wiki/State_Rights_and_Byron_Paine. Schurz later wrote that this speech was the most enthusiastically received of all his speeches. However, in his later reminiscences, he explained that the reason for its exclusion from his subsequently published collected works was because "a more matured judgment had convinced me that . . . the conclusions drawn from it as to the functions and necessary powers of government, were unsound": Carl L. Schurz, *The Reminiscences of Carl Schurz*, vol. 2, *1852–1863* (Garden City, NY: Doubleday, Page & Company, 1913), 113. Nor was a second and similar speech in support of Paine, delivered on 31 March 1859, included in his published collected works. As Schmitt pointedly observes, for Republicans, Lincoln's electoral success meant that "a political theory that vested supreme political power in the states was no longer in their interests": Schmitt, "Rethinking *Ableman v. Booth*," 1349. Wisconsin's governor, Alexander W. Randall, made a similar conversion from advocating the compact theory of the Constitution in 1859, to, in 1861, professing the nationalist theory: Shearer Davis Bowman, *At the Precipice: Americans North and South During the Secession Crisis* (Chapel Hill, NC: University of North Carolina Press, 2010), 58. This opportunistic reliance on opposing constitutional theories was common during the antebellum period. As Ames points out, although "[a]lmost every state in the Union at some time declared its own sovereignty . . . on other occasions [they] denounced as treasonable similar declarations by other states": Herman V. Ames, "John C. Calhoun and the Secession Movement of 1850," *Proceedings of the American Antiquarian Society* 28, no. 1 (April 1918): 19.
131. Baker, *The Rescue of Joshua Glover*, 159.
132. "Massachusetts on the Fugitive Slave Law," 6 April 1855, Ames, 288.
133. Schmitt, "Rethinking *Ableman v. Booth*," 1352.
134. Schmitt, "Rethinking *Ableman v. Booth*," 1349.
135. "Address, To the Citizens of Massachusetts," in *A Memoir of Benjamin Robbins Curtis With Some of His Professional and Miscellaneous Writings*, vol. 1, Benjamin R. Curtis (Boston: Little, Brown, & Company, 1879), 329–335. See also George Ticknor Curtis, *Letter to the Editor of the (Philadelphia) Times*, 20 August 1883, in Moore, *The Works of James Buchanan*, vol. 11, 48–49.
136. Morris, *Free Men All*, 208–211.
137. James Buchanan, "Fourth Annual Message," 12.
138. William Henry Seward, "State of the Union," 12 January 1861, in *The Works of William H. Seward*, vol. 4, ed. George E. Baker (New York: Houghton, Mifflin & Company, 1884), 666. Abraham Lincoln, no doubt with his upcoming inauguration in mind and hoping to defuse the secession crisis, was publicly silent on this issue and less forceful about the repeal of state personal liberty laws. In private communication in mid-December 1860, he expressed his agreement with the proposition that "[i]f any of them are in conflict with the fugitive slave clause, or any other part of the constitution, I certainly should be glad of their repeal." However, he expressed his reluctance to publicly say so because

he "could hardly be justified, as a citizen of Illinois," which had no such law, "or as President of the United States, to recommend the repeal of a statute of Vermont, or South Carolina": Abraham Lincoln, "To John A. Gilmer," 15 December 1860, CWAL 4:152.

139. Morris, *Free Men All*, 218. See also Norman L. Rosenberg, "Personal Liberty Laws and Sectional Crisis: 1850-1861," *Civil War History* 17, no. 1 (March 1971): 40-43.
140. "Joseph E. Brown's Secessionist Public Letter, December 7, from Milledgeville," in Freehling and Simpson, *Secession Debated*, 157–158.
141. "Hon. David Clopton to the Governor of Delaware," 1 January 1861, JSCAL, 442.
142. L. E. Crittenden, *A Report on the Debates and Proceedings in the Secret Sessions of the Conference Convention, for Proposing Amendments to the Constitution of the United States, Held at Washington D.C., in February, A.D. 1861* (New York: D. Appleton & Company, 1864), 430.
143. Lincoln, "First Inaugural Address," 264.
144. Lincoln, "First Inaugural Address," 269.
145. "Declaration of the Immediate Causes," 465; "Declaration of the Immediate Causes Which Induce and Justify the Secession of Mississippi from the Federal Union," 87; "A Declaration of the Causes which Impel the State of Texas to Secede from the Federal Union," 64.
146. Earl M. Maltz, *Slavery and the Supreme Court, 1825–1861* (Lawrence, KS: University Press of Kansas, 2009), 301. Federal fugitive slave legislation was enforced during the Civil War in the border slave states that remained with the Union: Stanley W. Campbell, *The Slave Catchers: Enforcement of the Fugitive Slave Law, 1850–1860* (Chapel Hill, NC: University of North Carolina Press, 1968), 192. However, Sections 3 and 4 of the Fugitive Slave law of 1793 and the Fugitive Slave Law of 1850 were repealed on 28 June 1864: "An Act to repeal the Fugitive Slave Act of eighteen hundred and fifty, and all Acts and Parts of Acts for the Rendition of Fugitive Slaves," 28 June 1850, USSL 13:200.
147. Abraham Lincoln, "To John A. Gilmer," 152.
148. Thomas Jefferson, "To Wilson Cary Nicholas," 5 September 1799, PTJ 31:179.
149. James H. Read and Neal Allen, "Living, Dead, and Undead: Nullification Past and Present," in *Nullification and Secession in Modern Constitutional Thought*, ed. Sanford Levinson (Lawrence, KS: University Press of Kansas, 2016), 112.
150. G. Edward White, *Law in American History*, vol. 1, *From the Colonial Years Through the Civil War* (Oxford: Oxford University Press, 2012), 381.

CHAPTER 5: THE FINAL WORD

1. *Texas v. White*, 74 U.S. 700, 724 (1869).
2. *Texas v. White*, 74 U.S. 700, 725 (1869).
3. In 1909, Basil Lanneau Gildersleeve, a classical scholar, grammarian, and former Confederate soldier, wrote that it "was a point of grammatical concord that was at the bottom of the Civil War—'United States are,' said one, 'United States is,' said another:'" Basil Lanneau Gildersleeve, *Hellas and Hesperia or The Vitality of Greek Studies in America* (New York: Henry Holt & Company, 1909), 16. A number of scholars have asserted that the Civil War marked the turning point

during which the Union was no longer referred to in the plural as "these United States," but in the singular as "the United States": James M. McPherson, *Battle Cry Freedom: The Civil War Era* (New York: Oxford University Press, 1988), 859; Gary Wills, *Lincoln at Gettysburg* (New York: Simon & Schuster, 1992), 145; Susan A. Ehrlich, "The Increasing Federalization of Crime," *Arizona State Law Journal* 32, no. 3 (Fall 2000): 831; Jack N. Rakove, "American Federalism: Was There an Original Understanding?" in *The Tenth Amendment and State Sovereignty: Constitutional History and Contemporary Issues*, ed. Mark R. Killenbeck (Lanham, MD: Rowman & Littlefield Publisher, Inc., 2002), 128; Sean Wilentz, *The Rise of American Democracy: Jefferson to Lincoln* (New York: W. W. Norton & Company, 2005), 790; William Michael Treanor, "Taking Text Too Seriously: Modern Textualism, Original Meaning, and the Case of Amar's *Bill of Rights*," *Michigan Law Review* 106, no. 3 (December 2007): 489. However, evidence indicates otherwise. For example, in Supreme Court opinions, the use of the United States as a plural noun predominated until the 1890s, although with slowly declining margins: Minor Myers, "Supreme Court Usage & the Making of an 'Is,'" *The Green Bag: An Entertaining Journal of Law* 11, no. 4 (Winter 2008): 457–465.

4. John C. Calhoun, "A Discourse on the Constitution and Government of the United States," in *Union and Liberty: The Political Philosophy of John C. Calhoun*, ed. Ross M. Lence (Indianapolis, IN: Liberty Fund, 1992), 212.
5. Akhil Reed Amar, *The Words That Made Us: America's Constitutional Conversation, 1760–1840* (New York: Basic Books, 2021), 594.
6. 41 U.S. 539 (1842).
7. 60 U.S. 393 (1857).
8. 41 U.S. 539 (1842).
9. DHRC 10:1507.
10. For accounts of the facts of *Texas v. White*, see William Whatley Pierson, Jr., *Texas versus White: A Study in Legal History* (Durham, NC: The Seeman Printery, 1916), 11–31; John J. Templin, "Texas v. White: A Study on the Merits of the Case," *Southwestern Law Journal* 6, no. 4 (Fall 1952): 467-489.
11. Charles Fairman, *Reconstruction and Reunion, 1864–1888*, part 1 (London: Macmillan Company, 1971), 628.
12. *Texas v. White*, 74 U.S. 700, 725 (1869).
13. *Texas v. White*, 74 U.S. 700, 726 (1869).
14. *Texas v. White*, 74 U.S. 700, 726 (1869).
15. *Texas v. White*, 74 U.S. 700, 727 (1869).
16. *Texas v. White*, 74 U.S. 700, 729 (1869).
17. *Texas v. White*, 74 U.S. 700, 732 (1869).
18. *Texas v. White*, 74 U.S. 700, 733 (1869).
19. *Texas v. White*, 74 U.S. 700, 734 (1869).
20. Pierson, *Texas versus White*, 45.
21. Timothy S. Huebner, *Liberty and Union: The Civil War Era and American Constitutionalism* (Lawrence, KS: University Press of Kansas, 2016), 389. Other favorable assessments of *Texas v. White* include Templin, "Texas v. White," 499; Harold M. Hyman, *The Reconstruction of Justice Salmon P Chase: In re Turner and Texas v. White* (Lawrence, KS: University of Kansas Press, 1997), 140–150.

However, Chase's opinion in *Texas v. White* has not met with universal acclaim. An anonymous reviewer, in 1911, asserted that Chase's opinion "must be pronounced unsatisfactory," given that some of its reasoning was "ludicrous" and because its account of the creation of the Constitution constituted a "venerable perversion of history": Anon., "Texas v. White," *Dickinson Law Review* 15, no. 6 (March 1911): 165, 166, 175. Brandon sees it as being "so riddled with contradiction . . . that it is an unreliable foundation for any coherent principle on whether secession is constitutionally justifiable": Mark E. Brandon, "Secession and Nullification in the Twenty-First Century," *Arkansas Law Review* 67, no. 1 (2014): 99. Elsewhere, Brandon describes Chase's opinion as "fundamentally incoherent and—putting aside questions of bindingness of judicial precedent—of little value": Mark E. Brandon, *Free in the World: American Slavery and Constitutional Failure* (Princeton, NJ: Princeton University Press, 1998), 168. Neff describes Chase's reasoning on the issue of secession as "somewhat opaque": Stephen C. Neff, *Justice in Blue and Gray: A Legal History of the Civil War* (Cambridge, MA: Harvard University Press, 2010), 21.3 Miller and Howell are somewhat more strident than Neff in their description of the case as one based upon "patently fallacious logic": Arthur S. Miller and Ronald F. Howell, "Interposition, Nullification and the Delicate Division of Power in a Federal System," *Journal of Public Law* 5, no. 1 (1956): 3.3 Currie, in dismissing the authority of *Texas v. White*, writes that "its reasoning was superficial at best": David P. Currie, "Prolegomena for a Sampler, Extrajudicial Interpretation of the Constitution, 1789–1861," in *Congress and the Constitution*, eds. Neal Devins and Keith E. Whittington (Durham. NC: Duke University Press, 2005), 28. Elsewhere, he writes that Chase's opinion is "hardly . . . an adequate treatment of an issue in which reasonable people had differed to the point of war" and one which was reached "without serious consideration of opposing arguments": David P. Currie, "The Constitution in the Supreme Court: Civil War and Reconstruction, 1865–1873," *University of Chicago Law Review* 51, no. 1 (Winter 1984): 163, 168. On the little, but varied, public attention given to the decision in *Texas v. White*, see Cynthia Nicoletti, *Secession on Trial: The Treason Prosecution of Jefferson Davis* (New York: Cambridge University Press, 2018), 318–321.

22. *Texas v. White*, 74 U.S. 700, 724–725 (1869).
23. *Texas v. White*, 74 U.S. 700, 725–726 (1869).
24. *Texas v. White*, 74 U.S. 700, 725 (1869). In a speech in November 1860, on the eve of the 1860 elections, Chase was adamant in his view that no state could secede from the Union: Walter Stahr, *Salmon P. Chase: Lincoln's Vital Rival* (New York: Simon & Schuster, 2021), 309.
25. G. Edward White, "Recovering the Legal History of the Confederacy," *Washington and Lee Law Review* 68, no. 2 (Spring 2011): 482.
26. Akhil Reed Amar, *The Law of the Land: A Grand Tour of Our Constitutional Republic* (New York: Basic Books, 2015), 15.
27. Amar, *Law of the Land*, 15. Notwithstanding his recognition of weaknesses in Lincoln's arguments, Amar suggests that Lincoln's arguments against secession contributed to establishing him as "the most significant constitutional interpreter and decision-maker of the past two centuries" and that "[n]o one else

in America's history, with the exception of George Washington, comes close" (p. 3).

28. *The State of Texas v. White & Chiles*, 25 Texas Reports (Supplement) 465, 520–539 (1869).
29. *The State of Texas v. White & Chiles*, 25 Texas Reports (Supplement) 465, 499–500 (1869). See also Walter Lee Brown, *A Life of Albert Pike* (Fayetteville, AR: University of Arkansas Press, 1997), 445.
30. Brandon, *Free in the World*, 173–174.
31. James Madison, "To Lafayette," 25 November 1820, PJMRS 2:159.
32. The only other instance of part of a state being admitted to the Union as a separate state is that West Virginia out of Virginia in 1863.
33. *Texas v. White*, 74 U.S. 700, 726 (1869).
34. Herman Belz, "Deep-conviction Jurisprudence and *Texas v. White*: A Comment on G. Edward White's Historicist Interpretation of Chief Justice Chase," *Northern Kentucky Law Review* 21, no. 1 (Fall 1993): 129.
35. *Texas v. White*, 74 U.S. 700, 715 (1869).
36. Pierson, *Texas versus White*," 58.
37. Abraham Lincoln, "First Inaugural Address," 4 March 1861, CWAL 4:269.
38. Lincoln, "First Inaugural Address," 270.
39. Abraham Lincoln, "Message to Congress in Special Session," 4 July 1861, CWAL 4:43.3
40. Lincoln, "Message to Congress," 435.
41. Brandon, *Free in the World*, 178.
42. Abraham Lincoln, "To Thurlow Weed," 17 December 1860, CWAL 4:154.
43. Thomas N. Bonner, "Horace Greeley and the Secession Movement, 1860–1861," *Mississippi Valley Historical Review* 38, no. 3 (December 1951): 428–429.
44. Brandon, *Free in the World*, 179.
45. Lincoln, "First Inaugural Address," 269.
46. Michael Burlingame, ed., *With Lincoln in the White House: Letters, Memoranda, and Other Writings of John G Nicolay, 1860–1865* (Carbondale and Edwardsville, IL: Southern Illinois University Press, 2000), 17.
47. Lincoln, "Message to Congress in Special Session," 437.
48. A variation of the constitutional amendment process to regulate secession was proposals by three Representatives during the great secession winter of 1860–1861. Each of them proposed an amendment to the Constitution that would prohibit secession unless achieved by consent. The amendment proposed by Daniel E. Sickles (Democrat) of New York would have required the approval of the president and "ratification by two thirds of the Senators present": CG, 36th Congress, 2nd Session, 107. That of Pennsylvania's Thomas B. Florence (Democrat) would have required "the consent of three fourths of all the States": CG, 36th Congress, 2nd Session, 598. And that of Connecticut's Orris S. Ferry (Republican) would have required "the consent of two thirds of both Houses of Congress, the approval of the President, and the consent of all the States": CG, 36th Congress, 2nd Session, 854.
49. *Reference re: Secession of Quebec* [1998] 2 S.C.R. 217, 240.
50. *Reference re: Secession of Quebec* [1998] 2 S.C.R. 217, 240.
51. *Reference re: Secession of Quebec* [1998] 2 S.C.R. 217, 265.

52. *Reference re: Secession of Quebec* [1998] 2 S.C.R. 217, 265, 294.
53. *Reference re: Secession of Quebec* [1998] 2 S.C.R. 217, 266.
54. *Reference re: Secession of Quebec* [1998] 2 S.C.R. 217, 263, 271, 27.3
55. *Reference re: Secession of Quebec* [1998] 2 S.C.R. 217, 274–275.
56. Douglas G. Smith, "An Analysis of Two Federal Structures: The Articles of Confederation and the Constitution," *San Diego Law Review* 34, no. 1 (Winter 1997): 337–338.
57. Akhil Reed Amar, "Abraham Lincoln and the American Union," 2001, no. 5 (2001): 1115.
58. Lincoln, "First Inaugural Address," 270.
59. In December 2021, a report, published by the Brookings Institution, stated that opinion polls in 2020 revealed that approximately 40 percent of likely voters in the forthcoming 2020 elections supported the secession of their state if their favored candidate lost the election. Furthermore, a poll conducted in July 2021 revealed that 41 percent of supporters of President Joseph Biden and 52 percent of supporters of former President Donald Trump agreed, to some degree, "that it's time to split the country": William G. Gale and Darrell M. West, "How seriously should we take talk of U.S. state secession," 13 December 2021, https://www.brookings.edu/blog/fixgov/2021/12/13/how-seriously-should-we-take-talk-of-us-state-secession/.
60. 44 U.S. 212, 230 (1845), (see also 223–224).
61. *The State of Texas v. White & Chiles*, 25 Texas Reports (Supplement) 465, 488 (1869).
62. *The State of Texas v. White & Chiles*, 25 Texas Reports (Supplement) 465, 500 (1869).
63. Pierson, *Texas versus White*," 34.
64. "An Act to provide for the more efficient Government of the Rebel States," Section 6, 2 March 1867, USSL 14:429.
65. *The State of Texas v. White & Chiles*, 25 Texas Reports (Supplement) 465, 533 (1869).
66. Brown, *A Life of Albert Pike*, 446.
67. *Texas v. White*, 74 U.S. 700, 737 (1869).
68. *Texas v. White*, 74 U.S. 700, 738–739 (1869).
69. *Texas v. White*, 74 U.S. 700, 737 (1869).
70. Nicoletti, *Secession on Trial*, 317.
71. Brown, *A Life of Albert Pike*, 446.
72. Quoted in Nicoletti, *Secession on Trial*, 321.
73. See for example, *Thomas v. City of Richmond*, 79 U.S. 349, 357–358 (1871); *White v. Hart*, 80 U.S. 646, 650–651 (1871); *Sprott v. United States*, 87 U.S. 459, 464–465 (1874); *Dewing v. Perdicaries*, 96 U.S. 193, 195 (1877); *Keith v. Clark*, 97 U.S. 454, 461–462 (1878); *Daniels v. Tearney*, 102 U.S. 415, 418 (1880); *Poindexter v. Greenhow*, 114 U.S. 270, 290–291 (1885); *United States v. Louisiana*, 363 U.S. 121, 131–132 (1960); *Gregory v. Ashcroft*, 501 U.S. 452, 457 (1991); *New York v. United States*, 505 U.S. 144, 162 (1992). In *Hickman v. Jones*, Justice Swayne, in delivering the opinion of the Court, but without citing *Texas v. White*, said: "The union of the States for all the purposes of the Constitution, is as perfect and indissoluble as the union of the integral parts of the States

themselves; and nothing but revolutionary violence can, in either case, destroy the ties which hold the parts together": *Hickman v. Jones*, 76 U.S. 197, 200 (1869).

74. See, for example, Sanford Levinson, Jack M. Balkin, Akhil Reed Amar, Reva B. Siegel, and Christina M. Rodriguez, eds., *Processes of Constitutional Decision-making: Cases and Materials*, 8th ed. (Frederick, MD: Aspen Publishing, 2022), 310.
75. Charles E. Larsen, "Nationalism and States' Rights in Commentaries on the Constitution After the Civil War," *American Journal of Legal History* 3, no. 4 (October 1959): 363–364.
76. Nicoletti, *Secession on Trial*, 324. Buchheit writes in a similar vein when he states that "the issue [of secession] was decided upon the battlefields of the American Civil War . . . [and] was given judicial recognition at the war's end [in *Texas v. White*]": Lee C. Buchheit, *Secession: The Legitimacy of Self-Determination* (New Haven, CT: Yale University Press, 1978), 111–112. Furthermore, as Nicoletti also points out, "if the verdict in [*Texas v. White*] had not matched the results of the war," Americans would have been confronted with having to "acknowledge that war was ultimately more powerful than law": Nicoletti, *Secession on Trial*, 325.
77. O. W. Holmes, Jr., *The Common Law* (Boston: Little, Brown, and Company, 1881), 1–2.
78. Cass R. Sunstein, "Constitutionalism and Secession," *University of Chicago Law Review* 58, no. 2 (Spring 1991) 633 (n. 33).
79. Sanford Levinson, "The 21st Century Rediscovery of Nullification and Secession in American Political Rhetoric: Frivolousness Incarnate, or Serious Arguments to Be Wrestled With?" in *Nullification and Secession in Modern Constitutional Thought*, ed. Sanford Levinson (Lawrence, KS: University Press of Kansas, 2016), 37–38.
80. See for example F. H. Buckley, *American Secession: The Looming Threat of a National Breakup* (New York: Encounter Books, 2020); David French, *Divided We Fall: America's Secession Threat and How to Restore our Nation* (New York: St Martin's Press, 2020); Richard Kreitner, *Break It Up: Secession, Division, and The Secret History of America's Imperfect Union* (New York: Little, Brown & Company, 2020).
81. *Kohlhaas v. Alaska*, 147 P. 3d. 714, 719–720 (2006).
82. *Kohlhaas v. Alaska*, 147 P. 3d. 714, 716 (2006).
83. Following the Alaskan Supreme Court decision, in 2007, the AIP submitted another proposal for a referendum on a reworded question. The proposal proceeded on the basis that, as held in *Kohlhaas v. Alaska*, "secession was clearly unconstitutional." The proposed question was whether or not Alaska should "seek changes in existing law and Constitutional provisions to authorize it to obtain independence from the United States of America": *Kohlhaas v. Alaska*, 223 P. 3d. 105, 108 (2010). The Alaskan Supreme Court again ruled that a popular referendum on this question could not proceed. The court's reasoning was based upon two possible interpretations of the question. The court held that if the question was, in substance, the same as the 2003 proposed question, then, on the basis of Lincoln's First Inaugural Address and the decision in *Texas v.*

White, it could not be put to a popular vote for the reason that "secession is clearly unconstitutional": *Kohlhaas v. Alaska*, 223 P. 3d. 105, 110, 113 (2010). However, if the question was one that sought a change to Alaska's Constitution, it could not be put to a popular vote because a referendum was not a means by which amendments to its Constitution could be initiated: *Kohlhaas v. Alaska*, 223 P. 3d. 105, 111–113 (2010).

84. Sunstein, "Constitutionalism and Secession," 633.
85. Daniel Farber, "The Fourteenth Amendment and the Unconstitutionality of Secession," *Akron Law Review* 45, no. 2 (2012): 480–483.
86. CG, 39th Congress, 1st Session, 2918.
87. CG, 39th Congress, 1st Session, 2918.
88. Tennessee was excluded from this process because it had already been readmitted to the Union on 24 July 1866, following its ratification of the Thirteenth and Fourteenth Amendments to the Constitution, on 7 April 1865 and 18 July 1866 respectively: Huebner, *Liberty and Union*, 361, 370.
89. Mark A. Graber, "Constructing Constitutional Politics: the Reconstruction Strategy for Protecting Rights," 2013, https://digitalcommons.law.umaryland.edu/fac_pubs/1390/, 5. See also Levinson et. al, *Processes of Constitutional Decisionmaking*, 366–367.
90. Not even Amar, who confesses to having "long been obsessed by the secession question," raises Section 3 as an argument against unilateral secession: Akhil Reed Amar, *The Constitution Today: Timeless Lessons for the Issues of Our Era* (New York: Basic Books, 2016, 402.
91. James MacGregor Burns, *The Vineyard of Liberty: The American Experiment* (New York: Alfred A. Knopf, 1991), 3.3
92. It has often been argued that the charge of hypocrisy against the founding generation is unwarranted and simply a case of presentism, that is, analyzing past events in terms of contemporary sensibilities. For example, Alf J. Mapp Jr. argues that Thomas Jefferson cannot be charged with hypocrisy in relation to slavery because it would be "extremely naive for us to judge him in the context of our time": quoted in Paul Finkelman, "Thomas Jefferson and Antislavery: The Myth Goes On," *Virginia Magazine of History and Biography* 102, no. 2 (April 1994): 197. However, to label men such as Jefferson as hypocrites is not to engage in presentism because they recognized and conceded that slavery was an immoral institution, but nevertheless chose to continue to participate in, and profit from, the practice of race-based human bondage.
93. Edward J. Larson, *American Inheritance: Liberty and Slavery in the Birth of a Nation, 1765-1795* (New York: W. W. Norton & Company, 2023), 175.
94. Joseph J. Ellis, *The Cause: The American Revolution and its Discontents, 1773–1783* (New York: Liveright Publishing Corporation, 2021), 87.
95. W. E. Burghardt Du Bois, *Black Reconstruction: An Essay Toward a History of the Part Which Black Folk Played in the Attempt to Reconstruct Democracy in America*, 1860–1880 (New York: Harcourt Brace & Company, 1935), 83.
96. Mark Antony, "*Independent Chronicle*," 10 January 1788, DHRC 5:676.
97. John Adams to Jeremy Belknap, 22 October 1795, https://founders.archives.gov/documents/Adams/99–02–02–1696.

98. Noah Feldman, *The Broken Constitution: Lincoln, Slavery, and the Founding of America* (New York: Farrar, Straus & Giroux, 2021), 4.
99. Feldman, *The Broken Constitution*, 7.
100. Jonathan B. Crider, "De Bow's Revolution: The Memory of the American Revolution on the Politics of the Sectional Crisis, 1850-1861," *American Nineteenth Century History* 10, no. 3 (September 2009): 321-322.
101. William Lloyd Garrison, "The United States Constitution," in *Selections from the Writings and Speeches of William Lloyd Garrison* (Boston: R. F. Wallcut, 1852), 308.
102. William J. Cooper Jr., *Jefferson Davis: American* (New York: Vintage Books, 2000), 705.
103. DHRC 23:2290, 2555–2556.
104. "From Charles Thomson," 2 November 1785, PTJ 9:9.
105. Abraham Lincoln, "Emancipation Proclamation," 1 January 1863, CWAL 6:28–30.
106. Lincoln, "Emancipation Proclamation," 29–30.
107. Abraham Lincoln, "Proclamation Admitting West Virginia into the Union," 20 April 1863, CWAL 6:181.
108. Delaware, Kentucky, Maryland, and Missouri.
109. Although Douglass had long supported voting rights for women, he was adamant that suffrage rights for African American men was a more important issue: David W. Blight, *Frederick Douglass: Prophet of Freedom* (New York: Simon & Schuster, 2018), 196–197, 488–493.
110. Frederick Douglass, "The Mission of the War," 13 January 1864, in *Frederick Douglass: Selected Speeches and Writings*, ed. Philip S. Foner (Chicago: Lawrence Hill Books, 1999), 626. See also Blight, *Frederick Douglass*, 454–455, 480–481.
111. Feldman, *The Broken Constitution*, 319.
112. James M. McPherson, *Abraham Lincoln and the Second American Revolution* (New York: Oxford University Press, 1991, 22; Sean Wilentz, *The Rise of American Democracy: Jefferson to Lincoln* (New York: W. W. Norton & Company, 2005), 790; David J. Bodenhamer, *The Revolutionary Constitution* (Oxford: Oxford University Press, 2012), 172; Gregory P. Downs, *The Second American Revolution: The Civil War-Era Struggle over Cuba and the Rebirth of the American Republic* (Chapel Hill, NC: University of North Carolina Press, 2019), 4; Kermit Roosevelt III, *The Nation That Never Was: Reconstructing America's Story* (Chicago: University of Chicago Press, 2022), 153. Others refers to "the second founding": Eric Foner, *The Second Founding: How the Civil War and Reconstruction Remade the Constitution* (New York: W. W. Norton & Company, 2019), xx; James W. Fox Jr., "The Constitution of Black Abolitionism: Reframing the Second Founding," *University of Pennsylvania Journal of Constitutional Law* 23, no. 2 (April 2021) 23(2) 267–350; Joseph Fishkin and William E. Forbath, *The Anti-Oligarchy Constitution: Reconstructing the Economic Foundations of American Democracy* (Cambridge, MA: Harvard University Press, 2022), 109. Morone refers to "a second American founding": James A. Morone, *Republic of Wrath: How American Politics Turned Tribal, from George Washington to Donald Trump* (New York: Basic

Books, 2020), 96. In the Senate, on 19 May 1870, Senator Carl Schurz from Missouri said that "the Republic has passed through a revolutionary process of tremendous significance" and that "the Constitution . . . has been changed in some essential points" and that "that change does amount to great revolution": CG, 41st Congress, 2nd Session, 3607. Wood makes, in substance, the same statement when he writes that the abolition of slavery at the end of the Civil War meant that the "Northern success in the Civil War was the culmination of the [American] Revolution": Gordon S. Wood, "The Revolutionary Origins of the Civil War," *Northwestern University Law* 114, no. 2 (2019): 541. Feldman puts it another way when he writes that "the Constitution, drafted in 1787 and ratified over the next two years, had a fundamentally different moral character from the post-Civil War Constitution": Feldman, *The Broken Constitution*, 7. To similar effect Justice Thurgood Marshall, writing extrajudicially on the occasion of the Bicentennial of the Constitution, wrote as follows: "While the Union survived the Civil War, the Constitution did not. In its place arose as new, more promising basis for justice and equality, the fourteenth amendment, ensuring protection of the life, liberty, and property of all persons against deprivations without due process and guaranteeing equal protection of the laws": The Honorable Thurgood Marshall, "The Constitution's Bicentennial: Commemorating the Wrong Document?" *Vanderbilt Law Review* 40, no. 6 (November 1987): 1340–1341.

113. Thomas Paine, *Rights of Man—Common Sense* (New York: Alfred A. Knopf, 1994), 265.
114. Douglass, "The Mission of the War," 628.
115. Paul Finkelman, "The Founders and Slavery: Little Ventured, Little Gained," *Yale Journal of Law and the Humanities* 13, no. 2 (Summer 2001): 417. Elsewhere, Finkleman reiterated this as follows: "We have come a long way since 1775, when slavery was legal in all the thirteen new states and equality was unknown. But we are not there yet": Paul Finkelman, "The First Civil Rights Movement: Black Rights in the Age of the Revolution and Chief Justice Taney's Originalism in *Dred Scott*," *University of Pennsylvania Journal of Constitutional La*w 24, no. 3 (June 2022): 728. The historian Eric Foner, writing in 2005, states that "[n]o one can argue, at the dawn of the twenty-first century, that America's long struggle with racial inequality has ended or that the contradictions created by the existence of slavery in a country that considers itself an embodiment of freedom have been fully resolved": Eric Foner, *Forever Free: The Story of Emancipation and Reconstruction* (New York: Alfred A. Knopf, 2005), xix.
116. "Gen. Milley's Message to the National Defense University Class of 2020," 11 June 2020, https://www.facebook.com/notes/2524982331096064/.

SELECTED BIBLIOGRAPHY

PRIMARY SOURCES

Abbot, W. W., ed. *The Papers of George Washington: Revolutionary War Series*, vols. 2–3, and 5. Charlottesville, VA: University of Virginia Press, 1987–1993.

Abbot, W. W., ed. *The Papers of George Washington: Confederation Series*, vols. 2 and 4–6. Charlottesville, VA: University of Virginia Press, 1987–1997.

Adams, Charles Francis, ed. *The Works of John Adams, Second President of the United States*, vols. 2, 9, and 10. Boston: Little, Brown & Co., 1850–1856.

Adams, Charles Francis, ed. *Memoirs of John Quincy Adams, Comprising Portions of His Diary from 1795 to 1848*, vols. 5, 8–9, and 11–12. Philadelphia: J. B. Lippincott & Co., 1875–1877.

Ames, Herman V., ed. *State Documents on Federal Relations: The States and the United States*. Philadelphia: University of Pennsylvania, 1911.

Annals of Congress: Debates and Proceedings, 1789–1824. http://memory.loc.gov/ammem/amlaw/lwaclink.html.

Baker, George E., ed. *The Works of William H. Seward*, vol. 4. Boston: Houghton, Mifflin & Company, 1884.

Ball, Terence, ed. *Hamilton, Madison, and Jay: The Federalist with Letters of "Brutus."* Cambridge, UK: Cambridge University Press, 2003.

Basler, Roy P., ed. *The Collected Works of Abraham Lincoln*, vols.1–8. New Brunswick, NJ: Rutgers University Press, 1953.

Belz, Herman, ed. *The Webster-Hayne Debate on the Nature of the Union: Selected Documents*. Indianapolis, IN: Liberty Fund, 2000.

Boyd, Julian P., et al., eds. *The Papers of Thomas Jefferson*, vols. 1–2, 6–7, 9–12, and 30–31. Princeton, NJ: Princeton University Press, 1950–2004.

Cain, William E., ed., *William Lloyd Garrison and the Fight Against Slavery: Selections from The Liberator*. Boston: Bedford/St Martin's, 1995.

Carter, Clarence Edwin, ed. *The Territorial Papers of the United States*, vols. 2 and 4. Washington: Government Printing Office, 1934–1936.

Coles, Edward. *History of the Ordinance of 1787*. Philadelphia: Historical Society of Pennsylvania, 1856.

Congressional Globe: Debates and Proceedings, 1833–1873. https://memory.loc.gov/ammem/amlaw/lwcglink.html.

Davis, Jefferson. *The Rise and Fall of the Confederate Government*, vols. 1–2. New York: D. Appleton & Company, 1881.

Documentary History of the Constitution of the United States of America, 1787–1870, Vol. 2. Washington: Department of State, 1894.

Elliot, Jonathan, ed. *The Debates in the Several State Conventions on the Adoption of the Federal Constitution as Recommended by the General Convention at Philadelphia in 1787*, vols. 1–4. Washington: Published Under the Sanction of Congress, 1836.

Farrand, Max, ed. *The Records of the Federal Convention of 1787, Revised Edition in Four Volumes*, vols. 1–4. New Haven, CT: Yale University Press, 1966.

Fisher, Sidney George. *The Trial of the Constitution*. Philadelphia: J. B. Lippincott & Co., 1862.

Forbes, Robert Pierce, ed. *Notes on the State of Virginia: An Annotated Edition*. New Haven, CT: Yale University Press, 2022.

Force, Peter, ed. *American Archives: Fourth Series*, vols. 5–6. Washington: M. St. Clair Clarke and Peter Force, 1844–1846.

Foner, Philip S., ed. *Frederick Douglass: Selected Speeches and Writings*. Chicago: Lawrence Hill Books, 1999.

Freehling, William W. and Craig M. Simpson, eds. *Secession Debated, Georgia's Showdown in 1860*. New York: Oxford University Press, 1992.

Gigantino II, James J., ed. *Slavery and Secession in Arkansas: A Documentary History*. Fayettville, AR: University of Arkansas Press, 2015.

Hall, Mark David, ed. *Collected Works of Roger Sherman*. Indianapolis, IN: Liberty Fund, 2016,

Hunt, Gaillard, ed. *The Writings of James Madison*, vols. 2, 6, and 9. New York: G. P. Putnam's Sons, 1901–1910.

Hutchinson, William T., et al., eds. *The Papers of James Madison*, vols. 1, 8–12, and 17, Charlottesville, VA: University of Virginia Press, 1962–1991.

Hutson, James H. ed. *Supplement to Max Farrand's The Records of the Federal Convention of 1787*. New Haven, CT: Yale University Press, 1987.

Jensen, Merrill, et al., eds. *The Documentary History of the Ratification of the Constitution: The Ratification of the Constitution by the States*, vols. 2, 5, 8–10 and 22–23. Madison, WI: State Historical Society of Wisconsin, 1976–2009.

Journal of Both Sessions of the Convention of the State of Arkansas Which were Begun and Held in the Capital, in the City of Little Rock. Little Rock, AR: Johnson & Yerkes, State Printers, 1861.

Journal of the Convention of South Carolina; Together With The Resolution and Ordinance. Columbia, SC: Johnston & Cavis, Printers to the Convention, 1852.

Journal of the Convention of the People of North Carolina, Held on the 20th day of May, A.D., 1861. Raleigh, NC: J .W. Syme, 1862.

Journal of the Convention of the People of South Carolina, Held in 1860, 1861 and 1862, Together With The Ordinances, Reports, Resolutions, etc., Columbia, SC: R. W. Gibbes, Printer to the Convention, 1862.

Journal of the Proceedings of the Convention of the People of Florida Begun and Held at the Capitol in the City of Tallahassee on Thursday, January 3, A.D. 1861. Tallahassee, FL: Dyke & Carlisle, 1861.

Journal of the Public and Secret Proceedings of the Convention of the People of Georgia Held in Milledgeville and Savannah in 1861, Together With the Ordinances Adopted. Milledgeville, GA: Boughton, Nisbet & Barnes, 1861.

Journal of the State Convention and Ordinances and Resolutions Adopted in January, 1861, With An Appendix. Jackson, MS: E. Barkdale, State Printer, 1861.

Journals of the Continental Congress 1774–1789, vols. 1, 4–5, 8, 26–29, and 32–34, Washington: Government Printing Office, 1904–1937.

Looney, J. Jefferson, ed. *The Papers of Thomas Jefferson: Retirement Series*, vols. 7, and 15–16. Princeton, NJ: Princeton University Press, 2010–1019.

Lence, Ross M., ed. *Union and Liberty: The Political Philosophy of John C Calhoun.* Indianapolis, IN: Liberty Fund, 1992.

Letters and Other Writings of James Madison, Fourth President of the United States, vols. 3–4. Philadelphia: J. B. Lippincott & Co., 1865–1867.

Mattern, David B., et al., eds. *The Papers of James Madison: Retirement Series*, vols. 1–3. Charlottesville, VA: University of Virginia Press, 2009–2016.

Moore, Frank, ed. *The Rebellion Record: A Diary of American Events, with Documents, Narratives, Illustrative Incidents, Poetry, etc*, vol. 1. New York: G. P. Putnam, 1861.

Official Journal of the Proceedings of the Convention of the State of Louisiana. New Orleans, LA: J. O. Nixon, Printer to the State Convention, 1861.

Orations and Speeches on Various Occasions by Edward Everett, vol.4. Boston: Little, Brown, & Company, 1879.

Pitcaithley, Dwight T., ed. *The US Constitution and Secession: A Documentary Anthology of Slavery and Supremacy.* Lawrence, KS: University Press of Kansas, 2018.

Register of Debates: Debates and Proceedings, 1824–1837. http://memory.loc.gov/ammem/amlaw/lwrdlink.html.

Reese, George H., ed. *Proceedings of the Virginia State Convention of 1861*, 4 vols. Richmond, VA: Virginia State Library, 1965.

Rowland, Dunbar, ed. *Jefferson Davis, Constitutionalist: His Letters, Papers and Speeches*, vols. 2 and 5. Jackson, MS: Mississippi Department of Archives & History, 1923.

Selections from the Writings and Speeches of William Lloyd Garrison. Boston: R. F. Wallcut, 1852.

Senate Journal of the Extra Session of the Thirty-Third General Assembly of the State of Tennessee Which Convened at Nashville, on the First Monday in January A.D. 1861. Nashville, TN: J. O. Griffith & Company, Public Printers, 1861.

Senate Journal of the Second Extra Session of the Thirty-Third General Assembly of the State of Tennessee Which Convened at Nashville on Thursday, the 25th Day of April, A.D. 1861. Nashville, TN: J. O. Griffith & Company, Public Printers, 1861.

Smith, Paul H. ed. *Letters of Delegates to Congress, 1774–1789*, vols. 1, 4, and 22–25, Washington: Library of Congress, 1976–1996.

Smith, William R., ed. *The History and Debates of the Convention of the People of Alabama.* Tuscaloosa, AL: White, Pfister & Co., 1861.

Stephens, Alexander H, *A Constitutional View of the Late War Between the States: Its Causes, Character, Conduct and Results*, vols. 1–2, Philadelphia: National Publishing Company, 1885.

Story, Joseph. *Commentaries on the Constitution of the United States With a Preliminary Review of the Constitutional History of the Colonies and States, Before the Adoption of the Constitution*, 3 vols. Boston: Hilliard, Gray, & Company, 1833.

Syrett, Harold C., ed. *The Papers of Alexander Hamilton*, vols. 2 and 4–5. New York: Columbia University Press, 1961–1962.

Tansill, Charles C. ed. *Documents Illustrative of the Formation of the Union of the American States.* Washington: Government Printing Office, 1927.

The Constitution of the State of Texas, as Amended in 1861. The Constitution of the

Confederate States of America. The Ordinances of the Texas Convention: and An Address to the People of Texas. Austin, TX: Printed by Order of the Convention & Senate, 1861.

Thorpe, Francis Newton, ed. *The Federal and State Constitutions, Colonial Charters, and Other Organic Laws of the States, Territories, and Colonies Now or Heretofore Forming the United States of America*, 7 vols. Washington: Government Printing Office, 1909.

de Tocqueville, Alexis. *Democracy in America*, vol. 1, trans. Francis Bowen. New York: Everyman's Library, 1994.

United States Statutes at Large, vols. 1–15, 1850–1869. https://memory.loc.gov/ammem/amlaw/lwsllink.html

Wilson, Clyde N. et.al. eds. *The Papers of John C. Calhoun*, vols. 1010–12, 14, and 24–27. Columbia, SC: University of South Carolina Press, 1977–2003.

Wiltse, Charles M. and Michael J. Birkner, eds. *The Papers of Daniel Webster: Correspondence*, vols. 1 and 7. Hanover, NH: University Press of New England, 1974–1986.

Wiltse, Charles M., ed. *The Papers of Daniel Webster: Speeches and Formal Writings*, vols. 1–2, Hanover, NH: University Press of New England, 1986–1988.

Winkler, Ernest William, ed. *Journal of the Secession Convention of Texas 1861*. Austin, TX: Austin Printing Co, 1912.

CASES

Ableman v. Booth, 62 U.S. 506 (1859).

Barron v. Mayor and City Council of Baltimore, 32 U.S. 243 (1833).

Calder v. Bull, 3 U.S. 386 (1798).

Chisholm v. Georgia, 2 U.S. 419 (1793).

Dred Scott v. Sandford, 60 U.S. 393 (1857).

Fletcher v. Peck, 10 U.S. 87 (1810).

Gibbons v. Ogden, 22 U.S. 1 (1824).

Groves v. Slaughter, 40 U.S. 449 (1841).

Jones v. Van Zandt, 46 U.S. 215 (1847).

Kentucky v. Dennison, 65 U.S. 66 (1861).

Kohlhaas v. Alaska, 147 P. 3d. 714 (2006).

Kohlhaas v. Alaska, 223 P. 3d. 105 (2010).

Lane County v. Oregon, 74 U.S. 71 (1869).

Martin v. Hunter's Lessee, 14 U.S. 304 (1816).

McCulloch v. Maryland, 17 U.S. 316 (1819).

McIlvaine v. Coxe's Lessee, 8 U.S. 209 (1808).

Moore v. Illinois, 55 U.S. 13 (1852).

Penhallow v. Doane, 3 U.S. 54 (1795).

Pollard's Lessee v. Hagan, 44 U.S. 212 (1845).

Prigg v. Pennsylvania, 41 U.S. 539 (1842).

Reference re: Secession of Quebec [1998] 2 S.C.R. 217.

Shortridge v. Macon, 22 Fed. Cas. 20 (1867).

Somerset v. Stewart (1772) 98 E.R. 499.

Strader v. Graham, 51 U.S. 82 (1851).

Texas v. White, 74 U.S. 700 (1869).

The State of Texas v. White & Chiles, 25 Texas Reports (Supplement) 465 (1869).
Ware v. Hylton, 3 U.S. 199 (1796).
Williams v. Bruffy, 96 U.S. 176 (1877).

SECONDARY SOURCES

Adams, Henry. *History of the United States of America During the Administrations of James Madison*. New York: Library of America, 1986.

Adams, Henry. *History of the United States of America During the Administrations of Thomas Jefferson*. New York: Library of America, 1986.

Adams, William Howard. *Gouverneur Morris: An Independent Life*. New Haven, CT: Yale University Press, 2003.

Alexander, Robert. *The Northwest Ordinance: Constitutional Politics and the Theft of Native Land*. Jefferson, NC: McFarland & Company, 2017.

Allen, Michael. "The Mississippi River Debate, 1785–1787." *Tennessee Historical Quarterly* 36, no. 4 (Winter 1977): 447–467.

Alpaugh, Micah. *Friends of Freedom: The Rise of Social Movements in the Age of Atlantic Revolutions*. Cambridge, UK: Cambridge University Press, 2022.

Amar, Akhil Reed. "Of Sovereignty and Federalism." *Yale Law Journal* 96, no. 7 (June 1987): 1425–1520.

Amar, Akhil Reed. "Philadelphia Revisited: Amending the Constitution Outside Article V." *University of Chicago Law Review* 55, no. 4 (Autumn 1988): 1043–1104.

Amar, Akhil Reed. "Some New World Lessons for the Old World." *University of Chicago Law Review* 58, no. 2 (Spring 1991): 483–510.

Amar, Akhil Reed. "The Consent of the Governed: Constitutional Amendment Outside Article V." *Columbia Law Review* 94, no. 2 (March 1994): 457–508.

Amar, Akhil Reed. "Abraham Lincoln and the American Union." *University of Illinois Law Review* [2001], no. 5 (2001): 1109–1134.

Amar, Akhil Reed. *America's Constitution: A Biography*. New York: Random House, 2005.

Amar, Akhil Reed. *America's Unwritten Constitution: The Precedents and Principles We Live By*. New York: Basic Books, 2012.

Amar, Akhil Reed. *The Law of the Land: A Grand Tour of Our Constitutional Republic*. New York: Basic Books, 2015.

Amar, Akhil Reed. *The Constitution Today: Timeless Lessons for the Issues of Our Era*. New York: Basic Books, 2016.

Amar, Akhil Reed. "Electoral College Reform, Lincoln-Style." *Northwestern University Law Review* 112, no. 1 (2017): 63–82.

Amar, Akhil Reed. *The Words That Made Us: America's Constitutional Conversation, 1760–1840*. New York: Basic Books, 2021.

Anastaplo, George. *Reflections on Slavery and the Constitution*. Lanham, MD: Lexington Books, 2012.

Anderson, Lawrence M. *Federalism, Secession and the American State: Divided, We Secede*. New York: Routledge, 2013.

Baker, H. Robert. *Prigg v. Pennsylvania: Slavery, the Supreme Court, and the Ambivalent Constitution*. Lawrence, KS: University of Kansas Press, 2012.

Banner Jr., James M. *To the Hartford Convention: The Federalists and the Origins of Party Politics in Massachusetts, 1789–1815*. New York: Alfred A. Knopf, 1970.

Barksdale, Kevin T. "The Spanish Conspiracy on the Trans-Appalachian Borderlands, 1786–1789." *Journal of Appalachian Studies* 12, nos. 1–2 (Spring 2007): 96–123.

Bauer, Elizabeth Kelley. *Commentaries on the Constitution, 1790–1860*. New York: Russell & Russell Inc., 1965.

Beach, Jr., Edward C. "'The Good of Each of the Parts': A Collective Action Understanding of the Treaty Clause." *Duke Journal of Constitutional Law and Public Policy* 16 (2021): 279–305.

Beckert, Sven. *Empire of Cotton: A New History of Global Capitalism*. London: Penguin Books, 2015.

Beeman, Richard. *Plain, Honest Men: The Making of the American Constitution*. New York: Random House, 2009.

Belz, Herman. "Deep-conviction Jurisprudence and *Texas v. White*: A Comment on G Edward White's Historicist Interpretation of Chief Justice Chase." *Northern Kentucky Law Review* 21, no. 1 (Fall 1993): 117–132.

Bestor, Arthur. "The American Civil War as a Constitutional Crisis." *The American Historical Review* 69, no. 2 (January 1964): 327–352.

Bird, Wendell. "Reassessing Responses to the Virginia and Kentucky Resolutions: New Evidence from the Tennessee and Georgia Resolutions and from Other States." *Journal of the Early Republic* 35, no. 4 (Winter 2015): 519–551.

Blackett, R. J. M. *The Captive's Quest for Freedom: Fugitive Slaves, the 1850 Fugitive Slave Law, and the Politics of Slavery*. New York: Cambridge University Press, 2018.

Blight, David W. *Frederick Douglass: Prophet of Freedom*. New York: Simon & Schuster, 2018.

Boonshoft, Mark. "Doughfaces at the Founding: Federalists, Anti-Federalists, Slavery, and the Ratification of the Constitution in New York." *New York History* 93, no. 3 (Summer 2012): 187–218.

Bowman, Shearer Davis. *At the Precipice: Americans North and South During the Secession Crisis*. Chapel Hill, NC: University of North Carolina Press, 2010.

Brandon, Mark E. *Free in the World: American Slavery and Constitutional Failure*. Princeton, NJ: Princeton University Press, 1998.

Brandon, Mark E. "Secession, Constitutionalism, and American Experience." In *Secession and Self-Determination*, ed. Stephen Macedo and Allen Buchanan, 272–314. New York: New York University Press, 2003.

Brandon, Mark E. "Secession and Nullification in the Twenty-First Century." *Arkansas Law Review* 67, no. 1 (2014): 91–102.

Campbell, Stanley W. *The Slave Catchers: Enforcement of the Fugitive Slave Law, 1850–1860*. Chapel Hill, NC: University of North Carolina Press, 1968.

Cohen, Andrew Wender. *Contraband: Smuggling and the Birth of the American Century*. New York: W. W. Norton & Company, 2015.

Conlin, Michael F. *The Constitutional Origins of the American Civil War*. Cambridge, UK: Cambridge University Press, 2019.

Crofts, Daniel W. *Lincoln and the Politics of Slavery: The Other Thirteenth Amendment and the Struggle to Save the Union*. Chapel Hill, NC: University of North Carolina Press, 2016.

Currie, David P. "The Constitution in the Supreme Court: Civil War and

Reconstruction, 1865–1873." *University of Chicago Law Review* 51, no. 1 (Winter 1984): 131–186.
Currie, David P. *The Constitution in Congress, 1789–1801: The Federalist Period.* Chicago: University of Chicago Press, 1997.
Currie, David P. *The Constitution in Congress, 1801–1829: The Jeffersonians.* Chicago: University of Chicago Press, 2001.
Currie, David P. *The Constitution in Congress, 1829–1861: Democrats and Whigs.* Chicago: University of Chicago Press, 2005.
Currie, David P. "Prolegomena for a Sampler, Extrajudicial Interpretation of the Constitution, 1789–1861." In *Congress and the Constitution*, ed. Neal Devins and Keith E Whittington, 18–38. Durham, NC: Duke University Press, 2005.
Curtis, George Ticknor. *Constitutional History of the United States from their Declaration of Independence to the Close of their Civil War*, vol. 2. New York: Harper & Brothers, 1896.
Davis, David Brion. "The Significance of Excluding Slavery from the Old Northwest in 1787." *Indiana Magazine of History* 84, no. 1 (March 1988): 75–89.
Denman, Clarence Phillips. *The Secession Movement in Alabama.* Montgomery, AL: Alabama State Department of Archives & History, 1933.
Delbanco, Andrew. *The War Before the War: Fugitive Slaves and the Struggle for America's Soul from the Revolution to the Civil War.* New York: Penguin Press, 2018.
Deyle, Steven. "'By far the most profitable trade': Slave Trading in British Colonial North America." *Slavery and Abolition* 10, no. 2 (1989): 107–125.
Deyle, Steven. *Carry Me Back: The Domestic Slave Trade in American Life.* Oxford, UK: Oxford University Press, 2005.
Deyle, Steven. "An 'Abominable' New Trade: The Closing of the African Slave Trade and the Changing Patterns of US Political Power, 1808–60." *The William and Mary Quarterly* 66, no. 4 (October 2009): 833–850.
Deyle, Steven. "An Ambiguous Legacy: The Closing of the African Slave Trade and America's Own Middle Passage." In *Ambiguous Anniversary: The Bicentennial of the International Slave Trade Bans*, ed. David T. Gleeson & Simon Lewis, 138–152. Columbia, SC: University of South Carolina Press, 2012.
Dew, Charles B. *Apostles of Disunion: Southern Secession Commissioners and the Causes of the Civil War.* Charlottesville, VA: University Press of Virginia, 2001.
Egerton, Douglas R. *Death or Liberty: African Americans and Revolutionary America.* Oxford, UK: Oxford University Press, 2009.
Egnal, Marc. *Clash of Extremes: The Economic Origins of the Civil War.* New York: Hill & Wang, 2009.
Elder, Robert. *Calhoun: American Heretic.* New York: Basic Books, 2021.
Ericson, David F. *Slavery in the American Republic: Developing the Federal Government, 1791–1861.* Lawrence, KS: University of Kansas Press, 2011.
Farber, Daniel. *Lincoln's Constitution.* Chicago: University of Chicago Press, 2003.
Farber, Daniel A. "The Story of *McCulloch*: Banking on National Power." *Constitutional Commentary* 20, no. 3 (Winter 2003–2004): 679–716.
Farber, Daniel. "The Fourteenth Amendment and the Unconstitutionality of Secession." *Akron Law Review* 45, no. 2 (2012): 479–512.

Farrand, Max. *The Framing of the Constitution of the United States*. New Haven, CT: Yale University Press, 1913.

Fehrenbacher, Don E. *The Dred Scott Case: Its Significance in American Law and Politics*. New York: Oxford University Press, 1978.

Fehrenbacher, Don E. *The Slaveholding Republic: An Account of the United States Government's Relations to Slavery*. New York: Oxford University Press, 2001.

Feldman, Noah. *The Broken Constitution: Lincoln, Slavery, and the Founding of America*. New York: Farrar, Straus & Giroux, 2021.

Finkelman, Paul. "*Prigg v. Pennsylvania* and Northern State Courts: Anti-Slavery Use of a Pro-Slavery Decision." *Civil War History* 25, no. 1 (March 1979): 5–35.

Finkelman, Paul, "Evading the Ordinance: The Persistence of Bondage in Indiana and Illinois." *Journal of the Early Republic* 9, no. 1 (Spring 1989): 21–51.

Finkelman, Paul. "The Kidnapping of John Davis and the Adoption of the Fugitive Slave Law of 1793." *Journal of Southern History* 56, no. 3 (August 1990): 397–422.

Finkelman, Paul. "Jefferson and Slavery: 'Treason Against the Hopes of the World.'" In *Jeffersonian Legacies*, ed. Peter S. Onuf, 181–221. Charlottesville, VA: University Press of Virginia, 1993.

Finkelman, Paul. "Thomas Jefferson and Antislavery: The Myth Goes On." *Virginia Magazine of History and Biography* 102, no. 2 (April 1994): 193–228.

Finkelman, Paul. "Slavery and Bondage in the 'Empire of Liberty.'" In *The Northwest Ordinance: Essays on Its Formation, Provisions, and Legacy*, ed. Frederick D. Williams, 61–95. East Lansing, MI: Michigan State University Press, 1988.

Finkelman, Paul. "The Founders and Slavery: Little Ventured, Little Gained." *Yale Journal of Law & the Humanities* 13, no. 2 (Summer 2001): 413–449.

Finkelman, Paul. *Slavery and the Founders: Race and Liberty in the Age of Jefferson*, 2nd ed. New York, M. E. Sharpe Inc., 2001.

Finkelman, Paul. "The American Suppression of the African Slave Trade: Lessons on Legal Change, Social Policy and Legislation." *Akron Law Review* 42, no. 2 (2009): 431–467.

Finkelman, Paul. "Slavery in the United States: Persons or Property?" In *The Legal Understanding of Slavery: From the Historical to the Contemporary*, ed. Jean Allain, 105–134. Oxford, UK: Oxford University Press, 2012.

Finkelman, Paul. "States' Rights, Southern Hypocrisy, and the Crisis of the Union." *Akron Law Review* 45, no. 2 (2012): 449–478.

Finkelman, Paul. *Supreme Injustice: Slavery in the Nation's Highest Court*. Harvard Cambridge, MA: University Press, 2018.

Finkelman, Paul. "The First Civil Rights Movement: Black Rights in the Age of the Revolution and Chief Justice Taney's Originalism in *Dred Scott*." *University of Pennsylvania Journal of Constitutional Law* 24, no. 3 (June 2022): 676–728.

Fishkin, Joseph, and William E. Forbath. *The Anti-Oligarchy Constitution: Reconstructing the Economic Foundations of American Democracy*. Cambridge, MA: Harvard University Press, 2022.

Fogel, Robert William and Stanley L. Engerman. *Time on the Cross: The Economics of Negro Slavery*. Boston: Little, Brown & Company, 1974.

Forbes, Robert Pierce. *The Missouri Compromise and Its Aftermath: Slavery and *the Meaning of America*. Chapel Hill, NC: University of North Carolina Press, 2007.

Freehling, William W. *The Road to Disunion*, vol. 1: *Secessionists at Bay 1776–1854*. New York: Oxford University Press, 1990.

Freehling, William W. *The Road to Disunion*, vol. 2: *Secessionists Triumphant, 1854–1861*. New York: Oxford University Press, 2007.

Gilbert, Alan. *Fighting for Emancipation in the War for Independence*. Chicago: University of Chicago Press, 2012.

Gilmore, W. E. "The Ordinance of 1787: Some Investigations as to the Authorship of the Famous Sixth Article." *Ohio History Journal* 14, no. 2 (April 1905): 148–157.

Graber, Mark A. *Dred Scott and the Problem of Constitutional Evil*. Cambridge, UK: Cambridge University Press, 2006.

Hacker, J. David, "A Census-Based Count of the Civil War Dead," *Civil War History* 57, no. 4 (December 2011): 307–348

Hendrickson, David C. *Peace Pact: The Lost World of the American Founding*. Lawrence, KS: University of Kansas Press, 2003.

Hendrickson, David C. *Union, Nation, or Empire: The American Debate over International Relations, 1789–1941*. Lawrence, KS: University Press of Kansas, 2009.

Hirschfeld, Fritz. *George Washington and Slavery: A Documentary Portrayal*. Columbia, MO: University of Missouri Press, 1997.

Horne, Gerald. *The Counter-Revolution of 1776: Slave Resistance and the Origins of the United States of America*. New York: New York University Press, 2014.

Huebner, Timothy S. *Liberty and Union: The Civil War Era and American Constitutionalism*. Lawrence, KS: University Press of Kansas, 2016.

Huston, James L. *Calculating the Value of the Union: Slavery, Property Rights, and the Economic Origins of the Civil War*. Chapel Hill, NC: University of North Carolina Press, 2003.

Hyman, Harold M. *The Reconstruction of Justice Salmon P. Chase: In Re Turner and Texas v. White*. Lawrence, KS: University Press of Kansas, 1997.

Jackman, Alexander. "Judging a Judge: A Reappraisal of Lord Mansfield and *Somerset's* Case." *Journal of Legal History* 39, no. 2 (August 2018): 140–156.

Karp, Matthew. *This Vast Southern Empire: Slaveholders at the Helm of American Foreign Policy*. Cambridge, MA: Harvard University Press, 2016.

Kerber, Linda K. "The Abolitionist Perception of the Indian." *Journal of American History* 62, no. 2 (September 1975): 271–295.

Kilberg, Andrew G. I. "We the People: The Original meaning of Popular Sovereignty." *Virginia Law Review* 100, no. 5 (September 2014): 1061–1109.

Klarman, Michael J. *The Framers' Coup: The Making of the United States Constitution*. New York: Oxford University Press, 2016.

Kornblith, Gary J. *Slavery and Sectional Strife in the Early American Republic, 1776–1871*. Lanham, MD: Rowman & Littlefield Publishers, Inc., 2010.

Larson, Edward J. *American Inheritance: Liberty and Slavery in the Birth of a Nation, 1765-1795*. New York: W. W. Norton & Company, 2023.

Levinson, Sanford. "'Perpetual Union,' 'Free Love,' and Secession: On the Limits of the "Consent of the Governed.'" *Tulsa Law Review* 39, no. 3 (Spring 2004): 457–483.

Levinson, Sanford. "The Ten Year War: What if Lincoln Had Not Exited After Four Years?" *Tulsa Law Review* 51, no. 2 (Winter 2016): 313–338.

Levinson, Sanford. "The 21st Century Rediscovery of Nullification and Secession in American Political Rhetoric: Frivolousness Incarnate, or Serious Arguments to Be Wrestled With?" In *Nullification and Secession in Modern Constitutional Thought*, ed. Sanford Levinson, 10–52. Lawrence, KS: University Press of Kansas, 2016.

Levinson, Sanford. *Written in Stone: Public Monuments in Changing Societies.* Twentieth Anniversary ed. Durham, NC: Duke University Press, 2018.

Lichtman, Allan J. *The Embattled Vote in America: From the Founding to the Present.* Cambridge, MA: Harvard University Press, 2018.

Lightner, David L. *Slavery and the Commerce Power: How the Struggle Against the Interstate Slave Trade Led to the Civil War.* New Haven, CT: Yale University Press, 2006.

Lind, Michael. *Land of Promise: An Economic History of the United States.* New York: HarperCollins, 2012.

Litwack, Leon F. *North of Slavery: The Negro in the Free States, 1790–1860.* Chicago: University of Chicago Press, 1961.

Lufkin, Charles L. "Secession and Coercion in Tennessee, the Spring of 1861." *Tennessee Historical Quarterly* 50, no. 2 (Summer 1991): 98–109.

Maier, Pauline. *American Scripture: Making the Declaration of Independence.* New York: Alfred A. Knopf, 1997.

Maier, Pauline. *Ratification: The People Debate the Constitution, 1787–1788.* New York: Simon & Schuster, 2010.

Majewski, John. *Modernizing a Slave Economy: The Economic Vision of the Confederate Nation.* Chapel Hill, NC: University of North Carolina Press, 2009.

Manjapra, Kris. *Black Ghost of Empire: The Long Death of Slavery and the Failure of Emancipation.* London: Allen Lane, 2022.

Mannix, Richard. "Gallatin, Jefferson, and the Embargo of 1808." *Diplomatic History* 3, no. 2 (April 1979): 151–172.

Masur, Kate. *Until Justice Be Done: America's First Civil Rights Movement, from Revolution to Reconstruction.* New York: W. W. Norton & Company, 2021.

Mayer, Henry. *All on Fire: William Lloyd Garrison and the Abolition of Slavery.* New York: St. Martin's Press, 1998.

Mayo-Bobee, Dinah. *New England Federalists: Widening the Sectional Divide in Jeffersonian America.* Madison, NJ: Fairleigh Dickinson University Press, 2017.

Mercantini, Jonathan, "'Most Contemptible in the Union': South Carolina, Slavery and the Constitution." In *Ambiguous Anniversary: The Bicentennial of the International Slave Trade Bans*, ed. David T. Gleeson and Simon Lewis, 35–51. Columbia, SC: University of South Carolina Press, 2012.

Merritt, Eli. "Sectional Conflict and Secret Compromise: The Mississippi River Question and the United States Constitution." *American Journal of Legal History* 35, no. 2 (April 1991): 117–171.

Meyler, Bernadette, "Between the States and the Signers: The Politics of the Declaration of Independence Before the Civil War." *Southern California Law Review* 89, no. 3 (March 2016): 541–573.

Miller, Arthur S. and Ronald F. Howell. "Interposition, Nullification and the Delicate Division of Power in a Federal System." *Journal of Public Law* 5, no. 1 (1956): 2–48.

Monaghan, Henry Paul. "We the People(s), Original Understanding, and Constitutional Amendment." *Columbia Law Review* 96, no. 1 (January 1996): 121–177.

Morgan, Edmund S. *American Slavery, American Freedom: The Ordeal of Colonial Virginia*. New York: W. W. Norton & Company, 1975.

Morgan, Edmund S. *Inventing the People: The Rise of Popular Sovereignty in England and America*. New York: W. W. Norton & Company, 1988.

Morone, James A. *Republic of Wrath: How American Politics Turned Tribal, from George Washington to Donald Trump*. New York: Basic Books, 2020.

Morris, Richard B. *The Forging of the Union, 1781–1789*. Harper & Row, Publishers, 1987.

Morris, Thomas D. *Free Men All: The Personal Liberty Law of the North 1780–1861*. Baltimore, MD: Johns Hopkins University Press, 1974.

Morris, Thomas D. *Southern Slavery and the Law, 1619–1860*. Chapel Hill, NC: University of North Carolina Press, 1996.

Morse, H. Newcomb. "The Foundations and Meaning of Secession." *Stetson Law Review* 15, no. 2 (Spring 1986): 419–436.

Nash, Gary B. *The Forgotten Fifth: African Americans in the Age of Revolution*. Cambridge, MA: Harvard University Press, 2006.

Nash, Gary B. *The Unknown American Revolution: The Unruly Birth of Democracy and the Struggle to Create America*. London: Jonathan Cape, 2006.

Nicoletti, Cynthia. *Secession on Trial: The Treason Prosecution of Jefferson Davis*. New York: Cambridge University Press, 2018.

Oakes, James. *The Scorpion's Sting: Antislavery and the Coming of the Civil War*. New York: W. W. Norton & Company, 2014.

Oakes, James. *The Crooked Path to Abolition: Abraham Lincoln and the Antislavery Constitution*. New York: W. W. Norton & Company, 2021.

Onuf, Peter. *Statehood and Union: A History of the Northwest Ordinance*. Bloomington, IN: Indiana University Press, 1987.

Parkinson, Robert G. *The Common Cause: Creating Race and Nation in the American Revolution*. Chapel Hill, NC: University of North Carolina Press, 2016.

Parkinson, Robert G. *Thirteen Clocks: How Race United the Colonies and Made the Declaration of Independence*, Chapel Hill, NC: University of North Carolina Press, 2021.

Peart, Daniel. *Lobbyists and the Making of US Tariff Policy, 1816–1861*. Baltimore, MD: Johns Hopkins University Press, 2018.

Pierson Jr., William Whatley. *Texas versus White: A Study in Legal History*, Durham, NC: The Seeman Printery, 1916.

Pohjankoski, Pekka. "Federal Coercion and National Constitutional Identity in the United States 1776–1861." *American Journal of Legal History* 56, no. 3. (September 2016): 326–358.

Poole, William Frederick. "Dr. Cutler and the Ordinance of 1787." *The North American Review* 122, no. 251 (April 1876): 229–265.

Potter, David. *The Impending Crisis, 1848–1861*. New York: Harper & Row Publishers, 1976.

Rakove, Jack N. "Ambiguous Achievement: The Northwest Ordinance." In Frederick D Williams (ed), *The Northwest Ordinance: Essays on Its Formation, Provisions, and Legacy*, Michigan State University Press, East Lansing MI, 1988, 1–19.

Rakove, Jack N. *Original Meanings: Politics and Ideas in the Making of the Constitution*. New York: Alfred A. Knopf, 1997.

Rasmussen, Dennis C. *Fears of a Setting Sun: The Disillusionment of America's Founders*. Princeton, NJ: Princeton University Press, 2021.

Rawley, James A with Behrendt, Stephen D, *The Transatlantic Slave Trade: A History*. Revised edition. Lincoln: University of Nebraska Press, 2005.

Robinson, Donald L. *Slavery in American Politics, 1765–1820*. New York: Harcourt Brace Jovanovich Inc., 1971.

Roosevelt III, Kermit. *The Nation That Never Was: Reconstructing America's Story*. Chicago: University of Chicago Press, 2022.

Rosenthal, Caitlin. *Accounting for Slavery: Masters and Management*. Cambridge, MA: Harvard University Press, 2018.

Rothman, Adam. *Slave Country: American Expansion and the Origins of the Deep South*. Cambridge, MA: Harvard University Press, 2005.

Rothman, Joshua D. *The Ledger and the Chain: How Domestic Slave Traders Shaped America*. New York: Basic Books, 2021.

Schmitt, Jeffery, "Rethinking *Ableman v. Booth* and States' Rights in Wisconsin." *Virginia Law Review* 95, no. 3 (September 2007): 1315–1354.

Sinha, Manisha. *The Slave's Cause: A History of Abolition*. New Haven, CT: Yale University Press, 2016.

Smith, Timothy B. *The Mississippi Secession Convention: Delegates and Deliberations in Politics and War, 1861–1865*. Jackson, MS: University Press of Mississippi, 2015.

Stampp, Kenneth M. "The Concept of a Perpetual Union." *Journal of American History* 65, no. 1 (June 1978): 5–33.

Sunstein, Cass R. "Constitutionalism and Secession." *University of Chicago Law Review* 58, no. 2 (Spring 1991): 633–670.

Taylor, Alan. *American Revolutions: A Continental History, 1750–1804*. New York: W. W. Norton & Company, 2016.

Taylor, Alan. *American Republics: A Continental History of the United States*, 1783–1850. New York: W. W. Norton & Company, 2021.

Taylor, John M. *William Henry Seward: Lincoln's Right Hand*. New York: HarperCollins Publishers, 1991.

Treanor, William Michael. "The Case of the Dishonest Scrivener: Gouverneur Morris and the Creation of the Federalist Constitution." *Michigan Law Review* 120, no. 1 (October 2021): 1–124.

Tribe, Laurence H. *The Invisible Constitution*. New York: Oxford University Press, 2008.

Van Cleve, George William. *A Slaveholders' Union: Slavery, Politics, and the Constitution in the Early American Republic*. Chicago: University of Chicago Press, 2010.

Van Cleve, George William. *We Have Not A Government: The Articles of Confederation and the Road to the Constitution*. Chicago: University of Chicago Press, 2017.

Varon, Elizabeth R. *Disunion! The Coming of the American Civil War, 1789–1859*. Chapel Hill, NC: University of North Carolina Press, 2008.

Vile, John R. *The Constitutional Convention: A Comprehensive Encyclopedia of America's Founding*. Vols. 1–2. Rev. second ed. Clark, NJ: Talbot Publishing, 2016.

Warren, Charles. "The Mississippi River and the Treaty Clause of the Constitution." *George Washington Law Review* 2, no. 3 (March 1934): 271–302.

White, G. Edward. *Law in American History*, vol. 1, *From the Colonial Years Through the Civil War*. New York: Oxford University Press, 2012.

Wiecek, William M. "*Somerset*: Lord Mansfield and the Legitimacy of Slavery in the Anglo-American World." *University of Chicago Law Review* 42, no. 1 (Autumn 1974): 86–146.

Wilentz, Sean. *No Property in Man: Slavery and Antislavery at the Nation's Founding*. Cambridge, MA: Harvard University Press, 2018.

Wood, Gordon S. *The Creation of the American Republic, 1776–1787*. Chapel Hill, NC: University of North Carolina Press, 1998.

Wood, Gordon S. "The Revolutionary Origins of the Civil War." *Northwestern University Law Review* 114, no. 2 (2019): 539–553

Wood, Gordon S. *Power and Liberty: Constitutionalism in the American Revolution*. New York: Oxford University Press, 2021.

Wright, Gavin. *Slavery and American Economic Development*. Baton Rouge, LA: Louisiana State University Press, 2006.

Yacovone, Donald. *Teaching White Supremacy: America's Democratic Ordeal and the Forging of Our National Identity*. New York: Pantheon Books, 2022.

INDEX